THE **BUSN** SOLUTION

KELLY • WILLIAMS

BUSN⁹

INTRODUCTION TO BUSINESS

4LTR PRESS | NOW WITH BUSN ONLINE
$19 US SUGGESTED RETAIL PRICE

Print
+
Online

Business Now: Change is
the Only Constant

CHAPTER **2**

Economics: The Framework
for Business

BUSN⁹ delivers all the key terms and
core concepts for the **Introduction
to Business** course.

BUSN Online provides the complete
narrative from the printed text with
additional interactive media and the unique
functionality of **StudyBits**—all available
on nearly any device!

What is a StudyBit™? Created through a deep investigation of students' challenges and workflows,
the StudyBit™ functionality of **BUSN Online** enables students of different generations and learning
styles to study more effectively by allowing them to learn their way. Here's how they work:

**COLLECT
WHAT'S
IMPORTANT**
Create
StudyBits
as you highlight
text, images or
take notes!

WEAK

FAIR

STRONG

UNASSIGNED

**RATE AND ORGANIZE
STUDYBITS**
Rate your
understanding and
use the color-coding
to quickly organize
your study time
and personalize
your flashcards
and quizzes.

StudyBit™

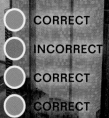

CORRECT

INCORRECT

CORRECT

CORRECT

**TRACK/MONITOR
PROGRESS**
Use Concept
Tracker to decide
how you'll spend
study time and
study YOUR way!

85%

PERSONALIZE QUIZZES
Filter by your StudyBits
to personalize quizzes or
just take chapter quizzes
off-the-shelf.

BUSN9

Marce Kelly and Chuck Williams

Vice President, General Manager, 4LTR Press: Neil Marquardt

Product Director, 4LTR Press: Steven E. Joos

Product Manager: Laura Redden

Content/Media Developer: Daniel Celenza

Product Assistant: Lauren Dame

Marketing Manager: Jeff Tousignant

Marketing Coordinator: Christopher Walz

Sr. Content Project Manager: Martha Conway

Manufacturing Planner: Ron Montgomery

Production Service: MPS Limited

Sr. Art Director: Bethany Casey

Internal Designer: Lou Ann Thesing

Cover Designer: Curio Press, LLC/Lisa Kuhn

Cover Image: Collage Photography/Veer.com

Title page and back cover images:

Computer and tablet illustration:
©iStockphoto.com/furtaev

Smart Phone illustration:
©iStockphoto.com/dashadima

Intellectual Property Analyst: Diane Garrity

Intellectual Property Project Manager:
Betsy Hathaway

For product information and technology assistance, contact us at
Cengage Learning Customer & Sales Support, 1-800-354-9706

For permission to use material from this text or product,
submit all requests online at **www.cengage.com/permissions**
Further permissions questions can be emailed to
permissionrequest@cengage.com

Library of Congress Control Number: 2015953549

Student Edition ISBN: 978-1-305-49695-8

Student Edition with Online ISBN: 978-1-305-49732-0

Cengage Learning
20 Channel Center Street
Boston, MA 02210
USA

Cengage Learning is a leading provider of customized learning solutions with employees residing in nearly 40 different countries and sales in more than 125 countries around the world. Find your local representative at **www.cengage.com**

Cengage Learning products are represented in Canada by Nelson Education, Ltd.

To learn more about Cengage Learning Solutions, visit **www.cengage.com**

Purchase any of our products at your local college store or at our preferred online store **www.cengagebrain.com**

Printed in the United States of America
Print Number: 01   Print Year: 2015

KELLY / WILLIAMS

BUSN⁹

BRIEF CONTENTS

Collage Photography/Veer.com

PART 1   THE BUSINESS ENVIRONMENT

1 Business Now: Change Is the Only Constant   2
2 Economics: The Framework for Business   18
3 The World Marketplace: Business without Borders   38
4 Business Ethics and Social Responsibility: Doing Well by Doing Good   56
5 Business Communication: Creating and Delivering Messages that Matter   74

PART 2   CREATING A BUSINESS

6 Business Formation: Choosing the Form that Fits   90
7 Small Business and Entrepreneurship: Economic Rocket Fuel   110

PART 3   FINANCING A BUSINESS

8 Accounting: Decision Making by the Numbers   126
9 Finance: Acquiring and Using Funds to Maximize Value   146
10 Financial Markets: Allocating Financial Resources   166

PART 4   MARKETING A BUSINESS

11 Marketing: Building Profitable Customer Connections   186
12 Product and Promotion: Creating and Communicating Value   204
13 Distribution and Pricing: Right Product, Right Person, Right Place, Right Price   230

PART 5   MANAGING A BUSINESS

14 Management, Motivation, and Leadership: Bringing Business to Life   246
15 Human Resource Management: Building a Top-Quality Workforce   264
16 Managing Information and Technology: Finding New Ways to Learn and Link   282
17 Operations Management: Putting It All Together   300

Personal Finance Appendix   320
Endnotes   332
Glossary   350
Index   362
Tear-out cards
Online Appendices
   Appendix 1: Labor Unions and Collective Bargaining
   Appendix 2: Business Law

CONTENTS

Letter to Students ix

Part 1
THE BUSINESS ENVIRONMENT

Klaus Tiedge/Getty Images

1 Business Now: Change Is the Only Constant 2

1-1 Business Now: Moving at Breakneck Speed 2

1-2 The History of Business: Putting It All in Context 4

1-3 Nonprofits and the Economy: The Business of Doing Good 6

1-4 Factors of Production: The Basic Building Blocks 7

1-5 The Business Environment: The Context for Success 8

1-6 Business and You: Making It Personal 15

2 Economics: The Framework for Business 18

2-1 Economics: Navigating a Crisis 18

2-2 Managing the Economy Through Fiscal and Monetary Policy 21

2-3 Capitalism: The Free Market System 26

2-4 Planned Economies: Socialism and Communism 30

2-5 Mixed Economies: The Story of the Future 31

2-6 Evaluating Economic Performance: What's Working? 32

3 The World Marketplace: Business without Borders 38

3-1 An Unprecedented Opportunity 38

3-2 Key Reasons for International Trade 41

3-3 Global Trade: Taking Measure 42

3-4 Seizing the Opportunity: Strategies for Reaching Global Markets 43

3-5 Barriers to International Trade 46

3-6 Free Trade: The Movement Gains Momentum 50

4 Business Ethics and Social Responsibility: Doing Well by Doing Good 56

4-1 Ethics and Social Responsibility: A Close Relationship 56

4-2 Business Ethics: Not an Oxymoron 58

4-3 Ethics: Multiple Touchpoints 60

4-4 Defining Social Responsibility: Making the World a Better Place 62

4-5 Ethics and Social Responsibility in the Global Arena: A House of Mirrors? 68

4-6 Monitoring Ethics and Social Responsibility: Who Is Minding the Store? 71

5 Business Communication: Creating and Delivering Messages that Matter 74

5-1 Excellent Communication Skills: Your Invisible Advantage 74

5-2 Nonverbal Communication: Beyond the Words 76

5-3 Choose the Right Channel: A Rich Array of Options 78

5-4 Pick the Right Words: Is That Car Pre-Loved or Just Plain Used?! 78

5-5 Write High-Impact Messages: Breaking through the Clutter 82

5-6 Create and Deliver Successful Verbal Presentations: Hook 'Em and Reel 'Em In! 85

Part 2
CREATING A BUSINESS

Everything Possible/Shutterstock.com

Part 3
FINANCING A BUSINESS

Khakimullin Aleksandr/Shutterstock.com

6 Business Formation: Choosing the Form that Fits 90

6-1 Business Ownership Options: The Big Four 90

6-2 Advantages and Disadvantages of Sole Proprietorships 93

6-3 Partnerships: Two Heads (and Bankrolls) Can Be Better Than One 94

6-4 Corporations: The Advantages and Disadvantages of Being an Artificial Person 96

6-5 The Limited Liability Company: The New Kid on the Block 102

6-6 Franchising: Proven Methods for a Price 104

7 Small Business and Entrepreneurship: Economic Rocket Fuel 110

7-1 Launching a New Venture: What's in It for Me? 110

7-2 The Entrepreneur: A Distinctive Profile 112

7-3 Finding the Money: Funding Options for Small Businesses 115

7-4 Opportunities and Threats for Small Business: A Two-Sided Coin 117

7-5 Launch Options: Reviewing the Pros and Cons 119

7-6 Small Business and the Economy: An Outsized Impact 121

8 Accounting: Decision Making by the Numbers 126

8-1 Accounting: Who Needs It—and Who Does It? 126

8-2 Financial Accounting: Intended for Those on the Outside Looking In 128

8-3 Financial Statements: Read All About Us 130

8-4 Interpreting Financial Statements: Digging Beneath the Surface 135

8-5 Budgeting: Planning for Accountability 139

8-6 Inside Intelligence: The Role of Managerial Accounting 141

9 Finance: Acquiring and Using Funds to Maximize Value 146

9-1 What Motivates Financial Decisions? 146

9-2 Identifying Financial Needs: Evaluation and Planning 149

9-3 Finding Funds: What Are the Options? 153

9-4 Leverage and Capital Structure: How Much Debt Is Too Much Debt? 156

9-5 Acquiring and Managing Current Assets 160

9-6 Capital Budgeting: In It for the Long Haul 162

10 Financial Markets: Allocating Financial Resources 166

10-1 The Role of Financial Markets and Their Key Players 166

10-2 Regulating Financial Markets to Protect Investors and Improve Stability 169

10-3 Investing in Financial Securities: What Are the Options? 171

10-4 Issuing and Trading Securities: The Primary and Secondary Markets 176

10-5 Personal Investing 178

10-6 Keeping Tabs on the Market 181

Part 4
MARKETING A BUSINESS

11 Marketing: Building Profitable Customer Connections 186

11-1 Marketing: Getting Value by Giving Value 186

11-2 The Customer: Front and Center 190

11-3 Marketing Strategy: Where Are You Going, and How Will You Get There? 191

11-4 Customer Behavior: Decisions, Decisions, Decisions! 197

11-5 Marketing Research: So What Do They Really Think? 198

11-6 Social Responsibility and Technology: A Major Marketing Shift 201

12 Product and Promotion: Creating and Communicating Value 204

12-1 Product: It's Probably More Than You Thought 204

12-2 Product Differentiation and Planning: A Meaningful Difference 207

12-3 Innovation and the Product Life Cycle: Nuts, Bolts, and a Spark of Brilliance 212

12-4 Promotion: Influencing Consumer Decisions 216

12-5 A Meaningful Message: Finding the Big Idea 217

12-6 The Promotional Mix: Communicating the Big Idea 218

13 Distribution and Pricing: Right Product, Right Person, Right Place, Right Price 230

13-1 Distribution: Getting Your Product to Your Customer 230

13-2 Wholesalers: Sorting Out the Options 233

13-3 Retailers: The Consumer Connection 234

13-4 Physical Distribution: Planes, Trains, and Much, Much More 237

13-5 Pricing Objectives and Strategies: A High-Stakes Game 238

13-6 Pricing in Practice: A Real-World Approach 241

Part 5
MANAGING A BUSINESS

14 Management, Motivation, and Leadership: Bringing Business to Life 246

14-1 Bringing Resources to Life 246

14-2 Motivation: Lighting the Fire 249

14-3 Planning: Figuring Out Where to Go and How to Get There 253

14-4 Organizing: Fitting Together the Puzzle Pieces 257

14-5 Leadership: Directing and Inspiring 260

14-6 Controlling: Making Sure It All Works 262

15 Human Resource Management: Building a Top-Quality Workforce 264

15-1 Human Resource Management: Bringing Business to Life 264

15-2 Human Resource Management Challenges: Major Hurdles 265

15-3 Human Resources Managers: Corporate Black Sheep? 267

15-4 Human Resource Planning: Drawing the Map 268

15-5 Legal Issues: HR and the Long Arm of the Law 277

16 Managing Information and Technology: Finding New Ways to Learn and Link 282

16-1 Information Technology: Explosive Change 282

16-2 Cloud Computing: The Sky's the Limit! 286

16-3 Information Technology and Decision Making: A Crucial Aid 287

16-4 Information Technology and the World of E-Commerce 289

16-5 Challenges and Concerns Arising from New Technologies 293

17 Operations Management: Putting It All Together 300

17-1 Operations Management: Producing Value in a Changing Environment 300

17-2 What Do Operations Managers Do? 303

17-3 Implications of a Service-Based Economy: Responding to Different Challenges 309

17-4 The Technology of Operations 310

17-5 Focus on Quality 311

17-6 The Move to Be Lean and Green: Cutting Cost and Cutting Waste 315

Personal Finance Appendix 320

Endnotes 332

Glossary 350

Index 362

Tear-out cards

Online Appendices

    Appendix 1: Labor Unions and Collective Bargaining

    Appendix 2: Business Law

With love and
appreciation
to Kathy,
the best friend imaginable!

—Marce Kelly

To Jenny,
the book is done, let's play!

—Chuck Williams

The idea for this book—a whole new way of learning—began with students like you across the country. We paid attention to students who wanted to learn about business without slogging through endless pages of dry text. We listened to students who wanted to sit through class without craving a triple espresso. We responded to students who wanted to use their favorite gadgets to prepare for tests.

So we are confident that BUSN will meet your needs. The short, lively text covers all the key concepts without the fluff. The examples are relevant and engaging, and the visual style makes the book fun to read. But the text is only part of the package. You can access a rich variety of study tools via computer or iPad—the choice is yours.

We did one other thing we hope you'll like. We paid a lot of attention to students' concerns about the high price of college textbooks. We made it our mission to ensure that our package not only meets your needs but does so without busting your budget!

This innovative, student-focused package was developed by the authors—Marce Kelly and Chuck Williams—and the experienced Cengage Learning publishers. The Cengage team contributed a deep understanding of students and professors across the nation, and the authors brought years of teaching and business experience.

Marce Kelly, who earned her MBA from UCLA's Anderson School of Management, spent the first 14 years of her career in marketing, building brands for Neutrogena and The Walt Disney Corporation. But her true love is teaching, so in 2000 she accepted a full-time teaching position at Santa Monica College. Professor Kelly has received seven Outstanding Instructor awards from the International Education Center and has been named four times to *Who's Who Among American Teachers*.

Chuck Williams' interests include employee recruitment and turnover, performance appraisal, and employee training and goal setting. Most recently, he was the Dean of Butler University's College of Business. He has taught in executive development programs at Oklahoma State University, the University of Oklahoma, Texas Christian University, and the University of the Pacific. Dr. Williams was honored by TCU's M.J. Neeley School of Business with the undergraduate Outstanding Faculty Teaching Award, was a recipient of TCU's Dean's Teaching Award, and was TCU's nominee for the U.S. Professor of the Year competition sponsored by the Carnegie Foundation for the Advancement of Teaching. He has written three other textbooks: *Management, Effective Management: A Multimedia Approach*, and *MGMT*.

We would appreciate any comments or suggestions you want to offer about this package. You can reach Chuck Williams at crwillia@butler.edu, and Marce Kelly at marcella.kelly@gmail.com. We wish you a fun, positive, productive term, and look forward to your feedback!

Marce Kelly

© Cengage Learning®

Chuck Williams

© Brent Smith, Butler University

1 | Business Now:
Change Is the Only Constant

LEARNING OBJECTIVES

After studying this chapter, you will be able to:

1-1 Define business and discuss the role of business in the economy

1-2 Explain the evolution of modern business

1-3 Discuss the role of nonprofit organizations in the economy

1-4 Outline the core factors of production and how they affect the economy

1-5 Describe today's business environment and discuss each key dimension

1-6 Explain how current business trends might affect your career choices

"YOU MISS **100%** OF THE SHOTS YOU DON'T TAKE."
—WAYNE GRETZY, HOCKEY STAR

Klaus Tiedge/Getty Images

will care less about what they *have or buy* and more about what they can *do or create*"—seeking services that eliminate time and learning barriers to their creation of professional quality output.

■ **Fast-Laning:** No one likes to wait on line. But if you invest your time and money in your favorite brand, you may not need to. A growing number of firms are finding creative ways to speed their loyal time-crunched consumers to the front of the queue, ideally without annoying everyone else, or without calling attention to the slow speed of "normal" service. For example, Starwood, Hyatt, and Hilton hotel chains have all tested programs allowing frequent guests to check in via their apps and use their cell phones as room keys, to avoid wait lines at the front desk. And in Sweden, amusement park Liseberg released an app to accompany its new Helix roller coaster. Attendees could play the free Helix Game while waiting in line for the attraction. Every 15 minutes, the player with the highest score got a pass to skip the line—creative and fun!

■ **Branded Governments:** Do you believe that governments alone can solve today's problems? Most millennials don't. In fact, 73% of millennials don't

believe governments can solve today's issues alone, and 83% want businesses to get more involved. That's why leading-edge brands will step up to civic challenges in a meaningful way. For example, when Ebola swept across West Africa in 2014, mobile app Easy Taxi partnered with Dettol to offer Nigerian cab drivers lessons on how to diagnose and prevent the disease, encouraging drivers to pass their knowledge onto passengers.

■ **Sympathetic Pricing:** Do the brands you buy really, truly feel your pain? Hard to know. But one good way for companies to show that they care is via imaginative discounts that demonstrate compassion or alleviate customer pain. Examples abound. PareUp, for instance, allows New York–based restaurants, coffee shops, and grocery stores to offer soon-to-be-wasted food at a discounted price. Participating merchants can send alerts to users detailing what is available, and the discounted price. Also, during the FIFA World Cup in July 2014, Brazilian publisher Lote 42 offered customers a 10% discount for every goal scored against the national team during the soccer championship. After Brazil lost 7–1 to Germany, customers were offered a 70% discount for 24 hours, catapulting the brand to national attention, and solidifying bonds with passionate fans.

- **Robolove:** Everyone knows that robots can save time and money—and who doesn't like efficiency? But do we like the robots themselves? Many people imagine a bleak robotic future with robocops out of control and robo-workers putting human workers out of work. That may well happen, but Trendwatching.com predicts that many of us will thoroughly enjoy our early contacts with robots. For instance, Düsseldorf Airport in Germany recently unveiled the world's first robotic parking valet. Customers leave their car, and a robot picks it up and positions the vehicle in one of 249 dedicated spaces. The system connects to the airport's flight database, meaning that customers find their vehicle ready and waiting for them upon their return. Hard to get more convenient than that—and the robotic valet doesn't even expect a tip![1]

1-1a Business Basics: Some Key Definitions

While you can certainly recognize a business when you see one, more formal definitions may help as you read through this book. A **business** is any organization or activity that provides goods and services in an effort to earn a profit. **Profit** is the financial reward that comes from starting and running a business. More specifically, profit is the money that a business earns in sales (or revenue), minus expenses such as the cost of goods and the cost of salaries. But clearly, not every business earns a profit all the time. When a business brings in less money than it needs to cover expenses, it incurs a **loss**. If you launch a music label, for instance, you'll need to pay your artists, lease a studio, and purchase equipment, among other expenses. If your label generates hits, you'll earn more than enough to cover all your expenses and make yourself rich. But a series of duds could leave you holding the bag. Just the possibility of earning a profit

business Any organization or activity that provides goods and services in an effort to earn a profit.

profit The money that a business earns in sales (or revenue), minus expenses, such as the cost of goods, and the cost of salaries. Revenue – Expenses = Profit (or Loss).

loss When a business incurs expenses that are greater than its revenue.

entrepreneurs People who risk their time, money, and other resources to start and manage a business.

standard of living The quality and quantity of goods and services available to a population.

quality of life The overall sense of well-being experienced by either an individual or a group.

provides a powerful incentive for people of all backgrounds to launch their own enterprises. But unfortunately, the rate of new business startups has been decreasing over the past few years. As the economy has finally emerged from the Great Recession, and unemployment and financial ruin are less of a threat, fewer people have been motivated to risk starting new businesses.[2] People who do risk their time, money, and other resources to start and manage a business are called **entrepreneurs**.

Interestingly, as entrepreneurs create wealth for themselves, they produce a ripple effect that enriches everyone around them. For instance, if your new website becomes the next Facebook, who will benefit? Clearly, *you* will. And you'll probably spend at least some of that money enriching your local clubs, clothing stores, and car dealerships. But others will benefit, too, including your members, advertisers on your site and the staff who support them, contractors who build your facilities, and the government that collects your taxes. The impact of one successful entrepreneur can extend to the far reaches of the economy. In fact, fast-growing new firms generate about 10% of all new jobs in any given year.[3] Multiply the impact by thousands of entrepreneurs—each working in his or her own self-interest—and you can see how the profit motive benefits virtually everyone.

From a bigger-picture perspective, business drives up the **standard of living** for people worldwide, contributing to a higher **quality of life**. Businesses not only provide the products and services that people enjoy but also provide the jobs that people need. Beyond the obvious, business contributes to society through innovation—think cars, TVs, and tablet computers. Business also helps raise the standard of living through taxes, which the government spends on projects that range from streetlights to environmental cleanup. Socially responsible firms contribute even more by actively advocating for the well-being of the society that feeds their success.

1-2 THE HISTORY OF BUSINESS: PUTTING IT ALL IN CONTEXT

You may be surprised to learn that—unlike today—business hasn't always been focused on what the customer wants. In fact, business in the United States has changed rather dramatically over the past 200–300 years. Most business historians divide the history of American business into five distinct eras, which overlap during the periods of transition:

- **The Industrial Revolution:** Technological advances fueled a period of rapid industrialization in America from the mid-1700s to the mid-1800s. As

Not Every Dumb Move Is an Utter Disaster...

In the wake of disastrous mistakes and outrageous mismanagement across our economy, it might be tough to remember that some mistakes are actually pretty amusing. Several examples might help remind you.[4]

- **Bad fabric, not fat thighs:** In early 2013, Lululemon Athletica was forced to recall its popular (and expensive) yoga pants, because many women found them utterly see-through. Later in the year, the founder of the firm was forced to resign after blaming the problem on women with fat thighs who rubbed the fabric too sheer with multiple uses.

- **Apple angst:** In a rare display of new product development weakness, Apple released its Maps program before it was ready for the Big Time. Mostly harmless, the program baffled millions of trusting consumers. But in Fairbanks, Alaska, it directed hapless users onto active runways of the international airport. Fortunately, there were no collisions—the worst harm done was to Siri's reputation as a navigator.[5]

- **Accidental cyber-snooping:** As Google sent its "Street View" cars all over the world, collecting panoramic images for uploading into GoogleMaps, the firm "unintentionally" collected and retained, among other things, passwords and complete email messages picked up from unsecured Wi-Fi networks.

- **Thank you, Captain Obvious!** A surprising number of firms just can't seem to credit their customers with even basic intelligence. Marks & Spencer's labeled one of their Bread Puddings, PRODUCT WILL BE HOT AFTER HEATING. On a Sears hairdryer, DO NOT USE WHILE SLEEPING. And on packaging for a Rowenta iron, DO NOT IRON CLOTHES ON BODY. While these warnings most likely have a legal backstory, it's hard for a reasonable consumer not to see them as silly goofs.[6]

---

mass production took hold, huge factories replaced skilled artisan workshops. The factories hired large numbers of semiskilled workers who specialized in a limited number of tasks. The result was unprecedented production efficiency but also a loss of individual ownership and personal pride in the production process.

- **The Entrepreneurship Era:** Building on the foundation of the industrial revolution, large-scale entrepreneurs emerged in the second half of the 1800s, building business empires. These industrial titans created enormous wealth, raising the overall standard of living across the country. But many also dominated their markets, forcing out competitors, manipulating prices, exploiting workers, and decimating the environment. Toward the end of the 1800s, the government stepped into the business realm, passing laws to regulate business and protect consumers and workers, creating more balance in the economy.

- **The Production Era:** In the early part of the 1900s, major businesses focused on further refining the production process and creating greater efficiencies. Jobs became even more specialized, increasing productivity and lowering costs and prices. In 1913, Henry Ford introduced the assembly line, which quickly became standard across

Hulton Collection/Hulton Archive/Getty Images

major manufacturing industries. With managers focused on efficiency, the customer was an afterthought. But when customers tightened their belts during the Great Depression and World War II, businesses took notice. The "hard sell" emerged: aggressive persuasion designed to separate consumers from their cash.

- **The Marketing Era:** After WWII, the balance of power shifted away from producers and toward consumers, flooding the market with enticing choices. To differentiate themselves from their competitors,

Traffic Jams and Parking Woes—A Problem of the Past?

Nobody likes to fight traffic at the end of the day. And it's no fun starting an evening trolling for parking or shelling out big bucks for a valet or space in a nearby lot. But when you call an Uber, you don't need to worry about any of that. More and more people are choosing the ultra-popular, relatively cheap car-hailing service, which some experts believe may eventually ease urban congestion and parking problems as millions of consumers *may* decide that using Uber is cheaper than owning a car. Meanwhile, despite some "significant growing pains," Uber is growing in leaps and bounds. By 2014, Uber was serving 250 cities in 53 countries, and was worth $40 billion, more than Delta Airlines ($37 billion) and less than Starbucks ($60 billion). Google's closest competitors, such as Sidecar and Lyft, are eating its dust (Lyft is worth about $700 million). Uber's "growing pains," such as a supposedly misogynistic culture and pushback from the taxi industry, which feels threatened by Uber, haven't hurt it much so far. In fact, the editor of *Fortune* magazine has recently

posited that the Uber model—connecting individual users and independent providers via app for a share of the take on a large-scale basis—will actually reshape the entire economy in the decade to come.[7]

Andrew Harrer/Bloomberg/Getty Images

---

businesses began to develop brands, or distinctive identities, to help consumers understand the differences among various products. *The marketing concept* emerged: a consumer focus that permeates successful companies in every department, at every level. This approach continues to influence business decisions today as global competition heats up to unprecedented levels.

- **The Relationship Era:** Building on the marketing concept, today, leading-edge firms look beyond each immediate transaction with a customer and aim to build long-term relationships. Satisfied customers can become advocates for a business, spreading the word with more speed and credibility than even the best promotional campaign. And cultivating current customers is more profitable than constantly seeking new ones. One key tool is technology. Using the Web and other digital resources, businesses gather detailed information about their customers and use these data to serve them better, "bringing a level of customer centricity that we've never seen before," according to Graeme Noseworthy, marketing director for IBM.

nonprofits Business-*like* establishments that employ people and produce goods and services with the fundamental goal of contributing to the community rather than generating financial gain.

1-3   NONPROFITS AND THE ECONOMY: THE BUSINESS OF DOING GOOD

Nonprofit organizations play a critical role in the economy, often working hand-in-hand with businesses to improve the quality of life in our society. Focusing on areas such as health, human services, education, art, religion, and culture, **nonprofits** are business-*like* establishments, but their primary goals do not include profits. Chuck Bean, Executive Director of the Nonprofit Roundtable, explains: "By definition, nonprofits are not in the business of financial gain. We're in the business of doing good. However, nonprofits are still businesses in every other sense—they employ people, they take in revenue, they produce goods and services and contribute in significant ways to our region's economic stability and growth." Nationwide, nonprofits employ about one in ten workers, accounting for more paid workers than the entire construction industry and more than the finance, insurance, and real-estate sectors combined. And nonprofit museums, schools, theaters, and orchestras have become economic magnets for many communities, drawing additional investment.[8]

1-4 FACTORS OF PRODUCTION: THE BASIC BUILDING BLOCKS

Both businesses and nonprofits rely on **factors of production**—four fundamental resources—to achieve their objectives. Some combination of these factors is crucial for an economic system to work and create wealth. As you read through the factors, keep in mind that they don't come free of charge. Human resources, for instance, require wages, while entrepreneurs need a profit incentive.

- **Natural Resources:** This factor includes all inputs that offer value in their natural state, such as land, fresh water, wind, and mineral deposits. Most natural resources must be extracted, purified, or harnessed; people cannot actually create them. (Note that agricultural products, which people do create through planting and tending, are not a natural resource.) The value of all natural resources tends to rise with high demand, low supply, or both.

- **Capital:** This factor includes machines, tools, buildings, information, and technology—the synthetic resources that a business needs to produce goods or services. Computers and telecommunications capability have become pivotal elements of capital across a surprising range of industries, from financial services to professional sports. You may be surprised to learn that in this context, capital does not include money, but, clearly, businesses use money to acquire, maintain, and upgrade their capital.

- **Human Resources:** This factor encompasses the physical, intellectual, and creative contributions of everyone who works within an economy. As technology replaces a growing number of manual labor jobs, education and motivation have become increasingly important to human resource development. Given the importance of knowledge to workforce effectiveness, some business experts, such as management guru Peter Drucker, break out knowledge as its own category, separate from human resources.

- **Entrepreneurship:** Entrepreneurs are people who take the risk of launching and operating their own businesses, largely in response to the profit incentive. They tend to see opportunities where others don't, and they use their own resources to capitalize on that potential. Entrepreneurial enterprises can kick-start an economy, creating a tidal wave of opportunity by harnessing the other factors of production. But entrepreneurs don't thrive in an environment that doesn't support them. The key ingredient is economic freedom: freedom of choice (whom to hire, for instance, or what to produce), freedom from excess regulation, and freedom from too much taxation. Protection from corruption and unfair competition is another entrepreneurial "must."

Clearly, all of these factors must be in place for an economy to thrive. But which factor is most important? One way to answer that question is to examine current economies around the world. Russia and China are both rich in natural resources and human resources, and both countries have a solid level of capital (growing in China, and deteriorating in Russia). Yet, neither country is wealthy; both rank relatively low in terms of gross national income per person. The missing ingredient seems to be entrepreneurship, limited in Russia largely through corruption and in China through government interference and taxes. Contrast those examples with, say, Hong Kong. The population is small, and the natural resources are severely limited, yet Hong Kong has consistently ranked among the richest regions in Asia. The reason: operating for many years under the British legal and economic system, the government actively encouraged entrepreneurship, which fueled the creation of wealth. Recognizing the potential of entrepreneurship, China has recently done more to relax

Many businesses work with nonprofits to boost their impact in the community.

kojoku/Shutterstock.com

factors of production Four fundamental elements—natural resources, capital, human resources, and entrepreneurship—that businesses need to achieve their objectives.

regulations and support free enterprise. The result has been tremendous growth, which may yet bring China into the ranks of the wealthier nations.[9]

1-5 THE BUSINESS ENVIRONMENT: THE CONTEXT FOR SUCCESS

No business operates in a vacuum. Outside factors play a vital role in determining whether each individual business succeeds or fails. Likewise, the broader **business environment** can make the critical difference in whether an overall economy thrives or disintegrates. The five key dimensions of the business environment are the economic environment, the competitive environment, the technological environment, the social environment, and the global environment, as shown in Exhibit 1.1.

1-5a The Economic Environment

In September 2008, the U.S. economy plunged into the worst fiscal crisis since the Great Depression. Huge, venerable financial institutions faced collapse, spurring unprecedented bailouts by the federal government and the Federal Reserve. By the end of the year, the stock market had lost more than a third of its value, and 11.1 million Americans were out of work. Housing prices fell precipitously, and foreclosure rates reached record levels. As fear swept through the banking industry, neither businesses nor individuals could borrow money to meet their needs. Economic turmoil in the United States spread quickly around the world, fueling a global economic crisis.

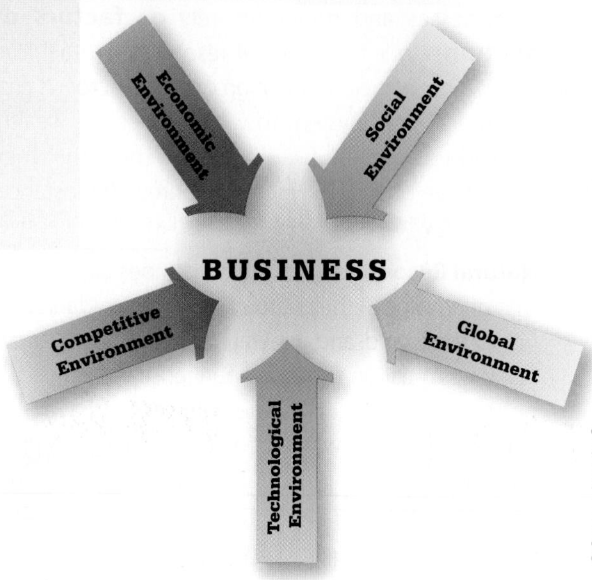

The U.S. economy continued to stagger through 2010 and 2011, with unemployment remaining stubbornly high, although signs of recovery began to emerge in late 2012, and certainly in 2013. The Federal Reserve—the U.S. central banking system—took unprecedented, proactive steps to encourage an economic turnaround. And President Barack Obama spearheaded passage of a massive economic stimulus package, designed not only to create jobs but also to build infrastructure—with a focus on renewable energy—to position the U.S. economy for stability and growth in the decades to come. (The price, of course, was more national debt, which will ultimately counterbalance some of the benefits.)

The government also takes active steps on an ongoing basis to reduce the risks of starting and running a business. The result: free enterprise and fair competition flourish. Despite the economic crisis, research suggests that most budding entrepreneurs still plan to launch their firms in the next three years. One government policy that supports business is the relatively low federal tax rate, both for individuals and businesses. A number of states—from Alabama to Nevada—make their local economies even more appealing by providing special tax deals to attract new firms. The federal government also runs entire

Exhibit 1.1
The Business Environment

Each dimension of the business environment affects both individual businesses and the economy in general.

© Cengage Learning®

> "A BANKER IS A FELLOW WHO LENDS YOU HIS UMBRELLA WHEN THE SUN IS SHINING, BUT WANTS IT BACK THE MINUTE IT BEGINS TO RAIN."
> —MARK TWAIN, AMERICAN AUTHOR

business environment The setting in which business operates. The five key components are: economic environment, competitive environment, technological environment, social environment, and global environment.

agencies that support business, such as the Small Business Administration. Other branches of the government, such as the Federal Trade Commission, actively promote fair competitive practices, which help give every enterprise a chance to succeed.

Another key element of the U.S. economic environment is legislation that supports enforceable contracts. For instance, if you contract a baker to supply your health food company with 10,000 pounds of raw kale chips at $1.00 per pound, that firm must comply or face legal consequences. The firm can't wait until a day before delivery and jack up the price to $10.00 per pound because you would almost certainly respond with a successful lawsuit. Many U.S. businesspeople take enforceable contracts for granted, but in a number of developing countries—which offer some of today's largest business opportunities—contracts are often not enforceable (at least not in day-to-day practice).

Corruption also affects the economic environment. A low level of corruption and bribery dramatically reduces the risks of running a business by ensuring that everyone plays by the same set of rules—rules that are clearly visible to every player. Fortunately, U.S. laws keep domestic corruption mostly—but not completely—at bay. Other ethical lapses, such as shady accounting, can also increase the cost of doing business for everyone involved. But in the wake of corporate ethical meltdowns such as Enron, the federal government has passed tough-minded new regulations to increase corporate accountability. If the new legislation effectively curbs illegal and unethical practices, every business will have a fair chance at success.

Upcoming chapters on economics and ethics will address these economic challenges and their significance in more depth. But bottom line, we have reason for cautious (some would say very cautious) optimism. The American economy has a proven track record of flexibility and resilience, which will surely help us navigate this crisis and uncover new opportunities.

1-5b The Competitive Environment

As global competition intensifies yet further, leading-edge companies have focused on customer satisfaction like never before. The goal: to develop long-term, mutually beneficial relationships with customers. Getting current customers to buy more of your product is a lot less expensive than convincing potential customers to try your product for the first time. And if you transform your current customers into loyal advocates—vocal promoters of your product or service—they'll get those new customers for you more effectively than any advertising or discount program. Companies such as Amazon, Coca-Cola, and

Northwestern Mutual life insurance lead their industries in customer satisfaction, which translates into higher profits even when the competition is tough.[10]

Customer satisfaction comes in large part from delivering unsurpassed value. The best measure of value is the size of the gap between product benefits and price. A product has value when its benefits to the customer are equal to or greater than the price that the customer pays. Keep in mind that the cheapest product doesn't necessarily represent the best value. If a 99-cent toy from Big Lots breaks in a day, customers may be willing to pay several dollars more for a similar toy from somewhere else. But if that 99-cent toy lasts all year, customers will be delighted by the value and will likely encourage their friends and family to shop at Big Lots. The key to value is quality, and virtually all successful firms offer top-quality products relative to their direct competitors.

A recent ranking study by consulting firm Interbrand highlights brands that use imagination and innovation to deliver value to their customers. Exhibit 1.2 shows the winners and the up-and-comers in the race to capture the hearts, minds, and dollars of consumers around the world.

EXHIBIT 1.2	2014 GLOBAL BRAND CHAMPIONS AND THE ONES TO WATCH, INTERBRAND	
Most Valuable	**Biggest Gainer**	**Percentage Growth**
Apple	Facebook	+86%
Google	Audi	+27%
Coca-Cola	Amazon	+25%
IBM	Nissan	+23%
Microsoft	Volkswagon	+23%
GE	Starbucks	+22%
Samsung	Apple	+21%
Toyota	Toyota	+20%
McDonald's	Ford	+18%
Mercedes-Benz	Hermes	+18%

Source: Best Global Brands 2014, Interbrand Website, http://www.bestglobalbrands.com/2014/ranking/, accessed February 5, 2015.

LEADING EDGE VERSUS BLEEDING EDGE

Speed-to-market—the rate at which a firm transforms concepts into actual products—can be another key source of competitive advantage. And the pace of change just keeps getting faster. In this tumultuous setting, companies that stay ahead of the pack often enjoy a distinct advantage. But keep in mind that there's a difference between leading edge and bleeding edge. Bleeding-edge firms launch products that fail because they're too far ahead of the market. During the late 1990s, for example, in the heart of the dot.com boom, WebVan, a grocery delivery service, launched to huge fanfare. But the firm went bankrupt just a few years later in 2001, partly because customers weren't yet ready to dump traditional grocery stores in favor of cyber-shopping. Leading-edge firms, on the other hand, offer products just as the market becomes ready to embrace them.[11]

Apple provides an excellent example of leading edge. You may be surprised to learn that Apple—which controls about 70%[12] of the digital music player market—did not offer the first MP3 player. Instead, it surveyed the existing market to help develop a new product, the iPod, which was far superior in terms of design and ease-of-use. But Apple didn't stop with one successful MP3 player. Racing to stay ahead, they soon introduced the colorful, more affordable iPod mini. And before sales reached their peak, they launched the iPod Nano, which essentially pulled the rug from under the blockbuster iPod mini just a few short months before the holiday selling season. Why? If they hadn't done it, someone else may well have done it instead. And Apple is almost maniacally focused on maintaining its competitive lead.[13]

1-5c The Workforce Advantage

Employees can contribute another key dimension to a firm's competitive edge. Recent research suggests that investing in worker satisfaction yields tangible, bottom-line results. The researchers evaluated the stock price of *Fortune* magazine's annual list of the "100 Best Companies to Work for in America" to the S&P 500, which reflects the overall market. From 1997 through 2012, cumulative stock market returns for the "100 Best" were up +366%, compared to +93% for the S&P 500. On an annualized basis, this translates to a return of about 10.6% per year for the "100 Best," and about 4.5% per year for the S&P 500 over the same time period. While the critical difference in performance most likely stemmed from employee satisfaction, other factors—such as excellent product and superb top management—likely *also* played a role in both employee satisfaction and strong stock performance.[14]

Finding and holding the best talent will likely become a crucial competitive issue in the next decade, as the baby boom generation begins to retire. The 500 largest U.S. companies anticipate losing about half of their senior managers over the next five to six years. Since January 1, 2011, approximately 10,000 baby boomers began to turn 65 (the traditional retirement age) every day, and the Pew Research Center anticipates that this trend will continue for 19 years. Replacing the skills and experience these workers bring to their jobs may be tough: baby boomers include about 77 million people, while the generation that follows includes only 46 million. Firms that cultivate human resources now will find themselves better able to compete as the market for top talent tightens.[15] However, job market contraction may

Google continues to be a powerhouse of innovation, in terms of both product development and employee benefits.

Simon Dawson/Bloomberg/Getty Images

speed-to-market The rate at which a new product moves from conception to commercialization.

10   PART ONE: The Business Environment

High-Level Worries

Even the masters of the universe get worried sometimes. And Dominic Barton, global managing director of elite management consulting firm McKinsey would know, since he talks regularly with CEOs of the world's largest firms, which are among his clients. In a recent interview, he reported that top CEOs around the globe seem to share four fairly consistent worries:

1. **Geopolitics:** The world simply isn't a stable place, and big shifts have a big impact on business.

2. **Technology:** Barton claims that technology is moving two to three times faster than management, which is both an opportunity and a huge potential threat.

3. **Cybersecurity:** CEOs have begun to realize just how vulnerable their systems really are.

4. **The Global Shift in Economic Power:** 2.2 billion new middle-class consumers will emerge in the next 15 years, many of them in Africa and Asia, and CEOs want to be ready.

But despite the prevailing concerns—perhaps even *because* of them—Barton believes there will always be room for savvy leadership. He says, "In a world that's more volatile, judgment is going to be a premium." So the more you learn and the better you prepare, the more value you will add to the constantly changing world of business.[16]

BARTON

Plus Utomi ekoei/AFP/Getty Images

---

not be an issue, because a growing number of baby boomers opt to either postpone retirement or continue working part-time during retirement, in the face of inadequate financial resources.

1-5d The Technological Environment

The broad definition of **business technology** includes any tools that businesses can use to become more efficient and effective. But more specifically, in today's world, business technology usually refers to computers, telecommunications, and other digital tools. Over the past few decades, the impact of digital technology on business has been utterly transformative. New industries have emerged, while others have disappeared. And some fields—such as travel, banking, and music—have changed dramatically. Even in categories with relatively unchanged products, companies have leveraged technology to streamline production and create new efficiencies. Examples include new processes such as computerized billing, digital animation, and robotic manufacturing. For fast-moving firms, the technological environment represents a rich source of competitive advantage, but it clearly can be

a major threat for companies that are slow to adopt or to integrate new approaches.

The creation of the **World Wide Web** has transformed not only business, but also people's lives. Anyone, anywhere, anytime can use the Web to send and receive images and data (as long as access is available). One result is the rise of **e-commerce** or online sales, which allow businesses to tap into a worldwide community of potential customers. In the wake of the global economic crisis, e-commerce has slowed from the breakneck 20%+ growth rates of the past five years, but even so, analysts predict that solid growth will continue. Business-to-business selling comprises the vast majority of total e-commerce sales (and an even larger share

Joachim Wendler/Shutterstock.com

> **business technology** Any tools—especially computers, telecommunications, and other digital products—that businesses can use to become more efficient and effective.
>
> **World Wide Web** The service that allows computer users to easily access and share information on the Internet in the form of text, graphics, video, apps, and animation.
>
> **e-commerce** Business transactions conducted online, typically via the Internet.

of the profits). A growing number of businesses have also connected their digital networks with suppliers and distributors to create a more seamless flow of goods and services.[17]

Alternative selling strategies thrive on the Internet, giving rise to a more individualized buying experience. If you've browsed seller reviews on eBay or received shopping recommendations from Amazon, you'll have a sense of how personal web marketing can feel. Online technology also allows leading-edge firms to offer customized products at prices that are comparable to standardized products. On the Burton website, for instance, customers can "custom build" professional quality "Custom X" snowboards, while sitting at home in their pajamas. Nike offers a similar service for NikeID shoes, clothing, and gear.

As technology continues to evolve at breakneck speed, the scope of change—both in everyday life and business operations—is almost unimaginable. In this environment, companies that welcome change and manage it well will clearly be the winners.

1-5e The Social Environment

The social environment embodies the values, attitudes, customs, and beliefs shared by groups of people. It also covers **demographics**, or the measurable characteristics of a population. Demographic factors include population size and density and specific traits such as age, gender, race, education, and income. Clearly, given all these influences, the social environment changes dramatically from country to country. And a nation as diverse as the United States features a number of different social environments. Rather than cover the full spectrum, this section will focus on the broad social trends that have the strongest impact on American business. Understanding the various dimensions of the social environment is crucial since successful businesses must offer goods and services that respond to it.

DIVERSITY While the American population has always included an array of different cultures, the United States has become more ethnically diverse in recent years. Caucasians continue to represent the largest chunk of the population at 63%, but according to the Director

demographics The measurable characteristics of a population. Demographic factors include population size and density, as well as specific traits such as age, gender, and race.

FAST FASHION— DOESN'T LOOK SO HOT LINING OUR LANDFILLS

Many college students love to find vintage clothing gems that set their style apart from everyone else's, especially for special events. Yet some of those same students also find their closets overflowing with "landfill fashion," trendy garments sold for rock bottom prices by fast fashion retailers, such as H&M and Zara. The garments aren't either purchased or designed to last. The average American throws away 68 pounds of clothing per year (perhaps because it's so cheap that if you get home and decide you don't want something, it's not worth going back to return it). Some people do by all means donate used clothing to charity, but fast fashion tends to be so cheaply made that no one wants to buy it. Instead, it gets recycled into industrial rags and insulation, or sits for years in landfills, since it's often made with synthetic, petroleum-based fibers that take decades to decompose. The products are so trendy, and the prices are so cheap, that sometimes it feels virtually impossible to leave a fast fashion retailer empty-handed, but next time you do, remember that you're scoring points not only for space in your closet, but also for space in the landfills.[18]

> INTERNET USAGE IN AFRICA IS GROWING MORE RAPIDLY THAN IN ANY OTHER REGION OF THE WORLD.
> —WORLD INTERNET STATISTICS

of the U.S. Census Bureau, "The next half century marks a turning point in continuing trends—the U.S. will become a plurality nation, where the non-Hispanic white population remains the largest single group, but no group is in the majority." This will probably happen in about 2043. The Hispanic and Asian populations will probably continue to grow faster than any other ethnic groups. By 2060, nearly one in three U.S. residents will be Hispanic, up from about one in six today. This will happen even though the overwhelming wave of immigration from Mexico to the United States has stalled and even begun to reverse in the past few years; nevertheless, among Mexican-born people worldwide, one in ten currently lives in the United States.[19] Exhibit 1.3 demonstrates the shifting population breakdown.

But the national statistics are somewhat misleading, since ethnic groups tend to cluster together. African Americans, for example, currently comprise about 37% of

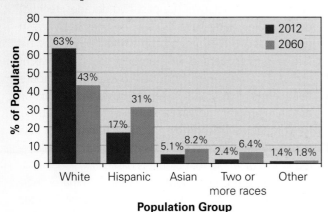

Exhibit 1.3

U.S. Population Estimates

Source: Population by Race and Hispanic Origin, U.S. Census Bureau, December 2012, http://www.census.gov/newsroom/releases/img/racehispanic_graph.jpg, accessed January 9, 2013.

the Mississippi population, Asians comprise about 39% of the Hawaii population, and Hispanics comprise about 47% of the New Mexico population.[20]

So what does this mean for business? Growing ethnic populations offer robust profit potential for firms that pursue them. For instance, a number of major brands such as Coca-Cola, General Mills, Ford, Nestlé, Purina, and Toyota have invested heavily in the Hispanic market over the past five years. Recognizing the potential of the Hispanic market, Universal Pictures launched *Dr. Seuss's The Lorax* with a high-profile multipronged campaign targeted to Hispanic consumers. *The Lorax* debuted at #1 at the box office; Hispanics accounted for 28% of those ticket sales, even though they accounted for only 17% of the population. Targeting an ethnic market can also yield remarkable results for products that cross over into mainstream culture. Music mogul and entrepreneur Russell Simmons, for example, initially targeted his music and clothing to the African American market, but his success quickly spilled over to mainstream culture, helping him build a hip-hop empire.[21]

Growing diversity also affects the workforce. A diverse staff—one that reflects an increasingly diverse marketplace—can yield a powerful competitive advantage in terms of both innovation and ability to reach a broad customer base. From global behemoths such as Coca-Cola and Verizon, to local corner stores, companies have taken proactive steps to hire and nurture people from a broad range of backgrounds. And that doesn't just reflect racial or ethnic roots. True diversity also includes differences in gender, age, religion, and nationality, among other areas. Leading-edge firms have also taken proactive steps to train their entire workforce to manage diversity for top performance.[22]

Effectively managing diversity should only become easier as time goes by. Multiple studies demonstrate that young American adults are the most tolerant age group, and they are moving in a more tolerant direction than earlier generations regarding racial differences, immigrants, and homosexuality. As this generation gathers influence and experience in the workforce, they are likely to leverage diversity in their organizations to hone their edge in a fiercely competitive marketplace.[23]

AGING POPULATION As life spans increase and birthrates decrease, the American population is rapidly aging. The U.S. Census Bureau projects that the nation's population age 65 and older will more than double between 2005 and 2060. By 2060, older Americans will represent just over one in five residents, up from one in seven today. Also, the number of working-age Americans will shrink from 63% to 57% of the population, dramatically increasing the number of people who are depending on each working American. And the United States isn't alone in this trend. The population is aging across the developed world, from Western Europe to Japan. China faces the same issue, magnified by its huge population. Demographers estimate that in the next 20 years the number of people in China over the age of 60 will double, leading to a nation where the retired will outnumber the entire population of Western Europe. There are currently six workers to every retiree, but China's one-child policy suggests that the number of people providing for the old will rapidly collapse.[24]

The rapidly aging population brings opportunities and threats for business. Companies in fields that cater to the elderly—such as healthcare, pharmaceuticals, travel, recreation, and financial management—will clearly boom. But creative companies in other fields will capitalize on the trend as well by reimagining their current products to serve older clients. Possibilities include books, movies—maybe even video games—with mature characters; low-impact fitness programs such as water aerobics; and cell phones and PDAs with more readable screens. Again, the potential payoff of age diversity is clear: companies with

> "WASTING RESOURCES COSTS THE EARTH—AND LOWERS YOUR COMPETITIVE EDGE."
>
> —PHIL HARDING, HEAD/ SUSTAINABLE BUSINESS TEAM

older employees are more likely to find innovative ways to reach the aging consumer market.

But the larger numbers of retired people also pose significant threats to overall business success. With a smaller labor pool, companies will need to compete even harder for top talent, driving up recruitment and payroll costs. As state and federal governments stretch to serve the aging population, taxes may increase, putting an additional burden on business. And as mid-career workers spend more on elder care, they may find themselves with less to spend on other goods and services, shrinking the size of the consumer market.

RISING WORKER EXPECTATIONS Workers of all ages continue to seek flexibility from their employers. Moreover, following massive corporate layoffs in the early 2000s, employees are much less apt to be loyal to their firms. A study released in 2013 showed that on average, employees in Fortune 500 firms have a median tenure of only 3.68 years. As young people today enter the workforce, they bring higher expectations for their employers in terms of salary, job responsibility, and flexibility—and less willingness to pay dues by working extra-long hours or doing a high volume of "grunt work." Smart firms are responding to the change in worker expectations by forging a new partnership with their employees. The goal is a greater level of mutual respect through open communication, information sharing, and training. And the not-so-hidden agenda, of course, is stronger long-term performance.[25]

ETHICS AND SOCIAL RESPONSIBILITY With high-profile ethical meltdowns dominating the headlines in the past few years, workers, consumers, and government alike have begun to hold businesses—and the people who run them—to a higher standard. Federal legislation, passed in the wake of the Enron fiasco, demands transparent financial management and more accountability from senior executives. And recognizing their key role in business success, a growing number of consumers and workers have begun to insist that companies play a proactive role in making their communities—and often the world community—better places. Sustainability—doing business today without harming the ability of future generations to meet their needs—has become a core issue in the marketplace, driving business policies, investment decisions, and consumer purchases on an unprecedented scale.[26]

free trade An international economic and political movement designed to help goods and services flow more freely across international boundaries.

General Agreement on Tariffs and Trade (GATT) An international trade agreement that has taken bold steps to lower tariffs and promote free trade worldwide.

1-5f The Global Environment

The U.S. economy operates within the context of the global environment, interacting continually with other economies. In fact, over the past two decades, technology and free trade have blurred the lines between individual economies around the world. Technology has forged unprecedented links among countries, making it cost effective—even efficient—to establish computer help centers in Mumbai to service customers in Boston, or to hire programmers in Buenos Aires to make websites for companies in Stockholm. Not surprisingly, jobs have migrated to the lowest bidder with the highest quality—regardless of where that bidder is based.

Often, the lowest bidder is based in China or India. Both economies are growing at breakneck speed, largely because they attract enormous foreign investment. Over the past couple of decades, China has been a magnet for manufacturing jobs because of the high population and low wages—about $3.50 per hour (including government-mandated benefits) versus about $19.50 in the United States—although the gap is rapidly closing due to double-digit annual wage inflation in China. And India has been especially adept at attracting high-tech jobs, in part because of their world-class, English-speaking university graduates who are willing to work for less than their counterparts around the globe.[27]

The migration of jobs relates closely to the global movement toward **free trade**. In 1995, a renegotiation of the **General Agreement on Tariffs and Trade (GATT)**—signed by 125 countries—took bold steps to lower tariffs (taxes on imports) and to reduce trade restrictions worldwide. The result: goods move more freely than

Global trade has forged unprecedented links among nations.

ever across international boundaries. Individual groups of countries have gone even further, creating blocs of nations with virtually unrestricted trade. Mexico, Canada, and the United States have laid the groundwork for a free-trade mega-market through the North American Free Trade Agreement (NAFTA), and 25 European countries have created a powerful free-trading bloc through the European Union, which has been weakened by a severe, ongoing financial crisis. The free-trade movement has lowered prices and increased quality across virtually every product category, as competition becomes truly global. We'll discuss these issues and their implications in more depth in Chapter 3.

A MULTI-PRONGED THREAT In the past decade alone, war, terrorism, disease, and natural disasters have taken a horrific toll in human lives across the globe. The economic toll has been devastating as well, affecting businesses around the world. The 9/11 terrorist attacks in New York and Washington, D.C., decimated the travel industry and led to multibillion-dollar government outlays for Homeland Security. In 2002, a terrorist bombing at an Indonesian nightclub killed nearly 200 people, destroying tourism on the holiday island of Bali. The 2003 deadly epidemic of the SARS flu dealt a powerful blow to the economies of Hong Kong, Beijing, and Toronto. And the Ebola outbreak of 2014 had a catastrophic impact on several impoverished African economies that could least afford the hit. Less than two years later, the Indian Ocean tsunami wiped out the fishing industry on long swaths of the Indian and Sri Lankan coastlines and crippled the booming Thai tourism industry. That same year, in 2005, Hurricane Katrina destroyed homes and businesses alike

> IN ASIA, THE AVERAGE PERSON'S LIVING STANDARDS ARE CURRENTLY SET TO RISE BY **10,000%** IN ONE LIFETIME!
> —*NEWSWEEK*

and brought the Gulf Coast oil industry to a virtual standstill. In 2012, Hurricane Sandy wreaked $50 billion of economic damage on the eastern seaboard states. And in 2013, Typhoon Haiyan decimated the Philippines. The wars in Afganistan and Iraq—while a boon to the defense industry—have dampened the economic potential of both areas. With nationalism on the rise, and growing religious and ethnic tensions around the world, the global economy may continue to suffer collateral damage.[28]

1-6 BUSINESS AND YOU: MAKING IT PERSONAL

Whatever your career choice—from video game developer, to real-estate agent, to web designer—business will affect your life. Both the broader economy and your own business skills will influence the level of your personal financial success. In light of these factors, making the right career choice can be a bit scary. But the good news is that experts advise graduating students to "Do what you love." This is a hardheaded strategy, not softhearted puffery. Following your passion makes dollars and sense in today's environment, which values less-routine abilities such as creativity, communication, and caring. These abilities tend to be more rewarding for most people than routine, programmable skills that computers can easily emulate. Following your passion doesn't guarantee a fat paycheck, but it does boost your chances of both financial and personal success.[29]

The BIG Picture

Business today is complex, global, and faster-moving than ever before. Looking forward, the rate of change seems likely to accelerate yet further. Although the full impact of the global economic crisis is still unclear, China and India seem poised to gain economic clout, raising worldwide competition to a whole new level. Technology will continue to change the business landscape. And a new focus on ethics and social responsibility will likely transform the role of business in society. This book will focus on the impact of change in every facet of business, from management to marketing to money, with an emphasis on how the elements of business relate to each other, and how business as a whole relates to you.

Careers in Business

Manager of New Media

Work with marketing team to determine what motivates and inspires consumers. Lead development and execution of digital marketing campaigns across a variety of platforms to build a deep, meaningful, and genuine relationship with consumers. Develop and manage interactive viral campaigns, integrate interactive media into the overall business strategy. According to Salary.com, the median base salary for social media marketing managers in 2014 was $105,151, although there was significant variation based on company, location, industry, experience, and benefits. Most new media positions require experience in the field and a four-year degree in either business or communication. Many also prefer a master's degree in business (an MBA). For more information on this career and other possible careers in business, check out Career Transitions.

STUDY TOOLS 1

LOCATED AT BACK OF THE TEXTBOOK

☐ Rip Out Chapter Review Card

LOCATED AT WWW.CENGAGE.COM/LOGIN

☐ Review key term flashcards and create your own using StudyBits

☐ Create and complete practice quizzes based off of your notes and StudyBits

☐ Complete Online activities such as Matching, Fill-in-the-Blank and Drag and Drop exercises

☐ View chapter highlight box content, including CEO Profiles, What Would You Do Cases and chapter videos

☐ Track your knowledge and understanding of key concepts in business using 4LTR Online

YOUR FEEDBACK MATTERS.

2 | Economics:
The Framework for Business

LEARNING OBJECTIVES
After studying this chapter, you will be able to:

2-1 Define economics and discuss the evolving global economic crisis

2-2 Analyze the impact of fiscal and monetary policy on the economy

2-3 Explain and evaluate the free market system and supply and demand

2-4 Explain and evaluate planned market systems

2-5 Describe the trend toward mixed market systems

2-6 Discuss key terms and tools to evaluate economic performance

Remember to visit
PAGE 37
for additional
STUDY TOOLS

2-1 ECONOMICS: NAVIGATING A CRISIS

In September 2008, the United States plunged into a deep economic crisis. The banking system hovered on the edge of collapse. Property values plummeted, and home foreclosure rates soared. Massive layoffs put more than a million Americans out of work. By the end of the year, the stock market had lost more than a third of its value, and financial turmoil in the United States had sparked sequential economic shocks from Europe, to South America, to Asia, and beyond. The outlook was grim.

economy A financial and social system of how resources flow through society, from production, to distribution, to consumption.

economics The study of the choices that people, companies, and governments make in allocating society's resources.

macroeconomics The study of a country's overall economic dynamics, such as the employment rate, the gross domestic product, and taxation policies.

How did this happen? Why? How could the economy get back on track?

Understanding these issues—and how the government, businesses, and individuals responded to them—requires understanding some basic definitions: The **economy** is essentially a financial and social system. It represents the flow of resources through society, from production, to distribution, to consumption. **Economics** is the study of the choices that people, companies, and governments make in allocating those resources. The field of economics falls into two core categories: macroeconomics and microeconomics. **Macroeconomics** is the study of a country's overall economic dynamics, such as the employment rate, the gross domestic product, and taxation policies. While

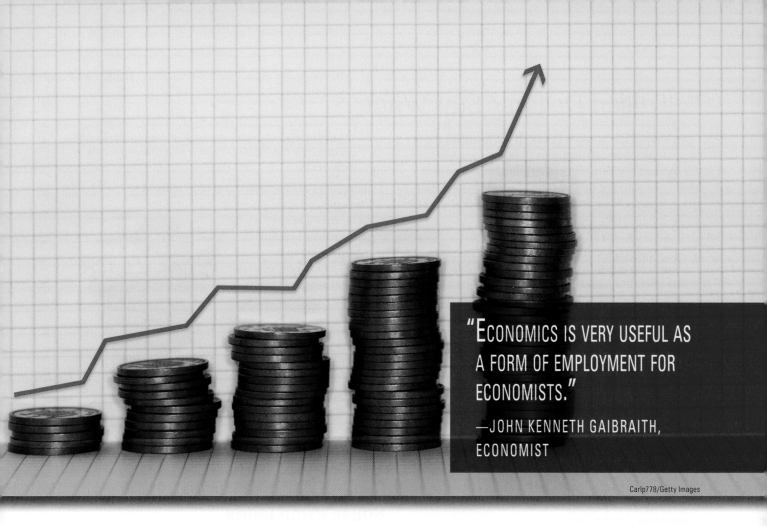

> "ECONOMICS IS VERY USEFUL AS A FORM OF EMPLOYMENT FOR ECONOMISTS."
>
> —JOHN KENNETH GAIBRAITH, ECONOMIST

macroeconomic issues may seem abstract, they directly affect your day-to-day life, influencing key variables such as what jobs will be available for you, how much cash you'll actually take home after taxes, or how much you can buy with that cash in any given month. **Microeconomics** focuses on smaller economic units such as individual consumers, families, and individual businesses. Both macroeconomics and microeconomics have played an integral role in the global economic crisis.

2-1a Global Economic Crisis: How Did This Happen?

The seeds of the crisis were planted more than a decade ago, during a time of prosperity. Through the last half of the 1990s, America enjoyed unprecedented growth. Unemployment was low, productivity was high, inflation was low, and the real standard of living for the average American rose significantly. The American economy grew by more than $2.4 trillion, a jump of nearly 33% in just five years. But the scene changed for the worse when the dot-com bubble burst in 2000, followed by the 9/11 terrorist attacks in 2001. As the stock market dropped and unemployment rose, economic experts

feared that the country was hovering on the brink of a full-blown recession.[1]

In an effort to avert recession by increasing the money supply and encouraging investment, the Federal Reserve—the nation's central bank—decreased interest rates from 6.5% in mid-2000 to 1.25% by the end of 2002. As a result, the economy was awash with money, but opportunities to invest yielded paltry returns. This is when *subprime mortgage loans* came into play. Most experts define subprime mortgages as loans to borrowers with low credit scores, high debt-to-income ratios, or other signs of a reduced ability to repay the money they borrow.

These subprime mortgage loans were attractive to borrowers and lenders alike. For the borrowers, getting a loan suddenly became a cinch, and for the first time ever, hundreds of thousands of people could afford homes. The lenders were all too willing to give them mortgage loans, sometimes with little or no documentation (such as proof of income), and sometimes with little or no money down. As demand for homes skyrocketed, prices continued to rise year after year. Borrowers took on adjustable-rate loans

microeconomics The study of smaller economic units such as individual consumers, families, and individual businesses.

A Trillion Dollars? Say What??

Between stimulating the economy and managing the federal debt, "a trillion dollars" is a figure you may have heard a lot lately. But getting your mind around what that actually means may be a little tricky, since it's just so much money. To understand the true magnitude of a trillion dollars, consider this:

- If you had started spending a million dollars a day—every day, without fail—at the start of the Roman Empire, you still wouldn't have spent a trillion dollars by 2012; in fact, you'd have more than $250 billion left over.

- One trillion dollars, laid end-to-end, would stretch farther than the distance from the earth to the sun. You could also wrap your chain of bills more than 12,000 times around the earth's equator.

- If you were to fly a jet at the speed of sound, spooling out a roll of dollar bills behind you, it would take you more than 14 years to release a trillion dollars. But your plane probably couldn't carry the roll, since it would weigh more than one million tons.

Turning the economy around may take even more than a trillion dollars, but make no mistake when you hear those numbers thrown around on the news—a trillion dollars is an awful lot of money![2]

Selensergen/iStockphoto.com

---

assuming that when their loans adjusted up—usually sharply up—they could simply refinance their now-more-valuable homes for a new low starter rate and maybe even pull out some cash.

Subprime loans were attractive to lenders because they provided a higher return than many other investments, and—given the growth in housing prices—they seemed relatively low risk. Banks and investment houses invented a range of stunningly complex financial instruments to slice up and resell the mortgages as specialized securities. Hedge funds swapped the new securities, convinced that they were virtually risk-free. With a lack of regulation—or any other government oversight—financial institutions did *not* maintain sufficient reserves in case those mortgage-backed funds lost value.

And they did indeed lose value. In 2006, housing prices peaked, and in the months that followed, prices began falling precipitously (see Exhibit 2.1), dropping nearly 35% from the market peak in 2006 through the market trough in 2009. Increasing numbers of subprime borrowers found themselves "upside down"—they owed their lenders more than the value of their homes. Once this happened, they couldn't refinance to lower their payments. Foreclosure rates climbed at an increasing pace. RealtyTrac, a leading online marketplace for foreclosure properties, reported that foreclosure rates were 33% higher in 2010 than they were in all of 2009. In 2011, the foreclosure rate dropped to the lowest level since 2007, when the recession began. And by January 2014, the inventory

Exhibit 2.1
House Price Index

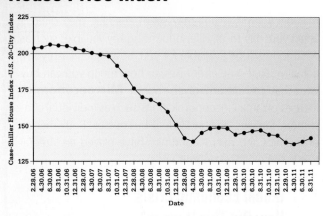

Source: Housing's Rise and Fall in 20 Cities, December 27, 2011, *The New York Times* website, http://www.nytimes.com/interactive/2011/05/31/business/economy/case-shiller-index.html#city/IND20, accessed January 25, 2012.

> "A BILLION HERE AND A BILLION THERE, AND PRETTY SOON YOU'RE TALKING REAL MONEY."
> —U.S. SENATOR EVERETT DIRKSEN

of foreclosed homes had experienced 16 consecutive months of year-to-year double-digit declines, signaling that the fragile economic recovery had finally taken hold.[3]

As mortgage values dropped, financial institutions began to feel the pressure—especially firms such as Bear Stearns that specialized in trading mortgage-backed securities, and firms such as Washington Mutual that focused on selling subprime mortgages. When financial institutions actually began to face collapse, a wave of fear washed over the entire banking industry. Banks became unwilling to lend money to each other or to clients, which meant that funds were not available for businesses to finance either day-to-day operations or longer-term growth. Company after company—from General Motors, to Yahoo!, to American Express, to countless small employers—began to announce layoffs. The December 2008 unemployment rate hit 7.2%. About 2.6 million Americans lost their jobs in 2008, making 2008 the worst year for jobs since 1945. And the unemployment rate continued to rise, hitting 9.3% in 2009 and 9.6% in 2010, leading to total Great Recession job losses of nearly 8 million, many of which will never come back as the economy continues to change and old skills become obsolete.[4] The national average unemployment rate began to drop in late 2011 and continued to trend down throughout 2014, another sign that the economic recovery has taken hold.

2-1b Moving in a Better Direction

Although the benefits were not immediately obvious in the face of a downward trend, the federal government and the Federal Reserve—known as "the Fed"—intervened in the economy at an unprecedented level to prevent total financial disaster. In March 2008, the Fed staved off bankruptcy at Bear Stearns. In early September 2008, the U.S. Department of the Treasury seized Fannie Mae and Freddie Mac, which owned about half of the U.S. mortgage market. A week later, the Fed bailed out tottering global insurance giant AIG with an $85 billion loan. But the bleeding continued.

The negative spiral spurred Congress to pass a controversial $700 billion economic bailout plan in early October 2008, called TARP (the Troubled Assets Relief Program). By the end of the year, the Treasury had spent the first half of that money investing in banks, although early results were imperceptible for the economy. Just as the Treasury began to release funds to the banks, GM and Chrysler, two of the Big Three U.S. automakers, announced they also desperately needed a bailout. Both firms suggested that bankruptcy was imminent without government assistance. (Ford, the other member of the Big Three, also admitted to financial problems but claimed that it was not in the dire straits faced by its domestic competitors.) Facing the loss of more than 2.5 million jobs related to the auto industry, the Treasury agreed to spend a portion of what remained of the $700 billion in a partial auto industry bailout.[5] Although much of the public railed against the expensive government bailout program, by 2010 it appeared likely that TARP could end up costing taxpayers far less than anticipated, or even nothing, as insurance companies and banks began to break even, or in many cases earn profits, and pay back their government loans.[6]

As the new administration began, President Obama proposed, and Congress passed, an $825 billion economic stimulus package called the American Recovery and Reinvestment Act, designed to turn the economy around over the next two years. The plan included cutting taxes, building infrastructure, and investing $150 billion in green energy. By late 2011, the economy had begun to turn around at a very slow pace, although unemployment remained high, and economists predicted that the jobless rate would remain painfully high through the middle of the decade.[7]

All of these moves by the federal government and the Federal Reserve are part of fiscal and monetary policy.

2-2 MANAGING THE ECONOMY THROUGH FISCAL AND MONETARY POLICY

While the free market drives performance in the American economy, the federal government and the Federal Reserve can help *shape* performance. During the recent crisis, both the government and the Fed have taken proactive—some say heavy-handed—roles to mitigate this economic contraction. The overarching goal is controlled, sustained growth, and both fiscal and monetary policy can help achieve this objective.

> "GOVERNMENT DOES NOT SOLVE PROBLEMS; IT SUBSIDIZES THEM."
> —U.S. PRESIDENT RONALD REAGAN

2-2a Fiscal Policy

Fiscal policy refers to government efforts to influence the economy through taxation and spending

> **fiscal policy** Government efforts to influence the economy through taxation and spending.

decisions that are designed to encourage growth, boost employment, and curb inflation. Clearly, fiscal strategies are closely tied to political philosophy. But regardless of politics, most economists agree that lower taxes can boost the economy by leaving more money in people's pockets for them to spend or invest. Most also agree that government spending can boost the economy in the short term by providing jobs, such as mail carrier, bridge repairer, or park ranger; and in the long term by investing in critical public assets, such as a national renewable energy grid. Done well, both taxation and spending can offer economic benefits. The tricky part is finding the right balance between the two approaches. As American economist Henry Hazlitt pointed out, it's important to keep in mind that "Either immediately or ultimately, every dollar of government spending must be raised through a dollar of taxation; once we look at the matter in this way, the supposed miracles of government spending will appear in another light."

2-2b Debt Ceiling/Fiscal Cliff

In mid-2011, the U.S. economy shuddered again as the news headlines screamed with dire warnings about a national or even international economic meltdown when we hit the federal *debt ceiling*. What did this mean? The debt ceiling is the maximum amount Congress lets the government borrow. In theory, this is meant to limit the amount that the government can borrow, but in practice, voting on the debt ceiling happens separately from voting on taxes and spending, so the debt ceiling ends up being mostly about whether or not the federal government can pay for debts that it has already incurred. Typically, debt ceiling hikes are fairly routine; in fact, Congress has raised the debt ceiling 74 times since 1962, and 10 times since 2001, all with little or no notice. But as federal debt began to nudge the ceiling in 2011, it garnered unprecedented political and journalistic attention because various political groups saw the issue as an opportunity to further their political agenda. Those who wanted to raise the debt ceiling portrayed others as irresponsible buffoons who were willing to shut down the government simply to make

budget surplus Overage that occurs when revenue is higher than expenses over a given period of time.

budget deficit Shortfall that occurs when expenses are higher than revenue over a given period of time.

federal debt The sum of all the money that the federal government has borrowed over the years and not yet repaid.

a point without any real long-term change in spending. Those who did not want to raise the debt ceiling argued that the others are spendthrift bureaucrats who must learn to live within their means like the Americans who elected them.

After weeks of high-profile wrangling, Congress finally agreed to raise the debt ceiling, which temporarily averted a shutdown crisis, but the deal they reached to do so created the fiscal cliff. The *fiscal cliff* was a package of draconian across-the-board spending cuts and sharp tax hikes scheduled to hit at the same time that could dramatically decrease the U.S. budget deficit. Going over the *fiscal cliff* could potentially cripple the U.S. economy, and possibly even cause the United States to default on some of its debt, which could send world markets into a tailspin. But once again, Congress could not reach a reasonable long-term agreement, so they simply passed last-minute legislation that pushed the really tough tax and spending decisions farther down the road. The federal government actually did shut down for 16 days in October 2013 after much Congressional squabbling failed to produce a budget agreement. The government reopened with passage of another temporary agreement that again delayed the tough fiscal choices.[8]

Every year, the government must create a budget, or a financial plan, that outlines expected revenue from taxes and fees, and expected spending. If revenue is higher than spending, the government incurs a **budget surplus** (rare in recent years, but usually quite welcome!). If spending is higher than revenue, the government incurs a **budget deficit** and must borrow money to cover the shortfall. The sum of all the money borrowed over the years and not yet repaid is the total **federal debt**. Exhibit 2.2 shows key sources of revenue and key expenses for the federal government in 2011. Note that spending significantly outstrips receipts, creating a one-year budget deficit of more than a trillion dollars. Clearly, any additional spending without corresponding tax increases could dramatically increase the shortfall.

As of January, 2014, the total U.S. federal debt stood at more than $18 trillion, a staggering $56,660.91 for every U.S. citizen (see an online national debt clock at http://brillig.com/debt_clock/ for the latest figures).

The debt has only grown bigger every year since 1957, and the pace of growth will likely increase further in the wake of the economic crisis. This matters to each taxpayer because as the government repays the debt—not

Talaj/iStockphoto.com

Exhibit 2.2
Federal Government Revenue and Expenses

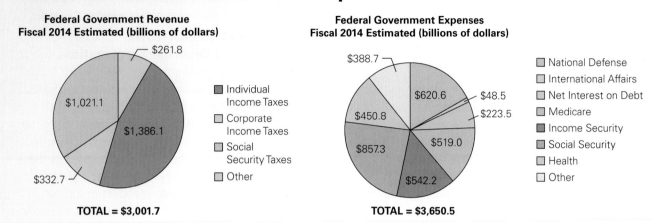

Federal Government Revenue
Fiscal 2014 Estimated (billions of dollars)

$261.8
$1,021.1
$1,386.1
$332.7

- ■ Individual Income Taxes
- □ Corporate Income Taxes
- ■ Social Security Taxes
- □ Other

TOTAL = $3,001.7

Federal Government Expenses
Fiscal 2014 Estimated (billions of dollars)

$388.7
$620.6
$48.5
$450.8
$223.5
$857.3
$519.0
$542.2

- ■ National Defense
- □ International Affairs
- ■ Net Interest on Debt
- □ Medicare
- ■ Income Security
- ■ Social Security
- □ Health
- □ Other

TOTAL = $3,650.5

Economic Report of the president, 2014, Table B-21. Federal receipts and outlays, by major category, and surplus or deficit, fiscal years 1947-2015, http://www.gpo.gov/fdsys/pkg/ERP-2014/html/ERP-2014-table21.htm, accessed June 2015.

to mention paying the skyrocketing interest to finance this debt—less and less money will be available for other uses; services may be eliminated (e.g., student loans, veterans' benefits, housing subsidies), or taxes will soar, or perhaps even both.

2-2c Monetary Policy

Monetary policy refers to actions that shape the economy by influencing interest rates and the supply of money. The Federal Reserve—essentially the central bank of the United States—manages U.S. monetary policy. For the first time in its history, the Fed has also taken an activist role in bailing out and propping up shaky financial firms during the economic crisis. Other Fed functions include banking services for member banks and the federal government.

The Fed is headed by a seven-member Board of Governors. The president appoints each member of the Board to serve a single 14-year term—though a member can also complete a former member's unexpired term and still be appointed to a full term of his or her own. These terms are staggered, with one expiring every two years, so that no single president can appoint all of the members. This structure helps ensure that the Fed can act independently of political pressure.

In addition to setting monetary policy, the Board of Governors oversees the operation of the 12 Federal Reserve Banks that carry out Fed policies and perform banking services for **commercial banks** in their districts.

Interestingly, the federal government does not own these Federal Reserve Banks. Instead, they're owned by the member commercial banks in their individual districts.

The president appoints one of the seven members of the Board of Governors to serve as its chair—a position so powerful that many consider him or her the second most powerful person on earth. For nearly 19 years, the chair was Alan Greenspan. When Greenspan retired in early 2006, President Bush appointed economist Ben Bernanke to the chair role. Bernanke led the Fed's proactive efforts to turn the ailing economy around. In early 2014, the Senate confirmed economist Janet Yellen as new chair of the Fed. Yellen is the first female chair, and in light of her track record, most experts anticipate that she will continue to focus primarily on fighting unemployment by encouraging economic expansion.

The core purpose of the Fed is to influence the size of the **money supply**—or the total amount of money within the overall economy. Clearly, you know what money is. But the formal definition of **money** is anything generally accepted as a medium of exchange, a measure of value, or a means of payment. The two most

monetary policy Federal Reserve decisions that shape the economy by influencing interest rates and the supply of money.

commercial banks Privately owned financial institutions that accept demand deposits and make loans and provide other services for the public.

money supply The total amount of money within the overall economy.

money Anything generally accepted as a medium of exchange, a measure of value, or a means of payment.

commonly used definitions of the money supply are M1 and M2:

- **M1:** All currency—paper bills and metal coins—plus checking accounts and traveler's checks.

- **M2:** All of M1 plus most savings accounts, money market accounts, and certificates of deposit (low-risk savings vehicles with a fixed term, typically less than one year).

By mid-2014, the M1 money supply totaled about $2.84 billion, and the M2 version of the money supply totaled about $11.6 billion. In practice, the term "money supply" most often refers to M2. (Note that credit cards are not part of the money supply, although they do have an unmistakable impact on the flow of money through the economy.)[9]

> **M1 money supply** Includes all currency plus checking accounts and traveler's checks.
>
> **M2 money supply** Includes all of M1 money supply plus most savings accounts, money market accounts, and certificates of deposit.
>
> **open market operations** The Federal Reserve function of buying and selling government securities, which include treasury bonds, notes, and bills.

When the economy contracts, the Fed typically increases the money supply. If more money is available, interest rates usually drop, encouraging businesses to expand and consumers to spend. But when prices begin to rise, the Fed attempts to reduce the money supply. Ideally, if less money is available, interest rates will rise. This will reduce spending, which should bring inflation under control. Specifically, the Fed uses three key tools to expand and contract the money supply: open market operations, discount rate changes, and reserve requirement changes.

OPEN MARKET OPERATIONS This is the Fed's most frequently used tool. **Open market operations** involve buying and selling government securities, which include treasury bonds, notes, and bills. These securities are the IOUs the government issues to finance its deficit spending.

How do open market operations work? When the economy is weak, the Fed *buys* government securities on the open market. When the Fed pays the sellers of these securities, money previously held by the Fed is put into circulation. This directly stimulates spending. In addition, any of the additional funds supplied by the Fed that are deposited in banks will allow banks to make more loans, making credit more readily available. This encourages even more spending and further stimulates the economy.

When inflation is a concern, the Fed *sells* securities. Buyers of the securities write checks to the Fed to pay for securities they bought, and the Fed withdraws these funds from banks. With fewer funds, banks must cut back on the loans they make, credit becomes tighter, and the money supply shrinks. This reduces spending and cools off the inflationary pressures in the economy.

Open market operations are set by the aptly named Federal Open Market Committee, which consists of the

Are Bad Roads Driving you Around the Bend?

Few other nations in the world are as dependent on their cars as the United States, yet across the United States, many roads are downright shoddy. One reason is that public spending on roads got stuck in a pothole after the interstate highway system was built in the 1950s and 1960s. It's not just roads—other elements of our infrastructure are suffering, too. According to the Federal Highway Administration, there are more deficient bridges in the 102 largest U.S. metropolitan regions than there are McDonald's restaurants in the entire country. And anyone who has traveled by air lately knows that everything about America's major airports is too small. Frighteningly, according to *Economist* magazine, most air traffic control systems are less advanced than the technology found in the average smartphone. The solution to these infrastructure shortfalls is unclear. Some experts maintain that the problems are so big that big government must be involved. Others have argued that the best solutions will come from local governments raising local taxes to solve local problems. And many believe that now is the time for private firms to step up and join with government to solve civic infrastructure issues in mutually beneficial partnerships. One way or the other let's hope that the problem gets fixed before an infrastructure disaster costs lives and forces action.[10]

Patti Sapone/The Star-Ledger/The Image Works

Looking to Multiply Your Money? Look No Further Than Your Local Bank!

Everyone knows that banks help people save money, but most people don't realize that banks actually create money. While the process is complex, a simplified example illustrates the point. Say you deposit $5,000 in the bank. How much money do you have? Obviously, $5,000. Now imagine that your neighbor Anne goes to the bank for a loan. In line with Federal Reserve requirements, the bank must hold onto about 10% of its funds, so it loans Anne $4,500. She uses the money to buy a used car from your neighbor Jake, who deposits the $4,500 in the bank. How much money does Jake have? Clearly, $4,500. How much money do you have? Still, $5,000. Thanks to the banking system, our "money supply" has increased from $5,000 to $9,500. Multiply this phenomenon times millions of banking transactions, and you can see why cold, hard cash accounts for only about 10% of the total U.S. M2 money supply. But what happens if everyone goes to the bank at once to withdraw their money? The banking system would clearly collapse. And in fact, in 1930 and 1931, a run on the banks caused wave after wave of devastating bank failures. Panicked customers lost all their savings, ushering in the worst years of the Great Depression. To restore public confidence in the banking system, in 1933 Congress established the **Federal Deposit Insurance Corporation (FDIC)**. The FDIC insures deposits in banks and thrift institutions for up to $100,000 per customer, per bank. In the wake of the banking crisis, the FDIC temporarily increased its coverage to $250,000 per depositor at the end of 2008. Since the FDIC began operations on January 1, 1934, no depositor has lost a single cent of insured funds as a result of a bank failure.

Keith Brofsky/Photodisc/Getty Images

seven members of the Board of Governors and five of the twelve presidents of the Federal Reserve district banks. Each year, the Federal Open Market Committee holds eight regularly scheduled meetings to make decisions about open market operations, although they do hold additional meetings when the need arises. Both businesses and markets closely watch Open Market Committee rate setting and outlook statements in order to guide decision making.

DISCOUNT RATE CHANGES Just as you can borrow money from your bank, your bank can borrow funds from the Fed. And, just as you must pay interest on your loan, your bank must pay interest on loans from the Fed. The **discount rate** is the interest rate the Fed charges on its loans to commercial banks. When the Fed reduces the discount rate, banks can obtain funds at a lower cost and use these funds to make more loans to their own customers. With the cost of acquiring funds from the Fed lower, interest rates on bank loans also tend to fall. The result: businesses and individuals are more likely to borrow money and spend it, which stimulates the economy. Clearly, the Fed is most likely to reduce the discount rate during recessions. In fact, during the early months of the financial crisis, the Fed cut the rate to less than 1%. But in response to inflation—usually a sign of a rapidly expanding economy—the Fed usually increases the discount rate. In response, banks raise the interest rates they charge their customers. Fewer businesses and individuals are willing to take loans, which ultimately slows down the economy and reduces inflation.[11]

RESERVE REQUIREMENT CHANGES The Fed requires that all of its member banks hold funds called "reserves," equal to a stated percentage of the deposits held by their customers. This percentage is called the **reserve requirement** (or required reserve ratio). The reserve requirement helps protect depositors who may want to withdraw their money without notice. Currently, the reserve requirement stands at about 10%,

Federal Deposit Insurance Corporation (FDIC) A federal agency that insures deposits in banks and thrift institutions for up to $250,000 per customer, per bank.

discount rate The rate of interest that the Federal Reserve charges when it loans funds to banks.

reserve requirement A rule set by the Fed, which specifies the minimum amount of reserves (or funds) a bank must hold, expressed as a percentage of the bank's deposits.

depending on the size and type of a bank's deposits. If the Fed increases the reserve requirement, banks must hold more funds, meaning they will have fewer funds available to make loans. This makes credit tighter and causes interest rates to rise. If the Fed decreases the reserve requirement, some of the funds that banks were required to hold become available for loans. This increases the availability of credit and causes interest rates to drop. Since changes in the reserve requirement can have a dramatic impact on both the economy and the financial health of individual banks, the Fed uses this tool quite infrequently.

OTHER FED FUNCTIONS In addition to monetary policy, the Fed has several other core functions, including regulating financial institutions and providing banking services both for the government and for banks. In its role as a regulator, the Fed sets and enforces rules of conduct for banks and oversees mergers and acquisitions to ensure fairness and compliance with government policy. The Fed will likely become even more proactive regarding regulation in the wake of the financial crisis. In its role as a banker for banks, the Fed coordinates the check-clearing process for checks on behalf of any banks that are willing to pay its fees. And as the government's bank, the Fed maintains the federal government's checking account and keeps the U.S. currency supply in good condition.

> THE U.S. ECONOMY IS 70% BASED ON CONSUMER SPENDING.
>
> —*TIME* MAGAZINE

determine how to distribute resources among their members. An **economic system** is a structure for allocating limited resources. Over time and around the globe, nations have instituted different economic systems. But a careful analysis suggests that no system is perfect, which may explain why there isn't one standard approach. The next sections of this chapter examine each basic type of economic system and explore the trend toward mixed economies.

The economic system of the United States is called **capitalism**, also known as a "private enterprise system" or a "free market system." Brought to prominence by Adam Smith in the 1700s, capitalism is based on private ownership, economic freedom, and fair competition. One core capitalist principle is the paramount importance of individuals, innovation, and hard work. In a capitalist economy, individuals, businesses, or nonprofit organizations privately own the vast majority of enterprises (with only a small fraction owned by the government). These private-sector businesses are free to make their own choices regarding everything from what they will produce, to how much they will charge, to whom they will hire and fire. Correspondingly, individuals are free to choose what they will buy, how much they are willing to pay, and where they will work.

To thrive in a free enterprise system, companies must offer value to their customers—otherwise, their customers will choose to go elsewhere. Businesses must also offer value to their employees and suppliers in order to attract top-quality talent and supplies. As companies compete to attract the best resources and offer the best values, quality goes up, prices remain reasonable, and choices proliferate, raising the standard of living in the economy as a whole.

2-3 CAPITALISM: THE FREE MARKET SYSTEM

It's a simple fact—more clear now than ever before—no one can get everything they want all of the time. We live in a world of finite resources, which means that societies must

economic system A structure for allocating limited resources.

capitalism An economic system—also known as the private enterprise or free market system—based on private ownership, economic freedom, and fair competition.

Adam Smith (1723–1790) has often been called the "father of modern economics."

2-3a The Fundamental Rights of Capitalism

For capitalism to succeed, the system must ensure some fundamental rights—or freedoms—to all of the people who live within the economy.

Georgios Kollidas/Shutterstock.com

- *The right to own a business and keep after-tax profits:* Remember that capitalism doesn't guarantee that anyone will actually *earn* profits. Nor does it promise that there won't be taxes. But if you do earn profits, you get to keep your after-tax income and spend it however you see fit (within the limits of the law, of course). This right acts as a powerful motivator for business owners in a capitalist economy; the lower the tax rate, the higher the motivation. The U.S. government strives to maintain low tax rates to preserve the after-tax profit incentive that plays such a pivotal role in the free enterprise system.

- *The right to private property:* This means that individuals and private businesses can buy, sell, and use property—which includes land, machines, and buildings—in any way that makes sense to them. This right also includes the right to will property to family members. The only exceptions to private property rights are minimal government restrictions designed to protect the greater good. You can't, for instance, use your home or business to produce cocaine, abuse children, or spew toxic smoke into the air.

- *The right to free choice:* Capitalism relies on economic freedom. People and businesses must be free to buy (or not buy) according to their wishes. They must be free to choose where to work (or not work) and where to live (or not live). Freedom of choice directly feeds competition, creating a compelling incentive for business owners to offer the best goods and services at the lowest prices. U.S. government trade policies boost freedom of choice by encouraging a wide array of both domestic and foreign producers to compete freely for our dollars.

- *The right to fair competition:* A capitalist system depends on fair competition among businesses to drive higher quality, lower prices, and more choices. Capitalism can't achieve its potential if unfair practices—such as deceptive advertising, predatory pricing, and broken contracts—mar the free competitive environment. The government's role is to create a level playing field by establishing regulations and monitoring the competition to ensure compliance.

2-3b Four Degrees of Competition

Although competition is essential for the free market system to function, not all competition works the same. Different industries experience different degrees of competition, ranging from pure competition to monopolies.

Ira Berger/Alamy

- **Pure competition** is a market structure with many competitors selling virtually identical products. Since customers can't (or won't) distinguish one product from another, no single producer has any control over the price. And new producers can easily enter and leave purely competitive markets. In today's U.S. economy, examples of pure competition have virtually disappeared. Agriculture probably comes closest— corn is basically corn, for example—but with the dramatic growth of huge corporate farms and the success of major agricultural cooperatives such as Sunkist and Sun-Maid, the number of competitors in agriculture has dwindled, and new farmers have trouble entering the market. Not only that, segments of the agriculture market—such as organic farms and hormone-free dairies—have emerged with hit products that command much higher prices than the competition.

- **Monopolistic competition** is a market structure with many competitors selling differentiated products. (Caution! Monopolistic competition is quite different from a *monopoly*, which we will cover shortly.) Producers have some control over the price of their wares, depending on the value that they offer their customers. And new producers can fairly easily enter categories marked by monopolistic competition. In fact, in monopolistic competition, a successful product

pure competition A market structure with many competitors selling virtually identical products. Barriers to entry are quite low.

monopolistic competition A market structure with many competitors selling differentiated products. Barriers to entry are low.

usually attracts new suppliers quite quickly. Examples of monopolistic competition include the clothing industry and the restaurant business.

Think about the clothing business, for a moment, in local terms. How many firms do you know that sell tee shirts? You could probably think of at least 50 without too much trouble. And the quality and price are all over the board: designer tee shirts can sell for well over $100, but plenty of options go for less than $10. How hard would it be to start your own tee shirt business? Probably not hard at all. In fact, chances are strong that you know at least one person who sells tee shirts on the side. In terms of product and price variation, number of firms, and ease of entry, the tee shirt business clearly demonstrates the characteristics of monopolistic competition.

■ **Oligopoly** is a market structure with only a handful of competitors selling products that can be similar or different. The retail gasoline business and the car manufacturing industry, for instance, are both oligopolies, even though gas stations offer very similar products, and car companies offer quite different models and features. Other examples of oligopoly include the soft drink industry, the computer business, and network television. Breaking into a market characterized by oligopoly can be tough because it typically requires a huge upfront investment.

You could start making tee shirts in your kitchen, for instance, but you'd need a pretty expensive facility to start manufacturing cars. Oligopolies typically avoid intense price competition, since they have nothing to gain—every competitor simply makes less money. When price wars do flare up, the results can be devastating for entire industries.

Comstock Images/Jupiter Images

oligopoly A market structure with only a handful of competitors selling products that can be similar or different. Barriers to entry are typically high.

monopoly A market structure with one producer completely dominating the industry, leaving no room for any significant competitors. Barriers to entry tend to be virtually insurmountable.

natural monopoly A market structure with one company as the supplier of a product because the nature of that product makes a single supplier more efficient than multiple, competing ones. Most natural monopolies are government sanctioned and regulated.

■ **Monopoly** is a market structure with just a single producer completely dominating the industry, leaving no room for any significant competitors. Monopolies usually aren't good for anyone but the company that has control since without competition there isn't any incentive to hold down prices or increase quality and choices. Because monopolies can harm the economy, most are illegal according to federal legislation, such as the Sherman Antitrust Act of 1890 and the Clayton Antitrust Act of 1914. Microsoft is the latest example of an industry giant that ran afoul of antimonopoly laws due to its position and policies in the software business. Even though Microsoft is not an actual monopoly, it was convicted of "monopolistic practices" that undermined fair competition.

However, in a few instances, the government not only allows monopolies but actually encourages them. This usually occurs when it would be too inefficient for each competitor to build its own infrastructure to serve the public. A **natural monopoly** arises. Public utilities offer a clear example. Would it really make sense for even a handful of competitors to pipe neighborhoods separately for water? Clearly, that's not practical. Just imagine the chaos! Instead, the government has granted exclusive rights—or monopolies—to individual companies for limited geographic areas and then regulated them (with mixed results) to ensure that they don't abuse the privilege. In addition to natural monopolies, the government grants patents and copyrights, which create artificial monopoly situations (at least temporarily) to encourage innovation.

2-3c Supply and Demand: Fundamental Principles of a Free Market System

In a free market system, the continual interplay between buyers and sellers determines the selection of products and prices available in the economy. If a business makes something that few people actually want, sales will be low, and the firm will typically yank the product from the market. Similarly, if the price of a product is too high, low sales will dictate a price cut. But if a new good or service becomes a hit, you can bet that similar offerings from other firms will pop up almost immediately (unless barriers—such as government-granted patents—prevent new entrants). The concepts of supply and demand explain how the dynamic interaction between buyers and sellers directly affects the range of products and prices in the free market.

SUPPLY **Supply** refers to the quantity of products that producers are willing to offer for sale at different market prices. Since businesses seek to make as much profit as possible, they are likely to produce more of a product that commands a higher market price and less of a product that commands a lower price. Think about it in terms of pizza. Assume it costs a local restaurant about $5 to make a pizza. If the market price for pizza hits, say, $20, you can bet that restaurant will start cranking out pizza. But if the price drops to $6, the restaurant has much less incentive to focus on pizza and will probably invest its limited resources in cooking other, more pricy, dishes.

The relationship between price and quantity from a supplier standpoint can be shown on a graph called the **supply curve**. The supply curve maps quantity on the x-axis (or horizontal axis) and price on the y-axis (or vertical axis). In most categories, as the price rises, the quantity produced rises correspondingly, yielding a graph that curves up as it moves to the right. Exhibit 2.3 shows a possible supply curve for pizza.

DEMAND **Demand** refers to the quantity of products that consumers are willing to buy at different market prices. Since consumers generally seek to get the products they need (or want) at the lowest possible prices, they tend to buy more products with lower prices and fewer products with higher prices. Pizza and tacos, for

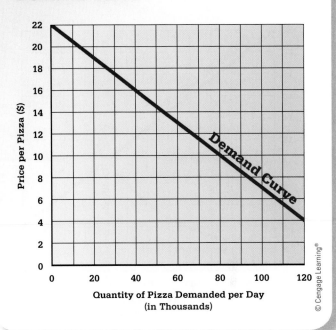

Exhibit 2.4
Demand Curve

instance, are both popular meals. But if pizza costs a lot less than tacos, most people will get pizza more often than tacos. Likewise, if the price of pizza were out of hand, people would probably order tacos (or some other option) more often, reserving their pizza-eating for special occasions.

The relationship between price and quantity from a demand standpoint can be shown on a graph called the **demand curve**. Like the supply curve, the demand curve maps quantity on the x-axis and price on the y-axis. But different from the supply curve, the demand curve for most goods and services slopes downward as it moves to the right, since the quantity demanded tends to drop as prices rise. Exhibit 2.4 shows how a demand curve for pizza could look.

EQUILIBRIUM PRICE It's important to remember that supply and demand don't operate in a vacuum. The constant interaction between the two forces helps determine the market price in any given category. In theory, market prices

supply The quantity of products that producers are willing to offer for sale at different market prices.

supply curve The graphed relationship between price and quantity from a supplier standpoint.

demand The quantity of products that consumers are willing to buy at different market prices.

demand curve The graphed relationship between price and quantity from a customer demand standpoint.

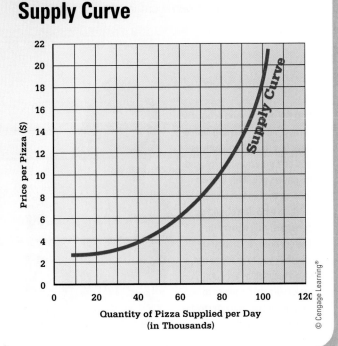

Exhibit 2.3
Supply Curve

Exhibit 2.5
Equilibrium

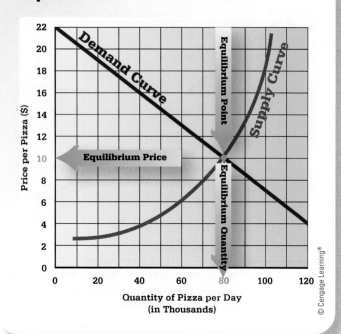

Price per Pizza ($) vs Quantity of Pizza per Day (in Thousands)

Demand Curve
Supply Curve
Equilibrium Point
Equilibrium Price
Equilibrium Quantity

Quantity of Pizza per Day
(in Thousands)

© Cengage Learning®

equilibrium price The price associated with the point at which the quantity demanded of a product equals the quantity supplied.

socialism An economic system based on the principle that the government should own and operate key enterprises that directly affect public welfare.

quantity demanded equals the quantity supplied—is called the **equilibrium price**, and the quantity associated with this point is called the "equilibrium quantity."

2-4 PLANNED ECONOMIES: SOCIALISM AND COMMUNISM

In capitalist economies, private ownership is paramount. Individuals own businesses, and their personal fortunes depend on their success in the free market. But in planned economies, the government plays a more heavy-handed role in controlling the economy. The two key categories of planned economies are socialism and communism.

2-4a Socialism

Socialism is an economic system based on the principle that the government should own and operate key enterprises that directly affect public welfare, such as utilities, telecommunications, and healthcare. Although the official government goal is to run these enterprises in the best interest of the overall public, inefficiencies and corruption often interfere with effectiveness. Socialist economies also tend to have higher taxes, which are designed to distribute wealth more evenly through society. Tax revenues typically fund services that citizens in free enterprise systems would have to pay for themselves in countries with lower tax rates. Examples range from free childcare to free university education to free public healthcare systems. Critics of the recent government intervention in the U.S.

adjust toward the point where the supply curve and the demand curve intersect (see Exhibit 2.5). The price associated with this point of intersection—the point where the

Waste Not, Want Not

Parents and grandparents across the years have counseled their children with this sage advice. Yet somewhat ironically, this same age old wisdom applies to the cutting edge of the on-demand economy, which puts idle resources to work for the benefit of society. If your car just sits in the garage all day, you can put it to use and make some money as an Uber driver, a Lyft driver, or both. If you are lucky enough to own more than one home—rent the extras on Abnb. And if you have spare brain cells, rent them out to do project work in your area of expertise. The options are limitless. The growing on-demand economy is very exciting for workers who value flexibility over security, workers who are ready and able to master multiple skill sets (and keep them updated), and workers who are savvy and skilled about selling themselves via networking and social media. But many others

find the on-demand economy somewhat threatening. Workers have few (if any) guarantees—and certainly no security. And taxpayers will likely end up footing the bill for contract workers who don't build up pensions, which isn't fair. The economy is changing, whether you're ready or not, so do yourself a favor and make sure you're ready to change with it, and effectively manage BRAND YOU.[12]

Catherine Lane/iStockphoto.com

"The Sky is Falling! The Sky is Falling!"

Or is it? Every few years, the popular press and social media reverberate with dire warnings that the world is running out of something crucial—soybeans, chocolate, fresh water, space, oil…yikes! The doomsday warnings create a temporary panic, and then blow over. Take oil, for instance. In 2010, economist Paul Krugman declared, "Peak oil has arrived." We're living in a finite world, in which the rapid growth of emerging economies is placing pressure on limited supplies of raw materials, pushing up their prices. But in January 2015 oil prices hit a new low of $49 per barrel. One reason may be the U.S. fracking boom, which dramatically increased supply. And as another renowned economist, Daniel Yergin, pointed out, "Technology responds to need and to price." *The Wall Street Journal* concluded, "The notion that the world is running out of resources always fails because the ingenuity of entrepreneurs, spurred by necessity and incentive, always exceeds the imagination of doomsayers." So stop hording that chocolate![13]

Acestock/Alamy

economy believe that the new moves have pushed us too far in a socialist direction.

Most Western European countries—from Sweden, to Germany, to the United Kingdom—developed powerful socialist economies in the decades after World War II. But more recently, growth in these countries has languished. Although many factors have contributed to the slow-down, the impact of high taxes on the profit incentive and lavish social programs on the work incentive has clearly played a role. Potential entrepreneurs may migrate to countries that let them keep more of their profits, and workers with abundant benefits may find themselves losing motivation. In late 2010, many of these economies imposed stiff austerity measures to control government spending, eliminating some public benefits many took for granted.

2-4b Communism

Communism is an economic and political system that calls for public ownership of virtually all enterprises, under the direction of a strong central government. The communist concept was the brainchild of political philosopher Karl Marx, who outlined its core principles in his 1848 *Communist Manifesto*. The communism that Marx envisioned was supposed to dramatically improve the lot of the worker at the expense of the super-rich.

But countries that adopted communism in the 1900s—most notably the former Soviet Union, China, Cuba, North Korea, and Vietnam—did not thrive. Most imposed authoritarian governments that suspended individual rights and

choices. People were unable to make even basic choices such as where to work or what to buy. Without the free market to establish what to produce, crippling shortages and surpluses developed. Corruption infected every level of government. Under enormous pressure from their own people and the rest of the world, communism began to collapse across the Soviet Union and its satellite nations. At the end of the 1980s, it was replaced with democracy and the free market. Over the past two decades, China has also introduced significant free market reforms across much of the country, fueling its torrid growth rate. And in the 1990s, Vietnam launched free market reforms, stimulating rapid, sustained growth. The remaining communist economic systems—North Korea and Cuba—continue to falter, their people facing drastic shortages and even starvation.

2-5 MIXED ECONOMIES: THE STORY OF THE FUTURE

In today's world, pure economies—market or planned—are practically nonexistent, since each would fall far short of meeting the needs of its citizens. A pure market economy would make insufficient provision for the old, the young, the sick, and the environment. A pure planned economy would not create

> **communism** An economic and political system that calls for public ownership of virtually all enterprises, under the direction of a strong central government.

enough value to support its people over the long term. Instead, most of today's nations have **mixed economies**, falling somewhere along a spectrum that ranges from pure planned at one extreme to pure market at the other.

Even the United States—one of the most market-oriented economies in the world—does not have a *pure* market economy. The various departments of the government own a number of major enterprises, including the postal service, schools, parks, libraries, entire systems of universities, and the military. In fact, the federal government is the nation's largest employer, providing jobs for more than 4 million Americans. And—although the government does not directly *operate* firms in the financial sector—the federal government has become part owner in a number of financial institutions as part of the recent bailouts. The government also intervenes extensively in the free market by creating regulations that stimulate competition and protect both consumers and workers. Regulations are likely to become stronger in the wake of the economic crisis.[14]

Over the past 30 years, most economies of the world have begun moving toward the market end of the spectrum. Government-owned businesses have converted to private ownership via a process called **privatization**. Socialist governments have reduced red tape, cracked down on corruption, and created new laws to protect economic rights. Extravagant human services—from free healthcare to education subsidies—have shrunk. And far-reaching tax reform has created new incentives for both domestic and foreign investment in once-stagnant planned economies.[15]

Unfortunately, the price of economic restructuring has been a fair amount of social turmoil in many nations undergoing market reforms. Countries from France to China have experienced sometimes violent demonstrations in response to social and employment program cutbacks. Change is challenging, especially when it redefines economic winners and losers. But countries that have taken strides toward the market end of the spectrum—from small players such as the Czech Republic, to large players such as China—have seen the payoff in rejuvenated growth rates that have raised the standard of living for millions of people.

mixed economies Economies that embody elements of both planned and market-based economic systems.

privatization The process of converting government-owned businesses to private ownership.

gross domestic product (GDP) The total value of all final goods and services produced within a nation's physical boundaries over a given period of time.

unemployment rate The percentage of people in the labor force over age 16 who do not have jobs and are actively seeking employment.

2-6 EVALUATING ECONOMIC PERFORMANCE: WHAT'S WORKING?

Clearly, economic systems are complex—very complex. So you probably won't be surprised to learn that no single measure captures all the dimensions of economic performance. To get the full picture, you need to understand a range of terms and measures, including gross domestic product, employment level, the business cycle, inflation rate, and productivity.

2-6a Gross Domestic Product

Real **gross domestic product**, or GDP, measures the total value of all final goods and services produced within a nation's physical boundaries over a given period of time, adjusted for inflation. (Nominal GDP does not include an inflation adjustment.) All domestic production is included in the GDP, even when the producer is foreign-owned. The U.S. GDP, for instance, includes the value of Hyundai Sonatas built in Alabama, even though Hyundai is a Korean firm. Likewise, the Indonesian GDP includes the value of Gap clothing manufactured in Indonesian factories, even though Gap is an American firm.

GDP is a vital measure of economic health. Business people, economists, and political leaders use GDP to measure the economic performance of individual nations and to compare the growth among nations. Interestingly, GDP levels tend to be somewhat understated, since they don't include any illegal activities—such as paying undocumented nannies and gardeners, or selling illegal drugs—which can represent a significant portion of some countries' production. The GDP also ignores legal goods that are not reported to avoid taxation, plus output produced within households. In 2014, the GDP of the United states was about $17.42 trillion, reflecting an encouraging +2.4% growth rate versus 2013.[16] Check out Chapter 3 for a survey of the world's key economies according to total GDP and GDP growth rate.

2-6b Employment Level

The overall level of employment is another key element of economic health. When people have jobs, they have money, which allows them to spend and invest, fueling economic growth. Most nations track employment levels largely through the **unemployment rate**, which includes everyone age 16 and older who doesn't have a job and is actively seeking one. The U.S. unemployment rate climbed precipitously through the Great Recession, rising from 5.8% in 2008 to 9.3% in 2009, to then dropping to 8.1% in 2012, as the economy began its glacially slow turnaround. Unemployment didn't move below 8% until September of 2012, and then it dropped slowly throughout 2013 to end the year at an annual average of 7.4% as the recovery began to take hold. Unemployment continued dropping, hitting a low of 5.6% by December 2014. But unfortunately, about half of the 8 million jobs lost during the recession were middle-income jobs, and about half of the new jobs created since have been in low-wage sectors of the economy, leading to stagnant household incomes.[17]

Interestingly, some unemployment is actually good—it reflects your freedom to change jobs. If you have an awful boss, for instance, you may just quit. If you quit, are you unemployed? Of course you are. Are you glad? You probably are, and in normal times, the chances are good that you'll find another position that's a better fit for you. This type of job loss is called *frictional unemployment*, and it tends to be ultimately positive. *Structural unemployment*, on the other hand, is usually longer term. This category encompasses people who don't have jobs because the economy no longer needs their skills. In the United States, growing numbers of workers in the past decade have found themselves victims of structural unemployment as manufacturing jobs have moved overseas. Often their only option is expensive retraining. Two other categories of unemployment are *cyclical*, which involves layoffs during recessions, and *seasonal*, which involves job loss related to the time of year. In some areas of the country, construction and agricultural workers are seasonally unemployed, but the best example may be the department-store Santa who has a job only during the holiday season!

2-6c The Business Cycle

The **business cycle** is the periodic contraction and expansion that occur over time in virtually every economy. But the word "cycle" may be a little misleading, since it implies that the economy contracts and expands in a predictable pattern. In reality, the phases of the cycle are different each time they happen, and—despite the efforts of countless experts—no one can accurately predict when changes will occur or how long they will last. Those who make the best guesses stand to make fortunes, but bad bets can be financially devastating. The two key phases of the business cycle are contraction and expansion, shown in Exhibit 2.6.

■ **Contraction** is a period of economic downturn, marked by rising unemployment. Businesses cut back on production, and consumers shift their buying patterns to more basic products and fewer luxuries. The economic "feel-good factor" simply disappears. Economists declare an official **recession** when GDP decreases for two consecutive quarters. A **depression** is an especially deep and long-lasting recession. Fortunately, economies seldom spiral into severe depressions, thanks in large part to proactive intervention from the government. The last depression in the United States was the Great Depression of the 1930s. Whether a downturn is mild or severe, the very bottom of the contraction is called the "trough," as shown in Exhibit 2.6.

■ **Recovery** is a period of rising economic growth and increasing employment following a contraction. Businesses begin to expand. Consumers start to regain confidence, and spending begins to rise. The recovery is essentially the transition period between contraction and expansion.

business cycle The periodic contraction and expansion that occur over time in virtually every economy.

contraction A period of economic downturn, marked by rising unemployment and falling business production.

recession An economic downturn marked by a decrease in the GDP for two consecutive quarters.

depression An especially deep and long-lasting recession.

recovery A period of rising economic growth and employment.

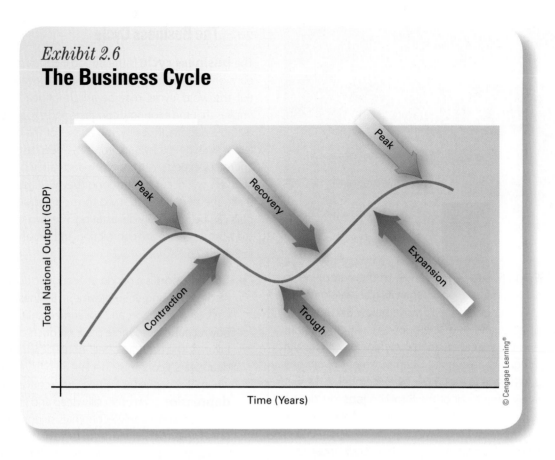

Exhibit 2.6

The Business Cycle

Peak

Recovery

Peak

Contraction

Expansion

Trough

Total National Output (GDP)

Time (Years)

© Cengage Learning®

■ **Expansion** is a period of robust economic growth and high employment. Businesses expand to capitalize on emerging opportunities. Consumers are optimistic and confident, which fuels purchasing, which fuels production, which fuels further hiring. As Exhibit 2.6 demonstrates, the height of economic growth is called the peak of the expansion. The U.S. economy had the longest growth spurt on record during the ten-year period from 1991 to 2001. After a relatively mild slowdown in 2001–2002, the U.S. economy again expanded for several years before it plunged into a full-blown recession in 2008.[18]

expansion A period of robust economic growth and high employment.

inflation A period of rising average prices across the economy.

hyperinflation An average monthly inflation rate of more than 50%.

disinflation A period of slowing average price increases across the economy.

deflation A period of falling average prices across the economy.

2-6d Price Levels

The rate of price changes across the economy is another basic measure of economic well-being. **Inflation** means that prices, on average, are rising. Similar to unemployment, a low level of inflation is not so bad. It reflects a healthy economy—people have money, and they are willing to spend it. But when the Federal Reserve—the nation's central bank—manages the economy poorly, inflation can spiral out of control, which can lead to **hyperinflation**, when average prices increase more than 50% per month. In Hungary, for example, inflation in its unstable, post–World War II economy climbed so quickly that prices doubled every 15 hours from 1945 to 1946. More recently, prices in the war-torn former Yugoslavia doubled every 16 hours between October 1993 and January 1994.

When the rate of price increases slows down, the economy is experiencing **disinflation**, which was the situation in the United States in the mid-1990s and more recently in the second half of 2008. But when prices actually decrease, the economy is experiencing **deflation**, typically a sign of economic trouble that goes hand-in-hand with very high unemployment. People don't have money and simply won't spend unless prices drop. During the Great Depression in the 1930s, the U.S. economy experienced deflation, with prices dropping 9% in 1931 and nearly 10% in 1932. Despite some economic turmoil, inflation in the United States was relatively low from 2000 to 2007, hovering at around 3%. But inflation picked up in the first half of 2008, only

Twohumans/iStockphoto.com

Many consumers keep careful track of inflation, since it directly impacts their standard of living.

The PPI measures the change over time in weighted-average wholesale prices, or the prices that businesses pay each other for goods and services. Changes in the PPI can sometimes predict changes in the CPI because producers tend to pass on price increases (and sometimes also price decreases) to consumers within a month or two of the changes.

2-6e Productivity

Productivity refers to the relationship between the goods and services that an economy produces and the resources needed to produce them. The amount of output—goods and services—divided by the amount of input (e.g., hours worked) equals productivity. The goal, of course, is to produce more goods and services, using fewer hours and other inputs. A high level of productivity typically correlates with healthy GDP growth, while low productivity tends to correlate with a more stagnant economy.

Over the past couple of decades, the United States has experienced strong productivity growth, due largely to infusions of technology that help workers produce more output, more quickly. But keep in mind that productivity doesn't measure quality. That's why it's so important to examine multiple measures of economic health rather than relying on simply one or two dimensions.

to fall during the first months of the economic crisis, remaining low throughout 2009 and 2010, picking back up to an annual average of 3.2% for 2011, and dropping yet further to an annual average of 1.5% for 2013 and 0.08% for 2014.[19]

The government uses two major price indexes to evaluate inflation: the **consumer price index (CPI)** and the **producer price index (PPI)**. The CPI measures the change in weighted-average price over time in a consumer "market basket" of goods and services that the average person buys each month. The U.S. Bureau of Labor Statistics creates the basket—which includes hundreds of items such as housing, transportation, haircuts, wine, and pet care—using data from more than 30,000 consumers. Although the market basket is meant to represent the average consumer, keep in mind that the "average" includes a lot of variation, so the CPI may not reflect your personal experience. For example, as a college student, you may be painfully sensitive to increases in tuition and the price of textbooks—a fact the authors of this particular textbook fully realize! But tuition and textbook prices aren't a big part of the "average" consumer's budget, so increases in these prices have a relatively small impact on the CPI.

consumer price index (CPI)
A measure of inflation that evaluates the change in the weighted-average price of goods and services that the average consumer buys each month.

producer price index (PPI)
A measure of inflation that evaluates the change over time in the weighted-average wholesale prices.

productivity The basic relationship between the production of goods and services (output) and the resources needed to produce them (input) calculated via the following equation: output/input = productivity.

The BIG Picture

From a business standpoint, one key goal of economics is to guide your decision making by offering a deeper understanding of the broad forces that affect both your business and your personal life. Knowing even basic economic principles can help you make better business decisions in virtually every area—from production, to marketing, to accounting, to name just a few—regardless of your specific function or level within an organization.

But you won't find an economics department within many (if any) businesses—rather, you'll find people across the organization applying economic theories and trends to their work, even in the face of continual economic flux. As you read through the other chapters in this book, take a moment to consider both the macroeconomic and microeconomic forces that affect each area you study. You're likely to find a surprising number of examples.

Careers in Economics

Business Economist

Collect, analyze, and distribute data to explain economic phenomenon and forecast economic trends, particularly with regard to supply and demand. Create and present clear, concise reports on economic trends to senior management on a monthly basis. Manage and motivate a small team of financial analysts and statisticians. For more information on this career and other possible careers in economics, check out Career Transitions.

STUDY TOOLS 2

LOCATED AT BACK OF THE TEXTBOOK

☐ Rip Out Chapter Review Card

LOCATED AT WWW.CENGAGE.COM/LOGIN

☐ Review key term flashcards and create your own using StudyBits

☐ Create and complete practice quizzes based off of your notes and StudyBits

☐ Complete Online activities such as Matching, Fill-in-the-Blank, and Drag and Drop exercises

☐ View chapter highlight box content, including CEO Profiles, What Would You Do Cases, and chapter videos

☐ Track your knowledge and understanding of key concepts in business using 4LTR Online

3 | The World Marketplace:
Business without Borders

LEARNING OBJECTIVES

After studying this chapter, you will be able to:

3-1 Discuss business opportunities in the world economy

3-2 Explain the key reasons for international trade

3-3 Describe the tools for measuring international trade

3-4 Analyze strategies for reaching global markets

3-5 Discuss barriers to international trade and strategies to surmount them

3-6 Describe the free-trade movement and discuss key benefits and criticisms

Remember to visit
PAGE 54
for additional
STUDY TOOLS

3-1 AN UNPRECEDENTED OPPORTUNITY

As access to technology skyrockets and barriers to trade continue to fall, individual economies around the world have become more interdependent than ever before. The result is a tightly woven global economy marked by intense competition and huge, shifting opportunities. The long-term potential for U.S. business is enormous. Although the global economic crisis caused the world GDP to contract in 2009 for the first time since World War II, compared with average increases of about 3.5% per year since 1946, world GDP growth turned positive again in 2010 and 2011, continuing a slow, steady pace through 2014.[1] See Exhibit 3.1 for a sampling of some specific higher- and lower-growth countries.

A quick look at population trends validates the global business opportunity, especially in developing nations. In October 2011, the world's population surpassed seven billion people. With 321 million people, the United States accounts for less than 4.5% of the world's total population. More than 6.9 billion people live beyond our borders, representing more than 95% of potential customers for U.S. firms. But even though the growth rates in many high-population countries are strong, most of these nations remain behind the United States in terms of development and prosperity, posing considerable challenges for foreign firms. (In other words, most of their populations may not have the resources

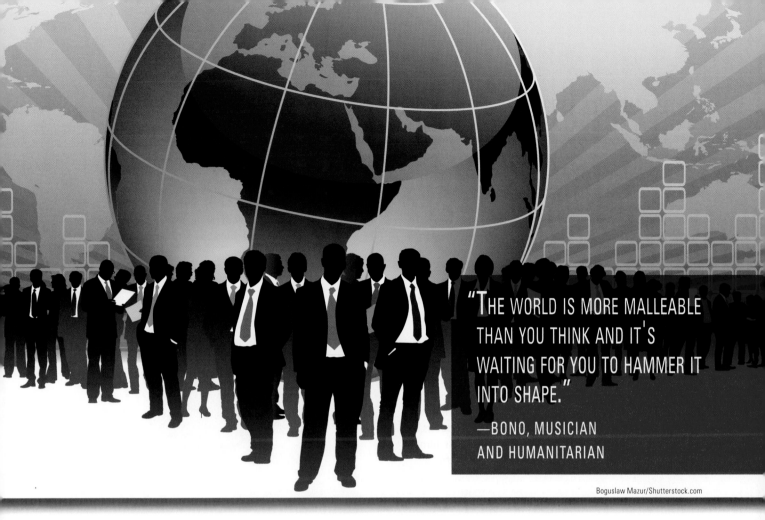

"THE WORLD IS MORE MALLEABLE THAN YOU THINK AND IT'S WAITING FOR YOU TO HAMMER IT INTO SHAPE."

—BONO, MUSICIAN AND HUMANITARIAN

to buy even basic goods and services.) The issue is likely to become even more severe in the wake of the global economic crisis. Exhibit 3.1, a comparison of population, GDP growth rate, and per capita GDP for the world's six largest nations, highlights some of the discrepancies. Note that even though U.S. consumers clearly have money, China and

India represent a much bigger opportunity in terms of both sheer size and economic growth.

The growing number of people with cell phones offers an interesting indicator of economic growth. Several recent studies have found that if a country increases cell phone penetration by 10 percentage points, GDP will

EXHIBIT 3.1	SELECTED POPULATION AND GDP FIGURES		
Nation	**Population***	**Per Capita GDP (U.S. Dollars)****	**GDP Growth Rate****
China	1,361,512,535	$9,800	+7.7%
India	1,251,695,584	$4,000	+3.2%
European Union	511,434,812	$34,500	+0.1%
United States	321,362,789	$52,800	+1.6%
Indonesia	255,993,674	$5,200	+5.3%
Brazil	204,259,812	$12,100	+2.3%

* U.S. Census Bureau 2015 Estimates.
** *CIA World Factbook* GDP 2013 Estimates.
*** *CIA World Factbook* GDP 2013 Growth Estimates.[2]

The world isn't every company's oyster

For the past couple of decades, corporations in virtually every country have been boosting profits by making the momentum of globalization work for them. But world markets don't work out for every corporation (at least not all the time). Walmart, for instance, with sales of more than $135 billion in 26 countries outside the United States, was forced to withdraw from Germany in 2006, and hasn't reopened since. Many Europeans prefer to shop daily at local markets, and Germans did not appreciate Walmart employees handling their groceries at the checkout line.

Male customers apparently thought the smiling clerks were flirting in an unwelcome manner. Even McDonald's, isn't "lovin' it" all over the world—105 countries don't have the Golden Arches. The reason is economic in Iceland. Imported burgers were just too pricey after the Great Recession. The reason is more political in Bolivia. According to the Bolivian president: "The major multinational food companies seek to control the production of food and to dominate global markets by imposing their customs and foods. The only goal of such producers is to generate profits. So they standardize food and drinks, turning them into global foods produced on a massive scale with the same formula. They are not interested in the health of human beings, only in their earnings and corporate profits." Bolivia's last McDonald's closed in 2002. So how can corporations avoid pricey globalization gaffes? The experts suggest that a deep dive into local culture plays a crucial role in long-term success across national borders." So with careful planning and thorough research, perhaps the world could be every company's oyster.[3]

Christos Georghiou/Shutterstock.com

likely increase by anywhere from +.5% to +1.2%. That may seem small, but it equates to somewhere between $49 and $118 billion for an economy the size of China. In other words, when the percentage of the population with cell phones goes up, the entire economy benefits.

Not surprisingly, cell phone penetration in India and China is skyrocketing. China currently boasts the world's largest base of cell phone users—more than one billion—and the growth will likely continue. India's current subscriber base is over 900 million; it has grown explosively over the past five years and seems likely to follow suit in the next decade. The growth may well continue until China and India hit the 100%+ cell phone penetration rates that characterize a number of developed nations, such as Taiwan, Hong Kong, Germany, and Argentina, which have more than one phone per person. In the United States, Europe, and Japan, cell phones followed landlines, but large swaths of developing nations aren't bothering to build conventional phone service. Rather, they're moving directly to cell phone networks. This trend is particularly marked across Africa, where cell phone penetration rates continue to grow explosively.

Most of the penetration growth involves basic-function phones, but smartphone penetration is growing as well, providing access to the Internet for the first time ever to huge swaths of the population. David Knapp, general director of Motorola Vietnam, points out that many developing nations "can leapfrog technology." And Vietnamese microentrepreneur Nguyen Huu Truc says, "It's no longer something that only the rich can afford. Now, it's a basic means of communication." As more people get the chance to get connected, better communication will likely feed economic growth. According to Muhammad Yunis, founder of Grameen Bank in Bangladesh, "a mobile phone is almost like having a card to get you out of poverty in a couple of years." The upshot is that millions of people worldwide will have a higher standard of living.[4]

> **49.9% OF HOUSEHOLDS IN INDIA HAVE A TOILET, WHILE MORE THAN 53% OWN A MOBILE PHONE.**
> —CNN

3-2 KEY REASONS FOR INTERNATIONAL TRADE

Companies engage in global trade for a range of reasons beyond the obvious opportunity to tap into huge and growing new markets. The benefits include better access to factors of production, reduced risk, and an inflow of new ideas.

■ *Access to factors of production:* International trade offers a valuable opportunity for individual firms to capitalize on factors of production that simply aren't present in the right amount for the right price in each individual country. India, China, and the Philippines, for example, attract multibillion-dollar investments because of their large cohort of technically skilled university graduates who work for about one-fifth the pay of comparable American workers. Russia and the OPEC nations offer a rich supply of oil, and Canada, like other forested nations, boasts an abundant supply of timber. The United States offers plentiful capital, which is less available in other parts of the world. International trade helps even out some of the resource imbalances among nations.

■ *Reduced risk:* Global trade reduces dependence on one economy, lowering the economic risk for multinational firms. When the Japanese economy entered a deep, sustained slump in the 1990s, for instance, Sony and Toyota thrived through their focus on other, healthier markets around the world. But a word of caution is key: as national economies continue to integrate, an economic meltdown in one part of the world can have far-reaching impact. Major foreign banks, for example, were badly burned by the U.S. subprime market mess, due to heavy investments in U.S. mortgage markets.

■ *Inflow of innovation:* International trade can also offer companies an invaluable source of new ideas. Japan, for instance, is far ahead of the curve regarding cell phone service. Japanese cell phone "extras," including games, ringtones, videos, and stylish new accessories, set the standard for cell service around the world. In Europe, meanwhile, consumers are showing a growing interest in traditional and regional foods, which allow them to picture where

their ingredients come from. Companies with a presence in foreign markets experience budding trends like these firsthand, giving them a jump in other markets around the world.[5]

3-2a Competitive Advantage

Beyond individual companies, industries tend to succeed on a worldwide basis in countries that enjoy a competitive advantage. But to understand competitive advantage, you need to first understand how **opportunity cost** relates to international trade. When a country produces more of one good, it must produce less of another good (assuming that resources are finite). The value of the second-best choice—the value of the production that a country gives up in order to produce the first product—represents the opportunity cost of producing the first product.

A country has an **absolute advantage** when it can produce more of a good than other nations, using the same amount of resources. China, for example, has an absolute advantage in terms of clothing production, relative to the United States. But having an absolute advantage isn't always enough. Unless they face major trade barriers, the industries in any country tend to produce products for which they have a **comparative advantage**—meaning that they tend to turn out those goods that have the lowest opportunity cost compared to other countries. The United States, for instance, boasts a comparative advantage versus most countries in movie and television program production; Germany has a comparative advantage in the production of high-performance cars; and South Korea enjoys a comparative advantage in electronics.

But keep in mind that comparative advantage seldom remains static. As technology changes and the workforce evolves (through factors such as education and experience), nations may gain or lose comparative advantage in various industries. China and India, for example,

> NEW YORK, MOSCOW, HONG KONG, LONDON, AND BEIJING WERE THE TOP FIVE CITIES IN THE WORLD FOR BILLIONAIRES IN 2014.
> —*FINANCIAL TIMES*

opportunity cost The opportunity of giving up the second-best choice when making a decision.

absolute advantage The benefit a country has in a given industry when it can produce more of a product than other nations using the same amount of resources.

comparative advantage The benefit a country has in a given industry if it can make products at a lower opportunity cost than other countries.

Most apparel today is produced outside of the United States.

are both seeking to build a comparative advantage versus other nations in technology production by investing in their infrastructure and their institutions of higher education.

3-3 GLOBAL TRADE: TAKING MEASURE

After a decade of robust growth, global trade began slowing in 2007, due largely to turbulence in the worldwide financial markets. In 2008, the rate of growth in world trade slid below 5%, as the global recession tightened its grip. In 2009, global trade plummeted nearly 25% in U.S. dollar terms, and 12% in terms of overall volume from the 2008 level, the largest single-year drop since World War II. In 2010, global trade volume surged 13.8%, but expanded a more modest +5.0% in 2011. In 2012, the growth rate dropped to +2.3%, but increased a modest +2.1% in 2013. Economists anticipate an increase of +4.7% in 2014 and an increase of +5.3% in 2015, which would still lag behind the turbo-charged growth rates of much of the past two decades. Measuring the impact of international trade on individual nations requires a clear understanding of balance of trade, balance of payments, and exchange rates.[6]

3-3a Balance of Trade

The **balance of trade** is a basic measure of the difference between a nation's exports and imports. If the total value of exports is higher than the total value of imports, the country has a **trade surplus**. If the total value of imports is higher than the total value of exports, the country has a **trade deficit**. Balance of trade includes the value of both goods and services, and it incorporates trade with all foreign nations. Although a trade deficit signals the wealth of an economy that can afford to buy huge amounts of foreign products, a large deficit can be destabilizing. It indicates, after all, that as goods and services flow into a nation, money flows out—a challenge with regard to long-term economic health. The United States has had an overall trade deficit since 1976, and as the American appetite for foreign goods has grown, the trade deficit has ballooned. But that growth may slow over the next few years if demand remains sluggish in response to the global economic crisis.

3-3b Balance of Payments

Balance of payments is a measure of the total flow of money into or out of a country. Clearly, the balance of trade plays a central role in determining the balance of payments. But the balance of payments also includes other financial flows such as foreign borrowing and lending, foreign aid payments and receipts, and foreign investments. A **balance of payments surplus** means that more money flows in than out, while a **balance of payments deficit** means that more money flows out than in. Keep in mind that the balance of payments typically corresponds to the balance of trade because trade is, in general, the largest component.

3-3c Exchange Rates

Exchange rates measure the value of one nation's currency relative to the currency of other nations. While the exchange rate does not directly measure global commerce, it certainly has a powerful influence on how global trade affects individual nations and their trading partners. The exchange rate of a given currency must be expressed in terms of another currency. The table below shows some examples of how the exchange rate can influence the economy, using the dollar and the euro. In 2012, for

balance of trade A basic measure of the difference in value between a nation's exports and imports, including both goods and services.

trade surplus Overage that occurs when the total value of a nation's exports is higher than the total value of its imports.

trade deficit Shortfall that occurs when the total value of a nation's imports is higher than the total value of its exports.

balance of payments A measure of the total flow of money into or out of a country.

balance of payments surplus Overage that occurs when more money flows into a nation than out of that nation.

balance of payments deficit Shortfall that occurs when more money flows out of a nation than into that nation.

exchange rate A measurement of the value of one nation's currency relative to the currency of other nations.

example, a number of currencies underwent value swings versus the U.S. dollar (e.g., the E.U. euro, the Japanese yen, the Brazilian real, the Indian rupee, the Australian dollar, and the Venezuelan bolivar). One result was multi billion dollar earnings hits against U.S. corporations with a strong international presence, including automotive giants, Ford and General Motors. Many firms opt to present their earnings reports stripped of the effects of currency translations, but in today's global economy, that clearly offers a misleading picture of performance.[7]

STRONG DOLLAR VERSUS EURO: WHO BENEFITS? (EXAMPLE: $1.00 = 1.20 EUROS)	WEAK DOLLAR VERSUS EURO: WHO BENEFITS? (EXAMPLE: $1.00 = .60 EUROS)
U.S. travelers to Europe: Their dollars can buy more European goods and services.	*European travelers to the United States:* Their dollars buy more American goods and services.
American firms with European operations: Operating costs— from buying products to paying workers—are lower.	*European firms with American operations:* Operating costs— from buying products to paying workers—are lower.
European exporters: Their products are less expensive in the United States, so Europe exports more, and we import more.	*American exporters:* Their products are less expensive in Europe, so we export more, and Europe imports more.

© 2015 Cengage Learning®

3-3d Countertrade

A complete evaluation of global trade must also consider exchanges that don't actually involve money. A surprisingly large chunk of international commerce—possibly as much as 25%—involves the barter of products for products rather than for currency. Companies typically engage in **countertrade** to meet the needs of customers that don't have access to hard currency or credit, usually in developing countries. Individual countertrade agreements range from simple barter to a complex web of exchanges that end up meeting the needs of multiple parties. Done poorly, countertrading can be a confusing nightmare for everyone involved. But done well, countertrading is a powerful tool for gaining customers and products that would not otherwise be available.[8] Not surprisingly, barter opportunities tend to increase during economic downturns. In 2009, for example, ads began to appear both in Russian newspapers and online, such as one that offered "2,500,000 rubles' worth of premium underwear for any automobile," and another that offered "lumber in Krasnoyarsk for food or medicine."[9]

SEIZING THE OPPORTUNITY: STRATEGIES FOR REACHING GLOBAL MARKETS

There is no one "right way" to seize the opportunity in global markets. In fact, the opportunity may not even make sense for every firm. While international trade can offer new profit streams and lower costs, it also introduces a higher level of risk and complexity to running a business. Being ready to take on the challenge can mean the difference between success and failure.

Firms ready to tap the opportunity have a number of options for how to move forward. One way is to seek foreign suppliers through outsourcing and importing. Another possibility is to seek foreign customers through exporting, licensing, franchising, and direct investment. These market development options fall in a spectrum from low cost–low control to high cost–high control, as shown in Exhibit 3.2. In other words, companies that choose to export products to a foreign country spend less to enter that market than companies that choose to build their own factories. But companies that build their own factories have a lot more control than exporters over how their business unfolds. Keep in mind that profit opportunity and risk—which vary along with cost and control—also play a critical role in how firms approach international markets.

Smaller firms tend to begin with exporting and move along the spectrum as the business develops. But larger firms may jump straight to the strategies that give them more control over their operations. Large firms are also likely to use a number of different approaches in different countries, depending on the goals of the firm and the structure of the foreign market. Regardless of the specific strategy, most large companies—such as General Electric, Nike, and Disney—both outsource with foreign suppliers and sell their products to foreign markets.

3-4a Foreign Outsourcing and Importing

Foreign outsourcing means contracting with foreign suppliers to produce products, usually at a fraction of the cost of domestic production. H&M, for instance, relies on a network for manufacturers around the globe, mostly in less developed parts of the world, including Kenya, Cambodia, Indonesia, Myanmar, Sri Lanka, and

countertrade International trade that involves the barter of products for products rather than for currency.

foreign outsourcing (also contract manufacturing) Contracting with foreign suppliers to produce products, usually at a fraction of the cost of domestic production.

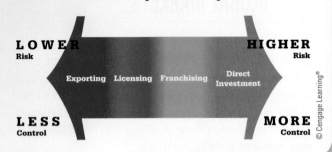

Exhibit 3.2
Market Development Options

LOWER Risk   HIGHER Risk

Exporting   Licensing   Franchising   Direct Investment

LESS Control   MORE Control

© Cengage Learning®

Bangladesh. Apple depends on firms in China and Taiwan to produce the iPhone. And countless small companies contract with foreign manufacturers as well. The key benefit, of course, is dramatically lower wages, which drive down the cost of production.

But while foreign outsourcing lowers costs, it also involves significant risk. Quality control typically requires very detailed specifications to ensure that a company gets what it actually needs. Another key risk of foreign outsourcing involves social responsibility. A firm that contracts with foreign producers has an obligation to ensure that those factories adhere to ethical standards. Deciding what those standards should be is often quite tricky, given different cultures, expectations, and laws in different countries. And policing the factories on an ongoing basis can be even harder than determining the standards. But companies that don't get it right face the threat of significant consumer backlash in the United States and Europe. This has been a particular issue with products produced in China. In the recent past, for instance, product defects forced U.S. firms to recall a host of Chinese-produced toys, including Thomas the Tank Engine trains that were coated with toxic lead paint, ghoulish fake eyeballs that were filled with kerosene, and Polly Pocket dolls that posed a swallowing hazard. And in 2013, Greenpeace released a study that showed that the bulk of children's clothing produced in China—the world's largest exporter of textiles—contains hazardous levels of toxic chemicals.[10]

Many Americans have become personally familiar with the quality/cost tradeoff as a growing number of companies have outsourced customer service to foreign call centers.

importing Buying products domestically that have been produced or grown in foreign nations.

exporting Selling products in foreign nations that have been produced or grown domestically.

Research suggests that the approximate cost of offering a live, American-based, customer service agent averages about $7.50 per call, while outsourcing those calls to live agents in another country drops the average cost down to about $3.25 per call. But customers end up paying the difference in terms of satisfaction, reporting high levels of misunderstanding, frustration, and inefficiency. A number of firms—such as jetBlue and Amazon.com—have enjoyed the best of both worlds by outsourcing customer service calls to U.S. agents who work from their own homes.[11]

Importing means buying products from overseas that have already been produced, rather than contracting with overseas manufacturers to produce special orders. Imported products, of course, don't carry the brand name of the importer, but they also don't carry as much risk. Pier 1 Imports, a large retail chain, has built a powerful brand around the importing concept, creating stores that give the customer the sense of a global shopping trip without the cost or hassle of actually leaving the country.

3-4b Exporting

Exporting is the most basic level of international market development. It simply means producing products domestically and selling them abroad. Exporting represents an especially strong opportunity for small and mid-sized companies. In Tennessee, for instance, Heritage Glass, a small firm that has manufactured glass since the Civil War, plans to reopen a factory that was shuttered for two years, to capitalize on strong demand for patterned glass from the Philippines, Europe, and South America.[12]

JuliusKielaitis/Shutterstock.com

Businesses expand through foreign franchising. They offer franchisees the right to produce and market its products.

3-4c Foreign Licensing and Foreign Franchising

Foreign licensing and foreign franchising, the next level of commitment to international markets, are quite similar. **Foreign licensing** involves a domestic firm granting a foreign firm the rights to produce and market its product or to use its trademark/patent rights in a defined geographical area. The company that offers the rights, or the *licensor*, receives a fee from the company that buys the rights, or the *licensee*. This approach allows firms to expand into foreign markets with little or no investment, and it also helps circumvent government restrictions on importing in closed markets. But maintaining control of licensees can be a significant challenge. Licensors also run the risk that unethical licensees may become their competitors, using information that they gained from the licensing agreement. Foreign licensing is especially common in the food and beverage industry. The most high-profile examples include Coke and Pepsi, which grant licenses to foreign bottlers all over the world.

Foreign franchising is a specialized type of licensing. A firm that expands through foreign franchising, called a *franchisor*, offers other businesses, or *franchisees*, the right to produce and market its products if the franchisee agrees to specific operating requirements—a complete package of how to do business. Franchisors also often offer their franchisees management guidance, marketing support, and even financing. In return, franchisees pay both a start-up fee and an ongoing percentage of sales to the franchisor. One key difference between franchising and licensing is that franchisees assume the identity of the franchisor. A McDonald's franchise in Paris, for instance, is clearly a McDonald's, not, say, a Pierre's Baguette outlet that also carries McDonald's products.

3-4d Foreign Direct Investment

Direct investment in foreign production and marketing facilities represents the deepest level of global involvement. The cost is high, but companies with direct investments have more control over how their business operates in a given country. The high-dollar commitment also represents significant risk if the business doesn't go well. Most direct investment takes the form of either acquiring foreign firms or developing new facilities from the ground up. Another increasingly popular approach is strategic alliances or partnerships that allow multiple firms to share risks and resources for mutual benefit.

Foreign acquisitions enable companies to gain a foothold quickly in new markets. In 2009, for example, Italian carmaker Fiat took over struggling U.S. auto giant Chrysler, with plans to more fully exploit the American market in the wake of the Great Recession. A number of other global giants, such as Microsoft, General Electric, and Nestlé, tend to follow a foreign acquisition strategy.[13]

Developing new facilities from scratch—or "offshoring"—is the most costly form of direct investment. It also involves significant risk. But the benefits include complete control over how the facility develops and the potential for high profits, which makes the approach attractive for corporations that can afford it. Intel, for instance, built a $2.5 billion specialized computer chip manufacturing plant in northeastern China. And foreign car companies, from German Daimler-Benz, to Korean Hyundai, to Japanese Toyota, have built factories in the southern United States.[14]

Joint ventures involve two or more companies joining forces—sharing resources, risks, and profits, but not merging companies—to pursue specific opportunities. A formal, long-term agreement is usually called a **partnership**, while a less formal, less encompassing agreement is usually called a **strategic alliance**. Joint ventures are a popular, though controversial, means of entering foreign markets. Often a foreign company connects with a local firm to ease its way into the market. In fact, some countries, such as India and Malaysia, require that foreign investors have local partners. But

---

foreign licensing Authority granted by a domestic firm to a foreign firm for the rights to produce and market its product or to use its trademark/patent rights in a defined geographical area.

foreign franchising A specialized type of foreign licensing in which a firm expands by offering businesses in other countries the right to produce and market its products according to specific operating requirements.

direct investment (or foreign direct investment) When firms either acquire foreign firms or develop new facilities from the ground up in foreign countries.

joint ventures When two or more companies join forces—sharing resources, risks, and profits, but not actually merging companies—to pursue specific opportunities.

partnership A voluntary agreement under which two or more people act as co-owners of a business for profit.

strategic alliance An agreement between two or more firms to jointly pursue a specific opportunity without actually merging their businesses. Strategic alliances typically involve less formal, less encompassing agreements than partnerships.

© Dmitry Melnikov/Shutterstock.com

Santa's Workshop—Chinese Style

Most Americans envision Santa's workshop as an idyllic village nestled in the North Pole, surrounded by drifts of soft, white snow, sheltered by pine trees, and inhabited by cheerful little elves, busily constructing the bounty for Santa to deliver next Christmas.   That may well be, but a very different Santa's workshop—600 factories in the Chinese city of Yiwu (dubbed "China's Christmas village")—churn out 60% of all the world's Christmas decorations and accessories. Ironically, the poorly paid workers who produce the holiday goods barely know what Christmas is—they're more concerned with minimizing their inhalation of various toxins. So when you enjoy your holiday decorations next season, remember to spare a thought for the workers in China who likely created them.[15]

AP Images/Yang guang/Imaginechina

research from Harvard finance professor Mihir Desai finds that joint ventures between multinational firms and domestic partners can be more costly and less rewarding than they initially appear. He and his team suggest that they make sense only in countries that require local political and cultural knowledge as a core element of doing business.[16]

3-5 BARRIERS TO INTERNATIONAL TRADE

Every business faces challenges, but international firms face more hurdles than domestic firms. Understanding and surmounting those hurdles is the key to success in global markets. Most barriers to trade fall into the following categories: sociocultural differences, economic differences, and legal/political differences. As you think about these barriers, keep in mind that each country has a different mix of barriers. Often countries with the highest barriers have the least competition, which can be a real opportunity for the first international firms to break through.

> "OBSTACLES ARE THOSE FRIGHTFUL THINGS YOU SEE WHEN YOU TAKE YOUR EYES OFF YOUR GOAL."
>
> —HENRY FORD, FOUNDER OF FORD MOTOR COMPANY

sociocultural differences Differences among cultures in language, attitudes, and values.

3-5a Sociocultural Differences

Sociocultural differences include differences among countries in language, attitudes, and values. Some specific, and perhaps surprising, elements that affect business include nonverbal communication, forms of address, attitudes toward punctuality, religious celebrations and customs, business practices, and expectations regarding meals and gifts. Understanding and responding to sociocultural factors are vital for firms that operate in multiple countries. But since the differences often operate at a subtle level, they can undermine relationships before anyone is aware that it's happening. The best way to jump over sociocultural barriers is to conduct thorough consumer research, cultivate firsthand knowledge, and practice extreme sensitivity. The payoff can be a sharp competitive edge. Hyundai, for instance, enjoys a whopping 18% share of the passenger car market in India. It beats the competition with custom features that reflect Indian culture, such as elevated rooflines to provide more headroom for turban-wearing motorists.[17]

3-5b Economic Differences

Before entering a foreign market, it's critical to understand and evaluate the local economic conditions. Key factors to consider include population, per capita income, economic

Veggie Surprise, Anyone?

Travel around the world, and you're likely to see American fast-food franchisees in virtually every city. Although you'll surely recognize the names of these fast-food behemoths, you may not be as familiar with the food that they serve, since many of the dishes have been completely changed in response to local culture.

Burger King:

- **Japan:** a limited time offer of a Whopper with 15 strips of bacon added. Soon after, pigs were listed in the Endangered Species Registry in Japan (just kidding).

- **Austria:** X-tra Long Burger (sub sandwich length burger with three beef patties topped with either chilli cheese or BBQ sauce AND onion rings)

- **Egypt:** Cheesy Whopper (a Whopper with a patty of deep-fried, breaded cheese on the beef)

Joe Raedle/Getty Images

Pizza Hut:

- **Japan:** crust stuffed with shrimp nuggets and injected with mayonnaise

- **South Korea:** crust filled with sweet potato mousse

- **China:** lemon-flavored salmon pastry roll and scallop croquettes with crushed seaweed

- **Middle East:** "Crown Crust": a pizza/cheeseburger hybrid studded with "cheeseburger gems," which are cheeseburger sliders attached to the outside of a meaty pizza that's topped with lettuce and tomato and drizzled with "special sauce," served with a side of Pepto Bismol

KFC:

- **China:** spicy tofu chicken rice, rice porridge breakfast (congee)

- **India:** Chana Snacker (a chickpea burger topped with thousand island sauce)

McDonald's:

- **India:** Paneer Salsa Wrap (cottage cheese with Mexican-Cajun coating)

- **Australia:** Bacon and Egg Roll ("rashers of quality bacon and fried egg")

- **Brazil:** Cheese Quiche

- **Kuwait:** Veggie Surprise Burger (no detailed description... yikes!)[18]

- **Austria:** McItaly Adagio burger topped with "eggplant mousse" and chopped almonds

---

growth rate, currency exchange rate, and stage of economic development. But keep in mind that low scores for any of these measures don't necessarily equal a lack of opportunity. In fact, some of today's biggest opportunities are in countries with low per capita income. For example, the Indian division of global giant Unilever gets 50% of its sales from rural India by selling products to individual consumers in tiny quantities, such as two-cent sachets of shampoo. The rural Indian market has been growing so dramatically that in 2010, the chairman of Hindustan Unilever declared, "What we have done in the last 25 years we want to do it in the next two years," scaling up the reach of its consumer products from about 250,000 rural retail outlets to about 750,000. And Hewlett-Packard has recently joined forces with Unilever to give microdistributors in rural India the ability to check prices and place orders online from "what are now distinctively offline villages and regions." Also capitalizing on the rapid growth and increased demand, Samsung has introduced Guru, a mobile phone that can be charged with solar power, to rural India. Other mobile companies are scrambling to keep up.[19]

Effectively serving less-developed markets requires innovation and efficiency. Emerging consumers often need different product features, and they almost always need lower costs. C. K. Prahalad, an influential business scholar, believed that forward-thinking companies can make a profit in developing countries if they make advanced technology affordable. Many markets are simply so large that high-volume sales can make up for low profit margins.

Overall, the profit potential is clear and growing. And as consumers in developing countries continue to gain income—although at a much slower pace in the wake of the economic crisis—companies that established their brands early will have a critical edge over firms that enter the market after them.

The elements of infrastructure may differ dramatically in different countries.

Dmitry Ersler/Fotolia

Infrastructure should be another key economic consideration when entering a foreign market. Infrastructure refers to a country's physical facilities that support economic activity. It includes basic systems in each of the following areas:

- Transportation (e.g., roads, airports, railroads, and ports)
- Communication (e.g., TV, radio, Internet, and cell phone coverage)
- Energy (e.g., utilities and power plants)
- Finance (e.g., banking, checking, and credit)

The level of infrastructure can vary dramatically among countries. In Africa, for instance, only 26.5% of the population has Internet access, compared to 87.7% in North America. In Vietnam and Thailand, many consumers buy products directly from vendors in small boats, compared to firmly grounded stores in Europe. Although credit card purchases are still relatively low in much of the world, particularly in Asia, recent growth has been explosive and will probably continue for the next few years.[20]

3-5c Political and Legal Differences

Political regimes obviously differ around the world, and their policies have a dramatic impact on business. The specific laws and regulations that governments create around business are often less obvious, yet they can still represent a significant barrier to international trade. To compete

infrastructure A country's physical facilities that support economic activity.

effectively—and to reduce risk—managers must carefully evaluate these factors and make plans to respond to them both now and as they change.

LAWS AND REGULATIONS International businesses must comply with international legal standards, the laws of their own countries, and the laws of their host countries. This can be a real challenge, since many developing countries change business regulations with little notice and less publicity. The justice system can pose another key challenge, particularly with regard to legal enforcement of ownership and contract rights. Since 2003, the World Bank has published a "Doing Business" report that ranks the ease of doing business for small and medium-sized companies in 189 different countries. The 2015 "Doing Business" report showed that for the seventh year running, Singapore leads in the ease of doing business, followed by New Zealand, Hong Kong SAR China, Denmark, South Korea, Norway, and the United States. As an individual country, Tajikistan improved the most in the ease of doing business. Overall, the Eastern Europe and Central Asia regions continue to show a faster rate of improvement than any other regions according to "Doing Business" indicators. The "Doing Business" project examines the ease of doing business from ten different angles, including the ease of dealing with construction permits, paying taxes, and enforcing contracts.[21] The key benefit of an effective legal system is that it reduces risk for both domestic and foreign businesses.

Bribery, the payment of money for favorable treatment, and corruption, the solicitation of money for favorable treatment, are also major issues throughout the world. While bribery and corruption are technically illegal in virtually every major country, they are often accepted as a standard way of doing business. Regardless, U.S. corporations and American citizens are subject to prosecution by U.S. authorities for offering bribes in any nation. See Chapter 4 for more details.

POLITICAL CLIMATE The political climate of any country deeply influences whether that nation is attractive to foreign business. Stability is crucial. A country subject to strife from civil war, riots, or other violence creates huge additional risk for foreign business. Yet, figuring out how to operate in an unstable environment, such as Russia, Bolivia, or the Middle East, can give early movers a real advantage. Grant Winterton, Coca-Cola's regional manager for Russia, commented to *Time* magazine that "the politics do concern us." But having snagged 50% of the $1.9 billion carbonated-soft-drink market, he concludes that "the opportunity far outweighs the risk." Poor enforcement of intellectual property rights across international borders is another tough issue for business. The Business Software Alliance's piracy-tracking study found that worldwide piracy rates hover at about 42%, with piracy rates in emerging markets towering over those in mature markets—68% versus 24%. The total value of software theft hit a record $63.4 billion. The highest-piracy countries are Georgia, Zimbabwe, Moldava, and Libya, all 90% or higher. Somewhat ironically, business decision makers admit to pirating software more frequently than other computer users do.[23]

INTERNATIONAL TRADE RESTRICTIONS National governments also have the power to erect barriers to international business through a variety of international trade restrictions. The arguments for and against trade restrictions—also called **protectionism**—are summarized below. As you read, note that most economists find the reasons to eliminate trade restrictions much more compelling than the reasons to create them.

Just as trade restrictions have a range of motivations, they can take a number of different forms. The most common trade restrictions are tariffs, quotas, voluntary export restraints, and embargoes.

- **Tariffs** are taxes levied against imports. Governments tend to use protective tariffs either to shelter fledgling industries that couldn't compete without help, or to shelter industries that are crucial to the domestic economy. In 2009, Egypt imposed tariffs on sugar and the United States levied new tariffs on Chinese goods—including mattress springs and electrodes—that it contended were being dumped on the market at below-cost prices. In late 2014, the United States took steps towards imposing steep tariffs on Chinese-made tires, which it claimed were unfairly subsidized by the government.[24]

- **Quotas** are limitations on the amount of specific products that may be imported from certain countries during a given time period. Russia, for instance, has specific quotas for U.S. meat imports.

- **Voluntary export restraints (VERs)** are limitations on the amount of specific products that one nation will export to another nation. Although the government of the exporting country typically imposes VERs, they usually do so out of fear that the importing country would impose even more onerous restrictions. As a result, VERs often aren't as "voluntary" as the name suggests. The United States, for instance, insisted on VERs with Japanese auto exports in the early 1980s (which many economists believe ultimately precipitated the decline of the U.S. auto industry).

- An **embargo** is a total ban on the international trade of a certain item, or a total halt in trade with a particular nation. The intention of most embargoes is to pressure the targeted country to change political policies or to protect national security. The U.S. embargo against trade with Cuba offers a high-profile example.

protectionism National policies designed to restrict international trade, usually with the goal of protecting domestic businesses.

tariffs Taxes levied against imports.

quotas Limitations on the amount of specific products that may be imported from certain countries during a given time period.

voluntary export restraints (VERs) Limitations on the amount of specific products that one nation will export to another nation.

embargo A complete ban on international trade of a certain item, or a total halt in trade with a particular nation.

Quotas, VERs, and embargoes are relatively rare compared to tariffs, and tariffs are falling to new lows. But as tariffs decrease, some nations are seeking to control imports through nontariff barriers such as:

- Requiring red-tape-intensive import licenses for certain categories

- Establishing nonstandard packaging requirements for certain products

- Offering less-favorable exchange rates to certain importers

- Establishing standards on how certain products are produced or grown

- Promoting a "buy national" consumer attitude among local people

Nontariff barriers tend to be fairly effective because complaints about them can be hard to prove and easy to counter.[25]

3-6 FREE TRADE: THE MOVEMENT GAINS MOMENTUM

Perhaps the most dramatic change in the world economy has been the global move toward **free trade**—the unrestricted movement of goods and services across international borders. Even though *complete* free trade is not a reality, the emergence of regional trading blocks, common markets, and international trade agreements has moved the world economy much closer to that goal.

3-6a GATT and the World Trade Organization

The **General Agreement on Tariffs and Trade (GATT)** is an international trade accord designed to encourage worldwide trade among its members. Established in 1948 by 23 nations, GATT has undergone a number of revisions. The most significant changes stemmed from the 1986–1994 Uruguay Round of negotiations, which took bold steps to slash average tariffs by about 30% and to reduce other trade barriers among the 125 nations that signed.

The Uruguay Round also created the **World Trade Organization (WTO)**, a permanent global institution to promote international trade and to settle international trade disputes. The WTO monitors provisions of the GATT agreements, promotes further reduction of trade barriers, and mediates disputes among members. The decisions of the WTO are binding, which means that all parties involved in disputes must comply to maintain good standing in the organization.

Ministers of the WTO meet every two years to address current world trade issues. As the world economy has shifted toward services rather than goods, the emphasis of WTO meetings has followed suit. Controlling rampant piracy of intellectual property is a key concern for developed countries. For less-developed countries, one central issue is U.S. and European agricultural subsidies, which may unfairly distort agricultural prices worldwide.

In fact, both the broader agenda and the individual decisions of the WTO have become increasingly controversial over the past ten years. Advocates for less-developed nations are deeply concerned that free trade clears the path for major multinational corporations to push local businesses into economic failure. A local food stand, for instance, probably won't have the resources to compete with a global giant such as McDonald's. If the food stand closes, the community has gained inexpensive hamburgers, but the entrepreneur has lost his livelihood, and the community has lost the local flavor that contributes to its unique culture. Other opponents of the WTO worry that the acceleration of global trade encourages developing countries to fight laws that protect the environment and workers' rights, for fear of losing their low-cost advantage on the world market. The concerns have sparked significant protests during the past few meetings of the WTO ministers, and the outcry may well grow louder as developing nations gain economic clout.

3-6b The World Bank

Established in the aftermath of World War II, the **World Bank** is an international cooperative of 188 member countries, working together to reduce poverty in the developing world. The World Bank influences the global economy by providing financial and technical advice to the governments of developing countries for projects in a range of areas, including infrastructure, communications, health, and education. The financial assistance usually comes in the form of low-interest loans. But to secure a

free trade The unrestricted movement of goods and services across international borders.

General Agreement on Tariffs and Trade (GATT) An international trade treaty designed to encourage worldwide trade among its members.

World Trade Organization (WTO) A permanent global institution to promote international trade and to settle international trade disputes.

World Bank An international cooperative of 188 member countries, working together to reduce poverty in the developing world.

The World Bank and the IMF both require a remarkable degree of international communication.

Stephen Jaffe/Handout/IMF/Getty Images

loan, the borrowing nation must often agree to conditions that can involve rather arduous economic reform.

3-6c The International Monetary Fund

Like the World Bank, the **International Monetary Fund (IMF)** is an international organization accountable to the governments of its 188 member nations. The basic mission of the IMF is to promote international economic cooperation and stable growth. Funding comes from the member nations, with the United States contributing more than twice as much as any other country. To achieve these goals, the IMF:

- Supports stable exchange rates
- Facilitates a smooth system of international payments
- Encourages member nations to adopt sound economic policies
- Promotes international trade
- Lends money to member nations to address economic problems

Although all of its functions are important, the IMF is best known as a lender of last resort to nations in financial trouble. This policy has come under fire in the past few years. Critics accuse the IMF of encouraging poor countries to borrow more money than they can ever hope to repay, which actually cripples their economies over the long term, creating even deeper poverty.

At the end of 2005, the IMF responded to its critics by implementing a historic debt relief program for poor countries. Under this program, which has since been expanded to include other agencies, the IMF and its partners have extended 100% debt forgiveness to 35 poor countries, erasing about $76 billion in debt. The managing director of the IMF pointed out that the canceled debt will allow these countries to increase spending in priority areas to reduce poverty and promote growth (although some experts worry that debt cancellation sets a troubling precedent for future lending). The result should be a higher standard of living for some of the poorest people in the world.[26]

3-6d Trading Blocs and Common Markets

Another major development in the past decade is the emergence of regional **trading blocs**, or groups of countries that have reduced or even eliminated all tariffs, allowing the free flow of goods among the member nations. A **common market** goes even further than a trading bloc by attempting to harmonize all trading rules. The United States, Mexico, and Canada have formed the largest trading bloc in the world, and the 28 countries of the European Union have formed the largest common market.

NAFTA The **North American Free Trade Agreement (NAFTA)** is the treaty that created the free-trading zone among the United States, Mexico, and Canada. The agreement took effect in 1994, gradually eliminating trade barriers and investment

> "WE MUST CREATE A KIND OF GLOBALIZATION THAT WORKS FOR EVERYONE... AND NOT JUST FOR A FEW."
>
> —NESTOR KIRCHNER, ARGENTINE STATESMAN

International Monetary Fund (IMF) An international organization of 188 member nations that promotes international economic cooperation and stable growth.

trading bloc A group of countries that have reduced or even eliminated tariffs, allowing for the free flow of goods among the member nations.

common market A group of countries that have eliminated tariffs and harmonized trading rules to facilitate the free flow of goods among the member nations.

North American Free Trade Agreement (NAFTA) The treaty among the United States, Mexico, and Canada that eliminated trade barriers and investment restrictions over a 15-year period starting in 1994.

REASONS TO CREATE TRADE RESTRICTIONS	REASONS TO ELIMINATE TRADE RESTRICTIONS
Protect domestic industry (e.g., the U.S. steel industry)	Reduce prices and increase choices for consumers by encouraging competition from around the world
Protect domestic jobs in key industries (but perhaps at the cost of domestic jobs in other industries)	Increase domestic jobs in industries with a comparative advantage versus other countries
Protect national security interests	Increase jobs—both at home and abroad—from foreign companies
Retaliate against countries who have engaged in unfair trade practices	Build exporting opportunities through better relationships with other countries
Pressure other countries to change their policies and practices	Use resources more efficiently on a worldwide basis

© 2015 Cengage Learning®

restrictions over a 15-year period. Despite dire predictions of American jobs flowing to Mexico, the U.S. economy has grown significantly since the implementation of NAFTA. The Canadian and Mexican economies have thrived as well (although all three economies have slowed significantly during the global economic crisis).

But NAFTA critics point out that the U.S. trade deficit with both Mexico and Canada has skyrocketed. While exports to both nations have increased, imports have grown far faster; both countries are among the top ten contributors to the total U.S. trade deficit, threatening the long-term health of the American economy. Other criticisms of NAFTA include increased pollution and worker abuse. Companies that move their factories to Mexico to capitalize on lower costs also take advantage of looser environmental and worker-protection laws, creating major ethical concerns. But the full impact of NAFTA—for better or for worse—is tough to evaluate because so many other variables affect all three economies.[27]

EUROPEAN UNION Composed of 28 nations and more than half a billion people, and boasting a combined GDP of nearly $17 trillion, the **European Union (EU)** is the world's largest common market. Exhibit 3.3 shows a map of the 2014 EU countries plus six countries which have applied to join.[28]

The overarching goal of the EU is to bolster Europe's trade position and to increase its international political and economic power. To help make this happen, the EU has removed all trade restrictions among member nations and unified internal trade rules, allowing goods

> **ALMOST HALF THE WORLD—OVER THREE BILLION PEOPLE—LIVE ON LESS THAN $2.50 A DAY.**
> —GLOBALISSUES.ORG

and people to move freely among EU countries. The EU has also created standardized policies for import and export between EU countries and the rest of the world, giving the member nations more clout as a bloc than each would have had on its own. Perhaps the EU's most economically significant move was the introduction of a single currency, the euro, in 2002. Of the 15 EU members at the time, 12 adopted

European Union (EU) The world's largest common market, composed of 28 European nations.

Exhibit 3.3
European Union 2015

© 2016 Cengage Learning®

GOLDEN STATE OR LEADEN WEIGHT?

Conventional wisdom has long held that "As California goes, so goes the nation." If that is indeed the case, the nation is on track for either wild success or massive failure, depending on who you ask.

Golden State detractors point out that more than 30% of the nation's welfare recipients are Californians—even though California has just 12% of the nation's population—ranking California number one in terms of poverty. They also cite high taxes, high debt, high regulation, and severe drought as causes for an overwhelmingly negative outlook. But Golden State boosters are quick to point out that in early 2015, California was overtaking Brazil as the world's seventh largest economy, having surpassed Russia and Italy in 2014. Causes for optimism include rising employment, home values, and personal and corporate income. According to Governor Jerry Brown, "It's the diversity of the California business environment, from movies to the Internet to agriculture—the incredible array of businesses that make up the state…the new investments in our schools; solid universities; investments in water and energy. All this gives security and keeps California very much in the forefront of investment, change, cultural adaptation and leadership."

California's economic well-being may or may not actually predict the health of other markets, but for everyone's sake, let's hope that the Golden State rocks good vibrations around the world.[29]

the euro (exceptions were the United Kingdom, Sweden, and Denmark). The EU also affects the global economy with its leading-edge approach to environmental protection, quality production, and human rights.

In 2010 and 2011, hobbled by overwhelming debt and slow growth, several of the weaker EU countries—most notably Greece—spiraled into economic crisis. Fearing a financial domino effect, due to the close ties among the nations, the economically stronger EU countries cobbled together several bailout packages. But many economists still fear that its weaker members could drag the EU overall into a deep, damaging recession, and that one or more countries could default on its debt, withdraw from using the euro as currency, or both, with devastating financial consequences for both the EU and the world economy.

The BIG Picture

The past decade has been marked by extraordinary changes in the world economy. The boundaries between individual countries have fallen lower than ever before, creating a new level of economic connectedness. The growing integration has created huge opportunities for visionary companies of every size. But integration also means risk. The dangers became clear in 2008, when the economic crisis in the United States rapidly reverberated around the globe, fueling a deep, worldwide recession.

To succeed abroad—especially in tough economic times—individual firms must make the right choices about how to structure their operations, surmount barriers to trade, meet diverse customer needs, manage a global workforce, and handle complex logistics. Human rights and environmental protection continue to be especially critical for international businesses. Both are vital components of social responsibility and will only gain importance as advocates raise awareness around the world. In the face of economic, political, and social flux, effective global business leaders must master both strategy and implementation at a deeper level than ever before.

Careers in International Business

International Sports Marketing Manager

Implement marketing plans outside the United States with a focus on Europe, Australia, and New Zealand. Work with global brand marketing team to develop and execute events that incorporate athletes. Participate in the scouting process to identify and pursue up-and-coming athletes in relevant sports. Provide support for the endorsement contract negotiation process. For more information on this career and other possible careers in international business, check out Career Transitions.

STUDY TOOLS 3

LOCATED AT BACK OF THE TEXTBOOK

☐ Rip Out Chapter Review Card

LOCATED AT WWW.CENGAGE.COM/LOGIN

☐ Review key term flashcards and create your own using StudyBits

☐ Create and complete practice quizzes based off of your notes and StudyBits

☐ Complete Online activities such as Matching, Fill-in-the-Blank and Drag and Drop exercises

☐ View chapter highlight box content, including CEO Profiles, What Would You Do Cases and chapter videos

☐ Track your knowledge and understanding of key concepts in business using 4LTR Online

YOUR
FEED-
BACK
YOUR
BOOK

Our research never ends. Continual feedback from you ensures that we keep up with your changing needs.

4 | Business Ethics and Social Responsibility:
Doing Well by Doing Good

LEARNING OBJECTIVES
After studying this chapter, you will be able to:

4-1 Define ethics and explain the concept of universal ethical standards

4-2 Describe business ethics and ethical dilemmas

4-3 Discuss how ethics relates to both the individual and the organization

4-4 Define social responsibility and examine the impact on stakeholder groups

4-5 Explain the role of social responsibility in the global arena

4-6 Describe how companies evaluate their efforts to be socially responsible

Remember to visit
PAGE 72
for additional
STUDY TOOLS

4-1 ETHICS AND SOCIAL RESPONSIBILITY: A CLOSE RELATIONSHIP

Ethics and social responsibility—often discussed in the same breath—are closely related, but they are definitely not the same. Ethics refers to sets of beliefs about right and wrong, good and bad; business ethics involve the application of these issues in the workplace. Clearly, ethics relate to individuals and their day-to-day decision making. Just as clearly, the decisions of each individual can affect the entire organization.

Social responsibility is the obligation of a business to contribute to society. The most socially responsible firms feature proactive policies that focus on meeting the needs of all their stakeholders—not just investors but also employees, customers, the broader community, and the environment. The stance of a company regarding social responsibility sets the tone for the organization and clearly influences the decisions of individual employees.

Although this chapter discusses ethics and social responsibility separately, keep in mind that

the two areas have a dynamic, interactive relationship that plays a vital role in building both profitable businesses and a vibrant community.

4-1a Defining Ethics: Murkier Than You'd Think

In the most general sense, **ethics** refer to sets of beliefs about right and wrong, good and bad. While your individual ethics stem from who you are as a human being, your family, your social group, and your culture also play a significant role in shaping your ethics. And therein lies the

ethics A set of beliefs about right and wrong, good and bad.

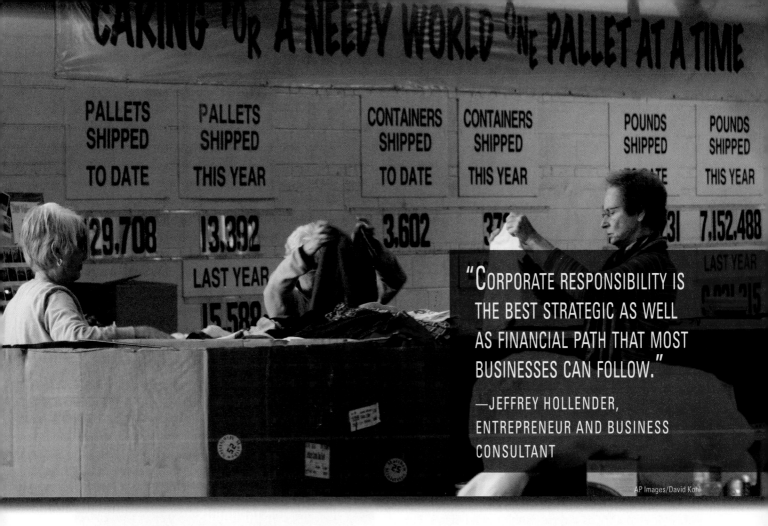

CARING FOR A NEEDY WORLD ONE PALLET AT A TIME

| PALLETS SHIPPED TO DATE | PALLETS SHIPPED THIS YEAR | CONTAINERS SHIPPED TO DATE | CONTAINERS SHIPPED THIS YEAR | POUNDS SHIPPED | POUNDS SHIPPED THIS YEAR |

"CORPORATE RESPONSIBILITY IS THE BEST STRATEGIC AS WELL AS FINANCIAL PATH THAT MOST BUSINESSES CAN FOLLOW."

—JEFFREY HOLLENDER, ENTREPRENEUR AND BUSINESS CONSULTANT

AP Images/David Kohl

challenge: in the United States, people come from such diverse backgrounds that establishing broad agreement on specific ethical standards can be daunting. The global arena only amplifies the challenge.

A given country's legal system provides a solid starting point for examining ethical standards. The function of laws in the United States (and elsewhere) is to establish and enforce ethical norms that apply to everyone within our society. Laws provide basic standards of behavior. But truly ethical behavior goes beyond the basics. In other words, your actions can be completely legal, yet still unethical. But since the legal system is far from perfect, in rare instances your actions can be illegal, yet still ethical. Exhibit 4.1 shows some examples of how business conduct can fall within legal and ethical dimensions. Clearly, legal and ethical actions should be your goal. Legality should be the floor—not the ceiling—for how to behave in business and elsewhere.

Do all actions have ethical implications? Clearly not. Some decisions fall within the realm of free choice with no direct link to right and wrong, good and bad. Examples might include what color tee shirt you choose to wear, what levels your game development company includes in its new video game, or what sunglasses you decide to purchase.

4-1b Universal Ethical Standards: A Reasonable Goal or Wishful Thinking?

Too many people view ethics as relative. In other words, their ethical standards shift depending on the situation and how it relates to them. Here are a few examples:

- "It's not okay to steal paper from the office supply store…*but* it's perfectly fine to 'borrow' supplies from the storage closet at work to use at home. Why? The company owes me a bigger salary."

- "It's wrong to lie…*but* it's okay to call in sick when I have personal business to take care of. Why? I don't want to burn through my limited vacation days."

- "Everyone should have a level playing field…*but* it's fine to give my brother the first shot at my company's contract. Why? I know he really needs the work."

This kind of two-faced thinking is dangerous because it can help people rationalize bigger and bigger ethical deviations. But the problem can be fixed by identifying **universal ethical standards** that apply

universal ethical standards
Ethical norms that apply to all people across a broad spectrum of situations.

EXHIBIT 4.1 LEGAL-ETHICAL MATRIX

Legal and Unethical	Legal and Ethical
Promoting high-calorie/low-nutrient foods with inadequate information about the risks	Producing high-quality products
Producing products that you know will break before their time	Rewarding integrity Leading by example
Paying non-living wages to workers in developing countries	Treating employees fairly Contributing to the community Respecting the environment
Illegal and Unethical	**Illegal and Ethical**
Embezzling money	Providing rock-bottom prices *only* to distributors in underserved areas
Engaging in sexual harassment	Collaborating with other medical clinics to guarantee low prices in low-income counties (collusion)
Practicing collusion with competitors	
Encouraging fraudulent accounting	

© Cengage Learning®

to everyone across a broad spectrum of situations. Some people argue that we could never find universal standards for a country as diverse as the United States. But the nonprofit, nonpartisan Character Counts organization has worked with a diverse group of educators, community leaders, and ethicists to identify six core values, listed in Exhibit 4.2, that transcend political, religious, class, and ethnic divisions.

4-2 BUSINESS ETHICS: NOT AN OXYMORON

Quite simply, **business ethics** is the application of right and wrong, good and bad in a business setting. But this isn't as straightforward as it may initially seem. The most challenging business decisions seem to arise when values are in conflict... when whatever you do will have negative consequences, forcing you to choose among bad options. These are true **ethical dilemmas**. (Keep in mind that ethical *dilemmas* differ from

business ethics The application of right and wrong, good and bad, in a business setting.

ethical dilemma A decision that involves a conflict of values; every potential course of action has some significant negative consequences.

EXHIBIT 4.2 UNIVERSAL ETHICAL STANDARDS

Trustworthiness	Be honest. Don't deceive, cheat, or steal. Do what you say you'll do.
Respect	Treat others how you'd like to be treated. Be considerate. Be tolerant of differences.
Responsibility	Persevere. Be self-controlled and self-disciplined. Be accountable for your choices.
Fairness	Provide equal opportunity. Be open-minded. Don't take advantage of others.
Caring	Be kind. Be compassionate. Express gratitude.
Citizenship	Contribute to the community. Protect the environment. Cooperate whenever feasible.

Source: © 2009 Josephson Institute. Reprinted from the Josephson Institute's Report Card on the Ethics of American Youth Summary with permission.

An A for Ethics?

Not quite. Every two years, the Josephson Institute Center for Youth Ethics produces a Report Card on the Ethics of American Youth, based on a survey of thousands of students in high schools across the United States. The 2012 results suggested that students are disturbingly willing to lie, cheat, or steal, despite significant improvement versus previous years. Some highlights from the institute:

- **Lying:** Students who admitted that they lied to a teacher in the past year about *something significant* dropped from 61% in 2010 to 55% in 2012. Those who admitted that they lied to their parents in the past year about *something significant* dropped from 80% in 2010 to 76% in 2012.

- **Cheating:** Students who admitted that they cheated on an exam in the past year dropped from 59% in 2010 to 51% in 2012.

- **Stealing:** Students who admitted that they stole something from a store in the past year dropped from 27% in 2010 to 20% in 2012.

Interestingly, boys are much more likely than girls to engage in ethical misconduct.

- Twenty-three percent of boys admitted to stealing from a store in the past year, compared to 17% of girls.

- Nineteen percent of boys had stolen from a friend versus 10% of girls.

If teenage behavior predicts adult behavior, and if the 2012 Ethics Report Card results indicate the start of a trend, we have every reason to hope that tomorrow's adults will make the grade in terms of ethical behavior.[1]

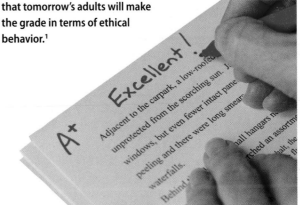

Pixsooz/Shutterstock.com

---

ethical *lapses*, which involve clear misconduct.) Here are three hypothetical examples of ethical dilemmas:

- You've just done a great job on a recent project at your company. Your boss has been very vocal about acknowledging your work and the increased revenue that resulted from it. Privately, she said that you clearly earned a bonus of at least 10%, but due to company politics, she was unable to secure the bonus for you. She also implied that if you were to submit inflated expense reports for the next few months, she would look the other way, and you could pocket the extra cash as well-deserved compensation for your contributions.

- You run a medium-sized publishing firm, and you pride yourself on offering your employees cutting-edge benefits. One of the new benefits that you are planning to propose to your board is six months paid maternity/paternity leave. You happen to know—because they told you in confidence—that two of your top team members are currently pregnant, and would almost certainly take advantage of the new policy if it were in place. Without the new policy, they would have to take three months unpaid leave. You also know that if these women were each gone for six months, the workload would increase dramatically for the rest of the senior staff members (yourself included). To make matters even more complicated, you and your spouse are hoping to start your own family in about a year, and would certainly benefit from the paid leave.

- Facebook: For one week in 2012, Facebook changed the content mix in the News Feeds of more than half a million users—without asking their permission—in an effort to gauge their emotional response. While the manipulation was covered under Facebook's terms of service, many users were outraged at what they considered an unethical psychological experiment without their permission. Facebook COO Sheryl Sandberg issued a classic nonapology: "It was poorly communicated. And for that communication we apologize." In actuality, the experiment was not communicated at all.

Juli Hansen/Shutterstock.com

4-3 ETHICS: MULTIPLE TOUCHPOINTS

Although each person must make his or her own ethical choices, the organization can have a significant influence on the quality of those decisions.

4-3a Ethics and the Individual: The Power of One

Ethical choices begin with ethical individuals. Your personal needs, your family, your culture, and your religion all influence your value system. Your personality traits—self-esteem, self-confidence, independence, and sense of humor—play a significant role as well. A recent study suggested that personal empathy—"identification with and understanding of another's situation, feelings, and motives"—is another strong predictor of ethical leadership. In fact, business leaders who scored highest on empathy also exhibited the highest levels of ethical leadership. These factors all come into play as you face ethical dilemmas. The challenge can be overwhelming, which has led a range of experts to develop frameworks for reaching ethical decisions. While the specifics vary, the key principles of most decision guides are very similar[2]:

- Do you fully understand each dimension of the problem?

- Who would benefit? Who would suffer?

- Are the alternative solutions legal? Are they fair?

- Does your decision make you comfortable at a "gut feel" level?

- Could you defend your decision on the nightly TV news?

- Have you considered and reconsidered your responses to each question?

The approach seems simple, but in practice it really isn't. Workers—and managers, too—often face enormous pressure to do what's right for the company or right for their career, rather than simply what's right. And keep in mind that it's completely possible for two people to follow the framework and arrive at completely different decisions, each feeling confident that he or she has made the right choice.

> "I KNOW IT SOUNDS CORNY, BUT I'D LOVE TO IMPROVE PEOPLE'S LIVES."
>
> —MARK ZUCKERBERG, FACEBOOK FOUNDER

4-3b Ethics and the Organization: It Takes a Village

Although each person is clearly responsible for his or her own actions, the organization can influence those actions to a startling degree. Not surprisingly, that influence starts at the top, and actions matter far more than words. The president of the Ethics Resource Center states, "CEOs in particular must communicate their personal commitment to high ethical standards and consistently drive the message down to employees through their actions." Any other approach—even just the *appearance* of shaky ethics—can be deeply damaging to a company's ethical climate. Here are a couple of examples from the wake of the Great Recession:

- High Flyers: When the CEOs of the Big Three automakers—two of them hovering on the edge of bankruptcy—went to Washington to request a $25 billion bailout package, they flew in three separate corporate jets at an estimated cost of $20,000 per round-trip flight. All three were operating in line with official corporate travel policies, but it just didn't look right. One lawmaker pointedly asked, "Couldn't you all have downgraded to first class or jet-pooled or something to get here? It would have at least sent a message that you do get it." Not surprisingly, the execs left empty-handed.[3]

- Beach Junket: A few days after the Fed committed $85 billion to keep AIG out of bankruptcy, the insurer spent more than $440,000 on a sales "retreat" at a luxury resort in California. Expenditures included $150,000 for food, $23,000 in spa charges, and $7,000 for golf. Rather than apologizing, CEO Edward Liddy only committed that the company would examine its expenses.[4]

- Gross Excess: In 2009, ousted Merrill Lynch CEO John Thain agreed—under pressure from President Obama—to reimburse federal bailout recipient Bank of America for an expensive, and fully approved, renovation of his office that had been done before the crisis hit. The somewhat outrageous expenses included an $87,000 area rug, a $5,000 mirror, and a $35,000 commode.

Are these decisions wrong? Unethical?[5] How do you feel about the business decisions described in Exhibit 4.3?

4-3c Creating and Maintaining an Ethical Organization

Research from the Ethics Resource Center (ERC) suggests that organizational culture has more influence than any other variable on the ethical conduct of individual employees. According to the ERC, key elements of a strong culture include displays of ethics-related actions at all levels of an organization and accountability for actions. The impact of these elements can be dramatic. Consider, for example, the following research results:

- A 61-percentage-point favorable difference in the level of observed misconduct when employees say they work in a strong ethical culture.

- When employees felt that the Great Recession negatively impacted the ethical culture of their company, misconduct rose by 16 percentage points.

- ERC research showed that companies behave differently during economic difficulties.

PlusONE/Shutterstock.com

Business ethics are a top priority in most companies.

The decisions and behaviors of their leaders are perceived by employees as a heightened commitment to ethics. As a result, employees adopt a higher standard of conduct for themselves.[7]

Robert Lane, former CEO of Deere, a highly performing, highly ethical corporation, believes in the importance of senior management commitment to ethics, but he points out that the "tone at the top" must be reinforced by the actual behavior observed by suppliers, dealers, customers, and employees. At Deere, this is summed up in highly visible, frequently referenced shorthand known as "the how." Lane declares that to establish an ethical culture, ethical words must be "backed up with documented practices, processes, and procedures, all understood around the globe."[8]

ERC research further supports the need for senior manager commitment by showing that when employees perceive more management commitment, they tend to be more fully engaged. More-engaged employees are much less likely to behave badly, and much more likely to report others who do, which dramatically lowers the risk for the company.[9]

A strong organizational culture works in tandem with formal ethics programs to create and maintain ethical work environments. A written **code of ethics** is the cornerstone of any formal ethics program. The purpose of a written code is to give employees the information they need to make ethical decisions across a range of situations. Clearly, an ethics code becomes even more important for multinational companies, since it lays out unifying values and priorities for divisions that are rooted in different cultures. But a written code is worthless if it doesn't reflect living principles. An effective code of ethics flows directly from ethical corporate values and leads directly to ongoing communication, training, and action.

Specific codes of ethics vary greatly among organizations. Perhaps the best-known code is the Johnson & Johnson Credo, which has guided the company profitably—with a soaring reputation—through a number of crises that would have sunk lesser organizations. One of the striking elements of the credo is the firm focus on fairness. It carefully refrains from overpromising financial rewards, committing instead to a "fair return" for stockholders.

To bring a code of ethics to life, experts advocate a forceful, integrated approach to ethics that virtually always includes the following steps:

1. Get executive buy-in and commitment to follow through. Top managers need to communicate—even overcommunicate—about the importance of ethics. But talking works only when it's backed up by action: senior management must give priority to keeping promises and leading by example.

2. Establish expectations for ethical behavior at all levels of the organization, from the CEO to the nighttime cleaning crew. Be sure that outside parties such as suppliers, distributors, and customers understand the standards.

3. Integrate ethics into mandatory staff training. From new-employee orientation to ongoing training, ethics must play a role. Additional, more specialized training helps employees who face more temptation (e.g., purchasing agents, overseas sales reps).

4. Ensure that your ethics code is both global and local in scope. Employees in every country should understand both the general principles and the specific applications. Be sure to translate it into as many languages as necessary.

5. Build and maintain a clear, trusted reporting structure for ethical concerns and violations. The structure should allow employees to seek anonymous guidance for ethical concerns and to report ethics violations anonymously.

6. Establish protection for **whistle-blowers**, people who report illegal or unethical behavior. Be sure that no retaliation occurs, in compliance with both ethics and the Sarbanes-Oxley Act (see discussion later in the chapter). Some have even suggested that whistle-blowers should receive a portion of the penalties levied against firms that violate the law.

7. Enforce the code of ethics. When people violate ethical norms, companies must respond immediately and—whenever appropriate—publicly to retain employee trust. Without enforcement, the code of ethics becomes meaningless.

4-4 DEFINING SOCIAL RESPONSIBILITY: MAKING THE WORLD A BETTER PLACE

Social responsibility is the obligation of a business to contribute to society. Similar to ethics, the broad definition is clear, but specific implementation can be complex. Obviously, the number-one goal of any business is long-term profits; without profits, other contributions are impossible. But once a firm achieves a reasonable return, the balancing act begins: how can a company balance the need to contribute against the need to boost profits, especially when the two conflict? The answer depends on the business's values, mission, resources, and management philosophy, which lead in turn to its position on social responsibility. Business approaches fall across the spectrum, from no contribution to proactive contribution, as shown in Exhibit 4.4.

BortN66/Shutterstock.com

code of ethics A formal, written document that defines the ethical standards of an organization and gives employees the information they need to make ethical decisions across a range of situations.

whistle-blowers Employees who report their employer's illegal or unethical behavior to either the authorities or the media.

social responsibility The obligation of a business to contribute to society.

Exhibit 4.4
The Spectrum of Social Responsibility

LESS
Responsible

No Contribution

Some businesses do not recognize an obligation to society and do only what's legally required.

Responsive Contributions

Some businesses choose to respond on a case-by-case basis to market requests for contributions.

Proactive Contributions

Some businesses choose to integrate social responsibility into their strategic plans, contributing as part of their business goals.

MORE
Responsible

© Cengage Learning®

4-4a The Stakeholder Approach: Responsibility to Whom?

Stakeholders are any groups that have a stake—or a personal interest—in the performance and actions of an organization. Different stakeholders have different needs, expectations, and levels of interest. The federal government, for instance, is a key stakeholder in pharmaceutical companies but a very minor stakeholder in local art studios. The community at large is a key stakeholder for a coffee shop chain but a minor stakeholder for a web design firm. Enlightened organizations identify key stakeholders for their business and consider stakeholder priorities in their decision making. The goal is to balance their needs and priorities as effectively as possible, with an eye toward building their business over the long term. Core stakeholder groups for most businesses are employees, customers, investors, and the broader community.

RESPONSIBILITY TO EMPLOYEES: CREATING JOBS THAT WORK Jobs alone aren't enough. The starting point for socially responsible employers is to meet legal standards, and the requirements are significant. How would you judge the social responsibility of the firms listed in Exhibit 4.5? Employers must comply with laws that include equal opportunity, workplace safety, minimum-wage and overtime requirements, protection from sexual harassment, and family and medical unpaid leaves. We will discuss these legal requirements (and others) in Chapter 15 on Human Resource Management.

But socially responsible employers go far beyond the law. They create a workplace environment that respects the dignity and value of each employee. They ensure that hard work, commitment, and talent pay off. They move beyond minimal safety requirements to establish proactive protections, such as ergonomically correct chairs and computer screens that reduce eyestrain. And the best employers respond to the ongoing employee search for a balance between work and personal life. With an increasing number of workers facing challenges such as raising kids and caring for elderly parents, responsible companies are stepping in with programs such as on-site day care, company-sponsored day camp, and referral services for elder care.

RESPONSIBILITY TO CUSTOMERS: VALUE, HONESTY, AND COMMUNICATION One core responsibility of business is to deliver consumer value by providing quality products at fair prices. Honesty and communication are critical components of this equation. **Consumerism**—a widely accepted social movement—suggests that consumer rights should be the starting point. In the early 1960s, President Kennedy defined these rights, which most businesses respect in response to both consumer expectations and legal requirements:

■ The Right to Be Safe: Businesses are

> **stakeholders** Any groups that have a stake—or a personal interest—in the performance and actions of an organization.
>
> **consumerism** A social movement that focuses on four key consumer rights: (1) the right to be safe, (2) the right to be informed, (3) the right to choose, and (4) the right to be heard.

EXHIBIT 4.5   SOCIAL RESPONSIBILITY AT WORK

How Would You Judge the Actions of These Firms?[10]

The Clorox Company In early 2008, Clorox introduced a line of "99% natural" cleaning products called Green Works. This was the first such effort from a major consumer products company, and also the first time that the Sierra Club endorsed a product line by allowing the use of its logo on the labels. In return, Clorox makes an annual contribution to the Sierra Club, the amount based on total Green Works sales.

Enron/Arthur Andersen (now defunct) Enron, once hailed as a shining example of corporate excellence, collapsed in late 2001 due to massive accounting fraud, which bilked employees and other small investors out of millions of dollars. Arthur Andersen, hired to audit Enron's accountings, participated in the scandal by masking the issues and shredding documents containing potential evidence.

Facebook For one week in 2012, Facebook changed the content mix in the News Feeds of more than half a million users—without asking their permission—in an effort to gauge their emotional response. While the manipulation was covered under Facebook's terms of service, many users were outraged at what they considered an unethical psychological experiment without their permission. Facebook COO Sheryl Sandberg issued a classic nonapology: "It was poorly communicated. And for that communication we apologize." In actuality, the experiment was not communicated at all.

Bank of America After receiving $45 billion in taxpayer bailout funds, Bank of America sponsored a five-day carnival-like event outside the 2009 Super Bowl stadium called the NFL Experience. The high-profile attraction included 850,000 square feet of sports games, plus marketing solicitations for football-themed B of A banking products. The bank defended the event as an effective growth strategy, while critics blasted it as an abuse of taxpayer dollars.

Kraft As obesity among kids spirals out of control, Kraft has taken a brave stand: a pledge to stop advertising unhealthy—yet highly profitable—foods to young children. Kraft also plans to eliminate in-school marketing and drop some unhealthy snacks from school vending machines. As the king of the food business, Kraft has chosen what's right for kids over what's right for its own short-term profits.

AIG: After the U.S. government pulled AIG from the brink of bankruptcy in 2008 with a bailout that topped $182 billion, the AIG board of directors voted in early 2013 about whether to join a lawsuit against the government, which claimed that the interest rate on the initial loan was excessive and the rescue was unfair to shareholders. Faced with public wrath and ridicule, they ultimately opted out of the lawsuit, but not before they further damaged their reputation among the general public.

legally responsible for injuries and damages caused by their products—even if they have no reason to suspect that their products might cause harm. This makes it easy for consumers to file suits. In some cases, the drive to avert lawsuits has led to absurdities such as the warning on some coffee cups: "Caution! Hot coffee is hot!" (No kidding…)

- The Right to Be Informed: The law requires firms in a range of industries—from mutual funds, to groceries, to pharmaceuticals—to provide the public with extensive information. The Food and Drug Administration, for instance, mandates that most grocery

foods feature a very specific "Nutrition Facts" label. Beyond legal requirements, many firms use the Web to provide a wealth of extra information about their products. KFC, for example, offers an interactive Nutrition Calculator that works with all of its menu items (and it's fun to use, too).

- The Right to Choose: Freedom of choice is a fundamental element of the capitalist U.S. economy. Our economic system works largely because consumers freely choose to purchase the products that best meet their needs. As businesses compete, consumer value increases. Socially responsible firms support consumer choice by following the laws that prevent anticompetitive behavior such as predatory pricing, collusion, and monopolies.

- The Right to Be Heard: Socially responsible companies make it easy for consumers to express legitimate complaints. They also develop highly trained customer service people to respond to complaints. In fact, smart businesses view customer complaints as an opportunity to create better products and stronger relationships. Statistics suggest that 1 in 50 dissatisfied customers takes the time to complain. The other 49 quietly switch brands. By soliciting feedback, you're not only being responsible, but also building your business.[11]

> "IN THIS ERA OF CORPORATE SCANDALS, WE MUST REFOCUS OUR ENERGIES ON CORPORATE ETHICS AND ENCOURAGE INDIVIDUALS TO REPORT WRONGDOING."
>
> —JORDAN THOMAS, CHAIR, WHISTLEBLOWER REPRESENTATION PRACTICE, LABATON SUCHAROW

Delivering quality products is another key component of social responsibility to consumers. **Planned obsolescence**—deliberately designing products to fail in order to shorten the time between consumer repurchases—represents a clear violation of social responsibility. In the long term, the market itself weeds out offenders. After all, who would repurchase a product that meets a premature end? But in the short term, planned obsolescence thins consumer wallets and abuses consumer trust.

When businesses do make mistakes, apologizing to consumers won't guarantee renewed sales. But a sincere apology can definitely restore a company's reputation, which can ultimately lead to greater profits. Three examples make this point clear:

- *Going with the Flow*: In late 2010, Johnson & Johnson discontinued the popular o.b. Ultra tampons. Loyal users stripped the shelves of remaining stock (bidding the price of a box of Ultras up to more than $100 on eBay) and bombarded the manufacturer with complaints. In late 2011, Johnson & Johnson announced that Ultras would be back on shelf by late 2012, and offered an apology video rife with every cliché imaginable, including a handsome, male singer. The music video was customizable; viewer names appeared throughout in the video, and the video closed with a coupon offer. The video represented a masterful attempt to regain loyalty for a product that had yet to reappear on the shelf.[12]

Investors count on companies to spend money wisely and fully disclose all key facts.

- *Apple Angst*: Apple introduced the iPhone on June 29, 2007, to rave reviews and stellar sales, despite the $599 price tag. But two months later, Apple dropped the price of the phone by $200, in order to expand the user base yet further. Not surprisingly, early adopters were livid—why, they demanded, did Apple repay their trust and support by ripping them off? CEO Steve Jobs quickly apologized and offered every $599 iPhone customer a $100 Apple store credit. The response seemed to work. In 2008, Apple's ranking in the American Customer Satisfaction Index climbed 8%, a full ten percentage points ahead of its nearest competitor, maintaining a dramatic lead through 2011.[13]

Investors count on companies to spend money wisely and fully disclose all key facts.

- *More Apple Angst:* In September 2012, Apple released an updated version of its moble Maps program, which iPhone users quickly realized was a hot mess that featured too many wrong directions, misplaced locations, and bizarre satellite images. CEO Tim Cook sent a contrite apology to customers, but basically referred them to archrival Google Maps, after acknowledging that Apple's Maps was not up to par. He ended the apology with some puffery about how Apple aims to make all their products "the best in the world." The following Christmas, iPhone sales underperformed analyst expectations, and the stock price plummeted, which may have been completely unrelated to the Maps debacle.[14]

RESPONSIBILITY TO INVESTORS: FAIR STEWARDSHIP AND FULL DISCLOSURE The primary responsibility of business to investors is clearly to make money—to create an ongoing stream of profits. But companies achieve and maintain long-term earnings in the context of responsibility to *all* stakeholders, which may mean trading short-term profits for long-term success. Responsibility to investors starts by meeting legal requirements, and in the wake of recent corporate scandals, the bar is higher than ever. The 2002 **Sarbanes-Oxley Act** limits conflict-of-interest issues by restricting the consulting services that accounting firms can provide for the companies they audit. Sarbanes-Oxley also requires that financial officers and CEOs personally certify the validity of their financial statements. (See Chapter 8 for more detail on the Sarbanes-Oxley Act.)

But beyond legal requirements, companies

planned obsolescence The strategy of deliberately designing products to fail in order to shorten the time between purchases.

Sarbanes-Oxley Act Federal legislation passed in 2002 that sets higher ethical standards for public corporations and accounting firms. Key provisions limit conflict-of-interest issues and require financial officers and CEOs to certify the validity of their financial statements.

Profits and Then Some

If the corporation you're dealing with does not have profits as a first priority, it may well be a B-Corp, or benefit corporation. B-Corps are a new corporate structure that value profits, but not more than other priorities such as employees, suppliers, the community, and the environment. Benefit corporations do not receive special tax treatment, but B-Corp status, like the food producer's organic certification, can offer a real advantage, especially for firms competing in crowded markets. It can also keep companies focused on what makes them different, especially since firms must undergo comprehensive annual audits to keep their status. Current B-Corps fall across a range of industries and include businesses of all different sizes. One example is Green Mountain Power of Vermont, which generates most of its power with renewable energy such as hydroelectric and wind power. It pays its employees more than 25% above the living wage and covers 80% of their health care premiums.

More than 25% of its managers are women or minorities. And Green Mountain pays workers to do volunteer work in their communities. Sounds like a benefit corporation that puts workers at the top of its priority list.[15]

Source: Green Mountain Power

---

have a number of additional responsibilities to investors. Spending money wisely would be near the top of the list. For instance, are executive retreats to the South Pacific on the company tab legal? They probably are. Do they represent a responsible use of corporate dollars? Now that seems unlikely. Honesty is another key responsibility that relates directly to financial predictions. No one can anticipate exactly how a company will perform, and an overly optimistic or pessimistic assessment is perfectly legal. But is it socially responsible? It probably isn't, especially if it departs too far from the objective facts—which is, of course, a subjective call.

RESPONSIBILITY TO THE COMMUNITY: BUSINESS AND THE GREATER GOOD

Beyond increasing everyone's standard of living, businesses can contribute to society in two main ways: philanthropy and responsibility. **Corporate philanthropy** includes all business donations to nonprofit groups, including both money and products. The Giving USA Foundation reported that total corporate donations dropped −1.9% in 2013, versus +4.4% overall growth during the same period.[16] Corporate philanthropy also includes donations of employee time; in other words, some companies pay their employees to spend time volunteering at nonprofits. Patagonia, for example, allows workers after one year of service to apply for two-month internships with environmental not-for-profits, during which time they're still paid by Patagonia.[17]

Some companies contribute to nonprofits through **cause-related marketing**. This involves a partnership between a business and a nonprofit, designed to spike sales for the company and raise money for the nonprofit. Unlike outright gifts, these dollars are not tax deductible for the company, but they can certainly build the company's brands.

Corporate responsibility relates closely to philanthropy but focuses on the actions of the business itself rather than donations of money and time. In 2013, Starbucks announced a strategic commitment to hire and develop at least 10,000 U.S. military veterans and active-duty spouses over the next five years, in response to its record growth. Taking a different approach to corporate responsibility, A to Z Wineworks in Oregon pays its workers 43% over the local living wage and guarantees its growers fair prices in both good and bad years. Starbucks pays its suppliers a premium for "ethically sourced" coffee. A fair portion of the price must get to the farmers, and measures are in place to ensure safe and humane working conditions. The policies of each of these corporations ultimately benefit society as a whole.[18]

RESPONSIBILITY TO THE ENVIRONMENT

Protecting the environment is perhaps the most crucial element of responsibility to the community. Business is

corporate philanthropy
All business donations to nonprofit groups, including money, products, and employee time.

cause-related marketing
Marketing partnerships between businesses and nonprofit organizations, designed to spike sales for the company and raise money for the nonprofit.

corporate responsibility
Business contributions to the community through the actions of the business itself rather than donations of money and time.

a huge consumer of the world's limited resources, from oil, to timber, to fresh water, to minerals. In some cases, the production process decimates the environment and spews pollution into the air, land, and water, sometimes causing irreversible damage. And the products created by business can cause pollution as well, such as the smog generated by cars, and the sometimes-toxic waste caused by junked electronic parts.

The government sets minimum standards for environmental protection at the federal, state, and local levels. But a growing number of companies are going further, developing innovative strategies to build their businesses while protecting the environment. Many have embraced the idea of **sustainable development**: doing business to meet the needs of this generation without harming the ability of future generations to meet their needs. This means weaving environmentalism throughout the business decision-making process. Since sustainable development can mean significant long-term cost savings, the economic crisis may even push forward environmentally friendly programs.

> "ULTIMATELY, THE PROFIT MOTIVE AND THE REVENUE GENERATION MODEL IS THE ONLY WAY TO BE TRULY SUSTAINABLE WITHIN A LARGE COMPANY."
>
> —AMY CHEN, PEPSICO

The results of sustainability programs have been impressive across a range of industries. McDonald's, for instance, produces mountains of garbage each year, as do virtually all major fast-food chains. But the Golden Arches stands above the others in its attempts to reduce the problem. Following are some encouraging statistics:

- By the end of 2008, McDonald's UK was recycling 100% of its used cooking oil for biodiesel to fuel delivery trucks. This equates to 1,500 family cars being removed from the road each year.

- On average, U.S. company-owned McDonald's restaurant recycles more than 17 tons of corrugated cardboard per year and approximately 13,000 pounds of used cooking oil per year.[19]

Reducing the *amount* of trash is better than recycling, but recycling trash clearly beats dumping it in a landfill. McDonald's participates in this arena as well, through their extensive recycling programs, but more importantly as a big buyer of recycled products.

Taking an even broader perspective, some firms have started to measure their carbon footprint, with an eye toward reducing it. **Carbon footprint** refers to the amount of harmful greenhouse gases that a firm emits throughout its operations, both directly and indirectly. The ultimate goal is to become carbon neutral—either to emit zero harmful gases or to counteract the impact of emissions by removing a comparable amount from the atmosphere through projects such as planting trees. Dell Inc. became fully carbon neutral in mid-2008, fulfilling its quest to become "the greenest technology on the planet." More recently, PepsiCo calculated the carbon footprint for its Tropicana orange juice brand and was surprised to learn that about a third of its emissions came from applying fertilizer to the orange groves. According to the Conference Board, business leaders have begun to see their carbon footprint—both measurement and reduction—as a burgeoning opportunity.[20] Many large corporations track three different types of emissions. The first, called Scope 1, refers to direct

Crosstudio/iStockphoto.com

Protecting the environment has become the most crucial element of responsibility to businesses across the globe.

sustainable development
Doing business to meet the needs of the current generation, without harming the ability of future generations to meet their needs.

carbon footprint Refers to the amount of harmful greenhouse gases that a firm emits throughout its operations, both directly and indirectly.

SORRY! SO, SO SORRY!

Why is it so compelling to watch the rich and powerful squirm? It's hard to explain, but when CEOs of big companies apologize for their mistakes, people love to watch, and their apologies often go viral. Sometimes the apologies are sincere and heartfelt and everyone moves on, and sometimes they become targets of ridicule. Here are a few noteworthy examples. You be the judge.

■ In 2013, Chip Wilson, former CEO and co-founder of Lululemon stated to the press that "some women's bodies just don't actually work" for Lululemon's yoga pants. He apologized via YouTube video in which he declared, "I'm really sad. I'm sad for the repercussions of my actions." He didn't even bother to address his offended customers.

■ In mid-2014, Snapchat founder and CEO Evan Spiegel was dismayed to learn that graphic emails from his party days as a Stanford undergrad were published online. In them, Spiegel wrote about getting sorority girls drunk and peeing on his date, among other offensive stories. In response, he issued a statement saying, "I'm obviously mortified and embarrassed that my idiotic emails during my fraternity days were made public. I have no excuse. I'm sorry I wrote them at the time and I was jerk to have written them. They in no way reflect who I am today or my views towards women."

■ Also in mid-2014, T-Mobile CEO John Legere used obscene language to trash talk competitors at a company event. He tweeted an apology the next day, when his comments went public, and drew criticism: "I know I have a Rated R vocabulary, but even I can go too far. Sincere apologies to anyone offended last night."[21]

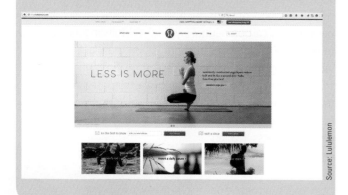

Source: Lululemon

emissions produced by corporate operations. The second, called Scope 2, refers to emissions that result from purchased electricity, heat, and steam. Scope 3 emissions, which are more complex to track, are emissions that occur outside a company's boundary, but over which it has some control. This category includes areas such as employee commutes, supplier emissions, and product-use emissions. When Stoneyfield Farms, maker of organic yogurt and other dairy products, examined their Scope 3 emissions, they came to the rather startling (and somewhat gross!) conclusion that most of their emissions did not come from manufacturing or transporting their products, but from the methane gas produced by the cows back at their suppliers' farms! Interest in Scope 3 emissions is still somewhat new, but seems sure to grow as environmental accounting methods become more sophisticated.[22]

A growing number of companies use **green marketing** to promote their businesses. This means marketing environmental products and practices to gain a competitive edge. Patagonia, for example, markets outdoor clothing using 100% organic cotton and natural fibers such as hemp. But green marketing represents a tough challenge: while most people support the idea of green products, the vast majority won't sacrifice price, performance, or convenience to actually buy those products. Sometimes, however, green marketing can be quite consistent with profitability. The Toyota Prius hybrid car offers an interesting example. The Prius costs several thousand dollars more than a standard car, but as gas prices skyrocketed through the summer of 2008, consumers flooded the dealerships, snapping up Prius hybrids faster than Toyota could ship them. Yet, when the economy dropped in late 2008, Toyota sales plummeted along with the rest of the industry, suggesting that the environment may be a fair-weather priority for consumers. But by 2012, Prius sales again were soaring, especially with the introduction of the plug-in hybrid version.[23]

4-5 ETHICS AND SOCIAL RESPONSIBILITY IN THE GLOBAL ARENA: A HOUSE OF MIRRORS?

Globalization has made ethics and social responsibility even more complicated for workers at every level. Bribery and corruption are among the most challenging issues faced by companies and individuals that are involved in international business. Transparency International, a leading anti-corruption organization, published its yearly index of "perceived corruption" across 175 countries in 2014. No country scored a completely clean 100 out of 100, and the United States scored a troubling 74 which was quite a bit higher

Cheaters might not prosper, but they do seem to feel pretty good

A series of recent studies showed that counter their own expectations, people who cheat tend to experience a "cheaters' high," an unanticipated emotional boost that may result from self-congratulation on their perceived cleverness in "getting away with it." The good news was that

B Christopher/Alamy

people are not monsters—the cheaters' high was smallest when there were no victims. But clearly, no crime is truly victimless. According to the IRS, for example, tax evasion costs the U.S. government nearly $350 billion annually, and according to the Business Software Alliance, global piracy costs the software industry more than $60 billion annually. Inflated expense reports and bogus insurance claims are other seemingly victimless crimes that can be outrageously costly for business. Researchers suggested that there are several steps companies can take to weaken the cheaters' high and lend more weight to guilt and shame that might counterbalance it:

- remove any "cloak of anonymity"
- "undercut cheating as clever"
- identify the victims of the cheating[24]
- celebrate individuals who bypass opportunities to cheat, to help remove the "sucker" stigma
- give workers opportunities (perhaps via training) to assert that they are good people

than India at 38 and China at 36, but lower than most of the European countries that dominated the top of the list. Not surprisingly, the world's poorest countries fall largely in the bottom half of the index, with African and Central Asian countries clustered at the very bottom, suggesting that rampant corruption is part of their business culture.[25]

Corruption wouldn't be possible if companies didn't offer bribes, so Transparency International also researched the likelihood of firms from industrialized countries to pay bribes abroad. The 2011 results indicated that firms from export powers Russia, China, and Mexico rank among the worst, with India following close behind. U.S. corporations, forbidden to offer bribes since 1977 under the Foreign Corrupt Practices Act, showed a disturbing inclination to flout the law. In fact, in 2012, Avon Corporation was accused of bribing Chinese officials to gain a permit to engage in direct sales, Walmart was accused of bribing Mexican officials to speed development of their stores in Mexico, and Ralph Lauren Corporation was accused of bribing Argentine customs officials to allow merchandise into that country. Other U.S. corporations that have recently found themselves in the crosshairs of government bribery investigations include Johnson & Johnson, Hewlett-Packard, and Disney. Overall, The United

States scored 8.1 out of a possible 10, falling well below many Western European countries.[26]

These statistics raise some thought-provoking questions:

- When does a gift become a bribe? The law is unclear, and perceptions differ from country to country.
- How can corporations monitor corruption and enforce corporate policies in their foreign branches?
- What are other ways to gain a competitive edge in countries where bribes are both accepted and expected?

Other challenging issues revolve around business responsibility to workers abroad. At minimum, businesses should pay a living wage for reasonable hours in a safe working environment. But exactly what this means is less clear-cut. Does a living wage mean enough to support an individual or a family? Does "support" mean enough to subsist day to day or enough to live in modest comfort? Should American businesses ban child labor in countries where families depend on their children's wages to survive? Companies must address these questions individually, bringing together their own values with the laws of both the United States and their host countries.

Choosing Between a Loaf of Bread and a Packet of Shampoo

Three-quarters of the world's population—nearly 4 billion people—earn less than $2 per day. But C. K. Prahalad, a well-respected consultant and economist, claims that if the "aspirational poor" had a chance to consume, they could add about $13 trillion in annual sales to the global economy. Unilever, a global marketing company headquartered in Europe, has aggressively pursued this market with consumer products. Their customers might not have electricity, running water, or even enough for dinner, but many of them do have packets of Sunsilk shampoo and Omo detergent. Unilever's success stems from local knowledge gained over decades operating in developing markets—Unilever has been in Indonesia since 1933, and India since 1888. Electronics

Sheriar Irani/iStockphoto.com

companies have experienced marketing success as well. In Dharavi, for instance—one of the largest urban slums in India—more than 85% of households own a television.

Critics suggest that the corporate push to reach impoverished consumers will enrich multinationals at the expense of their customers, representing exploitation of the world's poorest people. Ashvin Dayal, East Asia director for the antipoverty group Oxfam UK, expressed concern to *Time* magazine that corporate marketing might unseat locally produced products or encourage overspending by those who truly can't afford it. Citing heavily marketed candy and soda, he points out that "companies have the power to create needs rather than respond to needs."

But Prahalad counters that many people at the bottom of the economic pyramid accept that some of the basics—running water, for instance—are not likely to ever come their way. Instead, they opt to improve their quality of life through affordable "luxuries," such as single-use sachets of fragrant shampoo. He argues that "It's absolutely possible to do very well while doing good." Furthermore, he suggests that corporate marketing may kick-start the poorest economies, triggering entrepreneurial activity and economic growth. Since globalization shows no signs of slowing, let's hope that he's right.[27]

What do you think? Is targeting the poor with consumer goods exploitation or simply smart marketing?

The most socially responsible companies establish codes of conduct for their vendors, setting clear policies for human rights, wages, safety, and environmental impact. In 1991, Levi Strauss became the first global company to establish a comprehensive code of conduct for its contractors. Over the years, creative thinking has helped it maintain its high standards, even in the face of cultural clashes. An example from Bangladesh, outlined in the *Harvard Business Review*, illustrates its preference for win-win solutions. In the early 1990s, Levi Strauss "discovered that two of its suppliers in Bangladesh were employing children under the age of 14—a practice that violated the company's principles but was tolerated in Bangladesh. Forcing the

> **40% OF PAPER COLLECTED IN THE US FOR RECYCLING IN THE US IN 2013 WAS EXPORTED TO CHINA AND OTHER NATIONS.**
>
> —AMERICAN FOREST AND PAPER ASSOCIATION

suppliers to fire the children would not have ensured that the children received an education, and it would have caused serious hardship for the families depending on the children's wages. In a creative arrangement, the suppliers agreed to pay the children's regular wages while they attended school and to offer each child a job at age 14. Levi Strauss, in turn, agreed to pay the children's tuition and provide books and uniforms." This creative solution allowed the suppliers to maintain their valuable contracts from Levi Strauss, while Levi Strauss upheld its values and improved the quality of life for its most vulnerable workers.[28]

Clearly, codes of conduct work best with monitoring, enforcement, and a commitment to finding solutions that work for all parties involved. Gap Inc. offers an encouraging example. In 1996, Gap published a rigorous Code of Vendor Conduct and required compliance from all of its vendors. Its vendor-compliance officers strive to visit each of its 3,000 factories at least once a year. The company has uncovered a troubling number of violations, proactively pulling contracts from serious violators and rejecting bids from suppliers who don't meet its standards.

Gap and Levi Strauss seem to be doing their part, but the world clearly needs universal standards and universal enforcement to ensure that the benefits of globalization don't come at the expense of the world's most vulnerable people.[29]

4-6 MONITORING ETHICS AND SOCIAL RESPONSIBILITY: WHO IS MINDING THE STORE?

Actually, many firms are monitoring themselves. The process is called a **social audit**, which is a systematic evaluation of how well a firm is meeting its ethics and social responsibility objectives. Establishing goals is the starting point for a social audit, but the next step is to determine how to measure the achievement of those goals, and measurement can be a bit tricky. As You Sow, an organization dedicated to promoting corporate social responsibility, recommends that companies measure their success by evaluating a "double bottom line," one that accounts for traditional financial indicators, such as earnings, and one that accounts for social-responsibility indicators, such as community involvement.

Other groups are watching as well, which helps keep businesses on a positive track. Activist customers, investors, unions, environmentalists, and community groups all play a role. In addition, the threat of government legislation keeps some industries motivated to self-regulate. One example is the entertainment industry, which uses a self-imposed rating system for both movies and TV, largely to fend off regulation. Many people argue that the emergence of salads at fast-food restaurants represents an effort to avoid regulation as well.

> **social audit** A systematic evaluation of how well a firm is meeting its ethics and social responsibility goals.

The BIG Picture

Clearly, the primary goal of any business is to earn long-term profits for its investors. But profits alone are not enough. As active participants in society, firms must also promote ethical actions and social responsibility throughout their organizations and their corresponding customer and supplier networks. Although every area matters, a few warrant special mention:

- In tough economic times, effective business leaders focus more than ever on integrity, transparency, and a humane approach to managing the workforce—especially during cutbacks.

- Building or maintaining a presence in foreign markets requires particularly careful attention to human rights and local issues.

- Sustainable development and other environmentally sound practices are not only fiscally prudent and customer-friendly but also crucial for the health of our planet.

Careers in Business Ethics and Social Responsibility

Ethics Officer

Work with senior management to provide leadership, advice, and guidance in all matters pertaining to ethics, including training, enforcement, financial disclosure, and gift rules. Ensure that the company's code of ethics remains in strict compliance with all relevant laws. Model the highest standards of honesty and personal ethics at all times to foster an ethical climate in the organization. Arrange and facilitate employee ethics training. Work with HR to examine ethics complaints and to ensure that all investigations of employee misconduct are handled fairly and promptly. Assist in the resolution of ethical dilemmas wherever needed throughout the organization. For more information on this career and other possible careers in ethics, check out Career Transitions.

STUDY TOOLS 4

LOCATED AT BACK OF THE TEXTBOOK

☐ Rip Out Chapter Review Card

LOCATED AT WWW.CENGAGE.COM/LOGIN

☐ Review key term flashcards and create your own using StudyBits

☐ Create and complete practice quizzes based off of your notes and StudyBits

☐ Complete Online activities such as Matching, Fill-in-the-Blank and Drag and Drop exercises

☐ View chapter highlight box content, including CEO Profiles, What Would You Do Cases and chapter videos

☐ Track your knowledge and understanding of key concepts in business using 4LTR Online

YOUR FEED-BACK YOUR BOOK

Our research never ends. Continual feedback from you ensures that we keep up with your changing needs.

5 | Business Communication: Creating and Delivering Messages that Matter

LEARNING OBJECTIVES

After studying this chapter, you will be able to:

- **5-1** Explain the importance of excellent business communication
- **5-2** Describe the key elements of nonverbal communication
- **5-3** Compare, contrast, and choose effective communication channels
- **5-4** Choose the right words for effective communication
- **5-5** Write more effective business memos, letters, and emails
- **5-6** Create and deliver successful verbal presentations

Remember to visit **PAGE 89** for additional **STUDY TOOLS**

5-1 EXCELLENT COMMUNICATION SKILLS: YOUR INVISIBLE ADVANTAGE

Much of your success in business will depend on your ability to influence the people around you. Can you land the right job? Close the deal that makes the difference? Convince the boss to adopt your idea? Motivate people to buy your products? Excellent communicators are not only influential but also well liked, efficient, and effective. Great communication skills can dramatically boost your chance for success, while poor communication skills can bury even the most talented people.

So what exactly are "excellent communication skills"? Many students believe that great business communication equates to a knack for speaking or a flair for writing. But if that's where you stop, you're likely to hit a brick wall again and again as you attempt to achieve your goals. Effective **communication** happens only when you transmit meaning—*relevant* meaning—to your audience.

communication The transmission of information between a sender and a recipient.

Communication must be dynamic, fluid, and two-way, which includes listening. Seeking and understanding feedback from your audience—and responding appropriately—form the core of successful business communication. And it isn't as easy as you may think. American novelist Russell Hoban neatly summarized the issue: "When you come right down to it, how many people speak the same language even when they speak the same language?"

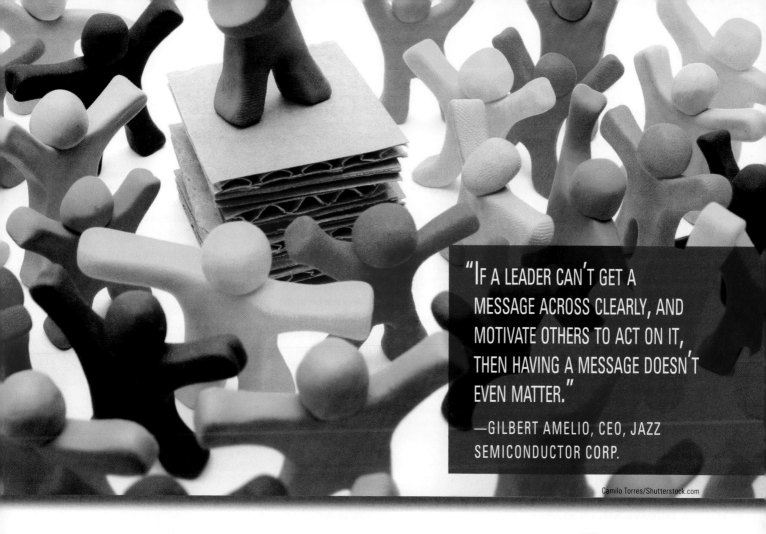

"IF A LEADER CAN'T GET A MESSAGE ACROSS CLEARLY, AND MOTIVATE OTHERS TO ACT ON IT, THEN HAVING A MESSAGE DOESN'T EVEN MATTER."

—GILBERT AMELIO, CEO, JAZZ SEMICONDUCTOR CORP.

Camilo Torres/Shutterstock.com

5-1a Communication Barriers: "That's Not What I Meant!"

Why is effective communication so challenging? The key issue is **noise**, which is any interference that causes the message you send to be different from the message your audience understands. Some experts define noise in terms of **communication barriers**, which arise in a number of different forms. As you read the definitions, keep in mind that with a bit of extra effort, most are surmountable, and we'll discuss strategies and tips as we move through the chapter.

- **Physical Barriers:** These can range from a document that looks like a wall of type, to a room that's freezing cold, to chairs in your office that force your visitors to sit at a lower level than you.

- **Language Barriers:** Clearly, if you don't speak the language, you'll have trouble communicating. But even among people who do share the same language, slang, jargon, and regional accents can interfere with meaning.

- **Body Language Barriers:** Even if your words are inviting, the wrong body language can alienate and distract your audience so completely that they simply won't absorb the content of your message.

- **Perceptual Barriers:** How your audience perceives you and your agenda can create a significant obstacle to effective communication. If possible, explore their perceptions—both positive and negative—in advance!

- **Organizational Barriers:** Some companies have built-in barriers to effective communication, such as an unspoken rule that the people at the top of the organization don't talk to the people at the bottom. These barriers are important to understand but hard to change.

- **Cultural Barriers:** These can include everything from how you greet colleagues and establish eye contact to how you handle disagreement, eat business meals, and make small talk at meetings. As globalization gains speed, **intercultural communication** will become increasingly pivotal to long-term business success. Identifying and understanding

noise Any interference that causes the message you send to be different from the message your audience understands.

communication barriers Obstacles to effective communication, typically defined in terms of physical, language, body language, cultural, perceptual, and organizational barriers.

intercultural communication Communication among people with differing cultural backgrounds.

If You See It in the News, It's Got to Be True...Psych!!!

With increased globalization, more and more businesses depend on world events, filtered through the news to guide their decision making. Millions of dollars hang in the balance, so the credibility of the news is crucial. But since mock news programs and websites enjoy more popularity than ever, business decision makers must make sure that they are in on the joke instead of the butt of the joke, which can't be as easy as it sounds, given the number of times legitimate news outlets and high-profile individuals have mistaken stories on *The Onion* website, a blatantly farcical mock news site, as real news. Some examples:

- China's *People's Daily Online* exuberantly reported that North Korea's short, pudgy leader, Kim Jong-un, was the "Sexiest Man Alive" based on a fake story in *The Onion*.

- *Fox News'* sister website, *Fox Nation*, excerpted several paragraphs from a satirical *Onion* piece called "Frustrated Obama sends nations a rambling 75,000-word email,"

eliciting a flurry of outraged comments from readers who obviously didn't get the joke.

- During the government shutdown of 2013, a Fox News co-host falsely stated that President Obama offered to pay out of his own pocket for the museum of Muslim culture, a claim that originated from another satire website called the *National Report*.

The lesson here is NOT that you shouldn't believe everything you read, but rather that if something seems too silly to be true, it may not be, and it certainly merits further investigation. Otherwise, it may be the jokers who get the last laugh![1]

Skylines/Shutterstock.com

---

communication barriers is a vital first step toward dismantling them in order to communicate more effectively with any audience.

5-2 NONVERBAL COMMUNICATION: BEYOND THE WORDS

Most of us focus on what we want to say, but *how* we say it matters even more. In fact, studies cited in *The Wall Street Journal's Career Journal* suggest that during face-to-face communication, only 7% of meaning comes from the verbal content of the message—38% comes from tone of voice, and 55% comes from body language such as facial expressions, gestures, and posture.[2]

The goal of **nonverbal communication** should be to reinforce the meaning of your message. Random facial expressions and disconnected body language—arbitrary arm thrusts, for example—are at best distracting, and at worst clownish. But strong, deliberate non-verbal communication can dramatically magnify the impact of your messages. Here are a few examples of how this can work (but keep in mind that these examples do not necessarily translate from culture to culture):

- **Eye Contact:** Within American culture, sustained eye contact (different from a constant cold stare) indicates integrity, trust, and respectful attention, whether you're communicating with a subordinate, a superior, or a peer.

- **Tone of Voice:** Variation is the key to effectiveness, since paying attention to a monotone takes more concentration than most people are willing to muster. Also, even when you're angry or frustrated, try to keep your voice in a lower pitch to encourage listeners to stay with your message.

- **Facial Expressions:** People vary widely in terms of how much emotion they show on their faces, but virtually everyone communicates, whether or not they know it, through a wide range of expressions that include shy smiles, focused frowns, clenched jaws, squinted eyes, and furrowed brows.

- **Gestures and Posture:** How you handle your body speaks for you. For example, leaning forward can indicate interest, shrugging can suggest a lack of authority, and fidgeting can imply either impatience or nervousness. To increase the power of your message, both your gestures and your posture should be confident, open, and coherent.

nonverbal communication
Communication that does not use words. Common forms of nonverbal communication include gestures, posture, facial expressions, tone of voice, and eye contact.

Sometimes You've Just Gotta Stick with the Man...

Not so long ago, postmen delivered the mail, waitresses served restaurant food, and stewardesses staffed airplanes. But today we have mail carriers, food servers, and flight attendants. In a sweeping effort to be more inclusive, entire industries and state governments have revamped their language to be more gender neutral, rather than assuming that certain positions or words are gender specific. Typically, the first step is to replace every "he" with "he or she"; then "he or she" must be interchanged with "she or he" to ensure that neither gender gets precedence. The final step is to replace words that are unnecessarily gender specific. A few more examples:

- Policeman becomes police officer
- Fisherman becomes fisher
- Congresssman becomes congressional representative
- Mailman becomes letter carrier
- Chairman becomes chair
- Penmanship becomes handwriting
- Freshman becomes first-year student
- Watchman becomes security guard

But not every word has an easy fix. When Washington state officials revamped the Washington state code, they could not find a suitable replacement for manhole, airman, or man lock, so they left them as is, for the time being. Many people object to spending time and money on this kind of project in a time of many other pressing needs, but advocate Liz Watson explains, "Words matter. Words help shape our perceptions about what opportunities are available to women and men."[3]

DoublePhoto studio/Shutterstock.com

When disgraced cyclist Lance Armstrong confessed to doping in a 2013 interview with Oprah Winfrey, body language expert Tonya Reiman noticed that despite the confidence of his words, he betrayed anxiety nonverbally by not meeting Ms. Winfrey's eye's, biting his lip, and repeatedly touching his face. She also pointed out that he "'fig-leafed,' or nervously covered his groin with his hands, several different times…That's a sign of somebody who's under pressure."[4] Reiman has also pointed out that when people swallow hard after making strong assertions, they are clearly lying. As silly as it sounds, one of the easiest, most effective ways to improve your body language is to practice nonverbal communication in front of the mirror. Check out your gestures, notice your facial expressions, and focus on eye contact. If you have the time and ability, it's also helpful (though humbling!) to videotape yourself delivering both a formal and informal message, and ask a trusted friend to dissect the results with you.

Accurately discerning the body language of others is another powerful business communication tool. But keep in mind that you must evaluate others in the context of common sense. When your boss keeps yawning, she may be bored, *or* she may just be tired. When your colleague crosses his arms, he may be indicating defensiveness, *or* he might just normally stand that way.

5-2a Active Listening: The Great Divider

How we listen (or don't listen) also sends a high-impact, nonverbal message. In fact, an old Chinese proverb asserts that to listen well is as powerful a means of influence as to talk well. Those who do both are unstoppable.

Strong listening skills—**active listening**—play an obvious role in business success. The higher you go in an organization, the more you find that people are listening. Hourly employees may spend 30% of their time listening, while managers often spend 60%, and executives might spend 75% or more. Interestingly, top salespeople also tend to spend about 75% of their communication time listening.[5]

According to the International Listening Association website, 85% of our learning is derived from listening, yet listeners are distracted, forgetful, and preoccupied 75% of the time. If listening is so crucial, why do most of us have such a hard time engaging completely? One reason may be that people *listen* at about 125 to 250 words per minute, but *think* at about 1,000 to 3,000 words per minute— that's a significant gap.

> **active listening** Attentive listening that occurs when the listener focuses his or her complete attention on the speaker.

EXHIBIT 5.1 TIPS FOR BETTER LISTENING

Listening Dos	Listening Don'ts
Use your extra mental capacity to summarize (to yourself!) what the speaker is saying. Ask yourself: Why does this matter? What's the key point?	Don't even glance at your emails or text messages. You won't fool anyone with those surreptitious peeks.
Take a few notes. It will not only help you concentrate but will also communicate to the speaker that his or her thoughts really matter.	Don't begin speaking the moment the person stops talking. Take a brief pause to indicate that you're absorbing the message.
Listen with both your ears and your eyes. Notice any inconsistency between the speaker's words and body language.	Don't get overly comfortable. If your body is too relaxed, your mind may wander more easily.
Use nonverbal communication—nods, smiles, leaning forward—to indicate interest in the speaker.	Don't pick up your phone—or even look at your phone—when you're listening. And whenever it's practical, set your cell phone to vibrate when others are speaking.
Use verbal feedback and questions to indicate understanding and empathy: "So you're saying that…," or "Why do you think that?"	Don't interrupt or finish other people's sentences. There are few better ways to cut off future communication.

© Cengage Learning®

Common ways to fill the void include daydreaming, thinking about the past (e.g., last night), and planning for the future (e.g., later in the day).[6]

When you listen, try to use the extra thinking time to make yourself pay closer attention to the speaker. You'll find that people tend to tell more to those who listen better, so if you polish your listening skills, you're also likely to buff up the quality of what you know and when you know it. Exhibit 5.1 highlights some listening dos and don'ts (specific to American culture).[7]

5-3 CHOOSE THE RIGHT CHANNEL: A RICH ARRAY OF OPTIONS

Figuring out the right way to send a message can be a daunting challenge, especially in light of the growing number of choices. The various options are called **communication channels**. Understanding the impact of each channel will help you make the best decision regarding which to use.

Communication channels differ from one another in terms of how much information—or richness—they communicate to the recipient. Exhibit 5.2 provides a brief overview of key channels. Other channels might include intranet postings, WebEx, Facebook, and instant messaging. Where would these additional channels fall on the spectrum? Why?

communication channels
The various ways in which a message can be sent, ranging from one-on-one in-person meetings to Internet message boards.

5-3a Consider the Audience: It's Not about You!

Clearly, the needs and expectations of your audience play a crucial role in your choice of communication channel. Even if the recipient's preferences seem absurd—for example, we probably all know someone who refuses to check email or voice mail—remember that your first priority is to communicate your message. If you send it through a channel that the audience doesn't expect, understand, or like, you've crippled your chance for successful communication.

Analysis and consideration of your audience should also be a top priority after you choose your communication channel. Meeting the needs of your audience will give you a crucial edge in developing a message that works.

5-4 PICK THE RIGHT WORDS: IS THAT CAR PRE-LOVED OR JUST PLAIN USED?!

Mark Twain once said, "The difference between the right word and almost the right word is the difference between lightning and the lightning bug." Perhaps that's a little extreme, but it may not be too far from the truth. In the business world, where your messages are competing with so many others for the all-too-limited attention of the recipient, the right words can encourage your audience to stay with you long enough to absorb your message.

EXHIBIT 5.2   COMMUNICATION CHANNELS

Communication Channel	Channel Richness	When Should You Use This Channel?
Texting	Very low: Because so many of us text with as few words as possible, your audience will pick up only the basics.	When your content is uncontroversial When you want a quick response regarding relatively simple issues When you know that your audience won't be annoyed by it
Memos/Reports	Very low: Your audience won't gain any information from your tone or your body language.	When your content is uncontroversial When you must reach a number of people with the same message When you must communicate lengthy or detailed information
Email	Very low: Here, too, your audience learns nothing beyond your words themselves.	When your content is uncontroversial When you must reach a number of people with the same message
Voice Mail	Low: Your audience has the benefit of hearing your tone but not seeing your body language.	When your content is uncontroversial When you don't need a record of your message (but don't forget that the recipient can easily save or forward your voice mail)
Telephone Conversation	Moderate: Your audience benefits from hearing your tone and how it changes through the call.	When you need to either deliver your message or get a response quickly When your content is more personal or controversial When you need or want a spontaneous, dynamic dialogue with the recipient
Videoconferencing	High: Especially with state-of-the-art equipment, the channel conveys much of the richness of actually being there.	When you need to reach multiple people with complex or high-priority content When you need or want a spontaneous, dynamic dialogue with an audience that you cannot reach in person
In-Person Presentation	High: Your audience directly experiences every element of your communication, from verbal content, to tone, to body language.	When you need to reach a large audience with an important message When you need or want to experience the immediate response of your audience
Face-to-Face Meeting	Very high: Your audience experiences your full message even more directly.	When your message is personal, emotional, complex, or high-priority (but if the recipient might be volatile, consider using a less-immediate channel) When you need or want instant feedback from your audience

© Cengage Learning®

5-4a Analyze Your Audience

To find the right words, begin with the needs of your audience. Consider:

- **Expectations:** What kind of language do most people use in the organization? Is it formal or informal? Is it direct or roundabout? Should you differ from the norm? Why or why not?

- **Education:** The education level of the audience should drive the level of vocabulary and the complexity of the message.

- **Profession:** Some professions (e.g., website development) are rife with jargon and acronyms. How should this influence your message?

5-4b Be Concise

Comedian Jerry Seinfeld once said, "I will spend an hour editing an eight-word sentence into five." While Jerry might be going a bit too far, it pays to be clear and concise in business communication. But don't be concise at the expense of completeness; include all information that your audience may need. (It'll save you time down the road.)

5-4c Avoid Slang

Unless you're absolutely certain that your audience will understand and appreciate it, do not use slang in either written or verbal communication. The risk of unintentionally alienating yourself from your audience is simply too high.

Ooops! Flushthatjobdownthetoilet

Common sense dictates that your work friends should not be your Facebook friends, especially if your private life is not suitable for your work realm (and in most cases—even if it isn't as racy as you might prefer—it simply isn't appropriate), but you might be surprised to learn that Twitter grew more than 60% between 2012 and 2014. And unlike Facebook posts, tweets are in the public arena, which means that workers must know, understand, and carefully follow their companies' social media policies, or risk fairly certain consequences. Job seekers should be particularly careful about what they post on social media.

Forty-three percent of employers use social networking sites to research job candidates, according to a 2014 Career-Builders.com national survey, and 51% of them said they've found content that caused them to not hire the candidate. Here are some of the key reasons:

- Job candidate posted provocative or inappropriate photographs or information (46%).
- Job candidate posted information about them drinking or using drugs (41%).
- Job candidates bad-mouthed their previous company or fellow employee (36%).
- Job candidate had poor communication skills (32%).
- Job candidate had discriminatory comments related to race, gender, religion, etc. (28%).

Potential employers also found some items that were just plain strange:

- Candidate's profile included links to an escort service.
- Candidate posted a photo of a warrant for his arrest.
- Candidate posted an exercise video for grandmothers.
- Candidate had sued his wife for shooting him in the head.
- Candidate featured a pig as his closest friend.
- Candidate posted his dental exam results.
- Candidate bragged about driving drunk and not getting caught on several occasions.
- Candidate was actively involved in a demonic cult.
- Candidate posted Sasquatch pictures he had taken.[8]

What do you think? Is it reasonable for employers to use social media to screen applicants? Why or why not? Does it represent a violation of privacy?

PiXXart/Shutterstock.com

---

bias A preconception about members of a particular group. Common forms of bias include gender bias; age bias; and race, ethnicity, or nationality bias.

5-4d Avoid Bias

Intentionally or unintentionally, words can communicate biases that can interfere with your message, alienate your audience, and call your own character into question. As a result, you will be less effective in achieving the immediate goals of your communication (and possibly any future communication as well). Three kinds of **bias** are common.

GENDER BIAS Gender bias consists of words that suggest stereotypical attitudes toward a specific gender. Avoiding bias becomes tricky when you simply don't know the gender of your audience, which often happens when you apply for a job in writing. The best solution, of course, is to find out the recipient's name, but if you can't do that, do not address your message to "Dear Sir" or "Dear Madam"; rather, use the title of the position (e.g., "Dear Hiring Manager").

Another common challenge is to establish agreement in your sentences without creating gender bias. Consider the following example:

The manager who loses his temper must apologize.

Effective business communication requires an analysis of the audience.

RACE, ETHNICITY, AND NATIONALITY BIAS Words can also suggest stereotypical attitudes toward specific races, ethnicities, and nationalities. Leaving aside prejudice—which is clearly wrong—the problems in this area are usually unintentional and stem from unarticulated assumptions about a person's attitudes, opinions, and experiences. Your best plan for avoiding bias is to forgo any references to race, ethnicity, or nationality unless they are directly relevant and clearly necessary. And, of course, never simply assume that one person embodies the attitudes, opinions, and experiences of a larger group. If you communicate with each person as an individual, you will not only avoid bias but also develop deeper, more effective channels of communication.

Technically, this sentence is correct, but it implies that all managers are men. A simple solution would be to convert to plural:

Managers who lose their temper must apologize.

This approach almost always works to help you sidestep the gender bias issue. In the rare case that it doesn't, you can simply use the "his or her" option:

The manager who loses his or her temper must apologize.

AGE BIAS Age bias refers to words that suggest stereotypical attitudes toward people of specific ages. In American culture, older people tend to experience negative age bias much more often than younger people. This happens despite specific federal legislation outlawing employment discrimination against people over 40 years old. The reason may be that American culture associates youth with highly valued qualities such as creativity, speed, independence, and individualism. This bias will become increasingly detrimental as the workforce ages. Here is an example of age bias:

We need someone young and dynamic in this position!

You could easily eliminate the negative bias by simply deleting the word "young" or by replacing it with the word "energetic." One clear benefit of eliminating bias in this case would be a broader applicant pool that might include an older person who is more dynamic than any of the younger applicants.

> "WHAT YOU DO SPEAKS SO LOUD THAT I CANNOT HEAR WHAT YOU SAY."
> —RALPH WALDO EMERSON

5-4e Use the Active Voice Whenever Possible

Active voice facilitates direct, powerful, concise communication. You have used the **active voice** when the subject of your sentence *is* doing the action described by the verb. You have used the **passive voice** when the subject of your sentence *is not* doing the action described by the verb.

Here's an example of a sentence that uses the active voice:

Our team did not hit our sales goal.

Our team, the subject of the sentence, did the action described by the verb (missing the sales goal). The same sentence in the passive voice would read as follows:

The sales goal was not reached.

In this version, the subject of the sentence is the sales goal, which clearly did not do the action. As you can see from these examples, another benefit of active voice is accountability, which can create deeper trust between you and your audience.

active voice Sentence construction in which the subject performs the action expressed by the verb (e.g., The accountant did the taxes.). The active voice works better for the vast majority of business communication.

passive voice Sentence construction in which the subject does not do the action expressed by the verb; rather the subject is acted upon (e.g., The taxes were done by our accountant.). The passive voice tends to be less effective for business communication.

Say What??!!

Between the Beijing Olympics in 2008 and the Shanghai World Expo in 2010, China has gained an increasingly high profile on the world stage, and so has Chinglish, a sometimes-bizarre blend of Chinese and mangled English language that seems to pop up on signs, menus, and labels throughout the tourist-heavy cities of China. For example:

- Plus-sized shoppers at the Scat clothing chain might find themselves needing to buy "fatso" or "lard-bucket" sizes.

- Before the Beijing Olympics, tourists could visit Racist Park, later rechristened Minorities Park to avoid sending a misleadingly negative message to visitors about Chinese culture.

- A sign at the Terracotta Warriors Museum in Xi'an reads "Cherishing Flowers and Trees" rather than "Keep Off the Grass."

- Until recently, Chinglish has been especially common on menus in China, including such gems as, "casserole with children's bone soup," "weeds blasting duck intestines," and "old pickle fry eggs soil." No wonder so many tourists came home slimmer!

- In the past, the sick may have sought treatment at the Dongda Anus Hospital, now called the Dongda Proctology Hospital.

Although many of these language goofs are highly amusing, a number of Chinese find the snickers humiliating rather than funny. In fact, as the World Expo approached in 2010, the Chinese government established the Shanghai Commission for the Management of Language Use to eradicate by fiat the worst examples of mangled English. By 2012, officials in Shanghai claimed to have won the battle, announcing that the accuracy of English language signs in public spaces had improved 85% since it took action. But a number of gaffes still remain, including a sign that points tourists to the "Garden of Curled Poo." No thanks. Although government officials are understandably proud of the progress, a number of Shanghai's English-speaking residents are a bit disappointed that the entertaining, mangled-language signs are on the wane.[9]

此段200米,当心落石,请靠岩壁行走,快速通过请勿逗留.
Within 200 meters,notice the rockslide,please is run about by cliff.

John Henshall/Alamy

5-5 WRITE HIGH-IMPACT MESSAGES: BREAKING THROUGH THE CLUTTER

For many businesspeople, checking email—or even regular mail—is like approaching a fire hose for a sip of water. Goal number one is to crank down the pressure to get what you need without being knocked over by all the rest. To attain this goal, many people simply press the delete button.

Your challenge as a writer is to make your message a must-read, and the starting point should be the needs of your audience. Consider how the audience will respond to your message—think about how they will feel, not what they will do—and use that information to guide your writing. But keep in mind that it's hard to know for sure how the recipient will respond. For instance, each of the responses in Exhibit 5.3 could be reasonable for different people.

How do you know how your audience will respond? In most cases, you must simply guess based on as much evidence as you can find. The value of making a thoughtful guess is that the chances of achieving your goal will soar if you happen to be correct.

EXHIBIT 5.3	MESSAGES AND RESPONSES
Message	**Possible Responses**
Please note the new computer password procedures.	**Positive:** *Great! We've really needed this.*
	Neutral: *OK, no big deal.*
	Negative: *Not another change…*
The company plans to reassign your project team at the end of the year.	**Positive:** *I can hardly wait to work with new people!*
	Neutral: *It's all part of the job…*
	Negative: *Not another change!*

© Cengage Learning®

Mind Your Digital Manners! Not As Easy As You Might Think...

Technology today makes almost everything easier. We can use navigation programs to find even the most obscure address and never struggle with an uncooperative paper map. We can use cheap or free video chat programs to see the faces of friends and family around the world. We can use health apps to monitor our own heart rate and sleeping patterns.

But technology doesn't make it easier to mind our manners as we communicate with each other—or with our devices—in the rapidly changing digital world. In fact, Kevin Sintumuang, columnist for *The Wall Street Journal*, noted that, "More devices will have us talking (or yelling) into the air—crying out, as if to the Almighty, 'Please play the workout mix!'" Sintumuang points out that it's rude to text at a nice restaurant, and to take selfies at disaster sites. He also comments that while some people are absolutely fluent in emojis, others swear that the cute cartoon symbols are destroying "real" human language.

So what are the right answers? Well until technology stops— which we hope won't be anytime soon—and the proper etiquette sorts itself out, all of us should probably let common sense and old-fashioned consideration be our guides.[10]

The anticipated audience response should directly affect how you structure your writing.

- If the recipient will feel positive or neutral about your message, the memo or email should begin with your bottom line. What is your request or recommendation or conclusion? Why should the audience care? After you've clarified those points, follow up with your rationale and explanations (keeping in mind that less is usually more for time-starved businesspeople).

- If the recipient will feel negative about your message, start the memo or email with a couple of lines that present the rationale before you give the bottom line. Follow up with alternatives if there are any, and be sure to end on a positive note (rather than an apology). This structure is less straightforward, but it's a more effective way to communicate your message.

See Exhibit 5.4 for sample emails based on different anticipated responses to messages in an Internet game development firm.

5-5a Strike the Right Tone

Good business writing sounds natural—it flows like spoken language and reads like a conversation on paper. To strike the right tone for any given message, remember that you can choose from a wide variety of conversational styles, from formal to chatty. Imagine yourself speaking to the recipient of your message, and you'll find that the right tone emerges naturally. A few guidelines will also help:

- Use common words in most situations (e.g., *use* versus *utilize*).

- Use the active voice (e.g., *We made a mistake* versus *A mistake was made*).

- Use personal pronouns (*I, you*) whenever appropriate.

- Use contractions (*I'll, don't, here's*) as often as you would when speaking.

5-5b Don't Make Grammar Goofs

Grammatical errors will distract your reader from your writing and undermine your credibility. Most businesspeople are aware of the more common grammatical errors, so they tend to jump off the page before the content of the message. But if you're uncertain about a particular point, look at how professionally edited publications handle similar issues. Finally, don't be afraid to do a common-sense check on any grammatical question.

Edward P. Bailey, noted professor and business communication author, points out that many writers make

Exhibit 5.4

Sample Emails: Same Message, Different Approach

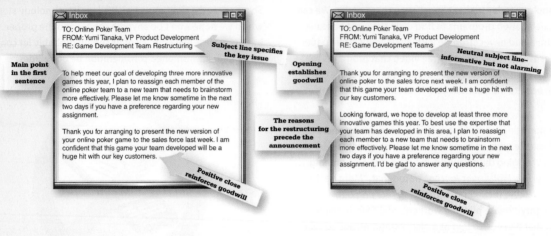

If the recipient will feel neutral...

If the recipient will feel negative...

Main point in the first sentence

Subject line specifies the key issue

Opening establishes goodwill

The reasons for the restructuring precede the announcement

Neutral subject line—informative but not alarming

Positive close reinforces goodwill

Positive close reinforces goodwill

Inbox

TO: Online Poker Team
FROM: Yumi Tanaka, VP Product Development
RE: Game Development Team Restructuring

To help meet our goal of developing three more innovative games this year, I plan to reassign each member of the online poker team to a new team that needs to brainstorm more effectively. Please let me know sometime in the next two days if you have a preference regarding your new assignment.

Thank you for arranging to present the new version of your online poker game to the sales force last week. I am confident that this game your team developed will be a huge hit with our key customers.

Inbox

TO: Online Poker Team
FROM: Yumi Tanaka, VP Product Development
RE: Game Development Teams

Thank you for arranging to present the new version of online poker to the sales force next week. I am confident that this game your team developed will be a huge hit with our key customers.

Looking forward, we hope to develop at least three more innovative games this year. To best use the expertise that your team has developed in this area, I plan to reassign each member to a new team that needs to brainstorm more effectively. Please let me know sometime in the next two days if you have a preference regarding your new assignment. I'd be glad to answer any questions.

© Cengage Learning®

---

grammar mistakes based on phantom knowledge—"mythical" grammar rules that aren't even in grammar handbooks. His research firmly reassures us that:

- It is OK to end a sentence with a preposition when doing so sounds natural and does not involve excess words (e.g., *Where is this book from?* is much better than *From where is this book?*).

- It is OK to begin sentences with "And" or "But" (e.g., *Most teens enjoy video games with a moderate level of violence. But a small, vocal minority strongly advocates a more clean-cut approach.*).

- It is OK to split infinitives (e.g., *Try to effectively film the next scene* is a perfectly acceptable sentence, even though "effectively" is inserted between "to" and "film.").

If you follow these principles, your writing not only will sound more natural but also will flow more easily. Winston Churchill, a renowned writer and speaker, was onboard with this common-sense approach decades ago, as we can see from his joking comment that poked fun at tortured writing: "From now on, ending a sentence with a preposition is something up with which I will not put."[11]

> "TECHNOLOGY OF LATE HAS BEEN SO FUN, SO EASILY ENGROSSING, THAT IT'S AMPLIFIED THE JERKITUDE OF THE AVERAGE AMERICAN."
>
> —KEVIN SINTUMUANG, *WALL STREET JOURNAL*

5-5c Use Block Paragraphs

There are three elements to block paragraphs: (1) use single spacing, (2) double space between paragraphs, and (3) do not indent the first sentence of your paragraphs. This approach has become standard for business writing over the past decade, as writers have begun to include an increasing number of additional elements such as headings and illustrations. The block paragraphs create a more organized look for your page, guiding the reader's eye through the key elements of your structure.

5-5d Use Headings and Bulleted Lists Wherever Appropriate

Both headings and bulleted lists will guide your reader more easily through your writing. And the easier it is for your reader, the more likely that he or she will absorb your message, which is, of course, your ultimate goal.

- **Headings:** A heading is not a title; rather, it is a label for one of several parts. If you have only one part, skip the heading and use a title or a subject line. Consider using informative headings (e.g., "Recruitment has

EXHIBIT 5.5 — TEN TIPS FOR EXCELLENT EMAIL

1. Consider both your primary and secondary readers. In other words, never forget that your reader may forward your email without considering the potential impact on you.

2. Keep it short! Many readers won't scroll down past whatever shows on their screen, so be sure to get your bottom line close to the top of your message.

3. Don't forget to proofread. This is especially important if you're asking someone to do something for you. And remember that your spell checker won't catch every mistake.

4. Use standard writing. Smiley faces, abbreviations, and five exclamation points are all fine if you're emailing your buddies, but in more formal messages they can make you look silly (or like you just don't care).

5. Avoid attachments if possible. They take time and space to open, and they don't always translate well to cell phones and PDAs. Instead, cut and paste relevant sections of the attachment into your email.

6. Don't assume privacy. Think of your emails as postcards that anyone (especially computer system administrators and managers) can read along the way. In that light, try not to use email to communicate negative or critical messages.

7. Respond promptly to emails. If you don't have time to respond to the email itself, consider sending a message such as "Sorry, but I'm swamped right now—will get back to you early next week."

8. Assume the best. Because emails are often brief, they can cause unintentional offense. If you receive an off-key message, don't be afraid to inquire: "I'm not sure what you mean... could you please explain?"

9. Create a compelling subject line. Make your reader want to open your message. Briefly communicate the topic of your message and why your reader should care.

10. Think before you write, and think again before you send! Too many people send messages in an emotional moment that they later regret. Take time to think and think again.

stalled," rather than simply "Recruitment"), or question headings (e.g., "Have we met our recruitment goals for this campaign?"). And remember, headings are just as effective for letters and emails as they are for memos, and they are perfectly OK in one-page documents.

- **Bulleted Lists:** A bulleted list is an invaluable tool that you can use to engage your reader's attention whenever you have more than one of anything in your writing (e.g., next steps, similar sections, questions). By formatting your lists with bullets, you are directing your reader's eye through your writing.

> "THE SINGLE BIGGEST PROBLEM IN COMMUNICATION IS THE ILLUSION THAT IT HAS TAKEN PLACE."
> —GEORGE BERNARD SHAW

5-6 CREATE AND DELIVER SUCCESSFUL VERBAL PRESENTATIONS: HOOK 'EM AND REEL 'EM IN!

What do people fear most? The *Book of Lists* asserts that public speaking ranks number one for the majority of people, high above the fear of death at number four. So, when people say they would rather die than give a speech, they may really mean it! This section is designed to mitigate any fear you might have about public speaking by giving you guidance on how to create and deliver a high-impact verbal presentation.

As with most communication, the needs of the audience are the best place to begin. How does your audience feel about you and your topic? Are they interested? Hostile? Positive? What were they doing before your presentation? Dragging themselves out of bed after a late night at a sales meeting? Eating lunch? Use this information to guide how you develop your presentation. For instance, an eager, educated audience might not need as much background as a more lethargic, less-interested audience.

5-6a Opening

The opening of your presentation gives you a chance to grab the attention of the audience. If your opening hooks them, you've boosted the likelihood that you will hold their attention throughout the presentation. But developing that hook can be a challenge. The following are some suggestions for effective hooks:

■ **An Interesting or Startling Statistic:** In a presentation from a nonprofit foodbank seeking to partner with a grocery chain, you could open by sharing that "the U.S. has the largest number of homeless women and children of any industrialized nation, and 57% of homeless kids spend at least one day a month completely without food. How could we improve these devastating numbers?"

■ **Audience Involvement:** Pulling the audience into your opening can be very effective. For instance, in a presentation for a clothing company: "Imagine yourself with me at 11 P.M. on a Friday night, standing in line for admission to the hottest club in New York. As we inch forward, we suddenly realize that three other women in line are wearing the exact same dress as you…."

■ **A Compelling Story or Anecdote:** This approach works best when it's completely genuine, using specific details that are directly relevant to the audience. For instance, in a presentation about employee benefits, you might want to share the story of a colleague who beat cancer using the company's innovative healthcare program.

■ **A Relevant Simile or Metaphor:** Patricia Fripp, an award-winning keynote speaker, shares a simile that worked well to open a presentation for a colleague: "Being a scientist is like doing a jigsaw puzzle in a snowstorm at night… you don't have all the pieces… and you don't have the picture to work from."

■ **Engaging Questions:** In a presentation about customer service, you could open by asking: "How many of you have spent far too long waiting on hold for customer service that was finally delivered by a surly agent who clearly knew nothing about your question?"

5-6b Body

The most common presentation mistake is to include too many key ideas in the body of your presentation. Audiences simply cannot absorb more than two to four main points, and three are ideal. Specific examples and vivid comparisons will illustrate your points and bring them to life, while trusted sources, specific data, and expert quotations will increase your credibility and persuasiveness. Regardless of the length of your presentation, be sure to use clear transitions as you move from point to point.

Just before launching into the body of your presentation, you should tell the audience your key points, ideally with visual reinforcement. Then as you move to each new point, you can refer to the blueprint that you established upfront. A clear, explicit structure will help the audience track with you as you move through your material.

5-6c Close

Ideally, the close of your presentation will summarize your key points. Then circle back to your introduction, so that the beginning and the end serve as "bookends" for the body of your presentation. For instance, if you began by asking questions, end by answering them. If you began with an anecdote, end by referring to the same story. As an alternative (or maybe an addition), consider sharing a quotation or a bit of humor relevant to your content.

Also, keep in mind that you should verbally signal to your audience that you are about to conclude. After you do so—by saying, "In summary," for instance—be sure that you actually do conclude. Nothing alienates an audience

Giving great presentations may be easier than you think.

Goldmund Lukic/iStockphoto.com

more quickly than launching into another point after you've told them you're finished! Your body language will support your conclusion if you turn off your projector and move toward the audience to answer questions. And even if you aren't so eager to field questions, try to paste a receptive look on your face—it'll increase your credibility and set a positive tone for the Q&A session.

Bikeriderlondon/Shutterstock.com

5-6d Questions

At the start of your presentation, decide whether you want to handle questions throughout your talk or save them for the end. Tell your audience your preference upfront; most of the time they will respect it. But if you do receive unwanted questions in the middle of your presentation, don't ignore them. Simply remind the questioner that you'll leave plenty of time for questions at the end.

Not surprisingly, the best tip for handling questions is to be prepared. Since it's tough to anticipate questions for your own presentation, you may want to enlist the help of a trusted colleague to brainstorm the possibilities. And don't just come up with the questions—prepare the answers, too!

5-6e Visual Aids

Studies suggest that three days after a presentation, people retain 10% of what they heard from an oral presentation, 35% from a visual presentation, and 65% from a combined visual and oral presentation. The numbers are compelling: visual aids matter. Depending on your audience, effective, high-impact visual aids could range from props to charts to mounted boards. But in business communication, PowerPoint slides are the most common option. If you use PowerPoint, consider these suggestions:

- **Showing Works Better Than Simply Telling:** Use pictures and other graphics whenever possible.

- **Less Is More:** Keep this helpful guideline in mind: no more than seven words per line, no more than seven lines per slide.

- **Don't Just Read Your Slides Aloud:** Instead, paraphrase, add examples, and offer analysis and interpretation.

- **Go Easy on the Special Effects:** Too many sounds and too much animation can be painfully distracting.

- **Don't Let Your Slides Upstage You:** Look at your audience, not at the slides. And dim the screen when you're not specifically using it.[12]

5-6f Google Presentations

Although Microsoft PowerPoint remains the software option of choice for business presentations, Google Presentations software is swiftly gaining ground. Google Presentations is one of a growing number of applications based in "the cloud." Another popular option is Prezi, which includes pan and zoom features that give presentations an engaging cinematic feel. Cloud-based presentation software means that when you buy a new computer, you don't need to spend hundreds of dollars buying PowerPoint. You simply log into your Google account, for instance, use the Google Presentations software, and save your finished product on Google's servers. Since your work is stored on the Internet, you can access it from any device with a web connection—you don't need to email it to yourself, or store it on a temperamental local drive, or worry about saving your changes as you move from work to home to school.

But cloud-based software is far from perfect. If you temporarily lose your Internet connection—while on a plane or a bus, for instance—you cannot access your work. Security might be a worry, since web-based data may be vulnerable to hackers. If Google disables your account for any reason, your work is lost. And Google Presentations does not yet include all the features available in PowerPoint, such as chart-making tools and advanced slide animations. The price, though, for both Google Presentations and Prezi is pretty attractive: free! And that includes new versions and updates.

From a long-term perspective, another key benefit of Google Presentations—and all other cloud computing applications—is environmental. *Newsweek* writer Brian Braiker points out that "conducting affairs in the cloud is not only convenient, it's also greener: less capital and fewer printouts means less waste." All of which suggests that the forecast for Google Presentations is far from cloudy.[13]

5-6g Handling Nerves

Believe it or not, most experts agree that nervousness can be useful before a presentation. A little adrenalin can help you perform better, think faster, and focus more completely. But we all know that out-of-control nerves can interfere with effectiveness. Here are some ideas to mitigate speech anxiety:

- Send yourself positive messages; visualize success. Examples: "I will be dynamic and engaging." "They will completely support my new product idea."

- Take ten slow, deep breaths—use the yoga approach of breathing in through your nose and out through your mouth.

- Take a sip of water to loosen your throat muscles and mitigate a shaking voice. (Water also gives you a way to fill pauses.)

- Pick a friendly face or two in the audience, and imagine yourself speaking only to those people (but don't fix them down with a cold stare!).

- Remind yourself that the audience wants you to succeed. Focus on their needs rather than your own nerves.

If possible, have a handful of one-on-one conversations with audience members before your presentation. This will almost certainly reinforce that they want you to succeed, which will likely take the edge off your nerves.

5-6h Handling Hostility

We've all seen hostile questioners who seem determined to undermine presenters. It can be awful to watch, but it's surprisingly easy to handle. Here are a few tips:

- Stay calm and professional. Rightly or wrongly, the hostile questioner has won the day if you get defensive or nervous.

- Don't be afraid to pause before you answer to gather your thoughts and allow the hostility to diffuse. (A sip of water can provide good cover for a thought-gathering moment.)

- Once you've answered the question, don't reestablish eye contact with the questioner. Doing so would suggest that you are seeking approval for your response, which only invites further hostile follow-up.

- If the questioner insists on follow-up, you may need to agree to disagree. If so, be decisive: "Sounds like we have two different points of view on this complex issue."

- Use body language to reinforce that you are done interacting with the questioner. Take a couple of steps away, and ask another part of the group whether they have any questions.

5-6i Incorporating Humor

Everyone likes to be funny, but incorporating humor in a business presentation can be risky. Only do it if you're very, very sure that it's funny. Even so, double-check that your jokes are appropriate and relevant. You should never, ever

dynamic delivery Vibrant, compelling presentation delivery style that grabs and holds the attention of the audience.

laugh at the expense of any member of your audience. Even laughing at yourself is chancy, since you risk diminishing your credibility. (But a joke at your own expense is always effective if you make a mistake; there's no better way to recover the goodwill of your audience.)

5-6j A Spot on the Back Wall?

Many people have heard the old myth that no one will know the difference if you calm your nerves by looking at a spot on the back wall rather than at the audience. Don't do it! While *you* may be more comfortable, your audience will be mystified . . . more often than not, they'll keep turning around to find out what's so interesting back there!

5-6k Delivery

Some people are naturals, but for the rest of us, **dynamic delivery** is a learned skill. It begins and ends with preparation, but keep in mind that practice doesn't always make perfect—in fact, practice more often just makes permanent. So be sure that you practice with an eye toward improvement. If possible, you should set up a practice situation that's close to the real thing. If you'll be standing to present, stand while you practice, since standing makes many people feel more vulnerable. Consider practicing in front of a mirror to work on eye contact and gestures. Also, try recording your voice to work on a lively tone.

Finally, practice in front of a trusted friend or two who can give you valuable feedback. See Exhibit 5.6 for Ten Tips for Dynamic Delivery.

EXHIBIT 5.6   TEN TIPS FOR DYNAMIC DELIVERY

1. PRACTICE!

2. Know your material, but never memorize it word for word.

3. Look directly at members of your audience at least 50% of the time.

4. Vary your voice, your facial expressions, and your body language.

5. Use selective notes (but keep them inconspicuous).

6. Stick to your allotted time.

7. Slow down and listen to yourself.

8. Don't apologize (unless you really did something wrong!).

9. Remember to use natural gestures.

10. PRACTICE!

ffective communication saves time and money—boosting performance and morale—across every area of business. But one vital principle holds true regardless of the more specific nature of your communication: the best way to achieve your goals is to focus on your audience, not on yourself. If you understand the goals, expectations, and needs of your audience, you can tailor your communication to boost your chances (sometimes dramatically) of accomplishing your objectives.

As globalization and technological change continue to accelerate, new communication challenges will likely develop across the spectrum of business. To ensure that your communication continues to be effective, keep an open mind. Pay attention to differences among cultures, to language usage in professional publications, and to new communication technology. And don't be afraid to consult an up-to-date communication website or handbook every so often. When other resources aren't available, rely on courtesy, consideration, and common sense—valuable tools to guide your communication in any situation.

Careers in Business Communication

Public Relations Manager

lan and implement strategies to build and maintain a positive image for the organization. Build strong relationships and open channels of communication with relevant members of the press. Write and distribute compelling press releases about the organization via both traditional and digital media. Respond to requests for information from the media. Work with senior management to develop crisis management plans when necessary. Work with marketing to create events and stunts that build the company's public image. Perform an effective liaison role with an outside public relations agency when there is one. For more information on this career and other possible careers in business communications, check out Career Transitions.

STUDY TOOLS 5

LOCATED AT BACK OF THE TEXTBOOK

☐ Rip Out Chapter Review Card

LOCATED AT WWW.CENGAGE.COM/LOGIN

☐ Review key term flashcards and create your own using StudyBits

☐ Create and complete practice quizzes based off of your notes and StudyBits

☐ Complete Online activities such as Matching, Fill-in-the-Blank and Drag and Drop exercises

☐ View chapter highlight box content, including CEO Profiles, What Would You Do Cases and chapter videos

☐ Track your knowledge and understanding of key concepts in business using 4LTR Online

6 | Business Formation:
Choosing the Form that Fits

LEARNING OBJECTIVES
After studying this chapter, you will be able to:

6-1 Describe the characteristics of the four basic forms of business ownership

6-2 Discuss the advantages and disadvantages of a sole proprietorship

6-3 Evaluate the pros and cons of the partnership as a form of business ownership

6-4 Explain why corporations have become the dominant form of business ownership

6-5 Explain why limited liability companies are becoming an increasingly popular form of business ownership

6-6 Evaluate the advantages and disadvantages of franchising

Remember to visit
PAGE 109
for additional
STUDY TOOLS

6-1 BUSINESS OWNERSHIP OPTIONS: THE BIG FOUR

One of the most important decisions entrepreneurs make when they start a new business is the form of ownership they'll use. The form they choose affects virtually every aspect of establishing and operating their firm, including the initial cost of setting up the business, the way the profits are distributed, the types of taxes (if any) the business must pay, and the types of regulations it must follow. Choice of ownership also determines the degree to which each owner is personally liable for the firm's debts and the sources of funds available to the firm to finance future expansion.

sole proprietorship A form of business ownership with a single owner who usually actively manages the company.

partnership A voluntary agreement under which two or more people act as co-owners of a business for profit.

The vast majority of businesses in the United States are owned and organized under one of the four forms:

1. A **sole proprietor-ship** is a business that is owned, and usually managed, by a single individual. As far as the law is concerned, a sole proprietorship is simply an extension of the owner. Company earnings are treated just like the owner's income; likewise, any debts the company incurs are considered to be the owner's personal debts.

2. A **partnership** is a voluntary agreement under which two or more people act as co-owners of a

Startup

> "THE LIMITED LIABILITY CORPORATION IS THE *GREATEST* SINGLE DISCOVERY OF MODERN TIMES."
>
> —NICHOLAS MURRAY BUTLER PRESIDENT OF COLUMBIA UNIVERSITY, 1902–1945

Everything Possible/Shutterstock.com

business for profit. As we'll see later in the chapter, there are several types of partnerships. In its most basic form, known as a **general partnership**, each partner has the right to participate in the company's management and share in profits—but also has unlimited liability for any debts the company incurs.

3. A **corporation** is a business entity created by filing a form (known in most states as the **articles of incorporation**) with the appropriate state agency, paying the state's incorporation fees, and meeting other requirements. (The specifics vary among states.) Unlike a sole proprietorship or a partnership, a corporation is considered to be a legal entity that is separate and distinct from its owners. In many ways, a corporation is like an artificial person. It can legally engage in virtually any business activity a natural person can pursue. For example, a corporation can enter into binding contracts, borrow money, own property, pay taxes, and initiate legal actions (such as lawsuits) in its own name. It can even be a partner in a partnership or an owner of another corporation. Because of a corporation's status as a separate legal entity, the owners of a corporation have **limited liability**—meaning they aren't personally responsible for the debts and obligations of their company.

4. A **limited liability company (LLC)** is a hybrid form of business ownership that is similar in some respects to a corporation while having other characteristics that are similar to a partnership. Like a corporation, a limited liability company is considered a legal entity separate from its owners. Also like

general partnership A partnership in which all partners can take an active role in managing the business and have unlimited liability for any claims against the firm.

corporation A form of business ownership in which the business is considered a legal entity that is separate and distinct from its owners.

articles of incorporation The document filed with a state government to establish the existence of a new corporation.

limited liability When owners are not personally liable for claims against their firm. Owners with limited liability may lose their investment in the company, but their other personal assets are protected.

limited liability company (LLC) A form of business ownership that offers both limited liability to its owners and flexible tax treatment.

a corporation—and as its name implies—an LLC offers its owners limited liability for the debts of their business. But it offers more flexibility than a corporation in terms of tax treatment; in fact, one of the most interesting characteristics of an LLC is that its owners can elect to have their business taxed either as a corporation *or* a partnership. Many states even allow individuals to form single-person LLCs that are taxed as if they were sole proprietorships.

Sole proprietorships, partnerships, and corporations have been around in some form since the beginning of our nation's history, but limited liability companies are a relatively new form of ownership in the United States. In 1977, Wyoming passed the first state statute allowing LLCs, and Florida became the second state to do so in 1982. But it wasn't until a ruling by the Internal Revenue Service (IRS) in 1988 clarifying the tax treatment of LLCs that most other states followed suit. Today every state has enacted LLC legislation, and the LLC has become a very popular ownership option. In many states, filings to form LLCs now outnumber filings to form corporations.[1]

Exhibits 6.1 and 6.2 provide some interesting insights about the relative importance of each form of ownership. As shown in Exhibit 6.1, the sole proprietorship is by far the most common type of business organization in the

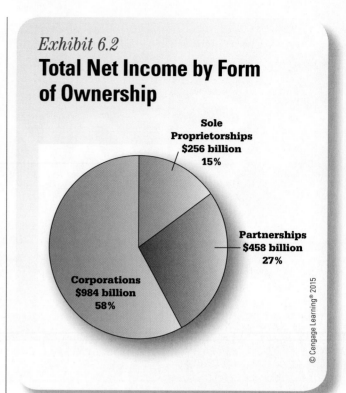

Exhibit 6.2
Total Net Income by Form of Ownership

Sole Proprietorships $256 billion 15%

Partnerships $458 billion 27%

Corporations $984 billion 58%

© Cengage Learning® 2015

Source: 2012 Statistical Abstract of the United States Table 744: U.S. Census Bureau. The 2012 Statistical Abstract of the United States Table 744: http://www.census.gov/compendia/statab/2012/tables/12s0744.pdf, accessed April 6, 2015.

United States. In 2008, 22.6 million individuals reported operating nonfarm sole proprietorships. This represented more than 71% of the total number of business enterprises. As a group, these sole proprietorships reported $1.37 trillion in revenue and $256 billion in net income (profit). But while these figures are impressive in the aggregate, most individual sole proprietorships are quite small. According to the U.S. Census Bureau's *2012 Statistical Abstract*, more than two-thirds of all sole proprietorships reported annual revenue of less than $25,000, while less than 1% reported receipts in excess of $1 million.[2]

As Exhibit 6.2 shows, when it comes to economic impact, the corporate form of ownership rules. Though

Exhibit 6.1
Total Number of Businesses by Form of Ownership

Corporations 5.85 million 18.5%

Partnerships 3.15 million 10%

Sole Proprietorships 22.61 million 71.5%

© Cengage Learning® 2015

Source: 2012 Statistical Abstract of the United States Table 744: U.S. Census Bureau. The 2012 Statistical Abstract of the United States Table 744: http://www.census.gov/compendia/statab/2012/tables/12s0744.pdf, accessed April 6, 2015.

"CORPORATION: AN INGENIOUS DEVICE FOR OBTAINING PROFIT WITHOUT INDIVIDUAL RESPONSIBILITY."

—AMBROSE BIERCE, 19TH-CENTURY COMPILER OF *THE DEVIL'S DICTIONARY*

corporations comprised only 18.5% of all business entities, in 2008 they reported about 58% of all business profits. Corporations such as Walmart, ExxonMobil, General Electric, Apple, and Boeing have annual sales revenues measured in the billions (sometimes hundreds of billions) of dollars. But not all corporations are multibillion-dollar enterprises. In fact, about 25% of all corporations reported total revenues of less than $25,000.[3]

As you can see from Exhibit 6.1, partnerships are less common than sole proprietorships or corporations. Still, more than 3.1 million businesses were classified as partnerships in the United States. And partnerships tend to be both larger and more profitable than sole proprietorships. As Exhibit 6.2 shows, in the aggregate, partnerships earned 1.8 times more total net income than sole proprietorships, despite the fact that sole proprietorships outnumbered partnerships by a ratio of almost seven to one![4]

You've probably noticed that Exhibits 6.1 and 6.2 don't include specific information about limited liability companies. That's because these exhibits are based on information taken from annual tax returns submitted to the Internal Revenue Service (IRS). The IRS doesn't track LLC information separately. Instead, it classifies each LLC based on the tax treatment the company selects. LLCs that choose to be taxed as partnerships are classified as partnerships, while those choosing to be taxed as corporations are classified as corporations. (The vast majority of LLCs elect to be taxed as partnerships, so most LLC earnings are reported in the partnership category.)

We'll see that each form of ownership has distinct advantages and disadvantages. As a company grows and matures, the form of ownership that's best suited to its needs may change. Fortunately, the form of ownership for a business isn't set in stone. For example, it is possible—and in fact quite common—for business owners to convert from a sole proprietorship to a corporation, or from a corporation to a limited liability company.

6-2 ADVANTAGES AND DISADVANTAGES OF SOLE PROPRIETORSHIPS

Our look at Exhibits 6.1 and 6.2 raises two questions about sole proprietorships. First, why is this form of ownership so popular? Second, why do sole proprietorships usually remain relatively small? A look at the advantages and disadvantages of sole proprietorships can help answer these questions.

Joe Seer/Shutterstock.com

6-2a Advantages

Sole proprietorships offer some very attractive advantages to people starting a business:

- **Ease of Formation:** Compared to the other forms of ownership we'll discuss, the paperwork and costs involved in forming a sole proprietorship are minimal. No special forms must be filed, and no special fees must be paid. Entrepreneurs who are eager to get a business up and running quickly can find this a compelling advantage.

- **Retention of Control:** As the only owner of a sole proprietorship, you're in control. You have the ability to manage your business the way you want. If you want to "be your own boss," a sole proprietorship might look very attractive.

- **Pride of Ownership:** One of the main reasons many people prefer a sole proprietorship is the feeling of pride and the personal satisfaction they gain from owning and running their own business.

- **Retention of Profits:** If your business is successful, all the profits go to you—minus your personal taxes, of course.

- **Possible Tax Advantage:** No taxes are levied directly on the earnings of sole proprietorships as a business. Instead, the earnings are taxed only as income of the proprietor. As we'll see when we discuss corporations, this avoids the undesirable possibility of double taxation of earnings.

6-2b Disadvantages

Entrepreneurs thinking about forming sole proprietorships should also be aware of some serious drawbacks:

- **Limited Financial Resources:** Raising money to finance growth can be tough for sole proprietors. With only one owner responsible for a sole proprietorship's debts, banks and other financial institutions are often reluctant to lend it money. Likewise, suppliers may be unwilling to provide supplies on credit. This leaves sole proprietors dependent on their own wealth plus the money that their firms generate.

- **Unlimited Liability:** Because the law views a sole proprietorship as an extension of its owner, the debts of the firm become the owner's personal debts. If someone sues your business and wins, the court can seize your personal possessions—even those that have nothing to do with your business—and sell them to pay the damages. This unlimited personal liability means that operating as a sole proprietorship is a risky endeavor.

- **Limited Ability to Attract and Maintain Talented Employees:** Most sole proprietors are unable to pay the high salaries and substantial perks that highly qualified, experienced employees get when they work for big, well-established companies.

- **Heavy Workload and Responsibilities:** Being your own boss can be very rewarding, but it can also mean very long hours and a lot of stress. Sole proprietors—as the ultimate authority in their business—often must perform tasks or make decisions in areas where they lack expertise.

- **Lack of Permanence:** Because sole proprietorships are just extensions of their owners, they lack permanence. If the owner dies, retires, or withdraws from the business for some other reason, the company legally ceases to exist. Even if the company continues to operate under new ownership, in the eyes of the law, it becomes a different firm.

6-3 PARTNERSHIPS: TWO HEADS (AND BANKROLLS) CAN BE BETTER THAN ONE

There are several types of partnerships, each with its own specific characteristics. We'll focus our discussion mainly on the most basic type, known as a general partnership. However, we'll also take a quick look at limited partnerships and limited liability partnerships.

6-3a Formation of General Partnerships

There is no limit on the number of partners who can participate in a general partnership, but most partnerships consist of only a few partners—often just two. The partnership is formed when the partners enter into a voluntary partnership agreement. It is legally possible to start a partnership on the basis of a verbal agreement, but doing so is often a recipe for disaster. It's much safer to get everything in writing and to seek expert legal assistance when drawing up the agreement. A typical partnership agreement spells out details, such as the initial financial contributions each partner will make, the specific duties and responsibilities each will assume, how they will share profits (and losses), how they will settle disagreements, and how they will deal with the death or withdrawal of one of the partners. Well-written agreements can prevent common misunderstandings.

6-3b Advantages of General Partnerships

Partnerships offer some key advantages relative to both sole proprietorships and corporations:

- **Ability to Pool Financial Resources:** With more owners investing in the company, a partnership is likely to have a stronger financial base than a sole proprietorship.

- **Ability to Share Responsibilities and Capitalize on Complementary Skills:** Partners can share the burden of running the business, which can ease the workload. Tasks and jobs can also be divided based on complementary skills, using each partner's talents to best advantage.

- **Ease of Formation:** In theory, forming a partnership is easy. As we've already noted, it's possible (but not advisable) to establish a partnership based on a

Sharing responsibilities and complementary skills are one of the advantages of general business partnerships.

simple verbal agreement. But we shouldn't overemphasize this advantage. Working out all of the details of a partnership agreement can sometimes be a complex and time-consuming process.

- **Possible Tax Advantages:** Similar to a sole proprietorship, the earnings of a partnership "pass through" the business—untouched by the Internal Revenue Service (IRS)—and are taxed only as the partners' personal income. Again, this avoids the potential for double taxation endemic to corporations.

6-3c Disadvantages of General Partnerships

General partnerships also have some serious disadvantages. Well-written partnership agreements, however, can mitigate some of these major drawbacks:

- **Unlimited Liability:** As a general partner, you're not only liable for your own mistakes but also for those of your partners. In fact, all general partners have unlimited liability for the debts and obligations of their business. So, if the assets they've invested in the business aren't sufficient to meet these claims, the personal assets of the partners are at risk. When someone sues a general partnership, the lawsuit can target *any* individual partner or group of partners. In fact, lawsuits often go after the partners with the deepest pockets, even if they did not personally participate in the act that caused the legal action. In other words, if you have more personal wealth than the other partners, you could lose more than they do even if they were the ones at fault!

- **Potential for Disagreements:** If general partners can't agree on how to run the business, the conflict can complicate and delay decision making. A well-drafted partnership agreement usually specifies how disputes will be resolved, but disagreements among partners can create friction and hard feelings that harm morale and undermine the cooperation needed to keep the business on track.

- **Lack of Continuity:** If a current partner withdraws from the partnership, the relationships among the participants will clearly change, potentially ending the partnership. This creates uncertainty about how long a partnership will remain in business.

- **Difficulty in Withdrawing from a Partnership:** A partner who withdraws from a partnership remains personally liable for any debts or obligations the firm had *at the time of withdrawal*—even if those obligations were incurred by the actions of other partners.

6-3d Limited Partnerships

The risks associated with unlimited liability make general partnerships unattractive to many individuals who would otherwise be interested in joining a business partnership. Fortunately, two other types of partnerships allow some partners to limit their personal liability to some extent, although each comes with particular requirements.

The first of these, known as a **limited partnership**, is a partnership arrangement that includes at least one general partner *and* at least one limited partner. Both types of partners contribute financially to the company and share in its profits. But in other respects they play different roles:

- General partners have the right to participate fully in managing their partnership, but they also assume unlimited personal liability for any of its debts—just like the partners in a general partnership.

- Limited partners *cannot* actively participate in its management, but they have the protection of limited liability. This means that, as long as they do not actively participate in managing the company, their personal wealth is not at risk.

6-3e Limited Liability Partnerships

The **limited liability partnership (LLP)** is another partnership arrangement that is attractive to partners who want to limit their personal risk. It is similar to a limited partnership in some ways, but it

limited partnership A partnership that includes at least one general partner who actively manages the company and accepts unlimited liability and one limited partner who gives up the right to actively manage the company in exchange for limited liability.

limited liability partnership (LLP) A form of partnership in which all partners have the right to participate in management and have limited liability for company debts.

When It Comes to Boards, Bigger Isn't Always Better

Size matters. Ask anyone who has tried to watch a sporting event or a movie on a smartphone. Bigger *is* better because it brings more clarity, more perspectives, and more detail. For decades, the same logic applied to corporate governance—the bigger the company, the bigger its board of directors should be. After all, effectively governing firms with billions of dollars in revenue and stock value, tens (or hundreds) of thousands of employees, and dozens (or thousands) of locations, should require more people at the top. Industry giants like Eli Lilly, Bank of America, and Walmart have 14, 15, and 16 directors, respectively, on their boards of directors. Indeed, the rule of thumb was that board size should grow with company size.

It makes sense that it should—but it doesn't. Recent research shows that smaller boards are actually more effective. A three-year

Hxdbzxy/Shutterstock.com

study found that, for companies with at least $10 billion in market capitalization, those with smaller boards increased stock values by 8.5% compared to similar-sized peers with bigger boards. And companies with large boards trailed the performance of their peers by nearly 11%!

Those findings strongly support the trend toward reducing the number of members on a company's board of directors. According to the research, smaller boards are more cohesive and more nimble. Because of the small numbers, there are fewer committees, and members tend to be more decisive. Netflix and Apple are two high-performing, high-capitalization companies with small boards. Jay Hoag, one of Netflix's seven directors, says that with such a tight-knit group, the board can afford to go through business decisions in depth. Tim Cook, Apple's CEO, likes that he can reach out to board members informally and thinks that a smaller group inspires greater candor. During the period covering the study, Netflix outperformed its sector peers by 32%, and Apple outperformed its peers by 37%.

For companies wanting to shrink their boards, the bad news is that doing it through attrition can take years (as each members' term on the board ends). For example, Time Warner has a 10-year term limit, and Ingredion, a food ingredient company, has a 12-year limit. At General Motors, the mandatory retirement age from the board is 72. So, with five directors who are 67 years old, the board may shrink according to Chair Tim Solso, because, "Through natural attrition, we may not replace all of the directors."[5]

---

has the advantage of allowing *all* partners to take an active role in management, while also offering *all* partners some form of limited liability. In other words, there's no need to distinguish between limited and general partners in an LLP.

The amount of liability protection offered by LLPs varies among states. In some states, LLPs offer "full-shield" protection, meaning that partners have limited liability for all claims against their company, except those resulting from *their own* negligence or malpractice. In other states, partners in LLPs have a lesser "partial-shield" protection. In these states, each partner has limited liability for the negligence or malpractice of other partners but still has unlimited liability for any other debts. Another drawback is that some states only allow specific types of professional businesses to form limited liability partnerships. For example, California law allows only accountants, lawyers, and architects to form LLPs.

C corporation The most common type of corporation, which is a legal business entity that offers limited liability to all of its owners, who are called stockholders.

 6-4

CORPORATIONS: THE ADVANTAGES AND DISADVANTAGES OF BEING AN ARTIFICIAL PERSON

There are several types of corporations. The most common is called a **C corporation**; when people use the term "corporation" without specifying which type, they are generally referring to a C corporation. Because it's the most common, we'll devote most of our discussion to

C corporations. However, we'll also describe three other types of corporations: S corporations, statutory close (or closed) corporations, and nonprofit corporations.

6-4a Forming a C Corporation

As mentioned earlier, the formation of a corporation requires filing articles of incorporation and paying filing fees. It also requires the adoption of **corporate bylaws**, which are detailed rules that govern the way the corporation is organized and managed. Because of these requirements, forming a corporation tends to be more expensive and complex than forming a sole proprietorship or partnership. The requirements, however, vary among the states. Some states are known for their simple forms, inexpensive fees, low corporate tax rates, and "corporation-friendly" laws and court systems. In those states, forming a corporation is not much harder or more expensive than setting up a sole proprietorship and sometimes can be simpler than forming a partnership. Not surprisingly, many large companies choose to incorporate in states with such favorable environments— even if they intend to do the majority of their business in other states. Delaware, in particular, has been very successful at attracting corporations. You may not think of Delaware as the home of corporate power, but more than half of all publicly traded corporations—and 64% of the firms listed in the *Fortune 500*—are incorporated in Delaware.[6]

6-4b Ownership of C Corporations

Ownership of C corporations is represented by shares of stock, so owners are called "**stockholders**" (or "shareholders"). Common stock represents the basic ownership interest in a corporation, but some firms also issue preferred stock. One key difference between the two types of stock involves voting rights; common stockholders normally have the right to vote in stockholders' meetings, while preferred stockholders do not. As shown in Exhibit 6.3, many large corporations issue billions of shares of stock and have hundreds of thousands—or even millions—of stockholders.

Stock in large corporations is usually publicly traded, meaning that anyone with the money and inclination to do so can buy shares—and that anyone who owns shares is free to sell them. But many smaller corporations are owned by just a handful of stockholders who don't actively trade their stock. It's even possible for individuals to incorporate their business and be the sole shareholder in their corporation.[7]

Stockholders don't have to be individuals. **Institutional investors**, such as mutual funds, insurance companies, pension funds, and endowment funds, pool money from a large number of individuals and use these funds to buy stocks and other securities. As Exhibit 6.3 illustrates, such institutional investors own the majority of stock in many large corporations.

6-4c The Role of the Board of Directors

It's not practical for all of the stockholders of a large corporation to actively participate in the management of their company. Besides, most stockholders don't have

corporate bylaws The basic rules governing how a corporation is organized and how it conducts its business.

stockholder An owner of a corporation.

institutional investor An organization that pools contributions from investors, clients, or depositors and uses these funds to buy stocks and other securities.

EXHIBIT 6.3	STOCK OWNERSHIP IN SELECTED MAJOR U.S. CORPORATIONS		
Corporation	**Shares of Common Stock Outstanding (Billions)**	**Total Number of Stockholders**	**Percentage of Shares Owned by Institutional Investors**
Apple	5.82	26,112	62.10
Coca-Cola	4.37	12,165	59.80
Ford	3.96	137,803	57.40
GE	10.06	490,000	54.20
IBM	0.988	458,306	59.30
McDonald's	0.961	1,663,000	65.30
Microsoft	8.20	113,923	71.30
Walmart	3.23	249,876	30.40

© Cengage Learning® 2015

Source: Shares outstanding and percentage of institutional ownership are from the Key Statistics for each corporation reported in Yahoo! Finance (http://finance.yahoo.com/); Information about the number of shareholders is found in Item 5 (Market for the Company's Common Equity) of each firm's 2014 10-K annual report filed with the SEC accessed through the Edgar database (http://www.sec.gov/edgar.shtml) accessed April 6, 2015.

the time, management skills, or desire to effectively manage such a complex business enterprise. Thus, in accordance with corporate bylaws, the stockholders elect a **board of directors** and rely on this board to oversee the operation of their company and protect their interests.

The board of directors establishes the corporation's mission and sets its broad objectives. But board members seldom take an active role in the day-to-day management of their company. Instead, again in accordance with corporate bylaws, the board appoints a chief executive officer (CEO) and other corporate officers to manage the company on a daily basis. The board also sets the level of compensation for these officers and monitors their performance to ensure that they act in a manner consistent with stockholder interests. It also provides advice to these officers on broad policy issues, approves their major proposals, and ensures that the company adheres to major regulatory requirements.

6-4d Advantages of C Corporations

Corporations have become the dominant form of business ownership for several reasons:

- **Limited Liability:** As already explained, stockholders are not personally liable for the debts of their company. If a corporation goes bankrupt, the stockholders might find that their stock is worthless, but their other personal assets are protected.

- **Permanence:** Unless the articles of incorporation specify a limited duration, corporations can continue operating as long as they remain financially viable and the majority of stockholders want the business to continue. Unlike a sole proprietorship or partnership, a general corporation is unaffected by the death or withdrawal of an owner.

- **Ease of Transfer of Ownership:** It's easy for stockholders of publicly traded C corporations to withdraw from ownership—they simply sell their shares of stock.

- **Ability to Raise Large Amounts of Financial Capital:** Corporations can raise large amounts of financial capital by issuing shares of stock or by selling formal IOUs called corporate bonds. The ability to raise money by issuing these securities gives corporations a major financial advantage over most other forms of ownership.

- **Ability to Make Use of Specialized Management:** Large corporations often find it easier to hire highly qualified professional managers than proprietorships and partnerships. Major corporations can typically offer attractive salaries and benefits, and their permanence and potential for growth offer managers opportunities for career advancement.

6-4e Disadvantages of C Corporations

In addition to their significant benefits, C corporations have a number of drawbacks:

- **Expense and Complexity of Formation and Operation:** As we've already seen, establishing a corporation can be more complex and expensive than forming a sole proprietorship or partnership. Corporations are also subject to more formal operating requirements. For example, they are required to hold regular board meetings and keep accurate minutes.

- **Complications When Operating in More Than One State:** When a business that's incorporated in one state does business in other states, it's called a "*domestic* corporation" in the state where it's incorporated, and a "*foreign* corporation" in the other states. A corporation must register (or "qualify") as a foreign corporation in order to do business in any state other than the one in which it incorporated. This typically requires additional paperwork, fees, and taxes. But registration as a foreign corporation is only necessary if the company is involved in substantial business activities within the state. Businesses that only engage in minor business activities typically are exempt from the registration requirement. For example, a firm operating a production facility or maintaining a district office in a state other than its corporate home would need to register as a foreign corporation, but a

---

board of directors The individuals who are elected by stockholders of a corporation to represent their interests.

"GENERAL ELECTRIC, ONE OF THE LARGEST CORPORATIONS IN AMERICA, FILED A WHOPPING 57,000-PAGE FEDERAL TAX RETURN... [WHICH] WOULD HAVE BEEN 19 FEET HIGH IF PRINTED OUT AND STACKED."

—WEEKLY STANDARD

A Spin-off for Time Warner

AP Images/Mark Lennihan

Time Warner, the world's second-largest media company, is successful in movies (Warner Bros. Pictures, DC Entertainment, and New Line Cinema), TV networks (HBO, Cinemax, Turner Broadcasting, CNN Headline News, and The Cartoon Channel), and video games (Lord of the Rings Online and LEGO Harry Potter: Years 1–4). However, its publishing division struggles because consumers are increasingly likely to read digital content on computers, smartphones, or tablets, rather than from printed books, magazines, or newspapers. Consequently, its publishing division, which makes up 12% of the company, saw revenues drop 6.5%, while operating income plunged 25%.

Because of declining performance, Time Warner is spinning off the publishing division into an independent, publicly traded company to be known as Time, Inc. Jeff Bewkes, Time Warner's CEO, says, "After a thorough review of options, we believe that a separation will better position both Time Warner and Time, Inc." Time, Inc. will become a completely independent company, publishing well-known magazines, such as *People*, *Sports Illustrated*, and *InStyle*, which rank, respectively, 1st, 3rd, and 5th in advertising revenue in the magazine industry. Furthermore, CEO Bewkes sees the spin-off as an opportunity to not only shed a struggling division, but also to establish a clear focus for Time Warner. Said Bewkes, "A complete spin-off of Time Inc. provides strategic clarity for Time Warner Inc., enabling us to focus entirely on our television networks and film and TV production businesses, and improves our growth profile."[8]

firm that simply held a bank account or solicited sales to customers in that state through the mail would not be required to do so.

- **Double Taxation of Earnings and Additional Taxes:** The IRS considers a C corporation to be a separate legal entity and taxes its earnings accordingly. Then, as shown in Exhibit 6.4, any dividends (earnings the corporation distributes to stockholders) are taxed *again* as the personal income of the stockholders.

This double taxation can take a big bite out of earnings that are distributed to shareholders. But note that corporations often reinvest some or all of their profits back into the business. Shareholders don't pay income taxes on these *retained earnings*. Many states also impose separate income taxes on corporations. Most states also impose an annual franchise tax on both domestic and foreign corporations that operate within their borders.

Exhibit 6.4
How Double Taxation Reduces Earnings for Stockholders

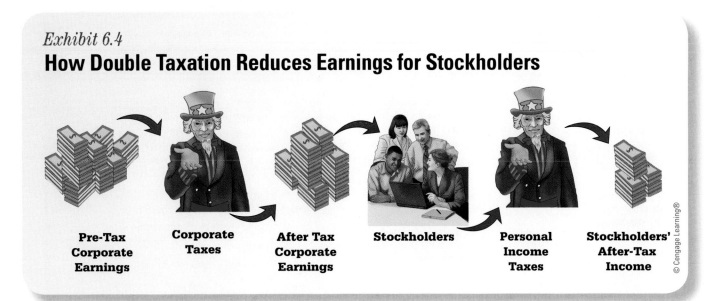

Pre-Tax Corporate Earnings → Corporate Taxes → After Tax Corporate Earnings → Stockholders → Personal Income Taxes → Stockholders' After-Tax Income

© Cengage Learning®

- **More Paperwork, More Regulation, and Less Secrecy:** Corporations are more closely regulated and are required to file more government paperwork than other forms of business. Large, publicly traded corporations are required to send annual statements to all shareholders and to file detailed quarterly and annual reports with the Securities and Exchange Commission (SEC). The annual report filed with the SEC (called a Form 10-K) is often hundreds of pages long and includes a wealth of information about the company's operations and financial condition. Anyone can look at these forms, making it difficult to keep key corporate information secret from competitors.

- **Possible Conflicts of Interest:** The corporate officers appointed by the board are supposed to further the interests of stockholders. But some top executives pursue policies that further their *own* interests (such as prestige, power, job security, high pay, and attractive perks) at the expense of the stockholders. The board of directors has an obligation to protect the interests of stockholders, but in recent years the boards of several major corporations have come under criticism for continuing to approve high compensation packages for top executives even when their companies performed poorly.

> **S corporation** A form of corporation that avoids double taxation by having its income taxed as if it were a partnership.
>
> **statutory close (or closed) corporation** A corporation with a limited number of owners that operates under simpler, less formal rules than a C corporation.
>
> **nonprofit corporation** A corporation that does not seek to earn a profit and differs in several fundamental respects from C corporations.

6-4f Other Types of Corporations: Same but Different

Now that we've described C corporations, let's take a quick look at three other types of corporations: **S corporations**, **statutory close corporations**, and **nonprofit corporations**. Like C corporations, each is created by filing the appropriate paperwork with a government agency. Also like general corporations, these corporations are considered legal entities that stand apart from their owners and can enter into contracts, own property, and take legal action in their own names. But in other key respects they are quite different from C corporations—and from each other. Exhibit 6.5 summarizes the basic features of these corporations.

6-4g Corporate Restructuring

Large corporations constantly look for ways to grow and achieve competitive advantages. Some corporations work to achieve these goals, at least in part, through mergers, acquisitions, and divestitures. We'll close our discussion of corporations by taking a quick look at these forms of corporate restructuring.

EXHIBIT 6.5	CHARACTERISTICS OF S, STATUTORY CLOSE, AND NONPROFIT CORPORATIONS	
Type	**Key Advantages**	**Limitations**
S Corporation	■ The IRS does not tax earnings of S corporations separately. Earnings pass through the company and are taxed only as income to stockholders, thus avoiding the problem of double taxation associated with C corporations. ■ Stockholders have limited liability.	■ It can have no more than 100 stockholders. ■ With only rare exceptions, each stockholder must be a U.S. citizen or permanent resident of the United States. (No ownership by foreigners or other corporations.)
Statutory Close (or Closed) Corporation	■ It can operate under simpler arrangements than conventional corporations. For example, it doesn't have to elect a board of directors or hold an annual stockholders' meeting. ■ All owners can actively participate in management while still having limited liability.	■ The number of stockholders is limited. (The number varies among states but is usually no more than 50.) ■ Stockholders normally can't sell their shares to the public without first offering the shares to existing owners. ■ Not all states allow formation of this type of corporation.
Nonprofit (or Not-for-Profit) Corporation	■ Earnings are exempt from federal and state income taxes. ■ Members and directors have limited liability. ■ Individuals who contribute money or property to the nonprofit can take a tax deduction, making it easier for these organizations to raise funds from donations.	■ It has members (who may pay dues) but cannot have stockholders. ■ It cannot distribute dividends to members. ■ It cannot contribute funds to a political campaign. ■ It must keep accurate records and file paperwork to document tax-exempt status.

© Cengage Learning®

EXHIBIT 6.6 TYPES OF MERGERS AND ACQUISITIONS

Type of Merger	Definition	Common Objective	Example
Horizontal Merger	A combination of firms in the same industry.	Increase size and market power within the industry. Improve efficiency by eliminating duplication of facilities and personnel.	Medtronic, a medical device company, acquires Covidien, which sells advanced medical supplies, solutions, and surgical technologies, for $42.9 billion.
Vertical Merger	A combination of firms that are at different stages in the production of a good or service, creating a "buyer-seller" relationship.	Provide tighter integration of production and increased control over the supply of crucial inputs.	AT&T acquires satellite TV subscription provider, DirecTV, for $49 billion.
Conglomerate Merger	A combination of firms in unrelated industries.	Reduce risk by making the firm less vulnerable to adverse conditions in any single market.	Anbang Insurance, a Chinese company, buys the famed New York City Waldorf Astoria Hotel from Hilton Worldwide Holdings for $1.95 billion.

© Cengage Learning®

MERGERS AND ACQUISITIONS In the news and casual conversation, the terms "merger" and "acquisition" are often used interchangeably. However, there's a difference between the two. An **acquisition** occurs when one firm buys another firm. The firm making the purchase is called the "acquiring firm," and the firm being purchased is called the "target firm." After the acquisition, the target firm ceases to exist as an independent entity while the purchasing firm continues in operation, and its stock is still traded. But not all acquisitions are on friendly terms. When the acquiring firm buys the target firm despite the opposition of the target's board and top management, the result is called a "hostile takeover."

In a **merger**, instead of one firm buying the other, the two companies agree to a combination of equals, joining together to form a new company out of the two previously independent firms. Exhibit 6.6 describes the three most common types of corporate combinations.

DIVESTITURES: WHEN LESS IS MORE
Sometimes corporations restructure by subtraction rather than by addition. A **divestiture** occurs when a firm transfers total or partial ownership of some of its operations to investors or to another company. Firms often use divestitures to rid themselves of a part of their company that no longer fits well with their strategic plans. This allows them to streamline their operations and focus on their core businesses. In many (but not all) cases, divestitures involve the sale of assets to outsiders, which raises financial capital for the firm.

One common type of divestiture, called a "spin-off," occurs when a company issues stock in one of its own divisions or operating units and sets it up as a separate company—complete with its own board of directors and corporate officers. It then distributes the stock in the new company to its existing stockholders. After the spin-off, the stockholders end up owning two separate companies rather than one. They can then buy, sell, or hold either (or both) stocks as they see fit. While a spin-off allows a corporation to eliminate a division that no longer fits in its plans, it doesn't actually generate any additional funds for the firm.

A "carve-out" is like a spin-off in that the firm converts a particular unit or division into a separate company and issues stock in the newly created corporation. However, instead of distributing the new stock to its current stockholders, it sells the stock to

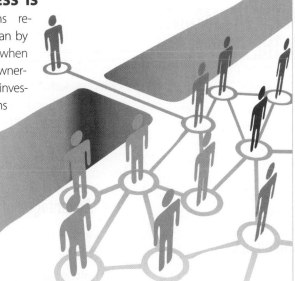

Michael D Brown/Shutterstock.com

horizontal merger A combination of two firms that are in the same industry.

vertical merger A combination of firms at different stages in the production of a good or service.

conglomerate merger A combination of two firms that are in unrelated industries.

acquisition A corporate restructuring in which one firm buys another.

merger A corporate restructuring that occurs when two formerly independent business entities combine to form a new organization.

divestiture The transfer of total or partial ownership of some of a firm's operations to investors or to another company.

Merger Makes for Unwelcome Competition

The trillion-dollar travel industry has experienced horizontal mergers for decades. Airlines, in particular, have long argued that they gain synergies from mergers by consolidating routes, fleets, and personnel, which make them more competitive in a highly dynamic industry.

Recently, however, an unanticipated—and unwelcome—new competitor entered the travel industry through a merger. When Google acquired ITA Software, Inc., it instantly became a powerful competitor among travel websites. ITA's software aggregates flight options for dozens of travel companies, including domestic and international airlines (Delta, American, Southwest, United, Air France, and more), online and traditional travel agents (Orbitz, Student Universe, and more), metasearch services (Kayak), and more. By purchasing the premier flight-search software company, Google instantly bolstered its own fledgling travel search service. Google can now rank its own flight search options higher than options from other online travel companies which get up to 20% of their business directly from Google searches.

Even more importantly, Google now controls access to the critical industry software on which its rivals rely.

Understandably, Google's acquisition of ITA also rankled the airlines which pay travel websites an average of $11 per booking compared to a cost of $1 per ticket purchased on their own websites. In other words, ITA, which was once their vendor was now a vendor and a direct competitor. The Department of Justice (DOJ) also recognized the threat that Google's acquisition posed to the industry. As a condition of the acquisition, the DOJ required Google to agree to a series of stringent conditions, including continuing to license ITA Software to airline and online travel sites until 2016.

With the DOJ licensing about to expire, Expedia began aggressively acquiring its competitors. In a matter of weeks, Expedia purchased Travelocity for $280 million *and* Orbitz for $1.34 billion. Following those mergers, the major online travel companies in the United States and Europe are controlled by one of two groups: Expedia (CheapTickets.com, Expedia.com, Hotels.com, Orbitz.com, and Travelocity) and Priceline (Booking.com, Kayak.com, Priceline.com, and rentalcars.com). But, even with Google's entry into this market via its acquisition of ITA, interesting startups continue to emerge in the online travel industry. Sites like Skyscanner, HomeAway, Stayful, Yapta, and AirBNB still apply independent competitive pressure on their larger competitors—for the moment, anyway.[9]

---

outside investors, thus raising additional financial capital. In many cases, the firm sells only a minority of the total shares, so that it maintains majority ownership.

6-5 THE LIMITED LIABILITY COMPANY: THE NEW KID ON THE BLOCK

As the newest form of business ownership, state laws concerning the legal status and formation of LLCs are still evolving. Several states have recently revised their statutes to make forming LLCs simpler and to make transfer of ownership easier. Other states have kept more restrictive requirements intact. This diversity of state requirements, and the continuing evolution of LLC statutes, makes it difficult to provide meaningful generalizations about this form of ownership.[10]

6-5a Forming and Managing an LLC

In many respects, forming an LLC is similar to forming a corporation. As with corporations, LLCs are created by filing a document (which goes by a variety of names, such as *certificate of organization* or *articles of organization*) and paying filing fees in the state where the business is organized. Organizers of most LLCs also draft an operating agreement, which is similar to the bylaws of a corporation. Some states also require LLCs to publish a notice of intent to operate as a limited liability company.

Because LLCs are neither corporations nor partnerships, their owners are called *members* rather than stockholders or partners. Members of LLCs often manage their own company under an arrangement similar to the relationship among general partners in a partnership. However, some LLCs hire professional managers who have responsibilities much like those of the CEO and other top officers of corporations.

6-5b Advantages of LLCs

Why are LLCs becoming so popular? This form of ownership offers significant advantages:

- **Limited Liability:** Similar to a corporation, all owners of an LLC have limited liability.

- **Tax Pass-Through:** As mentioned at the beginning of this chapter, for tax purposes the owners of LLCs may elect to have their companies treated as either a corporation or a partnership—or even as a sole proprietorship if owned by a single person. The default tax classification for LLCs with more than one owner—and the one most LLCs choose—is the partnership option. Under this arrangement, there is no separate tax on the earnings of the company. Instead, earnings "pass through" the company and are taxed only as income of the owners. This eliminates the double taxation of profits that is endemic to general corporations. However, there are some cases where it makes sense for LLCs to elect to be taxed as a corporation. For example, the owner of a single-person LLC can avoid paying self-employment taxes by electing to have the LLC treated as a corporation rather than as a sole proprietorship.

- **Simplicity and Flexibility in Management and Operation:** Unlike corporations, LLCs aren't required to hold regular board meetings. Also, LLCs are subject to less paperwork and fewer reporting requirements than corporations.

iQoncept/Shutterstock.com

- **Flexible Ownership:** Unlike S corporations, LLCs can have any number of owners. Also unlike S corporations, the owners of LLCs can include foreign investors and other corporations. However, some states do make it difficult to transfer ownership to outsiders.

6-5c Limitations and Disadvantages of LLCs

Despite their increasing popularity, LLCs have some limitations and drawbacks:

- **Complexity of Formation:** Because of the need to file articles of organization and pay filing fees, LLCs can take more time and effort to form than sole proprietorships. In general, forming an LLC is also more difficult than creating a partnership. But as we mentioned earlier, the formation of a partnership requires a "meeting of the minds" of the partners, which isn't always easy to achieve. So in some cases, the formation of a partnership can prove to be every bit as challenging as the formation of an LLC.

- **Annual Franchise Tax:** Even though they may be exempt from corporate income taxes, many states require LLCs to pay an annual franchise tax.

One Venti, Half-Caf, Non-Fat Franchise!

When Dunkin' Donuts decided to expand in California, where it had just one store for every 610,000 people, franchisees bought the right to open 100 new stores. Like Dunkin' Donuts, McDonald's uses franchising to grow around the world. When it recently opened its first restaurant in Vietnam in Ho Chi Minh City, 20,000 people ate there the first two days. Henry Nguyen, who owns the franchise for the Ho Chi Minh City McDonald's, plans to open another within three months.

Starbucks, by contrast, has never franchised any of its stores, instead choosing to own and run them itself so it could control the quality of its brand. Sometimes, however, that corporate-owned strategy hasn't worked. For instance, throughout Europe, Starbucks put stores in high-traffic, but very expensive, locations in major cities like London. As a result, its European profits

Sean Wandzilak/Shutterstock.com

have been 75% lower than in the United States. As a result, it is closing 72 stores throughout Europe.

But that hasn't stopped its European expansion plans. Kris Engskov, who heads Starbucks' European division, says, "We will definitely open more stores." But, for the first time, it will do so via franchising. So while you won't be able to buy a U.S. Starbucks franchise, you can buy Starbucks franchises in the United Kingdom, France, and Germany. Moving forward, 75% of its new stores in Europe will be franchised. In the United Kingdom, Starbucks will have no more than 25 franchise partners, all of whom will invest 500,000 pounds (about $805,000), sign ten-year contracts, and be expected to run ten stores or more. Engskov says, "I am certain that our new [franchising] strategy will lead to long-term profitability in Germany, France, and Britain."[11]

- **Foreign Status in Other States:** Like corporations, LLCs must register or qualify to operate as "foreign" companies when they do business in states other than the state in which they were organized. This results in additional paperwork, fees, and taxes.

- **Limits on Types of Firms that Can Form LLCs:** Most states do not permit banks, insurance companies, and nonprofit organizations to operate as LLCs.

- **Differences in State Laws:** As we've already mentioned, LLC laws are still evolving—and their specific requirements vary considerably among the states. In 2006, the National Conference of Commissioners on Uniform State Laws created a Revised Uniform Limited Liability Company Act that could be used as a model by all states. To date, only a few states have adopted this law. Until there is more uniformity in state laws, operating LLCs in more than one state is likely to remain a complex endeavor.[12]

6-6 FRANCHISING: PROVEN METHODS FOR A PRICE

A **franchise** is a licensing arrangement under which one party (the **franchisor**) allows another party (the **franchisee**) to use its name, trademark, patents, copyrights, business methods, and other property in exchange for monetary payments and other considerations. Franchising has become a very popular way to operate a business and an important source of employment and income. A 2013 study conducted by Global Insight for the International Franchising Association's Education Foundation reported that almost 760,000 franchise establishments operated in the United States, employing over 8.2 million workers. And according to another franchising study published by the Bureau of the Census in 2010, franchise establishments dominate several major markets such as fast food, auto dealerships, convenience stores, and private mail distribution centers.[13]

The two most popular types of franchise arrangements are **distributorships** and **business format franchises**. In a distributorship, the franchisor makes a product and grants distributors a license to sell it. The most common example of this type of franchise is the arrangement between automakers and the dealerships that sell their cars. In a business format franchise, the franchisor grants the franchisee the right to both make *and* sell its good or service. Under this arrangement, the franchisor usually provides a wide range of services to the franchisee, such as help with site selection, training, and help in obtaining financing, but also requires the franchisee to follow very specific guidelines while operating the business. You're no doubt very familiar with business format franchises; examples include Wendy's, Supercuts, Jiffy Lube, and Massage Envy.

6-6a Franchising in Today's Economy

Franchising is now a well-established method of operating a business—but that doesn't mean it's static. Let's look at some ways the world of franchising is changing.

One of the biggest trends in franchising for the past several years has been an expansion into foreign markets. Franchisors in a variety of industries have found that opportunities for franchise growth are greater in foreign countries because competition is less intense, and markets are less saturated than in the United States. In 2014, McDonald's had 15,527 franchise outlets in foreign countries (2,691 more than it had in the United States), Subway had 12,493, and 7–11 had 44,857.[14] Of course, operating in foreign countries can pose special challenges. Differences in culture, language, laws, demographics, and economic development mean that franchisors, like other types of business owners, must adjust their business methods—and the specific products they offer—to meet the needs of foreign consumers.

Another notable trend has been the growth in the number of women franchisees. Reliable statistics on women in franchising are difficult to find, but the International Franchising Association (IFA) estimates that women now own about 45% of all franchises, and anecdotal evidence suggests that the trend toward more women-owned franchises is continuing. A number of women, such as Dzana Homan (founder of School of Rock music lesson franchises), and Eileen Huntington, co-founder of Huntington Learning Centers, also have become very successful franchisors.[15] But, despite these highly visible success stories, the number of women franchisors hasn't grown nearly as fast as the number of women franchisees.[16]

franchise A licensing arrangement under which a franchisor allows franchisees to use its name, trademark, products, business methods, and other property in exchange for monetary payments and other considerations.

franchisor The business entity in a franchise relationship that allows others to operate its business using resources it supplies in exchange for money and other considerations.

franchisee The party in a franchise relationship that pays for the right to use resources supplied by the franchisor.

distributorship A type of franchising arrangement in which the franchisor makes a product and licenses the franchisee to sell it.

business format franchise A broad franchise agreement in which the franchisee pays for the right to use the name, trademark, and business and production methods of the franchisor.

Minority participation in franchises, both as franchisees and franchisors, has been relatively low. African Americans, Hispanics, Asian Americans, and Native Americans make up about a third of the population, and that share is expected to steadily grow over the next several decades. Indeed, 20.5% of franchises are minority-owned, which is roughly 50% higher than 14.2% for nonfranchised businesses.[17] One of the main reasons for such low minority involvement in franchising is a lack of awareness of franchising opportunities within minority communities. But many franchisors are now making a strong effort to actively recruit minority franchisees.[18]

Two major initiatives have given the efforts to reach minority franchising a boost in recent years. The first, known as the National Minority Franchising Initiative (NMFI), was founded in 2000. The NMFI's website currently maintains a directory of more than 500 franchisors who actively promote minority franchise ownership. The second initiative, called DiversityFran, was established in early 2006 by the IFA. This initiative has the cooperation of a variety of organizations interested in promoting minority business ownership, including the National Urban League, the Association of Small Business Development Centers, the U.S. Pan Asian American Chamber of Commerce, and the Minority Business Development Agency. Franchisors participating in the program receive information and marketing materials designed to help them reach potential minority franchisees more effectively. As of late 2014, DiversityFran had 118 participating franchisors, including such major players as Chick-fil-A, Dunkin' Donuts, and YUM! Brands (which owns KFC, Taco Bell, and Pizza Hut), all pledging to actively recruit minority franchisees.[19]

6-6b Advantages of Franchising

Both the franchisee and the franchisor must believe they'll benefit from the franchise arrangement; otherwise, they wouldn't participate. The advantages of franchising for the franchisor are fairly obvious. It allows the franchisor to expand the business and bring in additional revenue (in the form of franchising fees and royalties) without investing its own capital. Also, franchisees—business owners who are motivated to earn a profit—may have a greater incentive than salaried managers to do whatever it takes to maximize the success of their outlets.

From the franchisee's perspective, franchising offers several advantages:

- **Less Risk:** Franchises offer access to a proven business system and product. The systems and methods offered by franchisors have an established track record. People who are interested in buying a franchise can do research to see how stores in the franchise have performed and can talk to existing franchisees before investing.

- **Training and Support:** The franchisor normally provides the franchisee with extensive training and support. For example, Subway offers two weeks of training at its headquarters and additional training at meetings. The franchisor also sends out newsletters, provides Internet support, maintains a toll-free number for phone support, and provides on-site evaluations.[20]

- **Brand Recognition:** Operating a franchise gives the franchisee instant brand-name recognition, which can be a big help in attracting customers.

- **Easier Access to Funding:** Bankers and other lenders may be more willing to lend money if the business is part of an established franchise than if it is a new, unproven business.

6-6c Disadvantages of Franchising

Franchising also has some drawbacks. From the franchisor's perspective, operating a business with perhaps thousands of semi-independent owner–operators can be complex and challenging. With such a large number of owners, it can be difficult to keep all of the franchisees satisfied, and disappointed franchisees sometimes go public with their complaints, damaging the reputation of the franchisor. In fact, it isn't unusual for disgruntled franchisees to sue their franchisors.

Franchisees are also likely to find some disadvantages:

- **Costs:** The typical franchise agreement requires franchisees to pay an initial franchise fee when they enter into the franchise agreement and an ongoing royalty (usually a percentage of monthly sales revenues) to the franchisor. In addition, the franchisor may assess other fees to support national advertising campaigns

EXHIBIT 6.7 FRANCHISEE COSTS FOR SELECTED FRANCHISES

Franchise	Type of Business	Franchise Fee	Royalty*	Estimated Minimum Total Investment
Coffee News	Newspaper distributed at restaurants	$9,000	$80/wk.	$10,250
Anytime Fitness	24/7 Fitness club	$22,500	$549/mo.	$78,700
Subway	Fast food	$15,000	8%	$116,600
Papa John's	Pizza delivery	$25,000	5%	$129,910
Supercuts	Hair styling	$29,500	6%	$113,900
The UPS Store	Mailing and business	$29,950	8.5%	$150,152
The Joint	Chiropractic care	$29,000	7%	$130,625
Jiffy Lube	Automobile maintenance	$35,000	3%	$221,000

*Royalty is expressed as a percentage of gross revenues unless otherwise specified.

Source: Individual franchise opportunity pages for each listed franchise on the Entrepreneur.com website, http://www.entrepreneur.com/franchiseopportunities/index.html, accessed April 7, 2014/

© 2017 Cengage Learning®

or for other purposes. These costs vary considerably, but for high-profile franchises, they can be substantial. Exhibit 6.7 compares the franchise fees, royalties, and minimum total investment for several well-established franchises. (Total investment reflects the fact that the cost of starting a franchise generally requires the franchisee to invest in property, equipment, and inventory in addition to paying the franchise fee. The actual total investment that franchisees make is often substantially higher than the estimated minimum investment cited in Exhibit 6.7.)

■ **Lack of Control:** The franchise agreement usually requires the franchisee to follow the franchisor's procedures to the letter. People who want the freedom and flexibility to be their own boss can find these restrictions frustrating.

■ **Negative Halo Effect:** The irresponsible or incompetent behavior of a few franchisees can create a negative perception that adversely affects not only the franchise as a whole but also the success of other franchisees.

■ **Growth Challenges:** While growth and expansion are definitely possible in franchising (many franchisees own multiple

> "IN BUSINESS FOR YOURSELF, NOT BY YOURSELF."
>
> —RAY KROC, FOUNDER, MCDONALD'S RESTAURANTS

outlets), strings are attached. Franchise agreements usually limit the franchisee's territory and require franchisor approval before expanding into other areas.

■ **Restrictions on Sale:** Franchise agreements normally prevent franchisees from selling their franchises to other investors without prior approval from the franchisor.

■ **Poor Execution:** Not all franchisors live up to their promises. Sometimes the training and support are of poor quality, and sometimes the company does a poor job of screening franchisees, leading to the negative halo effect we mentioned previously.

These considerations suggest that before buying a franchise, potential owners should carefully research the franchise opportunity.

6-6d Entering into a Franchise Agreement

To obtain a franchise, the franchisee must sign a **franchise agreement**. This agreement is a legally binding contract that specifies the relationship between the franchisor and the franchisee in great detail. There's no standard form for the contract, but some of the key items normally covered include the following:

■ **Terms and Conditions:** The franchisee's rights to use the franchisor's trademarks, patents, and signage,

---

franchise agreement
The contractual arrangement between a franchisor and franchisee that spells out the duties and responsibilities of both parties.

Wendy's Restaurants and a 152-Store Franchisee Sue Each Other

To maintain quality across stores, franchise agreements require franchisees to strictly follow the franchisor's procedures for making or delivering a product or service. That consistency is why McDonald's fries or Wendy's Frosty™ shakes taste the same wherever you buy them. But what happens when franchisees don't want to follow the franchisor's requirements?

For example, increased competition from hamburger restaurants, such as Five Guys and Smashburger, prompted The Wendy's Company, which is the franchisor, to launch a store remodeling program called Image Activation. The program renovates dated-looking restaurants, while also upgrading their point-of-sale (POS) system to allow mobile payments and facilitate digital marketing campaigns. The overall goal of the program is to improve the customer experience and increase same store sales, something that Wendy's and its franchisees would both like to see. Wendy's CEO and President, Emil Brolick, says, "We are working to enhance the entire customer experience, including the restaurant design, inside environment, elevated food preparation standards and higher customer service standards."

One of Wendy's largest and oldest franchisors, however, didn't see it that way. DavCo, which owns and operates 152 restaurants in Maryland, Virginia, and Washington, D.C., refused to implement the Image Activation program. So in 2015 the Wendy's Company sued DavCo for breach of contract. DavCo immediately countersued, claiming that the design plans were too expensive and that it would not earn a sufficient return on investment from the remodeling costs. Indeed, DavCo estimated it would cost $55 million to remodel 90 of its oldest stores, and another $20 million to remodel the remaining 62 locations, which were less dated in appearance.

DavCo asserts that The Wendy's Company knows that the remodeling costs are a bad investment for its franchisee. Since the Image Activation program was launched in 2011, DavCo says that the company rolled out nine different designs trying to find a renovation plan franchisees could afford. Ironically, while The Wendy's Company was asking franchisees to pay for restaurant renovations, it was aggressively cutting its own expenses. Two years ago, Wendy's owned and operated nearly 1,200 of its 6,557 stores. In early 2015, it announced plans to sell 500 stores (to prospective franchisees) and said that it wants to own only 5% of its stores by mid-2016.

In theory, franchise agreements dictate nearly every way in which franchisors and franchisees work together. But, they can't anticipate everything. When conflicts occur, successful franchisors and franchisees strive for mutually beneficial solutions.[21] For Wendy's and DavCo, bringing in lawyers as hired guns to solve this dispute is a sure sign that the Wendy's franchise agreement is, for the moment, broken.

Ken Wolter/Shutterstock.com

and any restrictions on those rights. It also covers how long the agreement will last and under what terms (and at what cost) it can be renewed.

- **Fees and Other Payments:** The fees the franchisee must pay for the right to use the franchisor's products and methods, and when these payments are due.

- **Training and Support:** The types of training and support the franchisor will provide to the franchisee.

- **Specific Operational Requirements:** The methods and standards established by the franchisor that the franchisee is required to follow.

- **Conflict Resolution:** How the franchisor and franchisee will handle disputes.

- **Assigned Territory:** The geographic area in which the franchisee will operate and whether the franchisee has exclusive rights in that area.

It's vital for anyone thinking about entering into a franchise agreement to know all the facts before signing on the dotted line. Fortunately, the Federal Trade Commission (FTC) requires franchisors to provide potential franchisees with a document known as a **Franchise Disclosure Document (FDD)**. This long, complex document (covering 23 separate major topics and sometimes running well over 100 pages) can be an invaluable source of information about virtually every aspect of the franchise arrangement. For example, the FDD must provide contact information for at least 100 current franchisees. (If the franchisor has fewer than 100 current franchisees, it must list all of them.) This gives a potential franchisee the ability to contact other franchisees and ask them about their experiences with the franchisor. As an added bonus, the FTC requires the FDD to be written in "plain English" rather than in the complex legal jargon that often characterizes such documents. This rule means you actually have a chance to understand what you're reading![22]

Under FTC rules, the franchisor must give the franchisee at least 14 calendar days to review the FDD before the franchise agreement can be signed. A careful study of the FDD can go a long way toward ensuring that the franchisee makes an informed decision. Even though the FDD is written in "plain English," it's a good idea to have a lawyer who is knowledgeable about franchise law review it. You'll have to pay for any legal advice, but entering into a bad franchise agreement can be a lot more expensive (and stressful) than a lawyer's fees.

> **Franchise Disclosure Document (FDD)** A detailed description of all aspects of a franchise that the franchisor must provide to the franchisee at least 14 calendar days before the franchise agreement is signed.

The BIG Picture

This chapter discusses the four major forms of business ownership. Each form of ownership has both advantages and limitations, so no single form of ownership is the best in all situations.

Sole proprietorships are appealing to entrepreneurs who want to start a business quickly, with few formalities or fees, and who want to be their own boss. But sole proprietorships aren't well suited for raising financing from external sources, so growth opportunities are limited. And sole proprietors have unlimited liability for their company's debts and obligations.

General partnerships allow two or more owners to pool financial resources and take advantage of complementary skills. But each owner must assume the risk of unlimited liability,

and disagreements among partners can complicate and delay important decisions.

Corporations are more complex and expensive to create than other forms of business. Another potentially serious drawback is the double taxation of earnings. But corporations have the greatest potential for raising financial capital and provide owners with the protection of limited liability.

The limited liability company (LLC) is a relatively new form of business ownership that offers many of the advantages of corporations without as many regulations. One major advantage of LLCs compared to corporations is that its earnings can be taxed as if the company is a partnership, thus avoiding double taxation. But the laws governing limited liability companies vary considerably among states, making it a challenge to operate an LLC in multiple states.

Careers in Franchising

Franchise Store Manager

Responsible for running day-to-day retail store operations. Required to open and close the store, manage schedules and productivity, provide world-class customer service, monitor cost control, payroll, and expenses, provide weekly and monthly reports to the franchise owner, recruit, train, and coach employees, and develop and implement store marketing program. Ultimately accountable for profit/loss, continuous improvement, service delivery levels, personnel management, and business development. The ideal candidate has a college degree, a dynamic personality, two years retail store operations experience, strong management skills, excellent computer knowledge, and is a good listener who can motivate a team and run good meetings. For more information on this career and other possible careers in franchising, check out Career Transitions.

STUDY TOOLS 6

LOCATED AT BACK OF THE TEXTBOOK

☐ Rip Out Chapter Review Card

LOCATED AT WWW.CENGAGE.COM/LOGIN

☐ Review key term flashcards and create your own using StudyBits

☐ Create and complete practice quizzes based off of your notes and StudyBits

☐ Complete Online activities such as Matching, Fill-in-the-Blank, and Drag and Drop exercises

☐ View chapter highlight box content, including CEO Profiles, What Would You Do Cases, and chapter videos

☐ Track your knowledge and understanding of key concepts in business using 4LTR Online

7 | Small Business and Entrepreneurship:
Economic Rocket Fuel

LEARNING OBJECTIVES

After studying this chapter, you will be able to:

7-1 Explain the key reasons to launch a small business

7-2 Describe the typical entrepreneurial mindset and characteristics

7-3 Discuss funding options for small business

7-4 Analyze the opportunities and threats that small businesses face

7-5 Discuss ways to become a new business owner and tools to facilitate success

7-6 Explain the size, scope, and economic contributions of small business

Remember to visit
PAGE 125
for additional
STUDY TOOLS

7-1 LAUNCHING A NEW VENTURE: WHAT'S IN IT FOR ME?

Over time, the entrepreneurship rate has played a powerful, positive role in the U.S. economy. In 2013, the new business creation rate dipped slightly for the second year in a row, hitting a level more typically seen before the Great Recession. As the economy continued to gain momentum, unemployed workers were able to find jobs rather than turn to entrepreneurship.[1] The drop in entrepreneurship has been especially sharp among Generation Y (born between early 1980s and early 2000s), which is struggling with heavy student debt and a challenging job market. Since the prime age for entrepreneurship is late 30s to early 40s, a burst of entrepreneurial activity may lie ahead as the huge Generation Y reaches that age range.[2]

Starting a new business can be tough—very tough. Yet, for the right person, the advantages of business ownership far outweigh the risk and hard work. Although people start their own ventures for a variety of reasons, most are seeking some combination of greater financial success, independence, flexibility, and challenge. Others are simply seeking survival.

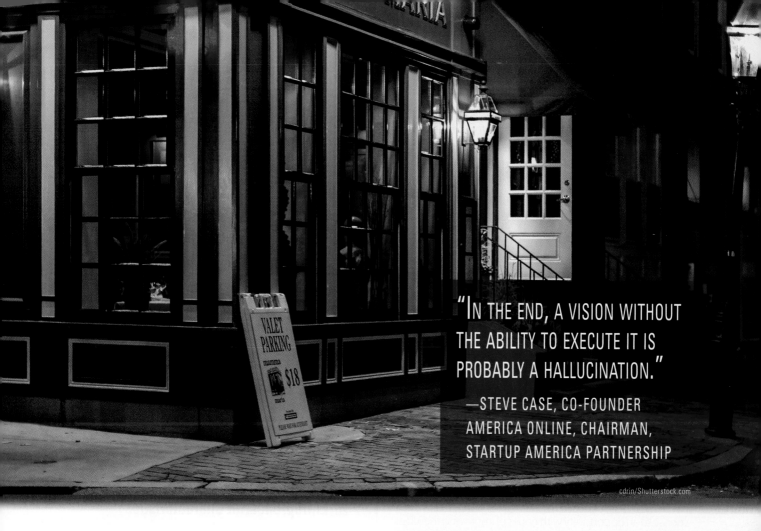

"IN THE END, A VISION WITHOUT THE ABILITY TO EXECUTE IT IS PROBABLY A HALLUCINATION."

—STEVE CASE, CO-FOUNDER AMERICA ONLINE, CHAIRMAN, STARTUP AMERICA PARTNERSHIP

7-1a Greater Financial Success

Although you can make a pretty good living working for someone else, your chances of getting really rich may be higher if you start your own business. The *Forbes* magazine annual list of the 400 richest Americans is dominated by **entrepreneurs**, such as Bill Gates and Paul Allen (founders of Microsoft), Phil Knight (founder of Nike), Michael Dell (founder of Dell Inc.), and Sergey Brin and Larry Page (founders of Google). And many people feel that their chances of even moderate financial success are higher if they're working for themselves rather than someone else. The opportunity to make more money is a primary motivator for many entrepreneurs, although other factors clearly play a role as well.[3]

7-1b Independence

Being your own boss is a huge benefit of starting your own business. You answer to no one other than yourself and any investors whom you invite to participate in your business. Bottom line: you are the only one who is ultimately responsible for your success or failure. This setup is especially compelling for people who have trouble being subordinates because of their personalities (and we probably all know

"OBVIOUSLY EVERYONE WANTS TO BE SUCCESSFUL, BUT I WANT TO BE LOOKED BACK ON AS BEING VERY INNOVATIVE, VERY TRUSTED AND ETHICAL AND ULTIMATELY MAKING A BIG DIFFERENCE IN THE WORLD."

—SERGEY BRIN, CO-FOUNDER, GOOGLE

someone who fits that description!). But while independence is nice, it's important to keep in mind that every business depends on meeting the needs of its customers, who can be even more demanding than the toughest boss.

7-1c Flexibility

The ability to set your own hours and control your own schedule is a

> **entrepreneurs** People who risk their time, money, and other resources to start and manage a business.

hugely appealing benefit for many business owners, especially parents seeking more time with their kids or retirees looking for extra income. Given current technological tools—from email to eBay—it's easy for small business owners to manage their firms on the go or after hours. Of course, there's often a correlation between hours worked and dollars earned. (It's rare to work less and earn more.) But when more money isn't the primary goal, the need for flexibility can be enough to motivate many entrepreneurs to launch their own enterprise.

7-1d Challenge

Running your own business provides a level of challenge unmatched by many other endeavors. Most business owners—especially new business owners—never find themselves bored! Starting a business also offers endless opportunities for learning that can provide more profound satisfaction for many people than grinding out the hours as an employee.

7-1e Survival

Although most entrepreneurs launch their business in response to an opportunity with hopes of improving their lives, some entrepreneurs—called "necessity entrepreneurs"—launch their business because they believe it is their *only* economic option. Necessity entrepreneurs range from middle-aged workers laid off from corporate jobs, to new immigrants with limited English and heavy accents, to those who experience discrimination in the standard workplace. For each of these types of people, small business ownership can be the right choice in the face of few other alternatives.

7-2 THE ENTREPRENEUR: A DISTINCTIVE PROFILE

Successful entrepreneurs tend to stand out from the crowd in terms of both their mindset and their personal characteristics. As you read this section, consider whether you fit the entrepreneurial profile.

7-2a The Entrepreneurial Mindset: A Matter of Attitude

Almost every entrepreneur starts as a small business-person—either launching a firm or buying a firm—but not every

small businessperson starts as an entrepreneur. The difference is a matter of attitude. From day one, a true entrepreneur—such as Sam Walton of Walmart, Steve Jobs of Apple, or Jeff Bezos of Amazon—aims to change the world through blockbuster goods or services. That isn't the case for all small business owners. Most people who launch new firms expect to better themselves, but they don't expect huge, transformative growth. In fact, nearly 70% of small business owners say they don't want to grow any larger.[4]

However, classic entrepreneurs who deliver on the promise of their best ideas can dramatically change the economic and social landscape worldwide. Examples of business owners who thought and delivered big include Henry Ford, founder of the Ford Motor Company and originator of assembly line production; Walt Disney, founder of The Walt Disney Company and creator of Mickey Mouse; Mary Kay Ash, founder of a cosmetics powerhouse; Martha Stewart, lifestyle innovator for the masses; Stephenie Meyer, creator of the *Twilight* franchise; and Mark Zuckerberg, founder of Facebook.

> "WHATEVER YOU'RE THINKING, THINK BIGGER."
> —TONY HSIEH, FOUNDER, ZAPPOS.COM

7-2b Entrepreneurial Characteristics

While experts sometimes disagree about the specific characteristics of successful entrepreneurs, virtually all include vision, self-reliance, energy, confidence, tolerance of uncertainty, and tolerance of failure. (See Exhibit 7.1.) Most successful entrepreneurs have all of these qualities and more, but they come in a huge variety of combinations that highlight the complexity of personality: there is no one successful entrepreneurial profile.

VISION Most entrepreneurs are wildly excited about their own new ideas, which many seem to draw from a bottomless well. Entrepreneurs find new solutions to old problems, and they develop new products that we didn't even know we needed until we had them. And entrepreneurs stay excited about their ideas, even when friends and relatives threaten to call the loony bin. For instance, Fred Smith, founder of the FedEx empire, traces the concept for his business to a term paper he wrote at Yale, which supposedly received a C from a skeptical professor. But that didn't stop him from creating a business logistics system that transformed the industry, and along with UPS, enabled e-commerce to flourish.

SELF-RELIANCE As an entrepreneur, the buck stops with you. New business owners typically need to do everything themselves, from getting permits, to motivating

Eccentric Entrepreneurs

Do quirky people become entrepreneurs, or does successful entrepreneurship breed quirkiness? Hard to know which comes first, but it's not hard to find quirky entrepreneurs. Some highlights:

- Mark Zuckerberg, founder of Facebook, personally butchers the animals he eats.

- Dustin Moscovitz, Zuckerberg's college roommate at Harvard and Facebook's third employee, still rides his bicycle to work despite being the world's youngest billionaire at age 29.

- Marc Andreessen, founder of Netscape, blogs in his underwear.

- David Karp, CEO of Tumblr, prides himself on ignoring email.

- Paul Graham, founder of Y Combinator, wrote an essay titled "Why Nerds Are Unpopular."

- John Harvey Kellogg (pictured), founder of the cereal empire, began his career as a medical doctor, and was once the chief physician at the Western Health Reform Institute of Battle Creek, where he argued that sex and masturbation cause cancer, epilepsy, and insanity, and that people should have yogurt enemas on a daily basis. Perhaps we should all be thankful that his corn flakes went mainstream, rather than his other ideas about health.

So if you're a quirky individual, you may want to consider nurturing your quirks, not hiding them. Who knows? Even if you're not the world's next billionaire, your quirks may give you a common interest with him or her, which could ultimately land you a great job![5]

AP Images

---

employees, to keeping the books—all in addition to producing the product or service that made them start the business in the first place. Self-reliance seems to come with an **internal locus of control**, or a deep-seated sense that the individual is personally responsible for what happens in his or her life. When things go well, people with an internal locus of control feel that their efforts have been validated, and when things go poorly, those same people feel that they need to do better next time. This sense of responsibility encourages positive action. In contrast, people with an **external locus of control** rely less on their own efforts, feeling buffeted by forces such as random luck and the actions of others, which they believe will ultimately control their fate.

ENERGY Entrepreneurs simply can't succeed without an enormous amount of energy. Six or seven 12-hour workdays are not atypical in the start-up phase of running a business. In fact, 61% of small business owners report working six or more days per week, compared to only 22% of workers in the general population. And

Exhibit 7.1
Entrepreneurial Characteristics

Vision · Self-Reliance · Energy · Confidence · Tolerance of Uncertainty · Tolerance of Failure

© Cengage Learning®

Arek Malang/Shutterstock.com

internal locus of control A deep-seated sense that the individual is personally responsible for what happens in his or her life.

external locus of control A deep-seated sense that forces other than the individual are responsible for what happens in his or her life.

for small business owners, even a day off isn't *really* off. Only 27% of small business owners define a day off as not working at all, while 57% of small business owners say they always or most of the time work on holidays. But Discover Financial Services also learned that many small business owners seem to find the grind worthwhile: 47% of small business owners said that if they won $10 million in the lottery, they would still work in their current job. Only 9% would stop working, and 8% would combine work, volunteering, and other areas of interest.[6]

CONFIDENCE Successful entrepreneurs typically have confidence in their own ability to achieve, and their confidence encourages them to act boldly. But too much confidence has a downside. Entrepreneurs must take care not to confuse likelihood with reality. In fact, many could benefit

> "I SUCK AT 99 PERCENT OF STUFF, BUT I GO ALL OUT ON THAT 1 PERCENT I'M GOOD AT."
>
> —GARY VAYNERCHUK, ENTREPRENEUR

from the old adage "Hope for the best and plan for the worst." A study for the Small Business Administration Office of Advocacy confirmed that entrepreneurs are typically overconfident regarding their own abilities. As a result they're sometimes willing to plunge into a new business, but they don't always have the skills to succeed.[7]

TOLERANCE OF UNCERTAINTY More often than others, entrepreneurs see the world in shades of gray, rather than simply black and white. They tend to embrace uncertainty in the business environment, turning it to their advantage rather than shying away. Uncertainty also relates to risk, and successful entrepreneurs tend to more willingly accept risk—financial risk, for instance, such as mortgaging their home for the business, and professional risk, such as staking their reputation on the success of an unproven product.

How to Make a Million Dollars

Clearly, if there were a proven way to make a million dollars, everyone would do it. Although there isn't a sure fire formula, there are certain characteristics that millionaire entrepreneurs have in common, which you can develop, too:

- **Cultivate Urgency:** Don't wait for "someday," do it now! Google, for instance, is hiring more teenagers than college graduates. Opportunities can evaporate in the mist if you wait for the perfect moment to jump on them.

- **Elevate Your Influence:** An exceptional network of wise and educated mentors can make all the difference, especially to a young entrepreneur with less experience. Since your time is a finite resource, be sure to spend it with the right people.

- **Maximize Your Strengths:** It never hurts to shore up your weakness or to delegate your

weak areas to someone else. But you'll never make a million by focusing on things you aren't good at. Figure out the one area where you can be exceptional, and master that area.

- **Never Trade Time for Money:** You'll only get rich by making your money work for you on its own. The power of scaling, leverage, and the Internet offer endless possibilities and upside, without forcing you to trade time for money.

- **Don't Worry What Others Think of You:** Forget needing to be liked—it just doesn't matter if you want to be extraordinary. You must trust your vision and stay fearless even when the rest of the world is doubting. Young millionaires are mentally tough.

- **Produce First, Consume Second:** For example, sell rather than buy, lend rather than borrow. According to millionaire M.J. Demarco, "Most people have it backward: consumption and no production. Producers get rich. Consumers get poor. Switch teams and reorient as a producer first, a consumer second. Make wealth attracted to you!"

While none of these characteristics will make you a million bucks, the mindset that they represent may set you well on your way. Good luck![8]

Tyler Boyes/Shutterstock.com

TOLERANCE OF FAILURE Even when they fail, entrepreneurs seldom label themselves losers. They tend to view failure as a chance to learn, rather than as a sign that they just can't do it (whatever "it" may be for them at any given moment). Interestingly, Isaac Fleischmann, director of the U.S. Patent Office for 36 years, pointed out that "During times of economic decline when unemployment increases, so does the number of patents. Dark days often force us to become more ingenious, to monitor and modify the ways we reached failure and reshape them into a new pattern of success." Failure can actually be an effective springboard for achievement.[9]

A surprising number of twentieth-century entrepreneurial stars experienced significant failure in their careers yet bounced back to create wildly successful ventures. Early in his career, for instance, Walt Disney was fired from an ad agency (in hindsight, a rather foolish ad agency) for a "singular lack of drawing ability." Ray Kroc, the man who made McDonald's into a fast-food empire, couldn't make a go of real estate, so he sold milkshake machines for much of his life. He was 52 years old, and in failing health, when he discovered the McDonald brothers' hamburger stand and transformed it into a fast-food empire. Steve Jobs, founder of Apple computer, found himself unceremoniously dumped by his board of directors less than ten years after introducing the world's first personal computer. After another decade, he returned in triumph, restoring Apple's polish with blockbuster new products such as the iPod

and the iPhone. And JK Rowling, creator of the $15 billion Harry Potter empire, had her initial book rejected by 12 shortsighted publishers. So next time you fail, keep your eyes open for opportunity—your failure may be the first step of the next big thing.[10]

7-3 FINDING THE MONEY: FUNDING OPTIONS FOR SMALL BUSINESSES

For many entrepreneurs, finding the money to fund their business is the top challenge of their start-up year. The vast majority of new firms are funded with the personal resources of their founder. In fact, about 95% of entrepreneurs raise start-up funds from personal accounts, family, and friends. Other key funding sources include bank loans, angel investors, and venture capital firms.[11]

7-3a Personal Resources

While the idea of using just your own money to open a business sounds great, and more than three-quarters of small business owners spend their own savings as a source of start-up funding,[12] the financial requirements of most new firms typically force entrepreneurs to also tap personal resources such as family, friends, and credit cards. According to *Consumer Reports*, 68% of total start-up financing comes

---

What Time of Day Are You Most Creative?

Probably not when you think you are…Research suggests that most people are best able to solve insight problems, the kind of problems where the answer comes in a single "aha" moment or flash of insight, or creativity, during the time of day when they are typically least alert. In other words, morning people tend to be most creative in the evening and vice versa.

Check out this insight problem. If you don't get the answer right away, try again during your least alert time of day, before you look at the answer at the bottom of the box.

Insight problem: A dealer in antique coins got an offer to buy a beautiful bronze coin. The coin had an emperor's head on one side and the date 544 BC stamped on the other. The dealer examined the coin, but instead of buying it, he called the police to report the forgery. What about the coin alerted him?

Clearly, entrepreneurship requires creativity. Knowing your most creative time of day may help you buff up your own creative prowess before you take the leap into small business ownership.

(Answer: Ancient coins were never dated BC, because no one knew with any certainty when Christ was coming.)[13]

from personal resources.[14] If you do borrow from family or friends, virtually every small business expert recommends that you keep the relationship as professional as possible. If the business fails, a professional agreement can preserve personal ties. And if the business succeeds, you'll need top-quality documentation of financing from family and friends to get larger-scale backing from outside sources.

Personal credit cards can be an especially handy—though highly risky—financing resource. In fact, a recent survey found that nearly half of all start-ups are funded with plastic. (It's no wonder, given that those solicitations just keep on coming.) Credit cards do provide fast, flexible money, but watch out—if you don't pay back your card company fast, you'll find yourself socked with financing fees that can take years to pay off.[15]

7-3b Loans

Getting commercial loans for a new venture can be tough. Banks and other lenders are understandably hesitant to fund a business that doesn't have a track record. And when they do, they require a lot of paperwork and often a fairly long waiting period. Given these hurdles, only 20% of new business owners launch with commercial loans. Unfortunately, small business lending fell 78% in the five years following the Great Recession.[16] And virtually no conventional lending source—private or government—will lend 100% of the start-up dollars for a new business. Most require that the entrepreneur provide a minimum of 25% to 30% of total start-up costs from personal resources.[17]

Another source for loans may be the U.S. Small Business Administration (SBA). The SBA doesn't give free money to start-up businesses—neither grants nor interest-free loans—but it does partially guarantee loans from local commercial lenders. This reduces risk for the lenders, who are, in turn, more likely to lend money to a new business owner. The SBA also has a microloan program that lends small amounts of money—$13,000 on average—to start-up businesses through community nonprofit organizations.[18]

Peer-to-peer lending offers yet another potential funding source for new business start-ups. Websites such as Prosper.com and LendingClub.com bring together borrowers and investors so that both can benefit financially. Many entrepreneurs have found this is an easier way to get money, at more favorable terms, than through more-established sources.

Finding funding is top-of-mind for many entrepreneurs.

7-3c Crowdfunding

Crowdfunding is the process of funding ventures by raising money from a large number of investors via the Internet. Crowdfunding began to appear in the mid-2000s, and quickly gained traction, becoming a $5+ billion funding source by 2013. Many crowdfunding sites are used to fund nonprofits. The largest crowdfunding sites in terms of traffic are gofundme.com, kickstarter.com, and indiegogo.com. Two examples of big crowdfunding successes are (1) the game *Star Citizen*, which apparently raised $70 million, and (2) the feature film *Veronica Mars*, which raised $4.7 million.

7-3d Angel Investors

Angel investors aren't as saintly—or as flighty—as they sound. They are wealthy individuals who invest in promising start-up companies for one basic reason: to make money for themselves. According to Jeffrey Sohl, director of the Center for Venture Research, angels look for companies that seem likely to grow at 30% to 40% per year and will then either be bought or go public. He estimates that 10% to 15% of private companies fit that description, but points out that finding those firms isn't easy. It doesn't help, he says, that "80% of entrepreneurs think they're in that 10% to 15%." In the first half of 2014, the number of ventures funded by angels increased +5.9% versus over 2013,[19] and Sohl expected that growth rate to continue throughout the year. And angels continued to focus on early-stage start-ups, an encouraging sign for long-term economic health.[20]

7-3e Venture Capital

Venture capital firms fund high-potential new companies in exchange for a share of ownership, which can sometimes be as high as 60%. These deals tend to be quite visible, but keep in mind that only a tiny fraction of new businesses receive any venture capital money. The advice and guidance

angel investors Individuals who invest in start-up companies with high growth potential in exchange for a share of ownership.

venture capital firms Companies that invest in start-up businesses with high growth potential in exchange for a share of ownership.

that come with the dollars can also be quite significant. David Barger, chief executive officer of jetBlue Airways, remembers that he and jetBlue's founder, David Neeleman, originally planned to call the airline Taxi and to fly bright yellow planes. But an influential venture capitalist changed their minds. He called them into his office and said, "If you call this airline Taxi, we're not going to invest." The name changed, and the venture capitalist stayed.[21]

firms can exploit narrow but profitable **market niches**, offer personal customer service, and maintain lower overhead costs. And due to advances in technology, small firms can compete more effectively than ever in both global and domestic markets.

MARKET NICHES Many small firms are uniquely positioned to exploit small, but profitable, market niches. These sparsely occupied spaces in the market tend to have fewer competitors because they simply aren't big enough—or high-profile enough—for large firms. They nonetheless offer more than enough potential for small, specialized companies. For example, Kazoo & Company, a relatively small toy store, competes effectively with Walmart, Target, and Kmart by stocking different—and complementary—products, deliberately zigging when the big players zag.[22]

PERSONAL CUSTOMER SERVICE With a smaller customer base, small firms can develop much more personal relationships with individual customers. Shel Weinstein, for instance, former owner of a Los Angeles corner pharmacy, knew his

7-4 OPPORTUNITIES AND THREATS FOR SMALL BUSINESS: A TWO-SIDED COIN

Most small businesses enjoy a number of advantages as they compete for customers. But they also must defuse a range of daunting potential threats in order to succeed over the long term.

7-4a Small Business Opportunities

Small businesses enjoy a real competitive edge across a range of different areas. Because of their size, many small

> **market niche** A small segment of a market with fewer competitors than the market as a whole. Market niches tend to be quite attractive to small firms.

Nutty Market Niches

Small businesses can do especially well in market niches, even niches that initially seem somewhat wacky. Here are a handful of wacky businesses that have really worked:

- **Neuticles:** Did you worry about your dog's self-esteem after he got neutered? Entrepreneur Greg Miller did, which was why he invented Neuticles, artificial testicular implants for dogs. Despite the giggle factor, Neuticles have become a huge commercial success, recently featured in *BusinessWeek* magazine, where he points out that at first, many people thought the idea was nuts.

- **The Smashing Place:** Ever been so mad you just wanted to smash something? If you live in Tokyo, you're in luck! You can just visit The Smashing Place, buy a plate or a cup of your choice, and smash it against a concrete wall—the staff will even cheer you on, and recycle the scraps afterwards.

- **Disposable Underwear:** Not to be confused with edible underwear, disposable underwear is a lightweight, single-use product, targeted at travelers who are seeking to lighten their load by lugging around as little as possible. Using disposable underwear means that they can leave their dirty underwear behind as they travel. According to Danita Harris, owner of disposable underwear firm, DNA products, the product has "proven appeal to women travelers overseas."[23]

So the next time inspiration strikes, you may want to write down your idea and get to work, no matter how wacky it may initially seem.

Maran Garai/Shutterstock.com

customers so well that they would call him at home in the middle of the night for help with medical emergencies. The personal touch can be especially beneficial in some foreign markets, where clients prize the chance to deal directly with top management.

LOWER OVERHEAD COSTS With entrepreneurs wearing so many hats, from CEO to customer service rep, many small firms have lower overhead costs. They can hire fewer managers and fewer specialized employees. Perhaps more importantly, smaller firms—due to a lack of resources—tend to work around costs with tactics such as establishing headquarters in the owner's garage or offering employees flexible schedules instead of costly health-care benefits.

TECHNOLOGY The Internet has played a powerful role in opening new opportunities for small businesses. Using a wealth of online tools, from eBay to eMachineshop, companies-of-one can create, sell, publish, and even manufacture goods and services more easily than ever before. The Internet has also created international opportunities, transforming small businesses into global marketers. The London-based Anything Left-Handed retail store, for instance, evolved into an award-winning global wholesaler of left-handed items within a year of launching its website. Founder Keith Milsom comments that "our website has allowed us to communicate with potential customers and market our business worldwide at very little cost, making international development possible."[24]

7-4b Small Business Threats

While small businesses do enjoy some advantages, they also face intimidating obstacles, from a high risk of failure to too much regulation.

HIGH RISK OF FAILURE Starting a new business involves risk—a lot of risk—but the odds improve significantly if you make it past the first five years. Check out the ten-year survival rate in Exhibit 7.2. Notice that it declines much more slowly in Years 7–10. Not surprisingly, new research also shows that the five-year survival rate depends fairly heavily on the industry, ranging from 51.3% at the high end for manufacturing to 36.4% at the low end for construction, as illustrated in Exhibit 7.3. So clearly, it pays to choose your industry carefully when you launch a new business.

Even though these numbers may look daunting, it's important to remember that owners shut down their businesses for many reasons other than the failure of the firm itself. The possibilities include poor health, divorce, better opportunities elsewhere, and interestingly, an unwillingness

EXHIBIT 7.2	NEW BUSINESS SURVIVAL RATES	
Year in Business	**Survival Rate**	**Change vs. Prior Year (percentage points)**
Year 1	80%	−20
Year 2	69%	−12
Year 3	61%	−8
Year 4	55%	−6
Year 5	50%	−5
Year 6	40%	−10
Year 7	42%	−2
Year 8	39%	−3
Year 9	36%	−3
Year 10	34%	−2

Source: Start-Up Failure Rates: The Definitive Numbers by Scott Shane, December 17, 2012, Small Business Trends website, http://smallbiztrends.com/2012/12/start-up-failure-rates-the-definitive-numbers.html, accessed March 15, 2013.

EXHIBIT 7.3	NEW BUSINESS 5-YEAR SURVIVAL RATES BY INDUSTRY
Mining	51.3%
Manufacturing	48.4%
Services	47.4%
Wholesaling and Agriculture	47.4%
Retailing	41.4%
Finance, Insurance, and Real Estate	39.6%
Transportation, Communications, and Utilities	39.4%
Construction	36.4%

Source: Small Business Failure rates by Industry: The real numbers by Scott Shane, September 24, 2012, Small Business Trends website, http://smallbiztrends.com/2012/09/failure-rates-by-sector-the-real-numbers.html, accessed March 15, 2013.

to make the enormous time commitment of running a business. Small business expert David Birch jokingly calls this last reason—which is remarkably common—the "I had no idea!" syndrome. It highlights the importance of anticipating what you're in for *before* you open your doors.[25]

LACK OF KNOWLEDGE AND EXPERIENCE People typically launch businesses because they either have expertise in a particular area—like designing websites or cooking Vietnamese food—or because they have a breakthrough idea—like a new way to develop computer chips or run an airline. But in-depth knowledge in a specific area doesn't necessarily mean expertise in running a business. Successful business owners must know everything from finance to human resources to marketing.

TOO LITTLE MONEY The media are filled with stories of business owners who made it on a shoestring, but lack of start-up money is a major issue for most new firms. Ongoing profits don't usually begin for a while, which means that entrepreneurs must plan on some lean months—or even years—as the business develops momentum. That means a real need to manage money wisely and to resist the temptation to invest in fixed assets, such as fancy offices and advanced electronics, before sufficient regular income warrants it. It also requires the nerve to stay the course despite initial losses.[26]

BIGGER REGULATORY BURDEN Complying with federal regulations can be challenging for any business, but it can be downright overwhelming for small firms. But relief may be on the way: Congress continues to examine ways to reduce the growing regulatory burden on small businesses—an urgent need in the face of the struggling economy.[27]

HIGHER HEALTH INSURANCE COSTS Administrative costs for small health plans are much higher than for large businesses, making it even tougher for small firms to offer coverage to their employees. Given skyrocketing healthcare costs in general, the best employees are likely to demand a great insurance plan, putting small business at a real disadvantage in terms of building a competitive workforce. But this may change as healthcare reform rolls out over the next couple of years; all but the very smallest businesses will be required to offer "affordable" health insurance to their full-time employees. Navigating the complexities of the legislation will be a significant challenge for many small business owners. And assuming the early implementation bugs are resolved, the legislation may also provide an opportunity to offer workers the top quality health insurance that the best employees seek, at competitive rates.[28]

7-5 LAUNCH OPTIONS: REVIEWING THE PROS AND CONS

When you imagine starting a new business, the first thought that comes to mind would probably be the process of developing your own big idea from an abstract concept to a thriving enterprise. But that's not the only option. In fact, it may make more sense to purchase an established business, or even buy a franchise such as a Pizza Hut or Subway restaurant. Each choice, of course, involves pros and cons. The trick is finding the best fit for you: the combination that offers you the least harmful downsides and the most meaningful upsides. Broadly speaking, it's less risky to buy an established business or franchise, but it can be more satisfying to start from scratch. Exhibit 7.4 offers a more detailed overview of the pros and cons.

7-5a Making It Happen: Tools for Business Success

Whatever way you choose to become a small business owner, several strategies can help you succeed over the long term: gain experience in your field, learn from others, educate yourself, access **Small Business Administration (SBA)** resources, and develop a business plan.

GAIN EXPERIENCE Getting roughly three years of experience working for someone else in the field that interests you is a good rule of thumb. That way, you can learn what does and doesn't fly in your industry with relatively low personal risk (and you'd be making any mistakes on someone else's dime). You can also start developing a vibrant, relevant network before you need to ask for favors. But if you stay much longer than three years, you may get too comfortable to take the plunge and launch your own venture.

LEARN FROM OTHERS You should actively seek opportunities to learn from people who've succeeded in your field. If you don't know anyone personally, use your network to get introductions. And don't forget industry associations, local events, and other opportunities to build relationships. Also, remember that people who failed in your field may be able to give you valuable insights (why make the same mistakes they did?). As a bonus, they may be more willing to share their ideas and their gaffes if they're no longer struggling to develop a business of their own.

EDUCATE YOURSELF The opportunities for entrepreneurial learning have exploded in the past decade. Many colleges and universities now offer full-blown entrepreneurship programs that help students both develop their plans and secure their initial funding. But education shouldn't stop there. Seek out relevant press articles, workshops, websites, and blogs so that your ongoing education will continue to boost your career.

Small Business Administration (SBA) An agency of the federal government designed to maintain and strengthen the nation's economy by aiding, counseling, assisting, and protecting the interests of small businesses.

EXHIBIT 7.4 PROS AND CONS OF STARTING A BUSINESS FROM SCRATCH VERSUS BUYING AN ESTABLISHED BUSINESS

Starting Your Business from Scratch

Key Pros	Key Cons
It's all *you*: Your concept, your decisions, your structure, and so on.	It's all *you*. That's a lot of pressure.
You don't have to deal with the prior owner's bad decisions.	It takes time, money, and sheer sweat equity to build a customer base.
	Without a track record, it's harder to get credit from both lenders and suppliers.
	From securing permits to hiring employees, the logistics of starting a business can be challenging.

Buying an Established Business

Key Pros	Key Cons
The concept, organizational structure, and operating practices are already in place.	Working with someone else's idea can be a lot less fun for some entrepreneurs.
Relationships with customers, suppliers, and other stakeholders are established.	You may inherit old mistakes that can range from poor employee relations to pending lawsuits.
Getting financing and credit is less challenging.	

Buying a Franchise

Key Pros	Key Cons
In most cases, you're buying your own piece of a well-known brand and proven way of doing business.	You have less opportunity for creativity since most agreements tie you to franchise requirements.
Typically, management expertise and consulting come with the franchise package.	If something goes wrong with the national brand (e.g., *E. coli* at a burger joint), your business will suffer, too.
Franchisers occasionally offer not just advice but also the financing that can make the purchase possible.	The initial purchase price can be steep, and that doesn't include the ongoing percent-of-sales royalty fee.
These advantages add up to a very low 5% first-year failure rate.	

Source: Five Reasons Why Franchises Flop, by Steve Strauss, February 28, 2005, *USA Today* Money website, http://www.usatoday.com/money/smallbusiness/columnist/strauss/2005-02-28-franchise_x.htm.

ACCESS SBA RESOURCES The SBA offers a number of resources beyond money (which we'll discuss in the next section). The SBA website, www.sba.gov, provides a wealth of information from industry-specific statistics, to general trends, to updates on small business regulations. The SBA also works hand in hand with individual states to fund local **Small Business Development Centers (SBDCs)**. SBDCs provide a range of free services for small businesses, from developing your concept, to consulting on your business plan, to helping with your loan applications. And the SBA supports **SCORE**, the **Service Corps of Retired Executives**, at www.score.org. They provide free, comprehensive counseling for small businesses from qualified volunteers.

DEVELOP A BUSINESS PLAN Can a business succeed without a plan? Of course. Many do just fine by simply seizing opportunity as it arises, and changing direction as

Small Business Development Centers (SBDCs) Local offices—affiliated with the Small Business Administration—that provide comprehensive management assistance to current and prospective small business owners.

SCORE (Service Corps of Retired Executives) An organization—affiliated with the Small Business Administration—that provides free, comprehensive business counseling for small business owners from qualified volunteers.

MORE THAN 30% OF THE RICHEST PEOPLE IN THE WORLD DO NOT HAVE A COLLEGE DEGREE, BUT 57% OF THOSE WHO START A BUSINESS IN HIGH-INCOME COUNTRIES DO HAVE A COLLEGE DEGREE.

—GLOBAL ENTREPRENEURSHIP MONITOR AND *FORBES*

needed. Some achieve significant growth without a plan. But a **business plan** does provide an invaluable way to keep you and your team focused on success. And it's absolutely crucial for obtaining outside funding, which is why many entrepreneurs write a business plan after they've used personal funding sources (such as savings, credit cards, and money from family and friends) to get themselves up and running. Even then, the plan may be continually in flux if the industry is rapidly changing.

An effective business plan, which is usually 25 to 50 pages long, takes about six months to write. While the specifics may change by industry, the basic elements of any business plan answer these core questions:

- What service or product does your business provide, and what needs does it fill?

- Who are the potential customers for your product or service, and why will they purchase it from you?

- How will you reach your potential customers?

- Where will you get the financial resources to start your business?

- When can you expect to achieve profitability?

The final document should include all of the following information:

- Executive summary (two to three pages)

- Description of business (include both risks and opportunities)

- Marketing

- Competition (don't underestimate the challenge)

- Operating procedures

- Personnel

A business plan can help entrepreneurs stay focused.

Peshkova/Shutterstock.com

- Complete financial data and plan, including sources of start-up money (be realistic!)

- Appendix (be sure to include all your research on your industry)[29]

Check out the SBA business-planning site for more information on how to write your own business plan and for samples of actual business plans (www.sba .gov/smallbusinessplanner/index.html). Other excellent resources (among many) on the Internet include the sample business plan resource center (www.bplans.com/) and the business plan pages of AllBusiness.com (www .allbusiness.com/).

7-6 SMALL BUSINESS AND THE ECONOMY: AN OUTSIZED IMPACT

The most successful entrepreneurs create goods and services that change the way people live. Many build blockbuster corporations that power the stock market and dominate pop culture through ubiquitous promotion. But small businesses—despite their lower profile—also play a vital role in the U.S. economy. Here are a few statistics from the U.S. Small Business Administration:

- In 2009, 99.9% of the 27,500,000 businesses in the United States had fewer than 500 employees.

- More than three-quarters of those business owners—21,400,000 people, totaling about 7% of the population—ran their businesses without any employees.

- Yet, these small businesses generate 46% of U.S. private sector output.

- Over the past 18 years, small businesses created 64% of the net new jobs in the United States.

- In total, small business provides jobs for about 43% the nation's private workforce.[30]

The statistics, of course, depend on the definition of small business. For research purposes, the SBA defines small business as companies with up to 500 employees, including the self-employed. But the SBA also points out that the meaning of small business differs across industries. To officially count as "small," the number of employees can range from fewer than 100 to 1,500, and the average revenue can range from

> **business plan** A formal document that describes a business concept, outlines core business objectives, and details strategies and timelines for achieving those objectives.

Accidental Inventions

Every new business begins with a great idea, but not all great ideas begin with careful planning—a number of successful businesses have been built on inventions that happened by accident. But that doesn't mean that you shouldn't be prepared; first-century philosopher Seneca said, "Luck is what happens when preparation meets opportunity." A sampling of "accidental inventions":

- **Microwave Ovens:** When World War II scientist Percy Spencer was inspecting a magnetron tube at a Raytheon lab, he noticed that a candy bar in his pocket had melted, which sparked the idea of using microwaves for cooking. Today, more than 90% of households have microwave ovens.

- **Viagra:** The pills failed to achieve their original goal, but clinical trials did yield some startling secondary benefits, which gave rise to a brand new multibillion-dollar business for Pfizer.

- **Post-it Notes:** 3M scientist Spencer Silver developed the repositionable adhesive for Post-it Notes. But they didn't become a product until his co-worker, Art Fry, was looking for a sticky, reusable bookmark to replace the paper bookmarks that kept slipping out of his church hymnal. Fry proposed the product, which quickly became a worldwide hit for 3M.[31]

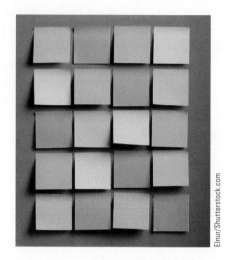

Elnur/Shutterstock.com

$0.75 million to $28.5 million, depending on the type of business. But regardless of the specific definition, the fact is clear: small business is a big player in the U.S. economy.

Beyond the sheer value of the goods and services they generate, small businesses make a powerful contribution to the U.S. economy in terms of creating new jobs, fueling innovation, and vitalizing inner cities.

- Creating New Jobs: Small businesses with employees start up at a rate of about 600,000 per year. Five years after they launch, about half of those businesses—and many of the jobs they create—remain viable. But while small businesses are quick to add new jobs, they're often the first to contract when times are tough; instability comes with the territory.[32]

- Fueling Innovation: Small businesses are much more likely to develop revolutionary new ideas. Small patenting firms produce about 16 times more patents per employee than their large-firm counterparts, and those patents are twice as likely to be found among the top 1% of highest-impact patents. Small firms tend to be effective innovators for a number of reasons. Perhaps most importantly, their very reason for being often ties to a brand new idea. In the early years, they need innovation in order to simply survive. And they often display a refreshing lack of bureaucracy that allows new thinking to take hold.[33]

- Vitalizing Inner Cities: New research shows that small businesses are the backbone of urban economies, finding opportunity in niches that may not be worthwhile for larger firms. Small business comprises more than 99% of inner-city business establishments. In addition to creating new jobs, these small businesses generate 80% of total employment in American inner cities, providing a springboard for economic development.[34]

7-6a Entrepreneurship Around the World

Research suggests that entrepreneurship has an economic impact in countries around the world. Societies need entrepreneurs to ensure that new ideas actualize and to ensure that people are able to self-employ when their

Nasirkhan/Shutterstock.com

economy does not provide for their basic needs. For the past 15 years, the Global Entrepreneurship Monitor (GEM) has measured the annual rate of new business start-ups across a range of countries across the globe. The fifteenth annual GEM study included 70 countries. According to GEM, the most effective way to evaluate entrepreneurship levels is by phase. A country's total early-phase entrepreneurship rate includes the percentage of adults who have been running their own business from three months to 3.5 years. The current entrepreneurship rate varies dramatically from country to country, ranging from a high of 39.9% in Nigeria and Zambia to a low of 3.4% in Italy, Russia, and Japan. (See Exhibit 7.5

> ## NEARLY HALF OF THE WORLD'S ENTREPRENEURS ARE BETWEEN THE AGES OF 25 AND 44.
> —GLOBAL ENTREPRENEURSHIP MONITOR

for the ten nations with the highest and lowest entrepreneurship rates.) The differences among countries seem to depend largely on several key factors: What is the national per capita income? What will the entrepreneur need to give up (i.e., the opportunity costs)? How high is the risk of failure? How strongly do the national culture and political environment support business start-ups?

PER CAPITA INCOME In lower-income countries, such as China and Chile, a high percentage of entrepreneurs start their own businesses because they simply have no other options. This contributes heavily to the startlingly high overall level of entrepreneurship. The rate of such "necessity entrepreneurship" declines in higher-income countries, such as the United States and Japan, where entrepreneurs are more likely to strike out on their own in response to an opportunity that they spot in the marketplace.

OPPORTUNITY COSTS Entrepreneurship rates are significantly lower in countries that provide a high level of employment protection (it's hard to get fired) and strong unemployment insurance (financial support if you do get fired). With these benefits in place, the sense of urgency regarding entrepreneurship tends to fall, in part because fear of failure is much lower. The European Union provides a number of clear examples.

CULTURAL/POLITICAL ENVIRONMENT Extensive, complex regulations can hinder entrepreneurship by raising daunting barriers. And a lack of cultural support only compounds the problem. These factors certainly contribute to the relatively low entrepreneurship rates in much of the European Union and Japan. Entrepreneurs in more supportive nations such as the United States and New Zealand get a boost from limited regulation and strong governmental support. A thriving "cowboy culture" helps, too—standout individuals who break free of old ways attract attention and admiration in many of the countries with higher entrepreneurship rates.[35]

EXHIBIT 7.5	EARLY PHASE ENTREPRENEURSHIP RATES 2013		
Top Ten Entrepreneurship Rates		**Bottom Ten Entrepreneurship Rates**	
Country	**Rate**	**Country**	**Rate**
Nigeria	39.9%	Italy	3.4%
Zambia	39.9%	Japan	3.7%
Ecuador	36.0%	France	4.6%
Malawi	28.1%	Algeria	4.9%
Ghana	25.8%	Belgium	4.9%
Indonesia	25.5%	Germany	5.0%
Uganda	25.2%	Suriname	5.1%
Chile	24.3%	Spain	5.2%
Colombia	23.7%	Finland	5.3%
Peru	23.4%	Greece	5.5%
Angola	22.2%		

Source: Global Entrepreneurship Monitor 2013 Global Report, by Jose Amoros and Niels Bosma, January 2014, Global Consortium website, http://www.16personalities.com/entp-parents, accessed January 2014.

The BIG Picture

Successful entrepreneurs need more than simply a great idea. Bringing that idea to market—and earning a profit in the process—requires deep knowledge of every area of business. Finding money, attracting customers, and absorbing risk are only some of the challenges. But for the right person, the payoff can be huge in terms of everything from financial success to scheduling flexibility. The key is finding something you love to do that offers value to others. While that doesn't guarantee success, building on a passion suggests that you'll at least enjoy the journey. Looking forward from the global economic crisis, entrepreneurship seems likely to become a way of life, either part-time or full-time, for a growing swath of the population. The ideal result would be a higher standard of living—and a higher quality of life—for business owners and their customers worldwide.

Careers in Entrepreneurship

Clothing Company Founder

Design unique items that appeal to young people via innovative styles, attention-grabbing slogans, and distinctive fabrics. Build relationships with business funders. Oversee suppliers to ensure timely order delivery and ethical manufacturing practices. Build solid base of retail accounts. Develop a creative social media marketing campaign to boost sales. Meet profitability goals every quarter. For more information on this career and other possible careers in entrepreneurship, check out Career Transitions.

STUDY TOOLS 7

LOCATED AT BACK OF THE TEXTBOOK

☐ Rip Out Chapter Review Card

LOCATED AT WWW.CENGAGE.COM/LOGIN

☐ Review key term flashcards and create your own using StudyBits

☐ Create and complete practice quizzes based off of your notes and StudyBits

☐ Complete Online activities such as Matching, Fill-in-the-Blank, and Drag and Drop exercises

☐ View chapter highlight box content, including CEO Profiles, What Would You Do Cases, and chapter videos

☐ Track your knowledge and understanding of key concepts in business using 4LTR Online

8 | Accounting: Decision Making by the Numbers

LEARNING OBJECTIVES

After studying this chapter, you will be able to:

8-1 Define accounting and describe how accounting information is used by a variety of stakeholders

8-2 Identify the purposes and goals of generally accepted accounting principles

8-3 Describe the key elements of the major financial statements

8-4 Describe several methods stakeholders can use to obtain useful insights from a company's financial statements

8-5 Explain how the budget process can help managers plan, motivate, and evaluate their organization's performance

8-6 Explain the role of managerial accounting and describe the various cost concepts identified by managerial accountants

Remember to visit **PAGE 144** for additional **STUDY TOOLS**

8-1 ACCOUNTING: WHO NEEDS IT—AND WHO DOES IT?

Accounting is a system for recognizing, organizing, analyzing, and reporting information about the financial transactions that affect an organization. The goal of this system is to provide its users with relevant, timely information that helps them make better economic decisions.

Who uses the information that accounting provides? It's a long list; after all, everyone wants to make good decisions! In fact, a variety of business stakeholders rely so heavily on accounting information that it's sometimes called the "language of business."

8-1a Accounting: Who Uses It?

accounting A system for recognizing, organizing, analyzing, and reporting information about the financial transactions that affect an organization.

Key users of accounting information include:

- Managers: Marketing managers, for instance, need information about sales in various regions and for various product lines. Financial managers need up-to-date facts about debt, cash, inventory, and capital.

- Stockholders: As owners of the company, most stockholders have a keen interest in its financial performance, especially as indicated by the firm's financial statements. Has management generated a strong-enough return on their investment?

- Employees: Strong financial performance would help employees make their case for nice pay raises and hefty bonuses. But if earnings drop—especially multiple times—layoffs might be in the

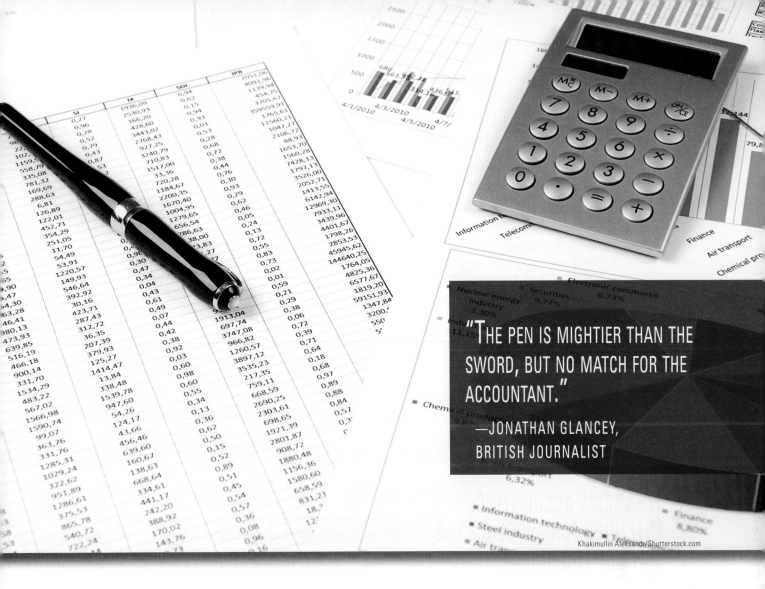

"THE PEN IS MIGHTIER THAN THE SWORD, BUT NO MATCH FOR THE ACCOUNTANT."

—JONATHAN GLANCEY, BRITISH JOURNALIST

offing, so many employees might decide to polish their résumés!

- Creditors: The late, great comedian Bob Hope once defined a bank as a place that would only lend you money if you could prove you didn't really need it. That's a bit of an exaggeration, but it is true that before granting a loan, responsible bankers and other lenders will want to assess a firm's creditworthiness by looking at its financial statements.

- Suppliers: Like bankers, companies that provide supplies want to know that the company can pay for the orders it places.

- Government agencies: Accurate accounting information is critical for meeting the reporting requirements of the Internal Revenue Service (IRS), the Securities and Exchange Commission (SEC), and other federal and state agencies.

A number of other groups—including the news media, competitors, and unions—might also have a real interest in a firm's accounting information—whether the firm wants them to have it or not! If you have any interest in managing, investing in, or working for a business, the ability to understand accounting information is extremely valuable.

8-1b Accounting: Who Does It?

Accountants work in a variety of positions to provide all of this information. Let's take a quick look at some of the roles accountants play:

- **Public accountants** provide services such as tax preparation, external auditing (a process we'll describe later in this chapter), or management consulting to clients on a fee basis.

- **Management accountants** work within a company and provide analysis, prepare reports and financial statements, and assist managers in their own organization. *Internal auditors* also work within their organizations to detect internal problems such as waste, mismanagement, embezzlement, and employee theft.

- **Government accountants** perform a variety of accounting functions for local, state, or federal government agencies. Some ensure that the government's own tax revenues and expenditures are recorded and reported in accordance with regulations and requirements. Others work for the IRS to audit tax returns or for other government agencies, such as the SEC or FDIC, to help ensure that our nation's banks and other financial institutions comply with the rules and regulations governing their behavior.

Many jobs performed by accountants require expertise in complex subject areas. For this reason, accountants who want to move up in their profession often seek certification in a particular field. But achieving such recognition isn't easy. For example, in order to be recognized as a *certified public accountant* in most states, a candidate must complete the equivalent of 150 semester hours (five years) of college education with a heavy emphasis in accounting and other business-related courses, must pass a rigorous two-day, four-part exam (very few candidates pass all four parts on their first try), and must complete at least one year of direct work experience in the field of accounting. Individuals seeking to become *certified management accountants* or *certified fraud examiners* must satisfy similarly challenging requirements.

8-2 FINANCIAL ACCOUNTING: INTENDED FOR THOSE ON THE OUTSIDE LOOKING IN

Financial accounting is the branch of accounting that addresses the needs of external stakeholders, including stockholders, creditors, and government regulators. These stakeholders are seldom interested in poring over detailed accounting information about the individual departments or divisions within a company. Instead, they're interested in the financial performance of the firm as a whole. They often want to know how a firm's financial condition has changed over a period of several years, or to compare its results to those of other firms in the same industry. The major output of financial accounting is a set of financial statements designed to provide this

financial accounting The branch of accounting that prepares financial statements for use by owners, creditors, suppliers, and other external stakeholders.

generally accepted accounting principles (GAAP) A set of accounting standards that is used in the preparation of financial statements.

Financial Accounting Standards Board (FASB) The private board that establishes the generally accepted accounting principles used in the practice of financial accounting.

broad type of information. We'll describe these statements in the next section.

8-2a Role of the Financial Standards Accounting Board

Imagine how confused and frustrated investors, creditors, and regulators would become if every firm could make its own financial accounting rules as it went along and change them whenever it wanted! To reduce confusion and provide external stakeholders with consistent and accurate financial statements, the accounting profession has adopted a set of **generally accepted accounting principles (GAAP)** that guide the practice of financial accounting. In the United States, the Securities and Exchange Commission (SEC) has the ultimate legal authority to set and enforce accounting standards. In practice, however, the SEC has delegated the responsibility for developing these rules to a private organization known as the **Financial Accounting Standards Board (FASB)**. This board consists of seven members appointed by the Financial Accounting Foundation. Each member serves a five-year term and can be reappointed to serve one additional term.

A variety of business stakeholders, managers, stockholders, employees, creditors, suppliers, and government agencies use accounting information.

Rawpixel/Shutterstock.com

Looking for Fraud? Call RoboCop

In 2009, Bernard Madoff was sentenced to a 150-year prison sentence after being convicted of running a decade-long Ponzi scheme that cheated investors, including charitable foundations, out of $65 billion. The U.S. Securities and Exchange Commission (SEC), which identifies and prosecutes corporate fraud, was criticized for not catching Madoff's crime much earlier. Many felt, however, that a Madoff-like crime was inevitable given that the SEC is overworked, underfunded, and understaffed.

In response to Madoff's historic crime, the SEC developed the Accounting Quality Model (AQM), a fully automated computer system known informally as RoboCop. The AQM performs detailed, customized analyses of financial documents that public companies are required to file with the SEC. It scans filings within 24 hours of being uploaded to SEC databases, marks financial results and activities that appear to be either high-risk or potentially fraudulent, and produces a final report with a "risk score" indicating the likelihood of fraud and misstated earnings. Those risk scores, in turn, help SEC auditors and lawyers decide where to investigate.

What factors lead to higher risk scores, and thus a greater likelihood of an SEC investigation? If a company's filings show a high number of off-balance sheet transactions, or accounting results in conflict with an independent auditor, the use of a high number of auditors within a short period, or numerous filing

delays, RoboCop yields a high-risk score that, in turn, prompts SEC agents to perform a more detailed investigation. The SEC's Craig Lewis says, "We're effectively going in…[and trying to] … maximize our ability to differentiate between fraudsters in the past and firms that haven't had fraud action brought against them yet."

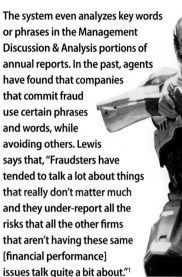

Photos 12/Columbia Pictures/MGM/Alamy

The system even analyzes key words or phrases in the Management Discussion & Analysis portions of annual reports. In the past, agents have found that companies that commit fraud use certain phrases and words, while avoiding others. Lewis says that, "Fraudsters have tended to talk a lot about things that really don't matter much and they under-report all the risks that all the other firms that aren't having these same [financial performance] issues talk quite a bit about."[1]

In order to preserve independence and impartiality, the members are required to sever all ties with any firms or institutions they served prior to joining the board.

Through GAAP, the FASB aims to ensure that financial statements are:

- Relevant: They must contain information that helps the user understand the firm's financial performance and condition.

- Reliable: They must provide information that is objective, accurate, and verifiable.

- Consistent: They must provide financial statements based on the same core assumptions and procedures over time; if a firm introduces any significant changes in how it prepares its financial statements, GAAP requires it to clearly identify and describe these changes.

- Comparable: They must present accounting statements in a reasonably standardized way, allowing users to track the firm's financial performance over a period of years and compare its results with those for other firms.

The FASB is constantly modifying, clarifying, and expanding GAAP as business practices evolve and new issues arise. Perhaps the most important focus in recent years has

been a move by the FASB and its international counterpart, the International Accounting Standards Board (IASB), to find ways to make U.S. accounting practices more consistent with those in other nations. This effort is likely to have far-reaching consequences.

8-2b Ethics in Accounting

Even clear and well-established accounting principles won't result in accurate and reliable information if managers and accountants flaunt them. Caterpillar, $580 million; Waste Management, $1.5 billion; Olympus, $1.7 billion; HealthSouth, $2.7 billion; Autonomy, a software company purchased by Hewlett-Packard, $8.8 billion; and the biggest of them all, WorldCom, $11 billion, are all unfortunate examples of exorbitant accounting fraud where debts were hidden or earnings overstated by a half a billion to $11 billion or more. Once their accounting improprieties became known, most of these firms suffered severe financial difficulties.[2]

These scandals served as a wake-up call to the accounting profession that their ethical training and standards needed major improvement. In the wake of the scandals, many state accounting boards passed new ethics-related requirements.

FINANCIAL STATEMENTS: READ ALL ABOUT US

One of the major responsibilities of financial accounting is the preparation of three basic financial statements: the balance sheet, income statement, and statement of cash flows. Taken together, these financial statements provide external stakeholders with a broad picture of an organization's financial condition and its recent financial performance. Large corporations with publicly traded stock must provide an annual report containing all three statements to all stockholders. They also must file quarterly and annual reports, including financial statements, with the SEC. Let's take a look at the information each statement provides.

balance sheet A financial statement that reports the financial position of a firm by identifying and reporting the value of the firm's assets, liabilities, and owners' equity.

accounting equation
Assets = Liabilities + Owners' Equity

8-3a The Balance Sheet: What We Own and How We Got It

The **balance sheet** summarizes a firm's financial position at a specific point in time. Though the balance sheets of different firms vary in specifics, all of them are organized to reflect the most famous equation in all of accounting—so famous that it is usually referred to simply as the **accounting equation**:

Assets = Liabilities + Owners' Equity

Exhibit 8.1 shows a simplified balance sheet for McDonald's Corporation, which we'll use to illustrate the information provided by financial statements. Notice that the three major sectors of this statement reflect the key terms in the accounting equation. Once we've defined

Exhibit 8.1
The Balance Sheet for McDonald's Corporation

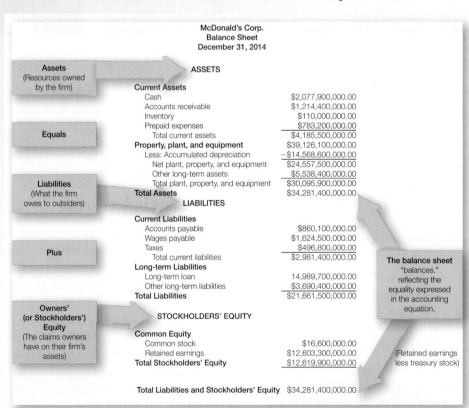

Adapted from "McDonald's Corporation 2014 Balance Sheet," http://finance.yahoo.com/q/bs?s=MCD+Balance+Sheet&annual, accessed April 9, 2015; and "McDonald's Corporation, Form 10-K, U.S. Securities and Exchange Commission, http://www.sec.gov/Archives/edgar/data/63908/000006390815000016/mcd-12312014x10k.htm#s7A53B72CBB24EE1BFF0C552128C24214, accessed April 9, 2015. Because the accounting information found in those sources is much more detailed than presented here, some of the accounting numbers in this balance sheet will differ from similar numbers shown in McDonald's balance sheets in those sources for the same time period.

Double-Entry Bookkeeping: "One of the Finest Inventions of Mankind"

The invention of double-entry bookkeeping, often attributed to Franciscan friar Luca Pacioli in 1494, was a key to the expanding trade of Italian merchants, as "it would be impossible for them to conduct their business, for they would have no rest and their minds would always be troubled."

Double-entry bookkeeping requires that every accounting transaction be in balance and have two entries, a debit on the left and a credit on the right. For example, a $1 million bank loan is recorded as a $1 million debit in cash and a $1 million credit for notes payable.

Ra2studio/Shutterstock.com

	Debit	Credit
Cash	$1,000,000	
Notes Payable		$1,000,000

As shown in the "T account" above, the transaction balances because the company has $1 million in cash, but owes $1 million to pay off the loan.

Likewise, if you sell $75,000 in goods and receive a cash payment, the balanced journal entry looks like this,

	Debit	Credit
Cash	$75,000	
Sales Revenue		$75,000

reflecting the increase in cash as a function of making the sale.

While most students find debits and credits confusing at first, the breakthrough that double-entry bookkeeping provided is that it facilitates error checking with every single accounting entry, and in so doing, according to Pacioli, allowed Italian merchants "to make a lawful and reasonable profit so as to keep up his business."

Goethe called double-entry bookkeeping one of "the finest inventions of mankind." Italian economist Antonio Martino agreed, saying that, "Without double-entry bookkeeping, the rational conduct of business, and the pursuit of profit, modern civilization would not exist."[3]

---

each of these terms, we'll explain the logic behind the accounting equation and how the balance sheet illustrates this logic.

- **Assets** are things of value that the firm owns. Balance sheets usually classify assets into at least two major categories. The first category, called *current assets,* consists of cash, $2.077 billion, and other assets that the firm expects to use up or convert into cash within a year. For example, in McDonald's balance sheet, the value for *accounts receivable,* $1.214 billion, refers to money owed to McDonald's by franchise restaurants who bought its goods on credit. (These receivables are converted into cash when the franchise restaurants pay their bills.) *Inventory*, also a current asset, represents the $110 million of burgers, fries, and other foods and ingredients used in McDonald's restaurants. If this strikes you as not very much, you're right. It isn't, because McDonald's never has more than three to four days of inventory on hand in

its restaurants. McDonald's has $783.2 million of *prepaid expenses*, such as insurance, or prepaid advertising, that have been paid before they are due.

The other major category of assets on McDonald's balance sheets is *Property, plant, and equipment*. It lists the value, in this case $39.12 billion, of the company's land, buildings, machinery, equipment, and other long-term assets. With the exception of land, these assets have a limited useful life, so accountants subtract *accumulated depreciation*, $14.5 billion, from the original value of these assets, to reflect the fact that these assets are being used up over time.

Though not shown here, some companies list a third category of assets, called *intangible assets*. These are assets that have no physical existence—you can't see or touch them—but they still have value. Examples include patents, copyrights, trademarks, and even the goodwill

assets Resources owned by a firm.

Just Because They Can, Doesn't Mean They Should.

One of the primary responsibilities in public companies is the fiduciary responsibility that managers have to the shareholders who own the firm. In other words, managers are expected to increase the value of the company by reducing expenses and minimizing taxes so as to maximize profits and increase dividends paid to shareholders.

The issue of tax liability is complex for multinational companies, given that they must pay corporate taxes in all the countries in which they operate, countries that may have vastly different tax structures and tax rates. To reduce their tax liabilities, many multinationals reconfigure their operating structures, or relocate to countries with more favorable tax environments. Indeed, favorable tax rates and structures are one of the most important ways in which governments encourage businesses to locate or invest more heavily in their countries.

Starbucks, for example, operates 817 stores in its European division. Of that number, 506 stores are in the United Kingdom and only 9 in the Netherlands, yet the company located its European headquarters in Amsterdam, where tax laws are more generous than in London. In 2014, Starbucks reported a profit in Europe of $446.6 million and paid taxes of $2.86 billion (0.06%) in the Netherlands. Similarly, over a three-year period, Apple transferred about $74 billion in sales to its Irish subsidiary and paid a negotiated tax rate under 2%.

Because the U.S. corporate tax rate, 35%, is the highest in the world, it is not surprising that many U.S.-based multinationals have located European headquarters in countries such as Ireland, Luxembourg, and the Netherlands to take advantage of lower taxes on their European earnings.

To be clear, moving to a location with a lower tax rate is not illegal, and Starbucks and Apple are not alone in this practice. Google, Facebook, Amazon, Fiat, Microsoft, and others have also used location strategies to minimize their tax burdens. And even though Starbucks paid only 0.06% of its European revenue in taxes, the company has said it pays "a global effective tax rate of 34 percent" when all of its taxes from all of its locations are tallied.[4]

What do YOU think?

- When it comes to paying taxes, how far should companies take their fiduciary responsibilities of increasing profit and shareholder value and minimizing expenses, including taxes?

- What impact do you think tax rates have on the overall business climate in a country—an adverse impact, a beneficial impact, or no impact at all? Explain.

- Starbucks ultimately moved its European headquarters to London as a result of backlash against its locating in Amsterdam to benefit from lower Dutch corporate tax rates. Do you think the company was right to move, or should it have stayed put in Amsterdam?

---

a company develops with its stakeholders. McDonald's trademarks, such as Ronald McDonald and the golden arches, clearly have tremendous value to the company.

- **Liabilities** indicate what the firm owes to nonowners—in other words, the claims nonowners have against the firm's assets. Balance sheets usually organize liabilities into two broad categories: current liabilities and long-term liabilities. *Current liabilities*, totaling $2.981 billion for McDonald's, are debts that come due within a year of the date on the balance sheet. McDonald's has, for example, $860.1 million in accounts payable, that is, how much it owes suppliers on credit. Wages payable, $1.624 billion for McDonald's, what the firm owes to workers for work they have already

liabilities Claims that outsiders have against a firm's assets.

> "IT SOUNDS EXTRAORDINARY, BUT IT'S A FACT THAT BALANCE SHEETS CAN MAKE FASCINATING READING."
>
> —BARONESS MARY ARCHER, CAMBRIDGE UNIVERSITY LECTURER AND CHAIRWOMAN OF THE NATIONAL ENERGY FOUNDATION

performed, is another current liability, as are taxes, which amount to $496.8 million for McDonald's. *Long-term liabilities* are debts that don't come due until more than a year after the date on the balance sheet. McDonald's has $14.9 billion in long-term loans and $3.69 billion in other long-term liabilities.

■ **Owners' (or Stockholders') equity** refers to the claims the owners have against their firm's assets. The specific accounts listed in the owners' equity section of a balance sheet depend on the form of business ownership. As Exhibit 8.1 shows, common stock is a key owners' equity account for corporations. For corporations like McDonald's, the owners' equity section is usually titled *stockholders' equity*. Also notice that retained earnings, which are the accumulated earnings reinvested in the company (rather than paid to owners), is another major component of the owners' equity section. McDonald's has $16.6 million in common stock and $12.6 billion in retained earnings, which it puts back into growing the company.

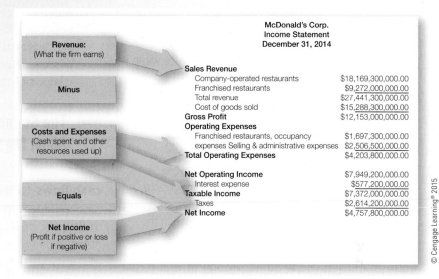

Exhibit 8.2
Income Statement for McDonald's

McDonald's Corp.
Income Statement
December 31, 2014

Revenue: (What the firm earns)

Minus

Costs and Expenses (Cash spent and other resources used up)

Equals

Net Income (Profit if positive or loss if negative)

Sales Revenue	
Company-operated restaurants	$18,169,300,000.00
Franchised restaurants	$9,272,000,000.00
Total revenue	$27,441,300,000.00
Cost of goods sold	$15,288,300,000.00
Gross Profit	$12,153,000,000.00
Operating Expenses	
Franchised restaurants, occupancy	$1,697,300,000.00
expenses Selling & administrative expenses	$2,506,500,000.00
Total Operating Expenses	$4,203,800,000.00
Net Operating Income	$7,949,200,000.00
Interest expense	$577,200,000.00
Taxable Income	$7,372,000,000.00
Taxes	$2,614,200,000.00
Net Income	$4,757,800,000.00

© Cengage Learning® 2015

Adapted from "McDonald's Corporation 2014 Income Statement," http://finance.yahoo.com/q/is?s=MCD+Income+Statement&annual, accessed April 9, 2015; and "McDonald's Corporation, Form 10-K, U.S. Securities and Exchange Commission, http://www.sec.gov/Archives/edgar/data/63908/000006390815000016/mcd-12312014x10k.htm#s7A53B72CBB24EE1BFF0C552128C24214, accessed April 9, 2015.

The logic behind the accounting equation is based on the fact that firms must finance the purchase of their assets, and owners and nonowners are the only two sources of funding. The accounting equation tells us that the value of a firm's assets must equal the amount of financing provided by owners (as measured by owners' equity) plus the amount provided by creditors (as indicated by the firm's liabilities) to purchase those assets. Because a balance sheet is based on this logic, it must *always* be in balance. In other words, the dollar value of the assets *must* equal the dollar value of the liabilities plus owners' equity. This is true for *all* firms, from the smallest sole proprietorship to the largest multinational corporation. Notice in Exhibit 8.1 that the $34.281 billion in total assets listed on McDonald's balance sheet matches the $34.281 billion in liabilities plus owners' equity.

8-3b The Income Statement: So, How Did We Do?

The **income statement** summarizes the financial results of a firm's operations over a given period of time. The figure that attracts the most attention on the income statement is net income, which measures the company's profit or loss. In fact, another name for the income statement is the *profit and loss statement* (or, informally, the *P&L*). Just as with the balance sheet, we can use a simple equation to illustrate the logic behind the organization of the income statement:

Revenue – Expenses = Net Income

In this equation:

■ **Revenue** represents the increase in the amount of cash and other assets (such as accounts receivable) the firm earns in a given time period as the result of its business activities. For example, Exhibit 8.2 shows that McDonald's has $27.4 billion in revenues, with $18.1 billion coming from company-owned restaurants and $9.2 billion coming from franchised restaurants. A firm normally earns revenue by selling goods or by charging fees for providing services (or both). Accountants

owners' equity The claims a firm's owners have against their company's assets (often called "stockholders' equity" on balance sheets of corporations).

income statement The financial statement that reports the revenues, expenses, and net income that resulted from a firm's operations over an accounting period.

revenue Increases in a firm's assets that result from the sale of goods, provision of services, or other activities intended to earn income.

use **accrual-basis accounting** when recognizing revenues. Under the accrual approach, revenues are recorded when they are earned, and payment is reasonably assured. It's important to realize that this is not always when the firm receives cash from its sales. For example, if a firm sells goods on credit, it reports revenue before it receives cash. (The revenue would show up initially as an increase in accounts receivable rather than as an increase in cash.)

- **Expenses** indicate the cash a firm spends, or other assets it uses up, to carry out the business activities necessary to generate its revenue. Under accrual-basis accounting, expenses aren't necessarily recorded when cash is paid. Instead, expenses are matched to the revenue they help generate. The specific titles given to the costs and expenses listed on an income statement vary among firms—as do the details provided. But the general approach remains the same: costs are deducted from revenue in several stages to show how net income is determined. The first step in this process is to deduct *costs of goods sold*, $15.2 billion for McDonald's, which are costs directly related to buying, manufacturing, or providing the goods and services the company sells. (Manufacturing companies often use the term *cost of goods manufactured* for these costs.) The difference between the firm's revenue and its cost of goods sold is its *gross profit*, which was $12.1 billion for McDonald's. The next step is to deduct *operating expenses*, totaling $4.2 billion for McDonald's, from gross profit. Operating expenses are costs the firm incurs in the regular operation of its business. Most income statements divide operating expenses into *selling expenses* (such as salaries and commissions to salespeople and advertising expenses) and *general* (or *administrative*) *expenses* (such as rent, insurance, utilities, and office supplies). McDonald's, however, typically owns the land and the building of franchised restaurants. So, it has another large, but specialized operating expense of $1.6 billion to pay for franchised restaurants' occupancy expenses. The difference between gross profit and operating expenses is *net operating income,* which is $7.9 billion for McDonald's. Finally, interest expenses and taxes are deducted from net operating income

to determine the firm's net income. After paying $577.2 million in interest expenses and $2.6 billion in taxes, McDonald's net income is $4.75 billion.

- **Net income** is the profit or loss the firm earns in the time period covered by the income statement. If net income is positive, the firm has earned a profit. If it's negative, the firm has suffered a loss. Net income is called the "bottom line" of the income statement because it is such an important measure of the firm's operating success.

8-3c The Statement of Cash Flows: Show Me the Money

The last major financial statement is the **statement of cash flows**. Cash is the lifeblood of any business organization. A firm must have enough cash to pay what it owes to workers, creditors, suppliers, and taxing authorities—hopefully, with enough left to pay a dividend to its owners! So it's not surprising that a firm's stakeholders are very interested in how and why a company's cash balance changed over the past year. Cash flow statements commonly begin with net income. Why? Because it represents an increase (or decrease in the case of a loss) to the cash available to the company. Indeed, since McDonald's net income was $4.75 billion in 2014, we see that amount at the beginning of cash flow statement in Exhibit 8.3. The statement of cash flows identifies the amount of cash that flowed into and out of the firm from three types of activities:

1. Cash flows from *operating activities* show the amount of cash that flowed into the company from the sale of goods or services, as well as cash from dividends and interest received from ownership of the financial securities of other firms. It also shows the amount of cash used to cover expenses resulting from operations and any cash payments to purchase securities held for short-term trading purposes. Remember that under the accrual method, not all revenues and expenses on the income statement represent cash flows, so operating cash flows may differ substantially from the revenues and expenses shown on the income statement. Exhibit 8.3 shows that McDonald's operating cash flow comes from three sources: $2.06 billion from cash payments from customers, less $4.9 billion spent on inventory purchases, and $85.7 million in cash expenditures to support its restaurants, all of which comes to $1.972 billion in net cash from operations.

2. Cash flows from *investing activities* show the amount of cash received from the sale of fixed assets (such as land and buildings) and financial assets bought as long-term investments. It also shows any cash used to buy fixed

accrual-basis accounting The method of accounting that recognizes revenue when it is earned and matches expenses to the revenues they helped produce.

expenses Resources that are used up as the result of business operations.

net income The difference between the revenue a firm earns and the expenses it incurs in a given time period.

statement of cash flows The financial statement that identifies a firm's sources and uses of cash in a given accounting period.

Exhibit 8.3
McDonald's Statement of Cash Flows

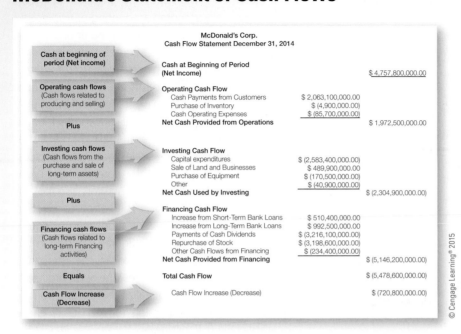

McDonald's Corp.
Cash Flow Statement December 31, 2014

Cash at Beginning of Period (Net Income)		$ 4,757,800,000.00
Operating Cash Flow		
Cash Payments from Customers	$ 2,063,100,000.00	
Purchase of Inventory	$ (4,900,000.00)	
Cash Operating Expenses	$ (85,700,000.00)	
Net Cash Provided from Operations		$ 1,972,500,000.00
Investing Cash Flow		
Capital expenditures	$ (2,583,400,000.00)	
Sale of Land and Businesses	$ 489,900,000.00	
Purchase of Equipment	$ (170,500,000.00)	
Other	$ (40,900,000.00)	
Net Cash Used by Investing		$ (2,304,900,000.00)
Financing Cash Flow		
Increase from Short-Term Bank Loans	$ 510,400,000.00	
Increase from Long-Term Bank Loans	$ 992,500,000.00	
Payments of Cash Dividends	$ (3,216,100,000.00)	
Repurchase of Stock	$ (3,198,600,000.00)	
Other Cash Flows from Financing	$ (234,400,000.00)	
Net Cash Provided from Financing		$ (5,146,200,000.00)
Total Cash Flow		$ (5,478,600,000.00)
Cash Flow Increase (Decrease)		$ (720,800,000.00)

Labels on left of diagram:
- Cash at beginning of period (Net income)
- Operating cash flows (Cash flows related to producing and selling)
- Plus
- Investing cash flows (Cash flows from the purchase and sale of long-term assets)
- Plus
- Financing cash flows (Cash flows related to long-term Financing activities)
- Equals
- Cash Flow Increase (Decrease)

© Cengage Learning® 2015

Sources: Adapted from "McDonald's Corporation 2014 Cash Flow Statement," http://finance.yahoo.com/q/cf?s=MCD+Cash+Flow&annual, accessed April 9, 2015; and "McDonald's Corporation, Form 10-K, U.S. Securities and Exchange Commission, http://www.sec.gov/Archives/edgar/data/63908/000006390815000016/mcd-12312014x10k.htm#s7A53B72CBB24EE1BFF0C552128C24214, accessed April 9, 2015. Because the accounting information found in those sources is much more detailed than presented here, some of the accounting numbers shown here will differ from similar numbers shown in McDonald's cash flow statements in those sources for the same time period.

assets or make long-term financial investments. McDonald's had $489.9 million from the sale of land and businesses, but spent $2.58 billion in cash on capital expenditures (primarily for building and opening new restaurants or remodeling existing restaurants) and an additional $170.5 million from cash on equipment for new restaurants or to upgrade existing restaurants, and an additional $40.9 million in cash on "other" investing activities.

3. Cash flows from *financing activities* show the cash the firm received from issuing additional shares of its own stock or from taking out short-term and long-term loans, which, increased McDonald's cash by $510.4 million and $999.25 million, respectively. It also shows cash outflows from payment of dividends to shareholders, $3.2 billion for McDonald's. McDonald's also decreased cash flow by spending $3.19 billion to repurchase shares of McDonald's stock. In all, cash flows from financing activities were negative for McDonald's at $5.16 billion more in cash outflows than inflows.

> "HAPPINESS IS A POSITIVE CASH FLOW."
> —FRED ADLER

Exhibit 8.3 shows that McDonald's cash flows declined from $5.58 billion to $3.07 billion in 2013, primarily because of large cash outflows for operating expenses, cash dividends to stockholders, and repurchasing stock.

8-3d Other Statements: What Happened to the Owners' Stake?

In addition to the three major statements we've just described, firms usually prepare either a statement of retained earnings or a stockholders' equity statement. Let's take a quick look at each of these statements.

The *statement of retained earnings* is a simple statement that shows how retained earnings have changed from one accounting period to the next. The change in retained earnings is found by subtracting dividends paid to shareholders from net income.

Firms that have more complex changes in the owners' equity section sometimes report these changes in notes to the financial statements in the annual report. But they often disclose these changes by providing a *stockholders' equity statement*. Like the statement of retained earnings, this statement shows how net income and dividends affect retained earnings. But it also shows other changes in stockholders' equity, such as those that arise from the issuance of additional shares of stock.

8-4 INTERPRETING FINANCIAL STATEMENTS: DIGGING BENEATH THE SURFACE

The financial statements we've just described contain a lot of important information. But they don't necessarily tell the whole story. In fact, the numbers they report can be misleading if they aren't put into proper context. Thus, in addition to looking at the statements, it's also important to check out the independent auditor's report and read the management discussion and footnotes that accompany these statements. It's also a good idea to compare the figures reported in current statements with those from earlier statements to see how key account values have changed.

8-4a The Independent Auditor's Report: Getting a Stamp of Approval

U.S. securities laws require publicly traded corporations in the United States to have an independent CPA firm (an accounting firm that specializes in providing public accounting services) perform an annual *external audit* of their financial statements. And many companies that aren't

External auditors carefully examine a company's financial records before rendering their opinion.

publicly traded also obtain external audits even though they aren't legally required to do so.

The purpose of an audit is to verify that the company's financial statements were properly prepared in accordance with generally accepted accounting principles and fairly present the financial condition of the firm. So external auditors don't just check the figures, they also examine the accounting *methods* the company used to *obtain* those figures. For example, auditors interview the company's accounting and bookkeeping staff to verify that they understand and properly implement procedures that are consistent with GAAP. They also examine a sample of specific source documents (such as sales receipts or invoices) and verify that the transactions they represent were properly posted to the correct accounts. Auditors also look for signs of fraud or falsified records. They often conduct an actual physical count of goods or supplies in inventory to determine the accuracy of the figures reported in the company's inventory records and contact the company's banker to verify its account balances. The audit process is rigorous, but it's important to realize that in large, public companies, it would be impossible for auditors to check the accuracy of every transaction.

The results of the audit are presented in an *independent auditor's report*, which is included in the annual report the firm sends to its stockholders. If the auditor doesn't find any problems with the way a firm's financial statements were prepared and presented, the report will offer an *unqualified* (or *"clean"*) *opinion*—which is by far the most common outcome. If the auditor identifies some minor concerns but believes that on balance the firm's statements remain a fair and accurate representation of the company's financial position, the report will offer a *qualified opinion*. But when auditors discover more serious and widespread problems with a firm's statements, they offer an *adverse opinion*. An adverse opinion indicates that the auditor believes the financial statements are seriously flawed and that they may be misleading and unreliable. (An adverse opinion must include an explanation of the specific reasons for the opinion.) Adverse opinions are very rare, so when an auditor renders one it should set off alarm bells, warning stakeholders to view the information in the firm's financial statements with real skepticism.

In order for CPA firms to perform audits with integrity, they must be independent of the firms they audit. During the 1990s, many of the major CPA firms entered into very lucrative consulting contracts with some of the businesses they were auditing. It became increasingly difficult for these CPA firms to risk losing these high-paying contracts by raising issues about accounting practices when

The End of "Free" Smartphones

Ken Wolter/Shutterstock.com

It's no wonder that nearly 60% of American adults own smartphones. Major phone carriers are quick to offer "free" smartphones "with a required two-year service contract." Carriers routinely subsidize phone costs, expecting to earn back the difference during the contract period. Subsidizing hides the phone's true price from consumers—and also contributes to hazy accounting practices that make it harder to determine a carrier's true financial performance.

In the fourth quarter of 2014, Verizon Communications posted an Ebitda (earnings before interest, taxes, depreciation, and amortization) margin of 48.5%. Although lower than analysts' projections, the margin would have been even lower had it not been significantly boosted by accounting changes related to Verizon's new Edge plan, which is its method of subsidizing subscribers' new phone purchases. Under its new Edge plan, rather than paying a single price each month, subscribers are billed for their service plans plus incremental installment payments to offset the phone's cost. Under the old Edge plan, customers were eligible for a trade-in upgrade after paying 60% of the phone's cost. The updated plan, however, requires customers to pay off 75% of the phone's cost before trading it in.

The accounting change (i.e., service plus installment payments) lowers Verizon's financial risk and allows the company to justify booking more upfront revenue from phone sales, which has the effect of increasing reported revenues and profits on each sale. Previously, Verizon would book about $400 upfront on a $600 smartphone, and then write off the remaining $200 as a reserve for losses on the phone's trade-in value. Now, however, Verizon books about $570 in upfront revenue, even though subscribers spread their phone payments across monthly installments.

Installment plans—straight or subsidized—are gaining momentum, as carriers move to shift more of the cost of expensive smartphones to customers. T-Mobile ended subsidies altogether in 2013, and Verizon's new Edge plan blends installments with subsidies. All carriers, however, will soon have to adjust their bookkeeping to comply with new accounting rules. Starting in 2017, the Financial Accounting Standards Board will require phone carriers to divide revenue into two categories: service and equipment, reporting the total cost of the latter up front. In doing so, carriers will report more immediate revenue, but less over time. Verizon will need to adjust its accounting practices before 2017, but investors, who want a more accurate assessment of Verizon's revenues, would prefer that it not wait to make those changes.[5]

---

they audited the books of their clients. In other words, the auditors ceased to be truly independent and objective. The lack of rigorous oversight by external auditors contributed to the accounting scandals we mentioned earlier in this chapter.

In the aftermath of the scandals, Congress passed the Sarbanes-Oxley Act of 2002 (commonly referred to as "SOX" or "Sarbox"). This law banned business relationships that might create conflicts of interest between CPA firms and the companies they audit. It also established a private-sector nonprofit corporation known as the Public Company Accounting Oversight Board (PCAOB). The PCAOB defines its mission as follows: "to protect the interests of investors and further the public interest in the preparation of informative, fair, and independent audit reports."[6]

8-4b Checking Out the Notes to Financial Statements: What's in the Fine Print?

Some types of information can't be adequately conveyed by numbers alone. Annual reports include notes (often *many* pages of notes) that disclose additional information about the firm's operations, accounting practices, and special circumstances that clarify and supplement the numbers reported on the financial statements. These notes can be *very* revealing. For example, GAAP often allows firms to choose among several options when it comes to certain accounting procedures—and the choices the firm makes can affect the value of assets, liabilities, and owners' equity on the balance sheet and the revenues, costs, and net income on the income statement. The notes to financial statements explain the specific accounting methods used

New Accounting Trend: Benefit Corporations, the Triple Bottom Line

Traditional corporate charters state that a company's board of directors and its management can only be concerned with one thing: maximizing the financial value of the company for its owners, the shareholders. Therefore, financial accounting exists to assess a firm's financial condition and compare its results to other firms in the same industry. Accounting, however, only measures financial success.

Today, six states offer an alternative charter, the benefit corporation, where firms are required to maximize the "general public benefit." According to B Lab, the nonprofit organization that authored benefit corporation laws, benefit corporations are identical to traditional corporations except for three key differences.

- A corporate purpose to create a material positive impact on society and the environment.

- Expanded fiduciary duty to require consideration of the interests of workers, community, and the environment.

- Annual public reports on overall social and environmental performance against a comprehensive, credible,

Feng Yu/Shutterstock.com

independent, and transparent third-party standard.

In short, benefit corporations give business leaders and their boards legal protection to pursue a "higher purpose than profit."

For example, Jonathan Harrison is CEO of Emerge Workplace Solutions, a payday lender that offers emergency loans to hourly workers. But unlike competitors who charge 400% interest on these short-term loans, his company charges only 9% to 19.99%. Benefit corporation status is important, says Harrison, because, "It's really important for us to have a designation that we're the good guys."

University of Delaware professor Charles Elson says, however, that benefit corporations are a "terrible idea" for investors because of a "lack of accountability." When traditional corporations mismanage resources, shareholders can sue. But, with benefit corporations, Elson says, "there's very little you can do about it as a shareholder" because nearly any decision can be seen as fulfilling the company's "triple bottom line"—social, environmental, and financial, all of which are equally important under a benefit corporation's charter.[7]

---

to recognize revenue, value inventory, and depreciate fixed assets. They might also provide details about the way the firm funds its pension plan or health insurance for its employees. They must also disclose *changes* in accounting methods that could affect the comparability of the current financial statements to those of previous years. Even more interesting, the notes might disclose important facts about the status of a lawsuit against the firm or other risks the firm faces. Stakeholders who ignore these notes are likely to miss out on important information.

Another important source of information is the section of the annual report usually titled "Management's Discussion and Analysis." As its name implies, this is where the top management team provides its take on the financial

> IN 2004 A HORSE NAMED "READ THE FOOTNOTES" RAN IN THE KENTUCKY DERBY.
>
> — SECURITIES AND EXCHANGE COMMISSION

condition of the company. SEC guidelines require top management to disclose any trends, events, or risks likely to have a significant impact on the firm's financial condition in this section of the report.

8-4c Looking for Trends in Comparative Statements

The SEC requires publicly traded corporations to provide *comparative financial statements*. This simply means that the balance sheet, income statement, and statement of cash flows must list two or more years of figures side by side, making it possible to see how account values have changed over a period of time. Many firms that aren't publicly traded also present comparative statements, even though they are not required to do so by GAAP.

Comparative balance sheets allow users to trace what has happened to key assets and liabilities over the past two or three years, and whether its owners' equity had increased. Comparative income statements show whether the firm's net income increased or decreased and what has happened to revenues and expenses over recent years. Using comparative statements to identify changes in key account values over time is called **horizontal analysis**.

8-5 BUDGETING: PLANNING FOR ACCOUNTABILITY

Management accountants also play an important role in the development of budgets. **Budgeting** is a management tool that explicitly shows how a firm will acquire and allocate the resources it needs to achieve its goals over a specific time period. The budgetary process facilitates planning by requiring managers to translate goals into measurable quantities and identify the specific resources needed to achieve these goals. But budgeting offers other advantages as well. If done well, budgeting:

- Helps managers clearly specify how they intend to achieve the goals they set during the planning process. This should lead to a better understanding of how the organization's limited resources will be allocated.

- Encourages communication and coordination among managers and employees in various departments within the organization. For example, the budget process can give middle and first-line managers and employees an opportunity to provide top managers with important insights about the challenges facing their specialized areas—and the resources they need to meet those challenges. But, as we will explain in the next section, the extent to which this advantage is realized depends on the specific approach used in the budgeting process.

- Serves as a motivational tool. Good budgets clearly identify goals *and* demonstrate a plan of action for acquiring the resources needed to achieve them. Employees tend to be more highly motivated when they understand the goals their managers expect them to accomplish and when they view these goals as ambitious but achievable.

- Helps managers evaluate progress and performance. Managers can compare actual performance to budgeted figures to determine whether various

Budgeting encourages communication and coordination among managers and employees.

departments and functional areas are making adequate progress toward achieving their organization's goals. If actual performance falls short of budgetary goals, managers can look for reasons and, if necessary, take corrective action.

8-5a Preparing the Budget: Top-Down or Bottom-Up?

There are two broad approaches to budget preparation. In some organizations, top management prepares the budget with little or no input from middle and supervisory managers—a process known as *top-down budgeting*. Supporters of this approach point out that top management knows the long-term strategic needs of the company and is in a better position to see the big picture when making budget decisions.

The other approach to budgeting is called *bottom-up* (or *participatory*) *budgeting*. Organizations that use a participatory process allow middle and supervisory managers to participate actively in the creation of the budget. Proponents

> **horizontal analysis** Analysis of financial statements that compares account values reported on these statements over two or more years to identify changes and trends.

> **budgeting** A management tool that explicitly shows how a firm will acquire and use the resources needed to achieve its goals over a specific time period.

of this approach maintain that it has two major advantages. First, middle and supervisory managers are likely to know more about the issues and challenges facing their departments—and the resources it will take to address them—than top management. Second, middle and first-line managers are likely to be more highly motivated to achieve budgetary goals when they have a say in how those goals are developed. On the negative side, the bottom-up approach is more time consuming and resource intensive to carry out than the top-down approach. Also, some middle managers may be tempted to overstate their needs or set low budget goals in order to make their jobs easier—an outcome known as *budgetary slack*.[8] Despite these drawbacks, the participatory approach currently is more common than the top-down process.

8-5b Developing the Key Budget Components: One Step at a Time

The budgeting process actually requires the preparation of several different types of budgets. But all of these individual budgets can be classified into two broad categories: operating budgets and financial budgets.

Operating budgets are budgets that identify projected sales and production goals and the various costs the firm will incur to meet these goals. These budgets are developed in a specific order, with the information from earlier budgets used in the preparation of later budgets.

The preparation of operating budgets begins with the development of a *sales budget* that provides quarterly estimates of the number of units of each product the firm expects to sell, the selling price, and the total dollar value of expected sales. The sales budget *must* be created first because many of the production and cost figures that go into other operating budgets depend on the level of sales. Once the sales budget is complete, the budgeted sales level can be used to develop the production budget, the administrative expenses, and the selling expenses budgets. And once the production budget is completed, the information it contains is used to prepare budgets for direct labor costs, direct materials costs, and manufacturing overhead. The final stage in the preparation of operating budgets is the creation of a *budgeted income statement*. This budget looks much like the income statement we described earlier, but instead of describing the actual results of the firm's

past operations, it combines the revenue projections from the sales budget and the cost projections from the other operating budgets to present a forecast of *expected* net income.

Financial budgets focus on the firm's financial goals and identify the resources needed to achieve these goals. The two main financial budget documents are the *cash budget* and the *capital expenditure budget*. The cash budget identifies short-term fluctuations in cash flows, helping managers identify times when the firm might face cash flow problems—or when it might have a temporary surplus of cash that it could invest. The capital expenditure budget identifies the firm's planned investments in major fixed assets and long-term projects. The information from these two financial budgets and the budgeted income statement are combined to construct the *budgeted balance sheet*. This is the last financial budget; it shows how the firm's operations, investing, and financing activities are expected to affect all of the asset, liability, and owners' equity accounts.

The firm's **master budget** organizes the operating and financial budgets into a unified whole, representing the firm's overall plan of action for a specified time period. In other words, the master budget shows how all of the pieces fit together to form a complete picture. Exhibit 8.4 shows all of the budget documents that are included in a typical master budget. The arrows indicate the order in which the budgets are developed, starting with the sales budget and ending with the budgeted balance sheet.

8-5c Being Flexible: Clearing Up Problems with Static

The budget process, as we've described it so far, results in a *static* budget, meaning that it is based on a single assumed level of sales. Static budgets are excellent tools for planning, but they have weaknesses when they are used to measure progress, evaluate performance, and identify problem areas that need correcting.

The problem with a static budget is that real-world sales can (and often do) vary considerably from their forecasted value—often for reasons that aren't under the control of the firm's management. For example, inconsistent job growth and a slow economic recovery led consumers to buy less during the 2013 "Black Friday" weekend, leading to a 2.9% drop in sales from the previous year.

As we mentioned earlier, many cost figures in budgets are based on the level of sales specified in the sales budget. When actual sales differ significantly from the sales volume assumed in a static budget, all of these related budget figures will be erroneous. Using these inaccurate figures to evaluate real-world performance is likely to result in very poor assessments!

operating budgets Budgets that communicate an organization's sales and production goals and the resources needed to achieve these goals.

financial budgets Budgets that focus on the firm's financial goals and identify the resources needed to achieve these goals.

master budget A presentation of an organization's operational and financial budgets that represents the firm's overall plan of action for a specified time period.

Exhibit 8.4
Development of the Master Budget

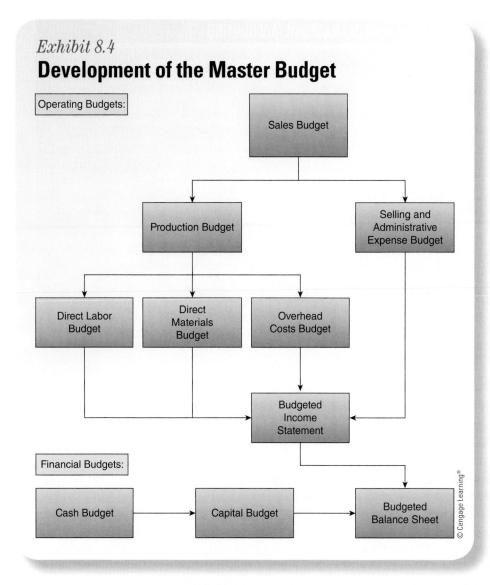

Operating Budgets:

- Sales Budget
- Production Budget
- Selling and Administrative Expense Budget
- Direct Labor Budget
- Direct Materials Budget
- Overhead Costs Budget
- Budgeted Income Statement

Financial Budgets:

- Cash Budget
- Capital Budget
- Budgeted Balance Sheet

© Cengage Learning®

One common way managerial accountants avoid this problem is to develop a *flexible budget* for control purposes. A flexible budget is one that isn't based on a single assumed level of sales. Instead, it is developed over a *range* of possible sales levels, and is designed to show the appropriate budgeted level of costs for each different level of sales. This flexibility enables managers to make more meaningful comparisons between actual costs and budgeted costs.

8-6 INSIDE INTELLIGENCE: THE ROLE OF MANAGERIAL ACCOUNTING

Now that we've looked at financial accounting, let's turn our attention to the other major branch of accounting, **managerial (or management) accounting**. As its name implies, this branch of accounting is designed to meet the needs of a company's managers, though in recent years many firms have empowered other employees and given them access to some of this information as well. Exhibit 8.5 identifies several ways that managerial accounting differs from financial accounting.

Managers throughout an organization rely on information created by managerial accountants to make important decisions. The accuracy and reliability of this information can make a huge difference in the performance of a firm. In fact, many firms view their management accounting systems as a source of competitive advantage and regard the specifics of these systems as highly valuable company secrets.[9]

It's impossible to describe all the functions performed by managerial accountants in a single chapter. So we'll be selective and focus on only two of them—but the two we'll discuss often play a crucial role in managerial decision making: measuring and assigning costs, and developing budgets.

8-6a Cost Concepts: A Cost for All Reasons

Without good information on costs, managers would be operating in the dark as they try to set prices, determine the most desirable mix of products, and locate areas where efficiency is lagging. A firm's management accounting system helps managers throughout an organization measure costs and assign them to products, activities, and even whole divisions.

Accountants define **cost** as the value of what is given up in exchange for something else. Depending on the type of problem they are analyzing, managerial accountants actually measure and evaluate

managerial (or management) accounting The branch of accounting that provides reports and analysis to managers to help them make informed business decisions.

cost The value of what is given up in exchange for something.

	Financial Accounting	Managerial Accounting
Purpose	Primarily intended to provide information to external stakeholders, such as stockholders, creditors, and government regulators. Information provided by financial accounting is available to the general public.	Primarily intended to provide information to internal stakeholders, such as the managers of specific divisions or departments. This information is proprietary—meaning that it isn't available to the general public.
Type of Information Presented	Focuses almost exclusively on financial information.	Provides both financial and nonfinancial information.
Nature of Reports	Prepares a standard set of financial statements.	Prepares customized reports to deal with specific problems or issues.
Timing of Reports	Presents financial statements on a predetermined schedule (usually quarterly and annually).	Creates reports upon request by management rather than according to a predetermined schedule.
Adherence to Accounting Standards?	Governed by a set of generally accepted accounting principles (GAAP).	Uses procedures developed internally that are not required to follow GAAP.
Time Period Focus	Summarizes past performance and its impact on the firm's present condition.	Provides reports dealing with past performance but also involves making projections about the future when dealing with planning issues.

© Cengage Learning®

several different types of costs. We'll begin our discussion by describing some of the cost concepts commonly used by managerial accountants.

At the most basic level, accountants distinguish between out-of-pocket costs and opportunity costs. **Out-of-pocket costs** (also called *explicit costs*) are usually easy to measure because they involve actual expenditures of money or other resources. The wages a company pays to its workers, the payments it makes to suppliers for raw materials, and the rent it pays for office space are examples.

But accountants realize that not all costs involve a monetary payment; sometimes what is given up is the *opportunity* to use an asset in some alternative way. Such costs are often referred to as **implicit costs**. For example, suppose a couple of lawyers form a partnership and set up their office in a building one of the partners already owns. They feel good about their decision because they don't have to make any out-of-pocket payments for rent. But a good managerial accountant would point out to the partners that they still incur an implicit cost, because by using the building themselves they forgo the opportunity to earn income by renting the office space to someone else.

Managerial accountants also distinguish between fixed costs and variable costs. As the name implies, **fixed costs** don't change when the firm changes its level of production. Examples of fixed costs include interest on a bank loan, property insurance premiums, rent on office space, and other payments that are set by a contract or by legal requirements. Many fixed costs

out-of-pocket cost A cost that involves the payment of money or other resources.

implicit cost The opportunity cost that arises when a firm uses owner-supplied resources.

fixed costs Costs that remain the same when the level of production changes within some relevant range.

Jetta Productions/Blend Images/GettyImages

A payment for materials to a supplier is an out-of-pocket cost.

are really only fixed for some "relevant range" of output. For example, if a company sees a dramatic rise in sales, it might have to move into bigger facilities, thus incurring a higher rent.

Variable costs are costs that rise (vary) when the firm produces more of its goods and services. As a company ramps up its production, it is likely to need more labor and materials and to use more electrical power. Thus payments for many types of labor, supplies, and utilities are variable costs.

8-6b Assigning Costs to Products: As (Not So) Simple as ABC?

Finally, accountants often want to assign costs to specific *cost objects*, such as one of the goods or services their firm produces. When they assign costs to specific cost objects, accountants distinguish between *direct costs* and *indirect costs*. **Direct costs** are those that can be directly traced to the production of the product. For example, the wage payments made to workers directly involved in producing a good or service would be a direct cost for that product. On the other hand, the costs a firm incurs for plant maintenance, quality control, or depreciation on office equipment are usually classified as **indirect costs** since they tend to be the result of the firm's general operation rather than the production of any specific product.

Direct costs for labor and materials are usually easy to measure and assign, since they have an easily identifiable link to the object. Unfortunately, indirect costs aren't tied in such a simple and direct way to the production of a specific product. In the past, managerial accountants usually relied on simple rules to assign indirect costs to different products—and in some cases they still do. One such approach is to allocate indirect costs in proportion

to the number of direct labor hours involved in the production of each product. Under this method, products that require the most labor to produce are assigned the most indirect costs. But, while this approach is simple, it can provide very misleading information. There is simply no logical reason for many types of indirect costs to be related to the amount of direct labor used to produce a product.

In recent years, managerial accountants have developed more sophisticated ways to allocate costs. One relatively new method is called **activity-based costing (ABC)**.

This approach is more complex and difficult to implement than the direct labor method. Basically, it involves a two-stage process. The first stage is to identify specific activities that create indirect costs and determine the factors that "drive" the costs of these activities. The second stage is to tie these cost drivers to the production of specific goods (or other cost objects). Once the relationships between cost drivers and specific products are identified, they can be used to determine how much of each indirect cost is assigned to each product.

Clearly, ABC is much more complex to implement than a system that assigns costs based on a simple "one size fits all" rule, such as the direct labor method. However, it's likely to provide more meaningful results because it is based on a systematic examination of how indirect costs are related to individual goods.

variable costs Costs that vary directly with the level of production.

direct cost Costs that are incurred directly as the result of some specific cost object.

indirect costs Costs that are the result of a firm's general operations and are not directly tied to any specific cost object.

activity-based costing (ABC) A technique to assign product costs based on links between activities that drive costs and the production of specific products.

The BIG Picture

Accounting provides vital information to both the internal and external stakeholders of a firm. The balance sheet, income statement, and statement of cash flows that are the main output of financial accounting help external stakeholders, such as owners and creditors, evaluate the financial performance of a firm.

And managerial accounting helps managers throughout an organization make better decisions by providing them with relevant and timely information about the costs and benefits of the choices they have to make. Clearly, a basic knowledge of accounting concepts will help you succeed in just about any career path you choose.

STUDY TOOLS 8

LOCATED AT BACK OF THE TEXTBOOK

☐ Rip Out Chapter Review Card

LOCATED AT WWW.CENGAGE.COM/LOGIN

☐ Review key term flashcards and create your own using StudyBits

☐ Create and complete practice quizzes based off of your notes and StudyBits

☐ Complete Online activities such as Matching, Fill-in-the-Blank, and Drag and Drop exercises

☐ View chapter highlight box content, including CEO Profiles, What Would You Do Cases, and chapter videos

☐ Track your knowledge and understanding of key concepts in business using 4LTR Online

ONE APPROACH.
70 UNIQUE SOLUTIONS.

CENGAGE
Learning·

www.cengage.com/4ltrpress

9 | Finance:
Acquiring and Using Funds to Maximize Value

LEARNING OBJECTIVES
After studying this chapter, you will be able to:

9-1 Identify the goal of financial management and explain the issues financial managers confront as they seek to achieve this goal

9-2 Describe the tools financial managers use to evaluate their company's current financial condition and develop financial plans

9-3 Evaluate the major sources of funds available to meet a firm's short-term and long-term financial needs

9-4 Identify the key issues involved in determining a firm's capital structure

9-5 Describe how financial managers acquire and manage current assets

9-6 Explain how financial managers evaluate capital budgeting proposals to identify the best long-term investment options for their company

Remember to visit
PAGE 165
for additional
STUDY TOOLS

9-1 WHAT MOTIVATES FINANCIAL DECISIONS?

Financial capital refers to the funds a firm uses to acquire its assets and finance its operations. Firms use some of their capital to meet short-term obligations, such as paying bills from suppliers, meeting payroll, repaying loans from banks, and paying taxes owed to the government. Other funds are used to finance major long-term investments, such as the purchase of a plant and equipment or the launch of a new product line. And, of course, firms need some funds to pay a return to the owners for their investment in the company.

Companies also have a variety of ways to acquire the financial capital they need: direct contributions by owners, reinvestment of earnings, loans from banks, credit provided by suppliers, and (for corporations) newly issued stocks or bonds. This isn't a complete list by any means—in fact, we'll discuss additional sources later in the chapter—but you get the idea: firms often have several ways to raise money.

financial capital The funds a firm uses to acquire its assets and finance its operations.

"MONEY IS LIKE A SIXTH SENSE—AND YOU CAN'T MAKE USE OF THE OTHER FIVE WITHOUT IT."

—WILLIAM SOMERSET MAUGHAM, ENGLISH PLAYWRIGHT, NOVELIST, AND SHORT STORY WRITER

In a nutshell, **finance** is the functional area of business that is responsible for finding, among all these alternatives, the best sources of funds and the best ways to use them. But which sources and uses are "best" depends on the goals of the financial managers. Historically, the most widely accepted goal of financial management has been to *maximize the value of the firm to its owners*. For corporations with publicly traded stock, this translates into finding the sources and uses of financial capital that will maximize the market price of the company's common stock.

Financial managers emphasize the goal of maximizing the market price of stock because they have a legal and ethical obligation (called a *fiduciary duty*) to make decisions consistent with the financial interests of their firm's owners. After all, the stockholders are the ones with their money at risk. The managers who work for the company have a fiduciary responsibility to act in the best interests of the stockholders, and that means increasing the value of their investment in the company.

Another reason for emphasizing shareholder wealth is more pragmatic. Firms that fail to create shareholder wealth are unlikely to be viewed as attractive investments. So, to continue attracting the financial capital needed to achieve its other goals, a firm must provide value to its stockholders.

But finding the mix of sources and uses of funds that maximize shareholder value isn't a simple process. Let's look at two major issues that confront financial managers as they seek to achieve their primary goal.

9-1a Shareholder Value and Social Responsibility: Does Good Behavior Pay Off?

The emphasis that financial managers place on maximizing shareholder value may seem to conflict with the modern view that a socially responsible firm has an obligation to respect the needs of *all* stakeholders—not just its owners, but also its employees, customers, creditors, suppliers, and even society as a whole.

finance The functional area of business that is concerned with finding the best sources and uses of financial capital.

PacificCare engages in social responsibility by letting its employees donate time to causes—in this case, building homes for people who lost theirs in Hurricane Katrina.

The good news is that being socially responsible *can* be (and often is) a good strategy for also achieving the goal of shareholder wealth maximization—especially if managers take a *long-term* perspective.

When a company respects the needs of customers by providing high-quality goods and services at competitive prices, and when it listens and responds fairly to their concerns, those customers are more likely to keep coming back—and to recommend the company to friends and relatives. Similarly, when a firm provides its employees with a good work environment, those employees are likely to have better morale and greater loyalty, resulting in higher productivity and lower employee turnover. And when a company supports its local community through corporate philanthropy or cause-related marketing, the resulting goodwill may boost sales and create a more favorable business climate. All of these outcomes suggest that a commitment to meeting social responsibilities can contribute to a more profitable company and an increase in shareholder value.[1]

But things aren't always that simple. Being socially responsible requires a long-term commitment to the needs of many different stakeholders. Unfortunately, the incentives of top executives (in the form of raises, bonuses, and other perks) are often tied to their firm's *short-term* performance. In such cases, some managers focus on policies that make their firm's stock price rise in the short run, but which are unsustainable over the long haul. And when managers fix their attention on raising the market price of the company's stock in the next year (or next quarter), concerns about social responsibility sometimes get lost in the shuffle.

It is also worth noting that responding to the needs of all stakeholders isn't always a simple and straightforward task. Diverse stakeholder groups can have very different goals, and finding the right balance among the competing interests of these groups can be difficult. For example, a firm's managers might believe they can increase profits (and the value of its stock) by shutting down a plant in the United States and outsourcing the work to China. While this might benefit shareholders, it would clearly be detrimental to its U.S. workforce and the community in which that current plant is located. When conflicts arise between the long-term interests of owners and those of other stakeholders, financial managers generally adopt the policies they believe are most consistent with the interests of ownership.

9-1b Risk and Return: A Fundamental Tradeoff in Financial Management

One of the most important lessons in financial management is that there is a tradeoff between risk and return. In financial management, **risk** refers to the degree of uncertainty about the actual outcome of a decision. The **risk-return tradeoff** suggests that sources and uses of funds that offer the potential for high rates of return tend to be riskier than sources and uses of funds that offer lower returns.

Financial managers want to earn an attractive rate of return for shareholders. But they also must realize that the higher the expected return they seek, the more they expose

risk The degree of uncertainty regarding the outcome of a decision.

risk-return tradeoff The observation that financial opportunities that offer high rates of return are generally riskier than opportunities that offer lower rates of return.

their company to risk. Our nation's recent economic history illustrates this point. In the years just prior to the Great Recession, many firms in the financial sector invested heavily in the housing market—a strategy that offered the potential for high returns but was very risky. Many of these same firms chose to finance most of their investments by increasing their own debt, which made the risk even greater.

When the housing market faltered, and prices dropped, these firms found themselves in serious trouble as their debts came due at the same time the value of their investments was falling.

Many of the companies who engaged in these risky strategies went belly-up during the early stages of the financial meltdown. The list of failures included some major banks and Wall Street firms that had been considered icons of free-market capitalism. Firms with almost $1.2 trillion in assets filed for bankruptcy in 2008. To put that in perspective, the total asset value of all of the firms that went bankrupt in the post-9/11 recession of 2001–2002 (a downturn that included the bankruptcies of Enron, WorldCom, and several other huge corporations) was less than $500 billion. And it could have been worse; without massive assistance (what some critics call a "bailout") by the federal government, many other major corporations might have suffered the same fate.[2]

9-2 IDENTIFYING FINANCIAL NEEDS: EVALUATION AND PLANNING

Before financial managers can determine the best financial strategies for their firm, they must identify existing strengths and weaknesses. Then they must devise financial plans that provide a roadmap the firm can use to improve financial performance and acquire the resources needed to achieve its short-term and long-term objectives.

9-2a Using Ratio Analysis to Identify Current Strengths and Weaknesses

One way financial managers evaluate a firm's current strengths and weaknesses is by computing ratios that compare values of key accounts listed on their firm's financial statements—mainly its balance sheet and income statement. This technique is called **financial ratio analysis**. Over the years, financial managers have developed an impressive array of specific ratios. The most important fall into four basic categories: liquidity, asset management, leverage, and profitability. Because financial needs differ across industries, for example, the automobile industry is capital intensive (it takes billions of dollars to

design new cars and build or refurbish factories) while the software industry is not (the marginal cost of producing another copy of a software program or app is close to zero), it's standard practice to compare a firm's financial ratios to industry averages. We'll do just that as we work through the financial ratios below by continuing our financial analysis of McDonald's, which we began in Chapter 8 on accounting where you learned the basics of income statements, balance sheets, and cash flows.[3]

1. **Liquidity ratios:** In finance, a **liquid asset** is one that can be quickly converted into cash with little risk of loss. **Liquidity ratios** measure the ability of an organization to convert assets into the cash it needs to pay off liabilities that come due in the next year.

   One of the simplest and most commonly used liquidity ratios is the *current ratio*, which is computed by dividing a firm's current assets by its current liabilities. Current assets include cash and other assets expected to be converted into cash in the next year, while current liabilities are the debts that must be repaid in the next year. The larger the current ratio, the easier it is for a firm to pay its short-term debts. A current ratio below 1.0 signifies that a company does not have enough current assets to pay short-term liabilities. In April 2015, McDonald's current ratio was 1.52 compared to the industry average of 1.52. While McDonald's current ratio is nearly identical to the industry, both share healthy financial liquidity ratios because they have 51% to 52% more current assets than current liabilities. But, as we'll explain when we discuss how firms manage cash and other liquid assets, it is also possible to have too much liquidity.

2. **Asset management ratios:** **Asset management ratios** (also sometimes called *activity ratios*) measure how effectively an organization uses its assets to generate net income. For example, the *inventory turnover ratio*—computed by dividing the firm's cost of goods sold by average inventory levels—measures how many times a firm's inventory is sold and replaced each year. For example, if

financial ratio analysis Computing ratios that compare values of key accounts listed on a firm's financial statements.

liquid asset An asset that can quickly be converted into cash with little risk of loss.

liquidity ratios Financial ratios that measure the ability of a firm to obtain the cash it needs to pay its short-term debt obligations as they come due.

asset management ratios Financial ratios that measure how effectively a firm is using its assets to generate revenues or cash.

a company keeps an average of 100 finished widgets in inventory each month, and it sold 1,000 widgets this year, then it turned its inventory ten times. A high turnover ratio is good because it indicates that a firm can continue its daily operations with a small amount of inventory on hand. It's expensive to have unsold inventory sitting on shelves, that is, low inventory turns. Companies with high inventory turns, which replenish inventory levels more frequently, have less cash tied up in inventory, which means those funds can be used elsewhere. However, inventory turnover ratios can be *too* high. When that happens, the company isn't keeping enough goods in stock, causing stockouts, which frustrates customers and results in lost sales if they take their business elsewhere.

In April 2015, McDonald's inventory turnover ratio of 145 was much stronger than the industry average of 29. In other words, McDonald's carries 2.5 days' worth of inventory on average, compared to the average fast-food restaurant, which carries 12.6 days of inventory.

For firms that sell a lot of goods on credit, the *average collection period* is another important asset management ratio. This ratio is computed by dividing accounts receivable by average daily credit sales. A value of 45 for this ratio means that customers take 45 days (on average) to pay for their credit purchases. In general, the smaller the ratio the better, since a lower value indicates that the firm's customers are paying for their purchases more quickly. But we'll see in our discussion of working capital management that low collection periods can also have drawbacks. In April 2015, McDonald's average collection period was 18 days, compared to the fast-food industry average of 9 days. Typically, average collection periods under 30 days are considered to be very strong.

3. **Leverage ratios: Financial leverage** is the use of debt to meet a firm's financing needs; a *highly leveraged* firm is one that relies heavily on debt. While the use of leverage can benefit a firm when times are good, a high degree of leverage is very risky. As we mentioned earlier, the extensive use of debt financing by big banks and major Wall Street firms played a major role in the financial

meltdown that began during the latter part of the past decade.

Leverage ratios measure the extent to which a firm uses financial leverage. One common measure of leverage is the *debt-to-asset ratio* (sometimes just called the *debt ratio*), which is computed by dividing a firm's total liabilities by its total assets. If a firm financed half its assets with debt and half with owners' equity, its debt ratio would be 0.5 (or 50%). The higher the debt-to-asset ratio, the more heavily leveraged the firm is. In April 2015, McDonald's debt-to-asset ratio was 43.7%, compared to an industry average of 24% indicating that McDonald's had nearly twice the debt of the typical fast-food company.

4. **Profitability ratios:** Firms are in business to earn a profit, and **profitability ratios** provide measures of how successful they are at achieving this goal. There are many different profitability ratios, but we'll look at just a couple of examples. *Return-on-equity* (ROE), calculated by dividing net income (profit) by owners' equity, measures the income earned per dollar invested by the stockholders. In April 2015, McDonald's ROE was 33%, compared to an industry average of 22.5%, so a dollar invested in McDonald's produces a larger return to shareholders than the fast-food industry on average.

Another profitability ratio, called *earnings per share* (EPS), indicates how much net income a firm earned per share of common stock outstanding. It is calculated by dividing net income minus preferred dividends by the average number of shares of common stock outstanding. In March 2015, McDonald's EPS was 4.85, compared to the industry average of 8.71. So EPS shows that McDonald's has been less profitable and a worse investment than the fast-food industry on average.

Exhibit 9.1 defines each of the ratios we've just described and shows how it is computed. As you look at the exhibit, keep in mind that it represents only a sample of the financial ratios used by financial managers.

9-2b Planning Tools: Creating a Road Map to the Future

Ratio analysis helps managers identify their firm's current financial strengths and weaknesses. The next step is to develop plans that build on the firm's strengths and correct its weaknesses. Financial planning is an important part of the firm's overall planning process. Assuming that the overall planning process has established appropriate goals and

financial leverage The use of debt in a firm's capital structure.

leverage ratios Ratios that measure the extent to which a firm relies on debt financing in its capital structure.

profitability ratios Ratios that measure the rate of return a firm is earning on various measures of investment.

EXHIBIT 9.1   KEY FINANCIAL RATIOS

Ratio Name	Type	What It Measures	How It Is Computed
Current	Liquidity: measures ability to pay short-term liabilities as they come due.	Compares current assets (assets that will provide cash in the next year) to current liabilities (debts that will come due in the next year).	$\dfrac{Current\ Assets}{Current\ Liabilities}$
Inventory Turnover	Asset management: measures how effectively a firm is using its assets to generate revenue.	How quickly a firm sells its inventory to generate revenue.	$\dfrac{Cost\ of\ Goods\ Sold}{Average\ Inventory}$
Average Collection Period	Asset management: measures how effectively a firm is using its assets to generate revenue.	How long it takes for a firm to collect from customers who buy on credit.	$\dfrac{Accounts\ Receivable}{\left(\dfrac{Annual\ Credit\ Sales}{365}\right)}$
Debt-to-Assets	Leverage: measures the extent to which a firm relies on debt to meet its financing needs.	Similar to debt-to-equity, but compares debt to assets rather than equity. This is another way of measuring the degree of financial leverage, or debt, the firm is using.	$\dfrac{Total\ Debt}{Total\ Assets}$
Return on Equity	Profitability: compares the amount of profit to some measure of resources invested.	Indicates earnings per dollar invested by the owners of the company. Since common stockholders are the true owners, preferred stockholders' dividends are deducted from net income before computing this ratio.	$\dfrac{Net\ Income - Preferred\ Dividend}{Average\ Common\ Stockholders\ Equity}$
Earnings per Share	Profitability: compares the amount of profit to some measure of resources invested.	Measures the net income per share of common stock outstanding.	$\dfrac{Net\ Income - Preferred\ Dividend}{Average\ Number\ of\ Common\ Shares\ Outstanding}$

© Cengage Learning®

objectives for the firm, financial planning must answer the following questions:

- What specific assets must the firm obtain to achieve its goals?

- How much additional financing will the firm need to acquire these assets?

- How much financing will the firm be able to generate internally (through additional earnings), and how much must it obtain from external sources?

- When will the firm need to acquire external financing?

- What is the best way to raise these funds?

The planning process involves input from a variety of areas. In addition to seeking input from managers in various functional areas of their business, financial managers usually work closely with the firm's accountants during the planning process.

Mgkaya/iStockphoto.com

9-2c Basic Planning Tools: Budgeted Financial Statements and the Cash Budget

The budgeting process provides financial managers with much of the information they need for financial planning. The **budgeted income statement** and **budgeted balance sheet** are

budgeted income statement A projection showing how a firm's budgeted sales and costs will affect expected net income. (Also called a pro forma income statement.)

budgeted balance sheet A projected financial statement that forecasts the types and amounts of assets a firm will need to implement its future plans and how the firm will finance those assets. (Also called a pro forma balance sheet.)

Exhibit 9.2

Cash Budget for Oze-Moore

Cash Budget for Oze-Moore

	February	March	April	May
Sales	$75,000	$110,000	$125,000	$90,000
Cash balance at beginning of month		$10,000	$10,000	$10,000
Receipts of Cash				
Cash sales		$16,500	$18,750	$13,500
Collection of accounts receivable from last month's sales		$63,750	$93,500	$106,250
Total Cash Available		$90,250	$122,250	$129,750
Disbursements of Cash				
Payment of accounts payable		$60,500	$68,750	$49,500
Wages and salaries		$27,500	$31,250	$22,500
Fixed costs (rent, interest on debt, etc.)		$8,000	$8,000	$8,000
Purchase of new computers			$6,500	
Total Cash Payments		$96,000	$114,500	$80,000
Excess or Deficit of Cash for Month		-$5,750	$7,750	$49,750
Loans needed to maintain cash balance of $10,000		$15,750	$2,250	$0
Amount of cash available to repay short-term loans		$0	$0	$39,750
Cash balance at end of month		$10,000	$10,000	$31,750
Cumulative loans		$15,750	$18,000	$0

Sales increase in both March and April. But since most of Oze-Moore's customers buy on credit, its receipt of cash lags behind these sales increases.

While receipts of cash lag behind sales, Oze-Moore's payments of wages and accounts payable are due in the same month as sales.

Despite big increases in sales in March and April, Oze-Moore suffers a shortfall of cash because of the difference in timing between cash receipts and cash payments.

Financial managers want to have at least $10,000 in the cash balance at the beginning of each month. When cash falls below this amount they take out a short-term loan.

In May, Oze-Moore has a surplus in cash. This gives it enough cash to pay off the loans from earlier months.

© Cengage Learning®

two key financial planning tools. Also called *pro forma financial statements*, they provide a framework for analyzing the impact of the firm's plans on the financing needs of the company.

- The budgeted income statement uses information from the sales budget and various cost budgets (as well as other assumptions) to develop a forecast of net income for the planning period. This can help the firm evaluate how much internal financing (funds generated by earnings) will be available.

- The budgeted balance sheet forecasts the types and amounts of assets a firm will need to implement its future plans. It also helps financial managers determine the amount of additional financing (liabilities and owners' equity) the firm must arrange to acquire those assets.

The **cash budget** is another important financial planning tool. Cash budgets normally cover a one-year period and show projected cash inflows and outflows for each month. Financial managers use cash budgets to get a better understanding of the *timing* of cash flows within the planning period. This is

cash budget A detailed forecast of future cash flows that helps financial managers identify when their firm is likely to experience temporary shortages or surpluses of cash.

important because most firms experience uneven inflows and outflows of cash over the course of a year, which can lead to cash shortages and cash surpluses. Projecting cash flows helps financial managers determine when the firm is likely to need additional funds to meet short-term cash shortages, and when surpluses of cash will be available to pay off loans or to invest in other assets.

Even firms with growing sales can experience cash flow problems, especially if many of their customers buy on credit. To meet increasing sales levels, a growing firm must hire more labor and buy more supplies. These workers and suppliers may expect to be paid well before the company's customers pay their bills, leading to a temporary cash crunch.

Exhibit 9.2 illustrates this type of situation by presenting a partial cash budget for a hypothetical firm called Oze-Moore. The cash budget shows that, despite its increasing sales, Oze-Moore will have cash shortages in March and April. Knowing this in advance gives financial managers time to find the best sources of short-term financing to cover these shortages. The cash budget also shows that Oze-Moore will experience a big cash surplus in May as the customers start paying for the purchases they made in March and April. Knowing this ahead of time helps managers forecast when they will be able to repay the loans they took out to cover their previous cash shortages. It also gives them time to evaluate short-term interest-earning investments they could make to temporarily "park" their surplus cash.

9-3 FINDING FUNDS: WHAT ARE THE OPTIONS?

Once financial managers have identified the amount of financial capital needed to carry out their firm's plans, the next step is to determine which sources of funds to tap. The most appropriate sources of funds for a business depend on several factors. One of the most important considerations is the firm's stage of development. Start-up firms face different challenges and have different needs than more established firms. Another factor is the reason the funds are needed. Funds used to meet short-term needs, such as meeting payroll, paying suppliers, or paying taxes, typically come from different sources than funds used to finance major investments in plants, property, and equipment.

The financing options available to new firms are generally much more limited than those available to more mature firms with an established track record. In fact, for start-up firms the main source of funds is likely to be the personal wealth of the owner (or owners), supplemented by loans from relatives and friends. Given how risky new business ventures are, banks and other established lenders often hesitate to make loans to new, unproven companies. (In some cases, the Small Business Administration overcomes this reluctance by guaranteeing loans for start-ups and other small businesses that satisfy its criteria.) As the firms grow and become more established, they typically are able to obtain financing from other sources.

Some start-ups with the potential for generating rapid growth may be able to attract funds from wealthy individuals, called *angel investors*, or from venture capital firms. Both angel investors and venture capitalists typically invest in risky opportunities that offer the possibility of high rates of return. Both also typically provide funds in exchange for a share of ownership.

9-3a Sources of Short-Term Financing: Meeting Needs for Cash

Firms that have survived the start-up phase of the business life cycle often have several sources of short-term financing. Let's take a look at some of the most common options.

TRADE CREDIT One of the most important sources of short-term financing for many firms is **trade credit**, which arises when suppliers ship materials, parts, or goods

to a firm without requiring payment at the time of delivery. By allowing the firms to "buy now, pay later," they help the firm conserve its existing cash, thus avoiding the need to acquire funds from other sources.

In most cases, the terms of trade credit are presented on the invoice the supplier

> **trade credit** Spontaneous financing granted by sellers when they deliver goods and services to customers without requiring immediate payment.

IS DONATING 5% OF PROFITS TO CHARITY SOCIALLY RESPONSIBLE OR GOOD FOR BUSINESS?

According to Nobel Prize–winning economist Milton Friedman, the only social responsibility organizations have is satisfying company shareholders by maximizing profits, the company's stock price, and the value of the firm.

If that's the case, then why does Whole Foods Market donate 5% of its profits to charity each year? Shouldn't it reinvest those funds back into the business (i.e., retained earnings) or distribute profits as dividends to shareholders? However, Whole Foods not only distributes 5% of its annual profits, it also holds "5% Days" in which each store donates 5% of daily total sales to nonprofit organizations.

Sounds warm and fuzzy, doesn't it? But CEO John Mackey believes that 5% Days are good business! Mackey says, "While our stores select worthwhile organizations to support, they also tend to focus on groups that have large membership lists, which are contacted and encouraged to shop our store that day to support the organization. This usually brings hundreds of new or lapsed customers into our stores, many of whom then become regular shoppers. So a 5% Day not only allows us to support worthwhile causes, but is an excellent marketing strategy that has benefited Whole Foods investors immensely."

Milton Friedman would say that while Whole Foods' 5% contributions look like social responsibility, they're really just a means to maximize profits by enhancing Whole Foods' reputation and to bring more customers into stores.

So is Whole Foods "doing good" or it is trying to increase profits? Which comes first, profits or social responsibility? What do you think?[4]

---

includes with the shipment. For example, the invoice might list the terms as 2/10 net 30. The "net 30" indicates that the supplier allows the buyer 30 days before payment is due. But the "2/10" tells the buyer that the supplier is offering a 2% discount off the invoice price if the buyer pays within 10 days.

At first glance, the 2% discount in our example may not seem like a big deal. But failing to take the discount can be very costly. Consider the terms we mentioned above: 2/10, net 30. If the firm fails to pay within 10 days, it loses the discount and must pay the full amount 20 days later. Paying 2% more for the use of funds for only 20 days is equivalent to an *annual* finance charge of over 37%![5]

Suppliers will grant trade credit only after they've evaluated the creditworthiness of the firm. But once they've granted this credit to a company, they generally continue offering it as long as the firm satisfies the terms of the credit arrangements. Trade credit is sometimes called **spontaneous financing** because it is granted when the company places its orders without requiring any additional paperwork or special arrangements. The level of trade credit automatically adjusts as business conditions change and the company places larger or smaller orders with its suppliers.

Although firms of all sizes use this type of financing, trade credit is a particularly important source of financing for small businesses. The Federal Reserve Board's *Survey of Small Business Finances* indicates that about 60% of small firms rely on trade credit as a major source of short-term financial capital.[6]

FACTORING The money that customers owe a firm when they buy on credit shows up in accounts receivable on the company's balance sheet. A **factor** buys the accounts receivables of other firms. The factor makes a profit by purchasing the receivables at a discount and collecting the full amount from the firm's customers.

Although firms that use factors don't receive the full amount their customers owe, factoring offers some definite advantages. Instead of having to wait for customers to pay, the firm gets its money almost immediately. Also, since the factor is responsible for collection efforts, the firm using the factor may be able to save money by eliminating its own collection department. Finally, the factor typically assumes the risk for bad debts on any receivables it buys. (However, factors typically perform a careful evaluation of the quality of accounts receivable before they buy them and may refuse to buy receivables that are high risk.) According to the Commercial Finance Association, factoring has typically provided more than $176.5 billion dollars in short-term funds on an annual basis to American businesses in recent years.[7]

SHORT-TERM BANK LOANS Banks are another common source of short-term business financing. Short-term bank loans are usually due in 30 to 90 days, though they can be up to a year in length. When a firm negotiates a loan with a bank, it signs a *promissory note*, which specifies the length of the loan, the rate of interest the firm must pay, and other terms and conditions of the loan. Banks sometimes require firms to pledge collateral, such as inventories or accounts receivable, to back the loan. That way, if the borrower fails to make the required payments, the bank has a claim on specific assets that can be used to pay off the amount due.

Rather than going through the hassle of negotiating a separate loan each time they need more funds, many firms work out arrangements with their bankers to obtain pre-approval so that they can draw on funds as needed. One way they do this is by establishing a **line of credit**. Under this arrangement, a bank agrees to provide the firm with funds up to some specified limit, as long as the borrower's credit situation doesn't deteriorate, and the bank has sufficient funds—conditions that aren't always met, as the recent financial meltdown clearly illustrated.

A **revolving credit agreement** is similar to a line of credit, except that the bank makes a formal, legally binding commitment to provide the agreed-upon funds. In essence, a revolving credit agreement is a *guaranteed* line of credit. In exchange for the binding commitment to provide the funds, the bank requires the borrowing firm to pay a commitment fee based on the *unused* amount of funds. Thus, under the terms of a revolving credit agreement, the

spontaneous financing
Financing that arises during the natural course of business without the need for special arrangements.

factor A company that provides short-term financing to firms by purchasing their accounts receivables at a discount.

line of credit A financial arrangement between a firm and a bank in which the bank pre-approves credit up to a specified limit, provided that the firm maintains an acceptable credit rating.

revolving credit agreement
A guaranteed line of credit in which a bank makes a binding commitment to provide a business with funds up to a specified credit limit at any time during the term of the agreement.

Gunnar Pippel/Shutterstock.com

firm will pay interest on any funds it borrows, and a commitment fee on any funds it does not borrow. The commitment fee is lower than the interest on the borrowed funds, but it can amount to a fairly hefty charge if the firm has a large unused balance.

COMMERCIAL PAPER Well-established corporations have some additional sources of short-term financial capital. For instance, many large corporations with strong credit ratings issue **commercial paper**, which consists of short-term promissory notes (IOUs). Historically, commercial paper issued by corporations has been unsecured—meaning it isn't backed by a pledge of collateral. Because it is normally unsecured, commercial paper is only offered by firms with excellent credit ratings; firms with less-than-stellar financial reputations that try to issue unsecured commercial paper are unlikely to find buyers. In recent years, a new class of commercial paper has emerged, called *asset-backed commercial paper*, which, as its name implies, is backed by some form of collateral.

Commercial paper can be issued for up to 270 days, but most firms typically issue it for much shorter periods— typically 30 days, but sometimes for as little as two days. One key reason commercial paper is popular with companies is that it typically carries a lower interest rate than commercial banks charge on short-term loans. By far the biggest issuers of commercial paper are financial institutions, but other large corporations also use this form of financing.

Why use commercial paper? According to the Consumerist, "The commercial paper market works like a credit card for big companies. Some days they have money, and some days they do not. So if they need money Tuesday, but will have money Friday, they'll go to the commercial paper market and borrow some money. Then on Friday they will pay back the money, plus interest."[8] Apple paid 0.15% interest, an extremely low rate, for commercial paper in 2013.[9] For $1 million of Apple 6-month commercial paper, Apple gets the $1 million for its own use for 6 months, after which it pays back $1,015,000 (0.15% of $1 million is $15,000). Commercial paper accounted for 8% of all short-term corporate cash assets in April 2015, down from 11% in 2013.[10]

9-3b Sources of Long-Term Funds: Providing a Strong Financial Base

The sources of financial capital we've looked at so far have been appropriate for dealing with cash needs that arise from short-term fluctuations in cash flows. But financial managers typically seek more permanent funding to finance major investments and provide a secure financial base for their company. Let's take a look at some of the more common sources of long-term funds.

DIRECT INVESTMENTS FROM OWNERS One key source of long-term funds for a firm is the money the owners themselves invest in their company. For corporations, this occurs when it sells *newly issued* stock—and it's important to realize that the *only* time the corporation receives financial capital from the sale of its stock is when it is initially issued. If Google issued new shares of stock which you bought, the funds would go to Google. But once you own Google's stock, if you decide to sell your shares to another investor, Google gets nothing.

Another way firms can meet long-term financial needs is by reinvesting their earnings. The profits that a firm reinvests are called **retained earnings**. This source isn't a pool of cash; it simply reflects the share of the firm's earnings used to finance the purchase of assets, pay off liabilities, and reinvest in the business. If you want to know how much cash a firm has, check the figure in the cash account at the top of its balance sheet. You'll typically find that the value in the firm's cash account is quite different from the amount listed as the retained earnings! For example, in 2014, Google had $75.7 billion in retained earnings compared to $8.5 billion in cash and cash equivalents.[11]

Retained earnings are a major source of long-term capital for many corporations, but the extent to which they are used depends on the state of the economy. When the economy is booming and profits are high, retained earnings tend to soar. But when the economy slides into a recession, most corporations find they have few earnings to reinvest. For instance, in the recession year of 2008, corporate retained earnings fell to $157 billion from $430 billion in 2006, and then rose to $737 billion in 2011 after the economy recovered—a drop of well over 60%.[12]

The decision to retain earnings involves a tradeoff because firms have another way to use their earnings: they can pay out some or all of their profits to their owners by declaring a dividend. You might think that stockholders would be unhappy with a firm that retained most of its earnings, since that would mean they would receive a smaller dividend. But many stockholders actually prefer their companies to reinvest earnings—at least if management invests them wisely—because doing so can help finance their firm's growth. And a growing, more profitable firm usually translates into an increase in the market price of the firm's stock.

> **commercial paper** Short-term (and usually unsecured) promissory notes issued by large corporations.
>
> **retained earnings** The part of a firm's net income it reinvests.

Billionaire Warren Buffet's company, Berkshire Hathaway, has never paid dividends, choosing to reinvest all of its substantial profits. This strategy paid off handsomely for stockholders. During the 12-year period between March 30, 2004, and March 24, 2015, Berkshire's stock soared from $93,000 to $217,005 per share.[13] Despite the fact that it paid them no dividend, you can bet that most of Berkshire's shareholders were pleased with the capital gains that resulted from this strategy!

LONG-TERM DEBT In addition to contributions from owners, firms can also raise long-term funds by borrowing from banks and other lenders or by issuing bonds.

TERM LOANS There are many different types of long-term loans, but the most typical arrangement—sometimes simply called a *term loan*—calls for a regular schedule of fixed payments sufficient to ensure that the principal (the amount initially borrowed) and interest are repaid by the end of the loan's term.

Lenders often impose requirements on long-term loans to ensure repayment. Most lenders require that the loans be backed by a pledge of some type of collateral. Banks and other lenders also often include *covenants* in their loan agreements. A **covenant** is a requirement a lender imposes on the borrower as a condition of the loan. One common covenant requires the borrower to carry a specified amount of liability insurance. Another requires the borrower to agree not to borrow any *additional* funds until the current loan is paid off. Covenants sometimes even restrict the size of bonuses or pay raises the firm can grant to employees. The purpose of covenants is to protect creditors by preventing the borrower from pursuing policies that might undermine its ability to repay the loan. While covenants are great for lenders, borrowers often view them as highly restrictive.[14]

CORPORATE BONDS Rather than borrow from banks or other lenders, corporations sometimes issue their own formal IOUs, called *corporate bonds*, which they sell to investors. Bonds often have due dates (maturities) of ten or more years after issuance. Like corporate stock, bonds are marketable, meaning that bondholders can sell them to other investors before they mature. But it is important to realize that unlike shares of stock, which represent ownership in a corporation, bonds are certificates of debt.

> "WHEN YOU COMBINE IGNORANCE AND LEVERAGE, YOU GET SOME PRETTY INTERESTING RESULTS."
>
> —WARREN BUFFET

covenant A restriction lenders impose on borrowers as a condition of providing long-term debt financing.

equity financing Funds provided by the owners of a company.

debt financing Funds provided by lenders (creditors).

capital structure The mix of equity and debt financing a firm uses to meet its permanent financing needs.

9-4 LEVERAGE AND CAPITAL STRUCTURE: HOW MUCH DEBT IS TOO MUCH DEBT?

Most firms use a combination of **equity** and **debt financing** to acquire needed assets and to finance their operations. Owners provide equity financing, while creditors (lenders) provide debt financing. Thus, when a company issues and sells new stock or uses retained earnings to meet its financial needs, it is using equity financing. But when it takes out a bank loan, or issues and sells corporate bonds, it is relying on debt financing.

Both equity and debt financing have advantages and drawbacks. The extent to which a firm relies on various forms of debt and equity to satisfy its financing needs is called that firm's **capital structure**. To simplify our discussion, we'll focus mainly on the capital structure of corporations, but many of the basic principles apply to other forms of ownership.

9-4a Pros and Cons of Debt Financing

When a firm borrows funds, it enters into a contractual agreement with the lenders. This arrangement creates a *legally binding* requirement to repay the money borrowed (called the principal) *plus interest*. These payments take precedence over any payments to owners. Lenders often require the firm to pledge collateral, such as real estate, financial securities, or equipment, to back the loan. Should the firm be unable to make the required payments, the lenders can use this collateral to recover what they are owed.

Debt financing offers some advantages to firms. For instance, the interest payments a firm makes on debt are a tax-deductible expense. So Uncle Sam (in the form of the IRS) subsidizes the interest payments. For example, if the corporation's tax rate is 30%, then each

The Stone Brewing Company of Escondido, California, is more than a brewery—it's a destination. The nearly 300,000 barrels of beer it produces annually are distributed to 40 states. Its two farm-to-table restaurant locations can seat over 1,200 people and welcome over half a million guests a year. For ten years in a row, Stone Brewing has made *Inc.* magazine's list of fastest-growing private companies, and, since its launch, the company boasts a regular annual growth rate of 50%.

So, when Stone Brewing was shopping for its first location east of the Mississippi River, hundreds of cities lined up for consideration. The brewery wanted to invest millions of dollars to open a new distribution hub and restaurant employing roughly 350 people. After reviewing hundreds of proposals and visiting 40 sites in about 20 different states, Stone Brewing made a deal with the city of Richmond, Virginia.

Why did Richmond win the deal? Financing. Municipalities commonly try to entice businesses to their cities by putting together attractive packages of tax incentives and debt forgiveness. The city of Richmond, however, went even further. The city will spend $8 million to build the company a new restaurant and will fund the construction of the distribution center and brewery

with $23 million in bonds backed by the city of Richmond. (Stone will pay back the total of $31 million through lease payments.) In addition, Stone Brewing will be receiving roughly $7 million in grants from the city and the state of Virginia. (Grants do not need to be repaid.)

Funding packages like the one Richmond is providing Stone Brewing are becoming increasingly common. Rather than offering tax incentives or debt forgiveness, municipalities are transforming subsidies into investments in the businesses they court.

Not all residents are toasting the public-private partnership, however. Richmond restaurant and bar owners object to the funding package, claiming that the city is directing their tax dollars into funding an enterprise that will compete with them directly. Some are frustrated at the proceeds of what they consider a high meals tax on restaurants (6%) going to underwrite the development of a strong competitor in an already saturated market.

Michael Byrne, who owned a brewery in Richmond for 17 years and now runs The Tobacco Company Restaurant, highlights the disparity between the city's support of Stone Brewing compared to its support for local breweries. He argues that the Stone Brewing Company will be "competing with us head-on, on a site that is going to get the kind of money that you don't see in a small-business loan."[15]

What do YOU think?

- When seeking financing, is there an ethical limit to how aggressively businesses should pursue public money to fund expansion?
- How far should municipalities go to finance the business activity of their city?
- What ethical responsibility do municipal and state governments have toward their current constituents relative to larger newcomers?

Source: Stone Brewing Co.

---

dollar of interest expense reduces the firm's taxes by $0.30—meaning the true cost to the firm of each dollar of interest is only $0.70.

Another advantage of debt is that it enables the firm to acquire additional funds without requiring existing stockholders to invest more of their own money or the sale of stock to new investors (which would dilute the ownership of existing owners). Moreover, if the firm invests the borrowed funds profitably, the use of debt can substantially improve the return on equity to the

shareholders. We'll illustrate this result in our discussion of financial leverage.

One obvious disadvantage of debt is the requirement to make fixed payments. This can create real problems when the firm finds itself in an unexpectedly tight financial situation. In bad times, required interest payments can eat up most (or all) of the earnings, leaving little or no return to the firm's owners. And if the firm is unable to meet these payments, its creditors can force it into bankruptcy.

As we mentioned earlier, another disadvantage of debt financing is that creditors often impose covenants on the borrower. These covenants can hamper the firm's flexibility and might result in unintended problems. For example, a covenant that restricts bonuses and pay raises to employees might undermine the morale of key workers and tempt them to seek employment elsewhere. Similarly, restrictions on dividends or on the ability of the firm to borrow additional funds may make it difficult for the firm to raise more money.

9-4b Pros and Cons of Equity Financing

For corporations, equity financing comes from two major sources: retained earnings and money directly invested by stockholders who purchase newly issued stock. Equity financing is more flexible and less risky than debt financing. Unlike debt, equity imposes no required payments. A firm can skip dividend payments to stockholders without having to worry that it will be pushed into bankruptcy. And a firm doesn't have to agree to burdensome covenants to acquire equity funds.

On the other hand, equity financing doesn't yield the same tax benefits as debt financing. In addition, existing owners might not want a firm to issue more stock, since doing so might dilute their share of ownership. Finally, a company that relies mainly on equity financing forgoes the opportunity to use financial leverage. But as we've already noted, leverage can be a two-edged sword. We'll illustrate the risks and rewards of leverage in our next section.

9-4c Financial Leverage: Using Debt to Magnify Gains (and Losses)

As mentioned in our discussion of ratios, firms that rely on a lot of debt in their capital structure are said to be *highly leveraged*. The main advantage of financial leverage is that it magnifies the return on the stockholders' investment when times are good. Its main disadvantage is that it also reduces the financial return to stockholders when times are bad.

Let's illustrate both the advantages and disadvantages of financial leverage with a simple example. Exhibit 9.3 shows the revenues, expenses, and earnings that two firms—Eck-Witty Corporation and Oze-Moore International—would experience for two different levels of sales, one representing a strong year and the other a weak year. To make the impact of leverage easy to see, we'll assume that Eck-Witty and Oze-Moore are *identical* in all respects *except* their capital structure. In particular, our example assumes that the two companies have the same amount of assets and experienced exactly the same *earnings before interest and taxes* (abbreviated as EBIT). Thus, any differences in the net income of these firms results from differences in their use of debt and equity financing. We'll use return on equity (ROE) to measure the financial return each firm offers its stockholders. (See Exhibit 9.1 if you need a reminder about how to interpret or compute this ratio.)

Note that *both* firms have a total of $1 million in assets, but they've financed the purchase of their assets in very different ways. Eck-Witty used only common stock

Exhibit 9.3
How Financial Leverage Affects the Return on Equity

Eck-Witty (Capital structure is all only equity)

Equity (Funds supplied by owners)		$1,000,000
Debt (Funds obtained by borrowing)		$0

	Strong Sales	Weak Sales
EBIT	$160,000	$80,000
Interest	0	0
Taxable income	160,000	80,000
Taxes	40,000	20,000
After Tax Earnings	120,000	60,000
ROE	12.0%	6%

Eck-Witty's use of only equity financing results in a lower ROE than Oze-Moore's when sales are strong. But it enjoys better ROE than Oze-Moore when sales are weak.

Oze-Moore (Capital structure is 20% equity and 80% debt)

Equity (Funds supplied by owners)		$200,000
Debt (Funds obtained by borrowing)		$800,000

	Strong Sales	Weak Sales
EBIT	$160,000	$80,000
Interest	80,000	80,000
Taxable income	80,000	0
Taxes	20,000	0
After Tax Earnings	60,000	0
ROE	30.0%	0.0%

Oze-Moore's use of leverage magnifies ROE when sales are strong. But the required interest payments of $80,000 completely wipes out taxable income and after-tax earnings.

© Cengage Learning®

Is Twitter Stock Worth Its "Innovation Premium"?

When Twitter announced that it would sell stock through an IPO, many investors were skeptical. Twitter has small revenues (about $665 million annually), doesn't produce anything, and hasn't turned a profit. So, by traditional financial measures, Twitter shouldn't be highly valued. Enthusiastic investors, however, turned Twitter, at $31 billion, into one of the world's most valuable companies. So, why is a company that isn't even profitable worth so much?

Cosmin – Constantin Sava/Dreamstime.com

According to GameChanger CEO Larry Popelka, the answer is "innovation." Twitter revolutionized how people share information, photos, videos, and breaking news. And in today's "ideas economy," companies that fundamentally change established ways of doing business can quickly turn that advantage to skyrocketing revenues. Stock market "innovation premiums," however, are always based on high growth, and in Twitter's case, that means expanding its user base. When more people establish Twitter accounts and send and read tweets, Twitter becomes more valuable.

Unfortunately, many people don't "get" Twitter. Christine Harsono, a 21-year-old waitress says that, with Facebook, "I feel like I already have a place for me to see all these things [i.e., news and celebrity gossip]. I don't really see a need for Twitter." While Twitter's active user base is growing at an annual rate of 30%, it will still take the company nearly 14 years to match Facebook's 1.23-billion user base.

Is Twitter worth an "innovation premium" without high growth? If Twitter's growth trends continue, it could be worth much less.[16]

---

and retained earnings in its capital structure, so it has $1 million in equity financing and no debt. Oze-Moore's capital structure consists of $200,000 in owners' equity and $800,000 in debt, so it is highly leveraged. The interest rate on its debt is 10%, so Oze-Moore has to make required interest payments of $80,000 per year to its lenders. Both companies must pay taxes equal to 25% of their earnings, but Oze-Moore's total tax bill will be lower than Eck-Witty's because its interest payments are tax-deductible.

As Exhibit 9.3 shows, when sales are strong, Oze-Moore's use of leverage really pays off. Eck-Witty's ROE of 12% under the strong sales scenario isn't bad, but it pales in comparison to the 30% return Oze-Moore generates for its owners under the same scenario. Oze-Moore's higher ROE occurs because its interest payments are *fixed*. It pays its creditors $80,000—no more, no less—whether EBIT is high or low. When Oze-Moore can borrow funds at an interest rate of 10% and invest them in assets that earn *more* than 10% (as it does in the strong sales scenario), the extra return goes to the *owners* even though creditors provided the funds. This clearly adds a significant boost to the returns enjoyed by the stockholders!

> **"DEBT IS ONE PERSON'S LIABILITY, BUT ANOTHER PERSON'S ASSET."**
>
> —NOBEL PRIZE–WINNING ECONOMIST PAUL KRUGMAN

But in the weak sales scenario, the results are quite different. In this case, the $80,000 of *required* interest payments eats up all of Oze-Moore's earnings, leaving it with no net income for its owners, so its ROE is zero. If EBIT had been anything less than $80,000, Oze-Moore wouldn't have had enough earnings to cover the interest—and if it failed to come up with the money to pay its creditors, they could force it into bankruptcy. This illustrates the risk associated with financial leverage. In comparison, notice that Eck-Witty still earns a positive ROE for its owners in the weak sales scenario; granted an ROE of 6% isn't spectacular, but it sure beats the 0% return Oze-Moore experienced!

Our leverage example contains important lessons for the real world—lessons that recent financial history clearly illustrates. During the economic boom between 2003 and early 2007, many companies found that the use of leverage magnified their ROEs. When the economy slowed, the required interest and principal payments on their debt became a heavy burden on highly leveraged firms. As we mentioned at the beginning of this chapter, many of these firms ended up in bankruptcy.

By late 2008, many of the highly leveraged firms that survived the initial carnage were frantically looking for ways to replace much of the debt in their capital structure with more equity—a strategy known as *deleveraging*. Unfortunately, most companies found deleveraging to be a slow and painful process. Their poor financial performance during the financial meltdown meant their earnings were low (or even negative), so they couldn't use retained earnings to build their equity capital. And the plummeting stock market and lack of investor confidence made it difficult to sell new stock. The moral of the story: if the financial returns of leverage seem too good to be true, over the long run they probably are. Sound financial management requires keeping a level head and considering the riskiness of financial decisions as well as their return.[17]

In the wake of the financial crisis, the federal government enacted new legislation designed to reduce the likelihood of similar meltdowns in the future. The **Dodd-Frank Act** included requirements for large firms in the financial sector to hold more equity and less debt in their capital structures and established a Financial Stability Oversight Council to monitor financial markets and to identify and respond to emerging risks. It also created a Consumer Financial Protection Bureau to protect consumers from predatory lending practices by financial institutions.[18]

9-5 ACQUIRING AND MANAGING CURRENT ASSETS

Let's turn our attention to how a firm determines the amount and type of current assets to hold. As we'll see, holding current assets involves tradeoff; either too much or too little of these assets can spell trouble.

9-5a Managing Cash: Is It Possible to Have Too Much Money?

A company must have cash to pay its workers, suppliers, creditors, and taxes. Many firms also need cash to pay dividends. And most firms also want to hold enough cash to meet unexpected contingencies. But cash has one serious shortcoming compared to other assets: it earns little or no return. If a firm holds much more cash

Dodd-Frank Act A law enacted in the aftermath of the financial crisis of 2008–2009 that strengthened government oversight of financial markets and placed limitations on risky financial strategies such as heavy reliance on leverage.

cash equivalents Safe and highly liquid assets that many firms list with their cash holdings on their balance sheet.

U.S. Treasury bills (T-bills) Short-term marketable IOUs issued by the U.S. federal government.

than needed to meet its required payments, stockholders are likely to ask why the excess cash isn't being invested in more profitable assets. And if the firm can't find a profitable way to invest the money, the stockholders are likely to ask management why it doesn't use the excess cash to pay them a higher dividend—most shareholders can think of plenty of ways *they'd* like to use the cash!

In the narrowest sense, a firm's cash refers to its holdings of currency (paper money and coins issued by the government) plus demand deposits (the balance in its checking account). However, when most firms report their cash holdings on their balance sheet, they take a broader view, including **cash equivalents** along with their actual cash. Cash equivalents are very safe and highly liquid assets that can be converted into cash quickly and easily. Commercial paper, U.S. Treasury Bills (T-bills), and money market mutual funds are among the most popular cash equivalents. The advantage of these cash equivalents is that they offer a better financial return (in the form of interest) than currency or demand deposits.

As we explained in our discussion of short-term sources of funds, major corporations with strong credit ratings often *sell* commercial paper to raise needed short-term funds. On the other side of such transactions are firms that *buy* commercial paper as part of their portfolio of cash equivalents because—at least under normal economic conditions—it is a safe and liquid way to earn some interest. But during economic downturns the appeal of commercial paper as a cash equivalent plummets due to increased risk.

U.S. Treasury bills, or "T-bills," are short-term IOUs issued by the U.S. government. Most T-bills mature (come due) in 4, 13, or 26 weeks. There is a very active secondary market for T-bills, meaning that their owners can sell them to other investors before they mature. Thus, T-bills are highly liquid. And, unlike commercial paper, T-bills are backed by the U.S. government, so they are

PrideBites Dog Toys "Factors" Accounts Receivable into Start-up Funds

PrideBites is an Austin, Texas-based company that sells durable, washable dog toys made of foam covered by two layers of fleece. PrideBites are light and soft, they float in water, and can withstand 55 pounds of "pull pressure" for games of doggie tug-of-war. And, like all good dog toys, they squeak! Furthermore, you can customize your PrideBites toy with pictures of people, your dog (or perhaps better, your cat), or in the shape of a dog bone with your dog's name on it. Indeed, PrideBites' founders knew their custom dogs toys were a great idea when they sold 50 in the shape of a

© Graphic design/Shutterstock.com

Trojan warrior in less than an hour at a University of Southern California football game. Furthermore, PrideBites received the 2012 award for "best dog toy" from *Pet Business*, as well as a similar award from Dogintonpost.com.

While founder Steven Blustein knew he had a great product, he and his partners didn't have enough cash to start their company. So, they turned to factors for funding. A "factor" is a company that provides short-term financing by purchasing accounts receivable at a discount. Blustein said, "It was expensive," because PrideBites paid 15% on every dollar of receivables for 16 large sales its first year of business. While expensive, the primary advantage is that instead of waiting for customers to pay, the firm gets its money immediately, and that gave PrideBites enough to pay operating expenses and start their business. Says Blustein, factoring "is an amazing strategy when you can't go to a bank and you're trying to get a product out there." PrideBite toys are now available at 3,100 retailers, and the company expects to earn a profit this year.[19]

essentially risk-free. The safety and liquidity of T-bills make them very attractive cash equivalents even in times of economic distress.

Money market mutual funds raise money by selling shares to large numbers of investors. They then pool these funds to purchase a portfolio of short-term, liquid securities. (In fact, money market mutual funds often include large holdings of commercial paper and T-bills.) Money market mutual funds are an affordable way for small investors to get into the market for securities, which would otherwise be beyond their means. This affordability also makes these funds a particularly attractive cash equivalent for smaller firms.

9-5b Managing Accounts Receivable: Pay Me Now or Pay Me Later

Accounts receivable represents what customers who buy on credit owe the firm. Allowing customers to buy on credit can significantly increase sales. However, as our discussion of the cash budget showed, credit sales can create cash flow problems because they delay the receipt of cash the firm needs to meet its financial obligations. Customers who pay late or don't pay at all only exacerbate the problem. So it's important for firms to have a well-thought-out policy that balances the advantages

of offering credit with the costs. The key elements of this policy should include:

- Setting credit terms: For how long should the firm extend credit? What type of cash discount should the firm offer to encourage early payments?

- Establishing credit standards: How should the firm decide which customers qualify for credit? What type of credit information should it require? How strict should its standards be?

- Deciding on an appropriate collection policy: How aggressive should the firm be at collecting past-due accounts? At what point does it make sense to take (or at least threaten to take) legal action against late-paying customers, or to turn over the accounts to collection agencies? When does it make sense to work out compromises?

In each area, financial managers face tradeoffs. For example, a firm that extends credit for only 30 days will receive its payments sooner than a firm that allows customers 90 days. But setting short credit periods may also result in lost sales. Similarly, setting high credit

money market mutual funds A mutual fund that pools funds from many investors and uses these funds to purchase very safe, highly liquid securities.

standards reduces the likelihood a firm will have problems with customers who pay late (or not at all). However, strict standards may prevent many good customers from getting credit, resulting in lower sales. Finally, an aggressive collection policy may help the firm collect payments that it would otherwise lose. But an aggressive policy is costly, and it might alienate customers who make honest mistakes, causing them to take future business to competitors.

Some small businesses have found that being flexible and creative about the form of payment can help them get at least some of what they are owed. Barter arrangements sometimes work better than demanding cash—especially in troubled times such as the recent recession. For example, a health spa took payments from one of its customers in the form of hundreds of granola bars. Similarly, the owner of a bookkeeping firm agreed to accept payment from a veterinarian in the form of emergency surgery on her pet cat![20]

9-5c Managing Inventories: Taking Stock of the Situation

Inventories are stocks of finished goods, work-in-process, parts, and materials that firms hold as a part of doing business. Clearly, businesses must hold inventories to operate. For example, you'd probably be disappointed if you visited a Best Buy store and were confronted with empty shelves rather than with a wide array of electronic gadgets to compare and try out. Similarly, a manufacturing firm wouldn't be able to assemble its products without an inventory of parts and materials.

Versusstudio/Shutterstock.com

But for many firms, the costs of storing, handling, and insuring inventory items are significant expenses. In recent years, many manufacturing firms have become very aggressive about keeping inventories as low as possible in an attempt to reduce costs and improve efficiency. Such "lean" inventory policies can be very effective, but they leave the firm vulnerable to supply disruptions. Honda had to shut down some of its Ohio assembly lines for eight days in late 2011 after 15 feet of floodwater swamped the Taiwanese factories of key suppliers, delaying shipments of four-wheel drive systems for its cars. If Honda held larger inventories, it might have been able to continue operating its assembly lines until its Taiwanese suppliers could resume shipments.[21]

capital budgeting The process a firm uses to evaluate long-term investment proposals.

9-6 CAPITAL BUDGETING: IN IT FOR THE LONG HAUL

We'll conclude the chapter with a look at how firms evaluate proposals to invest in long-term assets or undertake major new projects. **Capital budgeting** refers to the procedure a firm uses to plan for investments in assets or projects that it expects will yield benefits for more than a year. The capital budgeting process evaluates proposals such as:

■ Replacing old machinery and equipment with new models to reduce cost and improve the efficiency of current operations

■ Buying additional plant, machinery, and equipment to expand production capacity in *existing* markets

■ Investing in plant, property, and equipment needed to expand into *new* markets

■ Installing new, or modifying existing, plant and equipment to achieve goals not directly related to expanding production, such as reducing pollution or improving worker safety

The number of capital budgeting proposals a firm considers each year can be quite large. But it's unlikely that all proposals will be worth pursuing. How do financial managers decide whether or not to accept a proposal?

9-6a Evaluating Capital Budgeting Proposals

Financial managers measure the benefits and costs of long-term investment proposals in terms of the cash flows they generate. These cash flows are likely to be negative at the start of a project because money must be spent to get a long-term investment project up and running before it begins generating positive cash flows. But a project must eventually generate enough positive cash flows to more than offset these negative initial cash outflows if it is to benefit the company.

9-6b Accounting for the Time Value of Money

One of the most challenging aspects of the evaluation of a long-term project's cash flows is that they are spread out over a number of years. When financial managers compare cash flows that occur at different times, they

Decisions, Decisions—How Airlines Are Spending their Cash from Fuel Savings

There is no denying it—airlines have high operating costs. Their capital equipment (i.e., passenger jets) is expensive, they have tens of thousands of employees on their payrolls, and, until recently, oil prices had been high for decades. In fact, the airline industry, since inception, has been a money-losing business.

When it comes to jet fuel, airlines use hedges to control costs. Hedges are contracts that allow airlines to lock in prices. If prices rise above the agreed on prices in hedge contracts, airlines benefit by having purchased fuel more cheaply. Conversely, if prices drop, then airlines end up paying more, but still benefit because their fuel costs become predictable.

Given the volume of jet fuel used worldwide and the long-term increases in jet fuel costs, hedges have long been a critical

Chris Parypa Photography/Shutterstock.com

component of airlines' financial strategies. In 2013, over 528 million barrels of jet fuel were consumed in the United States, equating to roughly $65 billion in fuel expense. Starting in mid-2014, however, oil prices began dropping, first steadily then dramatically. Within nine months, the price of crude oil had dropped from $105 a barrel to $45, and prices for jet fuel had dropped a corresponding 40%. Because a 1-cent drop in oil prices equates to a $40 million savings in fuel costs for large carriers, even those that had long-term hedge contracts in place (airlines rarely hedge 100% of their jet fuel purchases) found themselves with billions in fuel savings. So while hedges ended up costing Delta $800 million, it will still save $1.7 billion from lower fuel costs since only 20% of its fuel is hedged. American Airlines, which quit using hedges in 2013, will realize $2.5 billion in savings from lower fuel costs.

So, what are airlines doing with their billions in fuel savings? What they are *not* doing is cutting fares or increasing service. Instead, airlines are using their surplus cash to strengthen their finances. American Airlines is directing its fuel savings toward higher profits. At United Continental, executives are using the savings to pay down debt and buy back stock. Delta Air Lines is also paying down debt, as well as increasing dividends to shareholders. Southwest's CEO Gary Kelly said, "If we are convinced that we're in for low energy prices for a while, we'll revisit 2016 and 2017 opportunities" for growth, or, "we'll just run a higher cash balance" or pay creditors or shareholders.[22]

must take the **time value of money** into account. The time value of money reflects the fact that, from a financial manager's perspective, a dollar received today is worth *more* than a dollar received in the future because the sooner you receive a sum of money, the sooner you can put that money to work to earn even *more* money.

Suppose, for example, that you were given the choice of receiving $1,000 either today or the same amount one year from today. If you think like a financial manager, this choice is a no-brainer! Let's be conservative and say that if you receive the money today you can deposit it in an insured one-year **certificate of deposit (CD)** at your local bank that pays 4% interest. (A CD is similar to a savings account, except that it requires the funds to remain on deposit for a fixed term; in our example, the term is one year. You would incur a penalty if you withdrew your funds early.) Investing in your 4% CD means that a year from today you would have $1,040 (the $1,000 you deposited plus

$40 in interest). But if you wait until next year to receive the $1,000, you'll lose the opportunity to earn that $40 in interest. Clearly, receiving the cash today is the better option.

Because money has a time value, a cash flow's value depends not only on the *amount* of cash received but also on *when* it is received. Financial managers compare cash flows occurring at different times by converting them to their present values. The **present value** of a cash flow received

> **time value of money** The principle that a dollar received today is worth more than a dollar received in the future.

> **certificate of deposit (CD)** An interest-earning deposit that requires the funds to remain deposited for a fixed term. Withdrawal of the funds before the term expires results in a financial penalty.

> **present value** The amount of money that, if invested today at a given rate of interest (called the discount rate), would grow to become some future amount in a specified number of time periods.

Exhibit 9.4

How a Present Value of $10,000 Grows to a Future Value of $11,255.09 in Four Years

Now
- Deposit $10,000.00 (Present value)
- Earn 3% per year

After 1 year you have
- $10,000 + $300 interest earned over first year (3% of 10,000) =
- $10,300.00

After 2 years you have
- $10,300.00 + $309 interest earned over second year (3% of $10,300) =
- $10,609.00

After 3 years you have
- $10,609.00 + $318.27 interest earned over third year (3% of $10,609) =
- $10,927.27

After 4 years you have
- $10,927.27 + $327.82 interest earned over fourth year (3% of $10,927.27) =
- $11,255.09 (Future value)

© Cengage Learning®

in a future time period is the amount of money that, if invested *today* at an assumed rate of interest (called the *discount rate*), would grow to become that future amount of money. Exhibit 9.4 shows that $10,000 invested today at 3% grows to a future value of $11,255.09 in four years. Thus, $10,000 is the present value of $11,255.09 received in four years.

9-6c The Risk-Return Tradeoff Revisited

Unfortunately, financial managers don't have crystal balls, so they don't know the *actual* cash flows a proposed project will generate. Instead, they base their analysis on the cash flows the proposal is *expected* to generate. Once a company actually invests in a project, it may find that the *actual* cash flows are quite different from these estimated flows. This uncertainty means that capital budgeting decisions must consider risk.

In general, projects with the potential for high returns are also the projects with a high degree of uncertainty and risk. This is another example of the risk-return tradeoff we introduced at the beginning of this

net present value (NPV) The sum of the present values of expected future cash flows from an investment, minus the cost of that investment.

chapter. Clearly, financial managers must take this tradeoff into account when they compare different capital budgeting proposals; they must determine whether riskier proposals generate a high enough expected return to justify their greater risk.

One common way financial managers try to do this is to use a higher discount rate when they compute the present values of cash flows for risky projects than when they compute present values for less risky projects. This reflects the idea that a higher return is required to compensate for the greater risk.

9-6d Net Present Value: A Decision Rule for Capital Budgeting

The most common method financial managers use to evaluate capital budgeting proposals is to compute their **net present value (NPV)**. The NPV of an investment proposal is found by adding the present values of *all* of its estimated future cash flows and subtracting the initial cost of the investment from the sum. A positive NPV means that the present value of the expected cash flows from the project is greater than the cost of the project. In other words, the benefits from the project exceed its cost even after accounting for the time value of money. Financial managers approve projects with positive NPVs. A negative NPV means that the present value of the expected future cash flows from the project is less than the cost of the investment. This would indicate that the cost of the project outweighs its cash flow benefits. Financial managers would reject proposals with negative NPVs. (See Exhibit 9.5.)

EXHIBIT 9.5	DECISION RULE FOR CAPITAL BUDGETING
Result of NPV Calculation	**Decision**
NPV ≥ 0	Accept proposal ✔
NPV < 0	Reject proposal ✗

© Cengage Learning®

The BIG Picture

In this chapter, we described the tasks financial managers perform as they attempt to find the "best" sources and uses of financial resources—meaning those that will maximize the value of the firm to its owners. We saw that in their attempts to achieve this goal, financial managers face two challenges. The first is to balance the needs of owners against those of the other stakeholders; the second is to balance the potential rewards of their decisions against the risks.

Recent history illustrates how important sound financial management is to the success of a firm—and how devastating poor financial decisions can be. Indeed, the recent decline and fall of some of the biggest and best-known U.S. corporations can be traced in large measure to poor financial decisions—especially

decisions that failed to adequately take risk into account, resulting in the use of too much leverage.

These lessons from the recent past will probably result in a different approach to financial management over the next several years. While memories of the Great Recession are still relatively fresh, firms may be more conservative in their view of what constitutes the best sources and uses of funds. In particular, they are likely to shy away from excessive debt and put more emphasis on equity financing. They also are less likely to use their funds to invest in highly risky or speculative assets. These more conservative tendencies are likely to be reinforced by the major regulatory reforms designed to curb aggressive (and risky) behavior introduced by the Dodd-Frank Act.

Careers in Finance

Financial Analyst

Responsible for financial planning; preparing complex financial analyses and recommendations; establishing and maintaining internal financial controls; creating and analyzing monthly, quarterly, and annual reports; and ensuring financial information has been recorded accurately, working closely with business unit leaders to align company and financial goals, and performing Sarbanes-Oxley assessments and testing. The ideal candidate has a bachelor's or master's degree in finance, expert spreadsheet and analytical skills, strong oral

and written communication skills, strong understanding of financial analysis and reporting, and effective time and project management skills including the ability to simultaneously manage multiple projects and priorities as well as to work under pressure to meet deadlines. For more information on this career and other possible careers in finance, check out Career Transitions.

STUDY TOOLS 9

LOCATED AT BACK OF THE TEXTBOOK

☐ Rip Out Chapter Review Card

LOCATED AT WWW.CENGAGE.COM/LOGIN

☐ Review key term flashcards and create your own using StudyBits

☐ Create and complete practice quizzes based off of your notes and StudyBits

☐ Complete Online activities such as Matching, Fill-in-the-Blank, and Drag and Drop exercises

☐ View chapter highlight box content, including CEO Profiles, What Would You Do Cases, and chapter videos

☐ Track your knowledge and understanding of key concepts in business using 4LTR Online

10 | Financial Markets:
Allocating Financial Resources

LEARNING OBJECTIVES
After studying this chapter, you will be able to:

10-1 Explain the role of financial markets in the U.S. economy and identify the key players in these markets

10-2 Identify the key laws that govern the way financial markets operate and explain the impact of each law

10-3 Describe and compare the major types of securities that are traded in securities markets

10-4 Explain how securities are issued in the primary market and traded on secondary markets

10-5 Compare several strategies that investors use to invest in securities

10-6 Interpret the information provided in the stock quotes available on financial websites

Remember to visit
PAGE 184
for additional
STUDY TOOLS

10-1 THE ROLE OF FINANCIAL MARKETS AND THEIR KEY PLAYERS

Financial markets perform a vital function: they transfer funds from savers (individuals and organizations willing to defer using some of their income to earn a financial return and build their wealth) to borrowers (individuals and organizations that need additional funds to achieve their financial goals). Without these markets, companies would find it difficult to obtain the financial resources needed to meet payrolls, invest in new facilities, develop new products, and compete effectively in global markets.

But it's not just businesses that benefit from these markets. You do, too, through your involvement in both sides of financial markets. You participate as a borrower when using your credit card to finance daily purchases or when taking out a loan for college tuition. You also participate as a saver when depositing money into a savings account to accumulate the down payment for your first house, or when investing in stocks and bonds to build a nest egg for your retirement years.

financial markets Markets that transfer funds from savers to borrowers.

"SOMETIMES YOUR BEST INVESTMENTS ARE THE ONES YOU DON'T MAKE."

—DONALD TRUMP

Pio3/Shutterstock.com

In the United States and other well-developed market economies, the vast majority of financing occurs indirectly, with *financial intermediaries* coming between the ultimate savers and borrowers. We'll see that they perform a variety of functions, but what they all have in common is that they help channel funds from savers to borrowers.

10-1a Depository Institutions

Depository institutions are financial intermediaries that obtain funds by accepting checking and savings deposits from individuals, businesses, and other institutions, and then lending those funds to borrowers.

- Commercial banks are the most common depository institutions. When you make a deposit into a checking or savings account at your bank, you are providing funds that the bank can use for making loans to businesses, governments, or other individuals.

    At the start of 2015, over half (53%) of total bank assets were in the form of loans, including over $4.5 trillion in real estate and mortgage loans, more than $1.6 trillion

in consumer loans, and over $2.8 trillion in commercial and other loans. And compared to historical trends, this was relatively high. In the immediate aftermath of the Great Recession, banks were still quite conservative in their loan-making decisions. For comparison, in 2007 loans comprised 57% of all bank assets.[1]

- **Credit unions** are cooperatives, meaning that they are not-for-profit organizations that are owned by their depositors. As not-for-profit organizations, they strive to pay higher interest rates on member deposits and charge lower interest rates on loans.

    Credit unions are open to individuals who belong to a specific "field of membership." For example, membership in some credit unions is limited to the employees who work for a specific

depository institution A financial intermediary that obtains funds by accepting checking and savings deposits and then lending those funds to borrowers.

credit union A depository institution that is organized as a cooperative, meaning that it is owned by its depositors.

Financial Information—Glitches and Outages Halt Trading Worldwide for Basic Investors

The securities information processor, or SIP, is a stock information database that is run by American stock exchanges, such as NASDAQ and the NYSE, to transmit data on stock prices to brokers, investors, and the media. Without the SIP, which executes a buy-sell order in just six-tenths of a millisecond and is the electronic backbone for nearly all stock trading, investors and traders would not have accurate information about stock prices, and major news channels would be unable to run stock price crawlers on the bottom of TV screens. In short, the SIP is a critical piece of technology, since it provides crucial information in an industry where tens of thousands of stocks are traded every second across the globe.

In the last year, the SIP has had several noteworthy glitches, one of which stopped stock trading at the NASDAQ stock exchange

Jean Miele/Corbis/Glow Images

for three hours, and another at the NYSE that halted trading in markets all over the world for 20 minutes. What's behind the recent glitches and shutdowns? One possibility—not enough money. Stock exchanges have not been maintaining the SIP as they have in the past, because people are investing less and overall trading volume has declined. Indeed, the exchanges are being paid much less each year for their basic SIP data feeds. By contrast, stock exchanges earn between $400 million and $600 million a year for direct "high-speed" stock feeds that not only arrive faster, but contain additional, propriety information that is not available in the standard SIP feed. NASDAQ, for example, saw its revenue from the SIP and SIP-derived sales fall by $32 million over a six-year period, while it more than doubled its revenue from selling proprietary high-speed data. Not surprisingly, these high-speed stock feeds have experienced fewer glitches and outages.

The Securities Exchange Commission (SEC), which regulates U.S. stock exchanges, told NASDAQ and the NYSE that they had just two months, working together, to come up with a way to make the SIP more reliable. NASDAQ's CEO Robert Greifeld said, "We know there's going to be issues with software. We know there's going to be bugs. We seek to get to perfection, but it's difficult." Despite the challenges, Laurence Fink, chairman and chief executive at BlackRock, a global investment firm, says, "We need to make sure as we think going forward that there are proper protections, proper investments in technology, so we don't have these glitches."[2]

---

employer and their family members; other credit unions base membership on church or union affiliation or are open to people living in a certain geographic area.[3]

Credit unions are a much smaller player in financial markets than commercial banks, but in early 2015 they held more than $371 billion in mortgage financing and $302 billion in consumer credit on their books.[4]

■ **Savings and loan associations** (also called "S&Ls" or "thrifts") traditionally accepted only savings account deposits and used them to make mortgage loans. During the early 1980s, regulations on S&Ls were relaxed, allowing them to accept checking account deposits and make a broader range of loans. Still, the major focus of the savings and loan industry remains mortgage loans.

■ At the end of 2013 S&Ls held about $452 billion in mortgage financing on their books—not a trivial sum by any means, but a big drop from 2006 when the figure peaked at $1.25 trillion.[5] In large part, this reflected the collapse of the housing market at the end of the past decade. But S&Ls began declining in importance well before the Great Recession.[6]

10-1b Nondepository Financial Institutions

In addition to banks and other depository institutions, a number of other financial intermediaries play important roles in financial markets.

- **Institutional investors** don't accept deposits but amass huge pools of financial capital from other sources and use these funds to acquire a portfolio of many different assets. Mutual funds obtain money by selling shares to investors; insurance companies obtain money by collecting premiums from policyholders; and pension funds obtain money by collecting funds employers and their employees contribute for the employees' retirement. These institutions invest heavily in corporate stock; institutional investors hold the majority of shares in most major U.S. corporations. They are also major holders of corporate bonds and government securities.

- **Securities brokers** act as agents for investors who want to buy or sell financial securities, such as corporate stocks or bonds. In addition to handling the trades, many brokers provide their clients with additional services, such as financial planning and market research. Brokers are compensated by charging fees and commissions for the services they provide.

- **Securities dealers** participate directly in securities markets, buying and selling stocks and bonds for their own account. They earn a profit by selling securities for higher prices than they paid to purchase them. (The difference between the prices at which they buy and sell a security is called the *spread*.)

- **Investment banks** are financial intermediaries that help firms issue new securities to raise financial capital. Sometimes investment banks actually buy the newly issued securities themselves; in other cases, they simply help arrange for their sale. Today's investment banks aren't actually independent companies. Instead, they are typically divisions of huge bank holding companies that also own commercial banks.

10-2 REGULATING FINANCIAL MARKETS TO PROTECT INVESTORS AND IMPROVE STABILITY

Financial markets work well only when savers and borrowers have confidence in the soundness of key financial institutions and in the fairness of the market outcomes.

When depositors lose confidence in their banks, or when investors discover that financial markets are rigged by practices such as insider trading or unethical and deceptive accounting, the financial system breaks down.

The financial crisis of 2008 is only the latest example of the disruptions that result when financial markets malfunction. From the early twentieth century to the present day, the U.S. economy has experienced several other major financial crises. The economy experienced massive bank failures in 1907 and in the early 1930s. It also weathered a savings and loan crisis in the late 1980s that brought the failure of over 1,000 S&Ls and required a federal bailout that cost over $120 billion.[7] And a variety of scandals involving ethical lapses (and in many cases outright fraud) roiled financial markets at the turn of the century.

10-2a Financial Regulation: Early Efforts

During most of the twentieth century, the federal government responded to financial upheavals by introducing new laws and regulations. This trend first emerged in the wake of the banking panic of 1907, which created pressure for Congress to find a way to stabilize the nation's banking system. The result was the **Federal Reserve Act of 1913**. As its name implies, this act created the Federal Reserve System (the Fed) to serve as the central bank in the United States. The law gave the Fed the primary responsibility for overseeing our nation's banking system.

Unfortunately, the creation of the Fed didn't solve all of the nation's banking problems. Another wave of bank failures occurred in the early 1930s as the economy sank into the Great Depression. Congress responded by passing the **Banking Act of 1933**, also known as the *Glass-Steagall Act*. This law established the Federal Deposit Insurance Corporation, which insured depositors against

securities broker A financial intermediary that acts as an agent for investors who want to buy and sell financial securities. Brokers earn commissions and fees for the services they provide.

securities dealer A financial intermediary that participates directly in securities markets, buying and selling stocks and other securities for its own account.

investment bank A financial intermediary that specializes in helping firms raise financial capital by issuing securities in primary markets.

Federal Reserve Act of 1913 The law that established the Federal Reserve System as the central bank of the United States.

Banking Act of 1933 The law that established the Federal Deposit Insurance Corporation (FDIC) to insure bank deposits. It also prohibited commercial banks from selling insurance or acting as investment banks.

financial losses when a bank failed. The insurance initially covered only $2,500 of deposits—but $2,500 bought a lot more in the 1930s than it does today! Over the years, coverage has been increased several times. Today, the FDIC insures up to $250,000 in deposits.[8]

Another major provision of the Glass-Steagall Act banned commercial banks from dealing in securities markets, selling insurance, or otherwise competing with nondepository institutions such as insurance companies and investment banks. The rationale for these restrictions was that involvement in such activities exposed banks and their depositors to higher levels of risk.

Congress responded to the stock market crash that occurred in 1929 with two laws that are still the foundation of U.S. securities markets regulation. The first of these was the **Securities Act of 1933**, which dealt mainly with the process of issuing new securities. It prohibited misrepresentation or other forms of fraud in the sale of newly issued stocks and bonds. It also required firms issuing new stock in a public offering to file a registration statement with the SEC. The next year, Congress passed the **Securities Exchange Act of 1934**, which regulated the trading of previously issued securities. This law created the **Securities and Exchange Commission** (SEC) and gave it broad powers to oversee the securities industry. The law required that all publicly traded firms with at least 500 shareholders and $10 million in assets file quarterly and annual financial reports with the SEC, and that brokers and dealers register with the SEC.

The Securities Exchange Act also gave the SEC the power to prosecute individuals and companies that engaged in fraudulent securities market activities. For example, the SEC has the authority to go after individuals who engage in illegal *insider trading*, which is the practice of using inside information (important information about a company that isn't available to the general investing public) to profit unfairly from trading in a company's securities.

Securities Act of 1933 The first major federal law regulating the securities industry. It requires firms issuing new stock in a public offering to file a registration statement with the SEC.

Securities and Exchange Act of 1934 A federal law dealing with securities regulation that established the Securities and Exchange Commission to regulate and oversee the securities industry.

Securities and Exchange Commission The federal agency with primary responsibility for regulating the securities industry.

Financial Services Modernization Act of 1999 An act that overturned the section of the Banking Act of 1933 that prohibited commercial banks from selling insurance or performing the functions of investment banks.

10-2b Deregulation During the 1980s and 1990s: Temporarily Reversing Course

The passage of these laws ushered in a period of more stable financial markets. But critics argued that the laws—especially the Glass-Steagall Act—represented an onerous government intrusion into the financial sector that stifled competition and impeded financial innovation. During the 1980s and 1990s Congress responded to these criticisms by easing restrictions on banks and other depository institutions. For instance, the **Financial Services Modernization Act of 1999**, also known as the *Gramm-Bliley-Leach Act*, reversed the Glass-Steagall Act's prohibition of banks selling insurance or acting as investment banks.

The financial sector initially seemed to prosper under its less regulated environment. It responded to its increased freedom with a variety of new services. Also, new technologies such as ATMs and online banking made financial transactions easier and more convenient.

10-2c Recent Developments: Reregulation in the Aftermath of Financial Turmoil

But the wave of deregulation didn't last. A series of accounting scandals at the beginning of the twenty-first century, followed by a near collapse of the financial system in 2008, created pressure for new laws.

Congress reacted to the accounting scandals in the first years of the new century by passing the Sarbanes-Oxley Act in 2002. This law included provisions to ensure that external auditors offered fair, unbiased opinions when they examined a company's financial statements. It also increased the SEC's authority to regulate financial markets and investigate charges of fraud and unethical behavior.[9]

In the wake of the financial crisis of 2008–2009 Congress passed the Dodd-Frank Act of 2010. This far-reaching law expanded the Fed's regulatory authority over nondepository financial institutions, such as hedge funds and mortgage brokers that had previously operated with little regulatory oversight or accountability. It also created the Financial Stability Oversight Council to identify emerging risks in the financial sector so that action could be taken to rein in risky practices *before* they led to a crisis. The council was given the authority to recommend new rules to the Federal Reserve that would limit risky practices of the nation's largest, most complex financial institutions.[10]

10-3 INVESTING IN FINANCIAL SECURITIES: WHAT ARE THE OPTIONS?

Financial securities markets are critical to corporations that rely on them to obtain much of their long-term financial capital. They also provide one of the most important venues that individuals can use to build their long-term wealth and earn significant financial returns.

10-3a Common Stock: Back to Basics

Common stock is the basic form of ownership in a corporation. Exhibit 10.1 shows a stock certificate for Berkshire Hathaway, Inc. As owners of corporations, common stockholders have certain basic rights:

- **Voting Rights:** Owners of common stock have the right to vote on important issues in the annual stockholders' meeting. Under the most common arrangement, stockholders can cast one vote for each share of stock they own. One of the key issues that stockholders vote on is the selection of members to the corporation's board of directors, but they also may vote on other major issues, such as the approval of a merger with another firm or a change in the corporation's by-laws. As you learned in Chapter 6, the

Exhibit 10.1
Stock Certificates Represent Shares of Ownership in a Corporation

Common stock is the basic form of ownership in a corporation.

James Colburn/Zuma Press/Newscom

Dodd-Frank Act of 2010 gives stockholders the right to vote on their company's executive compensation policies. While nonbinding, a "say on pay" vote gives shareholders a way to make their feelings known about executive compensation.[11]

- **Right to Dividends:** Dividends are a distribution of earnings to the corporation's stockholders. All common stockholders have the right to receive a dividend *if* their corporation's board of directors declares one. The "catch" is that the board has no legal obligation to declare a dividend. In fact, many rapidly growing companies routinely choose to skip dividends and reinvest most or all of their earnings to finance growth.

- **Capital Gains:** Stockholders receive another type of return on their investment, called a **capital gain**, *if* the price of the stock rises above the amount they paid for it. Capital gains can create very attractive financial returns for stockholders. Of course, there is no guarantee the stock's price will rise. If it falls, stockholders would experience a capital loss rather than a capital gain.

- **Preemptive Right:** If a corporation issues new stock, existing stockholders sometimes have a preemptive right to purchase new shares in proportion to their existing holdings before the stock is offered to the other investors. For example, if you own 5% of the existing shares of stock, then the preemptive right gives you the right to purchase 5% of the new shares. This could be important for large stockholders who want to maintain their share of ownership. However, the conditions under which existing stockholders have preemptive rights vary among the states. In several states, a preemptive right is only available if it is specifically identified in the corporation's charter.

- **Right to a Residual Claim on Assets:** The final stockholder right is a residual claim on assets. If the corporation goes out of business and liquidates its assets, stockholders have a right to share in the proceeds in proportion to their ownership. But note that this is a *residual* claim—it comes *after all other claims* have been satisfied. In other words, the firm must pay any back taxes, legal expenses, wages owed to workers, and debts owed to creditors before the owners get anything. By the time all of these other claims have been paid, nothing may be left for the owners.

> **common stock** The basic form of ownership in a corporation.
>
> **capital gain** The return on an asset that results when its market price rises above the price the investor paid for it.

10-3b Preferred Stock: Getting Preferential Treatment

Common stock is the basic form of corporate ownership, but some companies also issue **preferred stock**, so named because it offers its holders preferential treatment in two respects:

- **Claim on Assets:** Holders of preferred stock have a claim on assets that comes before common stockholders if the company goes out of business. This gives preferred stockholders a better chance than common stockholders of recovering their investment if the company goes bankrupt.

- **Payment of Dividends:** Unlike dividends on common stock, dividends on preferred stock are usually a stated amount. And a corporation can't pay *any* dividend to its common stockholders unless it pays the full stated dividend on its preferred stock. Still, it is important to note that a corporation has no *legal* obligation to pay a dividend to *any* stockholders, not even those who hold preferred stock.

Preferred stock sometimes includes a *cumulative feature*. This means that if the firm skips a preferred dividend in one period, the amount it must pay the next period is equal to the dividend for that period *plus* the amount of the dividend it skipped in the previous period. Additional skipped dividends continue to accumulate, and the firm can't pay *any* dividends to common stockholders until *all* accumulated dividends are paid to preferred stockholders.

Preferred stock isn't necessarily "preferred" to common stock in all respects. For instance, preferred stockholders normally don't have voting rights, so they can't vote on issues that come up during stockholders' meetings. And even though preferred stockholders are more likely to receive a dividend, they aren't guaranteed a *better* dividend; the board can declare a dividend to common stockholders that offers a higher return.[12] Finally, when a company experiences strong earnings, the market price of its common stock can—and often does—appreciate more in value than the price of its preferred shares, thus offering common shareholders a greater capital gain.

> "ONE OF THE FUNNY THINGS ABOUT THE STOCK MARKET IS THAT EVERY TIME ONE PERSON BUYS, ANOTHER SELLS, AND BOTH THINK THEY ARE ASTUTE."
>
> —WILLIAM FEATHER

10-3c Bonds: Earning Your Interest

A **bond** is a formal IOU issued by a corporation or government entity. Bonds come in many different varieties. Our discussion will focus on the basic characteristics of long-term bonds issued by corporations.

The date a bond comes due is called its **maturity date**, and the amount the issuer owes the bondholder at maturity is called the bond's **par value** (or face value). Long-term bonds issued by corporations usually mature ten to thirty years after issuance, but longer maturities are possible. In 2012, several major corporations, including IBM and Coca-Cola, issued *century bonds* that will mature 100 years after they were issued.[13]

Bondholders can sell their bonds to other investors before they mature, but the price they receive might not correspond to the bond's par value because bond prices fluctuate with conditions in the bond market. When a bond's market price is above its par value, it is selling at a *premium*; when its price is below par value, it is selling at a *discount*.

Most bonds require their issuers to pay a stated amount of interest to bondholders each year until the bond matures. The **coupon rate** on the bond expresses the annual interest payment as a percentage of the bond's par value. For example, investors who own a bond with a par value of $1,000 and a coupon rate of 7.5% receive $75 in interest (7.5% of $1,000) each year until the bond reaches maturity—or until they sell their bonds to someone else. But since bonds can sell at a premium or a discount, the coupon rate doesn't necessarily represent the rate of return that investors earn on the amount they actually *paid* for the bond. The **current yield** expresses a bond's interest payment as a percentage of the bond's *current market price* rather than its par value. If the market price of the

preferred stock A type of stock that gives its holder preference over common stockholders in terms of dividends and claims on assets.

bond A formal debt instrument issued by a corporation or government entity.

maturity date The date when a bond will come due.

par value (of a bond) The value of a bond at its maturity; what the issuer promises to pay the bondholder when the bond matures.

coupon rate The interest paid on a bond, expressed as a percentage of the bond's par value.

current yield The amount of interest earned on a bond, expressed as a percentage of the bond's current market price.

bond in our example was $833.33, then the current yield would be 9% (found by dividing the $75 interest payment by $833.33).

Unlike dividends on stock, a firm has a *legal obligation* to pay interest on bonds—and to pay the bondholder the par value of the bond when it matures. Thus, bondholders are more likely to receive a financial return than stockholders. But that doesn't mean that bonds are without risk. Corporations that get into serious financial difficulties sometimes *default* on their bonds, meaning that they are unable to make required payments. When that happens, bankruptcy proceedings usually allow bondholders to recover some (but not all) of what they are owed; historically, the average amount recovered has been about 72 cents on the dollar. While that is better than what stockholders can expect, it is far short of being risk free![14]

10-3d Convertible Securities: The Big Switch

Corporations sometimes issue **convertible securities**, which are bonds or shares of preferred stock that investors can exchange for a given number of shares of the issuing corporation's common stock. A *conversion ratio* indicates the number of shares of common stock exchanged for each convertible security. For example, if the conversion ratio is 20, then each convertible security can be exchanged for 20 shares of common stock. The ratio is set at the time the convertible securities are issued so that it is only financially desirable to convert the securities if the price of the common stock increases.

Owning a convertible security allows investors to gain from an increase in the price of common stock, while limiting their risk if the price of the stock falls. If the price of the common stock increases, the holders of convertible securities can convert them into the now more valuable stock. But if the price of the company's common stock falls, investors can continue to hold their convertible securities and collect their interest or preferred dividends.

The firm also can benefit from issuing convertible bonds, because the popularity of this feature with investors allows it to offer a lower coupon rate on convertible bonds (or a lower dividend on preferred stock), thus reducing its fixed payments. And if investors convert to common stock, the firm no longer has to make these fixed

> **convertible security** A bond or share of preferred stock that gives its holder the right to exchange it for a stated number of shares of common stock.

Are Stock Buybacks Good for Companies?

A stock buyback is when a company buys shares of its stock that it previously sold to investors to raise money to invest in growing its business. Apple, IBM, FedEx, Allstate, Motorola, eBay, and McDonald's have recently spent billions on share buybacks. Indeed, buybacks grew 25% in 2015 and 50% in 2014!

Home Depot Chief Financial Officer (CFO) Carol Tome says, "If you're cash rich, and you have no better place to put it," then stock buybacks make sense. Says Tome, "The last thing we're going to do is sit on cash. That is value-destroying to our shareholders." Because stock buybacks reduce the number of shares of stock in circulation, EPS rises because earnings are spread across fewer shares—not because earnings have improved. Since a higher EPS usually indicates better financial performance, it's not surprising that stock prices rise 4% on average after stock buybacks.

But, that increase may not be long lasting. Stanley Black & Decker's CFO, Donald Allan, Jr., says that buybacks "might help your stock price performance and your company's performance for a two- to three-year period, but it's not going to help the performance of the company over a decade." Furthermore, because executive pay often rises when share prices rise, particularly when executives hold stock options that allow them to buy stocks at lower prices, firm leaders often see substantial financial gains from share buybacks.

Critics argue that buybacks are the financial equivalent of a dog chasing its tail—the firm ends up going in financial circles and doesn't really get anywhere. They say instead that cash should either be reinvested in the business to improve long-term performance or paid to shareholders via dividends.[15]

AP Images/Richard Drew

payments at all. But there is one important group that may be unhappy with this arrangement; the corporation's existing stockholders may be displeased if the new stock issued to holders of convertible securities dilutes their share of ownership—and their share of profits!

MUTUAL FUNDS AND ETFs: DIVERSIFICATION MADE EASY **Financial diversification**—the practice of holding many different securities in many different sectors—is generally considered a desirable strategy because it helps reduce (but not completely eliminate) risk. If you hold many different securities in different sectors of the economy, then losses on some securities may be offset by gains on others.

Many investors who want to hold diversified portfolios find that investing in large numbers of individual stocks and bonds is prohibitively expensive. And even if they could afford to do so, investors often lack the time and expertise to select a large number of individual securities. Faced with these limitations, many investors find that **mutual funds** and exchange-traded funds are attractive options.

MUTUAL FUNDS: PORTFOLIOS MADE EASY

There are two ways mutual funds can be structured. A *closed-end fund* issues a fixed number of shares and invests the money received from selling these shares in a portfolio of assets. Shares of closed-end funds can be traded among investors much like stocks. An *open-end mutual fund* doesn't have a fixed number of shares, nor are its shares traded like stocks. Instead, the fund issues additional shares when demand increases and redeems (buys back) old shares when investors want to cash in.

The price at which shares of an open-end mutual fund are issued and redeemed is based on the fund's **net asset value per share** (NAVPS), which is computed by dividing the total value of the fund's cash, securities, and other assets (less any liabilities) by the number of fund shares outstanding. Though the NAVPS is the basis for the price of a fund's shares, investors often also pay commissions and purchase fees.

Several features make mutual funds a popular choice for investors:

- **Diversification at Relatively Low Cost:** By pooling the funds of thousands

financial diversification A strategy of investing in a wide variety of securities in order to reduce risk.

mutual fund An institutional investor that raises funds by selling shares to investors and uses the accumulated funds to buy a portfolio of many different securities.

net asset value per share The value of a mutual fund's securities and cash holdings minus any liabilities, divided by the number of shares of the fund outstanding.

HOW DOES "BEING GREEN" AFFECT COMPANY AND INVESTMENT PERFORMANCE AND INVESTOR BEHAVIOR?

Is it a good investment strategy to go "green"? Let's examine what the research tells us about company performance, investment performance, and how investors actually behave.

First, there is no tradeoff between social responsibility and company financial performance. The higher costs of being socially responsible can be offset by a better product or corporate reputation, leading to stronger sales or higher profit margins. Still, social responsibility doesn't guarantee profitability. All companies experience challenges and threats, and ups and downs. So while being socially responsible may be the right thing to do, it won't necessarily help or hurt business success.

Second, most examinations of the financial performance of green investment funds are limited to just a small number of mutual funds. However, a study comparing 131 green investment funds found they significantly underperformed average market returns over five-year (2.22% vs. 3.45%), and ten-year (3.92% vs. 5.10%) periods. The differences were smaller but similar over three-year (2.65% vs. 3.42%) and fifteen-year periods (6.53% vs. 6.93%). Green mutual funds also are more expensive to run. The authors concluded, "Green mutual funds have to date achieved relatively poor risk-adjusted returns."

Third, a study of individual investor behavior compared environmentalists, strong supporters of environmental issues, to typical investors. Environmentalists indicated it was important to invest in companies that don't sell weapons or experiment on animals or pollute. However, when asked to hypothetically invest up to $5,000 into 22 mutual funds, environmentalists, like typical investors, consistently ranked financial performance criteria as most important. This suggests that even environmentally minded investors are concerned foremost with earning good returns.

What's the takeaway? Socially responsible or environmentally minded companies are just as likely to be profitable— or unprofitable—as other companies. Green investment funds, so far, are more expensive and produce slightly lower returns. Even environmentalists want their portfolios to earn substantial returns.[16]

Mutual funds are one of the best ways for individual investors to diversify investment portfolios across different sectors of the economy.

of investors, mutual funds have the financial resources to invest in a broader portfolio of securities than individual investors could afford. This high level of diversification can help reduce risk.

- **Professional Management:** Most mutual funds are managed by a professional fund manager who selects the assets in the fund's portfolio. This can be appealing to investors who lack the time and expertise to make complex investment decisions.

- **Variety:** Whatever your investment goals and philosophy, you can probably find a fund that's a good match. There are many different types of funds; some invest only in certain types of securities (such as municipal bonds or stocks of large corporations), others invest in specific sectors of the economy (such as energy, technology, or healthcare), and yet others seek more balanced and broad-based portfolios. Some funds simply invest in a portfolio of stocks that matches those in a specific stock index, such as the Standard & Poor's 500 or the Wilshire 5000. These *index funds* have become very popular in recent years.

- **Liquidity:** It's easy to withdraw funds from a mutual fund. For a closed-end fund, you simply sell your shares. For an open-end fund, you redeem your shares from the fund itself. However, regardless of when you initiate your withdrawal, redemptions

> *"ALL I ASK IS THE CHANCE TO PROVE THAT MONEY CAN'T MAKE ME HAPPY."*
> —SPIKE MILLIGAN

of an open-end fund are not carried out until its NAVPS is determined after the *next* trading session is completed.

Mutual funds do have some drawbacks. Perhaps the most serious is that the professional management touted by many funds doesn't come cheap. Investors in mutual funds pay a variety of fees that typically range from 1% to 3% of the amount invested. The fees charged by mutual funds can make a serious dent in the overall return received by the fund's investors. And funds assess these fees even when they perform poorly. One reason for the popularity of index funds is that they don't require professional management, so their fees are lower.

Another drawback of actively managed funds is that when their professional managers engage in a lot of trading, significant tax consequences are associated with those financial gains. It is also important to realize that some of the specialized mutual funds that invest in only one sector of the economy or only one type of security may not provide enough diversification to reduce risk significantly.

10-3e Exchange Traded Funds: Real Basket Cases (and We Mean That in a Good Way)

An **exchange-traded fund (ETF)** is similar to a mutual fund in some respects but differs in how it is created and how its shares are initially distributed. ETFs allow investors to buy ownership in what is called a *market basket* of many different securities. In fact, the market basket for most ETFs reflects the composition of a broad-based stock index, much like an index mutual fund. But in recent years more specialized ETFs that focus on narrower market baskets of assets have appeared on the market. Like closed-end mutual funds—but unlike the more common open-end funds—ETFs are traded just like stocks. Thus, you can buy and sell ETFs any time of the day.

Compared to most actively managed mutual funds, ETFs usually have lower costs and fees. However, since ETFs are bought and sold like stocks, you do have to pay brokerage commissions every time you buy or sell shares.

> **exchange traded fund (ETF)** Shares traded on securities markets that represent the legal right of ownership over part of a basket of individual stock certificates or other securities.

ISSUING AND TRADING SECURITIES: THE PRIMARY AND SECONDARY MARKETS

There are two distinct types of securities markets: the primary securities market and the secondary securities market. The **primary securities market** is where corporations raise additional financial capital by selling *newly issued* securities. The **secondary securities market** is where *previously issued* securities are traded.

10-4a The Primary Securities Market: Where Securities Are Issued

There are two methods of issuing securities in the primary market:

- In a **public offering**, securities are sold (in concept, at least) to anyone in the investing public who is willing and financially able to buy them.

- In a **private placement**, securities are sold to one or more private investors (who may be individuals or institutions) under terms negotiated between the issuing firm and the private investors.

PUBLIC OFFERINGS

Many corporations are initially owned by a small number of people who don't sell the stock to outsiders. But growing corporations often need to obtain more financial capital than such a small group can provide. Such firms may *go public* by issuing additional stock and offering it to investors outside their group. The first time a corporation sells its stock in a public offering, the sale is called an **initial public offering (IPO)**.

Going public is a complicated and high-stakes process; obtaining sufficient funds in an IPO is often critical to the firm's success. So, almost all firms that go public enlist the help and advice of an investment bank that specializes in helping firms issue new securities. The investment bank assists the firm at every step of the IPO, from the planning and market assessment phase, until the actual securities are distributed to investors after the offering is conducted.

One of the key responsibilities of the investment bank is to arrange for the actual sale of the securities. The investment bank uses either a *best efforts* or a *firm commitment* approach. Under the best efforts approach the bank provides advice about pricing and marketing the securities and assists in finding potential buyers. But it doesn't guarantee that the firm will sell all of its securities at a high enough price to meet its financial goals. The investment bank earns a commission on all of the shares sold under a best efforts approach.

Under a *firm commitment* arrangement, the investment bank **underwrites** the issue. This means that the investment bank itself purchases *all* of the shares at a specified price, thus guaranteeing that the firm issuing the stock will receive a known amount of new funds. The investment bank that underwrites the offer seeks to earn a profit by reselling the stock to investors at a higher price. For large public offerings, a group of investment banks, called an *underwriting syndicate*, may temporarily work together to underwrite the securities.

Before going public, a firm must file a **registration statement** with the Securities and Exchange Commission (SEC). This long, complex document must include the firm's key financial statements plus additional information about the company's management, its properties, its competition, and the intended uses for the funds it plans to obtain from the offering. The corporation cannot legally offer its new securities for sale until the SEC has examined this statement and declared it effective.

---

primary securities market The market where newly issued securities are traded. The primary market is where the firms that issue securities raise additional financial capital.

secondary securities market The market where previously issued securities are traded.

public offering A primary market issue in which new securities are offered to any investors who are willing and able to purchase them.

private placement A primary market issue that is negotiated between the issuing corporation and a small group of accredited investors.

initial public offering (IPO) The first time a company issues stock that may be bought by the general public.

underwriting An arrangement under which an investment banker agrees to purchase all shares of a public offering at an agreed-upon price.

registration statement A long, complex document that firms must file with the SEC when they sell securities through a public offering.

"INVESTORS MUST KEEP IN MIND THAT THERE'S A DIFFERENCE BETWEEN A GOOD COMPANY AND A GOOD STOCK. AFTER ALL, YOU CAN BUY A GOOD CAR BUT PAY TOO MUCH FOR IT."

—RICHARD THALER, AMERICAN ECONOMIST

PRIVATE PLACEMENTS In a private placement, the issuing firm negotiates the terms of the offer directly with a small number of **accredited investors**. These are individuals, businesses, or other organizations that meet specific financial requirements set by the SEC. Private placements are usually quicker, simpler, and less expensive than public offerings. The investment bank often helps the firm identify and contact accredited investors and assists the firm as it negotiates the terms of the private placement.

The main reason private placements are simpler and less expensive than public offerings is that privately placed securities are exempt from the requirement to register with the SEC. The ability to obtain financing without having to prepare complex registration documents can be a real attraction. But because the pool of potential investors is limited to accredited investors, private placements normally don't have the potential to raise as much money as public offerings. Another drawback is that securities that haven't been registered with the SEC can't be sold to anyone except other accredited investors.

10-4b Secondary Securities Markets: Let's Make a Deal

The firms that issue stocks and bonds don't receive any additional funds when their securities are traded in the secondary markets. But few investors would want to buy securities issued in the primary markets without the liquidity and possibility of earning capital gains provided by the opportunity to sell these securities in the secondary markets.

STOCK (SECURITIES) EXCHANGES The stocks of most large publicly traded corporations are listed and traded on a **stock (or securities) exchange**. A securities exchange provides an organized venue for stockbrokers and securities dealers to trade listed stocks and other securities. Each exchange establishes its own requirements for the securities it lists. The requirements vary among the exchanges, but they're typically based on the earnings of the company, the number of shares of stock outstanding, and the number of shareholders. In addition to meeting listing requirements, exchanges require firms to pay an initial fee at the time their securities are first listed, and an annual listing fee to remain listed on the exchange.

The New York Stock Exchange, which is part of NYSE Euronext, is the largest in the world. Euronext exchanges in the United States and Europe represent one-third of equities trading worldwide. NASDAQ, the second-largest stock exchange, is part of NASDAQ OMX, which runs exchanges

Stockbrokers and securities dealers buy and sell stocks for individual and institutional investors at stock (securities) exchanges like this.

in the United States and seven in Europe. NASDAQ began 40 years ago as the National Association of Securities Dealers, or NASD.[17]

Trading on early stock exchanges occurred at physical locations where brokers met on trading floors to buy and sell securities for their clients. Some exchanges still maintain actual trading floors, but most trading on today's exchanges is done electronically. The participants in these markets carry out their trades mainly via computer networks.

The trend toward electronic trading began in 1971 with the establishment of NASDAQ, which initially was just a system used to report stock prices electronically. But over the years, it evolved into a complete market with formal listing requirements and fees. The stocks of many of today's high-profile technology companies, such as Apple, Google, and Microsoft, are traded on the NASDAQ market.

The key players in the NASDAQ market are known as **market makers**. These are securities dealers that make a commitment to continuously offer to buy and sell (make a market in) specific NASDAQ-listed stocks. Each NASDAQ stock has several market makers who compete against

accredited investor An organization or individual investor who meets certain criteria established by the SEC and so qualifies to invest in unregistered securities.

stock (or securities) exchange An organized venue for trading stocks and other securities that meet its listing requirements.

market makers Securities dealers that make a commitment to continuously offer to buy and sell the stock of a specific corporation listed on the NASDAQ exchange or traded in the OTC market.

each other by posting two prices for each stock: the *bid price* indicates how much the market maker will pay per share to buy a stated quantity of the stock, while the *ask price* indicates the price per share at which it will sell the same stock. The ask price is higher than the bid price; the difference is called the *bid/ask spread* (or just the *spread*) and is the source of the market maker's profit.

THE OVER-THE-COUNTER MARKET Many corporations with publicly traded stock don't meet the requirements to have their shares listed on an organized exchange; others choose not to list on exchanges because they don't want to pay the listing fees. The **over-the-counter market (OTC)** is where the stocks of such companies are traded. OTC stocks are traded through a system of market makers much like stocks are traded on the NASDAQ exchange. However, the market for most OTC stocks is much less active than for stocks listed on the major exchanges. Because of this, most stocks listed on the OTC have only a few market makers. The lack of competition often leads to much higher spreads between bid and ask prices for stocks traded in the OTC than normally exist for stocks traded on the NASDAQ exchange.

ELECTRONIC COMMUNICATIONS NETWORKS The newest development in stock market technology involves the rise of **electronic communications networks (ECNs)**. The SEC classifies ECNs as alternative trading systems because they represent an alternative to established stock exchanges as a venue for buying and selling securities. ECNs are entirely automated and computerized trading systems that allow traders to bypass the market makers used in the NASDAQ and OTC markets. However, individuals can only take advantage of this venue by opening an account with a broker-dealer that subscribes to an ECN.

If you place an order to buy a security on an ECN, the computer system checks to see if there is a matching order from another trader to sell the same security. If so, it immediately and automatically executes the transaction in a process that typically takes less than a second to complete. ECNs obviously speed up transactions. They also make it possible for investors to trade securities "after hours" when the U.S. exchanges are closed.

over-the-counter (OTC) market The market where securities that are not listed on exchanges are traded.

electronic communications network (ECN) An automated, computerized securities trading system that automatically matches buyers and sellers, executing trades quickly and allowing trading when securities exchanges are closed.

10-5 PERSONAL INVESTING

Would investing in stocks, bonds, and other securities make sense for you? If so, how could you get started? What are the potential risks and rewards of various investment strategies?

Investing in securities requires you to think carefully about your specific situation, your personal goals, and your attitudes:

- What are your short-term and long-term goals?
- Given your budget, how much are you able to invest?
- How long can you leave your money invested?
- How concerned are you about the tax implications of your investments?
- How much tolerance do you have for risk?

Notice that the last question deals with your attitudes toward risk. Most people are not comfortable with high levels of risk. But no investment strategy completely avoids risk. And in general, the riskier the approach, the greater the *potential* rewards. To achieve your goals, you'll need to find the balance between risk and return that works for you.

10-5a Choosing a Broker: Gaining Access to the Markets

Members of the general public cannot directly trade stocks and other securities on the exchanges, the over-the-counter market, or the ECNs we described earlier in the chapter. Thus, most investors enlist the services of a brokerage firm to carry out their trades. Choosing the right broker is the first step in implementing your investment plans.

A *full-service broker* provides a wide range of services—such as market research, investment advice, and tax planning—in addition to carrying out your trades. *Discount brokers* provide the basic services needed to buy and sell securities but offer fewer additional services. They may also restrict your ability to trade certain types of securities. For example, some discount brokers don't offer the ability to buy and sell foreign securities. Discount brokers tend to charge significantly lower commissions than full-service brokers. In fact, many discount brokers charge flat fees of only a few dollars per trade for basic transactions. But brokerage firms also charge a variety of fees—sometimes including "inactivity fees" if you don't place enough orders! Once these fees are considered, brokerage firms that offer low commissions may not be as inexpensive as they first appear!

Index Funds Certainly Aren't Average!

Index funds match or mirror the stock market, or a particular segment of it. For instance, Vanguard's Total Stock Market Index (VTSMI) fund holds 3,808 stocks that are weighted proportionally to the entire U.S. stock market. For example, 18.8% of VTSMI's holdings are financial stocks, just like in the overall U.S. market. Those weightings change, of course, as the overall market changes. Today, Apple's stock is VTSMI's largest holding. But that wasn't the case five years ago. So, when market weightings change, index funds buy and sell stocks proportionate to those changes.

Index funds provide three great benefits for investors.

Because they don't employ expensive fund managers to decide which stocks to buy or sell, costs are low. While professional money managers may charge fees up to 2% per year, VTSMI's charge is just 0.17% per year. For an investor with $100,000 invested, that's the difference between annual fees as high as $2,000 and as low as $170.

Next, compared to managed funds, which frequently buy and sell stocks (called turnover), index funds make infrequent and few changes to the stocks they hold. Since buying and selling stocks incurs capital gains taxes, this means that index funds are not only cheaper, they reduce capital gains taxes, which reduce investment returns.

Finally, because they mirror the market, index funds almost always match average market performance, something that 75% to 80% of managed funds fail to do every year.

Simple. Cheap. Low taxes. Superior investment performance year after year. Index funds should be a key part of every investor's portfolio.[18]

PeskyMonkey/iStockphoto.com

In recent years, competition among brokerage firms has blurred the distinction between full-service and discount brokers. To stop clients from defecting to discount brokers, many full-service firms have lowered their commissions. At the same time, many discount brokers have begun to offer a broader range of services to attract more clients. Now many brokerage firms offer investors the choice of discount or full-service accounts.

Once you've decided on a broker, you need to open an account. This is a fairly simple process; it requires filling out some forms (usually available online) and making an initial investment. The minimum initial investment varies, but $1,000 to $3,000 is fairly typical.

10-5b Buying Securities: Let's Make a Deal

Once you've set up your account, you can trade securities by contacting your broker and indicating the security you want to trade and the quantity you want to buy or sell. You can also specify the type of order you want to place. The most common types of orders are market orders and limit orders:

- **Market orders** instruct the broker to buy or sell a security at the current market price. Placing a market order virtually guarantees that your order will be executed. The downside is that you may end up buying at a higher price than you expected to pay (or selling your stock for less than you expected to receive).

- **Limit orders** place limits on the prices at which orders are executed. A buy limit order tells a broker to buy a stock *only* if its price is at or below a specified value. You'd use this approach if you wanted to make sure you didn't pay more for the stock than you thought it was worth. A sell limit order tells your broker to sell the shares only if the price is at or above a specified value. This prevents your broker from selling your stock at a price you believe is too low.

10-5c Strategies for Investing in Securities

There are several strategies you can use to guide your investment decisions. We'll provide an overview of the more

market order An order telling a broker to buy or sell a specific security at the best currently available price.

limit order An order to a broker to buy a specific stock only if its price is below a certain level, or to sell a specific stock only if its price is above a certain level.

Just Because They Can, Doesn't Mean They Should. ???

Activist investors typically purchase large blocks of stock in public companies and then attempt to use their position as large shareholders to obtain board seats or otherwise influence (or dictate) company strategy. Generally, they aim to quickly increase share prices and then sell to realize large gains. According to FactSet, 84% of activist-owned shares are indeed sold within two years.

When Sandra Cochran became CEO of Cracker Barrel (CB), she came ready with a six-point, long-term plan for improving the casual-dining restaurant chain's financial performance. Her plan included new marketing highlighting the chain's made-from-scratch cooking, a new menu adjusted for lower consumer spending, a reduced cost structure, and new board members.

Source: Cracker Barrel Old Country Store

But then Sardar Biglari, an activist investor who claimed success turning around Steak-N-Shake, bought 20% of the company. Biglari demanded a board seat, agitated for aggressive growth and overseas expansion, and even proposed buying the entire company to quick-start his plans. Cochran had a choice. Either she could revise her plan to align more closely with Biglari's, or she could stick to her plan and fend off his attempts to derail it.

Historically, activist investors like Biglari advocate for actions such as cutting costs, laying off employees, buying back shares, spinning off underperforming divisions, and even selling the entire company. For a company faced with chronically poor results, those choices may make sense, but they might also be short-term fixes to more complex problems.[19]

What do YOU think?

- What ethical responsibility does a CEO have to pursue strategies proposed by an activist investor?
- At what level of ownership, 5%, 10%, or more, are shareholders justified in demanding that company executives allow them to participate in setting company direction or strategy?
- How should executives handle activists while still pursuing the company's strategy? When and why should they keep them at arm's length or try to work with them?

---

common approaches, but none of these approaches is foolproof—alas, there is no known strategy that is guaranteed to earn you millions.

INVESTING FOR INCOME
Some investors focus on buying bonds and preferred stocks to generate a steady, predictable flow of income. This approach is popular with retirees who want to supplement their retirement income. But the return on such low-risk securities is relatively low, and their market value seldom increases much over time. Thus, it probably isn't the best strategy for younger investors who are trying to grow their wealth.

MARKET TIMING Investors who rely on *market timing* use a variety of analytical techniques to try to predict

> "I WILL TELL YOU HOW TO BECOME RICH. CLOSE THE DOORS. BE FEARFUL WHEN OTHERS ARE GREEDY. BE GREEDY WHEN OTHERS ARE FEARFUL."
>
> —WARREN BUFFETT

when prices of specific stocks are likely to rise and fall. Market timers try to make quick gains by buying low and selling high over a relatively short time horizon.

The problem with market timing is that so many factors can influence stock prices—some of them random in nature—that it's tough to consistently identify the timing and direction of changes in stock prices. Market timing also requires investors to make frequent trades. Given the commissions paid on trades and the taxes incurred on short-term capital gains, this approach may do a better job of enriching the broker than enriching the trader!

VALUE INVESTING Investors who favor *value investing* try to find stocks that are undervalued in the market.

Stockbrokers place orders to buy and sell stocks and other securities for their clients.

set of securities and holding them for a long period of time. Buy-and-hold investors put their faith in the ability of the *overall market* to continue the long-run upward trend it has exhibited throughout its history. One way that many buy-and-hold investors do this is by investing in index mutual funds and ETFs. The buy-and-hold strategy seldom allows investors to "get rich quick," but it usually results in a solid financial return over the long haul.

Obviously, the buy-and-hold strategy will work only if you can afford to leave your money invested for a long time. When the stock market takes a dive, it can sometimes take years for stocks to recover and start to show solid returns. Some people who think they're comfortable with a buy-and-hold strategy end up getting "happy feet" after a few weeks of declining stock prices. They panic and sell off their stocks at exactly the wrong time, locking in big losses. For the buy-and-hold strategy to work, you've got to have the patience—and mental toughness—to ride out short-term downturns in the market.

They believe that the market price will rise over time to reflect its true value, thus generating a capital gain. This approach requires intensive research to identify discrepancies between a company's true (or intrinsic) value and its current market price.

The drawback with value investing is that thousands of investors are all trying to do the same thing, so the competition to locate undervalued stocks is intense. Unless you're among the first to discover a good value, the investors who beat you to it will rush to buy up the stock, increasing demand and driving up the stock's price so that it is no longer undervalued.

INVESTING FOR GROWTH Investors who focus on growth look for companies that have the potential to grow much faster than average for a sustained time, which they believe will lead to a steady (and sometimes spectacular) rise in the stock's price. Investors using this strategy often invest in stocks of relatively new companies with innovative products in a hot sector of the economy.

Investing for growth entails significant risk. Small new companies lack established track records. And rapidly expanding industries tend to attract many start-up companies, so competition can be intense. Finally, given the rapid pace of technological change, today's hot prospects may soon be dethroned by the next big thing. It's hard to predict which firms will be winners; even experts often make the wrong choice.

BUYING AND HOLDING If you're a patient person with steady nerves, a buy-and-hold approach might appeal to you. This strategy involves purchasing a diversified

 10-6 KEEPING TABS ON THE MARKET

Once you've begun to invest in securities, you'll want to keep track of how your investments are doing. Using the Internet, you can easily find information about both general market trends and the performance of specific securities.

10-6a Stock Indices: Tracking the Trends

One of the most common ways to track general market conditions and trends is to follow what's happening to various stock indices. A **stock index** tracks the prices of a large group of stocks that meet certain defined criteria. Many investors like to compare how the stocks in their own portfolio compare to the performance of these broad indices. Two of the best-known indices are the Dow Jones Industrial Average and the S&P 500.

- The **Dow Jones Industrial Average (DJIA)**: Often called just "the Dow,"

> **stock index** A statistic that tracks how the prices of a specific set of stocks have changed.
>
> **Dow Jones Industrial Average (DJIA)** An index that tracks stock prices of 30 large, well-known U.S. corporations.

EXHIBIT 10.2 — MAJOR STOCK PRICE INDICES

Index	What It Tracks
NASDAQ Composite	All of the domestic and foreign common stocks traded on the NASDAQ exchange.
Wilshire 5000	Stock prices of all U.S. corporations with actively traded stock. Despite the 5,000 in its name, this index actually includes well over 6,000 stocks. (The exact number changes frequently.)
Russell 2000	Stock prices of 2,000 relatively small but actively traded U.S. corporations.
FTSE 100	Stock prices of 100 of the largest and most actively traded companies listed on the London Stock Exchange.
Nikkei 225	Stock prices of 225 of the largest and most actively traded companies listed on the Tokyo Stock Exchange.
SSE Composite	Stock prices of all stocks listed on the Shanghai Stock Exchange.

© Cengage Learning®

this is the most widely followed stock index. The Dow is based on the adjusted average price of 30 stocks picked by the editors of *The Wall Street Journal*. All of the Dow firms are large, well-established corporations, such as Apple, General Electric, Coca-Cola, McDonald's, and Disney.

- The **Standard & Poor's 500**: With 500 stocks instead of just 30, the S&P 500 is a much broader index than the DJIA. Still, like the Dow, the companies included in the S&P 500 are large, well-established American corporations.

Exhibit 10.2 identifies several other well-known indices, including some that track prices of stocks in foreign securities markets.

10-6b Tracking the Performance of Specific Securities

Many financial websites offer detailed stock quotes that provide the current price of a company's stock and a wealth of related information. To check out a specific stock, you simply type its *stock symbol*—a short combination of letters that uniquely identifies a corporate security—into a "Get Quote" box. (Most sites have a lookup feature that finds the symbol if you type in the company's name.)

Standard & Poor's 500 A stock index based on prices of 500 major U.S. corporations in a variety of industries and market sectors.

Exhibit 10.3 illustrates the information a popular financial website, Yahoo! Finance (http://finance.yahoo.com/), provides about McDonald's common stock. Some of the key figures reported for McDonald's include:

- *Last trade*: The price of McDonald's common stock for the most recent trade was $97.44.

- *Change*: The last trade of McDonald's stock was $0.36 lower than the closing price for the stock on the previous day.

- *Bid and Ask*: The highest price currently offered (bid) to buy McDonald's stock is $97.21 for 300 shares. The lowest price currently offered (asked) to sell the stock is $97.68 for 100 shares.

- *Day's range*: The highest price for the stock during the day was $97.75 and the lowest price was $97.07.

- *52-Week range*: The highest price for McDonald's stock over the previous 52 weeks was $103.78 while its lowest price was $87.62.

- *Volume*: 5,197,686 shares of the stock have been traded up to this point in the current trading session.

- *Market Cap*: The total market value of all shares of McDonald's common stock outstanding was $93.65 billion. This is found by multiplying the price per share times the number of shares of common stock outstanding.

- *P/E*: The price-to-earnings of 20.22 is found by dividing the stock's price per share by its earnings per

EXHIBIT 10.3 — YAHOO! FINANCE QUOTE FOR A STOCK

McDonald's Corp. Common St (NYSE: McD) Real-time 95.85 ↓ .69 (0.71%) 4:00 PM EDT

Last Trade:	97.44	Day's Range:	97.07–97.75
Trade Time:	4:00 pm EDT	52wk Range:	87.62–103.78
Change:	↓0.36 (0.37%)	Volume:	5,197,686
Prev Close:	97.80	Avg Vol (3m):	7,453,340
Open:	97.41	Market Cap:	93.65B
Bid:	97.21 × 300	P/E (ttm):	20.22
Ask:	97.68 × 100	EPS (ttm):	4.82
1y Target Est:	99.76	Div & Yield:	3.40 (3.50%)

Source: Yahoo! Finance stock quote, accessed April 13, 2015.

share. In general, a higher P/E ratio means investors expect a greater growth in earnings over time.

- *EPS (earnings per share)*: McDonald's earned $4.82 per share of common stock outstanding. EPS is computed by dividing the net income available to common stockholders by the number of shares of common stock outstanding.

- *Div & Yield*: The sum of dividends paid by McDonald's over the past 12 months was $3.40 per share. Yield is found by dividing the dividend per share by the previous day's price per share. It tells us that at that price the dividend paid by McDonald's represented a 3.50% return to the investor. (But since the total return to stockholders may also include a capital gain or loss, this yield doesn't tell us the whole story.)

Financial websites also provide information about other types of securities such as mutual funds, ETFs, and bonds.

The BIG Picture

Many different organizations participate in financial markets, including banks, finance companies, securities brokers and dealers, investment banks, and institutional investors such as mutual funds, insurance companies, and pension funds. Although they differ in their functions, each of these participants helps financial markets achieve their primary purpose of channeling funds from savers to borrowers.

In this chapter, we focused on one particular type of financial market, namely the market for financial securities. The financial capital that corporations raise when they issue stocks and bonds in these markets is critical to every functional area of their operations. Without these funds, the marketing department would lack the resources needed to develop new products, information technology professionals would be unable to update hardware and software, and operations managers would be unable to acquire the machinery and equipment needed to produce the goods and services the company sells to earn its profits.

On the other side of these markets, investors who buy corporate securities do so to acquire assets that they believe will help them achieve their own financial goals. But investing in securities involves risk. Over any short-run time period, there is simply no guarantee that stocks and bonds will provide investors with the returns they expect. The good news—at least if you plan to invest—is that history shows that, over the long run, the return on these securities is positive. Given enough time and patience, investing in stocks and other securities is likely to result in a substantial increase in wealth.

Careers in Business

Stock Broker

Responsible for meeting and getting to know clients and their financial needs, offering financial advice on investment recommendations (for a diversified mix of stocks, fixed-income investments including bonds and certificates of deposit, mutual funds and annuities, as well as a wide range of insurance options, including life insurance, long-term disability, and long-term care), and placing trades. The ideal candidate has a bachelor's or master's degree, Series 7 license, a strong sales and/or management background, strong interpersonal skills that provide the ability to develop meaningful relationships, the drive to set and achieve goals in a performance-driven atmosphere, and the ability to work autonomously from your own neighborhood office. For more information on this career and other possible careers in business, check out Career Transitions.

STUDY TOOLS 10

LOCATED AT BACK OF THE TEXTBOOK

☐ Rip Out Chapter Review Card

LOCATED AT WWW.CENGAGE.COM/LOGIN

☐ Review key term flashcards and create your own using StudyBits

☐ Create and complete practice quizzes based off of your notes and StudyBits

☐ Complete Online activities such as Matching, Fill-in-the-Blank, and Drag and Drop exercises

☐ View chapter highlight box content, including CEO Profiles, What Would You Do Cases, and chapter videos

☐ Track your knowledge and understanding of key concepts in business using 4LTR Online

LEARNING YOUR WAY

Go to **www.cengagebrain.com**
to access **BUSN Online!**

11 | Marketing: Building Profitable Customer Connections

LEARNING OBJECTIVES

After studying this chapter, you will be able to:

11-1 Discuss the objectives, the process, and the scope of marketing

11-2 Identify the role of the customer in marketing

11-3 Explain each element of marketing strategy

11-4 Describe the consumer and business decision-making process

11-5 Discuss the key elements of marketing research

11-6 Explain the roles of social responsibility and technology in marketing

Remember to visit **PAGE 203** for additional STUDY TOOLS

11-1 MARKETING: GETTING VALUE BY GIVING VALUE

What comes to mind when you hear the term **marketing**? Most people think of the radio ad they heard this morning, or the billboard they saw while driving to school. But advertising is only a small part of marketing; the whole story is much bigger. The American Marketing Association defines marketing as *the activity, set of institutions, and processes for creating, communicating, delivering, and exchanging offerings that have value for customers, clients, partners, and society at large.*

marketing An organizational function and a set of processes for creating, communicating, and delivering value to customers and for managing customer relationships in ways that benefit the organization and its stakeholders.

utility The ability of goods and services to satisfy consumer "wants."

The ultimate benefit that most businesses seek from marketing is long-term profitability. But attaining this benefit is impossible without first delivering value to customers and other stakeholders.

A successful marketer delivers value by filling customer needs in ways that exceed their expectations. As a result, you get sales today and sales tomorrow and sales the next day, which—across the days and months and years—can translate into long-term profitability. Alice Foote MacDougall, a successful entrepreneur in the 1920s, understood this thinking early on: "In business you get what you want by giving other people what they want." **Utility** is the ability of goods

"A THRILLED CUSTOMER IS THE MOST POTENT MARKETING ASSET YOUR ORGANIZATION CAN LEVERAGE."

—JOHN JANTSCH, AUTHOR, *DUCT TAPE MARKETING*

Rootstock/Shutterstock.com

and services to satisfy these wants. And since there is a wide range of wants, products can provide utility in a number of different ways:

- *Form utility* satisfies wants by converting inputs into a finished form. Clearly, the vast majority of products provide some kind of form utility. For example, McDonald's slices, dices, and fries potatoes into delicious french fries, and UGG Australia stretches, treats, and sews sheepskins and wool into comfortable, stylish boots.

- *Time utility* satisfies wants by providing goods and services at a convenient time for customers. For example, FedEx offers evening and Saturday residential delivery times, many dry cleaners offer one-hour service, 24 Hour Fitness is virtually always open, and most fast-food restaurants offer 24-hour drive-through windows.

- *Place utility* satisfies wants by providing goods and services at a convenient place for customers. For example, Redbox makes DVDs and games available in front of a growing number of retailers, Motel 6 offers budget lodging at the bottom of many freeway off ramps, and vending machines refuel tired students on virtually every college campus.

- *Ownership utility* satisfies wants by smoothly transferring ownership of goods and services from seller to buyer. Virtually every product provides some degree of ownership utility, but some offer more than others. Apple, for example, has created a hassle-free purchase process that customers can follow by phone, by computer, and in person. And many car dealerships offer financing options.

Satisfying customer wants—in a way that exceeds expectations—is a job that never ends. Jay Levinson, a recognized expert in breakthrough marketing, comments, "Marketing is…a process. You improve it, perfect it, change it, even pause it. But you never stop it completely."

11-1a The Scope of Marketing: It's Everywhere!

For many years, businesspeople have actively applied the principles of marketing to goods and services that range from cars, to fast food, to liquor, to computers, to movies.

But within the past decade or two, other organizations have successfully adopted marketing strategies and tactics to further their goals.

Nonprofit organizations—in both the private and public sectors—play a significant role in our economy, employing more people than the federal government and all 50 state governments combined (not to mention an army of volunteers!). These organizations use marketing, sometimes quite assertively, to achieve their objectives. The U.S. Army's marketing communications budget, for example, sometimes approaches as much as $200 million per year. Your own college probably markets itself to both prospective students and potential alumni donors. Private-sector nonprofit organizations also use marketing strategies for everything from marshalling AYSO soccer coaches for kids, to boosting attendance at the local zoo, to planning cultural events.[1]

Nonprofit organizations play a pivotal role in the expansion of marketing across our economy to include people, places, events, and ideas. But for-profit enterprises have also begun to apply marketing strategies and tactics beyond simply goods and services.

■ **People Marketing:** Sports, politics, and art dominate this category, but even some business-people merit mentioning. Top banking executives, for instance, took a beating from a marketing standpoint during the financial meltdown at the end of 2008. Also in 2008, President Barack Obama was named Ad Age Marketer of the Year, edging

Athletic, cultural and charitable events are all activities that rely on sponsorships as part of their event marketing approach.

out powerhouse consumer brands that were also on the short list, such as Apple, Nike, and Coors. He became a living symbol of change in the minds of his supporters. Countless entertainers and athletes have used people marketing to their advantage as well. Consider, for example, Paris Hilton, who appeared to build her early career on promotion alone, eventually parlaying the media attention into a successful line of perfumes and fashion items. Hilton clearly has no doubt about her abilities, declaring, "I am a marketing genius." In fact, as you pursue your personal goals—whether you seek a new job, university admission, or a Friday night date—people marketing principles can help you achieve your objective. Start by figuring out what your "customer" needs, and then ensure that your "product" (you!) delivers above and beyond expectations.[2]

■ **Place Marketing:** This category involves drawing people to a particular place. Cities and states use place marketing to attract businesses. Delaware, for instance, the second-smallest state in the Union, is home to more than half of the Fortune 500 firms because it deliberately developed a range of advantages for corporations. But more visibly, cities, states, and nations use place marketing to attract tourists. Thanks to powerful place marketing, most people have probably heard that "What happens in Vegas stays in Vegas." In late 2008, Las Vegas shelved the high-rolling campaign in favor of a more "recession-proof," but less successful strategy: the "Take a Break USA" campaign. By late 2009, Vegas had reverted to the "What Happens …" campaign that fueled visitors since its launch in 2003, leading to a record-breaking 41.1 million visitors in 2014.[3]

■ **Event Marketing:** This category includes marketing—or sponsoring—athletic, cultural, or charitable events. Partnerships between the public and private sectors are increasingly common. Examples include the Olympics, the Super Bowl, the FIFA World Cup, and NBC's 2012 benefit telethon concert to benefit the victims of Hurricane Sandy.

■ **Idea Marketing:** A whole range of public and private organizations market ideas that are meant to change how people think or act. Recycle, don't drink and drive, buckle your seatbelt, support our political party, donate blood, and don't smoke are all examples of popular causes. Often, idea

Exhibit 11.1
The Evolution of Marketing

The focus of marketing has evolved over time.

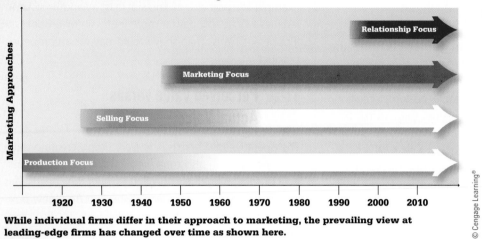

Marketing Approaches (vertical axis)

Relationship Focus

Marketing Focus

Selling Focus

Production Focus

1920 1930 1940 1950 1960 1970 1980 1990 2000 2010

© Cengage Learning®

While individual firms differ in their approach to marketing, the prevailing view at leading-edge firms has changed over time as shown here.

---

marketing and event marketing are combined, as we see in the annual Avon Walk for Breast Cancer. The planners actively market the idea of annual mammograms, as they solicit contributions for breast cancer research and participation in the event itself.

11-1b The Evolution of Marketing: From the Product to the Customer

The current approach to marketing evolved through a number of overlapping stages, as you'll see in Exhibit 11.1. But as you read about these eras, keep in mind that some businesses have remained lodged—with varying degrees of success—in the thinking of a past era.

PRODUCTION ERA Marketing didn't always begin with the customer. In fact, in the early 1900s, the customer was practically a joke. Henry Ford summed up the prevailing mindset when he reportedly said "You can have your Model T in any color you want as long as it's black." This attitude made sense from a historical perspective, since consumers didn't have the overwhelming number of choices that are currently available; most products were purchased as soon as they were produced and distributed to consumers. In this context, the top business priority was to produce large quantities of goods as efficiently as possible.

SELLING ERA By the 1920s, production capacity had increased dramatically. For the first time, supply in many categories exceeded demand, which caused the emergence of the hard sell. The selling focus gained momentum in the 1930s and 1940s, when the Depression and World War II made consumers even more reluctant to part with their limited money.

MARKETING ERA The landscape changed dramatically in the 1950s. Many factories that had churned out military supplies converted to consumer production, flooding the market with choices in virtually every product category. An era of relative peace and prosperity emerged, and—as soldiers returned from World War II—marriage and birthrates soared. To compete for the consumer's dollar, marketers attempted to provide goods and services that met customer needs better than anything else on the market. As a result, the marketing concept materialized in the 1950s. The **marketing concept** is a philosophy that makes customer satisfaction—now and in the future—the central focus of the entire organization. Companies that embrace this philosophy strive to delight customers, integrating this goal into all business activities. The marketing concept holds that delivering unmatched value to customers is the only effective way to achieve long-term profitability.

RELATIONSHIP ERA The marketing concept has gathered momentum across the economy, leading to the current era, unfolding over the last decade, which zeros in on long-term customer relationships. Acquiring a new customer can cost five times more than keeping an existing customer. Retaining your current customers—and getting them to spend additional dollars—is clearly cost-effective. Moreover, satisfied customers can develop into advocates for your business, becoming powerful generators of positive "word-of-mouth."

marketing concept A business philosophy that makes customer satisfaction—now and in the future—the central focus of the entire organization.

11-2 THE CUSTOMER: FRONT AND CENTER

11-2a Customer Relationship Management (CRM)

Customer relationship management (CRM) is the centerpiece of successful, twenty-first century marketing. Broadly defined, CRM is the ongoing process of acquiring, maintaining, and growing profitable customer relationships by delivering unmatched value. CRM works best when marketers combine marketing communication with one-on-one personalization. Amazon is a champion player at CRM, greeting customers by name, recommending specific products, and providing streamlined checkout. Clearly, information is an integral part of this process—you simply can't do CRM without collecting, managing, and applying the right data at the right time for the right person (and every repeat customer is the "right person"!).

LIMITED RELATIONSHIPS The scope of your relationships will depend not just on the data you gather but also on your industry. Colgate-Palmolive, for example, can't forge a close personal bond with every person who buys a bar of Irish Spring soap. However, the company does invite customers to call its toll-free line with questions or comments, and it maintains a vibrant website with music, an e-newsletter, special offers, and an invitation to contact the company. You can bet that the company actively gathers data and pursues a connection with customers who initiate contact.

FULL PARTNERSHIPS If you have a high-ticket product and a smaller customer base, you're much more likely to pursue a full partnership with each of your key clients. Colgate-Palmolive, for instance, has dedicated customer service teams working with key accounts such as Walmart and Costco. With a full partnership, the marketer gathers and leverages extensive information about each customer and often includes the customer in key aspects of the product development process.

VALUE You know you've delivered **value** when your customers believe that your product has a better relationship between the cost and the benefits than any competitor. By this definition, low cost does not always mean high value. In fact, a recent survey suggests that loyal customers are often willing to pay *more* for their products rather than switch to lower-cost competitors. Apple provides a clear example. We probably all know at least a handful of Apple fanatics who gladly pay far more for their PowerBooks (or iPhones or iPads) than they would pay for a competing product.

11-2b Perceived Value versus Actual Value

The operative idea here is *perceived*. Simply creating value isn't enough; you also must help customers believe that your product is uniquely qualified to meet their needs. This becomes a particular challenge when you're a new business competing against a market leader with disproportionately strong perceived value.

11-2c Customer Satisfaction

You know you've satisfied your customers when you deliver perceived value above and beyond their expectations. But achieving **customer satisfaction** can be tricky. Less savvy marketers frequently fall into one of two traps:

- The first trap is overpromising. Even if you deliver more value than anyone else, your customers will be disappointed if your product falls short of overly high expectations. The messages that you send regarding your product influence expectations—keep them real!

Perhaps in no other industry is there more customer loyalty than when purchasing a new vehicle.

Mangostock/Shutterstock.com

---

customer relationship management (CRM) The ongoing process of acquiring, maintaining, and growing profitable customer relationships by delivering unmatched value.

value A customer perception that a product has a better relationship than its competitors between the cost and the benefits.

customer satisfaction When customers perceive that a good or service delivers value above and beyond their expectations.

- The second trap is underpromising. If you don't set expectations high enough, too few customers will be willing to try your product. The result will be a tiny base of highly satisfied customers, which usually isn't enough to sustain a business.

Finding the right balance is tricky but clearly not impossible. Judging by their high scores on the American Customer Satisfaction Index, the following companies come close to mastering the art of customer satisfaction: Costco, Office Depot, Publix, Nordstrom, Amazon, Lexus, and Northwestern Mutual.[4]

11-2d Customer Loyalty

Customer loyalty is the payoff for delivering value and generating satisfaction. Loyal customers purchase from you again and again—and they sometimes even pay more for your product. They forgive your mistakes. They provide valuable feedback. They may require less service. They refer their friends (and sometimes even strangers). Moreover, studying your loyal customers can give you a competitive edge for acquiring new ones, since people with a similar profile would likely be a great fit for your products.[5]

 11-3

MARKETING STRATEGY: WHERE ARE YOU GOING, AND HOW WILL YOU GET THERE?

In marketing terms, the questions become: Who is your target audience, and how will you reach them? Many successful firms answer this question by developing a formal **marketing plan**, updated on a yearly basis; other firms handle their planning on a more informal basis. But regardless of the specific approach, the first step in planning your marketing strategy should be to determine where to target your efforts. Who are those people who are most likely to buy your products? The first step is **market segmentation**—dividing your marketing into groups of people, or segments, that are similar to one another and different from everyone else. One or more of these segments will be your target market. Once you've identified your target market, your next step is to determine how you can best use marketing tools to reach them. And finally, you need to anticipate and respond to changes in the external environment. This section will define target market, explain market segmentation, introduce the marketing mix, and review the key factors in the

Exhibit 11.2
Marketing Strategy

© Cengage Learning®

marketing environment. Taken together, these elements will shape an effective marketing strategy, as shown in Exhibit 11.2.

The marketer creates the marketing mix but responds to the marketing environment with a single-minded focus on the target market.

11-3a Target Market

Your **target market** is the group of people who are most likely to buy your product. This is where you should concentrate your marketing efforts. But why not target your efforts toward everyone? After all, even if most middle-aged moms wouldn't buy purple polka-dotted miniskirts, an adventurous few just might do it. Well, you can always hope for the adventurous few, but virtually every business has limited resources, and marketing toward the people who are most likely to

customer loyalty When customers buy a product from the same supplier again and again—sometimes paying even more for it than they would for a competitive product.

marketing plan A formal document that defines marketing objectives and the specific strategies for achieving those objectives.

market segmentation Dividing potential customers into groups of similar people, or segments.

target market The group of people who are most likely to buy a particular product.

buy your flamboyant minis—say, teenage girls—will maximize the impact of each dollar you spend. A well-chosen target market embodies the following characteristics:

- Size: There must be enough people in your target group to support a business.

- Profitability: The people must be willing and able to spend more than the cost of producing and marketing your product.

- Accessibility: Your target must be reachable through channels that your business can afford.

- Limited competition: Look for markets with limited competition; a crowded market is much tougher to crack.

11-3b Consumer Markets versus Business Markets

Consumer marketers (B2C) direct their efforts to people who are buying products for personal consumption (e.g., granola bars, toothpaste, and clothing), whereas **business marketers (B2B)** direct their efforts to customers who are buying products to use either directly or indirectly to produce other products (e.g., lumber, insulation, and robots). But keep in mind that the distinction between the market categories is not in the products themselves; rather, it lies in how the buyer will use the product. For instance, shoes that you buy for yourself are clearly a consumer product, but shoes that a bowling alley buys for its customers are a business product. Similarly, a computer that you buy for yourself is a consumer product, but a computer that your school buys for the computer lab is a business product. Both B2C and B2B marketers need to choose the best target, but they tend to follow slightly different approaches.

11-3c Consumer Market Segmentation

Choosing the best target market (or markets) for your product begins with dividing your market into segments, or groups of people who have similar characteristics. But people can be similar in a number of different ways, so, not surprisingly, marketers have several options for segmenting potential consumers.

DEMOGRAPHIC B2C **demographic segmentation** refers to dividing the market based on measurable characteristics about people such as age, income, ethnicity, and gender. Demographics are a vital starting point for most marketers. Chapstick, for instance, targets young women with the Shimmer version of its lip balm, and Chevy Camaro targets young men with money. Sometimes the demographic makeup of a given market is tough to discern; African American artists, for instance, create the bulk of rap music, yet Caucasian suburban males form the bulk of the rap music market.

GEOGRAPHIC B2C **geographic segmentation** refers to dividing the market based on where consumers live. This process can incorporate countries, or cities, or population density as key factors. For instance, Ford Expedition does not concentrate on European markets, where tiny, winding streets and nonexistent parking are common in many cities. Cosmetic surgeons tend to market their services more heavily in urban rather than rural areas. And finding the perfect surfboard is easy in Hawaii but more challenging in South Dakota.

PSYCHOGRAPHIC B2C **psychographic segmentation** refers to dividing the market based on consumer attitudes, interests, values, and lifestyles. Toyota Prius, for instance, targets consumers who care about protecting the

Surf board makers will use psychographic segmentation in order to determine their target market.

environment. A number of companies have found a highly profitable niche providing upscale wilderness experiences for people who seek all the pleasure with none of the pain (you enjoy the great outdoors, while someone else lugs your gear, pours your wine, slices your goat cheese, and inflates your extra-comfy air mattress). Both magazine racks and the Internet are filled with products geared toward psychographic segments, including adventure travel sites, Adventure Center .com, shoe-selling mega site Zappos.com, and business and financial powerhouse WallStreetJournal.com. NOTE: Marketers typically use psychographics to complement other segmentation approaches rather than to provide the core definition.

BEHAVIORAL B2C **behavioral segmentation** refers to dividing the market based on how people behave toward various products. This category includes both the benefits that consumers seek from products and how consumers use the product. The Neutrogena Corporation, for example, built a multimillion-dollar hair care business by targeting consumers who wanted an occasional break from their favorite shampoo. Countless products such as Miller Lite actively target the low-carbohydrate consumer. But perhaps the most common type of behavioral segmentation is based on usage patterns. Fast-food restaurants, for instance, actively target heavy users (who, ironically, tend to be slender): young men in their 20s and 30s. This group consumes about 17% of their total calories from fast food, compared to 12% for adults in general. Understanding the usage patterns of your customer base gives you the option of either focusing on your core users or trying to pull light users into your core market.

11-3d Business Market Segmentation

B2B marketers typically follow a similar process in segmenting their markets, but they use slightly different categories:

GEOGRAPHIC B2B geographic segmentation refers to dividing the market based on the concentration of customers. Many industries tend to be highly clustered in certain areas, such as technology in California, and auto suppliers in the "auto corridor" that stretches south from Michigan to Tennessee. Geographic segmentation, of course, is especially common on an international basis, where variables such as language, culture, income, and regulatory differences can play crucial roles.

CUSTOMER-BASED B2B customer-based segmentation refers to dividing the market based on the characteristics of customers. This approach includes a range of possibilities. Some B2B marketers segment based on customer size. Others segment based on customer type. Johnson & Johnson, for example, has a group of salespeople dedicated exclusively to retail accounts such as Target and Publix, while other

salespeople focus solely on motivating doctors to recommend their products. Other potential B2B markets include institutions—schools and hospitals, for instance, are key segments for Heinz Ketchup—and the government.

PRODUCT-USE–BASED B2B product-use–based segmentation refers to dividing the market based on how customers will use the product. Small and midsized companies find this strategy especially helpful in narrowing their target markets. Possibilities include the ability to support certain software packages or production systems or the desire to serve certain customer groups, such as long-distance truckers or restaurants that deliver food.

11-3e The Marketing Mix

Once you've clearly defined your target market, your next challenge is to develop compelling strategies for product, price, distribution, and promotion. The blending of these elements becomes your **marketing mix**, as shown in Exhibit 11.3.

- ■ **Product Strategy:** Your product involves far more than simply a

> **behavioral segmentation**
> Dividing the market based on how people behave toward various products. This category includes both the benefits that consumers seek from products and how consumers use the products.
>
> **marketing mix** The blend of marketing strategies for product, price, distribution, and promotion.

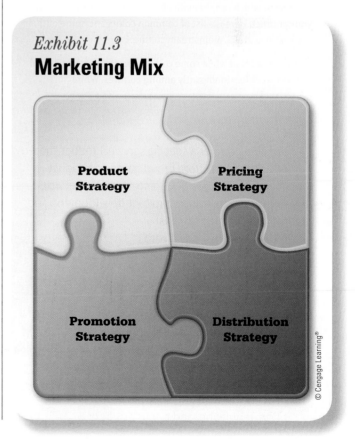

Exhibit 11.3
Marketing Mix

Product Strategy

Pricing Strategy

Promotion Strategy

Distribution Strategy

© Cengage Learning®

Color me... hungry?!

Have you ever noticed that fast-food restaurants typically feature vivid shades of red, yellow, and orange in both their logos and their décor? Think McDonald's, KFC, Burger King, and Pizza Hut. The color choice is no coincidence.

David P. Smith/Shutterstock.com

Marketing researchers have learned that consumers in the United States associate red with energy, passion, and speed. Yellow suggests happiness and warmth, while orange suggests playfulness, affordability, and fun. A simulated cocktail party study found that partygoers in red rooms reported feeling hungrier and thirstier than others, and guests in yellow rooms ate twice as much as others. The implication? Surrounding customers with red, yellow, and orange encourages them to eat a lot quickly and leave, which aligns nicely with the goals of most fast-food chains.

Color psychology is a powerful—though often overlooked—marketing tool. Colors evoke emotions and trigger specific behaviors, which can dramatically influence how people buy your product. Here is a list of common colors and some of their associations in U.S. mainstream culture.

Keep in mind that while some color associations are universal, others can differ significantly among cultures. White, for instance, signifies death and mourning in Chinese culture, while purple represents death in Brazil.

As a marketer, your goal should be to align your color choice with the perceptions of your target market and the features of your product. The result should be more green for your bottom line![6]

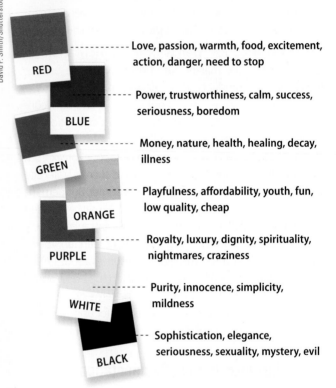

- **RED** — Love, passion, warmth, food, excitement, action, danger, need to stop
- **BLUE** — Power, trustworthiness, calm, success, seriousness, boredom
- **GREEN** — Money, nature, health, healing, decay, illness
- **ORANGE** — Playfulness, affordability, youth, fun, low quality, cheap
- **PURPLE** — Royalty, luxury, dignity, spirituality, nightmares, craziness
- **WHITE** — Purity, innocence, simplicity, mildness
- **BLACK** — Sophistication, elegance, seriousness, sexuality, mystery, evil

---

tangible good or a specific service. Product strategy decisions range from brand name, to product image, to package design, to customer service, to guarantees, to new product development, and more. Designing the best product clearly begins with understanding the needs of your target market.

- **Pricing Strategy:** Pricing is a challenging area of the marketing mix. To deliver customer value, your prices must be fair, relative to the benefits of your product. Other factors include competition, regulation, and public opinion. Your product category plays a critical role as well. A low-cost desk, for instance, might be appealing, but who would want discount-priced knee surgery?

> "DON'T FIND CUSTOMERS FOR YOUR PRODUCTS, FIND PRODUCTS FOR YOUR CUSTOMERS."
>
> —SETH GODIN, ENTREPRENEUR AND AUTHOR

- **Distribution Strategy:** The goal is to deliver your product to the right people, in the right quantities, at the right time, in the right place. The key decisions include shipping, warehousing, and selling outlets (e.g., the Web versus network marketing versus brick-and-mortar stores). The implications of these decisions for product image and customer satisfaction can be significant.

- **Promotion Strategy:** Promotion includes all of the ways that marketers communicate about their products. The list of possibilities is long and growing, especially as the Internet continues to evolve at breakneck speed. Key elements today include advertising, personal selling, sales promotion, public relations, word-of-mouth, and product placement. Successful promotional strategies typically evolve in response to both customer needs and competition. A number of innovative companies are even inviting their customers to participate in creating their advertising through venues such as YouTube. Check out Exhibit 11.4 to see how easily you can analyze promotional strategies.

Exhibit 11.4
Analyzing Promotional Strategies

Who is the target audience for each of these ads? How does each ad position the product relative to the competition? Which strategy is most effective? Why?

Source: Ford Motor Company

Source: General Motors

Source: BMW of North America

11-3f The Global Marketing Mix

As you decide to enter foreign markets, you'll need to reevaluate your marketing mix for each new country. Should it change? If so, how should it change? Many business goods simply don't require much change in the marketing mix, since their success isn't dependent on culture. Examples include heavy machinery, cement, and farming equipment. Consumer products, however, often require completely new marketing mixes to effectively reach their consumers.

Nike's approach to marketing in China offers an interesting example of how one firm managed the complex process of building a successful business in a foreign market. When Nike first entered China in the 1990s, the company seemed to face an insurmountable challenge: not only did a pair of Nike sneakers cost twice the Chinese average monthly salary, but most Chinese just didn't play sports, according to Terry Rhoads, then director of Nike sports marketing. So he boldly set out to change that. Rhoads created a Nike high-school basketball league, which has since spread to 17 cities. To loosen up fans, he blasted canned cheering during games and arranged for national TV coverage of the finals. He even leveraged connections with the NBA to bring Michael Jordan for visits.

The gamble quickly paid off, as the Chinese middle class emerged—along with more individualistic values, which are a strong fit with the Nike ethos. By 2001, Nike had dubbed its marketing approach "hip hoop," which they described as an effort to "connect Nike with a creative lifestyle." Sales in 2011 exceeded $2 billion, driven largely by basketball shoes, although sales began to soften in 2012 and 2013, due to fierce competition and deep discounting. In 2014, Nike continued to lose traction in China, due in part to fierce competition from Adidas. Analysts also pointed out that among other reasons, "Nike's branding is based on encouraging strong identification with iconic sports-stars it uses to endorse its products. In a culture where parents are excessively focused on academic achievement, such a strategy has limited appeal."[7]

11-3g The Marketing Environment

While marketers actively influence the elements of the marketing mix, they must anticipate and respond to the elements of the external environment, which they typically cannot control.

Smartphones Are So Yesterday—
Smart Fashion Is Truly Tomorrow

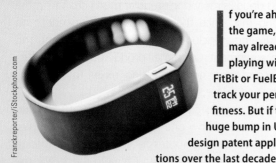

Franckreporter/iStockphoto.com

If you're ahead of the game, you may already be playing with a FitBit or FuelBand to track your personal fitness. But if the huge bump in U.S. design patent applications over the last decade can be trusted, smart fashion will be the next breakout hit. *Businessweek* recently highlighted four developments to watch:

- **Self-Lacing Sneakers:** Marty McFly sported a pair in *Back to the Future II* back in 1989, and Nike finally secured a patent for these gems, which will need their own docking station to recharge.

- **Smart Purses:** Wouldn't it be nice if your gadgets charged themselves without needing a plug? Or if your bag alerted you to forgotten keys or lost cards? The technology already exists, but will likely disseminate more widely over the next few years.

- **Body Scan Tailoring:** Hard-to-find clothes that fit perfectly? Soon it won't be an issue with computer scanning that collects more than 200,000 data points to help create clothes that skim your body perfectly in all the right places without ever breaking out a tape measure.

- **Wearable Chic:** The first generation of wearable technology seemed deliberately designed to look as clunky as possible. But the next generation may be more sophisticated. Google, for example, has recently addressed the dorkiness factor of Glass by introducing a stylish new line of frames, designed by Diane van Furstenburg. And frames by Oakley and Ray-Ban will likely infuse Glass with even more much-needed cool in the next year or two.[8]

- **Color Matching:** Have you ever wished that your shirt better matched your earrings? Or that your tie better matched your shirt? Sometime in the next few years, wearable technology should be able to color match your clothing, even to change temperature with minimal interference from you.

Environmental scanning is a key tool; the goal is simply to continually collect information from sources that range from informal networks, to industry newsletters, to the general press, to customers, to suppliers, to the competition, among others. The key elements of the external environment include the following components:

COMPETITIVE The dynamic competitive environment probably affects marketers on a day-to-day basis more than any other element. Understanding the competitive environment often begins with analysis of **market share**, or the percentage of the marketplace that each firm controls. To avoid ambushes—and to uncover new opportunities—you must continually monitor how both dominant and emerging competitors handle each element of their marketing mix. And don't forget indirect competitors, who meet the same consumer needs as you but with a completely different product (e.g., Altoids vs. Scope).

ECONOMIC The only certainty in the economic environment is change, but the timing of expansions and contractions is virtually impossible to predict. Your goal as a marketer is to identify and respond to changes as soon as possible, keeping in mind that a sharp eye sees opportunity even in economic downturns. For instance, affordable luxuries and do-it-yourself enterprises can thrive during recessions.

SOCIAL/CULTURAL The social/cultural element covers a vast array of factors, including lifestyle, customs, language, attitudes, interests, and population shifts. Trends can change rapidly, with a dramatic impact on marketing decisions. Anticipating and responding to trends can be especially important in industries such as entertainment, fashion, and technology. In late 2009, for instance, Facebook removed some key privacy controls from its News Feed. The social media giant did not anticipate the black eye it received from outraged consumers who believed that Facebook had violated their privacy.

environmental scanning
The process of continually collecting information from the external marketing environment.

market share The percentage of a market controlled by a given marketer.

Facebook was also surprised that the privacy controls it implemented in May 2010, which required consumers to opt out of sharing, would not be enough to appease privacy advocates.[9]

TECHNOLOGICAL Changes in technology can be very visible to consumers (e.g., the introduction of the iPhone). However, technology often affects marketers in ways that are less directly visible. For example, technology allows mass customization of Levi's blue jeans at a reasonable price and facilitates just-in-time inventory management for countless companies that see the results in their bottom lines.

POLITICAL/LEGAL The political/legal area includes laws, regulations, and political climate. Most U.S. laws and regulations are clear (e.g., those declaring dry counties in certain states), but others are complex and evolving (e.g., qualifications for certain tax breaks). Political climate includes changing levels of governmental support for various business categories. Clearly, the political/legal issues affect heavily regulated sectors (e.g., telecommunications and pharmaceuticals) more than others.

11-3h The Global Marketing Environment

As the Internet has grown, the world market has become accessible to virtually every business. This boosts the importance of understanding each element of the marketing environment—competitive, economic, social/cultural, technological, and political/legal—in each of your key markets. Among the biggest global challenges are researching opportunities in other countries and delivering your product to customers in other countries.

11-4 CUSTOMER BEHAVIOR: DECISIONS, DECISIONS, DECISIONS!

If successful marketing begins with the customer, then understanding the customer is critical. Why do people buy one product but not another? How do they use the products they buy? When do they get rid of them? Knowing the answers to these questions will clearly help you better meet customer needs.

11-4a Consumer Behavior

Consumer behavior refers specifically to how people act when they are buying products for their own personal consumption. The decisions they make often seem spontaneous (after all, how much thought do you give to buying a pack of gum?), but they often result from a complex set of influences, as shown in Exhibit 11.5.

Marketers, of course, add their own influence through the marketing mix. For instance, after smelling pretzels in the mall and tasting pretzel morsels from the sample tray, many of us would at least be tempted to cough up the cash for a hot, buttery pretzel of our own . . . regardless of any other factors! Similarly, changes in the external environment—for example, a series of hurricanes in Florida—dramatically affect consumer decisions about items such as flashlights, batteries, and plywood.

consumer behavior Description of how people act when they are buying, using, and discarding goods and services for their own personal consumption. Consumer behavior also explores the reasons behind people's actions.

EXHIBIT 11.5	ELEMENTS THAT INFLUENCE THE CONSUMER DECISION-MAKING PROCESS
Influence	**Description**
Cultural	*Culture:* The values, attitudes, and customs shared by members of a society
	Subculture: A smaller division of the broader culture
	Social Class: Societal position driven largely by income and occupation
Social	*Family:* A powerful force in consumption choices
	Friends: Another powerful force, especially for high-profile purchases
	Reference Groups: Groups that give consumers a point of comparison
Personal	*Demographics:* Measurable characteristics such as age, gender, or income
	Personality: The mix of traits that determines who you are
Psychological	*Motivation:* Pressing needs that tend to generate action
	Attitudes: Lasting evaluations of (or feelings about) objects or ideas
	Perceptions: How people select, organize, and interpret information
	Learning: Changes in behavior based on experience

© Cengage Learning®

Exhibit 11.6
Consumer Decision Process

Need Recognition

Your best friend suddenly notices that she is the only person she knows who still wears high-rise blue jeans to class...problem alert!

Information Search

Horrified, your friend not only checks out your style but also notices what the cool girls on campus are wearing. AND she snitches your copy of *Cosmo* to leaf through the ads.

Evaluation of Alternatives

Your friend compares the prices and styles of the various brands of blue jeans that she identifies.

Purchase Decision

After a number of conversations, your friend finally decides to buy True Religion jeans for $215.

Postpurchase Behavior

Three days later, she begins to kick herself for spending so much money on jeans because she can no longer afford her daily Starbucks habit.

© Cengage Learning®

All these forces shape consumer behavior in each step of the process regarding purchase decisions. Exhibit 11.6 shows how the consumer decision process works.

Clearly, marketing can influence the purchase decision every step of the way, from helping consumers identify needs (or problems), to resolving that awful feeling of **cognitive dissonance** (or kicking oneself) after a major purchase. Some marketers attempt to avoid cognitive dissonance altogether by developing specific programs to help customers validate their purchase choices. One example might be post-purchase mailings that highlight the accolades received by an expensive product.

But does every consumer go through every step of the process all the time? That's clearly not the case! People make low-involvement decisions (such as buying that candy bar) according to habit ... or even just on a whim. But when the stakes are high—either financially or socially—most people move through the five steps of the classic decision-making process. For example, most of us wouldn't think of buying a car, a computer, or the "right" pair of blue jeans without stepping through the decision-making process.

11-4b Business Buyer Behavior

Business buyer behavior refers to how people act when they're buying products to use either directly or indirectly to produce other products (e.g., chemicals, copy paper, computer servers). Business buyers typically have purchasing training and apply rational criteria to their decision-making process. They usually buy according to purchase specifications and objective standards, with a minimum of personal judgment or whim. Often, business buyers are integrating input from a number of internal sources, based on a relatively formal process. And finally, business buyers tend to seek (and often secure) highly customized goods, services, and prices.

11-5 MARKETING RESEARCH: SO WHAT DO THEY REALLY THINK?

If marketing begins with the customer, marketing research is the foundation of success. **Marketing research** involves gathering, interpreting, and applying information to uncover opportunities and challenges. The goal, of course, is better marketing decisions: more value for consumers and more profits for businesses that deliver. Companies use marketing research to:

- Identify external opportunities and threats (from social trends to competition).

- Monitor and predict customer behavior.

- Evaluate and improve each area of the marketing mix.

Most successful marketers rely on research to develop breakthrough products and effective marketing programs. But research will never replace the creative potential of the gifted individual. Steve Jobs, founder of Apple, famously declared, "A lot of times, people don't know what they want until you show it to them."

11-5a Types of Data

There are two main categories of marketing research data—**secondary data** and **primary data**—each with its own set of benefits and drawbacks, as shown in Exhibit 11.7.

---

cognitive dissonance Consumer discomfort with a purchase decision, typically for a higher-priced item.

business buyer behavior Describes how people act when they are buying products to use either directly or indirectly to produce other products.

marketing research The process of gathering, interpreting, and applying information to uncover marketing opportunities and challenges, and to make better marketing decisions.

secondary data Existing data that marketers gather or purchase for a research project.

primary data New data that marketers compile for a specific research project.

"If you can't be a good example, then you'll just have to serve as a horrible warning."

Even the heavy hitters make marketing gaffes. Their biggest mistakes are often entertaining, but they also serve as a powerful warning to consult with the customer *before* taking action. A few amusing examples:

- 2012 was a tough year for a number of brands in terms of fake tweets, accidental tweets, and just plain tasteless tweets. Both StubHub and Hale & Hearty sent obscene tweets when employees inadvertently tweeted private messages from the corporate account. Healthnet was busted featuring fake customer tweets gushing about their wonderful experiences with the firm on a series of billboards. Gap sent a peculiar tweet to East Coast residents during Hurricane Sandy, cautioning them to stay safe and urging them to shop on Gap.com while they were confined to their homes, as the storm caused $50 billion of damage.

- Polite men everywhere know it's never wise to talk to a woman about her weight. Too bad some big corporations don't seem to have gotten the message. In 2013, annoyed by the lack of larger clothing at retailer Abercrombie & Fitch, customers demanded an explanation. Apparently, the CEO "doesn't want his core customers to see people who aren't as hot as them wearing his clothing." Also in 2013, Target displayed a dress for sale, described as "Dark Heather Gray" for all but the plus size version, which was described as "manatee gray." Ouch!

- In late 2013, Burger King, in the wake of adding the French Fry Burger and reduced calorie Satisfries to their menu, pretended to change their name to Fries King, and uploaded a raft of photos to their Facebook page documenting the "new corporate I.D." The result was massive confusion, which mostly played out in a blizzard of baffled tweets.

- 2014 was another tough year for social media marketing. Union Street Guest House hotel in New York threatened to fine wedding parties $500 for every negative social media post and online review that their guests posted. And Minnesota retailer Global Village—showing a remarkable lack of sensitivity—commemorated Martin Luther King Day by offering "25% off everything black" via its Facebook page.

These fiascos only highlight the importance of *marketing research*. But sometimes, of course, even research isn't enough to identify marketing issues before they hit. At that point, the priority should shift to dealing with the mistake openly, honestly, and quickly, which can help a company win the game, despite the gaffe.[10]

Clearly, it makes sense to gather secondary data before you invest in primary research. Look at your company's internal information. What does previous research say? What does the press say? What can you find on the Web? Once you've looked at the secondary research, you may find that primary research is unnecessary. But if not, your secondary research will guide your primary research and make it more focused and relevant, which ends up saving time and money.

11-5b Primary Research Tools

There are two basic categories of primary research: observation and survey. **Observation research** happens when the researcher *does not* directly interact with the research subject. The key advantage of watching versus asking is that what

> **observation research**
> Marketing research that does not require the researcher to interact with the research subject.

EXHIBIT 11.7	RESEARCH DATA COMPARISON

Secondary Data	Primary Data
Existing data that marketers gather or purchase	New data that marketers compile for the first time
Tends to be lower cost	Tends to be more expensive
May not meet your specific needs	Customized to meet your needs
Frequently outdated	Fresh, new data
Available to your competitors	Proprietary—no one else has it
Examples: U.S. census, *The Wall Street Journal*, *Time* magazine, your product sales history	Examples: Your own surveys, focus groups, customer comments, mall interviews

© Cengage Learning®

people actually *do* often differs from what they *say*—sometimes quite innocently. For instance, if an amusement park employee stands outside an attraction and records which way people turn when they exit, he may be conducting observation research to determine where to place a new lemonade stand. Watching would be better than asking because many people could not honestly say which way they'd likely turn. Examples of observation research include:

- Scanner data from retail sales
- Traffic counters to determine where to place billboards
- Garbage analysis to measure recycling compliance

Observation research can be both cheap and amazingly effective. A car dealership, for instance, can survey the preset radio stations on every car that comes in for service. That information helps them choose which stations to use for advertising. But the biggest downside of observation research is that it doesn't yield any information on consumer motivation—the reasons behind consumer decisions. The preset radio stations wouldn't matter, for example, if the bulk of drivers listen only to their iPods in the car.

Survey research happens when the researcher *does* interact with research subjects. The key advantage is that you can secure information about what people are thinking and feeling, beyond what you can observe. For example, a carmaker might observe that the majority of its purchasers are men. They could use this information to tailor their advertising to men, or they could do survey research and possibly learn that even though men do the actual purchasing, women often make the purchase decision . . . a very different scenario! But the key downside of survey research is that many people aren't honest or accurate about their experiences, opinions, and motivations, which can make survey research quite misleading. Examples of survey research include:

- Telephone and online questionnaires
- Door-to-door interviews
- Mall-intercept interviews
- Focus groups
- Mail-in questionnaires

survey research Marketing research that requires the researcher to interact with the research subject.

WALMART AND THE WORLD

Well aware of its impact on the world, Walmart—the world's largest retailer—wraps sustainability into the heart of its marketing plans. In 2009, Walmart, along with several university partners and a number of corporate partners such as PepsiCo, P&G, J&J, Kellogg's, L'Oreal, and Unilever, founded The Sustainability Consortium (TSC), which has been working to figure out what makes certain products more sustainable than others, based on the best peer-reviewed science on the lifecycle impacts and "material" environmental and social issues for a given product category. The group identifies the "hot spots" in the value chain that create the most risk and footprint. So, for example, in the case of computers, key issues might be how much energy they consume during use, or the inclusion of metals in the design that come from controversial "conflict minerals" in the supply chain. For other product categories, the largest issues may be things like overall carbon footprint, water use, resource depletion, or worker health and safety. Each product from each firm receives a sustainability score from TSC, and brands with the top scores are now sold on Walmart's ecommerce site with a badge that reads "Made by a Sustainability Leader."

The big question is: Will it make any difference? Recent research suggests that a huge chunk of global consumers are finally ready to actively seek and purchase environmentally and socially conscious products—especially when the price and quality are equal to their competitors. Andrew Winston, writing for the *Harvard Business Review*, points out that even if the Walmart badges point consumers to the *best* products, Walmart is at the center of a "consumption-driven model of business that has enormous environmental impacts." So reduced consumption—which ultimately benefits the environment—really isn't in Walmart's best interest on a long-term basis.[11]

Ken Wolter/Shutterstock.com

Innovation: Unleashed!

I n today's hyper-competitive marketplace, businesses must differentiate their products from an astonishing array of alternatives. While life-changing innovation is rare, many successful products simply provide a new twist on an existing product. Examples include Wish-Bone's salad dressing spritzers, Nike's neon-colored Flyknit athletic shoes, and Yoplait's squeezable, Go-gurt yogurt snack tubes.

To help you make those kinds of jumps, the game in this box uses rebus puzzles to stretch your creativity. Rebus puzzles present common words and phrases in novel orientation to each other. The goal is to determine the meaning. The puzzles are below, and the answers are at the bottom of the box.

| ARREST YOU'RE | HISTORY HISTORY HISTORY | SK8 iiiiiiiiii iiiiiiiii | print | BAN ANA | Shut Sit |
| funny funny words words words words | ST4ANCE | herring | MEREPEAT | Jack | Symphon |

Answers: You're under arrest, too funny for words, history repeats itself, for instance, skate on thin ice, red herring, small print, repeat after me, banana split, Jack-in-the-Box, sit down and shut up, unfinished symphony

---

11-5c An International Perspective

Doing marketing research across multiple countries can be an overwhelming challenge. In parts of Latin America, for instance, many homes don't have telephone connections, so the results from telephone surveys could be very misleading. Door-to-door tends to be a better approach. But in parts of the Middle East, researchers could be arrested for knocking on a stranger's door, especially if they aren't dressed according to local standards. Because of these kinds of issues, many companies hire research firms with a strong local presence (often based in-country) to handle their international marketing research projects.

11-6 SOCIAL RESPONSIBILITY AND TECHNOLOGY: A MAJOR MARKETING SHIFT

Two key factors have had a dramatic impact on marketing in the past couple of decades: a surge in the social responsibility movement, and the dramatic emergence of

> ## 75% OF THE ENGAGEMENT ON A FACEBOOK POST HAPPENS IN THE FIRST FIVE HOURS.
> —DIGITAL INSIGHTS

the Internet and digital technology. This section will cover how each factor has influenced marketing.

11-6a Marketing and Society: It's Not Just about You!

Over the past couple of decades, the social responsibility movement has accelerated in the United States, demanding that marketers actively contribute to the needs of the broader community. Leading-edge marketers have responded by setting a higher standard in key areas such as environmentalism, abolishment of sweatshops, and involvement in the local community. Starbucks, Target, and General Electric, for instance, all publish corporate responsibility reports that evaluate the social impact of how the companies run their businesses, and all highlight their programs on their corporate websites.

GREEN MARKETING Companies employ **green marketing** when they actively promote the ecological benefits of their products. Toyota has been especially successful promoting the green benefits of its Prius (although, like all carmakers, Toyota has struggled during the global financial crisis and, more recently, during the Japanese earthquake and tsunami). Its strategy highlights fuel economy and performance, implying that consumers can "go green" without making any real sacrifices. Environmentally friendly fashion offers another emerging example of green marketing. Over the past few years, a number of designers have rolled out their versions of upscale ecofashion. In addition to clothing made of organic cotton, recent entries include vegan stilettos with four-inch heels, bamboo dresses, biodegradable umbrellas, and solar-powered jackets. (These jackets feature solar cells, integrated into the collar, that collect solar energy and route it to charge devices.) Green marketing items are aimed at a growing number of consumers who make purchase decisions based (at least in part) on their convictions. But reaching these consumers may be an increasing challenge in tough economic times, when low prices trump all other considerations for a growing swath of the population.[12]

> **green marketing** Developing and promoting environmentally sound products and practices to gain a competitive edge.
>
> **mass customization** The creation of products tailored for individual consumers on a mass basis.

11-6b Technology and Marketing: Power to the People!

The emergence of the digital age has revolutionized every element of marketing. Perhaps the most dramatic change has been a shift in power from producers to customers. The Internet gives customers 24/7 access to information and product choices from all over the world. In response, competition has intensified as marketers strive to meet an increasingly high standard of value.

But technology has also created opportunities for marketers. The Internet has opened the door for **mass customization**: creating products tailored for individual consumers on a mass basis. Using sophisticated data collection and management systems, marketers can now collect detailed information about each customer, which allows them to develop one-on-one relationships and to identify high-potential new customers. Through the Web, marketers can tap into (or even create) communities of users that yield valuable information about their goods and services. Technology also helps marketers lower costs, so they can deliver greater value to their customers.

The digital boom has also created an abundance of promotional opportunities, as marketers reach out to consumers via new tools, such as interactive advertising, virtual reality displays, text messaging, and video kiosks. We'll discuss these tools in more detail in Chapter 12.

The BIG Picture

Since the ultimate goal of most marketing is long-term profitability, a core marketing principle must infuse every facet of a successful organization: the need to deliver products that exceed customer expectations. The customer must come first for *every* department—including finance, accounting, engineering, manufacturing, and human resources—although the specifics of how that plays out will clearly differ for each organizational function. Competition in the future will only intensify. Customer choices will continue to multiply as globalization and technology march forward. While these forces will weed out the weaker players, firms with a deeply engrained marketing orientation and a strong customer focus will continue to flourish—delivering value to their stakeholders, and dollars to their bottom line.

Brand Manager

Drive the overall performance and profitability of a brand or group of brands. Establish the brand image and position in relation to competitors. Formulate and implement creative and effective marketing strategies. Manage and motivate creative teams that support the brand's development. Understand and integrate overall corporate goals into brand strategies.

Communicate brand performance to senior management. Communicate key brand information to both internal and external stakeholders. For more information on this career and other possible careers in marketing, check out Career Transitions.

STUDY TOOLS 11

LOCATED AT BACK OF THE TEXTBOOK

☐ Rip Out Chapter Review Card

LOCATED AT WWW.CENGAGE.COM/LOGIN

☐ Review key term flashcards and create your own using StudyBits

☐ Create and complete practice quizzes based off of your notes and StudyBits

☐ Complete Online activities such as Matching, Fill-in-the-Blank, and Drag and Drop exercises

☐ View chapter highlight box content, including CEO Profiles, What Would You Do Cases, and chapter videos

☐ Track your knowledge and understanding of key concepts in business using 4LTR Online

12 | Product and Promotion:
Creating and Communicating Value

LEARNING OBJECTIVES

After studying this chapter, you will be able to:

12-1 Explain "product" and identify product classifications

12-2 Describe product differentiation and the key elements of product planning

12-3 Discuss innovation and the product life cycle

12-4 Analyze and explain promotion and integrated marketing communications

12-5 Discuss development of the promotional message

12-6 Discuss the promotional mix and the various promotional tools

Remember to visit **PAGE 229** for additional STUDY TOOLS

12-1 PRODUCT: IT'S PROBABLY MORE THAN YOU THOUGHT

When most people hear the term "product," they immediately think of the material things that we buy, use, and consume every day: for example, a Samsung Galaxy, or a pair of True Religion jeans. But from a marketing standpoint, product means much more. A **product** can be anything that a company offers to satisfy consumer needs and wants; the possibilities include not only physical goods but also services and ideas. A charity event, cosmetic surgery, and a cooking lesson all qualify as products.

When you buy a product, you also "buy" all of the attributes associated with the product. These encompass a broad range of qualities, such as the brand name, the image, the packaging, the reputation, and the guarantee. From a consumer standpoint, these attributes (or the lack of these attributes) are part of the product purchase, even if they don't add to its value. As a marketer, it's worth your while to carefully consider each element of your product to ensure that you're maximizing value without sacrificing profitability. With the introduction of the translucent, multicolored iMac computers in 1998, Apple established its reputation for creating value through product design—an attribute that other PC manufacturers completely overlooked as they churned out their inventories of boring, beige boxes. Over the years, Apple has continued to polish its reputation by introducing sleek, elegantly designed products such as its iPad tablet computers and its iPhones.

product Anything that an organization offers to satisfy consumer needs and wants, including both goods and services.

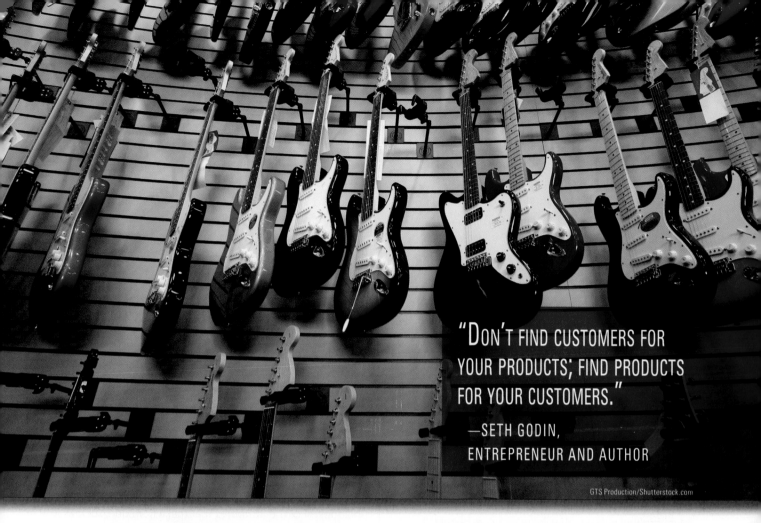

"DON'T FIND CUSTOMERS FOR YOUR PRODUCTS; FIND PRODUCTS FOR YOUR CUSTOMERS."

—SETH GODIN, ENTREPRENEUR AND AUTHOR

12-1a Services: A Product by Any Other Name

If a "product" includes anything that satisfies consumer needs, services clearly fit the bill. But services have some obvious differences from tangible goods. You often cannot see, hear, smell, taste, or touch a service, and you can virtually never "own" it. After math tutoring, for example, you might possess sharper algebra skills, but you don't own the tutoring experience (at least not literally). Most services embody these qualities:

- **Intangibility:** You typically cannot see, smell, taste, or touch a service before you buy it. Clearly, this creates a lot of uncertainty. Will the purchase really be worthwhile? Smart marketers mitigate the uncertainty by giving clues that suggest value. For example, the Formosa Café, a funky, old-time Hollywood bar and restaurant, plasters the walls with signed pictures of movie stars, providing "evidence" of its movie biz credentials.

- **Inseparability:** Try as you might, you simply can't separate the buyer of a service from the person who renders it. Delivery requires interaction between the buyer and the provider, and the customer directly contributes to the quality of the service. Consider a trip to the doctor. If you accurately describe your symptoms, you're likely to get a correct diagnosis. But if you simply say, "I just don't feel normal," the outcome will likely be different.

- **Variability:** This one ties closely to inseparability. A talented massage therapist would probably help you relax, whereas a mediocre one might actually create tension. And even the talented massage therapist might give better service at the end of the day than at the beginning, or worse service on the day she breaks up with her boyfriend. Variability also applies to the difference among providers. A massage at a top-notch spa is likely to be better than a massage at your local gym.

- **Perishability:** Marketers cannot store services for delivery at peak periods. A restaurant, for instance, only has so many seats; they can't (reasonably) tell their 8 P.M. dinner customers to come back the next day at 5 P.M. Similarly, major tourist destinations, such as Las Vegas, can't store an inventory of room service deliveries or performances of Cirque du Soleil. This creates obvious cost issues; is it worthwhile to prepare for a peak crowd but lose money when it's slow? The answer depends on the economics of your business.

12-1b Goods versus Services: A Mixed Bag

Identifying whether a product is a good or a service can pose a considerable challenge, since many products contain elements of both. A meal at your local Italian restaurant obviously includes tangible goods: you definitely own that calzone. But someone else took your order, brought it to the table, and (perhaps most importantly) did the dishes! Service was clearly a crucial part of the package.

A goods and services spectrum can provide a valuable tool for analyzing the relationship between the two. (See Exhibit 12.1.) At one extreme, **pure goods** don't include any services. Examples include a bottle of ketchup or a package of socks. At the other extreme, **pure services** don't include any goods. Examples include financial consulting or a piano lesson. Other products—such as a meal at Pizza Hut—fall somewhere between the poles.

Trubach/Shutterstock.com

12-1c Product Layers: Peeling the Onion

When customers buy products, they actually purchase more than just the good or service itself. They buy a complete product package that includes a core benefit, the actual product, and product augmentations. Understanding these layers is valuable, since the most successful products delight consumers at each one of them.

CORE BENEFIT At the most fundamental level, consumers buy a core benefit that satisfies their needs. When you go to a movie, the core benefit is entertainment. When you buy a smartphone, the core benefit is communication. And when you go to the doctor, the core benefit is better health. Most products also provide secondary benefits that help distinguish them from other goods and services that meet the same customer needs. A secondary benefit of a smartphone might include entertainment, since it probably plays your music, too.

---

pure goods Products that do not include any services.

pure services Products that do not include any goods.

consumer products Products purchased for personal use or consumption.

12-1d Actual Product

The *actual product* layer, of course, is the product itself: the physical good or the delivered service that provides the core benefit. *Furious 7* was the actual "service" that provided entertainment in 2015 to millions of fans of the Fast and Furious franchise. The HTC One is an actual smartphone that provides communication and entertainment services. Identifying the actual product is sometimes tough when the product is a service. For example, the core benefit of visiting a doctor might be better health, but the actual product may be someone in a white coat poking and prodding you. Keep in mind that the actual product includes all of the attributes that make it unique, such as the brand name, the features, and the packaging.

AUGMENTED PRODUCT Most marketers wrap their actual products in additional goods and services, called the *augmented product*, that sharpen their competitive edge. Augmentations come in a range of different forms. Many upscale movie theaters in L.A. display props from movies that have played in that theater. Most smartphones come with warranties or insurance and offer at least some customer service. And some doctors might give you sample pills until you can get your prescription filled.

12-1e Product Classification: It's a Bird, It's a Plane…

Products fall into two broad categories—consumer products and business products—depending on the reason for the purchase. **Consumer products** are purchased for personal use or consumption, while

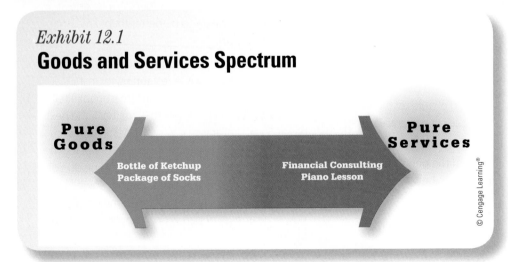

Exhibit 12.1
Goods and Services Spectrum

Pure Goods

Bottle of Ketchup
Package of Socks

Pure Services

Financial Consulting
Piano Lesson

© Cengage Learning®

business products are purchased to use either directly or indirectly in the production of another product. The shoes in your closet at home are a consumer product, while the shoes that you rent at the bowling alley are a business product.

CONSUMER PRODUCT CATEGORIES Marketers further divide consumer products into several different subcategories, as shown below. Understanding the characteristics of the subcategories can help marketers develop betterstrategies.

- *Convenience products* are the inexpensive goods and services that consumers buy frequently with limited consideration and analysis. Distribution tends to be widespread, with promotion by the producers. Examples include staples such as toothpaste and shampoo, impulse items such as magazines and candy bars, and emergency products such as headache tablets and plumbing services.

- *Shopping products* are the more expensive products that consumers buy less frequently. Typically, as consumers shop, they search for the best value and learn more about features and benefits through the shopping process. Distribution is widespread but more selective than for convenience products. Both producers and retailers tend to promote shopping products. Examples include cars, computers, and cell phone service.

- *Specialty products* are those much more expensive products that consumers seldom purchase. Most people perceive specialty products as being so important that they are unwilling to accept substitutes. Because of this, distribution tends to be highly selective. (Consumers are willing to go far out of their way for the "right" brand.) Both producers and retailers are apt to promote specialty products but to a highly targeted audience. Some specialty product examples are high-end sports cars, branded jewelry, and weight reduction surgery.

- *Unsought products* are the goods and services that hold little interest (or even negative interest) for consumers. Price and distribution vary wildly, but promotion tends to be aggressive to drum up consumer interest. Disability insurance and prepaid burial plots (especially for young people), and blood donations are some examples.

BUSINESS PRODUCT CATEGORIES Marketers also divide business products into subcategories. Here, too, understanding the subcategories can lead to better marketing strategies.

- *Installations* are large capital purchases designed for a long productive life. The marketing of installations emphasizes personal selling and customization. Examples include industrial robots, new buildings, airplanes, and railroad cars.

- *Accessory equipment* includes smaller, movable capital purchases, designed for a shorter productive life than installations. Marketing focuses on personal selling but includes less customization than installations. Examples include personal computers, power tools, and furniture.

- The *maintenance, repair, and operating products* category consists of small-ticket items that businesses consume on an ongoing basis but don't become part of the final product. Marketing tactics emphasize efficiency. Examples include cleaning supplies, lightbulbs, and copy paper.

- *Raw materials* include the farm and natural products used in producing other products. Marketing emphasizes price and service rather than product differentiation. Examples include cotton, timber, and wheat.

- *Component parts and processed materials* include finished (or partially finished) products used in producing other products. Marketing emphasizes product quality as well as price and service. Examples include batteries and spark plugs for cars, aluminum ingots for soda cans, and Intel computer chips.

- *Business services* are those services that businesses purchase to facilitate operations. Marketing focuses on quality and relationships; the role of price can vary. Examples include payroll services, janitorial services, and legal services.

 12-2 PRODUCT DIFFERENTIATION AND PLANNING: A MEANINGFUL DIFFERENCE

While some products have succeeded with little or no forethought, you'll dramatically boost your chance of a hit with careful planning. **Product differentiation** should be a key consideration. Winning products must embody a real

business products Products purchased to use either directly or indirectly in the production of other products.

product differentiation The attributes that make a good or service different from other products that compete to meet the same or similar customer needs.

or perceived difference versus the glut of goods and services that compete in virtually every corner of the market. But different alone isn't enough; different from, and better than, the competition are both critical in order to create the shortest path to success. A quick look at some high-profile product failures illustrates the point.

- **Vegetable Jello:** Few kids today would name Jello as their favorite dessert, and back in the 1960s, even fewer were fans of vegetable-flavored Jello (think celery, tomato, mixed vegetable, and Italian salad) which was soon yanked from the market.

- **Clear Beer:** In the 1990s, several companies introduced clear beers, reflecting an ill-fated obsession with clear products, including shampoo, soap, and the short-lived, clear Crystal Pepsi.

- **Lumia 900:** Nokia introduced the Lumia 900 phone in early 2012 for just $100 with a two-year contract. The price soon dropped to $50, but even that didn't spur sales, mostly due to a dearth of apps for its Windows operating system. By 2013, Nokia, once the dominant player in cell phones, had sold its entire handset business to Microsoft.

- **Funky French Fries:** In 2002, Ore-Ida introduced Funky Fries. The flavors included cinnamon-sugar, chocolate, and "radical blue." Not surprisingly, they were off the market in less than a year.

- **Cocaine Energy Drink:** In 2006, Redux Beverages brought Cocaine Energy Drink to market, calling it a "legal alternative" to the illegal drug in form of an energy drink, and describing the beverage, which had no actual cocaine in it as a "fruity, atomic fireball" drink. Redux was forced to pull Cocaine off the shelves in the U.S. in 2007 when the FDA declared that its producers were "illegally marketing their drink as an alternative to street drugs."[1]

12-2a Product Quality

Product quality relates directly to product value, which comes from understanding your customer. Peter Drucker, a noted business thinker, writer, and educator, declared:

Quality in a product or service is not what the supplier puts in. It's what

quality level How well a product performs its core functions.

product consistency How reliably a product delivers its promised level of quality.

EXHIBIT 12.2 PRODUCT QUALITY INDICATORS

Product Category	Some Quality Indicators
Cell Phones	Design, brand, number of apps, graphics, memory, battery life, memory, and customer service
Kids' Toys	Safety, expert endorsements, and educational and entertainment value
Cars	Horsepower, design, fuel efficiency, brand, resale value, reliability, and awards
Water Parks	Thrill factor, design, cleanliness, variety, and setting
Coffee	Taste, brand, price, country of origin, and additives (or lack of)

© Cengage Learning®

the customer gets out and is willing to pay for. A product is not quality because it is hard to make and costs a lot of money . . . this is incompetence. Customers pay only for what is of use to them and gives them value. Nothing else constitutes quality.

> "GIVE THEM QUALITY. THAT'S THE BEST KIND OF ADVERTISING."
> —MILTON HERSHEY

In other words, a high-quality product does a great job meeting customer needs. Siemens, a huge electronics conglomerate, embodies this thinking in its approach to quality: "Quality is when our customers come back and our products don't."

But the specific definition of quality—and the attributes that indicate quality—changes across product categories. See Exhibit 12.2 for a few examples.

Regardless of product category, the two key aspects of quality are level and consistency. **Quality level** refers to how well a product performs its core functions. You might think that smart companies deliver the highest possible level of performance, but this is seldom profitable, or even desirable. For instance, only a tiny group of consumers would pay for a speedboat to go 200 mph, when 80 mph offers a sufficient thrill (at least for most of us!). The right level of product performance is the level that meets the needs of your consumers, and those needs include price. Decisions about quality level must also consider the competition. The goal is to outperform the other players in your category while maintaining profitability.

The second dimension of quality is **product consistency**. How consistently does your product actually deliver the promised level of quality? With a positive

EXHIBIT 12.3 PRODUCT FEATURES AND CUSTOMER BENEFITS

Product	Product Feature	Customer Benefit
Subway Sandwiches	Lower fat	Looser pants
Costco	Rock-bottom prices on a huge range of higher end products and services	More cash for other needs
Whole Foods Market	Organic produce	A healthier planet
Stella McCartney Clutch	Highly fashionable	You feel chic
Triple Latte	Caffeine, caffeine, caffeine	More time to, uh, study

© Cengage Learning®

relationship between price and performance, consistent delivery can offer a competitive edge at almost any quality level.

Honda offers an excellent example. When most people consider the Accord, the Civic, and the CRV, all Honda-owned models, quality quickly comes to mind. And all three dominate their markets. But clearly, the quality *levels* (and price) are different for each. The Accord serves the upper, more conservative end of the market; the Civic tends to appeal to younger, hipper, more budget-minded consumers; the CRV tends to appeal to middle-of-the-road shoppers seeking a reliable, small SUV. In short, Honda succeeds at delivering product consistency at several markedly different quality levels.

12-2b Features and Benefits

Product features are the characteristics of the product you offer. If a product is well designed, each feature corresponds to a meaningful **customer benefit**. The marketer's challenge is to design a package of features that offers the highest level of value for an acceptable price. And the equation must also account for profitability goals.

One winning formula may be to offer at least some low-cost features that correspond to high-value benefits. Creating an "open kitchen" restaurant, for instance, has limited impact on costs but gives patrons an exciting, up-close view of the drama and hustle of professional food preparation. Exhibit 12.3 lists some other examples of product features and their corresponding customer benefits.

12-2c Product Lines and the Product Mix

Some companies focus all of their efforts on one product, but most offer a number of different products to enhance their revenue and profits. A **product line** is a group of products that are closely related to each other, in terms of

either how they work or the customers they serve. Sony, for example, carries a wide range of digital cameras and accessories, to meet the needs of as many different customers as possible. A **product mix** is the total number of product lines and individual items sold by a single firm. Sony's product mix ranges from cameras, to electronics, to phones, to music, to video game consoles, to entertainment (games, movies, music, and so on).

Decisions regarding how many items to include in each product line and in the overall product mix can have a huge impact on a firm's profits. With too few items in each line, the company may be leaving money on the table. With too many items, the company may be spending unnecessarily to support its weakest links.

One reason that firms add new product lines is to reach completely new customers. Gap, for instance, added Old Navy to reach younger, lower-income customers, and Banana Republic to reach older, higher-income customers. Each line includes a range of different products designed to meet the needs of their specific customers. But one risk of adding new lines—especially lower-priced lines—is **cannibalization**, which happens when a new entry "eats" the sales of an existing line. This is especially dangerous when the new products are lower-priced than the current ones. You could see the problem, for instance, if a $20 blue jean purchase from Old Navy replaces a $50 blue jean purchase from Gap; the company has

product features The specific characteristics of a product.

customer benefit The advantage that a customer gains from specific product features.

product line A group of products that are closely related to each other, either in terms of how they work, or the customers they serve.

product mix The total number of product lines and individual items sold by a single firm.

cannibalization When a producer offers a new product that takes sales away from its existing products.

lost more than half its revenue on the sale. Like other companies with multiple lines, Gap carefully monitors the cannibalization issue and works to differentiate its lines as fully as possible.

12-2d Branding

At the most basic level, a **brand** is a product's identity that sets it apart from other players in the same category. Typically, brands represent the combination of elements such as product name, symbol, design, reputation, and image. But today's most powerful emerging brands go far beyond the sum of their attributes. They project a compelling group identity that creates brand fanatics: loyal customers who advocate for the brand better than any advertising a marketer could buy. The overall value of a brand to an organization—the extra money that consumers will spend to buy that brand—is called **brand equity**.

Since 2001, *BusinessWeek* and Interbrand, a leading brand consultancy, have teamed up to publish a ranking of the 100 Best Global Brands by dollar value. The top ten brands are listed in Exhibit 12.4, but you can find the complete list at Interbrand's website.

BRAND NAME A catchy, memorable name is among the most powerful elements of your brand. While the right name will never save a bad business, it can launch a good business to new heights. But finding the right name can be tough. According to the respected Brighter Naming consulting group, the following characteristics can help:

1. Short, sweet, and easy to pronounce and spell: Examples include Sprite, H&M, GE, Nike, and Visa.

2. Unique within the industry: Think Caterpillar, Yahoo!, Starbucks, Zara, and Google.

3. Good alliteration, especially for long names: The words should roll off your tongue. Some examples are Coca-Cola, BlackBerry, Dunkin Donuts, Weight Watchers, and Minute Maid.[2]

Brand names typically fall into four categories, as described in Exhibit 12.5.

LINE EXTENSIONS VERSUS BRAND EXTENSIONS As companies grow, marketers look for opportunities to grow their businesses. **Line extensions** are similar

brand A product's identity—including product name, symbol, design, reputation, and image—that sets it apart from other players in the same category.

brand equity The overall value of a brand to an organization.

line extensions Similar products offered under the same brand name.

brand extension A new product, in a new category, introduced under an existing brand name.

licensing Purchasing the right to use another company's brand name or symbol.

EXHIBIT 12.4	BUSINESSWEEK/INTERBRAND TOP TEN GLOBAL BRANDS 2014
Brand	**Country of Ownership**
Apple	United States
Google	United States
Coca-Cola	United States
IBM	United States
Microsoft	United States
GE	United States
Samsung	South Korea
Toyota	Japan
McDonald's	United States
Mercedes-Benz	Germany

Source: Interbrand Website, http://www.bestglobalbrands.com/2014/ranking/, accessed July 2015

products offered under the same brand name. Possibilities include new flavors, sizes, colors, ingredients, and forms. One example is Lays potato chips, which offers more than 45 versions, including BBQ, Baked, Flamin Hot, Chili Limon, mustard flavored, and lightly salted. The marketing challenge is to ensure that line extensions steal market share from competitors rather than from the core brand.

Brand extensions, on the other hand, involve launching a product in a new category under an existing brand name. The Bic brand, for instance, is quite elastic, stretching nicely to include diverse products such as pens, glue, cigarette lighters, and disposable razors. The Virgin brand demonstrates similar elasticity, covering more than 350 companies that range from airlines, to cell phones, to soft drinks, to cars. But the concept of brand extension becomes most clear (and most entertaining) through examining brand extension failures. Examples include Bic perfume, Budweiser Dry, Colgate (yes, the toothpaste brand!) frozen dinners, and Harley-Davidson Cologne. Apparently there is some mysterious link between lighter fluid and perfume. Zippo offers perfume, too.[3]

LICENSING Some companies opt to license their brands from other businesses. **Licensing** means purchasing—often for a substantial fee—the right to use another company's brand name or symbol. The benefits,

EXHIBIT 12.5   BRAND NAME CATEGORIES

Category	Description	Examples
Location-Based	Refers to either the area served or the place of origin	Southwest Airlines, Bank of America, Best Western Hotels
Founder's Name	Can include first name, last name, or both	McDonald's, Dell Computer, Ford, Disney, Jenny Craig
Descriptive or Functional	Describes what the product is or how it works	eBay, U.S. News and World Report, Subway, Krispy Kreme
Evocative	Communicates an engaging image that resonates with consumers	Yahoo!, Craftsman, Virgin, Intel, Lunchables, Cosmopolitan, Starbucks, Apple

© Cengage Learning®

of course, are instant name recognition, an established reputation, and a proven track record. On a worldwide basis, the best-known licensing arrangements are probably character names, which range from Bart Simpson to SpongeBob and appear on everything from cereal, to toys, to underwear. Many movie producers also do high-profile licensing, turning out truckloads of merchandise that features movie properties such as *Batman* and *The Hunger Games*.

Another fast-growing area is the licensing of corporate or college names. Coca-Cola, for instance, claims to have more than 300 licensees who sell over a billion dollars of licensed merchandise each year. The potential benefits for Coca-Cola are clear: more promotion, increased exposure, and enhanced image. But the risk is significant. If licensed products are of poor quality or overpriced, the consumer backlash hits the core brand rather than the producer of the licensed product.

COBRANDING **Cobranding** is when established brands from different companies join forces to market the same product. This cooperative approach has a long history but is currently enjoying a new popularity. Examples include:

■ T.G.I. Friday's markets a broad (and very popular) range of Jack Daniel's-flavored foods.

■ Dairy Queen worked with Girl Scouts to offer the hugely popular limited-edition Thin Mint Blizzard.

■ As the official airline of SeaWorld, Southwest Airlines (LUV) has three Shamu planes in its fleet. Passengers are occasionally visited by penguins before takeoff.

GeorgeMPhotography/Shutterstock.com

Cobranding can offer huge advantages to both partners, by leveraging their strengths to enter new markets and gain more exposure. But cobranding can be risky. If one partner makes a major goof, the fallout can damage the reputation of the other partner as well.

NATIONAL BRANDS VERSUS STORE BRANDS **National brands**, also called *manufacturers' brands*, are brands that the producer owns and markets. Many are well known and widely available, such as Oreo cookies, Dial soaps, and Nutella. Although most retailers carry lots of national brands, an increasing number have opted to also carry their own versions of the same products, called **store brands**, or *private label*. Deep discounters, such as Walmart and Costco, have had particular success with their private-label brands (e.g., Sam's Choice and Kirkland). *Private labels* play a growing role in grocery stores as well. In the United States, more than one out of four grocery purchases is private label, and the numbers are even higher in Europe, hitting half of all grocery sales in a number of markets. Since the global recession, private-label brand sales have grown more than twice as fast as national brand sales. The growing influence and increasing quality of low-end private-label brands increase the pressure on national brands to continually innovate while holding down prices.[4]

At the upper end of the market—especially in the clothing business— key retailers specialize in

cobranding When established brands from different companies join forces to market the same product.

national brands Brands that the producer owns and markets.

store brands Brands that the retailer both produces and distributes (also called private-label brands).

private brands to create and protect a consistent, upscale image. Examples include Neiman Marcus, Coldwater Creek, and Saks Fifth Avenue.[5]

12-2e Packaging

Great packaging does more than just hold the product. It can protect the product, provide information, facilitate storage, suggest product uses, promote the product brand, and attract buyer attention. Great packaging is especially important in the crowded world of grocery stores and mass merchandisers. In the average supermarket, the typical shopper passes about 300 items per minute and makes anywhere from 20% to 70% of purchases on sheer impulse. In this environment, your package must call out to your target customers and differentiate your product from all the others lined up beside it. Yet, in attracting consumer attention, a good package cannot sacrifice the basics such as protecting the product.[6]

Bottom line: great packaging stems from consumer needs, but it usually includes at least a smidge of creative brilliance. Examples include yogurt in a pouch that doesn't need a spoon, soup-to-go that can be microwaved in the can, "anti-theft" clear sandwich bags printed with mold-like green splotches (seriously!), and single-serving baby carrot packets that moms can toss into kids' lunches.

12-3 INNOVATION AND THE PRODUCT LIFE CYCLE: NUTS, BOLTS, AND A SPARK OF BRILLIANCE

For a business to thrive long term, effective new product development is vital. And the process works only if it happens quickly. As technological advances hit the market at breakneck speed, current products are becoming obsolete faster than ever before. The need for speed compounds as hungry competitors crowd every niche of the market. But the rush is risky, since new product development costs can be in the millions, and the success rate is less than a third. Marketers who succeed in this challenging arena devote painstaking effort to understanding their customers, but they also nurture the creativity they need to generate new ideas. An example of how this can work: The 3M Corporation—makers of Post-It Notes and Scotch Tape—introduces about 500 new products per year by pushing its employees to "relentlessly ask, 'What if?'" Some innovative firms, such as Google, Facebook, and LinkedIn, also encourage workers to spend 20% of their work time (paid work time!) on projects of personal interest.[7]

12-3a Types of Innovation

Clearly, the first personal computer represented a higher degree of newness than the first personal computer with a color screen. And the computer with a color screen represented a higher degree of newness than the first low-cost knockoff. Levels of innovation fall along a spectrum, as shown in Exhibit 12.6.

DISCONTINUOUS INNOVATION *Discontinuous innovations* are brand-new ideas that radically change how people live. Examples include the first car, the first television, and the first computer. These dramatic innovations require extensive customer learning, which should guide the marketing process.

DYNAMICALLY CONTINUOUS INNOVATION *Dynamically continuous innovations* are characterized by marked changes to existing products. Examples include cell phones, Blu-ray discs, and digital cameras. These types of innovations require a moderate level of consumer learning in exchange for significant benefits.

CONTINUOUS INNOVATION A slight modification of an existing product is called a *continuous innovation*. Examples include new sizes, flavors, shapes, packaging, and design. The goal of continuous innovation is to distinguish a product from the competition. The goal of a knockoff is simply to copy a competitor and offer a lower price.

12-3b The New Product Development Process

An efficient, focused development process will boost your chances of new product success. The standard model includes six stages:

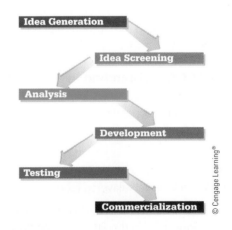

Each stage requires management to "green light" ideas before moving forward, to ensure that the company doesn't waste resources on marginal concepts.

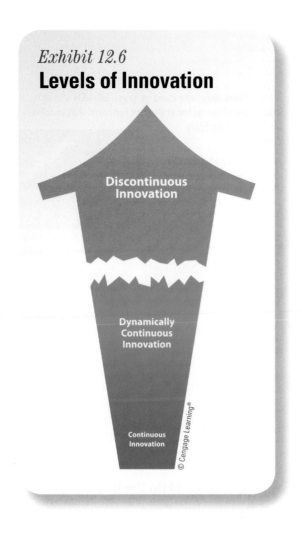

Exhibit 12.6
Levels of Innovation

Discontinuous Innovation

Dynamically Continuous Innovation

Continuous Innovation

© Cengage Learning®

- **Idea Generation:** Some experts estimate that it takes 50 ideas for each new product that makes it to market, so you should definitely cast a wide net. Ideas can come from almost anywhere, including customer research, customer complaints, salespeople, engineers, suppliers, and competitors.

- **Idea Screening:** The purpose of this stage is to weed out ideas that don't fit with the company's objectives and ideas that would clearly be too expensive to develop. The Walt Disney Company, for instance, would certainly eliminate the idea of a XXX cable channel because it just doesn't fit their mission.

- **Analysis:** The purpose of the analysis stage is to estimate costs and forecast sales for each idea to get a sense of the potential profit and of how the product might fit within the company's resources.

Each idea must meet rigorous standards to remain a contender.

- **Development:** The development process leads to detailed descriptions of each concept with specific product features. New product teams sometimes also make prototypes, or samples, that consumers can actually test. The results help fully refine the concept.

- **Testing:** This stage involves the formal process of soliciting feedback from consumers by testing the product concept. Do they like the features? Are the benefits meaningful? What price makes sense? Some companies also test-market their products or sell them in a limited area to evaluate the consumer response.

- **Commercialization:** This stage entails introducing the product to the general market. Two key success factors are gaining distribution and launching promotions. But a product that tested well doesn't always mean instant success. The VW Beetle, for example, sold only 330 cars during its first year in the United States, but it later became a hit.

12-3c New Product Adoption and Diffusion

In order to become a commercial success, new products must spread throughout a market after they are introduced. That process is called *diffusion*. But diffusion clearly happens at different speeds, depending on the individual consumer and on the product itself.

PRODUCT ADOPTION CATEGORIES Some consumers like to try new things; others seem terrified of change. These attitudes clearly affect the rate at which individual people are willing to adopt (or begin buying and using) new products. The first adopters, about 2.5% of the total, are adventurous risk takers. The laggards, about 16% of the total, sometimes adopt products so late that earlier adopters have already moved to the next new thing. The rest of the population falls somewhere in between. Keep in mind that individuals tend to adopt new products at different rates. For instance, we probably all know someone who is an innovator in technology but a laggard in fashion, or vice versa.

PRODUCT DIFFUSION RATES Some new products diffuse into the population much more quickly than others. For example, Apple iPods and Segway Human

"YOU CAN'T WAIT FOR INSPIRATION, YOU HAVE TO GO AFTER IT WITH A CLUB."

—JACK LONDON, AUTHOR

Wacky Warnings

As product lawsuits take on a life of their own, manufacturers are responding with warning labels that seem increasingly wacky. To call attention to this trend, a Michigan anti-lawsuit group called M-LAW sponsors the annual Wacky Warning Label Contest. Top finishers over the past few years have included the following gems:

- A toilet brush tag that says: "Do not use for personal hygiene."

- An electric razor for men warns: "Never use while sleeping."

- A can of self-defense pepper spray warns users: "May irritate eyes."

- A box of birthday cake candles says: "DO NOT use soft wax as ear plugs or for any other function that involves insertion into a body cavity."

- A label on a baby stroller with a small storage pouch warns: "Do not put child in bag."[8]

Transporters appeared on the market around the same time; iPods have become a pop culture icon, while Segways remain on the fringe. What accounts for the difference? Researchers have identified five product characteristics that affect the rate of adoption and diffusion. The more characteristics a product has, the faster it will diffuse into the population.

- **Observability:** How visible is the product to other potential consumers? Some product categories are easier to observe than others. If you adopt a new kind of car, the whole neighborhood will know, plus anyone else who sees you on the streets and highways.

- **Trialability:** How easily can potential consumers sample the new product? Trial can be a powerful way to create new consumers, which is why many markets fill their aisles with sample tables during popular shopping hours. Other examples of trial-boosting strategies include test-driving cars, sampling music, and testing new fragrances.

- **Complexity:** Can potential consumers easily understand what your product is and how it works? If your product confuses people—or if they find it hard to explain to others—adoption rates will slow. For example, many people who test-ride Segway Human Transporters love the experience, but they have trouble explaining to others how it works or why it beats other transportation options.

- **Compatibility:** How consistent is your product with the existing way of doing things? Cordless phones, for example, caught on almost instantly, since they were completely consistent with people's prior experiences—only better!

- **Relative Advantage:** How much better are the benefits of your new product compared to existing products? When gas prices climb, for example, the benefits of a hybrid car take on a much higher value relative to standard cars. As a result, demand skyrockets.

12-3d The Product Life Cycle: Maximizing Results over Time

When marketers introduce a new product, they hope it will last forever, generating sales and profits for years to come. But they also realize that all products go through a **product life cycle**: a pattern of sales and profits that typically changes over time. The life cycle can be dramatically different across individual products and product categories, and predicting the exact shape and length of the life cycle is virtually impossible. But most product categories do move through the four distinct stages shown in Exhibit 12.7.

- **Introduction:** This is a time of low sales and nonexistent profits as companies invest in raising awareness about the product and the product category. Some categories, such as the microwave, languish in this phase for years, while other categories, such as computer memory sticks, zoom through this phase. And some categories never get beyond introduction. (Think clear beers.)

- **Growth:** During the growth period, sales continue to rise, although profits usually peak. Typically, competitors begin to notice emerging categories in the growth phase. They enter the market—often with

product life cycle A pattern of sales and profits that typically changes over time.

Exhibit 12.7
Product Life Cycle for a Typical Product Category

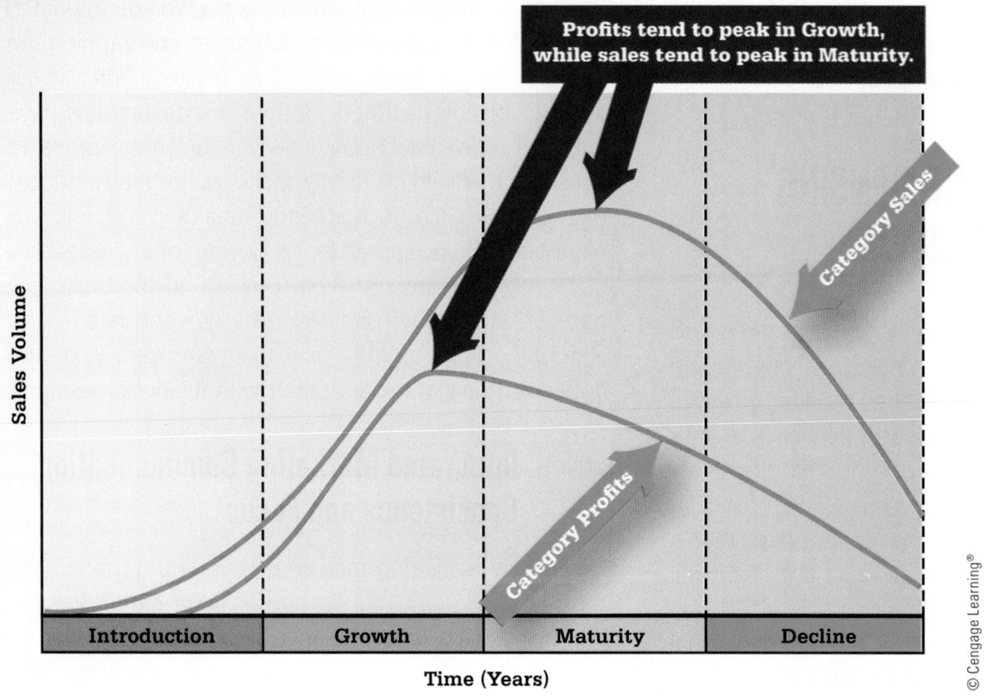

Profits tend to peak in Growth, while sales tend to peak in Maturity.

Sales Volume

Category Sales

Category Profits

| Introduction | Growth | Maturity | Decline |

Time (Years)

© Cengage Learning®

new variations of existing products—which further fuels the growth. Electric cars and plug-in hybrids are currently in the growth phase, and a number of competitors have recently entered the market.

- **Maturity:** During maturity, sales usually peak. Profits continue to decline as competition intensifies. Once a market is mature, the only way to gain more users is to steal them from competitors, rather than to bring new users into the category. Weaker players begin to drop out of the category. Gasoline-powered cars, sugared soda, and network TV are in maturity in the United States.

- **Decline:** During this period, sales and profits begin to decline, sometimes quite rapidly. The reasons usually relate to either technological change or change in consumer needs. For instance, the introduction of word processing pushed typewriters into decline, and a change in consumer taste and habits pushed hot cereal into decline. Competitors continue to drop out of the category.

Familiarity with the product life cycle helps marketers plan effective strategies for existing products and identify profitable categories for new products. Exhibit 12.8 summarizes typical marketing strategies and offers examples for each phase.

Individual products also have life cycles that usually follow the category growth pattern but sometimes vary

EXHIBIT 12.8	THE PRODUCT LIFE CYCLE AND MARKETING STRATEGIES		
Phase	**Examples**	**Sales/Profits**	**Key Marketing Strategies**
Introduction	Virtual reality games, fuel cell technology, "smart" glasses	Low sales, low profits	Build awareness, trial, and distribution
Growth	Electric cars, eBook readers, mini tablets, Blu-ray players	Rapidly increasing sales and profits	Reinforce brand positioning, often through heavy advertising
Maturity	Airlines, DVD players, personal computers, online stock trading, energy drinks	Flat sales and declining profits	Target competitors, while defending franchise with new product features, competitive advertising, promotion, and price cuts
Decline	Pagers, videocassettes	Declining sales and profits	Reduce spending and consider terminating the product

© Cengage Learning®

dramatically. Clearly, it's in the marketer's best interest to extend the profitable run of an individual brand as long as possible. There are several ways to make this happen: finding new uses for the product, changing the product, and changing the marketing mix. For example, *Dancing with the Stars* renews interest in their franchise by continually introducing new celebrity contestants.

 ## 12-4 PROMOTION: INFLUENCING CONSUMER DECISIONS

Promotion is the power to influence consumers—to remind them, to inform them, to persuade them. The best promotion goes one step further, building powerful consumer bonds that draw your customers back to your product again and again. But don't forget that great promotion only works with a great product. Bill Bernbach, an ad industry legend, captures this concept by noting that "A great ad campaign will make a bad product fail faster. It will get more people to know it's bad."

Marketers can directly control most promotional tools. From TV advertising to telephone sales, the marketer creates the message and communicates it directly to the target audience. But, ironically, marketers *cannot* directly control the most powerful promotional tools: publicity, such as a comment on *The View* or a review in *Consumer Reports*, and word-of-mouth, such as a recommendation from a close friend or even a casual acquaintance. Marketers can only influence these areas through creative promotional strategies.

12-4a Promotion in Chaos: Danger or Opportunity?

Not coincidentally, the Chinese symbol for crisis resembles the symbols for danger and opportunity—a perfect description of promotion in today's market. The pace of change is staggering. Technology has empowered consumers to choose how and when they interact with media, and they are grabbing control with dizzying speed. Digital TV and streaming movies continue to grow explosively. In 2013, consumers spent 5 hours per day online on nonvoice digital media (including mobile Internet usage on phones and tablets) versus 4 hours and 31 minutes per day watching TV. Meanwhile, more passive forms of entertainment, such as network television, are slowly losing their audience. And those people who do still watch TV are gleefully changing the schedules and zapping the ads with TiVo or similar devices. As media splinter across an array of entertainment options, usage patterns have changed as well: tech-savvy viewers are more prone to consume media in on-the-fly snacks rather than sit-down meals. Also, services such as Netflix streaming and Hulu Plus have led to an increase in binge viewing of entire seasons of TV shows. Rising consumer power and the breakneck pace of technology have created a growing need—and a stunning opportunity—for marketers to zero in on the right customers, at the right time, with the right message.[9]

12-4b Integrated Marketing Communication: Consistency and Focus

How many marketing messages have you gotten in the past 24 hours? Did you flip on the TV or radio? Surf the Web? Notice a billboard? Glance at the logo on a T-shirt or cap? Chat with a friend about some product he likes? Marketing exposure quickly snowballs: the typical consumer receives about 3,000 advertising messages each day. Some of those messages are hard to avoid as marketers find new, increasingly creative ways to promote their products to a captive audience. The venues include elevators, taxicabs, golf carts, and other surprising settings.[10]

Given the confounding level of clutter, smart companies use **integrated marketing communication** to coordinate their messages through every promotional vehicle—including their advertising, website, and salespeople—creating a coherent impression in the minds of their customers. Why bother coordinating all of these elements? The answer is clear. Consumers don't think about the specific source of the communication; instead, they combine—or integrate—the messages from *all* the sources to form a unified impression about your product. If the messages are out of sync or confusing, busy consumers won't bother to crack the code. They'll simply move on to the next best option.

Can you really control every message that every consumer sees or hears about your product? It's not likely. But if you accurately identify the key points of contact between your product and your target market, you can focus on those areas with remarkable effectiveness. For instance, the most common points of contact for McDonald's are probably advertising and the in-store experience. From upbeat commercials, to smiling employees, to brightly

promotion Marketing communication designed to influence consumer purchase decisions through information, persuasion, and reminders.

integrated marketing communication The coordination of marketing messages through every promotional vehicle to communicate a unified impression about a product.

striped uniforms, McDonald's spends millions of dollars to support its core message of fast, tasty food in a clean, friendly environment—heavily concentrated in the areas that are key to its brand.

Other companies are likely to encounter the bulk of their customers through different channels. You'd probably learn about Dell computers, for example, through either its website or word-of-mouth. Dell has invested heavily in both areas. The company maintains an innovative, user-friendly website that allows even novice users to create customized systems. And Dell delivers award-winning customer service and technical support, which gets its customers to recommend its products to family and friends.

12-4c Coordinating the Communication

Even after you've identified the key points of contact, coordinating the messages remains a challenge. In many companies, completely different teams develop the different promotional areas. Salespeople and brand managers often have separate agendas, even when the same executive manages both departments. Frequently, disconnected outside agencies handle advertising, web development, and sales promotion programs. Coordinating the messages will happen only with solid teamwork, which must begin at the top of the organization.

Information also plays a crucial role. To coordinate marketing messages, everyone who creates and manages them must have free access to knowledge about the customer, the product, the competition, the market, and the strategy of the organization. Some of this information, such as strategic goals, will come from the top down, but a fair amount, such as information about the customer, should come from the bottom up. Information must also flow laterally, across departments and agencies. The marketing research department, for instance, might have critical information about product performance, which might help the web management agency create a feature page that might respond to competitive threats identified by the sales force. When all parties have access to the same data, they are much more likely to remain on the same page.

12-5 A MEANINGFUL MESSAGE: FINDING THE BIG IDEA

Your promotional message begins with understanding how your product is different from and better than the competition. But your **positioning statement**—a brief statement that articulates how you want your target market to envision your product relative to the competition—seldom translates directly into the promotional message. Instead, it marks the beginning of the creative development process, often spearheaded by ad agency creative professionals. When it works, the creative development process yields a *big idea*—a meaningful, believable, and distinctive concept that cuts through the clutter. Big ideas are typically based on either a rational or an emotional premise. Here are a few examples from the last decade:

Rational:	Price:	Home Depot: "More saving. More doing."
	Engineering:	Bose: "Better sound through research"
	Ingredients:	Snapple: "Made from the best stuff on earth."
Emotional:	Imagination:	GE: "Imagination at work"
	Humor:	Virgin Atlantic: "More experience than our name suggests"
	Fun:	Nintendo: "Born to play"
	Fear:	Cancer Patient's Aid Association: "Cancer Cures Smoking"

© 2015 Cengage Learning®

Not surprisingly, funny ads are a consumer favorite, although humor can be risky. For a record ten years in a row, from 1998 through 2008, Budweiser—known for using humor effectively—nabbed the top spot in *USA Today's* annual Ad Meter consumer ranking of Super Bowl ads. But in 2009, a very funny

Ffooter/Shutterstock.com

With so much clutter in the marketplace, coordinating messages can be a real challenge.

positioning statement A brief statement that articulates how the marketer would like the target market to envision a product relative to the competition.

"Free Doritos" ad—created by talented amateurs in an on-line contest sponsored by Frito-Lay—knocked Budweiser off its pedestal. Budweiser regained the top spot in 2011, sharing the honor with Doritos, which, once again, took the top prize with a hilarious customer-created ad. Doritos used the same strategy to score a third win in 2012. In 2013, Budweiser held on to the top spot with a heart-warming spot about the bond between a trainer and his horse, while Doritos—again using the same strategy—fell to eighth place. In 2015, Budweiser again held the top spot with an ad about a puppy and a horse, while Doritos' customer-created ad took fifth place.[11]

The best big ideas have entrenched themselves in popular culture. A small sampling:

- The Energizer Bunny
- "Got Milk?"
- Budweiser: "Whassssuuuup?!?!"
- GE: "We bring good things to life."
- Motel 6: "We'll leave the light on for you."

12-5a An International Perspective

Some big ideas translate well across cultures. The Marlboro Man now promotes rugged individualism across the globe. But other big ideas don't travel as smoothly. DeBeers tried running ads in Japan using their proven strategy in the West: fabulously dressed women smiling and kissing their husbands who have just given them glittering diamonds. The ads failed in Japan because a Japanese woman would be more likely to shed a few tears and feign anger that her husband would spend so much money. The revised DeBeers campaign featured a hardworking husband and wife in their tiny apartment. Receiving a diamond, the wife chides her extravagant husband: "Oh, you stupid!" The campaign was a wild success. Taking a big idea to a for-eign market can mean big money and a powerful brand, but careful research should still be your first step.[12]

 ## 12-6 THE PROMOTIONAL MIX: COMMUNICATING THE BIG IDEA

promotional channels Specific marketing communication vehicles, including traditional tools, such as advertising, sales promotion, direct marketing, and personal selling, and newer tools such as product placement, advergaming, and Internet minimovies.

Once you've nailed your message, you need to communicate the big idea to your target market. The traditional communication tools—or **promotional channels**—include advertising, sales promotion, direct marketing, and personal selling. But more recently, a number of new tools have emerged, ranging from advergaming to Internet minimovies. The combination of communication tools that you choose to promote your product is called your "promotional mix."

12-6a Emerging Promotional Tools: The Leading Edge

In the past decade, the promotional landscape has changed dramatically. Consumer expectations and em-powerment have skyrocketed. Consumer tolerance for im-personal corporate communication has fallen. And digital technology has surged forward at breakneck speed. As a result, new promotional tools have emerged, and previously minor tools have burst into the mainstream. This section covers several leading-edge promotional tactics, but keep in mind that other tools—such as mobile phone promotion, social media marketing and widget-based marketing—are growing explosively, too.

INTERNET ADVERTISING Internet advertising has been highly visible for more than a decade. But the industry has moved far beyond simple banner ads and annoying pop-up ads. The highest growth areas include paid search advertising, search engine optimization, and online video advertising.

Paid search advertising includes both sponsored links on Google that relate to the topic you've searched, and targeted Google text ads on a number of different websites—both of which are at the heart of Google's outsized financial success. Industry expert *eMarketer* estimates that paid search advertising, including both Google and other similar services, will top $25 billion by 2017, with more than half of the spending going toward mobile. Paid search seems to be an especially attractive tactic during tough economic times, since it offers high accountability—marketers can tell exactly how well their limited advertising dollars are working.[13]

Search engine optimization (SEO) also demonstrated strong growth as the economy weakened. SEO involves taking specific steps to ensure that your website appears high on the list when customers look for your product or service via an Internet search engine such as Google or Yahoo!. Typically, the higher a firm appears, the more traffic that site will receive from potential customers. Analysis from *eMarketer* suggest that most marketers worldwide do desktop SEO as a matter of course, and will turn their efforts to mobile SEO over the next few years, since that is where consumers make most of their search queries.[14]

Online video advertising represents another high-growth area. This includes the increasingly popular "pre-roll" ads, the 15- to 30-second spots that viewers often sit through before watching an online video on YouTube, Hulu, or many other sites. According to *eMarketer* estimates, the growth will continue to increase at a spectacular rate, more than doubling from $4.14 billion in 2013 to $9.06 billion in 2017.[15]

SOCIAL MEDIA Clearly, social media—including Facebook, Twitter, Blogger, Tumblr, Foursquare, and many others—are not a fad, but rather, a paradigm shift in how successful businesses market themselves. According to advertising heavyweight Alex Bogusky, "You can't buy attention anymore. Having a huge budget doesn't mean anything in social media. . . The old media paradigm was PAY to play. Now you get back what you authentically put in." And the evidence is building that social media offer a truly impressive return on investment, especially compared to traditional media. A few examples compiled by social media expert Erik Qualman underscore the potential return on investment:

- Wetpaint/Altimeter Study found companies that are both deeply and widely engaged in social media significantly surpass their peers in both revenues and profits. The study also found the company sales with the highest levels of social media activity grew on average by +18%, while those companies with the least amount of social activity saw their sales decline by −6%.

- BlendTec increased its sales five times by running the often humorous "Will It Blend" videos on YouTube, blending everything from an iPhone to a sneaker.

- Dell sold $3,000,000 worth of computers on Twitter.

- Ford Motor Company gave away 100 Fiestas to influential bloggers, resulting in 37% of Generation Y

Social media offer marketers myriad opportunities to reach consumers.

learning of the Ford Fiesta before it was launched in the United States.

- Debt relief firm CareOne found that customers gained through social media completed their first payment through the company, at a higher rate of +732%.

- Web host provider Moonfruit more than recouped its $15,000 social media investment as its website traffic soared +300% while sales increased +20%.

Looking ahead, smart marketers of both large and small businesses are investing their limited resources in social marketing and reaping an unprecedented return, forging the future of marketing promotion.[16]

NATIVE ADVERTISING Across all media, but especially Internet advertising and social media, native advertising is a burgeoning category of advertising specifically designed to mimic the user experience into which it is placed in terms of form and function (picture the "suggested posts" in your Facebook newsfeed that you as a user are much more likely to read and click on than a typical banner ad, or similarly, any of the first few options that come up on a typical Google search). Native ads are often fully integrated into a specific delivery platform, and are not always identified as advertising. They *do* look like the surrounding editorial content and they typically *are* relevant to it. Market research firm Statista projected that native advertising spending of $4.3 billion in 2015 would more than double to $8.8 billion in 2018. But it's still the smallest part of marketers' spending plans, at only about 5%, due largely to concerns about ethics and budget.[17]

PRODUCT PLACEMENT Product placement—the paid integration of branded products into movies and TV—exploded into big-screen prominence in 1982, when Reese's Pieces played a highly visible role in Steven Spielberg's blockbuster film *E.T.* Reese's Pieces sales shot up 65% (a major embarrassment for the marketers of M&Ms, who had passed on the opportunity). Over the years, product placement in movies has moved rapidly into the limelight. A few notable examples are:

- "Walking Dead": Sponsor Hyundai plays a starring role in this series about the zombie apocalypse, and the car somewhat oddly remains incongruously clean as the rest of the world decays.

- "Modern Family" (2010): An entire episode of the hit TV show "Modern Family" revolved around the Apple iPad two days before the tablet hit the stores.

- James Bond: This long-standing movie icon hawked

product placement The paid integration of branded products into movies, television, and other media.

so many products in recent movies (e.g., Omega watches, Heineken beer, British Airways, and most recently, in *Skyfall*, Macallan whiskey) that it triggered a backlash from annoyed moviegoers and critics.[18]

For many years, Apple took top honors in the movie product placement sweepstakes, with products appearing in 34.3% of all films that were number one in the U.S. box office. But in 2012, Mercedes-Benz was the most frequently placed brand in hit films, knocking Apple from the top spot. One reason may be that in 2012, many more of the number-one films were produced by Sony Studios than in the previous year, and they all featured Sony electronics and shut out Apple completely. But in 2014, Apple was back, showing up in 9 of the 35 number-one films. Lego may have had the highest impact product placement, generating an 11% increase in sales in the 6 months after *The Lego Movie* (essentially a 2-hour ad for the product) was released.[19]

In an interesting combination of promotional tactics, product placement and online video have begun to merge. In 2010, Lady Gaga's YouTube smash hit video *Telephone* featured no fewer than ten product placements. Some of the placements, for instance, Miracle Whip, were paid, while others, such as Virgin Mobile and Polaroid, were extensions of existing partnerships with Gaga. In 2013, Avril Lavigne released her new single, "Rock N Roll", starting with a shot of her saying, "Oh, my new Sony phone is ringing." Fans of the Nexflix original series *House of Cards* have probably noticed placements for Samsung, Fiji water, and other products. Given its efficacy in reaching younger consumers, this approach seems sure to grow in the future.

Product placement on TV has catapulted into the mainstream in response to the growing prominence of digital video recorders (DVRs) such as TiVo. Nielsen estimates that nearly 40% of U.S. households had at least one DVR in 2011, 46% in 2013, up from fewer than 10% in 2005. DVRs allow consumers not only to watch on their own schedule but also to zap ads. Worried marketers see product placement as a chance to "TiVo-proof" their messages by integrating them into the programming. Worldwide, the United States is the largest product placement market, but China is fastest growing. One notable example: Analysts estimate the media value of Macallan whiskey's appearance in the 2012 Bond film *Skyfall* at well over $9 million—plus a permanent place in Bond lore, which many brands would consider priceless . . .[20]

Product placement works best for marketers if the product

seamlessly integrates into the show as a player rather than simply a prop. For instance, it's hard to miss Coke in *American Idol*. The judges are seldom without their Coca-Cola–emblazoned cups, and during the early years of the show a 'Coke Couch' was used onstage. The price tag for this exposure—including commercial time and online content—is about $35 million. Media buyers often negotiate product placement deals as part of a package that includes regular ads, which reinforce the product that appeared in the program (unless, of course, the ads are zapped).[21]

Whether in TV or movies, product placement offers marketers huge sales potential in a credible environment, which may account for its huge growth rate. But product placement is risky—if your show is a dud, your placement is worthless. And the cost is high and growing, which only increases the financial risk. The benefits of product placement are tough to measure as well, especially for existing brands. But in the end, the only measure that really counts is consumer acceptance, which may disappear if product placement intrudes too much on the entertainment value of movies and TV.

ADVERGAMING Interactive games have exploded into pop culture; about 67% of U.S. consumers play some kind of video game, and mobile gamers are the largest and most vibrant segment. Not surprisingly, marketers have followed closely behind, developing two promotional channels: **advergaming**, which involves video games created as a marketing tool, usually with brand awareness as the core goal; plus advertising in the video games themselves. The advergaming segment was estimated to be between $700 million and $1.8 billion by 2014, and analysts estimate that in-game advertising will hit $2.6 billion by 2017.[22]

According to Massive, an advertising network that specializes in video games, advergaming works for marketers. Gamers exposed to embedded ads show a 64% increase in brand familiarity, a 37% increase in brand rating, and a 41% increase in purchase consideration; furthermore, rather than despising the ads, 55% of gamers said they "look cool." But Massive isn't the only game in town. In early 2007, Google purchased AdScape, a nimble video game advertising company, and independent agency Double Fusion also provides fierce competition. Despite the strong research results, analysts anticipate that advergaming will move in a new direction over the next few years, with deals that link brands with tangible rewards for players. Dr. Pepper, for instance, seeded 500 million bottles and fountain drink cups in 2010 with special codes that allowed gamers to download content such as virtual weapons for EA games. This approach still leaves room for purely promotional in-game ads to

advergaming Video games created as a marketing tool, usually with brand awareness as the core goal.

International Intrigue—Not the 007 Kind!

For the past couple of decades, news headlines have been screaming about foreign countries as a seemingly endless source of cheap labor that sucks away American jobs. And millions of American jobs have indeed been exported overseas. But a closer look suggests that foreign markets may also be an intriguing source of new ideas—both new products and new customers. A couple of examples:

- **Crocs: Not the ultimate *Fashion Don't*?:** While many customers love their unsurpassed comfort level, the brightly colored rubber clogs have been roundly ridiculed in the U.S. for their silly appearance, even spawning their own "I Hate Crocs" website and online store. But Crocs don't suffer the same reputation issues overseas. In China, consumers see Crocs more as "an American brand similar to Starbucks," and in Russia, consumers tend to gravitate more toward the brand's fur-lined boots. Who knew?

- **Pizza and a movie: Press play, call Dominos, and pull out your wallet, right?** Not so fast… at least not in Brazil. You may be able to enjoy your pizza without spending an extra dollar. Ten video rental stores have partnered with Dominos to cover certain hit DVDs with thermal ink. As the disc spins, the ink melts to reveal the sight and smell of a Dominos pizza. Yum, yum!![23]

Minerva Studio/Shutterstock.com

support the out-of-game campaigns. Given the explosive growth of mobile gaming, and the growing willingness of gamers to buy virtual goods (e.g., access to better game levels, or to products for their online avatars), gamers may soon see a cyberworld filled with as much promotion as the real world.[24]

BUZZ MARKETING A recent study defined "buzz" as the transfer of information from someone who is in the know to someone who isn't. Buzz is essentially word-of-mouth, which now influences two-thirds of all consumer product purchases. And it makes sense. In a world that's increasingly complex, people turn to people they know and trust to help sort the garbage from the good stuff. Other popular terms for **buzz marketing** are "guerrilla marketing" and "viral marketing."

Not surprisingly, marketers have actively pursued buzz for their brands, especially with the rising cost and diminishing effectiveness of more traditional media channels. Innovative buzz campaigns are typically custom-designed to meet their objectives, and they often cost significantly less than more traditional approaches. Here are some notable examples:

- **Whopper Sacrifice:** Burger King has been among the most successful buzz marketers, using the Internet to develop quirky and creative campaigns that

> **90% OF PEOPLE TRUST ONLINE RECOMMENDATIONS FROM PEOPLE THEY KNOW. ONLY 14% TRUST TRADITIONAL TV ADVERTISEMENTS.**
> —SOCIALNOMICS

have quickly gone viral. In late 2009, Burger King invited customers to download their Whopper Sacrifice Facebook application and use it to drop ten Facebook friends in exchange for a free Angry Whopper coupon worth $3.69. The application then bluntly notified each friend that he or she had been dumped in exchange for about $.37 worth of burger. Consumers responded in droves, apparently thankful for the excuse to purge their friend lists. Burger King terminated the campaign when Facebook requested that they terminate the "de-friending" notification. But Burger King could still loudly proclaim, "Your love for the Whopper sandwich proved to be stronger than 233,906 friendships."

- **Fitness First:** This Dutch health club ambushed unsuspecting commuters by displaying their weight in neon lights when they took a seat at a bus bench in Rotterdam. Yikes. Chances are good that they both gained some new customers and scarred some other potential customers for life![25]

> **buzz marketing** The active stimulation of word-of-mouth via unconventional, and often relatively low-cost, tactics. Other terms for buzz marketing are "guerrilla marketing" and "viral marketing."

Manscape Maintenance

In late 2013, P&G, a personal care products giant, sales were shaved rather dramatically by fashion-forward facial hair. Each of the five contenders for the Best Actor Award rocked the hairy look in his role or on the red carpet. Not only that, facial hair became more accepted in workplaces, in industries from finance to fashion, with men of all ages sporting hipster-like "permastubble." P&G responded by marketing a new Gillette men's body razor in early 2014, calling it "the first tool of its kind built for the terrain of a man's body," aimed at the expanding market of "guys' holistic shaving needs," also known as manscaping, which is of particular interest to younger men, ages 18–24.[26]

lenetstan/Shutterstock.com

SPONSORSHIPS **Sponsorships** certainly aren't new, but they should experience healthy worldwide growth over the next few years, led by a vibrant emerging national sponsorship market, particularly in Central and South America, between the 2014 World Cup and the 2016 Olympic Games. Sponsorships provide a deep association between a marketer and a partner (usually a cultural or sporting event). Even though sponsors can't usually provide more than simply their logo or slogan, consumers tend to view them in a positive light, since they are clearly connected to events that matter to the target audience. The best sponsorship investments, of course, occur when the target audience for the marketer completely overlaps the target audience for the event. The high level of integration between the sponsors and events can provide millions of dollars in valuable media coverage, justifying the hefty price.[27]

12-6b Traditional Promotional Tools: A Marketing Mainstay

Although new tools are gaining prominence, traditional promotional tools—advertising, sales promotion, public relations, and personal selling—remain powerful. In fact, many marketers use the new tools in conjunction with the traditional to create a balanced, far-reaching promotional mix.

ADVERTISING The formal definition of **advertising** is paid, nonpersonal communication, designed to influence a target audience with regard to a product, service, organization, or idea. Most major brands use advertising not only to drive sales, but also to build their reputation, especially with a broad target market. Television (network broadcasts and cable combined) remains the number-one advertising medium, with magazines and newspapers following. As mass media prices increase and audiences fragment, fringe media are roaring toward the mainstream. But measurement is tough, since alternative media tactics are buried in other categories, including magazines, outdoor, and Internet. The overall media spending patterns for 2010 are shown in Exhibit 12.9. As you review the table, note that Internet spending does not include search advertising or online video advertising, which are typically tracked separately. Also note that overall media spending has dropped significantly in response to the recession.

Each type of media offers advantages and drawbacks, as summarized in Exhibit 12.10. Your goal as a marketer should be to determine which media options reach your target market efficiently and effectively, within the limits of your budget.

sponsorship A deep association between a marketer and a partner (usually a cultural or sporting event), which involves promotion of the sponsor in exchange for either payment or the provision of goods.

advertising Paid, nonpersonal communication, designed to influence a target audience with regard to a product, service, organization, or idea.

> "DOING BUSINESS WITHOUT ADVERTISING IS LIKE WINKING AT A GIRL IN THE DARK. YOU KNOW WHAT YOU ARE DOING BUT NOBODY ELSE DOES."
>
> —STEUART HENDERSON BRITT, MARKETING MANAGEMENT AND ADMINISTRATIVE ACTION

Right Idea. Wrong Places.

Finding the right Big Idea to promote a product can be an enormous challenge. But the work doesn't stop even after a great Big Idea becomes a brilliant ad. Even the best ad won't work if it doesn't find the right place in the clutter of the overcrowded promotional environment. Less vigilant marketers have found themselves stuck with some amusingly bad placement:

- If your Starbucks ad is designed for the side of a van, made sure that when the door slides open, the "S" doesn't join with the "UCKS."

- Don't put an ad for fancy underpants on the side of a bus unless you're sure that the mud flaps on the bus tires will *always* prevent *all* mud from splashing on the pristine image of the panties.

- Make sure that your billboard for *The Walking Dead* isn't anywhere near a funeral home. And if you run a funeral home, scour the area to make sure that no tasteless billboards are posted nearby.

- Make sure that your print or digital ad isn't placed near copy that undermines it, such as a recent ad for Folgers coffee that was on a website next to an article headlined "Coffee might trigger a first heart attack in some."

You can't always know what will be around your ad, but it's always possible —and certainly worthwhile—to at least ask the question... [28]

Roman Sigaev/Shutterstock.com

SALES PROMOTION Sales promotion stimulates immediate sales activity through specific short-term programs aimed at either consumers or distributors. Traditionally, sales promotion has been subordinate to other promotional tools, but spending has accelerated in the past decade. Sales promotion falls into two categories: consumer and trade.

Consumer promotion is designed to generate immediate sales. Consumer promotion tools include premiums, promotional products, samples, coupons, rebates, and displays.

- **Premiums** are items that consumers receive free of charge— or for a lower

sales promotion Marketing activities designed to stimulate immediate sales activity through specific short-term programs aimed at either consumers or distributors.

consumer promotion Marketing activities designed to generate immediate consumer sales, using tools such as premiums, promotional products, samples, coupons, rebates, and displays.

EXHIBIT 12.9	2013 MEASURED MEDIA SPENDING BY MEDIUM (BILLIONS)	
Measured Media	**2013 Spending**	**Percentage of Total**
Broadcast TV	$27,000	19.2%
Cable TV	$26,100	18.6%
Spot TV	$15,800	11.3%
Syndicated TV	$5,200	3.7%
Newspapers	$18,400	13.1%
Radio	$7,000	5.0%
Magazines	$23,700	16.9%
Outdoor	$4,400	3.1%
Internet*	$12,700	9.1%
Total	$140,300	100%

*Internet figures are based on display advertising. They do not include paid search or broadband video advertising.

Source: 100 Leading National Advertisers 2015 Marketing Fact Pack, December 29, 2014, *Advertising Age*.

EXHIBIT 12.10 **MAJOR MEDIA CATEGORIES**

Major Media	Advantages	Disadvantages
Broadcast TV	*Mass audience:* Top-rated shows garnered more than 20 million viewers in 2013. *High impact:* TV lends itself to vivid, complex messages that use sight, sound, and motion.	*Disappearing viewers:* The 100 million viewers for the top-rated show in 2012 was dwarfed by the 1983 record of 105 million viewers for the finale of M*A*S*H. *Jaded viewers:* Consumers who aren't zapping ads with their DVR are prone to simply tuning them out. *High cost:* A 30-second ad during Super Bowl 2013 cost a record $4 million, and a typical primetime ad cost $200,000 to $400,000, depending on the show.
Cable TV	*Targeted programming:* Cable helps advertisers target highly specialized markets (Zhong Tian Channel, anyone?). *Efficient:* The cost per contact is relatively low, especially for local buys. *High impact:* Cable offers the same sight, sound, and motion benefits as broadcast.	*DVRs:* As with broadcast TV, many viewers simply aren't watching ads. *Uneven quality:* Many cable ads are worse than mediocre, providing a seedy setting for quality products.
Newspapers	*Localized:* Advertisers can tailor their messages to meet local needs. *Flexible:* Turnaround time for placing and pulling ads is very short. *Consumer acceptance:* Readers expect, and even seek, newspaper ads.	*Short life span:* Readers quickly discard their papers. *Clutter:* It takes two or three hours to read the average metro paper from cover to cover. Almost no one does it. *Quality:* Even top-notch color newsprint leaves a lot to be desired.
Direct Mail	*Highly targeted:* Direct mail can reach very specific markets. *International opportunity:* Less jaded foreign customers respond well to direct mail. *Email option:* Opt-in email can lower direct mail costs.	*Wasted resources:* Direct mail uses a staggering amount of paper. And most recipients don't even read it before they toss it. *High cost:* Cost per contact can be high, although advertisers can limit the size of the campaign. *Spam:* Unsolicited email ads have undermined consumer tolerance for all email ads.
Radio	*Highly targeted:* In L.A., for example, the dial ranges from Vietnamese talk radio, to urban dance music, each station with dramatically different listeners. *Low cost:* Advertisers can control the cost by limiting the size of the buy. *Very flexible:* Changing the message is quick and easy.	*Low impact:* Radio relies only on listening. *Jaded listeners:* Many of us flip stations when the ads begin.
Magazines	*Highly targeted:* From *Cosmopolitan* to *Computerworld*, magazines reach very specialized markets. *Quality:* Glossy print sends a high-quality message. *Long life:* Magazines tend to stick around homes and offices.	*High cost:* A full-page, four-color ad in *People* can cost more than $300,000. *Inflexible:* Advertisers must submit artwork months before publication.
Outdoor	*High visibility:* Billboards and building sides are hard to miss. *Repeat exposure:* Popular locations garner daily viewers. *Breakthrough ideas:* Innovative approaches include cars and buses "wrapped" in ads, video billboards, and blimps.	*Simplistic messages:* More than an image and a few words will get lost. *Visual pollution:* Many consumers object to outdoor ads. *Limited targeting:* It's hard to ensure that the right people see your ad.
Internet	*24/7 global coverage:* Offers a remarkable level of exposure. *Highly targeted:* Search engines are especially strong at delivering the right ad to the right person at the right time. *Interactive:* Internet ads can empower consumers.	*Intrusive:* The annoyance factor from tough-to-close pop-ups alienates consumers, infuriating many. *Limited readership:* Web surfers simply ignore the vast majority of ads.

© Cengage Learning®

than normal cost—in return for making a purchase. Upscale cosmetics companies use the gift-with-purchase approach on a regular basis. Successful premiums create a sense of urgency—"Buy me now!"—while building the value of the brand.

- **Promotional** products are also essentially gifts to consumers of merchandise that advertise a brand name. Or pizza delivery places give away refrigerator magnets with their logo and phone number. Promotional products work best when the merchandise relates to the brand, and it's so useful or fun that consumers will opt to keep it around.

- **Samples** reduce the risk of purchasing something new by allowing consumers to try a product before committing their cash. From 2009 to 2011, Muscle Milk hired hundreds of personal trainers to conduct promotions and distribute samples. Sampling also drives immediate purchases. At one time or another, most of us have probably bought food we didn't need after tasting a delicious morsel in the supermarket aisle. Costco and Trader Joe's do especially well with this angle on sampling.

- **Coupons** offer immediate price reductions to consumers. Instant coupons require even less effort, since they are attached to the package right there in the store. The goal is to entice consumers to try new products. But the downside is huge. Marketers who depend on coupons encourage consumers to focus on price rather than value, which makes it harder to differentiate brands and build loyalty. In categories with frequent coupons (such as soap and cereal), too many consumers wait for the coupon in order to buy. They end up getting great deals, but marketers pay the price in reduced profits.

- **Rebates**, common in the car industry and the electronics business, entice consumers with cash-back offers. This is a powerful tactic for higher-priced items, since rebates offer an appealing purchase motivator. And rebates provide an incentive for marketers as well: breakage. Most people who buy a product because of the rebate don't actually follow through and do the paperwork to get the money (some estimates suggest that breakage rates are as high as 90 to 95%). This means that marketers can offer hefty discounts without actually coughing up the cash, so it isn't surprising that rebates are a popular promotional tool!

- **Displays** generate purchases in-store. Most experts agree that consumers make a hefty chunk of their

Pio3/Shutterstock.com

Companies and stores work together to create a positive message through store displays.

purchase decisions as they shop, which means that displays can play a crucial role in sales success. Marketers of consumer products often give prefabricated display materials to grocery stores and mass merchandisers to encourage promotion.

Trade promotion is designed to stimulate wholesalers and retailers to push specific products more aggressively. Special deals and allowances are the most common form of trade promotion, especially for consumer products. The idea is that if you give your distributors a temporary price cut, they will pass the savings on to consumers via a short-term "special."

Trade shows are another popular form of trade promotion. Usually organized by industry trade associations, trade shows give exhibitors a chance to display and promote their products to their distributors. They typically attract hundreds of exhibitors and thousands of attendees. Trade shows are especially common in rapidly changing industries such as toys and consumer electronics. Every year the Consumer Electronics Association hosts "The world's largest annual trade show for consumer electronics!" in Las Vegas.

Other forms of trade promotion include contests, sweepstakes, and special events for distributors. A soda company might sponsor a contest to see which grocery store can build the most creative summer display for its soda brands. Or a cable TV programmer might take a group of system managers to Key West to "learn more about their programming" (really an

> **trade promotion** Marketing activities designed to stimulate wholesalers and retailers to push specific products more aggressively over the short term.

DIFFERENT SHADES OF GREEN

With wacky weather ravaging countries around the world, it's no wonder that a large-scale global survey by Interbrand consulting firm found that more than half of the people questioned were concerned about environmental issues. And understanding exactly what this means is crucial, since so many people are finally willing to act according to their ideals. For instance, more than a third of people in most countries claim to be prepared to pay a little extra for environmentally responsible products or services. And about half claim they will not purchase products from companies that have a negative reputation regarding the environment. The meaning of the different shades of green must be folded into product strategy to ensure long-term global success. Interbrand notes that in Brazil, for example, recycling is a more relevant activity in many categories than launching flagship green products. In China, the opposite tends to be true, with green products more highly evaluated than recycling activities. The study found differences not only among countries but also among categories overall. Also, in China, the car industry, which has very strong green perceptions in the rest of the world, does not fare very well. So it makes sense not just to go green, but also to go the right shade of green at the right time in the right place.[29]

excuse for a great party that makes the system managers more open to the programmer's pitch).

PUBLIC RELATIONS In the broadest sense, **public relations (or PR)** involves the ongoing effort to create positive relationships with all of a firm's different "publics," including customers, employees, suppliers, the community, the general public, and the government. But in a more focused sense, PR aims to generate positive **publicity**, or unpaid stories in the media that create a favorable impression about a company or its products. The endgame, of course, is to boost demand.

For the most part, the media cover companies or products that they perceive as newsworthy. To get coverage,

public relations (PR) The ongoing effort to create positive relationships with all of a firm's different "publics," including customers, employees, suppliers, the community, the general public, and the government.

publicity Unpaid stories in the media that influence perceptions about a company or its products.

personal selling The person-to-person presentation of products to potential buyers.

smart firms continually scan their own companies for potential news—a hot product or a major corporate achievement—and present that news to the media. But finding news on a regular basis can be tough. To fill the gaps, innovative PR people sometimes simply create "news." PR guru Bill Stoller offers some interesting ideas for how to invent stories that will grab media attention:

- **Launch a Hall of Fame:** Induct some luminaries from your industry, create a simple website, and send your press release to the media. Repeat each year, building your reputation along the way.

- **Make a List:** The best, the worst, the top ten, the bottom ten—the media loves lists, and the possible topics are endless! Just make sure that your list is relevant to your business.

- **Create a Petition:** The Web makes this tactic easy. Harness a growing trend or identify a need in your industry, and launch your petition. The more signatures you get, the better your chances for publicity.[30]

The biggest advantage of publicity is that it is usually credible. Think about it: Are you more likely to buy a product featured on the news or a product featured in a 30-second ad? Are you more likely to read a book reviewed by *The New York Times* or featured on a billboard? Publicity is credible because most people believe that information presented by the media is based on legitimate opinions and facts rather than on the drive to make money. And it also helps that publicity is close to free (excluding any fees for a PR firm).

But publicity has a major downside: the marketer has no control over how the media present the company or its products. For example, in an effort to protect customers from a growing tide of solicitors in front of its stores, Target banned Salvation Army bell ringers in front of all its stores in 2004. The press cried foul, focusing not on the service to consumers, but rather on the disrespect to a venerable charity. Target's archrival Walmart, spotting an opportunity for itself at Target's expense, announced that it would match customer donations to the Salvation Army at all of its locations.

PERSONAL SELLING **Personal selling**—the world's oldest form of promotion—is person-to-person presentation of products to potential buyers. But successful selling typically begins long before the actual presentation and ends long afterward. In today's competitive environment, selling means building relationships on a long-term basis.

Creating and maintaining a quality sales force is expensive. Experts estimate that each business-to-business sales call costs nearly $400. So why are so many people employed in sales?[31] Because nothing works better than personal selling for high-ticket items, complex products, and high-volume customers. In some companies, the sales team works directly with customers; in other firms, the sales force works with distributors who buy large volumes of products for resale.

Salespeople fall along a spectrum that ranges from order takers who simply process sales to order seekers who use creative selling to persuade customers. Most department stores hire order takers who stand behind the counter and ring up sales. But Nordstrom hires creative order seekers who actively garner sales by offering extra services such as tasteful accessory recommendations for a clothing shopper.

A separate category of salespeople focuses on *missionary selling*, which means promoting goodwill for a company by providing information and assistance to customers. The pharmaceutical industry hires a small army of missionary salespeople who call on doctors to explain and promote its products, even though the actual sales move through pharmacies.

The sales process typically follows six key stages. Keep in mind that well before the process begins, effective salespeople seek a complete understanding of their products, their industry, and their competition. A high level of knowledge permeates the entire selling process.

1. **Prospect and Qualify:** Prospecting means identifying potential customers. Qualifying means choosing those who are most likely to buy your product. Choosing the right prospects makes salespeople more efficient, since it helps them focus their limited time in areas that will yield results. Companies find prospects in a number of different ways, from trade shows, to direct mail, to cold calling. In a retail environment, everyone who walks in the door is a prospect, so salespeople either ask questions or look for visual cues to qualify customers.

2. **Prepare:** Before making a sales call, research is critical, especially in a business-to-business environment. What are your prospect's wants and needs? What are his or her current product lines? Who are the key competitors? What are the biggest internal and external challenges? How much time is your prospect willing to give you? The answers to these

questions will help you customize your presentation for maximum effectiveness.

3. **Present:** You've probably heard that you don't get a second chance to make a good first impression, and that's especially true in sales. With so many options and so little time, buyers often look for reasons to eliminate choices; a weak first impression provides an easy reason to eliminate you. Your presentation itself should match the features of your product to the benefits that your customer seeks (a chance to use all that preparation). Testimonials, letters of praise from satisfied current customers, can push forward the sale by reducing risk for your prospect. A demonstration can be the clincher. When test-driving cars, a demonstration is a no-brainer. But in other categories, technology can help demonstrate products that are too big to move.

4. **Handle Objections:** The key to success here is to view objections as opportunities rather than criticism. Objections give you a chance to learn more about the needs of your prospects and to elaborate on the benefits of your product. You should definitely anticipate as many objections as possible and prepare responses. One response may be connecting prospects with others in your company who can better handle their concerns. This approach offers the additional benefit of deepening ties between your prospect and your company.

5. **Close Sale:** Closing the sale—or asking the prospect to buy—is at the heart of the selling process. The close should flow naturally from the prior steps, but often it doesn't—sealing the deal can be surprisingly tough. One approach may be a trial close: "Would you like the 15-inch screen or the 17-inch screen?" If your prospect is still reluctant to buy, you may want to offer another alternative, or a special financial incentive. Even if the prospect doesn't actually make the purchase, remember that he or she may be willing in the future, so keep the door open.

6. **Follow-up:** The sales process doesn't end when the customer pays. The quality of service and support plays a crucial role in future sales from the same customer, and getting those sales is much easier than finding brand-new prospects. Great relationships with current customers also lead

"MORE THAN 85 PERCENT OF CUSTOMERS HAVE A NEGATIVE VIEW OF ALL SALESPEOPLE."

—BILL BROOKS, THE BROOKS GROUP

to testimonials and referrals that build momentum for long-term sales success.

Two personal selling trends are gathering momentum in a number of organizations: consultative selling and team selling. *Consultative selling* involves shifting the focus from the products to the customers. On a day-to-day basis, the practice involves a deep understanding of customer needs. Through lots and lots of active listening, consultative salespeople offer practical solutions to customer problems—solutions that use their products. While consultative selling generates powerful customer loyalty, it involves a significant—and expensive—time investment from the sales force.

Team selling tends to be especially effective for large, complex accounts. The approach includes a group of specialists from key functional areas of the company—not just sales but also engineering, finance, customer service, and others. The goal is to uncover opportunities and respond to needs that would be beyond the capacity of a single salesperson. In these situations, a key part of the salesperson's role is to connect and coordinate the right network of contacts.

12-6c Choosing the Right Promotional Mix: Not Just a Science

There are no fail-safe rules for choosing the right combination of promotional tools. The mix varies dramatically among various industries but also within specific industry segments. The best approach may simply be to consider the following questions in developing the mix that works best for your products.

- **Product Characteristics:** How can you best communicate the features of your product? Is it simple or complex? Is it high-priced or inexpensive? A specialized, high-priced item, for example, might require an investment in personal selling, whereas a simple, low-cost product might lend itself to billboard advertising.

- **Product Life Cycle:** Where does your product stand in its life cycle? Are you developing awareness? Are you generating desire? What about driving purchases? And building loyalty? The answers will clearly affect your promotional focus. For instance, if you're developing awareness, you might focus more on advertising, but if you're aiming to drive immediate sales, you'll probably emphasize sales promotion.

- **Target Audience:** How big is your target audience? Where do they live and work? A small target audience—especially if it's geographically dispersed—would lend itself to personal selling or direct mail. A sizable target audience might suggest advertising as an effective way to reach large numbers. Audience expectations should also play a role in your promotional mix decisions.

- **Push versus Pull:** Does your industry emphasize push or pull strategies? A **push strategy** involves motivating distributors to "push" your product to the final consumers, usually through heavy trade promotion and personal selling. A **pull strategy** involves creating demand from your final consumers so that they "pull" your products through the distribution channels. Many successful brands use a combination of push and pull strategies to achieve their goals. P&G recently launched a consumer marketing campaign for Crest toothpaste featuring an "Irresistibility IQ" quiz for club-goers, but it also promotes heavily to dentists, hoping that those dentists will recommend Crest to their patients.

- **Competitive Environment:** How are your key competitors handling their promotional strategies? Would it make more sense for you to follow their lead or to forge your own promotional path? If all your competitors offer coupons, for instance, your customers may expect you to offer them as well. Or if the environment is cluttered, you might want to focus on emerging promotional approaches such as advergaming.

- **Budget:** What are your promotional goals? How much money will it take to achieve them? (Answering this question is tough, but it's clearly important.) How much are your competitors spending in each area of the mix? And how much money do you have for promotion? Even though available budget shouldn't drive the promotional mix, it plays a crucial role, especially for smaller businesses.

push strategy A marketing approach that involves motivating distributors to heavily promote—or "push"—a product to the final consumers, usually through heavy trade promotion and personal selling.

pull strategy A marketing approach that involves creating demand from the ultimate consumers so that they "pull" your products through the distribution channels by actively seeking them.

The possibilities in both product development and promotional strategy have rapidly multiplied in the past few years alone. But companies can't deliver on the potential without well-oiled teamwork throughout the organization. For instance, the operations group must focus on quality, the accounting group must focus on cost, and the finance group must focus on funding—but from a big-picture standpoint, all groups must work toward the same overarching goal: maximizing customer value. Promotion also requires coordination within the organization and among the outside suppliers who provide promotional services. Finally, the best ideas for both product and promotion can come from any department. Marketers who stay ahead of the curve will only sharpen their competitive edge in the decade to come.

Careers in Product and Promotion

Pharmaceutical Sales Representative

Build effective long-term business relationships with healthcare providers. Develop and deliver sales presentations to healthcare professionals. Distribute product information and samples in order to encourage more prescriptions and recommendations. Answer questions from healthcare professionals in a timely manner. Keep current about clinical data, competitive offerings, and healthcare organizations, issues, and events, particularly in area of specialty. Organize group events for healthcare professionals. Create and maintain detailed records of all contacts and meetings. For more information on this career and other possible careers in product management or marketing promotion, check out Career Transitions.

STUDY TOOLS 12

LOCATED AT BACK OF THE TEXTBOOK

☐ Rip Out Chapter Review Card

LOCATED AT WWW.CENGAGE.COM/LOGIN

☐ Review key term flashcards and create your own using StudyBits

☐ Create and complete practice quizzes based off of your notes and StudyBits

☐ Complete Online activities such as Matching, Fill-in-the-Blank, and Drag and Drop exercises

☐ View chapter highlight box content, including CEO Profiles, What Would You Do Cases, and chapter videos

☐ Track your knowledge and understanding of key concepts in business using 4LTR Online

13 | Distribution and Pricing:
Right Product, Right Person, Right Place, Right Price

LEARNING OBJECTIVES

After studying this chapter, you will be able to:

13-1 Define distribution and differentiate between channels of distribution and physical distribution

13-2 Describe the various types of wholesale distributors

13-3 Discuss strategies and trends in store and nonstore retailing

13-4 Explain the key factors in physical distribution

13-5 Outline core pricing objectives and strategies

13-6 Discuss pricing in practice, including the role of consumer perceptions

Remember to visit
PAGE 245
for additional
STUDY TOOLS

13-1 DISTRIBUTION: GETTING YOUR PRODUCT TO YOUR CUSTOMER

Next time you go to the grocery store, look around—the average U.S. supermarket carries about 50,000 different products.[1] Is your favorite brand of soda part of the mix? Why? How did it get from the factory to your neighborhood store? Where else could you find that soda? How far would you be willing to go to get it? These are marketing distribution questions that contribute directly to the **distribution strategy**: getting the right product to the right person at the right place at the right time.

The distribution strategy has two elements: channels of distribution and physical distribution. A **channel of distribution** is the path that a product takes from the producer to the consumer, while **physical distribution** is the actual movement of products along that path. Some producers choose to sell their products directly to their customers through a **direct channel**. No one stands between the producer and the customer. Examples range from Dell computers, to local

distribution strategy A plan for delivering the right product to the right person at the right place at the right time.

channel of distribution The network of organizations and processes that links producers to consumers.

physical distribution The actual, physical movement of products along the distribution pathway.

direct channel A distribution process that links the producer and the customer with no intermediaries.

"WE NOW LIVE IN AN AGE OF SURREAL ABUNDANCE."
—JONAH LEHRER, AUTHOR

Matushchak Anton/Shutterstock.com

farmers markets, to factory outlet stores. But most producers use **channel intermediaries** to help their products move more efficiently and effectively from their factories to their consumers. Hershey's, for example, sells chocolate bars to Sam's Club—a channel intermediary—which may, in turn, sell them to you.

13-1a The Role of Distributors: Adding Value

You might be asking yourself why we need distributors. Wouldn't it be a lot less expensive to buy directly from the producers? The answer, surprisingly, is no. Distributors add value—additional benefits—to products. They charge for adding that value, but typically they charge less than it would cost for consumers or producers to add that value on their own. When distributors add to the cost of a product without providing comparable benefits, the middlemen don't stay in business. Fifteen years ago, for instance, most people bought plane tickets from travel agents. But when the Internet reduced the cost and inconvenience of buying tickets directly from airlines, thousands of travel agencies lost their customers.

One core role of distributors is to reduce the number of transactions—and the associated costs—for goods to flow from producers to consumers. As you'll see in Exhibit 13.1, even one marketing intermediary in the distribution channel can funnel goods from producers to consumers with far fewer costly transactions.

Distributors add value, or utility, in a number of different ways: form, time, place, ownership, information, and service. Sometimes the distributors deliver the value (rather than adding it themselves), but often they add new utility that wouldn't otherwise be present. As you read through the various types of utility, keep in mind that they are often interrelated, building on each other to maximize value.

Form utility provides customer satisfaction by converting inputs into finished products. Clearly, form utility is primarily a part of manufacturing. Pepsico, for instance, provides form utility by transforming water, chemicals, and aluminum into cans of soda. But retailers can add form utility as well. McDonald's, for instance, converts syrup, bubbly water, and paper into cups of soda.

Time utility adds value by making products available at a convenient time for consumers. In our 24/7 society, consumers feel entitled to

channel intermediaries
Distribution organizations—informally called "middlemen"—that facilitate the movement of products from the producer to the consumer.

It's a Bird…It's a Plane…It's Superman…Wait, No—It's a Drone!

In 2013, Amazon CEO Jeff Bezos made a media splash by announcing that the online giant is developing Amazon Prime Air, 30 minute deliveries via drone-like "octocopters." He cautioned that the service would not be in action until 2015 at the very earliest. The plan was for the drones to initially carry items up to five pounds, which is roughly 86% of all deliveries Amazon makes. Initial reaction from the public was mixed. Much of the public was concerned about safety and theft. Would people be shooting drones from the sky? And what about privacy? Others seemed to find the whole concept downright hilarious. The jokes almost instantly rippled across Twitter, which almost inevitably spawned of parody accounts. A sampling of Tweets from the fictional Octobot to the Twitterverse:

- I see you have guests. You may also be interested in curtains.

- After your first drone arrives, five others will arrive bearing items we think you might also like.

- Want to show someone how much you hate them? Send me to their house with a Nickelback CD. #DroneRevenge

But not everyone was laughing. The Federal Aviation Administration has plans to integrate drones into U.S. national airspace by 2015. And industry expert Sebastian Valencia predicts that unmanned commercial drones will add over $82 billion to the U.S. GDP by 2025. So your next Amazon order may arrive a whole lot sooner than you think.[2]

AP Images/Peter Endig/Picture-Alliance/DPA

Exhibit 13.1
Reducing Transactions through Marketing Intermediaries

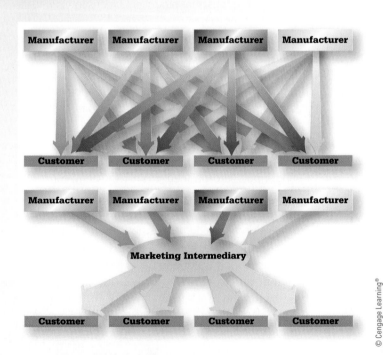

© Cengage Learning®

instant gratification, a benefit that distributors can provide more easily than most producers. Consider one-hour dry cleaning, or vending machines at your school. These distributors provide options for filling your needs at a time that works for you.

Place utility satisfies customer needs by providing the right products in the right place. Gas stations and fast food, for instance, often cluster conveniently at the bottom of freeway ramps. ATMs—essentially electronic distributors—are readily available in locations that range from grocery stores to college cafeterias.

Ownership utility adds value by making it easier for customers to actually possess the goods and services that they purchase. Providing credit, cashing checks, delivering goods, and installing products are all examples of how distributors make it easier for customers to own their products.

Information utility boosts customer satisfaction by providing helpful information. Zappos.com, for instance, hires customer service experts to guide its customers through its website to the perfect pair of shoes. Similarly, most skateboard stores

Zappos has built its brand around superb customer service.

360b/Shutterstock.com

hire skater salespeople who gladly help customers find the best board for them.

Service utility adds value by providing fast, friendly, personalized service. Examples include placing a special order for that part you need to customize your computer, or choosing just the right gift in your local clothing boutique. Distributors that provide service utility typically create a loyal base of customers.

THE MEMBERS OF THE CHANNEL: RETAILERS VERSUS WHOLESALERS Many producers sell their goods through multiple channels of distribution. Some channels have many members, while others have only a few. The main distinction among channel members is whether they are retailers or wholesalers. **Retailers** are the distributors that most of us know and use on a daily basis. They sell products directly to final consumers. Examples include 7-Eleven markets, Starbucks, and Urban Outfitters. **Wholesalers**, on the other hand, buy products from the producer and sell them to businesses (or other nonfinal users, such as hospitals, nonprofits, and the government). The businesses that buy from wholesalers can be retailers, other wholesalers, or business users. To complicate this fairly simple concept, some distributors act as both wholesalers and retailers. Costco, for example, sells directly to businesses *and* to consumers.

 13-2 ## WHOLESALERS: SORTING OUT THE OPTIONS

Some wholesalers are owned by producers, while others are owned by retailers, but the vast majority—accounting for about two-thirds of all the wholesale trade—are **independent wholesaling businesses**. These companies represent a number of different producers, distributing their goods to a range of customers. Independent wholesalers fall into two categories: (1) **merchant wholesalers**, who take legal possession, or title, of the goods they distribute, and (2) **agents/brokers**, who don't take title of the goods.

13-2a Merchant Wholesalers

Merchant wholesalers comprise about 80% of all wholesalers. By taking legal title to the goods they distribute, merchant wholesalers reduce the risk of producers' products being damaged or stolen—or even that they just won't sell. Taking title also allows merchant wholesalers to develop their own marketing strategies, including pricing.

- Full-service merchant wholesalers provide a complete array of services to the retailers or business users who typically purchase their goods. This includes warehousing, shipping, promotional assistance, product repairs, and credit.

- Limited-service merchant wholesalers provide fewer services to their customers. For example, some might warehouse products but not deliver them. Others might warehouse and deliver but not provide credit or marketing assistance. The specific categories of limited-service merchant wholesalers include the following:

  - *Drop Shippers:* Drop shippers take legal title of the merchandise, but they never physically process it. They simply organize and facilitate product shipments directly from the producer to their customers. Drop shippers are common in industries with bulky products, such as coal or timber. Amazon, however, successfully pioneered the use of drop shipping in e-commerce, where it has become a standard shipping method for a number of major websites.

retailers Distributors that sell products directly to the ultimate users, typically in small quantities, that are stored and merchandized on the premises.

wholesalers Distributors that buy products from producers and sell them to other businesses or nonfinal users such as hospitals, nonprofits, and the government.

independent wholesaling businesses Independent distributors that buy products from a range of different businesses and sell those products to a range of different customers.

merchant wholesalers Independent distributors who take legal possession, or title, of the goods they distribute.

agents/brokers Independent distributors who do not take title of the goods they distribute (even though they may take physical possession on a temporary basis before distribution).

- *Cash and Carry Wholesalers:* These distributors service customers who are too small to merit in-person sales calls from wholesaler reps. Customers must make the trip to the wholesaler themselves and cart their own products back to their stores. Costco and Staples are both examples.

- *Truck Jobbers:* Typically working with perishable goods such as bread, truck jobbers drive their products to their customers, who are usually smaller grocery stores. Their responsibilities often include checking the stock, suggesting reorder quantities, and removing out-of-date goods.

13-2b Agents and Brokers

Agents and brokers connect buyers and sellers and facilitate transactions in exchange for commissions. But they do not take legal ownership of the goods they distribute. Many insurance companies, for instance, distribute via agents, while brokers often handle real estate and seasonal products such as fruits and vegetables.

13-3 RETAILERS: THE CONSUMER CONNECTION

Retailers represent the last stop on the distribution path, since they sell goods and services directly to final consumers. Given their tight consumer connection, retailers must keep in especially close touch with rapidly changing consumer needs and wants.

Smart retailers gain a competitive edge by providing more utility, or added value, than their counterparts. Low prices are only part of the equation. Other elements clearly include customer service, product selection, advertising, and location. The look and feel of the retailer—whether online or on-ground—is another critical element.

Retailing falls into two main categories: store and non-store. But as we discuss each type, keep in mind that the lines between them are not always clear. In fact, **multichannel retailing**—or encouraging consumers to buy through different venues—is an emerging phenomenon. Some marketers have sold their products through multiple channels for many years. For example, on any given day, you could purchase a Coke from a grocery store, a restaurant, or a vending machine. But the emergence of the Internet has provided a host of new opportunities for firms that hadn't previously considered a

multichannel retailing
Providing multiple distribution channels for consumers to buy a product.

Radu Bercan/Shutterstock.com

multichannel approach. An active relationship between on-ground and online outlets has become pivotal for many retailers.

13-3a Store Retailers

While other retail channels are growing, traditional stores remain the 800-pound gorilla of the retail industry, accounting for well over 90% of total retail. Stores range in size from tiny mom-and-pop groceries to multi-acre superstores dwarfed only by their parking lots. Exhibit 13.2 highlights examples of different store types.

Both retailers and the producers who distribute through them must carefully consider their distribution strategy. The three key strategic options are intensive, selective, and exclusive.

INTENSIVE DISTRIBUTION Intensive distribution involves placing your products in as many stores as possible (or placing your stores themselves in as many locations as possible). This strategy makes the most sense for low-cost convenience goods that consumers won't travel too far to find. Marketers have chosen this strategy for Snickers candy bars, Dial soap, and Sports *Illustrated* magazine, among thousands of other items.

SELECTIVE DISTRIBUTION Selective distribution means placing your products only with preferred retailers (or establishing your stores only in limited locations). This approach tends to work best for medium- and higher-priced products or stores that consumers don't expect to find on every street corner. Marketers have chosen this strategy for Neiman Marcus, Jones Soda, and most brands of paintball equipment, for instance.

EXCLUSIVE DISTRIBUTION Exclusive distribution means establishing only one retail outlet in a given area. Typically, that one retailer has exclusive distribution rights and provides exceptional service and selection. This strategy tends to work for luxury-goods providers with a customer

EXHIBIT 13.2   RETAIL STORE CATEGORIES

Store Type	Store Description	Examples
Category Killer	Dominates its category by offering a huge variety of one type of product.	OfficeMax, Best Buy, Staples, PetSmart, Toys R Us, Big 5 Sporting Goods
Convenience Store	Sells a small range of everyday and impulse products at easy-to-access locations with long hours and quick checkout.	7-Eleven, AM/PM markets, Circle K, and a wide range of local stores
Department Store	Offers a wide variety of merchandise (e.g., clothes, furniture, cosmetics), plus (usually) a high level of service.	Nordstrom, Macy's, Neiman Marcus
Discount Store	Offers a wide array of merchandise at significantly lower prices and with less service than most department stores.	Target, Walmart, Kmart
Outlet Store	Producer-owned store sells directly to the public at a huge discount. May include discontinued, flawed, or overrun items.	Nike, Versace, Quicksilver, Calvin Klein, Converse, GUESS
Specialty Store	Sells a wide selection of merchandise within a narrow category, such as auto parts.	Barnes & Noble, Victoria's Secret, Claire's, AutoZone, Lenscrafter, Bath & Body Works
Supermarket	Offers a wide range of food products, plus limited nonfood items (e.g., toilet paper).	Kroger, Safeway, Albertson's, Whole Foods, Trader Joe's
Supercenter	Sells a complete selection of food and general merchandise at a steep discount in a single enormous location.	Walmart Supercenters, Super Target
Warehouse Club	Sells discounted food and general merchandise to club members in a large warehouse format.	Costco, Sam's Club

© Cengage Learning®

base that actively seeks their products. Examples include top-end cars such as Tesla and fashion trendsetters such as Jason Wu.

The **wheel of retailing** offers another key strategic consideration. The wheel is a classic theory that suggests retail firms—sometimes even entire retail categories—become more upscale as they go through their life cycles. For instance, it's easiest to enter a business on a shoestring, gaining customers by offering low prices. But eventually businesses trade up their selection, service, and facilities to maintain and build their customer base. Higher prices then follow, creating vulnerability to new, lower-priced competitors. And thus the wheel keeps rolling.

Although the wheel of retailing theory does describe many basic retail patterns, it doesn't account for stores that launch at the high end of the market (e.g., Whole Foods) and those that retain their niche as deep discounters (e.g., Dollar General or Taco Bell). But the wheel theory does underscore the core principle that retailers must meet changing consumer needs in a relentlessly competitive environment.

> IN 2013, THE AVERAGE U.S. SUPERMARKET CARRIED NEARLY 44,000 DIFFERENT ITEMS.
> —FOOD MARKETING INSTITUTE

13-3b Nonstore Retailers

While most retail dollars flow through brick-and-mortar stores, a growing number of sales go through other channels, or nonstore retailers. The key players represent online retailing, direct-response retailing, direct selling, and vending.

ONLINE RETAILING Also known as "e-tailing," online retailing grew at the astonishing rate of nearly 25% per year for most of the early 2000s. But the torrid pace began to slow in 2008 with the onset of the recession. Online retailing grew only 1.6% in 2009, but growth bounced back to over 12% in 2011. Looking forward, experts predict that annual growth will remain robust in the following years, even as e-commerce continues to mature. Much of the growth will likely come

> **wheel of retailing** A classic distribution theory that suggests that retail firms and retail categories become more upscale as they go through their life cycles.

at the expense of on-ground retail, as consumers continue to shift to online channels. The bigger name brands—including online-only brands, such as Amazon, and on-ground brands with a strong web presence, such as Best Buy—seem poised to benefit most, since cautious consumers are most familiar with them.[3]

Online retailers, like their on-ground counterparts, have learned that great customer service can be a powerful differentiator. Simply "getting eyeballs" isn't enough, since—depending on the industry—fewer than 5% of the people visiting a typical website convert into paying customers. Overstock.com, for instance, has been a pioneer in online customer service, hiring and training 60 specialists who engage customers in live chats, available 24/7. When a customer has a live chat with one of its specialists, the average purchase amount doubles. In fact, according to the National Retail Federation (NRF), shoppers have increasingly identified Internet-only retailers among those who offered the best customer service. In 2012, Amazon .com took top honors in the annual NRF/American Express Customers' Choice survey, and two other online retailers—Overstock.com and Zappos.com—placed in its top five positions for the fourth year in a row, for retailers that offer the best customer service in any retail format.[4]

Despite the advantages, online retailers face two major hurdles. The first is that products must be delivered, and even the fastest delivery services typically take at least a couple of days. But the truly daunting hurdle is the lack of security on the Web. As online retailers and software developers create increasingly secure systems, hackers develop more sophisticated tools to crack their new codes.

DIRECT RESPONSE RETAILING This category includes catalogs, telemarketing, and advertising (such as infomercials) meant to elicit direct consumer sales. While many traditional catalog retailers have also established successful websites, the catalog side of the business continues to thrive. Victoria's Secret, for instance, sends a mind-boggling 400 million catalogs each year—that's more than four catalogs for every American woman between the ages of 15 and 64. Telemarketing, both inbound and outbound, also remains a potent distribution channel, despite the popular National Do Not Call list established in 2003.

DIRECT SELLING This channel includes all methods of selling directly to customers in their homes or workplaces. Door-to-door sales has enjoyed a resurgence in the wake of the National Do Not Call list, but the real strength of direct selling lies in **multilevel marketing**, or **MLM**. Multilevel marketing involves hiring independent contractors to sell products to their personal network of friends and colleagues and to recruit new salespeople in return for a percentage of their commissions. Mary Kay Cosmetics and The Pampered Chef have both enjoyed enormous success in this arena, along with pioneering companies such as Tupperware.

VENDING Until about a decade ago, vending machines in the United States sold mostly soft drinks and snacks. But more recently, the selection has expanded (and the machines have gone more upscale) as marketers recognize the value of providing their products as conveniently as possible to their target consumers. The Maine Lobster Game, for example, allows customers to catch their own fresh lobster dinner with a metal claw in restaurants and bars. But other countries are far ahead of the

> "LEADERS WIN THROUGH LOGISTICS. VISION, SURE. STRATEGY, YES. BUT WHEN YOU GO TO WAR, YOU NEED TO HAVE BOTH TOILET PAPER AND BULLETS AT THE RIGHT PLACE AT THE RIGHT TIME. IN OTHER WORDS, YOU MUST WIN THROUGH SUPERIOR LOGISTICS."
>
> —TOM PETERS, BUSINESS WRITER

Selection in vending machines has recently expanded, as people want healthier options.

multilevel marketing (MLM) Involves hiring independent contractors to sell products to their personal network of friends and colleagues and to recruit new salespeople in return for a percentage of their commissions.

United States in the vending arena. In Japan, for instance, people buy everything from blue jeans to beef from vending machines. In China, a vending machine at a main subway station in Nanjing sells an average of 200 live hairy crabs every day. And vending machines in Puerto Rico dispense free tubes of Colgate along with candy bars, plus an LED message that says "Don't forget to brush."[5] As technology continues to roll forward, U.S. consumers are likely to see a growing number of vending ma-chines for products as diverse as "fresh-baked" pizza, digital cameras, and specialty coffee drinks.

13-4 PHYSICAL DISTRIBUTION: PLANES, TRAINS, AND MUCH, MUCH MORE

Determining the best distribution channels for your product is only the first half of your distribution strategy. The second half is the physical distribution strategy: determining how your product will flow through the channel from the producer to the consumer.

The **supply chain** for a product includes not only its distribution channels but also the string of suppliers who deliver products to the producers. (See Exhibit 13.3.) Planning and coordinating the movement of products along the supply chain—from the raw materials to the final consumers—is called **supply chain management** or **SCM**. **Logistics** is a subset of SCM that focuses more on tactics (the actual movement of products) than on strategy.

At one time, relationships among the members of the supply chain were contentious. But these days, companies that foster collaboration, rather than competition, have typically experienced more success. Vendor-managed inventory is an emerging strategy—pioneered by Walmart—that allows suppliers to determine buyer needs and automatically ship product. This strategy saves time and money but also requires an extraordinary level of trust and information-sharing among members of the supply chain.

In our turbocharged 24/7 society, supply chain management has become increasingly complex. Gap, for instance, contracts with more than 3,000 factories in more than 50 different countries, and distributes its products to about 3,000 stores in eight different countries. The coordination requirements are mind-boggling. Key management decisions include the following considerations:

Exhibit 13.3
Elements of the Supply Chain

The supply chain highlights the links among the various organizations in the production and distribution process.

Raw Materials → Logistics (transportation, coordination, etc.) → Warehouse/Storage → Production → Warehouse/Storage → Logistics (transportation, coordination, etc.) → Distributors—Marketing and Sales

© Cengage Learning®

- **Warehousing:** How many warehouses do we need? Where should we locate our warehouses?

- **Materials Handling:** How should we move products within our facilities? How can we best balance efficiency with effectiveness?

- **Inventory Control:** How much inventory should we keep on hand? How should we store and distribute it? What about costs such as taxes and insurance?

- **Order Processing:** How should we manage incoming and outgoing orders? What would be most efficient for our customers and suppliers?

- **Customer Service:** How can we serve our customers most effectively? How can we reduce waiting times and facilitate interactions?

- **Transportation:** How can we move products most

supply chain All organizations, processes, and activities involved in the flow of goods from the raw materials to the final consumer.

supply chain management (SCM) Planning and coordinating the movement of products along the supply chain, from the raw materials to the final consumers.

logistics A subset of supply chain management that focuses largely on the tactics involved in moving products along the supply chain.

EXHIBIT 13.4　MODES OF TRANSPORTATION

Mode	Percentage of U.S. Volume Based on 2007 Ton-Miles	Cost	Speed	On-Time Dependability	Flexibility in Handling	Frequency of Shipments	Availability
Rail	39.5%	Medium	Slow	Medium	Medium	Low	Extensive
Truck	28.6%	High	Fast	High	Medium	High	Most extensive
Ship	12.0%	Lowest	Slowest	Lowest	Highest	Lowest	Limited
Plane	0.3%	Highest	Fastest	Medium	Low	Medium	Medium
Pipeline	19.6%	Low	Slow	Highest	Lowest	Highest	Most limited

Source: Table 1-46b: U.S. Ton-Miles of Freight (BTS Special Tabulation), 2007 data, Bureau of Transportation website, http://www.bts.gov/publications/national_transportation_statistics/html/table_01_46b.html, accessed April 8, 2013.

efficiently through the supply chain? What are the key tradeoffs?

■ **Security:** How can we keep products safe from vandals, theft, and accidents every step of the way?

And fragile or perishable products, of course, require even more considerations.

13-4a　Transportation Decisions

Moving products through the supply chain is so important that it deserves its own section. The various options—trains, planes, and railroads, for instance—are called **modes of transportation**. To make smart decisions, marketers must consider what each mode offers in terms of cost, speed, dependability, flexibility, availability, and frequency of shipments. The right choice, of course, depends on the needs of the business and on the product itself. See Exhibit 13.4 for a description of the transportation options.

Depending on factors such as warehousing, docking facilities, and accessibility, many distributors use several different modes of transportation. If you owned a clothing boutique in Las Vegas, for example, chances are that much of your merchandise would travel by boat from China to Long Beach, California, and then by truck from Long Beach to Las Vegas.

13-4b　Proactive Supply Chain Management

A growing number of marketers have turned to supply chain management to build a competitive edge through greater efficiency. But given the complexity of the field, many firms choose to outsource this challenge to experts rather than handling it internally. Companies that specialize in helping other companies manage the supply chain—such as UPS—have done particularly well in today's market.

13-5　PRICING OBJECTIVES AND STRATEGIES: A HIGH-STAKES GAME

Pricing strategy clearly has a significant impact on the success of any organization. Price plays a key role in determining demand for your products, which directly influences a company's profitability. Most people, after all, have a limited amount of money and a practically infinite number of ways they could spend it. Price affects their spending choices at a more fundamental level than most other variables.

But ironically, price is perhaps the toughest variable for marketers to control. Both legal constraints and marketing intermediaries (distributors) play roles in determining the final price of most products. Marketers must also consider costs, competitors, investors, taxes, and product strategies.

In today's frenetic environment, stable pricing is no longer the norm. Smart marketers continually evaluate and refine their pricing strategies to ensure that they meet their goals. Even the goals themselves may shift in response to the changing market. Common objectives and strategies include building profitability, boosting volume, matching the competition, and creating prestige.

13-5a　Building Profitability

Since long-term profitability is a fundamental goal of most businesses, profitability targets are often the starting point for pricing strategies. Many firms express these goals in terms of either return on investment (ROI) or return on sales (ROS). Keep in mind that profitability is the positive

---

modes of transportation The various transportation options—such as planes, trains, and railroads—for moving products through the supply chain.

Many firms express long-term profitability goals in terms of either return on investment or return on sales.

difference between revenue (or total sales) and costs. Firms can boost profits by increasing prices or decreasing costs, since either strategy will lead to a greater spread between the two. Doing both, of course, is tricky, but companies that succeed—such as Apple—typically dominate their markets.

13-5b Boosting Volume

Companies usually express volume goals in terms of market share—the percentage of a market controlled by a company or a product. Amazon.com, for example, launched with volume objectives. Its goal was to capture as many "eyeballs" as possible, in hopes of later achieving profitability through programs that depend on volume, such as advertising on its site. A volume objective usually leads to one of the following strategies.

PENETRATION PRICING **Penetration pricing**, a strategy for pricing new products, aims to capture as much of the market as possible through rock-bottom prices. Each individual sale typically yields a tiny profit; the real money comes from the sheer volume of sales. One key benefit of this strategy is that it tends to discourage competitors, who may be scared off by the slim margins. But penetration pricing makes sense only in categories that don't have a significant group of consumers who would be willing to pay a premium (otherwise, the marketer would be leaving

money on the table). For obvious reasons, companies that use penetration pricing are usually focused on controlling costs. JetBlue is a key example. Its prices are often unbeatable, but it strictly controls costs by using a single kind of jet, optimizing turnaround times at the gate, and using many non-major airports.

EVERYDAY-LOW PRICING Also known as "sustained discount pricing," **everyday-low pricing (EDLP)** aims to achieve long-term profitability through volume. Walmart is clearly the king of EDLP with "Always low prices. *Always!*" But Costco uses the same strategy to attract a much more-upscale audience. The difference between the two customer groups quickly becomes apparent by glancing at the cars, while strolling through the two parking lots. Costco customers are typically seeking everyday discounts because they want to, not because they need to. The product mix—eclectic and upscale—reflects the customer base. (Costco sells discounted fine wine, low-priced rotisserie chickens, fresh king crab legs, and high-end electronics.) While Costco posted years of healthy, sustained growth, the firm ran into trouble at the end of 2008. As the recession tightened its grip, sales began to soften, especially in non-food categories, suggesting that EDLP may be most effective for less-upscale products.[6] By 2010, Costco had recovered and returned to its historical growth trajectory.

HIGH/LOW PRICING The **high/low pricing** strategy tries to increase traffic in retail stores by special sales on a limited number of products, and higher everyday prices on others. Often used—and overused—in grocery stores, drug stores, and department stores, this strategy can alienate customers who feel cheated when a product they bought for full price goes on sale soon afterward. High/low pricing can also train consumers to buy only when products are on sale.

LOSS-LEADER PRICING Closely related to high/low pricing, **loss-leader pricing** means pricing a handful of items—or loss leaders—temporarily below cost to drive traffic. The retailer loses money on the loss leaders but aims to make up the difference (and then some) on other purchases. To encourage other purchases, retailers

penetration pricing A new product pricing strategy that aims to capture as much of the market as possible through rock-bottom prices.

everyday-low pricing (EDLP) Long-term discount pricing, designed to achieve profitability through high sales volume.

high/low pricing A pricing strategy designed to drive traffic to retail stores by special sales on a limited number of products, and higher everyday prices on others.

loss-leader pricing Closely related to high/low pricing, loss-leader pricing means pricing a handful of items—or loss leaders—temporarily below cost to drive traffic.

Timing Is Everything!

At the *exact same time of day* that you might score free appetizers and a half-priced beverage at your local happy hour, you might pay double for a ride with Uber during surge pricing hours. While pricing in the United States appears to be fixed, it's flexible in more cases than you might initially think. Consider early bird specials at restaurants, Blue Light Specials at K-Mart, and Black Friday deals the day after Thanksgiving. Time is a consistent factor in every one of these deals. If you are interested in getting the best possible deals in the United States, you must plan your time accordingly. It all circles back to supply and demand. During windows of high demand, prices are likely to rise; when demand is low, prices will plummet. The opposite holds true for supply. So one way to keep an eye on your wallet is to keep a close eye on the clock and the calendar.

Justin Tallis/AFP/Getty Images

"IF AUTOMOBILES HAD FOLLOWED THE SAME DEVELOPMENT CYCLE AS THE COMPUTER, A ROLLS-ROYCE WOULD TODAY COST $100, GET A MILLION MILES PER GALLON, AND EXPLODE ONCE A YEAR, KILLING EVERYONE INSIDE."

—ROBERT CRINGELY, TECHNOLOGY JOURNALIST

typically place loss leaders at the back of the store, forcing customers to navigate past a tempting array of more profitable items. The loss-leader strategy has been used effectively by producers, as well. Gillette, for instance, gives away some shavers practically for free but reaps handsome profits as consumers buy replacement blades. Similarly, Microsoft has sold its Xbox systems at a loss in order to increase potential profits from high-margin video games. But the loss-leader strategy can't be used everywhere, since a number of states have made loss leaders illegal for anti-competitive reasons.[7]

skimming pricing A new product pricing strategy that aims to maximize profitability by offering new products at a premium price.

13-5c Matching the Competition

The key goal is to set prices based on what everyone else is doing. Usually, the idea is to wipe out price as a point of comparison, forcing customers to choose their product based on other factors. Examples include Coke and Pepsi, Honda and Toyota, Chevron and Mobil, and Delta and United. But sometimes one or two competitors emerge that drive pricing for entire industries. Marlboro, for instance, leads the pack in terms of cigarette pricing, with other brands falling into place behind.

13-5d Creating Prestige

The core goal is to use price to send consumers a message about the high quality and exclusivity of a product—the higher the price, the better the product. Of course, this strategy works only if the product actually delivers top quality; otherwise, nobody would buy more than once (and those who do so would clearly spread the word). Rolex watches, Mont Blanc pens, and Bentley cars all use prestige pricing to reinforce their image.

SKIMMING PRICING This new product pricing strategy is a subset of prestige pricing. **Skimming pricing** involves offering new products at a premium price. The idea is to entice price-insensitive consumers—music fanatics, for example—to buy high when a product first enters the market. Once these customers have made their purchases, marketers will often introduce lower-priced versions of the same product to capture the bottom of the market. Apple used this strategy with its iPod, introducing its premium

"Slippery Finger" Pricing Goofs

If a price seems too good to be true, it probably is. But seeking an incredible bargain can still make sense—dollars and cents. Due to "slippery finger" typos, frequent price changes, and programming glitches, online retailers are especially vulnerable to pricing mistakes. Without human cashier confirmation, it's tough to catch the goofs. And to magnify the problem, quick communication on the Web almost ensures a flood of customers placing orders as soon as the wrong price goes live.

A sampling of recent online "deals":

- Free flights from Los Angeles to Fiji
- Round-trip tickets from San Jose, CA, to Paris for $27.98
- $1,049 televisions wrongly listed for $99.99 on Amazon
- $588 Hitachi monitors mistakenly marked down to $164
- High-definition computer monitors and digital projectors, worth hundreds of dollars, wrongly priced at $8.85 on Walmart.com
- Five watches, worth $11,332, briefly sale-priced at $0.0 (with free shipping) on Ashford.com

After the first few high-profile pricing disasters, online retailers have taken steps to protect themselves through specific disclaimers in their terms of use. And the courts have generally ruled that a company need not honor an offer if a reasonable person would recognize that it was a mistake.

But disclaimers and legal protections won't protect a retailer from customers who feel cheated. So companies that post pricing mistakes must choose between losing money by honoring offers or losing customer goodwill by canceling them—there simply isn't a winning option. But Travelocity—home of those unintended free tickets from Los Angeles to Fiji—has at least found a way to handle snafus with grace. Its Travelocity Guarantee program notes "If, say, we inadvertently advertise a fare that's just 'too good to be true,' like a free trip to Fiji, we'll work with you and our travel partners to make it up to you and find a solution that puts a smile on your face." So—happy shopping![8]

---

version for a hefty price tag. Once it had secured the big spenders, Apple introduced the lower-priced iPod Nanos and Shuffles with a powerful market response. But keep in mind that skimming works only when a product is tough to copy in terms of design, brand image, technology, or some other attribute. Otherwise, the fat margins will attract a host of competitors.

13-6 PRICING IN PRACTICE: A REAL-WORLD APPROACH

At this point, you may be wondering about economic theory. How do concepts such as supply and demand and price elasticity affect pricing decisions?

Even though most marketers are familiar with economics, they often don't have the information they need to apply the theories to their specific pricing strategies. Collecting data for supply and demand curves is expensive and time consuming, which may be unrealistic for rapidly changing markets. From a real-world standpoint, most marketers consider market-based factors—especially customer expectations and competitive prices—but they rely on cost-based pricing. The key question is: What price levels will allow me to cover my costs and achieve my objectives?

13-6a Breakeven Analysis

Breakeven analysis is a relatively simple process that determines the number of units a firm must sell to cover all costs. Sales above the breakeven point will generate a profit; sales below the breakeven point will lead to a loss. The actual equation looks like this:

$$\text{Breakeven Point (BP)} = \frac{\text{Total fixed costs (FC)}}{\text{Price/unit (p)} - \text{Variable costs/unit (VC)}}$$

If you were selling customized nachos, for example, your fixed costs might be $400,000 per year. Fixed costs stay the same regardless of how many servings of nachos you sell. Specific fixed costs might include the mortgage, equipment payments, advertising, insurance, and taxes. Suppose your variable cost per serving—the cost of the ingredients and the cost of wages for the cook—were $5 per serving. If your customers would pay $12 per serving, you could use the breakeven equation to determine how

> **breakeven analysis** The process of determining the number of units a firm must sell to cover all costs.

Coca-Cola: It's Everywhere You Want to Be; and Some Places You May Not Want to Be...

You don't need to travel very far to find a Coca-Cola product. That's because the beverage behemoth has 17 brands with more than one billion dollars in annual retail sales and sells more than 500 different brands of soda, tea, and juice. In fact, Coke makes so many different beverages that if you drank one per day, it would take you over nine years to try them all. Coca-Cola has also developed an enviable distribution network. From the rugged mountains of Nepal to the remote villages of Zimbabwe, local vendors sell Coke. This distribution network is so comprehensive that philanthropic groups such as the Bill and Melinda Gates Foundation are testing it as a potential means to reach rural areas to deliver medicine and supplies alongside soda. Pretty impressive for a brand that's losing some of its fizzle in the United States. [9]

Attila Dudas/Shutterstock.com

---

many servings of nachos you'd need to sell in a year so that your total sales were equal to your total expenses. Remember: a company that is breaking even is not making a profit.

Here's how the breakeven analysis would work for our nacho business:

$$BP = \frac{FC}{P - VC} = \frac{\$400,000}{\$12 - \$5} = \frac{\$400,000}{\$7} = 57,143 \text{ Servings Nachos}$$

Over a one-year horizon, 57,143 servings of customized nachos would translate to about 157 servings per day. Is that reasonable? Could you do better? If so, start thinking of some creative names! If not, you have several choices, each with its own set of considerations:

- **Raise Prices:** How much do other snack-like meals in your neighborhood cost? Are your nachos better in some way? Would potential customers be willing to pay more?

- **Decrease Variable Costs:** Could you use less expensive ingredients? Is it possible to hire less expensive help? How would these changes affect quality and sales?

- **Decrease Fixed Costs:** Should you choose a different location? Can you lease cheaper equipment? Would it make sense to advertise less often? How would these changes affect your business?

> **profit margin** The gap between the cost and the price of an item on a per-product basis.

Clearly, there isn't one best strategy, but a breakeven analysis helps marketers get a sense of where they stand and the hurdles they need to clear before actually introducing a product.

13-6b Fixed Margin Pricing

Many firms determine upfront how much money they need to make for each item they sell. The **profit margin**—which is the gap between the cost and the price on a per-product basis—can be expressed as a dollar amount but more often is expressed as a percent. There are two key ways to determine margins.

1. **Cost-Based Pricing:** The most popular method of establishing a fixed margin starts with determining the actual cost of each product. The process is more complex than it may initially seem, since fixed costs must be allocated on a per-product basis, and some variable costs fluctuate dramatically on a daily or weekly basis. But once the per-product cost is set, the next step is to layer the margin on the cost to determine the price. Costco, for instance, has a strict policy that no branded

> THERE ARE TWO KINDS OF FOOLS IN ANY MARKET. ONE DOESN'T CHARGE ENOUGH. THE OTHER CHARGES TOO MUCH.
>
> —RUSSIAN PROVERB

item can be marked up by more than 14%, and no private-label item by more than 15%. Supermarkets, on the other hand, often mark up merchandise by 25%, and department stores by 50% or more. Margins in other industries can be much thinner.[11]

2. **Demand-Based Pricing:** This approach begins by determining what price consumers would be willing to pay. With that as a starting point, marketers subtract their desired margin, which yields their target costs. This method is more market-focused than cost-based pricing, but it's also more risky, since profits depend on achieving those target costs. A number of Japanese companies, such as Sony, have been very successful with this approach, achieving extraordinarily efficient production.

13-6c Consumer Pricing Perceptions: The Strategic Wild Card

You just don't know if you've found the right price until you figure out how consumers perceive it. And those perceptions can sometimes defy the straightforward logic of dollars and cents. Two key considerations are price–quality relationships and odd pricing.

The link between price and perceived quality can be powerful. Picture yourself walking into a local sporting goods store, looking for a new snowboard. They have several models of your favorite brand, most priced at around $450. But then you notice another option—same brand, same style—marked down to $79. Would you buy it? If you were like most consumers, you'd probably assume that something were wrong with a board that cheap. Would you be right? It's hard to know. Sometimes the relationship between price and quality is clear and direct, but that is not always the case. Regardless, consumers will use price as an indicator of quality unless they have additional information to guide their decision. Savvy marketers factor this tendency into their pricing strategies.

Marketers also must weigh the pros and cons of **odd pricing**, or ending prices in numbers below even dollars and cents. A micro stereo system at Target, for instance, costs $99.99. Gasoline, of course, uses odd pricing to 99/100ths of a cent. But wouldn't round numbers be easier? Does that extra penny really make a difference? While the research is inconclusive, many marketers believe that jumping up to the "next" round number sends a message that prices have hit a whole new level. In other words, they believe that the *perceived* gap between $99.99 and $100.00 is much greater than the *actual* gap of .0001%. And it certainly makes sense from an intuitive standpoint.

Odd prices have also come to signal a bargain, which is often—but not always—a benefit for the marketer.

> **odd pricing** The practice of ending prices in numbers below even dollars and cents in order to create a perception of greater value.

For instance, a big-screen TV for $999.99 might seem like a great deal, while knee surgery for $4,999.99 sounds kind of scary—you'd probably rather that your doctor charge $5,000. Likewise, a fast-food joint might charge $3.99 for its value meal, while fine restaurants almost always end their prices in zeros. Marketers can determine whether odd pricing would work for them by evaluating the strategy in light of the messages it sends to the target market.

The BIG Picture

Distribution and pricing are two fundamental elements of the marketing mix. In today's frenzied global economy, marketers are seeking a competitive edge through distribution management. Creating a profitable presence in multiple retail venues requires constant focus throughout the organization. And managing the supply chain—how products move along the path from raw materials to the final consumer—plays a crucial role in controlling costs and providing great customer service. Integrating effective technology during the entire process can separate the winners from the losers.

Pricing objectives and strategies are also pivotal since they directly impact both profitability and product image. As the market changes, successful companies continually reevaluate and modify their approach, working hand in hand with their accountants.

Looking ahead, a growing number of companies will probably move toward collaboration, rather than competition, as they manage their supply chains. And pricing will likely become even more dynamic in response to the changing market.

Careers in Distribution and Pricing

Warehouse Manager

Oversee the safe receipt, storage, retrieval, and timely transmission of goods. Oversee computerized inventory management system. Comply with federal, state, and local laws regarding warehousing, material handling, and shipping. Plan the arrangement of goods within the warehouse and handle requirements for specialized stock (e.g., chilled goods or fragile products). Keep current with all relevant legislation and industry trends. Ensure security in all aspects of warehouse operation. Maintain physical condition of warehouse. Create and track warehousing budget to meet financial objectives. Hire, manage, and motivate warehouse staff. For more information on this career and other possible careers in distribution or pricing, check out Career Transitions.

STUDY TOOLS 13

LOCATED AT BACK OF THE TEXTBOOK

☐ Rip Out Chapter Review Card

LOCATED AT WWW.CENGAGE.COM/LOGIN

☐ Review key term flashcards and create your own using StudyBits

☐ Create and complete practice quizzes based off of your notes and StudyBits

☐ Complete Online activities such as Matching, Fill-in-the-Blank, and Drag and Drop exercises

☐ View chapter highlight box content, including CEO Profiles, What Would You Do Cases, and chapter videos

☐ Track your knowledge and understanding of key concepts in business using 4LTR Online

14 | Management, Motivation, and Leadership:
Bringing Business to Life

LEARNING OBJECTIVES

After studying this chapter, you will be able to…

14-1 Discuss the role of management and its importance to organizational success

14-2 Explain key theories and current practices of motivation

14-3 Outline the categories of business planning and explain strategic planning

14-4 Discuss the organizing function of management

14-5 Explain the role of managerial leadership and the key leadership styles

14-6 Describe the management control process

Remember to visit **PAGE 263** for additional **STUDY TOOLS**

14-1 BRINGING RESOURCES TO LIFE

To grow and thrive, every business needs resources—money, technology, materials—and an economic system that helps enterprise flourish. But those resources, or factors of production, are nothing without **management** to bring them to life. Managers provide vision and direction for their organizations, they decide how to use resources to achieve goals, and they inspire others—both inside and outside their companies—to follow their lead. By formal definition, managers achieve the goals of an organization through planning, organizing, leading, and controlling organizational resources, including people, money, and time.

management Achieving the goals of an organization through planning, organizing, leading, and controlling organizational resources including people, money, and time.

planning Determining organizational goals and action plans for how to achieve those goals.

organizing Determining a structure for both individual jobs and the overall organization.

leading Directing and motivating people to achieve organizational goals.

In simple terms, **planning** means figuring out where to go and how to get there. **Organizing** means determining a structure for both individual jobs and the overall organization. **Leading** means directing and motivating people to

IT'S ALL IN YOUR HANDS!

"IF YOU CAN GET THOSE TWO THINGS RIGHT— HAVING A CLEAR DIRECTION ON WHAT YOU ARE TRYING TO DO AND BRINGING IN GREAT PEOPLE WHO CAN EXECUTE ON THE STUFF— THEN YOU CAN DO PRETTY WELL."

—MARK ZUCKERBERG, FOUNDER AND CEO, FACEBOOK

achieve organizational goals. And **controlling** means monitoring performance and making adjustments as needed. In today's chaotic, hyper-competitive business environment, managers face daunting challenges. But for the right people, management positions can provide an exhilarating—though sometimes exhausting—career.

As the business pace accelerates and the environment continues to morph—especially in the wake of economic turmoil—the role of management is also radically transforming. The successful manager has changed from boss to coach, from disciplinarian to motivator, from dictator to team builder. But the bottom-line goal remains the same: to create value for the organization.

14-1a Management Hierarchy: Levels of Responsibility

Most medium-sized and large companies have three basic levels of management: **top management**, **middle management**, and **first-line (or supervisory) management**. The levels typically fall into a pyramid of sorts, with a small number of top managers and a larger number of supervisory managers. Responsibilities shift as managers move up the hierarchy, and the skills that they use must shift accordingly. Here are the differences between three key levels:

- **Top management** sets the overall direction of the firm. Top managers must articulate a vision, establish priorities, and allocate time, money, and other resources. Typical titles include chief executive officer (CEO), president, and vice president.

- **Middle management** manages the managers. (Say that three times!) Middle managers must communicate up and down the pyramid, and their primary contribution often involves coordinating teams and special projects with their peers from other departments. Typical titles include director, division head, and branch manager.

controlling Monitoring performance and making adjustments as needed.

top management Managers who set the overall direction of the firm, articulating a vision, establishing priorities, and allocating time, money, and other resources.

middle management Managers who supervise lower-level managers and report to a higher-level manager.

first-line (supervisory) management Managers who directly supervise nonmanagement employees.

Starting Early and Staying Strong

Some people seem compelled to succeed no matter what ... and those are the folks who tend to drive the economy. A quick survey of some well-known super-achievers suggests that a high level of motivation was part of their personalities from the very beginning:

- *Mark Zuckerberg, Facebook founder:* Before he went to college, Mark was recruited to work for Microsoft and AOL. As a toddler, he found a screwdriver and dismantled his crib when he thought he was too old for a "baby bed."

- *Gene Simmons, frontman for flamboyant rock band Kiss:* Simmons, a.k.a. the Demon, began his career as a sixth-grade teacher in Spanish Harlem, and was reportedly fired for, among other things, replacing the Shakespearean play in the curriculum with Spiderman comics.

- *Jeff Bezos, Amazon founder:* As a teenager, Jeff built amateur robots and an assortment of other electronic inventions.

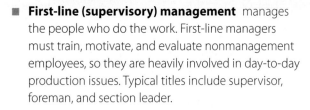

Brian Goff/Shutterstock.com

- Warren Buffet, founder of Berkshire Hathaway and one of the richest people in the world, began delivering papers on his bicycle at the age of 13. By the time he finished high school in 1947, Buffett had earned $5,000, which is the equivalent of $54,000 today.

- *Richard Branson, Virgin Group CEO:* Branson attributes at least some of his motivation to his mom: when he was six, she would shove him out of the car and tell him to find his own way home.

- *Chris Rock, comedian:* Chris' first job was at Red Lobster. "The thing about Red Lobster is that if you work there, you can't afford to eat there," he once told Jay Leno. "You're making minimum wage. A shrimp costs minimum wage."

But keep in mind that some high achievers don't gear up until well after childhood. True motivation requires clear goals, which people can develop at any point in their lives. When meaningful goals merge with energy and determination, anything becomes possible.[1]

- **First-line (supervisory) management** manages the people who do the work. First-line managers must train, motivate, and evaluate nonmanagement employees, so they are heavily involved in day-to-day production issues. Typical titles include supervisor, foreman, and section leader.

Smaller companies usually don't have a hierarchy of management. Often the owner must act as the top-, middle-, and first-line manager, all rolled into one. This clearly requires enormous flexibility and well-developed management skills.

14-1b Management Skills: Having What It Takes to Get the Job Done

technical skills Expertise in a specific functional area or department.

human skills The ability to work effectively with and through other people in a range of different relationships.

conceptual skills The ability to grasp a big-picture view of the overall organization, the relationships among its various parts, and its fit in the broader competitive environment.

Given the turbulence of today's business world, managers must draw on a staggering range of skills to do their jobs efficiently and effectively. Most of these abilities cluster into three broad categories: technical skills, human skills, and conceptual skills.

- **Technical Skills:** **Technical skills** refer to expertise in a specific functional area or department. Keep in mind that technical skills don't necessarily relate to technology. People can have technical skills—or specific expertise—in virtually any field, from sales, to copywriting, to accounting, to airplane repair, to computer programming.

- **Human Skills:** **Human skills** refer to the ability to work with and through other people in a range of different relationships. Human skills include communication, leadership, coaching, empathy, and team building. A manager with strong human skills can typically mobilize support for initiatives and find win–win solutions for conflicts.

- **Conceptual Skills:** **Conceptual skills** refer to the ability to grasp a big-picture view of the overall organization and the relationship between its various parts. Conceptual skills also help managers understand how their company fits into the broader competitive environment. Managers with strong conceptual skills typically excel at strategic planning.

All three categories of skill are essential for management success. But their importance varies according to the level of the manager. Front-line managers must have a high degree of technical skills, which help them hire, train, and evaluate employees; avoid mistakes; and ensure high-quality production. Middle-level managers need an especially high level of human skills. They typically act as the bridge between departments, co-ordinating people and projects that sometimes have mismatched priorities. Top-level managers must demonstrate excellent conceptual skills in order to formulate a vision, interpret marketplace trends, and plan for the future. To move up in an organization, managers must constantly learn and grow, nurturing skills that reflect their new tasks.

Across all three skill sets, critical thinking and decision-making abilities have become increasingly important. Critical thinking helps managers find value even in an overload of information. Part of how information overload plays out is in email management; according to *Fortune* magazine, the average knowledge worker now spends an astounding 28% of her work time managing email. Simply deleting unwanted emails could take more than 16 hours per year! Strong decision-making skills help managers respond wisely and rapidly to all this information, with an unwavering focus on customer satisfaction.

Managers who expect to grow in the company hierarchy must expect to foster new skills. Too often, workers get promotions because of great technical skills—e.g., the top salesperson lands the sales manager slot—but they struggle to move further because they don't fully develop their human and conceptual skills.

14-2 MOTIVATION: LIGHTING THE FIRE

Standout managers motivate others to reach for their best selves—to accomplish more than they ever thought possible. Motivated workers tend to feel great about their jobs, and workers who feel great tend to produce more. But the thinking about *how* to motivate workers has changed dramatically over time. In the early 1900s, key management thinkers focused on efficiency and productivity, dictating precisely how workers should do each element of their jobs. But more recent research suggests that people's thoughts and feelings play a vital role in motivation, which leads to a range of new theories.

 What Were They Thinking?

Bad Decisions, Big Impacts

Every day, managers around the globe make high-stakes decisions, from expanding overseas, to introducing new products, to closing factories. The great decisions have become the stuff of legends, shaping the business world as we know it today. Bad choices also abound. Consider these five business decisions that made history for their silliness:

- Faced with the opportunity to buy rights to the telephone in 1876, Western Union, the telegraph behemoth, rejected the newfangled device: "This 'telephone' has too many short-comings to be seriously considered as a means of communication. The device is inherently of no value to us."

- In 1899, two young attorneys approached Asa Candler—owner of the briskly selling new fountain drink Coca-Cola—with an innovative proposal to bottle the beverage. Chandler sold them exclusive rights to bottle Coke across most of the United States for the grand sum of $1. Oops.

- In 1977, the executives at 20th Century Fox exhibited overconfidence in their deal-making abilities, and far too little confidence in director George Lucas's filmmaking and

business savvy. In exchange for a paltry $20,000 pay cut, they signed over to Lucas all product merchandising rights for the current and all future *Star Wars* films. The combined revenue from merchandising is estimated to have exceeded $3 billion, and continues to grow annually, making it the most lucrative deal ever struck between an individual and a corporate studio in entertainment history. Seemed like a good idea at the time . . . .

- In 1999, fledgling search engine, Excite, rejected an offer to buy Google because it considered the $1 million asking price to be too high. Google is now worth nearly $300 billion, and Excite is defunct.

- Mike Smith, one of the executives in charge of evaluating new talent for the London office of Decca Records, rejected the Beatles in 1962 with the now infamous line: "Groups are out; four-piece groups with guitars particularly are finished." Not so much. . . .

With the help of hindsight, momentous decisions may seem almost inevitable. But these bloopers clearly show that in the fog of the moment, the right choice can be anything but clear.[2]

EXHIBIT 14.1 MASLOW'S HIERARCHY OF NEEDS AND THE WORKPLACE

Maslow's Need	Description	Workplace Examples
Self-Actualization	Need for fulfillment—the need to realize one's fullest potential	Challenging, creative jobs; meaningful work that ties to a greater good; volunteer opportunities
Safety	Need to feel secure—free of harm and free of fear	Safety equipment, healthcare plans, life insurance, retirement plans, job security, gym membership
Social (Belonging)	Need to feel connected to others—accepted by family and friends	Teamwork, positive corporate culture, company lunchroom, uniforms, department outings
Esteem	Need for self-respect and respect from others—recognition and status	Acknowledgment, feedback, promotions, perks, raises
Physiological	Need for basic survival—food, water, clothing, and shelter	A job with enough pay to buy the basics

© Cengage Learning®

14-2a Theories of Motivation

Maslow's Hierarchy of Needs Theory Noted psychologist Abraham Maslow theorized that people are motivated to satisfy only unmet needs. He proposed a hierarchy of human needs—from basic to abstract—suggesting that as each need is met, people become motivated to meet the next-highest need in the pyramid. Maslow's five specific needs are shown in Exhibit 14.1. While his theory was not based on the workplace, Maslow's ideas can illuminate the needs behind motivation at work.

From a workplace perspective, the idea that people are motivated only by unmet needs clearly holds true for the first two levels of the hierarchy. Finding a job that pays the bills, for instance, is the primary motivator for most people who don't have any job at all. People who have a job but no healthcare would find health insurance much more motivating than, say, a company picnic geared toward meeting social needs.

But after physiological and safety needs are met, the other needs are motivating to different degrees in different people. An employee with strong social connections outside work might be more motivated by a promotion that meets esteem needs than by a company outing that meets social needs. A number of firms actually use self-actualization needs as a starting point for motivating employees, by creating a mission statement that communicates the importance of the work. The House of Blues inspires employees through its lofty purpose: to promote racial and spiritual harmony through love, peace, truth, righteousness, and nonviolence.

14-2b Theory X and Theory Y

Psychologist Douglas McGregor, one of Maslow's students, studied workplace motivation from a different angle. He proposed that management attitudes toward workers would directly affect worker motivation. His research suggested that management attitudes fall into two opposing categories, which he called **Theory X and Theory Y**, described in Exhibit 14.2.

McGregor proposed that managers should employ Theory Y assumptions in order to capitalize on the imagination and intelligence of every worker. In American business today, some organizations use a Theory X approach, but a growing number have begun to at least experiment with Theory Y, tapping into a rich pool of employee input.

JOB ENRICHMENT A number of researchers have focused on creating jobs with more meaningful content, under the assumption that challenging, creative work will motivate employees to give their best effort. **Job enrichment** typically includes the following factors:

1. **Skill Variety:** Workers can use a range of different skills.

2. **Task Identity:** Workers complete tasks with clear beginnings and endings.

Maslow's hierarchy of needs theory A motivation theory that suggests that human needs fall into a hierarchy and that as each need is met, people become motivated to meet the next-highest need in the pyramid.

Theory X and Theory Y A motivation theory that suggests that management attitudes toward workers fall into two opposing categories based on management assumptions about worker capabilities and values.

job enrichment The creation of jobs with more meaningful content, under the assumption that challenging, creative work will motivate employees.

EXHIBIT 14.2 THEORY X AND THEORY Y

Theory X Assumptions about Workers	Theory Y Assumptions about Workers
■ Workers dislike work and will do everything they can to avoid it.	■ Work is as natural as play or rest—workers do not inherently dislike it.
■ Fear is motivating—coercion and threats are vital to get people to work toward company goals.	■ Different rewards can be motivating—people can exercise self-direction and self-control to meet company goals.
■ People prefer to be directed, avoiding responsibility and seeking security.	■ People can accept and even seek responsibility.
	■ The capacity for imagination, creativity, and ingenuity is widely distributed in the population.
	■ The intellectual capacity of the average worker is underutilized in the workplace.

© Cengage Learning®

3. **Task Significance:** Workers understand the impact of the task on others.

4. **Autonomy:** Workers have freedom and authority regarding their jobs.

5. **Feedback:** Workers receive clear, frequent information about their performance.

Richard Branson, maverick founder of the Virgin Group, relies on job enrichment, especially autonomy and feedback, to keep people motivated at his 350-company empire (which includes a startling range of firms, such as Virgin Atlantic Airlines, Virgin Music, Virgin mobile phones, and Virgin Galactic space travel). Branson gives his managers a stake in their companies and then tells them "to run it as if it's their own." He says, "I have to be good at helping people run the individual businesses, and I have to be willing to step back. The company must be set up so it can continue without me." According to Virgin's website, "we pretty much practice a collaborative and supportive style of custodianship." Due in large part to Branson's motivational approach, the Virgin workforce is fully engaged with the company, contributing to its remarkable long-term success.[3]

EXPECTANCY THEORY Usually attributed to researcher Victor Vroom, **expectancy theory** deals with the relationship among individual effort, individual performance, and individual reward. The key concept is that a worker will be motivated if he or she believes that effort will lead to performance, and performance will lead to a meaningful reward.

Effort →Performance →Reward

> "OUTSTANDING LEADERS GO OUT OF THEIR WAY TO BOOST THE SELF-ESTEEM OF THEIR PERSONNEL. IF PEOPLE BELIEVE IN THEMSELVES, IT'S AMAZING WHAT THEY CAN ACCOMPLISH."
>
> —SAM WALTON, FOUNDER, WAL-MART

The theory suggests that if any link in the chain is broken, the employee will not be motivated.

Imagine if your professor announced on the first day of class that he or she had never given any student an A, as a matter of principle. Would you be motivated to perform in class? Not likely—the link between performance and reward would be broken. Retailer Hot Topic has done a particularly strong job implementing the link between effort and performance. A Hot Topic employee describes the connection, saying, "I've worked for HT for five years, and the best thing I've learned is that if you work hard enough and dedicate enough of yourself to something, you can achieve your goals!" Hot Topic has also established strong links between performance and rewards. Perhaps it's no coincidence that Hot Topic was one of the few retail chains that continued to perform well, even as the recession tightened its grip in late 2008 and early 2009.[4]

EQUITY THEORY Pioneered by J. Stacy Adams, **equity theory** proposes that perceptions of fairness directly affect worker motivation. The key idea is that people won't be motivated if they believe that the relationship between what they contribute and what they earn is different from the relationship between what others contribute

expectancy theory A motivation theory that concerns the relationship among individual effort, individual performance, and individual reward.

equity theory A motivation theory that proposes that perceptions of fairness directly affect worker motivation.

and what others earn. For example, if you worked ten-hour days, and earned less than the guy in the next cube who works seven-hour days, you'd probably think it was pretty unfair. To restore a sense of balance, you might:

- Demand a raise
- Start coming in late, leaving early, and taking extra-long lunch hours
- Convince yourself that the other guy is about to be fired (or try to get him fired)
- Look for another job

The response to perceived inequity almost always involves trying to change the system, changing your own work habits, distorting your perceptions, or leaving the company.

But keep in mind that equity theory is based on perceptions, which are not always on the mark. People are all too prone to overestimate their own contributions, which throws perceived equity out of balance. The best way to combat equity issues is through clear, open communication from management.[5]

14-2c Motivation Today

Companies today use a range of approaches to motivation, although several key themes have emerged. Most firms no longer seek to make their employees happy; instead, they want their workers to be productive and engaged. Yet, for employees, work is about more than just productivity. University of Michigan business school professor David Ulrich points out that even in today's hyper-competitive environment, "people still want to find meaning in their work and in the institutions that employ them."[6]

A growing emphasis on corporate culture has captured the best of both worlds for companies that do it right. A look at *Fortune* magazine's 100 Best Companies to Work for in 2015 demonstrates that a distinctive, positive culture tends to create productive employees who are deeply attached to their work and their companies. The winners tend to emphasize the health and well-being of their employees and to offer strong commitments to make the world a better place. Google, which consistently earns the number-one slot, offers employees a famous set of perks at their Silicon Valley headquarters, including on-site haircutting, massage services, game facilities, and 25 cafés companywide, all free. As one happy Googler writes, "Employees are never more than 150 feet away from a well-stocked pantry." Despite—or perhaps in part

Many "Googlers" especially appreciate the top-quality free food that's always available for employees.

ERIN SIEGAL/Reuters/Landov

because of the pricey perks—everything at Google is up: revenue, profits, share price, paid search clicks, and hiring. Googlers nearly uniformly praise the competence of their leadership, the support they receive as professionals, and the pride they take in the challenging work they accomplish together. "Simply by being here, I feel very naturally motivated to be (and also very proud to be) my best possible self," explains one employee. The work-hard, play-hard culture at biotech giant Genentech is especially inspiring for employees who believe in helping others. Several have commented that they personally know people who are alive today due to Genentech drugs that they helped bring to market. CEO Paul Purcell of number five firm, Baird Investment advisor, sets the culture with his one rule: there are "no a**holes here." And he stands by it—over the years roughly two dozen people have been terminated for breaking that rule.

Many firms on the 2015 list give their employees generous sabbaticals. Adobe, for instance, gives four weeks paid time off after five years of service, five weeks for after ten years and six weeks after fifteen years. Genentech gives a six-week paid sabbatical after six years of service. Upscale home builder David Weekly Homes offers employees a four-week paid sabbatical after ten years of service, and throws in a grant of $2,000 for such things as travel and education expenses.[7]

A growing number of businesses have expanded their benefits to include a range of nontraditional programs that employees love. At W. L. Gore, leadership opportunities are based on how much of a "followership" a person has among co-workers. Gore also uses peer assessments to determine compensation. Design consulting firm Kimley

Horn encourages employees to nominate each other for an immediate $50 award each time they spot someone going "above and beyond." The firm approved 4,468 of these peer awards, which totaled $245,000 in bonuses, comprising more than two awards for every employee.[8]

Detroit-based Quicken Loans nurtures such an open culture that CEO Bill Emerson has given his personal cell phone number to each of the firm's 8,500 employees, and has not received any prank calls, only a handful of "pocket calls." When Facebook went public, Mark Zuckerberg described the firm's "hack culture" as one of its assets, more specifically, an approach to building that involves continuous improvement and iteration. He added that "hackers believe that something can always be better, and that nothing is ever complete. They just have to go fix it—often in the face of people who say it's impossible or are content with the status quo." With the "Hacker Way," the best idea and implementation should always win—not the person who is best at lobbying for an idea or the person who manages the most people.[9]

Effective planning can be complex and time-consuming.

 ## 14-3 PLANNING: FIGURING OUT WHERE TO GO AND HOW TO GET THERE

The planning function—figuring out where to go and how to get there—is the core of effective management. A survey in *The Wall Street Journal* found that 80% of executives identify planning as their most valuable management tool. But even though planning is critical, it's also highly risky in light of cutthroat competition, rapid change, and economic uncertainty. The best plans keep the organization on track without sacrificing flexibility and responsiveness; they incorporate ways to respond to change both inside and outside the organization.[10]

Although all managers engage in planning, the scope of the process changes according to the manager's position, as shown in Exhibit 14.3. Top-level managers focus on **strategic planning**. They establish a vision for the company, define long-term objectives and priorities, determine broad action steps, and allocate resources.

> **strategic planning** High-level, long-term planning that establishes a vision for the company, defines long-term objectives and priorities, determines broad action steps, and allocates resources.

EXHIBIT 14.3	MANAGERIAL PLANNING		
Type of Planning	**Management Level**	**Scope of Planning**	**Examples of Planning Questions and Concerns**
Strategic Planning	Senior management	Typically five-year time frame	Should we acquire a new company? Should we begin manufacturing in China? Should we expand to overseas markets? Should we take our company public?
Tactical Planning	Middle management	Typically one-year time frame	Should we spend more time servicing each customer? Should we hire a public relations agency to handle PR? Should we spend fewer ad dollars on TV and more on the Web?
Operational Planning	First-line management	Daily, weekly, and monthly time frame	How should we schedule employees this week? When should we schedule delivery for each batch of product? How should customer service people answer the phones?

© Cengage Learning®

Middle managers focus on **tactical planning**, or applying the strategic plan to their specific areas of responsibility. And first-line managers focus on **operational planning**, or applying the tactical plans to daily, weekly, and monthly operations. Successful firms often encourage a flow of feedback up and down the organization to ensure that all key plans are sound and that all key players "buy in." Some typical planning decisions and time frames are shown in Exhibit 14.3.

A fourth category of planning has gained new prominence in the past decade: **contingency planning**, or planning for unexpected events. Senior management usually spearheads contingency planning but with input from the other levels of management. Contingency plans consider what might go wrong—both inside the business and with the outside environment—and develop responses. Potential issues include:

- How should we respond if our competitors knock off our best-selling product?

- What should we do if the government regulates our industry?

- How should we respond if our data management/computer system fails?

- How can we restart our business if a natural disaster destroys our plant or supply channels?

- How will we evacuate employees if terrorists strike our headquarters?

Clearly, anticipating every potential problem is impossible (and impractical). Instead, effective contingency plans tend to focus only on the issues that are most probable, most potentially harmful, or both (see Exhibit 14.4). For example, a Southern California amusement park (e.g., Disneyland) might concentrate its contingency plans on earthquake response, while an online retailing firm might focus its plans on responding to a computer hacker attack.

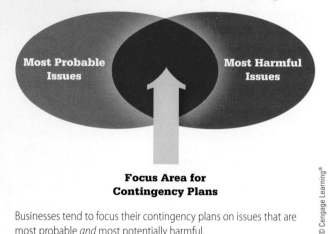

Exhibit 14.4
Contingency Planning Paradigm

Most Probable Issues

Most Harmful Issues

Focus Area for Contingency Plans

© Cengage Learning®

Businesses tend to focus their contingency plans on issues that are most probable *and* most potentially harmful.

14-3a Strategic Planning: Setting the Agenda

Strategic planning is the most fundamental part of the planning process, since all other plans—and most major management decisions—stem from the strategic plan. The strategic planning process typically includes these steps:

1. Define the mission of the organization.

2. Evaluate the organization's competitive position.

3. Set goals for the organization.

4. Create strategies for competitive differentiation.

5. Implement strategies.

6. Evaluate results, and incorporate lessons learned.

DEFINING YOUR MISSION The mission of an organization articulates its essential reason for being. The **mission** defines the organization's purpose, values, and core goals, providing the framework for all other plans (see Exhibit 14.5). Most large companies present their mission as a simple, vivid, compelling statement that everyone involved with the company—from the janitor to the CEO, from customers to investors—can easily understand. Mission statements tend to vary in their length, their language, and even their names, but they share a common goal: to provide a clear, long-term focus for the organization.

EVALUATING YOUR COMPETITIVE POSITION Strategy means nothing in a vacuum—every firm must plan in the context of the marketplace. Many companies use a **SWOT analysis** (strengths, weaknesses, opportunities, and

tactical planning More specific, shorter-term planning that applies strategic plans to specific functional areas.

operational planning Very specific, short-term planning that applies tactical plans to daily, weekly, and monthly operations.

contingency planning Planning for unexpected events, usually involving a range of scenarios and assumptions that differ from the assumptions behind the core plans.

mission The definition of an organization's purpose, values, and core goals, which provides the framework for all other plans.

SWOT analysis A strategic planning tool that helps management evaluate an organization in terms of internal strengths and weakness, and external opportunities and threats.

EXHIBIT 14.5 EXAMPLES OF MISSION STATEMENTS

Company	Mission Statement
Levi Strauss & Co.	We will market the most appealing and widely worn casual clothing in the world. We will clothe the world.
IKEA	To create a better everyday life for the many people. Our business idea supports this vision by offering a wide range of well-designed, functional home furnishing products at prices so low that as many people as possible will be able to afford them.
Google	To organize the world's information and make it universally accessible and useful.
Harley-Davidson, Inc.	We fulfill dreams through the experience of motorcycling.

© Cengage Learning®

threats) to evaluate where they stand relative to the competition. Strengths and weaknesses are internal to the organization, and they include factors that would either build up or drag down the firm's performance. Opportunities and threats are external, and they include factors that would affect the company's performance but are typically out of the company's control. Exhibit 14.6 offers some examples.

Initial information about internal strengths and weaknesses usually comes from careful analysis of internal reports on topics such as budget and profitability. But to

EXHIBIT 14.6 SWOT ANALYSIS

Potential Internal Strengths	Potential External Opportunities
Premium brand name	Higher consumer demand
Proven management team	Complacent competitors
Lower costs/higher margins	Growth in foreign markets
Diverse workforce	New social trends

Potential Internal Weaknesses	Potential External Threats
Low employee satisfaction	A powerful new competitor
Inadequate financial resources	A deep recession
Poor location	New government regulations
Bad safety record	Significant new taxes

© Cengage Learning®

better understand strengths and weaknesses, executives should actively seek firsthand information—on a personal basis—from key people throughout the company, from front-line workers to the board of directors.

Gathering information about external opportunities and threats can be more complex, since these areas include both current and potential issues (which can be tough to predict). Information about external factors can come from many different sources, including the news, government reports, customers, and competitors.

SETTING YOUR GOALS Strategic goals represent concrete benchmarks that managers can use to measure performance in each key area of the organization. They must fit the firm's mission and tie directly to its competitive position. The three most effective goals are:

1. **Specific and Measurable:** Whenever possible, managers should define goals in clear numerical terms that everyone understands.

2. **Tied to a Time Frame:** To create meaning and urgency, goals should be linked to a specific deadline.

3. **Realistic but Challenging:** Goals that make people stretch can motivate exceptional performance.

Exhibit 14.7 offers examples of how weak goals can transform into powerful goals.

CREATING YOUR STRATEGIES Strategies are action plans that help the organization achieve its goals by forging the best fit between the firm and the environment. The underlying aim, of course, is to create a significant advantage versus the competition. Sources of competitive advantage vary, ranging from better product quality, to better technology, to more motivated employees. The most successful companies build their advantage across several fronts. Southwest Airlines, for example, has a more motivated workforce and a lower cost structure. H&M has lower prices and more fashionable clothing choices. And Procter & Gamble has more innovative new products and strong core brands.

The specifics of strategy differ by industry and by company, but all strategies represent a roadmap. The SWOT analysis determines the starting point, and the objectives signify the immediate destination. Since speed matters, you must begin

strategic goals Concrete benchmarks that managers can use to measure performance in each key area of the organization.

strategies Action plans that help the organization achieve its goals by forging the best fit between the firm and the environment.

Slackers? Not so much...

Generation Y—which includes the 76 million kids born between 1978 and 1998—is changing the face of the workforce. These self-confident, outspoken young people have posed a new set of challenges for managers across the economy. A quick profile of Generation Y—also known as "millennials," "echo-boomers," and "Gen F" (for Facebook)—highlights their key characteristics. Keep in mind that no general overview can clearly describe each member of Generation Y. Yet, chances are strong that you recognize at least parts of yourself in this profile. Companies that understand you and your peers—and figure out how to harness your talents—will find themselves with a sharp competitive edge in the years to come.

Unfortunately, not all employers "get" Gen Y. According to a 2009 Pew Research Center study, three out of four Americans believe that today's youth are less virtuous and industrious than their elders. But the facts suggest otherwise. Volunteerism among young people has exploded. Between 1989 and 2006, the share of teenagers doing volunteer work doubled. Furthermore, millennials are more willing to accept that their work will bleed into evenings and weekends. Some experts also believe that millennials are better at switching quickly from one activity to another, a real plus in today's fast-paced work environment.[11] More Gen Y characteristics:

- **Goal Driven:** Gen Yers expect to perform for their rewards. But they tend to find smaller, short-term goals much more motivating than long-term goals. The reason: a week in their fast-paced world is more like a year was for their parents.

- **Facebook-Focused:** On average, Gen Yers have 696 Facebook friends, and 16 of them are work friends.

- **Change Oriented:** Gen Yers actively embrace change and excitement. Many anticipate—even hope—to change jobs frequently. They don't share the expectation of long-term employment that disillusioned so many of their parents.

- **Tech Savvy:** Gen Yers are masters of the Internet and the iPhone. They often expect top technology in the workplace, and they use virtually all of it (often at the same time!) to boost their performance.

- **Diverse:** Gen Y is among the most diverse demographic groups in America—one in three is a minority—and most don't believe that their ethnicity defines their character. Many were born in other countries and speak multiple languages fluently.

- **Neither Highly Ambitious nor Optimistic:** Although today's Gen Y young women are the first in modern history to start their work lives at near pay parity with men, many believe that they are paid less than men for doing the same job, and they see roadblocks to their success when they look ahead. Millennial men *and* women want a job they enjoy that provides security and flexibility, and they place relatively little importance on high pay. At the same time, however, young working women are less likely than men to aspire to top management jobs: 34% say they are *not* interested in becoming a boss or top manager, and 24% of young men say the same.

- **Fulfillment Focused:** Gen Yers tend to value their families and their personal lives deeply. They fully expect to achieve their lofty career goals without sacrificing time for themselves and the people they care about.[12]

Wavebreakmedia/Shutterstock.com

EXHIBIT 14.7	GOAL SETTING: GETTING IT RIGHT
Weak Goal	**Powerful Goal**
Become More innovative.	Introduce one new product each quarter for the next three years.
Reduce Delinquent Accounts.	Reduce delinquent accounts to no more than 1% of the total by the next quarter.
Increase Market Share.	Become the #1 or #2 brand in each market where we compete by the end of 2015.

© Cengage Learning®

mapping the next leg of the journey even before you arrive. For added complexity, you never know—given the turbulent environment—when you might hit roadblocks. This means that strategies must be dynamic and flexible. Top managers have responded to this challenge by encouraging front-line managers to participate in the process more than ever before.

IMPLEMENTING YOUR STRATEGIES Implementation should happen largely through tactical planning. Middle managers in each key area of the company must develop plans to carry out core strategies in their area. If the strategic plan, for example, calls for more new products, marketing would need to generate ideas, finance would need to find funding, and sales would need to prepare key accounts. And all of these steps would require tactical planning.

EVALUATING YOUR RESULTS AND INCORPORATING LESSONS LEARNED Evaluation of results should be a continual process, handled by managers at every level as part of their controlling function, covered further in this chapter. But for evaluation to be meaningful, the lessons learned must be analyzed objectively and factored back into the next planning cycle.

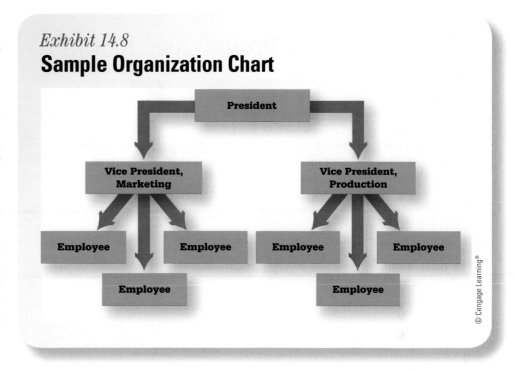

Exhibit 14.8
Sample Organization Chart

© Cengage Learning®

14-4 ORGANIZING: FITTING TOGETHER THE PUZZLE PIECES

The organizing function of management means creating a logical structure for people, their jobs, and their patterns of interaction. And clearly, the pieces can fit together in a number of different ways. In choosing the right structure for a specific company, management typically considers many factors, including the goals and strategies of the firm, its products, its use of technology, its size, and the structure of its competitors. Given the potential for rapid change in each of these factors, smart companies continually reexamine their structure and make changes whenever necessary. Microsoft, for instance, restructures its organization every couple of years as new challenges emerge.

But to be effective, reorganizations—and their purpose—must be clear to employees throughout the company. Xerox CEO Anne Mulcahy learned the hard way. Her comments: "During the 1990s, we had lots of consultants on organizational effectiveness. We sliced and diced the business into industries, product lines, and geographies … you name it. It looked good on paper, but fell apart in implementation. I found myself in a job where I couldn't look anybody in the eye and feel clear accountability for anything … I'll trade off organizational design for clarity and accountability any day of the week!"[13]

In order to help employees understand how they and their jobs fit within the broader organization, most firms issue an **organization chart**, or a visual representation of the company's formal structure, as shown in Exhibit 14.8.

Looking at the company represented by Exhibit 14.8, you would probably assume that the vice president of production has more power than a regular employee in the marketing department. And in terms of formal power, you'd be absolutely right. But if the marketing employee babysits on the weekend for the president's granddaughter, the balance of power may actually be a bit different than it seems. Make no mistake: the formal structure matters. But knowing how power flows on an informal basis could dramatically increase your effectiveness as well, by helping you target your ideas to the right managers and marshal the support of the most influential employees.

14-4a Key Organizing Considerations

In developing the organizational structure, management must make decisions about the degree of centralization, the span of management control, and the type of departmentalization that makes the most sense at any given time.

CENTRALIZATION The **degree of centralization** relates directly to the source of power and control. In

organization chart A visual representation of the company's formal structure.

degree of centralization The extent to which decision-making power is held by a small number of people at the top of the organization.

Wanna be more Productive? Relax!!

Ironically, a growing body of research suggests rather strongly that the best way to get more done may be to spend more time doing less, which may include daytime workouts, short afternoon naps, longer sleep hours at night, and longer, more frequent vacations. Despite misguided efforts to make it otherwise, time is definitely finite; energy, on the other hand, can be renewed, which is why a study by Harvard University estimated that sleep deprivation (less than six hours per night) costs American businesses $63.2 billion in lost productivity. Studies of vacation show that taking more vacation days has a dramatic positive impact on worker performance, *despite* the fact that in 2013, unused American

Warren Goldswain/Shutterstock.com

vacation days hit a 40-year high, with the average American essentially working for free for almost one week per year. CEO Tony Schwartz attempts to run his business on the principle that the energy people bring to their jobs is more important than the number of hours they work. He and his management team have policies in place that reflect the idea that, "When we're renewing, we're truly renewing, so when we're working, we can really work." In part because of this ethos, in the decade that his firm has been in business, no one has chosen to leave the company. Several firms, such as Virgin Group and Netflix, are offering employees unlimited or unmonitored vacation days to encourage time off and rejuvenation.[14]

centralized companies, a small number of people at the top of the organization have the power to make decisions. This approach is simple and efficient, and the result tends to be a strong corporate image and a uniform customer approach across the front lines. But the downside is that centralized companies typically respond more slowly to customer needs and have lower employee morale. The tradeoff may be worthwhile in steady, stable markets, but those are rare.

Faced with today's turbulent environment, most firms are moving toward greater decentralization, pushing power to the lower levels of the organization. Employees with the power to make decisions can respond to customer needs more quickly and effectively. They can also capitalize on opportunities that would likely vaporize in the time it would take to get permission to act. But for decentralization to work, every employee must fully understand the firm's mission, goals, and strategy; otherwise, the company could develop a fragmented image, which would undermine its long-term strength. Also, active communication across departments is essential so that all employees can benefit from innovations in other parts of the organization.

SPAN OF CONTROL The **span of control**, or span of management, refers to the number of people a manager supervises. There is no ideal number for every manager. The "right" span of control varies, based on the abilities of both the manager and the subordinates, the nature of the work being done, the location of the employees, and

the need for planning and coordination. Across industries, the general trend has moved toward wider spans of control as a growing number of companies have pruned layers of middle management to the bare minimum.

DEPARTMENTALIZATION Departmentalization means breaking workers into logical groups. A number of different options make sense, depending on the organization.

- **Functional:** Dividing employees into groups based on area of expertise, such as marketing, finance, and engineering, tends to be efficient and easy to coordinate. For those reasons, it works especially well for small- to medium-sized firms.

- **Product:** Dividing employees into groups based on the products that a company offers helps workers develop expertise about products that often results in especially strong customer relations.

- **Customer:** Dividing employees into groups based on the customers that a company serves helps companies focus on the needs of specific customer groups. Many companies have separate departments for meeting the needs of business and consumer users. This approach is related to product departmentalization.

- **Geographical:** Dividing employees into groups based on where customers are located can help different departments better serve specific regions within one country. Similarly, many international firms create a separate department for each different country they serve.

span of control Span of management; refers to the number of people a manager supervises.

departmentalization The division of workers into logical groups.

Exhibit 14.9
An Example of Hybrid Departmentalization

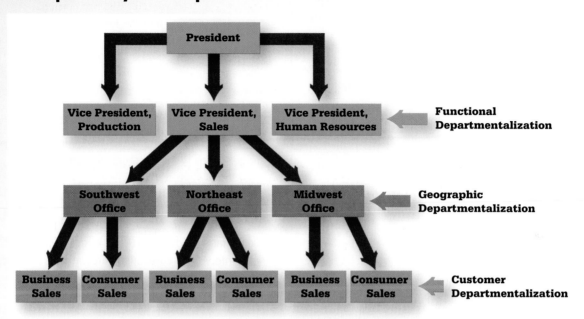

President

Vice President, Production — Vice President, Sales — Vice President, Human Resources ← **Functional Departmentalization**

Southwest Office — Northeast Office — Midwest Office ← **Geographic Departmentalization**

Business Sales — Consumer Sales — Business Sales — Consumer Sales — Business Sales — Consumer Sales ← **Customer Departmentalization**

© Cengage Learning®

■ **Process:** Dividing into groups based on what type of work employees do is common in manufacturing, where management may divide departments by processes such as cutting, dyeing, and sewing.

As companies get larger, they usually adopt several different types of departmentalization at different levels of the organization. This approach, shown in Exhibit 14.9, is called "hybrid departmentalization."

> "MANAGEMENT IS DOING THINGS RIGHT; LEADERSHIP IS DOING THE RIGHT THINGS."
>
> —PETER DRUCKER, MANAGEMENT RESEARCHER, WRITER, AND SPEAKER

immediately above, which means quick decision making and no fuzziness about who is responsible for what. The downside is a lack of specialists to provide advice or support for line managers. This approach tends to work well for small businesses, but for medium-sized and large companies, the result can be inflexibility, too much paperwork, and even incompetence, since experts aren't available to give their input on key decisions.

14-4b Organization Models

Company structures tend to follow one of three different patterns: line organizations, line-and-staff organizations, and matrix organizations. But these organizational models are not mutually exclusive. In fact, many management teams build their structure using elements of each model at different levels of the organization.

LINE ORGANIZATIONS A **line organization** typically has a clear, simple chain of command from top to bottom. Each person is directly accountable to the person

LINE-AND-STAFF ORGANIZATIONS A **line-and-staff organization** incorporates the benefits of a line organization without all the drawbacks. **Line managers** supervise the functions that contribute directly to profitability: production and

line organizations Organizations with a clear, simple chain of command from top to bottom.

line-and-staff organizations Organizations with line managers forming the primary chain of authority in the company, and staff departments working alongside line departments.

line managers Managers who supervise the functions that contribute directly to profitability: production and marketing.

marketin g. **Staff managers**, on the other hand, supervise the functions that provide advice and assistance to the line departments. Examples include legal, accounting, and human resources. In a line-and-staff organization, the line managers form the primary chain of authority in the company. Staff departments work alongside line departments, but there is no direct reporting relationship (except at the top of the company). Since staff people don't report to line people, their authority comes from their know-how. This approach, which overlays fast decision making with additional expertise, tends to work well for medium-sized and large companies. But in some firms, the staff departments gain so much power that they become dictatorial, imposing unreasonable limitations on the rest of the company.

MATRIX ORGANIZATIONS **Matrix organizations** build on the line-and-staff approach by adding a lot more flexibility. A matrix structure brings together specialists from different areas of the company to work on individual projects on a temporary basis. A new-product-development team, for instance, might include representatives from sales, engineering, finance, purchasing, and advertising. For the course of the project, each specialist reports to the project manager and to the head of his or her own department (e.g., the vice president of marketing). The matrix approach has been particularly popular in the high-tech and aerospace industries.

The matrix structure offers several key advantages. It encourages teamwork and communication across the organization. It offers flexibility in deploying key people. It lends itself to innovative solutions. And not surprisingly—when managed well—the matrix structure creates a higher level of motivation and satisfaction for employees. But these advantages have a clear flip side. The need for constant communication can bog down a company in too many meetings. The steady state of flux can be overwhelming for both managers and employees. And having two bosses can cause conflict and stress for everyone.

staff managers Managers who supervise the functions that provide advice and assistance to the line departments.

matrix organizations Organizations with a flexible structure that brings together specialists from different areas of the company to work on individual projects on a temporary basis.

autocratic leaders Leaders who hoard decision-making power for themselves and typically issue orders without consulting their followers.

democratic leaders Leaders who share power with their followers. While they still make final decisions, they typically solicit and incorporate input from their followers.

free-rein leaders Leaders who set objectives for their followers but give them freedom to choose how they will accomplish those goals.

14-5 LEADERSHIP: DIRECTING AND INSPIRING

While most people easily recognize a great leader, defining the qualities of leaders can be more complex since successful leaders have a staggering range of personalities, characteristics, and backgrounds. Most researchers agree that true leaders are trustworthy, visionary, and inspiring. After all, we don't follow people who don't know where they're going, and we definitely don't follow people we don't trust. Other key leadership traits include empathy, courage, creativity, intelligence, and fairness.

14-5a Leadership Style

How a leader uses power defines his or her leadership style. While the range of specific styles is huge, most seem to cluster into three broad categories: autocratic, democratic, and free-rein. The categories fall along a continuum of power, with the manager at one end and the employees at the other, as shown in Exhibit 14.10.

Autocratic leaders hoard decision-making power for themselves, and they typically issue orders without consulting their followers. **Democratic leaders** share power with their followers. Even though they still make final decisions, they typically solicit and incorporate input from their followers. **Free-rein leaders** set objectives for their followers but give them freedom to choose how they accomplish those goals.

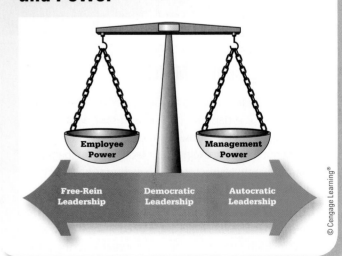

Exhibit 14.10
The Continuum of Leadership and Power

© Cengage Learning®

The most effective leaders are typically comfortable using a range of different leadership styles.

Raleigh News & Observer/Contributor/Tribune News Service/Getty Images

Interestingly, the most effective leaders don't use just one approach. They tend to shift their leadership style, depending on the followers and the situation. When a quick decision is paramount, autocratic leadership may make the most sense. An army officer, for example, probably shouldn't take a vote on whether to storm a hill in the middle of a firefight. But when creativity is the top priority—during new-product brainstorming, for instance—free-rein management would probably work best. Likewise, a brand-new worker might benefit from autocratic (but friendly) management, while a talented, experienced employee would probably work best under free-rein leadership.

Another vital consideration is the customer. When the customer seeks consistency in the delivery of the product—in fast food, for instance—the autocratic leadership style may be appropriate. But when the customer needs flexibility and problem-solving assistance—a consulting client, for example—the free-rein leadership style may be most effective. The democratic leadership style typically provides customers with a balance of consistency and flexibility, which works across a wide range of industries.

Power to the People!

How can a company boost sales by +600% and profitability by +500% over ten years through a severe economic downturn? Brazilian industrial manufacturing conglomerate Semco did it with a series of radical moves, masterminded by maverick CEO Ricardo Semler, who inherited the firm from his father when he was only 21 years old. Some of his more radical moves:

- Within a month, he fired more than half of the senior executives.

- Semco has no job titles, no organizational charts, and no headquarters.

- Many employees (including factory workers) set their own schedules and their own salaries, and all workers must reapply for their own jobs every six months, which provides strong incentive not to overpay themselves.

- Workers choose their managers and evaluate them twice a year. The results are publicly posted.

Source: Semco Partners

Ricardo Semler has been known to say: "The best way to invest corporate profits is to give them to the employees." So it's not surprising to also find that Semco has had less than 1 percent turnover among its 3,000 employees in the last six years.[15]

14-6 CONTROLLING: MAKING SURE IT ALL WORKS

Controlling may be the least glamorous of the management functions, but don't be fooled: it's critically important. Controlling means monitoring performance of the firm—or individuals within the firm—and making improvements when necessary. As the environment changes, plans change. And as plans change, the control process must change as well, to ensure that the company achieves its goals. The control process includes three key steps:

1. Establish clear performance standards.

2. Measure actual performance against standards.

3. Take corrective action if necessary.

Establishing clear standards—or performance goals—begins with planning. At every level of planning, objectives should emerge that are consistent with the company's mission and strategic plan. The objectives must be (1) specific and measurable, (2) realistic but challenging, and (3) tied to a time frame. Individual managers may need to break these goals into smaller parts for specific employees, but the subgoals should retain the same three qualities as the original objective.

Measuring performance against standards should happen well before the end of the time frame attached to the goal. A strong information-tracking system is probably management's best tool in this phase of the control process.

If the company or individual is not on track to meet the goals, management's first response should be communication. Employees with full information are far more likely to improve their performance than employees who never learn that they're falling behind. But sometimes workers need more than information—they may need additional resources or coaching in order to meet their goals. Apple's Steve Jobs was often accused of being a tyrannical boss—especially in the employee-evaluation process—but he defended himself by saying, "My job is not to be easy on people. My job is to make them better." If they still don't succeed, perhaps the goals themselves need reexamination as part of a dynamic planning process. Given the expense in both human and financial terms, disciplining employees for poor performance should come only after exploring the reasons for not meeting goals and making changes if necessary.

The BIG Picture

In the past decade, management has become more complex and demanding than ever before. Managers in every area of the business must carry out their roles—planning, organizing, leading, and controlling—in a relentlessly fast-paced world, seething with constant change. While management isn't for everyone, it's often a fit for people with vision, courage, integrity, energy, and a passionate commitment to their companies.

Looking forward, the role of management will continue to evolve in response to the environment. Regardless of how the changes unfold, several key factors will be absolutely vital for successful managers in the twenty-first century: a constant focus on the customer, a commitment to globalization, excellent judgment, and the right mix of talented, motivated employees.

Careers in Management

Manager

Define strategic and tactical objectives for the organization or business unit. Develop plans to meet those objectives. Coach, counsel, motivate, and develop employees. Maintain and allocate resources as necessary to attain goals. Monitor achievement of objectives and make changes as necessary. Create and oversee a business unit budget. Ensure product and service quality by setting and enforcing standards.

Foster a business culture that aligns with the broader organizational culture. Communicate and collaborate as appropriate throughout the organization. Maintain current professional and technical knowledge. For more information on careers in management, check out Career Transitions.

STUDY TOOLS 14

LOCATED AT BACK OF THE TEXTBOOK

☐ Rip Out Chapter Review Card

LOCATED AT WWW.CENGAGE.COM/LOGIN

☐ Review key term flashcards and create your own using StudyBits

☐ Create and complete practice quizzes based off of your notes and StudyBits

☐ Complete Online activities such as Matching, Fill-in-the-Blank, and Drag and Drop exercises

☐ View chapter highlight box content, including CEO Profiles, What Would You Do Cases, and chapter videos

☐ Track your knowledge and understanding of key concepts in business using 4LTR Online

15 | Human Resource Management:
Building a Top-Quality Workforce

LEARNING OBJECTIVES
After studying this chapter, you will be able to:

15-1 Explain the importance of human resources to business success

15-2 Discuss key human resource issues in today's economy

15-3 Outline challenges and opportunities that the human resources function faces

15-4 Discuss human resource planning and core human resources responsibilities

15-5 Explain the key federal legislation that affects human resources

Remember to visit **PAGE 280** for additional **STUDY TOOLS**

15-1 HUMAN RESOURCE MANAGEMENT: BRINGING BUSINESS TO LIFE

As competition accelerates across the globe, leading firms in every business category have recognized that a quality workforce can vault them over the competition. Southwest Airlines was early to recognize the untapped potential of its people. Executive Chairman Herb Kelleher declared, "We value our employees first. They're the most important, and if you treat them right, then they treat the customers right, and if you treat the customers right, then they keep coming back and shareholders are happy." His attitude has more than paid off. Southwest Airlines has posted profits for 41 consecutive years, even as other airlines have spiraled into decline.

As the Great Recession constricted the economy in 2009, managing human resources remained a top priority for Southwest CEO Gary Kelly. "We've never had a layoff. We've never had a pay cut. And we're going to strive mightily, especially this year, to avoid them once again . . ." Instead, he says, "We're being more creative about encouraging employees to move about the company. We are not threatening people with their jobs." He points out, "We're known for being the greatest company to work for and at the top of the customer service rankings." He maintains, "There is a devotion to the people and a commitment to our people, once we hire them, that we have lived up to. We have proven many times that we're going to be there for our employees in the bad times." Even the union supports management, describing the naturally confrontational relationship as one of "the loyal opposition as

"IF SOMETHING GOES WRONG, IT'S MY PROBLEM; IF SOMETHING GOES *RIGHT*, IT'S THEIR SUCCESS."

—PAMELA FIELDS, CEO, STETSON

opposed to death to the infidel. It's adversarial to get to a goal, not adversarial to hurt."[1]

Companies that get the most from their people often consider their human resources their biggest investment. They view the core goal of **human resource (HR) management** in a similar light: to nurture their human investment so that it yields the highest possible return. HR can achieve that goal by recruiting world-class talent, promoting career development, and boosting organizational effectiveness. But clearly, this can happen only in partnership with key managers throughout the company, especially senior executives. (In smaller companies, of course, the owners usually handle HR management in addition to their other responsibilities.)

15-2 HUMAN RESOURCE MANAGEMENT CHALLENGES: MAJOR HURDLES

Building a top-quality workforce can be tougher than it may initially seem. Human resource managers—and their counterparts throughout the company—face huge challenges. The best strategies still aren't clear, but forward-thinking firms tend to experiment with new approaches.

15-2a Layoffs and Outsourcing

As high-tech, high-end jobs follow low-tech, low-end jobs out of the country—or even just to local contractors—human resources find themselves in turmoil. Many jobs have disappeared altogether as companies have contracted in response to the Great Recession. In 2011 and 2012, many economists were concerned about a "jobless recovery," as labor markets faltered, and unemployment rates began to rise again. How can businesses boost the morale and the motivation level of the employees who are left behind? Does less job security translate to less worker loyalty? How can human resources continue to add value as the ground shifts beneath them—and as they wonder how long their own jobs will last?[2]

15-2b Wage Gap

Comparing CEO pay to worker pay demonstrates a startling wage gap, bigger in the United States than in any other developed country. In 2013, the average American CEO earned

human resource (HR) management The management function focused on maximizing the effectiveness of the workforce by recruiting world-class talent, promoting career development, and determining workforce strategies to boost organizational effectiveness.

Humble Beginnings

Everyone starts somewhere. Not even the rich and famous always had glamour jobs. In today's challenging economy, getting any job at all can be tough for young people, but whatever work you do get, consider that it might be the first step on the road to the next big thing. Some early job examples of the rich and famous:

- **Steve Jobs (Apple founder):** assembly line worker at HP. At age 13, Jobs put in screws on an HP assembly line. The young computer geek later described the first day of work as "bliss."

- **Suze Orman (personal finance guru):** During her early years, Orman bused tables and washed dishes to make a buck.

- **Oprah Winfrey (media mogul):** Oprah began working at the corner grocery store next to her father's barber shop ... and she hated every minute of it.

- **Jon Hamm (actor):** Set dresser for films. "Essentially, I had to move furniture around sweaty, naked people. It wasn't a great job but the money was useful," he said. "I had to get by—I wanted to be an actor.

- **Michael Dell (founder, Dell Computer Corporation):** dishwasher at a Chinese restaurant. Memorable proverb learned at work: "Do work you love and you'll never work a day in your life."

- **Whoopie Goldberg (actress):** After becoming a licensed beautician, Goldberg took a job as a mortuary beautician. Her boss played a welcoming prank on her by pretending to be dead and sitting upright to wave at her—yikes![4]

Who is Danny/Shutterstock.com

331 times the average American worker and a staggering 774 times the average American minimum wage worker.[3] As a point of comparison, 30 years ago, chief executives averaged only 30 to 40 times the average American worker's paycheck. In 2009, median CEO salaries at 200 large, publicly held U.S. firms fell by 0.9%, while net income decreased by 5%. Most observers don't object to the CEO-worker pay gap when top CEO pay is tied to top performance. But as the value of formerly high-flying corporations began to evaporate in 2008 and 2009, public rage over senior management salaries and bonuses hit new highs. But the tide turned in 2011, when data revealed CEO pay during 2011 was correlated to how well companies fared in the stock market, a change from 2010. Maintaining the link between pay and performance clearly represents a strategic challenge for HR management.[5]

> FORTUNE 500 FIRMS WITH THE MOST FEMALE BOARD MEMBERS OUTPERFORM THOSE WITH THE LEAST BY 26% ON RETURN ON INVESTED CAPITAL AND 16% ON RETURN ON SALES.
>
> —*WALL STREET JOURNAL*

15-2c Older Workers

As the oversized baby boomer generation begins turning 60, their employers—which include virtually every major American company—face a potential crisis: the loss of key talent and experience through massive retirements. Beginning January 1, 2011, every single day more than 10,000 baby boomers reached the age of 65, and that will continue to happen every single day until 2030.[6] Enlightened companies have responded with programs to retain their best employees through flexible schedules, training opportunities, and creative pay schedules. But as companies aggressively trimmed their payrolls in 2008 and 2009, the priority of these kinds of programs plummeted, which may leave some firms with a critical dearth of highly experienced workers when the economy revs back up.

15-2d Younger Workers

As twenty-somethings enter the workforce, they often bring optimism, open minds, technological know-how, a team orientation, a proven ability to multitask, and a multicultural perspective. But a number of them also bring an unprecedented sense of entitlement. This can translate into startlingly high expectations for their pay, their responsibilities, and their job flexibility, but little willingness to "pay dues."

Many have no expectation that their employers will be loyal to them, and they don't feel that they owe their companies strong loyalty. Managing this group can sometimes be a challenge, but companies that do it well stand to deliver results for years to come.[7]

15-2e Women Workers

Over the past few decades, women have made enormous strides in terms of workplace equality. But several large-scale studies confirm that women continue to face daunting discrimination in terms of both pay and promotions. While unfair treatment has been an issue for many years, recent legal changes have made it easier for women to sue, costing companies millions of dollars in the past decade alone. And the flood of lawsuits shows no signs of slowing. Many women have responded to the unfriendly business environment by leaving the workforce; droves of highly qualified, professional women step out of the workforce early—usually to raise children, start their own companies, or pursue other interests. As a result, we are experiencing a harmful, ongoing brain drain. Human resource managers can help mitigate this issue by implementing specific retention plans for valued women workers and by taking proactive steps to reintegrate returning women back into the workforce.[8]

15-2f Work–Life Balance

Over the past decade, workers across all ages and both genders have actively pursued more flexibility and work–life balance in their jobs. But as the recession deepened in 2009, companies began to cut back on these initiatives, describing them as "nice to have" programs in a time when "need to have" goals—such as meeting payroll each month—are tough to attain. Middle-level managers are also apt to demonstrate bias against worker flexibility, even when top management actively supports work–life balance programs. In spite of these issues, insightful HR managers try hard to offer enough flexibility to keep their best workers without jeopardizing their company's business goals.[9]

15-2g Lawsuits

The United States has become a wildly litigious society, with employees, customers, and shareholders levying lawsuit after lawsuit against firms of all sizes. Even though many of the lawsuits are legitimate—some profoundly important—a good number are just plain silly. But even if a lawsuit is frivolous, and even if it's thrown out of court, it can still cost a company millions of dollars. Even more importantly, a frivolous lawsuit can cost a business its reputation. Avoiding employee lawsuits by knowing the law and encouraging legal practices is a growing human resources challenge.

15-3 HUMAN RESOURCES MANAGERS: CORPORATE BLACK SHEEP?

15-3a The Problem

The human resource management function is clearly critical, but human resources departments—and the people who work in them—face major challenges. Leading-edge firms expect every department to offer "big picture," strategic contributions that boost company value. But a report in *Fast Company* suggests that most HR professionals lack sufficient strategic skills. Among other data, the report quotes a respected executive at a top U.S. company: "Business acumen is the single biggest factor that HR professionals in the U.S. lack today."[10]

But even highly qualified, strategically focused HR managers face daunting perception problems. A management professor at a leading school comments that "The best and the brightest just don't go into HR." Once in the workforce, many employees see the human resources department as irrelevant—or even worse, as the enemy. This perception clearly undermines their effectiveness.

15-3b The Solution

To gain respect from both senior management and their peers, human resources executives must earn a seat at the table. The first step is to know the company. What are the strategic goals? Who is the core customer? Who is the competition? Respected HR departments typically figure out ways to quantify their impact on the company in dollars and cents. They determine how to raise the value of the firm's human capital, which in turn increases the value of the firm itself. Effective HR people also remain open to exceptions even as they enforce broad company policies.

But clearly, these solutions will work only if senior management recognizes the potential value of effective human resource management. One simple test of senior management commitment is the reporting relationship. If the HR department reports to the CFO, it may be on the

Job Description	Job Specifications
Work with the music group to help make major decisions regarding the creative and business direction of the band	A bachelor's degree in music management
Negotiate recording contracts and engagement fees	A minimum of three years' experience managing a high-profile band
Help band members understand their rights and responsibilities	Excellent communication and networking skills

© Cengage Learning®

fast track to outsourcing. But if the HR department reports to the CEO, the strategic possibilities are unlimited.

15-4   HUMAN RESOURCE PLANNING: DRAWING THE MAP

Great human resource management begins with great planning: Where should you go? And how should you get there? Your objectives should flow from the company's master plan, and your strategies must reflect company priorities.

One of the first steps in the HR planning process should be to figure out where the company stands in terms of human resources. What skills does the workforce already have? What skills does it need? A company-wide **job analysis** often goes hand in hand with evaluating the current workforce. Job analysis examines what exactly needs to be done in each position to maximize the effectiveness of the organization—independent of who might be holding each job at any specific time. Smaller companies often handle job analysis on an informal basis, but larger companies typically specify a formal **job description** and **job specifications** (or "specs").

job analysis The examination of specific tasks that are assigned to each position, independent of who might be holding the job at any specific time.

job description An explanation of the responsibilities for a specific position.

job specifications The specific qualifications necessary to hold a particular position.

internal recruitment The process of seeking employees who are currently within the firm to fill open positions.

A job description defines the jobholder's responsibilities, and job specs define the qualifications for doing the job. Consider the job of band manager. The job description might include finding engagements for the band and settling disputes among band members. The job specs might include the type of education and experience required. Taken together, the two might look something like Exhibit 15.1.

The next step is to forecast future human resource requirements. The forecasting function requires a deep understanding of the company's goals and strategies. HR managers must also assess the future supply of workers. Assessing supply can be a real challenge, since the size and quality of the workforce shift continually. But key considerations should include retirement rates, graduation rates in relevant fields, and the pros and cons of the international labor market.

A complete HR plan—which falls under the company's strategic planning umbrella—must cover each core area of human resource management (see Exhibit 15.2):

- Recruitment
- Selection
- Training
- Evaluation
- Compensation
- Benefits
- Separation

15-4a   Recruitment: Finding the Right People

Finding people to hire is easy—especially when the unemployment rate is high—but finding *qualified* employees is almost always a daunting challenge. The U.S. Census Bureau points out that a college degree typically doubles earning power, and the U.S. Bureau of Labor Statistics attests that most of the fastest-growing fields in the next five years will require college graduates. But only one-third of adults in America ages 25–29 have a college degree. And as highly trained, highly educated baby boomers hit retirement, HR recruiters may face a hiring crunch. In addition to finding qualified hires, recruiters also must find new employees who fit with the company culture in terms of both personality and style.[11]

New employees come from two basic sources: internal and external. **Internal recruitment** involves

Exhibit 15.2
Human Resource Management

STRATEGIC PLANNING

Separation · Recruitment · Selection · Training · Evaluation · Compensation/Benefits

HUMAN RESOURCE MANAGEMENT

© Cengage Learning®

- Reduces risk for the firm, since current employees have a proven track record

- Lowers costs of both recruitment and training

But companies often find that they don't have the right person within their organization. The firm may be too small, or perhaps no one has the right set of skills to fill the immediate needs. Or maybe the firm needs the fresh thinking and energy that can come only from outside. When this is the case, companies turn to **external recruitment**.

External recruitment, or looking for employees outside the firm, usually means tapping into a range of different resources. The possibilities include employment websites, newspaper ads, trade associations, college and university employment centers, and employment agencies. But the most promising source of new hires may be referrals from current employees. A growing number of organizations offer their current employees a cash bonus—typically $1,000 to $2,000—for each person they refer to the company who makes it past a probationary period. As an added benefit, employees who come through referrals have an excellent chance at success, since the person who recommended them has a stake in their progress. Employee-referral programs also represent a real bargain for employers, compared to the average cost per new hire of more than $4,000. Not surprisingly, a higher level of employee referrals correlates to a higher level of shareholder returns, although lack of diversity may become a long-term problem with relying on employee referrals.[12]

transferring or promoting employees from other positions within the company. This approach offers several advantages:

- Boosts employee morale by reinforcing the value of experience within the firm

Pan_kung/Shutterstock.com

Selecting the best candidate for each job is much tougher than it may initially seem.

15-4b Selection: Making the Right Choice

Once you have a pool of qualified candidates, your next step is to choose the best person for the job. This, too, is more easily said than done, yet making the right selection is crucial. The costs of a bad hire—both the direct costs such as placing ads, and the intangibles such as lost productivity and morale—can drain company resources. A typical selection process includes accepting applications, interviewing, testing, checking references and background, and making the job offer. Keep in mind that small businesses often follow a more streamlined process.

APPLICATIONS Many companies use written applications simply as an initial screening mechanism. Questions about education and experience will determine whether a candidate gets any further consideration. In other words, the application is primarily a tool to reject unqualified candidates, rather than to actually choose qualified candidates.

> **external recruitment** The process of seeking new employees from outside the firm.

INTERVIEWS Virtually every company uses interviews as a central part of the selection process. In larger companies, the HR department does initial interviews and then sends qualified candidates to the hiring manager for the actual selection. The hiring manager usually recruits coworkers to participate in the process.

Although employers frequently give interviews heavy weight in hiring decisions, interviews often say surprisingly little about whether a candidate will perform on the job. Too many managers use the interview as a get-to-know-you session rather than focusing on the needs of the position. To help ensure that interviews better predict performance, experts recommend a **structured interview** process: developing a list of questions beforehand and asking the same questions to each candidate. The most effective questions are typically behavioral: they ask the candidate to describe a situation that he or she faced at a previous job—or a hypothetical situation at the new job—and to explain the resolution. Interviewers should gear the specific questions toward behaviors and experiences that are key for the new position. Consider the following examples of how these questions could be worded:

- Describe a time when you had to think "outside the box" to find a solution to a pressing problem.

- Describe a situation that required you to do a number of things at the same time. How did you handle it? What was the outcome?

- If you realized that a co-worker was cheating on his expense report, how would you handle the situation?

- What would you do if your boss asked you to complete a key project within an unreasonable time frame?

Cultural differences also affect interview

structured interviews An interviewing approach that involves developing a list of questions beforehand and asking the same questions in the same order to each candidate.

performance. As the U.S. labor pool becomes more diverse, even domestic companies must be aware of cultural differences. And it isn't simply a matter of legality or ethics. Firms that hire the best people regardless of cultural background will gain a critical edge in our increasingly competitive world.

Most colleges and universities offer comprehensive career services. Especially in today's competitive labor market, you would be wise to visit your career center early in your college career and use those services to prepare yourself for a smooth transition into the workforce.

TESTING Either before or after the interview process (and sometimes at both points), a growing number of companies have instituted employment testing of various sorts. The main categories include skills testing, personality testing, drug testing, and physical exams. Skills testing and personality testing carry a fair amount of legal risk, since these tests must measure skills and aptitudes that relate directly to the job itself. Virtually 100% of Fortune 500 companies conduct pre-employment drug testing, as do most other companies. Physical exams are also standard but are highly regulated by state and federal law to ensure that firms don't use them just to screen out certain individuals.

REFERENCES AND BACKGROUND CHECKS Even if you feel absolutely certain that a candidate is right for the job, don't skip the reference check before you make an offer. Research from the Society for Human Resource Managers suggests that more than 50% of job candidates lie on their résumé in some way. Although it may be tough to verify contributions and accomplishments at former jobs, it's pretty easy to uncover lies about education, job titles, and compensation. And it's quite worthwhile, given that the costs of bringing an unethical employee on board can be staggering. Furthermore, if you happen to hire a truly dangerous employee, you can open the door to negligent-hiring lawsuits for not taking "reasonable care." But surprisingly—despite the high risk—employment expert James Challenger estimates that only about 25% of candidates are thoroughly vetted by the companies that consider them.[13]

JOB OFFERS After you find the right person, the next hurdle is to design the right job offer and get your candidate to accept it. To hook an especially hot contender, you may need to get creative. A phone call from top management, the royal treatment, and special perks go a long way, but most superb candidates also want to know in very specific terms how their contributions would affect the business. And no matter how excited you are about your candidate, be certain to establish a **probationary period** up front. This means a specific time frame (typically three to six months) during which a new hire can prove his or her worth on the job. If everything works out, the employee will move from conditional to permanent status; if not, the company can fire the employee fairly easily.

CONTINGENT WORKERS Companies that experience a fluctuating need for workers sometimes opt to hire **contingent workers**—or employees who don't expect regular, full-time jobs—rather than permanent, full-time workers. Specifically, contingent employees include temporary full-time workers, independent contractors, on-call workers, and temporary agency or contract agency workers. As a group, these contingent workers account for more than 30% of U.S. employment.[14]

Employers appreciate contingent workers because they offer flexibility, which can lead to much lower costs. But the hidden downside can be workers who are less committed and less experienced. Too much reliance on contingent workers could unwittingly sabotage company productivity and the customer experience.

15-4c Training and Development: Honing the Competitive Edge

For successful companies in virtually every field, training and development have become an ongoing process rather than a one-time activity. Even in a recession, training and development must gather speed for companies and individuals to maintain their competitive edge. Experts offer five key reasons that relate directly to a healthy bottom line:

1. Increased innovation in strategies and products

2. Increased ability to adopt new technologies

3. Increased efficiency and productivity

4. Increased employee motivation and lower employee turnover

5. Decreased liability (e.g., sexual harassment lawsuits)

> **probationary period** A specific time frame (typically three to six months) during which a new hire can prove his or her worth on the job before he or she becomes permanent.
>
> **contingent workers** Employees who do not expect regular, full-time jobs, including temporary full-time workers, independent contractors, and temporary agency or contract agency workers.

What Were They Thinking?

Interview Gaffes: The Top Ten Things NOT to Do

As you get ready to interview for your dream job, you'll almost certainly find yourself awash in a torrent of advice from family and friends, and flooded with tips found on the Web and elsewhere. "Don't be late, don't be early … Don't ask too many questions, don't ask too few … Don't look too casual, don't look too stuffy …. And whatever you do, never let anyone see that you're nervous!" But however you actually feel—and whatever you actually say—take heart from knowing that you probably won't top these "real-life" interview-question blunders:

1. **Question:** "What five or six adjectives best describe you?"
   Answer: "Really, really, really, really, really cool!"

2. **Question:** "Were you late because you got lost?"
   Answer: "No. It was such a nice day that I didn't mind driving slowly."

3. **Question:** "Why should I hire you?"

Answer: "Because they say you should always hire people better than yourself."

4. **Question:** "What do you find interesting about this job?"
   Answer: "The money. I don't really care what your company does."

5. **Question:** "Is it important to you to get benefits right away?"
   Answer: "I don't believe in healthcare. If I broke my leg, I'd just live with it."

6. **Question:** "What is your greatest strength?"
   Answer: "I'm a quick learner if I'm in the mood to pay attention."

7. **Question:** "What can you tell me about your creative ability?"
   Answer: "My answers to most of your questions are pretty good indicators."

8. **Question:** "Would you be willing to take a drug test?"
   Answer: "Sure. What kind of drugs do I get to test?"

9. **Question:** "What would your boss say about you?"
   Answer: "That I'm insubordinate."

10. **Question:** "How would you define a 'problem person'?"
    Answer: "Anyone who disagrees with me."[15]

Training programs take a number of different forms, from orientation to skills training, to management development, depending on the specific employee and the needs of the organization.

ORIENTATION Once you hire new employees, **orientation** should be the first step in the training and development process. Effective orientation programs typically focus on introducing employees to the company culture (but without sacrificing need-to-know administrative information). Research consistently shows that strong orientation programs significantly reduce employee turnover, which lowers costs.

The Boeing aerospace company has mastered the art of employee orientation. Boeing Military Aircraft and Missile Systems revamped its orientation process to include mentoring, meetings with senior executives, and an after-work social program. One highlight of the orientation—meant to crystallize the "wow" factor of working at Boeing—is the chance to take the controls of an F/A-18 fighter plane flight simulator. Management rightfully sees the program as a chance to develop "future leaders … the ones who will make sure that Boeing continues to be a great place to work."[16]

ON-THE-JOB TRAINING **On-the-job training** is popular because it's very low-cost. Employees simply begin their jobs—sometimes under the guidance of more experienced employees—and learn as they go. For simple jobs, this can make sense, but simple jobs are disappearing from the U.S. market due to the combined impact of offshoring and technology. On-the-job training can also compromise the customer experience. Have you ever waited much too long in a short line at the grocery store because the clerk couldn't figure out how to use the cash register? Multiplied across hundreds of customers, this kind of experience undermines the value of a company's brand.

Formal apprenticeship programs tend to be a more effective way of handling on-the-job training. **Apprenticeship** programs mandate that each beginner serve as an assistant to a fully trained worker for a specified period of time before gaining full credentials to work in the field. In the United States, apprenticeships are fairly common in trades such as plumbing and bricklaying. But in Europe, apprenticeships are much more common across a wide range of professionals, from bankers to opticians.

OFF-THE-JOB TRAINING Classroom training happens away from the job setting but typically during work hours. Employers use classroom training—either on-site or off-site—to teach a wide variety of topics from new computer programming languages, to negotiation skills, to stress management, and more. Going one step further than classroom training, some employers train workers off-site on "real" equipment (e.g., robots) similar to what they would actually use on the job. This approach is called "vestibule training." Police academies often use vestibule training for firearms. Job simulation goes even further than vestibule training, by attempting to duplicate the exact conditions that the trainee will face on the job. This approach makes sense for complex, high-risk positions such as astronaut or airline pilot.

COMPUTER-BASED TRAINING Computer-based training—mostly delivered via the Web—now plays a crucial role in off-the-job training. Broadband technology has turbocharged audio and visual capabilities, which support engaging and interactive online training programs. Online training also standardizes the presentation

On-the-job training often works best for relatively simple jobs.

Jupiterimages/Stockbyte/Getty Images

orientation The first step in the training and development process, designed to introduce employees to the company culture and provide key administrative information.

on-the-job training A training approach that requires employees to simply begin their jobs—sometimes guided by more experienced employees—and to learn as they go.

apprenticeships Structured training programs that mandate that each beginner serve as an assistant to a fully trained worker before gaining full credentials to work in the field.

of the material, since it doesn't depend on the quality of the individual instructor. And the Web helps employers train employees wherever they may be in the world, at their own pace and convenience. But there is a key drawback: it takes a lot of discipline to complete an online program, and some people simply learn better through direct human interaction.

MANAGEMENT DEVELOPMENT

As the bulk of top-level U.S. executives move toward retirement (or lose their jobs in the recession), developing new leaders has become a priority in many organizations. **Management development** programs help current and potential executives develop the skills they need to move into leadership positions. These programs typically cover specific issues that the business faces but also less-tangible—yet equally important—topics, such as communication, planning, business-analysis, change-management, coaching, and team-building skills.

Evan Lorne/Shutterstock.com

15-4d Evaluation: Assessing Employee Performance

Straightforward, frequent feedback is a powerful tool to improve employee performance. The best managers provide informal feedback on a constant basis so that employees always know where they stand. But most companies also require that managers give formal feedback through periodic **performance appraisals**, usually every six months or once a year. Typically, managers conduct the appraisals by sitting down with each employee on a one-to-one basis and comparing actual results to expected results. The performance appraisal affects decisions regarding compensation, promotions, training, transfers, and terminations.

The HR role in performance appraisals begins with the strategic process of creating evaluation tools that tie directly into the company's big-picture objectives. Then, on a day-to-day basis, HR coordinates the actual appraisal process, which typically involves volumes of paperwork. HR must also ensure that managers are trained in providing relevant, honest, objective feedback, and that workers at every level know how to respond if they believe their appraisal is not fair.

Both giving and receiving evaluations tend to be awkward for everyone involved, and unfortunately, uncomfortable people tend to make mistakes. As you read the following list, you'll probably find that you've been on the receiving end of at least a couple of the most common appraisal goofs.

1. **Gotcha!** Too many managers use the performance appraisal as a chance to catch employees doing something wrong, rather than doing something right.

2. **The Once-a-Year Wonder** Many companies mandate annual reviews, but some managers use that as an excuse to give feedback only once a year.

3. **Straight from the Gut** Although "gut feel" can have real value, it's no substitute for honest, relevant documentation of both expectations and accomplishments.

4. **What Have You Done for Me Lately?** Many managers give far too much weight to recent accomplishments, discounting the early part of the review period.

5. **The "Me Filter"** While appraisals are a bit subjective by their very nature, some managers filter every comment through their personal biases. Here are some examples:

   - **Positive Leniency:** "I'm a nice guy, so I give everyone great scores."

   - **Negative Leniency:** "I have high expectations, so I give everyone low scores."

   - **Halo Effect:** "I like this employee so I'll give her top scores across the board."

For a performance appraisal to be effective, the manager must focus on fairness, relevance, objectivity, and balance. Equally important, the manager should give feedback on a continual basis to eliminate surprises and maximize performance.

15-4e Compensation: Show Me the Money

The term **compensation** covers both pay and benefits, but when most people think about compensation, they think about cash. Yet your paycheck is only part of the picture. Many companies also offer noncash benefits such as healthcare, which can be worth up to 30% of each employee's

management development Programs to help current and potential executives develop the skills they need to move into leadership positions.

performance appraisal A formal feedback process that requires managers to give their subordinates feedback on a one-to-one basis, typically by comparing actual results to expected results.

compensation The combination of pay and benefits that employees receive in exchange for their work.

pay. Researching, designing, and managing effective compensation systems are core HR functions.

From a company perspective, compensation—both cash and noncash—represents a big chunk of product costs, especially in labor-intensive businesses such as banks, restaurants, and airlines. Although many firms opt to cut labor costs as far as possible, others boost compensation above the norm to find and keep the best workers. In fact, research suggests that companies offering higher-than-average compensation generally outperform their competitors in terms of total return to shareholders—both stock price and dividend payouts.[17]

Regarding specific individuals and positions, companies typically base compensation on a balance of the following factors:

- **Competition:** How much do competing firms offer for similar positions?

- **Contribution:** How much does a specific person contribute to the bottom line?

- **Ability to Pay:** How much can the company afford?

- **Cost of Living:** What would be reasonable in light of the broader local economy?

- **Legislation:** What does the government mandate?

The most common compensation systems in the United States are wages and salaries. **Wages** refer to pay in exchange for the number of hours or days that an employee works. Variations can be huge, starting at the federal minimum wage of $7.25 per hour (as of early 2015) and ranging up to more than $50 per hour. Jobs that require less education—such as flipping burgers—typically pay hourly wages. Federal law requires companies to pay nonexempt wage earners overtime, 50% more than their standard wage, for every hour worked over 40 hours per week.

Salaries, on the other hand, cover a fixed period, most often weekly or monthly. Most professional, administrative, and managerial jobs pay salaries. While salaries are usually higher than wages, salaried workers do not qualify for overtime, which means that sometimes a low-level manager's overall pay may be less than the pay of wage-based employees who work for that manager.

PAY FOR PERFORMANCE In addition to wages and salaries, many organizations link some amount of worker pay directly to performance. The idea, of course, is to motivate

---

wages The pay that employees receive in exchange for the number of hours or days that they work.

salaries The pay that employees receive over a fixed period, most often weekly or monthly.

benefits Noncash compensation, including programs such as health insurance, vacation, and childcare.

EXHIBIT 15.3	PERFORMANCE PAY OPTIONS
Variable Pay System	**Description**
Commission	Commission involves payment as a percentage of sales. Usually, larger commissions go with smaller base pay.
Bonuses	Bonuses are lump-sum payments, typically to reward strong performance from individual employees.
Profit Sharing	Profit-sharing plans reward employees with a share of company profits above and beyond predetermined goals.
Stock Options	Stock options are the right to buy shares of company stock at some future date for the price of the shares on the day that the company awarded the options.
Pay for Knowledge	This approach involves awarding bonuses and pay increases in exchange for increases in knowledge such as earning an MBA.

© Cengage Learning®

employees to excel. Exhibit 15.3 lists some common approaches.

As you look over the range of variable pay options, which would you find most motivating? Why? What type of business might use each form of variable pay? Why?

15-4f Benefits: From Birthday Cakes to Death Benefits

Benefits represent a significant chunk of money for employers, but for many years, workers took benefits for granted. No longer. As the unemployment rate skyrocketed in 2009, employees began to appreciate their benefits more than ever, recognizing that healthcare, dental care, paid sick days, retirement plans, and other perks add enormous value to their paychecks—and can be yanked at the discretion of their employer.[18]

In fact, a number of budget-minded employers already stick to the legally mandated basics: Social Security and Medicare contributions, payments to state unemployment and workers' compensation programs, and job protection per the Federal Family and Medical Leave Act. However, socially responsible employers—and companies that seek a competitive advantage through a top-notch workforce—tend to offer far more. Optional benefits usually include some or all of the following:

- Paid vacation days and holidays
- Paid sick days

- Health insurance
- Retirement programs
- Product discounts

A smaller number of companies also offer less traditional benefits such as backup childcare options, free massage, pet health insurance, tuition reimbursement, and paid time off for volunteering. Since the recession of 2009, companies that offered "extras" have focused extra attention on perks that would boost morale without an outrageous price tag.[19]

In the past decade, a growing number of companies have begun to offer **cafeteria-style benefits**. This approach involves giving their employees a set dollar amount per person that they must spend on company benefits. The key to these plans is choice, which allows employees to tailor their benefits to their individual needs.

Over the past couple of decades, employees across the U.S. economy have demanded more flexibility from their employers, and companies have responded. Flexible scheduling options include flextime, telecommuting, and job-sharing plans, discussed in detail below. But unfortunately, as massive, widespread layoffs swept across the economy in 2009, workers began to give up flexible schedules—or to stop even asking about them in the first place—out of fear that they would appear less committed to their jobs.[20]

FLEXTIME A **flextime** plan gives workers some degree of freedom in terms of when they start and finish their workday, as long as they complete the required number of hours. Typically, companies with flextime scheduling oblige their employees to start work between mandated hours in the morning—say, anytime between 7 A.M. and 10 A.M.—to take lunch between certain hours in the middle of the day, and to complete work at the end of eight hours. This approach ensures that everyone is present during core hours for communication and coordination, but it provides choice outside those parameters. Flextime tends to increase employee morale and retention, but it makes less sense in jobs that entail extensive teamwork and customer interaction. It also requires careful management to avoid abuse.

The **compressed workweek**, another version of flextime scheduling, allows employees to work a full-time number of hours in less than the standard

cafeteria-style benefits An approach to employee benefits that gives all employees a set dollar amount that they must spend on company benefits, allocated however they wish within broad limitations.

flextime A scheduling option that allows workers to choose when they start and finish their workdays, as long as they complete the required number of hours.

compressed workweek A version of flextime scheduling that allows employees to work a full-time number of hours in less than the standard workweek.

Wacky Benefits

While most benefits are optional, you would not be unreasonable to expect your firm to offer standard perks, such as paid vacation days or sick time, but a handful of creative companies have developed a package of perks to create unique, compelling corporate cultures that seem especially appealing to millenial workers. Some examples:

- **Zappos.com:** Offers a full-time, on-site life coach who helps employees achieve work–life balance and "create fun and a little weirdness."

- **Sweetgreen:** This healthful-food-and-lifestyle firm rewards longtime employees with special tee shirts, among other perks, and over time they noticed that the tee shirt orders have gone down from larges and extra larges to smalls and mediums as the Sweetgreen lifestyle—which includes salads, frozen yogurts, and exercise—takes hold among employees.

- **AirBnB:** AirBNB has built "mini cultural destinations" throughout their San Francisco office. Millenial executive

Takek Pertew reports, "So if your team wanted to go to Bali for a week, they would book that trip and simply go the 3rd floor, where an entire area has been designed to feel like an AirBNB location in Bali." All the fun of an exotic vacation, without the hassle.

- **GoDaddy:** Every month the Internet domain and web-hosting firm holds team-boosting events on company time, including gems such as whitewater rafting, gold panning, competitive cooking courses, and trapeze classes.[21]

Source: GoDaddy

EXHIBIT 15.4   AN ANALYSIS OF TELECOMMUTING

	Benefits	Drawbacks
Organization	■ Lower costs for office space, equipment, and upkeep ■ Higher employee productivity due to better morale, fewer sick days, and more focused performance ■ Access to a broader talent pool (not everyone needs to be local)	■ Greater challenges maintaining a cohesive company culture ■ Greater challenges fostering teamwork ■ Greater challenges monitoring and managing far-flung employees
Employee	■ Much more flexibility ■ Zero commute time (less gas money) ■ Better work–family balance ■ Every day is casual Friday (or even pajama day!) ■ Fewer office politics and other distractions	■ Less fast-track career potential ■ Less influence within the organization ■ Weaker connection to the company culture ■ Isolation from the social structure at work

Source: Flexible Hours and Telecommuting—Not the Ticket to the Top of Corporate America, Five Questions for Susan DePhillips, Workforce Management, September 2005, http://www.workforce.com/section/02/article/24/14/66.html.

workweek. The most popular option is to work four ten-hour days rather than five eight-hour days. Major companies, such as Intel, have developed successful compressed workweek programs at a number of their facilities.

TELECOMMUTING Despite clear benefits for employees, the environment, and many employers, telecommuting has not fully permeated the American workplace. Booming technological advances make it possible for many employees to "commute" to the office via phones, fax machines, and broadband networks. More than 60% of companies allow **telecommuting**, and 20%–30% of Americans telecommute at least occasionally. The bottom-line benefits for companies that embrace the approach can be significant. Over two-thirds of employers report increased productivity among their telecommuters. Telecommuting employees are 35%–40% more productive than their office-bound colleagues. And direct savings from decreased costs add up fast, as well. By establishing telecommuting programs, employers can realize annual cost savings of $20,000–$37,000 per employee, which adds up to hundreds of millions of dollars each year for big players, such as IBM, Sun Microsystems, and AT&T. In fact, if every worker who *could* telecommute actually *did* telecommute, national productivity would increase by $334 billion to $467 billion a year through telecommuting.[22]

While telecommuting sounds great at first glance, it offers benefits and drawbacks for organizations and employees alike, as you'll see in Exhibit 15.4.

JOB SHARING Job sharing allows two or more employees to share

a single full-time job. Typically, job-share participants split the salary equally, but they often need to allocate full benefits to just one of the partners. On a nationwide basis, fewer than 20% of employers (e.g., American Express and Pricewater-houseCoopers) offer job-sharing programs and reap the benefits such as higher morale and better retention.[23]

15-4g Separation: Breaking Up Is Hard to Do

Employees leave jobs for a number of different reasons. Experiencing success, they may be promoted or lured to another firm. Experiencing failure, they may be fired. Or in response to changing business needs, their employer might transfer them or lay them off. And employees also leave jobs for completely personal reasons such as family needs, retirement, or a change in career aspirations.

When companies terminate employees, they must proceed very carefully to avoid wrongful-termination lawsuits. The best protection is honesty and documentation. Employers should always document sound business reasons for termination and share those reasons with the employee.

But employees can still lose their jobs for reasons that have little or nothing to do with their individual performance. In response to the recession, employers eliminated 5.1 million jobs between December 2007 and March 2009. And while the economy regained its footing by 2015, many experts anticipate that it will not fully rebound for many years. As companies have become leaner, the remaining workers have experienced enormous stress. Managers can mitigate the trauma most effectively by showing empathy and concern for their employees, and by treating any laid-off employees with visible compassion.[24]

telecommuting Working remotely—most often from home—and connecting to the office via phone lines, fax machines, or broadband networks.

Really Sick, or Not So Much?

A recent survey by CareerBuilder asked human resource managers to share the most unusual reasons they heard for employees to call in sick days. One employee couldn't come to work because he got bit by a deer during hunting season. Another worker couldn't come in because she got bats in her hair. Another was upset after watching *The Hunger Games* movie. And another's hair turned orange in a home dye job. The excuses are funny, but the lost productivity ... not so much. In fact, more than a quarter of employers' payroll expenses cover work time when employees aren't at work. More than a third of employees admitted in the survey that they called in sick simply because they "don't feel like going to work," and nearly a third called in sick because they "felt like they needed to relax." In response to these kinds of numbers, many human resource managers are making a point of checking up on suspected "fakers" by calling their home later in the day, or even driving by their home, which would seem to violate trust even further. Perhaps a more effective approach would be to create a more engaging workplace that generates less stress, which seems to compel employees to fake sick days.[25]

Subbotina Anna/Shutterstock.com

15-5 LEGAL ISSUES: HR AND THE LONG ARM OF THE LAW

Even when the company is right—even when the company wins—employment lawsuits can cost millions of dollars and deeply damage the reputation of an organization, as we briefly discussed earlier in this chapter. To avoid employment lawsuits, most firms rely on HR to digest the complex, evolving web of employment legislation and court decisions, and to ensure that management understands the key issues.

The bottom-line goal of most employment legislation is to protect employees from unfair treatment by employers. Some would argue that the legislation goes so far that it hinders the ability of companies to grow. But regardless of your personal perspective, the obligation of an ethical employer is to understand and abide by the law as it stands—even if you're working within the system to change it.

The most influential piece of employment law may be the **Civil Rights Act of 1964. Title VII** of this act—which applies only to employers with 15 or more workers—outlaws discrimination in hiring, firing, compensation, apprenticeships, training, terms, conditions, or privileges of employment based on race, color, religion, sex, or national origin. Over time, Congress has supplemented Title VII with legislation that prohibits discrimination based on pregnancy, age (40+), and disability.

Title VII also created the **Equal Employment Opportunity Commission (EEOC)** to enforce its provisions. And in 1972, Congress beefed up the EEOC with additional powers to regulate and to enforce its mandates, making the EEOC a powerful force in the human resources realm.

Here are some additional key pieces of employment legislation:

- **Fair Labor Standards Act of 1938:** Established a minimum wage and overtime pay for employees working more than 40 hours a week.

- **Equal Pay Act of 1963:** Mandated that men and women doing equal jobs receive equal pay.

Civil Rights Act of 1964 Federal legislation that prohibits discrimination in hiring, firing, compensation, apprenticeships, training, terms, conditions, or privileges of employment based on race, color, religion, sex, or national origin.

Title VII A portion of the Civil Rights Act of 1964 that prohibits discrimination in hiring, firing, compensation, apprenticeships, training, terms, conditions, or privileges of employment based on race, color, religion, sex, or national origin for employers with 15 or more workers.

Equal Employment Opportunity Commission (EEOC) A federal agency designed to regulate and enforce the provisions of Title VII.

- **Occupational Safety and Health Act of 1970:** Required safety equipment for employees and established maximum exposure limits for hazardous substances.

- **Immigration Reform and Control Act of 1986:** Required employers to verify employment eligibility for all new hires.

- **Americans with Disabilities Act of 1990:** Prohibited discrimination in hiring, promotion, and compensation against people with disabilities and required employers to make "reasonable" accommodations for them.

affirmative action Policies meant to increase employment and educational opportunities for minority groups—especially groups defined by race, ethnicity, or gender.

- **Family and Medical Leave Act of 1993:** Required firms with 50 or more employees to provide up to 12 weeks of job-secure, unpaid leave on the birth or adoption of a child or the serious illness of a spouse, child, or parent.

15-5a Affirmative Action: The Active Pursuit of Equal Opportunity

The term **affirmative action** refers to policies meant to increase employment and educational opportunities for minority groups—especially groups defined by race, ethnicity, or gender. Emerging during the American civil rights movement in the 1960s, affirmative action seeks to make up for the systematic discrimination of the past by creating more opportunities in the present.

Over the past couple of decades, affirmative action has become increasingly controversial. Opponents have raised concerns that giving preferential treatment to some groups amounts to "reverse discrimination" against groups who do not get the same benefits. They claim that affirmative action violates the principle that all individuals are equal under the law. But supporters counter that everyone who benefits from affirmative action must—by law—have relevant and valid qualifications. They argue that proactive measures are the only workable way to right past wrongs and to ensure truly equal opportunity.

Recent U.S. Supreme Court decisions have supported affirmative action, pointing out that government has a "compelling interest" in ensuring racial diversity. But the Court has rejected "mechanistic" affirmative action programs that amount to quota systems based on race, ethnicity, or gender.

Odd Jobs

As you contemplate your post-college career, chances are good that you are mostly considering the more typical fields, where people you know have built successful careers. Although there are many satisfying options, a number of folks have built rewarding careers in fields that initially appear somewhat odd. A few examples:

- **Flavorists:** Also known as flavor chemists, flavorists synthesize and re-create natural flavors. Average pay for these specialists is up to $100,000 per year.

- **Dog Food Taster:** Just like any other meals, dog food needs to be inspected too. Since they can't use dogs to test the food, this delicious cuisine requires a professional taste tester.

- **Hot dog vendor:** Busy hot dog vendors in New York can earn up to $100,000 a year—while those with a reasonably successful business in less trafficked areas can earn a profit of $30,000 to $80,000 a year.

- **Psychic:** If you want to earn between $60 and $110 per hour without any certification required, you should consider that psychics are in demand, especially when the world is experiencing any kind of turbulence or upheaval.[26]

Stuart Monk/Shutterstock.com

The long-term fate of affirmative action remains unclear, but achieving the underlying goal—a diverse workplace with equal opportunity for all—stands to benefit both business and society as a whole.

15-5b Sexual Harassment: Eliminating Hostility

Sexual harassment—which violates Title VII of the Civil Rights Act of 1964—involves discrimination against a person based on his or her gender. According to the EEOC, sexual harassment can range from requests for sexual favors to the presence of a hostile work environment. The EEOC also points out that a sexual harasser may be either a woman or a man, and the harasser doesn't need to be the victim's supervisor. The victim could be anyone affected—either directly or indirectly—by the offensive conduct. And clearly, to qualify as sexual harassment, the conduct must be unwelcome.

The total number of sexual harassment charges filed with the EEOC in the past decade dropped 27% from 2001 to 2011, but the number of charges filed by men rose from 13.7% to 16.3%.[27]

Not just the perpetrator is liable for sexual harassment; employers may share accountability if they did not take "reasonable care" to prevent and correct sexually harassing behavior, or if they did not provide a workable system for employee complaints. Simply adopting a written policy against sexual harassment is not enough. Taking "reasonable care" also means taking proactive steps—such as comprehensive training—to ensure that everyone in the organization understands 1) that the firm does not tolerate sexual harassment, and 2) that the firm has a system in place for complaints and will not tolerate retaliation against those who complain.[28]

> **sexual harassment** Workplace discrimination against a person based on his or her gender.

The BIG Picture

Effective human resource management can create an unbeatable competitive edge—a fair, productive, empowering workplace pays off in bottom-line results. In good times, one core HRM goal is to find, hire, and develop the best talent. While that function remains crucial in tough economic times, the focus changes to managing HR costs while maintaining morale. Looking forward, a growing number of firms will most likely outsource traditional HR tasks such as payroll and benefits administration to companies that specialize in these areas. HR departments could then focus on their core mission: working with senior management to achieve business goals by cultivating the firm's investment in human resources.

Careers in Human Resources

Human Resources Manager

Plan, organize, lead, and coordinate the personnel, or labor relations activities of an organization. Identify staff vacancies and recruit, interview, and select applicants, ensuring a strong match between personnel and positions. Establish, maintain, and implement a competitive pay and benefit structure, and insure that policies remain in compliance with federal, state, and local laws. Establish and conduct employee orientation and training programs. Provide current and prospective employees with information about company policies, pay, benefits, and promotional opportunities. Counsel and coach management as necessary on human resources issues. Maintain accurate human resources records. Keep current regarding professional and technical knowledge. For more information on this career and other possible careers in human resources, check out Career Transitions.

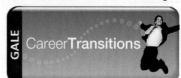

STUDY TOOLS 15

LOCATED AT BACK OF THE TEXTBOOK

☐ Rip Out Chapter Review Card

LOCATED AT WWW.CENGAGE.COM/LOGIN

☐ Review key term flashcards and create your own using StudyBits

☐ Create and complete practice quizzes based off of your notes and StudyBits

☐ Complete Online activities such as Matching, Fill-in-the-Blank, and Drag and Drop exercises

☐ View chapter highlight box content, including CEO Profiles, What Would You Do Cases, and chapter videos

☐ Track your knowledge and understanding of key concepts in business using 4LTR Online

YOUR FEEDBACK MATTERS.

f Follow us at
www.facebook.com/4ltrpress

16 | Managing Information and Technology:
Finding New Ways to Learn and Link

LEARNING OBJECTIVES
After studying this chapter, you will be able to:

16-1 Explain the basic elements of computer technology—including hardware, software, and networks—and describe key trends in each area

16-2 Discuss the reasons for the increasing popularity of cloud computing

16-3 Describe how data become information and how decision support systems can provide high-quality information that helps managers make better decisions

16-4 Explain how Internet-based technologies have changed business-to-consumer and business-to-business commerce

16-5 Describe the problems posed by the rapid changes in Internet-based technologies, and explain ways to address these problems

Remember to visit
PAGE 299
for additional
STUDY TOOLS

16-1 INFORMATION TECHNOLOGY: EXPLOSIVE CHANGE

Over the past few decades, computer and communications hardware and software have changed dramatically. The capabilities of hardware have increased by orders of magnitude. In the late 1950s, for example, you would have needed 50 24-inch disks—costing tens of thousands of dollars—to store 5 megabytes of data. Today you can buy a flash memory device, about the same size as a postage stamp, that stores 128 gigabytes of data—over 24,000 times more than that whole 1950s disk array—for under $75. And in terms of processing power and performance, Apple's iPad Air 2, which performs 3 billion mathematical operations per second, is not only faster than multimillion dollar super computers from the 1990s, it runs 11 hours on its battery, and can be controlled via dictation or easy-to-learn touch screen commands.[1] While more difficult to quantify with specific statistics, it's also clear that software has become more powerful, more flexible, and easier to use.

NETWORKING

WORLD
-EUROPE
-AMERICA
-ASIA
-AFRICA

-SHOW BUSINESS
-NETWORK
-MUSIC
-CINEMA
-BUSINESS/FINA
-WORLD NEWS

"THE INTERNET? IS THAT THING STILL AROUND?"

—HOMER SIMPSON

Sergey Nivens/Shutterstock.com

Perhaps an even more important development than the increased power of hardware and sophistication of software is the degree to which today's technology is linked by networks. These networks allow businesses to coordinate their internal functions, reach their customers, and collaborate with their suppliers and partners in ways that could not have been envisioned a quarter of a century ago. Networks have not only improved the efficiency and effectiveness of existing businesses, they've also opened up entirely new business opportunities. Of course, these new linkages pose challenges and threats as well as benefits and opportunities; a quarter of a century ago, people hadn't heard of computer viruses, spyware, phishing, or spam (except for the Hormel meat product variety). Over the course of this chapter, we'll take a look at both sides of this rapidly changing story.

16-1a Hardware and Software

Hardware refers to the physical components used to collect, input, store, and process data, and to display and distribute information. This hardware includes the various components of a computer system as well as communications and network equipment. Examples include barcode scanners, hard drives, printers, routers, and smartphones.

Software refers to the programs that provide instructions to a computer so that it can perform a desired task. There are two broad categories of software: system software and application software. Both types of software have used the tremendous increase in hardware capabilities to become more powerful and easier to use.

System software performs the critical functions necessary to operate a computer at the most basic level. The fundamental form of system software is the operating system, which controls the overall operation of the computer. It implements vital tasks, such as managing the file system, reading

---

hardware The physical tools and equipment used to collect, input, store, organize, and process data and to distribute information.

software Programs that provide instructions to a computer so that it can perform a desired task.

system software Software that performs the critical functions necessary to operate the computer at the most basic level.

programs and data into main memory, and allocating system memory among various tasks to avoid conflicts.

Operating system software also provides the interface that enables users to interact with their computers. Early operating systems required users to type complex commands with very precise syntax to carry out tasks such as running programs or opening, saving, or deleting files. If you made an error while typing a command, your computer would just sit there until you typed the correct command. Today's operating systems are much simpler and more intuitive. The *graphical user interface* (or GUI—pronounced "gooey") allows users to enter commands by clicking on icons on the computer screen or by tapping or swiping them on devices with a touch screen.

Utility programs supplement operating system software in ways that increase the security or abilities of the computer system. Examples include firewalls, antivirus software, and antispyware programs. Over the years, operating systems have incorporated many features that were originally provided by such utility programs.

Applications software is software that helps users perform a desired task. Horizontal applications software, such as word processing, spreadsheet, and personal information management software, is used by many different businesses and occupations. Vertical applications software is designed for a specific industry or profession. For example, brokerage firms have special software that allows them to transact business on the stock exchanges, and product designers have computer-aided design (CAD) software that enables them to produce technical drawings in three dimensions.

Angela Waye/Shutterstock.com

16-1b Networks

Today, most firms (and households) use networks that allow users to communicate with each other and share both files and hardware resources. A network links computer resources using either a wired or wireless connection. Firms usually want to prevent outsiders from obtaining access to their networks for privacy and security reasons, but they sometimes allow customers or suppliers partial access to their private networks to strengthen their relationships with these important stakeholders.

THE INTERNET AND THE WORLD WIDE WEB

The development and growth of the **Internet** is one of the great networking stories of the past two decades. The Internet is often referred to as the world's largest computer network. It's actually a network of networks, consisting of hundreds of thousands of smaller networks operating under a common set of protocols (rules) so that they can communicate with each other.

One common way to experience the Internet is through the World Wide Web. But while the Internet supports the Web and provides access to it, only about 13% of the traffic on the Internet involves the Web. (Other traffic includes, but isn't limited to, real time entertainment (59%) like NetFlix, YouTube and Amazon Prime streaming, to video and audio communication (13%) like Skype, to filesharing (6.75%) like Dropbox, to marketplaces (6.2%) like eBay and iTunes.)[2] Still, the Web is an incredibly rich environment; it consists of more than 45 billion pages of documents—the number grows every day—written and linked together using Hypertext Markup Language (HTML).[3]

The increased availability of broadband Internet connections has fueled the popularity of Internet applications. A **broadband Internet connection** has the capacity to transmit large amounts of data very quickly, allowing users to quickly download large files such as music, games, and movies. A survey by the Pew Internet and American Life Project, summarized in Exhibit 16.1, found that access to broadband Internet connections grew rapidly for much of the past decade. As Exhibit 16.1 shows, only 3% of American adults had access to high-speed Internet at home in 2000, but by 2013 that figure had climbed to 70%.[4] From a business perspective, the growth in broadband penetration allows companies to offer richer, more interactive experiences to customers who visit their websites or use their apps.

But even today's broadband connections are too slow and inefficient for many business and scientific applications. Such projects often require high-definition video and audio files to be shared among multiple sites at the same time. Beginning in 1996, several leading

Forget the Clouds—The Computing Forecast Calls for Fog

With 93% of organizations running cloud services and 25 billion connected devices worldwide (50 billion by 2020!), we're generating so much data that 3G and 4G cellular networks can't keep up. Today, those connected devices generate more than 2 exabytes (2 million terabytes) of data worldwide per day! One machine in a factory can generate 13 billion data points per day. One jet engine can produce 10 terabytes of data in a half hour. (There are 25,000 flights on average per day, and jets have two to four engines.) Once the Internet of Things is widespread, data volumes will explode, and cloud computing, by itself, won't be enough.

One answer is to offload data and processing power from the cloud to the "fog," meaning closer to the devices (smartphones, appliances, cars, street lights, thermostats, etc.) and people that use them. Cisco, IBM, EMC, and others are developing products to create fog systems that connect user devices at the edges of the network where the data processing, networking, and storage are actually needed and used without having to send data to the cloud. Indeed, smartphone apps already do this as the device itself handles some of the data processing. Not only do apps create a better user experience, but using a company's app is often faster than connecting to the company's website through a browser.

Cloud computing is today's solution, but the future seems to belong to the fog.[5]

Ollyy/Shutterstock.com

---

research universities, corporations, and other organizations formed a coalition to create a new generation of Internet technology in the United States based on fiber-optic cable. The resulting network became known as **Internet2** (or "**I2**").

Access to I2 was initially limited to dues-paying members of the Internet2 consortium, which today consists of over 250 major universities as well as 82 leading high-tech corporations, 68 government agencies, and about 65 international organizations.[6] But under an initiative begun in 2001, members of the I2 consortium can sponsor access to the network for other research and educational organizations that otherwise would be unable to qualify for membership. This initiative has given many elementary schools, high schools, community colleges, libraries, and museums access to I2 resources.[7]

Internet2 isn't simply a faster way to surf the Web or send email. In fact, such routine uses of the current Internet aren't even allowed. Instead, it is a noncommercial network that uses high-speed connectivity to improve education, research, and collaboration. Member organizations see Internet2 as a way to bring together their researchers, scientists, and engineers at various locations in a way that allows real-time

> **Internet2 (I2)** A new high-tech Internet with access limited to a consortium of member organizations (and other organizations these members sponsor). I2 utilizes technologies that give it a speed and capacity far exceeding the current Internet.

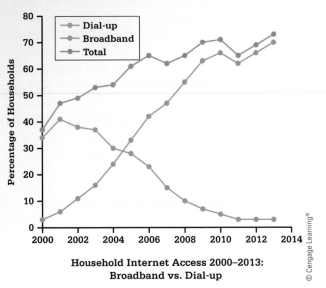

Exhibit 16.1
Growth in Broadband Internet Access

Household Internet Access 2000–2013: Broadband vs. Dial-up

*Source: K. Zichurh and A. Smith, "Home Broadband 2013," Pew Research Internet Project, August 26, 2013, http://www.pewinternet.org/2013/08/26/home-broadband-2013/, accessed March 31, 2014.

© Cengage Learning®

collaboration on complex and important topics. It also allows corporations to collaborate with other companies, universities, and organizations located thousands of miles apart. One of the missions of the Internet2 consortium is to "facilitate the development, deployment and use of revolutionary Internet technologies."[8] So, the benefits of Internet2 will eventually become commonplace on the Internet that the rest of us use.

INTRANETS AND EXTRANETS An **intranet** is a private network that has the same look and feel as the Web and uses the same web browser software to display documents, but limits access to the employees of a single firm (or members of a single organization). When properly implemented, intranets enhance communication and collaboration among employees and provide an effective way to distribute information and applications throughout the organization. Employees can usually log onto their company's intranet from remote locations using password-protected Internet access, allowing them to use company resources when working on the road or from home.

Firms sometimes also create **extranets** by giving key stakeholders, such as suppliers or customers, limited access to certain areas of their intranet. Extranets enable firms to provide additional services and information to their external stakeholders. For example, the firm might allow customers to check on the status of their order, or suppliers to check on the state of the firm's inventory to plan shipments of parts and materials.

16-1c The Role of the IT Department

intranet A private network that has the look and feel of the Internet and is navigated using a web browser, but which limits access to a single firm's employees (or a single organization's members).

extranet An intranet that allows limited access to a selected group of stakeholders, such as suppliers or customers.

cloud computing The use of Internet-based storage capacity, processing power, and computer applications to supplement or replace internally owned information technology resources.

Many business organizations have an information technology (IT) department to manage their information resources. But the role of this department varies significantly from one company to another. In some firms, the IT department plays a strategic role, making and implementing key decisions about the technologies the firm will use. In other organizations, the role of IT is largely operational; managers in functional departments make the key decisions about the computer and information resources their areas need, and the IT department simply maintains these resources and provides technical support to employees.

16-2 CLOUD COMPUTING: THE SKY'S THE LIMIT!

In most companies, employees use applications and access data stored on their own computers or their companies' servers. But "cloud computing" is challenging that approach. **Cloud computing** means using Internet-based storage capacity, applications, and processing power to supplement or replace internally owned computer resources.

You're already familiar with consumer-focused cloud computing services if you share photos on Shutterfly, store your music on Apple's iCloud storage services, or use a service like Dropbox or Google Docs to access and share documents and files. These services clearly offer significant benefits, such as the ability to store large files without taking up valuable space on your computer's hard drive and the convenience of being able to access your documents, music, or photos from anywhere via computer (and many mobile devices) with an Internet connection.

Until recently, most businesses were reluctant to embrace cloud computing, citing concerns about security and reliability. But the rapid increase in the number of firms using cloud-based services suggests that businesses are becoming convinced that the advantages of cloud computing outweigh its risks. John Engates, chief technology officer at Raskspace, a leading cloud data host, says, "We're definitely having more conversations about security with small- and medium-sized customers, and we're also selling more security services to those customers than ever before. It's on the rise."[9]

And for some organizations, moving to the cloud may actually increase data security. Jim Reavis, of Cloud Security Alliance, an industry group, says, "Small and medium businesses are insane not to leverage the advantages of cloud computing. It ends up being almost in all cases a security upgrade because they can't otherwise afford the practices." Eric Cooper, executive director of the San Antonio Food

> "THERE ARE ONLY TWO INDUSTRIES THAT REFER TO THEIR CUSTOMERS AS 'USERS.'"
>
> —EDWARD TUFTE, STATISTICIAN

If you share photos on Facebook, store your music on Apple's iCloud storage services, or use Dropbox to access and share documents and files, you're already using cloud computing.

Bank, works with 150 employees, 5,000 volunteers, and a small technology budget. He said that basic data security practices were "well above our [in-house] technological and intellectual capacity." So they put their critical data and supplier network in the cloud. He says, "It was a no-brainer. I can't be worried about whether there's someone hacking our system."[10] Now his cloud provider does that for him. More specifically, the cloud offers to its users the ability to:

- Access a vast array of computing resources without the need to invest heavily in expensive new hardware, software, and IT personnel.

- Allow lower costs and excess capacity by only paying for the computer resources they need or use. When *Conde Nast*, the travel publisher, moved all of its data online, data costs dropped by 40%. In general, firms that spend a million a month on data needs will cut costs significantly by switching to cloud computing.[11]

- Encourage collaboration among employees and business partners. Cloud resources aren't confined to a specific platform or operating system, so it is easy for people using different computer systems to share files and programs. In addition, many cloud-based applications include tools specifically designed to facilitate collaboration.

- Take advantage of incredible gains in processing speed via *massively parallel computing* that simultaneously combines the processing power of hundreds (or even thousands) of computers. By combining computing power, data processing projects can be completed in 70%–80% less time. For example, DNA2.0, using cloud computing and specialized software, can analyze and count the number of cells in 50,000 microscope images in just two years, a task that would have taken a team of scientists ten years to complete.[12]

16-3 INFORMATION TECHNOLOGY AND DECISION MAKING: A CRUCIAL AID

One of the vital functions of information technology—at least in relationship to business—is to transform data into useful information for decision makers. In order to make decisions, managers must have information about the current state of their business, their competitive environment, and the trends and market conditions that offer new opportunities. Where does this information come from? How can it be made more useful? How can managers process the information to make better decisions?

16-3a Data and Information

Let's start by distinguishing between data and information. **Data** are the facts and figures a firm collects. Data in their raw form have limited usefulness because they lack the context needed to give them meaning. Data become **information** when they are processed, organized, and presented in a way that makes them useful to a decision maker. Sometimes firms can obtain useful information from external sources, but sometimes they must create information by processing their own data. Given today's competitive environment, the speed with which managers obtain good-quality information can be a crucial competitive advantage.

Internally, every department of an organization generates facts and figures that the firm must store and track. Every time a financial transaction is completed, for example, the firm's accounting system must record the specific accounts affected. Similarly, a firm's human resources department must enter new data every time an employee is hired, fired, promoted, changes jobs, or retires. Firms must also keep track of the names, addresses, and credit information of

data Raw, unprocessed facts and figures.

information Data that have been processed in a way that make them meaningful to their user.

each customer. This is hardly a complete list, but you get the picture; firms must store mountains of data and convert them into useful information.

Typically, today's businesses store their data in **databases**, which are files of related data organized according to a logical system and stored on hard drives or some other computer-accessible storage media. It isn't unusual for a company to have many different databases, each maintained by a different department or functional area to meet its specific needs. For example, the human resources department might have a database of employee pay rates, and the marketing department may have another database of customer history.

Once all these data are stored, the firm must convert them into information. One common method is to query a database. A query is a request for the database management software to search the database for data that match criteria specified by the user. Suppose, for instance, that a marketing manager plans to introduce a product upgrade. She can enter a query that asks for the email addresses of all customers who have purchased the product in the past year. She can use this information to send a targeted email message, promoting the upgrade to the customers who are most likely to buy it.

16-3b Characteristics of Good Information

database A file consisting of related data organized according to a logical system and stored on a hard drive or some other computer-accessible media.

decision support system (DSS) A system that gives managers access to large amounts of data and the processing power to convert these data into high-quality information, thus improving the decision-making process.

business intelligence system A sophisticated form of decision support system that helps decision makers discover information that was previously hidden.

data warehouse A large, organization-wide database that stores data in a centralized location.

data mining The use of sophisticated statistical and mathematical techniques to analyze vast amounts of data to discover hidden patterns and relationships, thus creating valuable information.

We've seen that businesses have many sources of information. But not all information is of good quality. High-quality information is:

- Accurate: It should be free of errors and biases.

- Relevant: It should focus on issues that are important to decision makers.

- Timely: It should be available in time to make a difference.

- Understandable: It must help the user grasp its meaning.

- Secure: Confidential information must be secure from hackers and competitors.

16-3c Using Information Technology to Improve Decision Making

A company's information technology (IT) department frequently works closely with managers throughout the organization to support decision making. In fact, many companies develop **decision support systems (DSS)** that give managers access to large amounts of data and the processing power to convert the data into high-quality information quickly and efficiently.

Over the past two decades, a new class of decision support system has evolved to take advantage of the dramatic increase in data storage and processing capabilities. Called **business intelligence systems**, these systems help businesses discover subtle and complex relationships hidden in their data. Such systems can be a source of competitive advantage for the businesses that develop them.

One of the most common approaches to implementing a business intelligence system is to create a data warehouse and use data mining to discover unknown relationships. A **data warehouse** is a very large, organization-wide database that provides a centralized location for storing data from both the organization's own databases and external sources.

Data mining uses powerful statistical and mathematical techniques to analyze vast amounts of data to identify useful information that had been hidden. In recent years, data mining has had considerable success in areas as diverse as fraud and crime detection and quality control and scientific research. New York City's Human Resources Administration used data mining to identify $46.5 million in fraudulent welfare claims, up 60% from before. Commissioner Steven Banks says data mining "allows us to zero in on likely fraud so we don't divert resources to finding what otherwise might be a needle in a haystack."[13]

16-3d Expert Systems

Managers who use decision support systems usually already know quite a bit about the problem and how

An expert system helps managers make better decisions by asking a series of questions until enough information is gathered to reach a decision.

they want to solve it. They just need access to the right data and a system to "crunch the numbers" in a way that provides relevant, accurate, and timely information to help them make their decisions. But what happens when the problem is beyond the expertise of the manager? One way to deal with this problem is to set up an **expert system (ES)** to guide the manager through the decision-making process.

To develop expert systems, programmers ask experts in the relevant area to explain how they solve problems. They then devise a program to mimic the expert's approach, incorporating various rules or guidelines that the human expert uses. The finished program will ask a user a series of questions, basing each question on the response to the previous question. The program continues to ask questions until it has enough information to reach a decision and make a recommendation.

Expert systems routinely solve problems in areas as diverse as medical diagnoses, fraud detection, and consumer credit evaluation. The troubleshooting systems that many companies have on the customer-support pages of their websites are another type of expert system. If your product doesn't work, the troubleshooter will ask a series of questions designed to diagnose the problem and suggest solutions. Based on your responses to each question, the system selects the next question as it starts narrowing down the possible reasons for the problem until it identifies the cause and offers a solution. Often you can solve your problem without waiting on hold to talk to a human expert over the phone.[14]

Despite impressive results in many fields, expert systems have their limitations. Programming thousands of decision rules into the system can be time-consuming, complicated, and expensive. In fact, it's sometimes impossible because the experts themselves can't clearly explain how they make their decisions—they just "know" the answer based on their years of experience. If the experts can't clearly explain how they reach their conclusions, then programmers can't include the appropriate decision rules in the system. Finally, an expert system has little flexibility and no common sense. It probably won't be able to find a solution to a problem that deviates in any significant way from the specific type of problem it was programmed to solve.[15]

16-4 INFORMATION TECHNOLOGY AND THE WORLD OF E-COMMERCE

Over the past 20 years, advances in information technology have had a dramatic and widespread effect on how companies conduct their business. But in this chapter, we'll just concentrate on one key area: the growth and development of e-commerce.

E-commerce refers to marketing, buying, selling, and servicing of products over a network (usually the Internet). You're probably most familiar with **business-to-consumer (B2C) e-commerce**. You participate in this form of e-commerce when you purchase songs from iTunes, use Expedia to make travel arrangements, or buy stocks through an online broker such as Charles Schwab. However, **business-to-business (B2B) e-commerce**, which consists of markets where businesses sell supplies, components, machinery, equipment, or services to other businesses, actually accounts for a much larger volume of e-commerce.

While both B2C and B2B involve exchanging goods over the Internet, they differ in some important ways, as shown in Exhibit 16.2. Given these structural differences, it isn't surprising that the two markets operate so differently.

> **expert system (ES)** A decision support system that helps managers make better decisions in an area where they lack expertise.
>
> **e-commerce** The marketing, buying, selling, and servicing of products over a network (usually the Internet).
>
> **business-to-consumer (B2C) e-commerce** E-commerce in which businesses and final consumers interact.
>
> **business-to-business (B2B) e-commerce** E-commerce in markets where businesses buy from and sell to other businesses.

EXHIBIT 16.2   KEY DIFFERENCES BETWEEN B2C AND B2B E-COMMERCE

	B2C	B2B
Type of Customers	Individual final consumers	Other businesses
Number of Customers in Target Market	Very large	Often limited to a few major business customers
Size of Typical Individual Transaction	Relatively small (usually a few dollars to a few hundred dollars)	Potentially very large (often several thousand dollars, sometimes several million dollars)
Customer Behavior	May do some research, but many purchases may be based on impulse.	Usually does careful multiple research and compares vendors. May take bids.
Complexity of Negotiations	Purchase typically involves little or no negotiation. Customer usually buys a standard product and pays the listed price.	Often involves extensive negotiation over specifications, delivery, installation, support, and other issues.
Nature of Relationship with Customers	Firm wants to develop customer loyalty and repeat business but seldom develops a close working relationship with individual customers.	Buyers and sellers often eventually develop close and long-lasting relationships that allow them to coordinate their activities.

© Cengage Learning®

While B2B and B2C are the most obvious forms of e-commerce, they aren't the *only* forms. For example, in C2C (consumer-to-consumer) e-commerce, consumers buy from and sell to other consumers—think eBay and Craigslist. And in B2G (business-to-government), e-commerce businesses sell information, goods, and services to government agencies.

16-4a   Using Information Technology in the B2C Market

Firms in the B2C market use information technology in a variety of ways. In this section, we'll describe how firms use technology in general (and the Internet in particular) to attract new customers and strengthen the loyalty of existing customers.

WEB 2.0 One major goal for most firms today is to develop stronger relationships with their customers. The Internet has proven to be an excellent tool for fostering such relationships—though it took a while for businesses to discover the best way to do so. In the early days of e-commerce, most companies tried to maintain tight control over the content presented on their websites. These websites presented information about products and allowed customers to place orders for goods and services, but offered little opportunity for user participation or involvement. However, by the early years of the twenty-first century, innovative businesses were developing ways to make e-commerce more interactive and collaborative. In doing so, they not only forged

WANT TO GO GREEN? THERE ARE APPS FOR THAT!

Looking for ways to be more environmentally responsible? If you own a smartphone or tablet, a good strategy is to check out the "green" apps available for your device. Some help you find places to recycle, others help you identify "green" businesses, and yet others provide tips to improve your fuel economy while driving. These apps not only allow you to be "green," they also allow you to save some "green" (as in money). Most green apps are priced under $5, and several of them are free. Even the ones that cost a few bucks often quickly pay for themselves by helping you save on gasoline consumption or utility bills.

Numerous green apps are available for the iPhone and Android phones, as well as for other types of smartphones

Source: Think Dirty

and for tablets. Here's an "apps sampler" to illustrate some of the possibilities:

Good Guide: Provides ratings for thousands of products to help you pick the ones that are good for both you and the environment.

EcoChallenge: Presents two challenges a week, such as "Cook a meal for your friends using only local produce," that can easily be integrated into daily lives. Users can compare their progress with others on Facebook. Provides a calculator so you can measure your progress and impact and useful information and research related to each challenge.

Waterprint: Identifies how much water is used for daily activities, so you can minimize your water consumption. The Waterprint calculator can tell you how much water it takes to brush your teeth, grow the food you eat, and manufacture your blue jeans (and wash them).

Think Dirty: Identifies the ingredients in your personal care items (soap, shampoo, toothpaste, etc.) and assigns a score on its "Dirty Meter" for how toxic they are to the human body. The app recognizes bar codes for more than 60,000 products made by 1,600 brands.

Gas Manager: Monitors gas usage, cost per mile, and gas prices. The app also helps drivers track their vehicle's fuel economy and tracks its carbon footprint. Geolocation features help drivers locate mechanics and nearby gas stations as well.

Avego Driver: Dynamically matches drivers and riders who want to share rides. The app includes built-in safety and security measures. It uses GPS technology to measure the length of the shared ride, and electronically transfers micropayments from the rider to the driver.

Keep in mind that this is far from a complete list. There are hundreds of additional apps that can help you in your quest to be green—and more are being developed all the time. So be sure to check for new green apps on a regular basis.[16]

> ## IN 2013, EVERY DAY USERS SPENT AN AVERAGE OF 20 BILLION MINUTES ON FACEBOOK AND 2 BILLION MINUTES ON SKYPE.
>
> —ZDNET, *EWEEK*

networking sites such as Facebook and Twitter wouldn't exist without user-created material. The more users who participate on these sites, the more useful (and entertaining) they become—and the easier it is for them to attract even more visitors and contributors.

Interestingly, many companies have found that techniques used to encourage collaboration among their customers can be used to accomplish the same result with their employees. Major corporations such as HP, Wells Fargo, and Procter & Gamble now use Web 2.0 techniques to help their own employees work more effectively together. The use of Web 2.0 technologies within organizations is called Enterprise 2.0.[17]

ADVERTISING ON THE INTERNET Many B2C companies have large target markets, so advertising is an important part of their marketing strategy. Internet advertising revenue grew rapidly in the early twenty-first century, increasing almost fourfold from 2002 to 2008. It dropped slightly in early 2009 (as did most types of advertising expenditures during the onset of the recession) but began rising again later that year.

By the end of 2009, it surpassed magazine advertising revenue for the first time, and in 2014 it increased to over $47 billion. Annual Internet advertising revenues now exceed those from broadcast and cable TV, newspapers, radio and magazines. Ads placed on pages containing search results (such as those you see on Google or Bing) accounted for 38% of all Internet advertising revenues. Nonsearch websites accounted for 28% of Internet ad revenues, while ads targeted at mobile devices, such as tablets and smartphones, generated 24% of Internet ad revenues.[18]

Firms in B2C markets also use opt-in email as an advertising medium. Opt-in emails are messages that the receiver has explicitly chosen to receive. Customers often opt in when they register their products online and click to indicate that

stronger relationships with the customers who posted this content, they also created a richer, more interesting, and more useful experience for *others* who visited the site. This new approach became known as **Web 2.0**.

Many Web 2.0 sites rely on users (or members) to provide most of their content. For instance, the online encyclopedia Wikipedia uses wiki software to allow users to comment on and contribute to its articles. And social

> **Web 2.0** Websites that incorporate interactive and collaborative features to create a richer, more interesting, and more useful experience for their users.

they would like to receive product information from the company. Since the customer has agreed to receive the message, opt-in emails tend to reach interested consumers. And, because email requires no envelopes, paper, or postage, it's much less expensive than direct mail.

VIRAL MARKETING The Internet has also proven to be an effective medium for **viral marketing**, which attempts to get customers to communicate a firm's message to friends, family, and colleagues. Despite its name, legitimate viral marketing doesn't use computer viruses. Effective viral marketing campaigns can generate a substantial increase in consumer awareness of a product. As a strategy, viral marketing isn't unique to the Internet; even before the World Wide Web, marketers were adept at buzz marketing, the use of unconventional (and usually low-cost) tactics to stimulate word-of-mouth product promotion. But the Internet has made it possible to implement such strategies in clever ways and reach large numbers of people very quickly. Many viral marketing campaigns in recent years have used social media such as Facebook, Twitter, and YouTube.

HANDLING PAYMENTS ELECTRONICALLY

B2C e-commerce normally requires customers to pay at the time the purchase is made. Clearly, the use of cash and paper checks isn't practical. In the United States, most payments in the B2C market are made by credit cards. To ensure that such transactions are secure, most sites transmit payment information using a secure socket layer (SSL) protocol. You can tell if a site on which you're doing business is using SSL in two fairly subtle ways. First, the URL will begin with https:// instead of simply http://. (Note the "s" after http in the address.) Also, a small closed lock icon will appear near the bottom of your web browser (the exact location depends on the specific browser you are using).

Another common method of payment is to use a **cybermediary**—an Internet-based company that specializes in the secure electronic transfer of funds. By far the best-known cybermediary is PayPal. According to figures on its website, PayPal, which, in 2014, had 162 million active accounts that handled $228 billion in annual payments in 203 countries and 100 currencies.[19]

There are two kinds of **electronic bill presentment and payment**, which is another

Coca Cola Super Bowl ad 2014 Kid gets a Coca Cola. Coke is k...

> Viral marketing generates substantial increases in consumer awareness by getting people outside the company to help promote a product or service by forwarding interesting pictures.

form of electronic payments. With biller-direct, consumers receive email reminders and then pay their bills at the company website. But with bank-aggregator billing, you use the "bill-pay" service at your bank to automatically pay your monthly bills.

16-4b Using Information Technology in the B2B Market

B2B e-commerce generally requires a very different approach than B2C e-commerce. Not only do B2B transactions often involve much larger sums of money and require much more negotiation than B2C transactions, they also often result in long-term supply chain relationships that require close collaboration between buyer and seller. A *supply chain* is the network of organizations and activities needed to obtain materials and other resources, produce final products, and get those products to their final users. Forging tight and efficient supply chain relationships can be a key competitive advantage for firms.

An effective supply chain requires close coordination between a company and its suppliers. Information technology can provide the tools needed to foster this coordination. For example, the extranets we mentioned earlier

---

viral marketing An Internet marketing strategy that tries to involve customers and others not employed by the seller in activities that help promote the product.

cybermediary An Internet-based firm that specializes in the secure electronic transfer of funds.

electronic bill presentment and payment A method of bill payment that makes it easy for the customer to make a payment, often by simply clicking on a payment option contained in an email.

can allow suppliers to keep tabs on their customers' inventories, thus anticipating when to make shipments of parts or materials.

Many firms involved in B2B business also make use of specialized Internet sites, called **e-marketplaces**, which provide a platform for businesses in specific B2B markets to interact. These platforms generally allow buyers in the market to solicit bids by posting requests for proposals (RFPs) on the site. Suppliers can then respond by bidding on RFPs that interest them.

E-marketplaces provide a number of advantages to their participants:

- Compared to older methods, they reduce the time, effort, and cost of doing business for both buyers and sellers.

- Because they are Internet-based, they don't require expensive dedicated connections between firms, so even smaller firms can afford to participate.

- They enable sellers and buyers to contact and negotiate with a large number of market participants on the other side of the market, thus maximizing the chances of finding good matches.

- They often provide additional services—beyond simple trade—that allow firms to exchange information and collaborate, thus forging tighter supply chain relationships.

In recent years, many firms have begun using another information technology known as **radio frequency identification (RFID)** to improve the efficiency of their supply chains. This technology stores information on a microchip and transmits it to a reader when it's within range—up to several thousand feet. The chips can be extremely small—some are difficult to see with the naked eye—and can be embedded in most types of tangible products. The chips are usually powered by the energy in the radio signal sent by the reader, so they don't need batteries.

RFID chips can store and transmit all sorts of information, but most commonly they transmit a serial number that uniquely identifies a product, vehicle, or piece of equipment. This type of information can be used to help track goods and other resources as they move through a supply chain. Deliveries can be recorded automatically and electronically without the need to make manual records. The chips also can make taking inventory much quicker and simpler, since the items in stock identify themselves to readers. And the chips can be used to reduce the chances of theft. The results of these advantages are lower costs and a more efficient supply chain.

> ## "GETTING INFORMATION OFF THE INTERNET IS LIKE TAKING A DRINK FROM A FIRE HYDRANT."
> —MITCHELL KAPOR, ENTREPRENEUR, FOUNDER OF LOTUS DEVELOPMENT CORPORATION

Disney World uses RFID chips in MagicBands, bracelets that serve as park visitors' admission tickets, hotel keys, and credit cards at shops and restaurants. Because they contain RFID chips, Disney can track where the park is busy and then add more staff at those rides and restaurants. And with the ability to shift staff precisely where they are most needed, Disney World can now easily admit 3,000 more people to the park each day. One example is faster food service. For instance, after park guests Jason and Melissa McInerney entered their lunch orders into a touch screen kiosk, the screen directed them to sit wherever they liked. Just after they sat down at their table, their food server brought them their sandwiches and drinks. Thanks to the MagicBands, the kitchen and their server knew what they ordered and where they were sitting.[20]

16-5 CHALLENGES AND CONCERNS ARISING FROM NEW TECHNOLOGIES

So far, we've concentrated on the benefits of advances in information technology—and it's clear that these benefits are enormous. But rapid technological advances also pose challenges and create opportunities for abuse. These problems affect businesses, their customers, and their employees, as well as the general public. In this section, we'll look at annoyances, security concerns, and legal and ethical issues.

e-marketplace A specialized Internet site where buyers and sellers engaged in business-to-business e-commerce can communicate and conduct business.

radio frequency identification (RFID) A technology that stores information on small microchips that can transmit the information when they are within range of a special reader.

RFID: Good Idea, Bad Execution

After leaving Apple to come to JC Penney, CEO Ron Johnson tried to execute a radical remake of the company's stores, including replacing anti-theft tags with RFID tags that could wirelessly track every single item in stock in *all* JC Penney warehouses and stores. The tags were also supposed to allow customers to pay for items at self-service checkout stations, saving shoppers time and JC Penney money (because of reduced staffing). Financial analyst Paul Swinland said, "Johnson saw this as a cost saving that would save money right off the bat." The RFID-based system had the potential to revolutionize the company's inventory tracking and stocking processes, provide a high-tech and efficient shopping experience, and save millions of dollars.

So, a great, high-tech plan for saving money, right? Except that JC Penney made several critical mistakes. First, it removed all of the existing anti-theft tags on in-stock items *before* the new RFID tags and system were in place. Second, it implemented a customer-friendly "return any item, any time" return policy, even if you didn't have a receipt. Third, the company then decided that the RFID chips were too expensive, so it halted the program *after* asking vendors to stop attaching anti-theft tags to items shipped to JC Penney stores. The result of these mistakes, according to CEO Mike Ullman, who came out of retirement to become CEO after Johnson stepped down from the job, was that "most of the theft [in retail stores] comes to our place." Dishonest people came to JC Penney stores, grabbed goods off shelves, and then, without buying them, "returned" them to get "their money back."

Paula Rosenblum, a retail analyst at RST Research, said, "If someone eliminated the security tags for whatever reason, that was an egregious mistake. You don't leave a store unprotected." Indeed, former CEO Johnson's aggressive layoffs of store staff probably contributed to the situation, too. A former JC Penney executive stated, "The fact is they've fired everybody who was watching the stores. This is not rocket science."

So rather than save money, JC Penney's foray into RFID tags ended up in a $28 million loss in just three months.[21]

16-5a Malware

The Internet—for all its advantages—creates the possibility that unwanted files and programs may land on your computer. In many cases, this happens without your knowledge, much less your permission. Some of these files and programs are relatively benign (even useful), but others can create major problems. Software that is created and distributed with malicious intent is called **malware** (short for "malicious software"). Spyware, computer viruses, and worms are all examples of malware.

Spyware is software that installs itself on your computer without permission and then tracks your computer behavior in some way. It might track which Internet sites you visit to learn more about your interests and habits in order to send you targeted ads. Or, more alarmingly, it might log every keystroke (thus capturing passwords, account numbers, and user names to accounts as you enter them), allowing someone to steal your identity. Some spyware even goes beyond passive watching and takes control of your computer, perhaps sending you to websites you didn't want to visit.

Computer viruses are programs that install themselves on computers without the users' knowledge or permission and spread—sometimes very rapidly—by attaching themselves to other files that are transferred from computer to computer. Viruses are often attached to emails, instant messages, or files downloaded from the Internet. Some viruses are little more than pranks, but others can cause great harm. They can erase or modify data on your hard drive, prevent your computer from booting up, or find and send personal information you've stored on your computer to people who want to use it for identity theft. **Worms** are similar to viruses, except that they are independent

---

malware A general term for malicious software, such as spyware, computer viruses, and worms.

spyware Software that is installed on a computer without the user's knowledge or permission to track the user's behavior.

computer virus Computer software that can be spread from one computer to another without the knowledge or permission of the computer users by attaching itself to emails or other files.

worm Malicious computer software that, unlike viruses, can spread on its own without being attached to other files.

> "GOOD PASSWORDS ARE BAD FOR PEOPLE, AND BAD PASSWORDS ARE GOOD FOR CRIMINALS."
>
> —MICHAEL JONES, CHIEF TECHNOLOGY ADVOCATE, GOOGLE

programs that can spread across computer networks without being attached to other files.

How can you protect yourself from spyware, viruses, and worms? Take these common-sense steps:

- Perform regular backups. This can come in handy should a virus tamper with (or erase) the data on your hard drive. Store the backed-up data in a separate place.

- Install high-quality antivirus and antispyware software, and keep it updated. (Today's Internet security software usually has the ability to download and install updates automatically, but they may need to be configured to do so.)

- Update your operating system regularly so that any security holes it contains are patched as soon as possible.

- Don't open email messages or attachments if you don't know and trust the sender.

- Don't download files from websites unless you are sure they are legitimate. And be sure to read the licensing agreement of any programs you install—especially those of freeware you download from the Internet. The wording of these agreements will often indicate if other programs (such as spyware) will be installed along with your free program.

16-5b Spam, Phishing, and Pharming

Spam refers to unsolicited commercial emails, usually sent to huge numbers of people with little regard for whether they are interested in the product or not. It's hard to get exact measures of the amount of spam that is sent each year, but experts agree that it now comprises the vast majority of all email in the United States. It clogs email inboxes and makes it tough for people to find legitimate messages among all the junk. Spam filters exist that help detect and eliminate spam, but spammers are very good at eventually finding ways to fool these filters.[22]

The U.S. Congress enacted the Controlling the Assault of Non-Solicited Pornography and Marketing Act (usually called the CAN-SPAM Act) in 2003. This act requires senders of unsolicited commercial email to label their messages as ads and to tell the recipient how to decline further messages. It also prohibits the use of false or deceptive subject lines in email messages. But the rapid increase in the amount of spam in recent years suggests this law hasn't been an effective deterrent.

Phishing is another common use of spam. Phishers send email messages that appear to come from a legitimate business, such as a bank, credit card company, or retailer. The email attempts to get recipients to disclose personal information, such as their social security or credit card numbers, by claiming that there is a problem with their account—or sometimes simply that the account information needs to be verified or updated. The messages appear authentic; in addition to official-sounding language, they often include official-looking corporate logos. The email also usually provides a link to a website where the recipient is supposed to log in and enter the desired information. When the victims of the scam click on this link, they go to a website that can look amazingly like the site for the real company—but it's not. It's a clever spoof of the site where the phishers collect personal information and use it to steal identities.

One of the best ways to avoid such scams is to be skeptical of email requests for personal information; reputable businesses almost *never* ask you to divulge such information via email. Also, never click on a link in an email message to go to a website where you have financial accounts—if the message is from a phisher, that link is used to direct you to the fake site where the phishers hope that you'll mistakenly enter your username and password. Instead, use a link to the site that you've bookmarked, or type in the link to the real site yourself.

Not content with phishing expeditions, some scam artists have now taken to **pharming**. Like phishing, pharming uses fake websites to trick people into divulging personal information. But pharming is more sophisticated and difficult to detect than phishing because it doesn't require the intended victim to click on a bogus email link. Instead, it uses techniques to redirect Internet traffic to the fake sites. Thus, even if you type in the *correct* URL for a website you want to visit, you still might find yourself on a very realistic-looking pharming site. One way to check the validity of the site is to look for the indications that the site is secure, such as the https:// in the URL and the small closed lock icon mentioned earlier.[23]

Computers aren't the only devices plagued by these threats and annoyances. Cell phone users are facing increasing problems with spam delivered via text messaging. Even more alarming, some scammers have found ways to take their phishing expeditions to cell phones—a practice known as "SMiShing," or SMS phishing. One typical SMiShing ploy is to use text messaging to entice cell phone users to visit the scammer's fake website asking you to provide personal or financial information.[24]

spam Unsolicited email advertisements usually sent to very large numbers of recipients, many of whom may have no interest in the message.

phishing A scam in which official-looking emails are sent to individuals in an attempt to get them to divulge private information such as passwords, usernames, and account numbers.

pharming A scam that seeks to steal identities by routing Internet traffic to fake websites.

Scamming in a Winter Wonderland

The holidays are a great time for reuniting with loved ones and giving generously to those in need. Unfortunately, high-tech thieves take advantage of the holiday season by stealing cash, credit cards, or personal information. To make sure your holidays are indeed happy, avoid these common scams.

Fake email greeting cards contain malware-laced attachments or links to websites that infect computers with malware. While it's counter to the holiday spirit, you're best off not opening email greeting cards.

Then there are fake online stores with amazingly low prices and the promise of the most popular, hard-to-find toys and gifts. But, if it's too good to be true, meaning the prices are much lower than at traditional e-tailers like Amazon, and if they've got inventory when no one else does, then you're probably being scammed, especially if you've never heard of the website before.

Another popular scam is fake emails from UPS, FedEx, or the post office claiming a package is waiting for you. Like fake email greeting cards, fake delivery notifications may have dangerous attachments, ask you to share personal and financial information, or to link to websites that infect your computer.

Finally, watch out for fake charity websites, containing heartbreaking, but false, stories about poor, homeless children who will go without food and gifts without your help. Check with the Charity Navigator website to make sure your gift goes to those who really need it via a legitimate charity.[25]

Benoitb/iStockphoto.com

16-5c Hackers: Break-Ins in Cyberspace

Hackers are skilled computer users who have the expertise to gain unauthorized access to other people's computers. Not all hackers intend to do harm, but some—called "black hat hackers" (or "crackers")—definitely have malicious intent. They may attempt to break into a computer system to steal identities or to disrupt a business.

Protecting against hackers requires individuals and businesses to be security conscious. Some of the precautions used against hackers, such as making frequent backups, are similar to those used to protect against viruses. Another key to protecting against hackers is to make sure that all data transmitted over a network are encrypted, or sent in encoded form that can only be read by those who have access to a key. Security experts also suggest that organizations restrict access to computer resources by requiring users to have strong passwords. According to Microsoft, strong passwords are at least 14 characters in length; include a mix of letters, numbers and special characters; and don't contain any common words or personal information.[26]

Unfortunately, users struggle to remember strong passwords, so they reuse one or two passwords. "Having the same password for everything is like having the same key for your house, your car, your gym locker, your office," says PayPal's Michael

> **hacker** A skilled computer user who uses his or her expertise to gain unauthorized access to the computer (or computer system) of others, sometimes with malicious intent.

Stokkete/Shutterstock.com

Hackers use their computer expertise to gain unauthorized access to other people's computers, often for malicious purposes.

Just Because They Can, Doesn't Mean They Should. ???

On rainy days, the number of negatively worded Facebook posts increases 1.16%, while the number of positive posts drops 1.19%. In a process called social contagion, those positive and negative posts, in turn, affect what Facebook friends post where it isn't raining. A positive post generated 1.75 positive posts by friends, while a negative post generated 1.29 negative posts by friends. The study's lead researcher explained that, "We wanted to see if emotional changes in one person caused emotional changes in another person and that's exactly what we found."

In another study, Facebook then manipulated the news feeds of nearly 700,000 users to again study emotional contagion. In this one-week study, Facebook removed a small percentage of positive story feeds from half of the users, and small percentage of negative story feeds from the other half. As with the "rainy day" study, people were more likely to post happy (or sad) content upon seeing more positive (or negative) news feeds, suggesting again that emotions grow through social contagion.

Critics complained that it's one thing to study naturally occurring social contagion (i.e., rainy days), but it's another to manipulate what people see in their Facebook news feeds without first obtaining consent from the study participants.

University of Maryland Professor James Grimmelmann said, "If you are exposing people to something that causes changes in psychological status, that's experimentation. This is the kind of thing that would require informed consent."

Facebook explained that the research was consistent with the Data Use Policy its users agree to when establishing their Facebook accounts, namely, that it "may use the information we receive about you … For internal operations, including troubleshooting, data analysis, testing, research and service improvement."[27]

What do YOU think?

- How influential is a company's data usage policy in your decision to use their services? Is it troublesome that Facebook monitors almost everything you do online? Or, are you willing to let Facebook do that so it accurately tailors what you see when using your Facebook account?

- What sort of information – if any – do you believe should be totally exempt from data mining? What kind of data privacy are you unwilling to sacrifice to use Facebook?

- How would you feel if you learned Facebook had altered your news feed for its research? Would you be upset? Would you consider quitting the service?

Barrett. With password management software, such as 1Password, users memorize just one master password. 1Password works with any browser on any computer, tablet, or smartphone. It generates unique, strong passwords, synchronizes encrypted data across devices, and autofills forms so you don't have to manually enter personal information or passwords.[28]

Firewalls are another important tool to guard against hackers and other security threats. A firewall uses hardware or software (or sometimes both) to create a barrier that prevents unwanted messages or instructions from entering a computer system. As threats from spyware, hackers, and other sources have developed, the use of firewalls has become commonplace.

16-5d Ethical and Legal Issues

Information technology raises a number of legal and ethical challenges, such as the need to deal with privacy issues and to protect intellectual property rights. These issues are controversial and don't have simple solutions.

PERSONAL PRIVACY Firms now have the ability to track customer behavior in ways that were never before possible. This has advantages for you because it allows firms to offer better, more personalized service. But all this extra information comes at the expense of your privacy. Does the fact that firms know so much about your preferences and behavior make you a bit nervous?

Does it bother you that your email messages lack confidentiality? When you send an email, it could be stored on several computers: your personal computer, the server of your email provider, the server of your recipient's provider, and your recipient's own computer. If you send the email from your company's system, it's also likely to be stored when the company backs up its information. If you thought that deleting an email message from your own computer erased it permanently and completely, you need to think again.

The list of other ways in which information technology can erode your personal privacy is long and getting longer. For example, RFID chips are now embedded in U.S. passports and in many states' driver's licenses. Some privacy experts are concerned that such chips will make it easy for government organizations to track individuals. One

firewall Software and/or hardware designed to prevent unwanted access to a computer or computer system.

reason government officials gave for embedding RFID chips in passports and driver's licenses was to make it harder for criminals and terrorists to forge IDs. But in 2009, a hacker publicly demonstrated the ability to read the information in these chips from a distance of several yards, leading to fears that identity thieves could use similar techniques to obtain personal information and perhaps even create convincing copies of these important identification documents. Encryption and protective sleeves, however, can prevent unauthorized scanning. Thieves are more likely to be successful by stealing your actual ID or passport the old-fashioned way.[29]

The bottom line is that there's no simple way to solve privacy concerns. Privacy is an elusive concept, and there is no strong consensus about how much privacy is enough.

PROTECTING INTELLECTUAL PROPERTY RIGHTS Intellectual property refers to products that result from creative and intellectual efforts. There are many types of intellectual property, but we'll focus on forms of intellectual property that are protected by copyright law, such as books, musical works, computer programs, video games, and movies. Copyright law gives the creators of this property the exclusive right to produce, record, perform, and sell their work for a specified time period.

intellectual property
Property that is the result of creative or intellectual effort, such as books, musical works, inventions, and computer software.

Piracy of intellectual property occurs when someone reproduces and distributes copyrighted work without obtaining permission from—or providing

compensation to—the owner of the copyrighted material. When piracy becomes widespread, creators of intellectual property receive much less income for their efforts. This can substantially reduce their incentive to continue developing creative material.

The Business Software Alliance estimates that, globally, 42% of all business software installed on personal computers in 2013 was pirated, resulting in the loss of over $63 billion in revenue to software companies. In several smaller countries, including Georgia, Armenia, and Zimbabwe, the rate of piracy was over 90%. Among larger nations, the piracy rate in China exceeded 74%, while in India it was 60%. The good news is that the piracy rate was much lower in the United States at 18%. But given the huge size of the U.S. software market, even this relatively low rate of piracy still resulted in losses of over $9.7 billion in revenue for software companies. Faced with such a widespread problem, many software publishers have become very aggressive at prosecuting firms and individuals engaged in software piracy.[30]

Music studios, video game developers, and motion picture producers also face significant problems with piracy.[31] Furthermore, software piracy costs companies 1.2 billion hours and $25 billion per year to identify, repair, and recover pirated software that is usually infected with malware designed to steal your personal and financial information.[32]

Given how lucrative piracy can be, it's unlikely that this problem will go away anytime soon. You can expect the companies hurt by these practices to continue aggressively prosecuting pirates and to work on new technologies that make pirating digital media more difficult.

The BIG Picture

Information technology plays a vital role in virtually every aspect of business operations. For instance, marketing managers use information technology to learn more about customers, reach them in novel ways, and forge stronger relationships with them—as we showed in our discussion of Web 2.0. Operations managers use RFID technologies to coordinate the movement of goods within supply chains and to keep more accurate inventory records. And financial managers use IT to track financial conditions and identify investment opportunities. Managers in all areas of a business can use decision support systems to improve their decision making. They also can apply techniques such as data mining to obtain interesting new insights hidden in the vast streams of data that flow into their companies.

Cloud computing represents the newest and one of the most exciting new approaches to how companies acquire and utilize

IT resources. The use of cloud-based resources has the potential to not only lower costs and increase flexibility but also significantly magnify computation power. If cloud computing can overcome concerns about security and stability, it is likely to continue growing in popularity, which could result in significant changes to the role IT departments play within their organizations.

The rapid changes in IT in recent years—especially those related to the rise of the Internet as a business venue—have opened up exciting new commercial opportunities. But these changes have also created a host of legal and ethical challenges and security questions. One thing is certain: business organizations that find ways to leverage the advantages of new IT developments while minimizing the accompanying risks are most likely to enjoy competitive success.

Information Technology Support Specialist

Responsible for installing and configuring software, responding to employee and customer issues within the ticket management system, interacting with sales, engineering, and product managers to address complex customer issues, escalating relevant problems to appropriate functional and management teams, contributing potential technical workarounds, and acting as a technical expert for IT solutions within a global IT team. The ideal candidate has a bachelor's degree in computer science or information technology, at least one year of experience with Windows and Unix/Linux administrative services, web services, configuration and release management, possesses strong analytical, problem solving, and customer communication skills, and is self-motivated and works effectively with little instruction. For more information on this career and other possible careers in information technology, check out Career Transitions.

STUDY TOOLS 16

LOCATED AT BACK OF THE TEXTBOOK

☐ Rip Out Chapter Review Card

LOCATED AT WWW.CENGAGE.COM/LOGIN

☐ Review key term flashcards and create your own using StudyBits

☐ Create and complete practice quizzes based off of your notes and StudyBits

☐ Complete Online activities such as Matching, Fill-in-the-Blank, and Drag and Drop exercises

☐ View chapter highlight box content, including CEO Profiles, What Would You Do Cases, and chapter videos

☐ Track your knowledge and understanding of key concepts in business using 4LTR Online

17 | Operations Management:
Putting It All Together

Remember to visit **PAGE 318** for additional **STUDY TOOLS**

LEARNING OBJECTIVES

After studying this chapter, you will be able to:

17-1 Define operations management and describe how the role of operations management has changed over the past 50 years

17-2 Discuss the key responsibilities of operations managers

17-3 Describe how operations managers face the special challenges posed by the provision of services

17-4 Explain how changes in technology have revolutionized operations management

17-5 Describe the strategies operations managers have used to improve the quality of goods and services

17-6 Explain how lean and green practices can help both the organization and the environment

17-1 OPERATIONS MANAGEMENT: PRODUCING VALUE IN A CHANGING ENVIRONMENT

Operations management is concerned with managing all of the activities involved in creating value by producing goods and services and distributing them to customers. When operations managers do their job well, their firms produce the *right* goods and services in the *right* quantities and distribute them to the *right* customers at the *right* time—all the while keeping quality high and costs low. Obviously, the decisions of operations managers can have a major impact on a firm's revenues and its costs, and thus on its overall profitability.

17-1a Responding to a Changing Environment

The practice of operations management has changed dramatically over the past half century. New technologies, shifts in the structure of the economy, challenges posed by global competition, and concerns about the impact of production on the environment have fueled this revolution. Let's begin by identifying the key changes that have characterized the practice of operations management over the past 50 years.

> "SUCCESS IS SIMPLE. DO WHAT'S *RIGHT*, THE RIGHT WAY, AT THE RIGHT TIME."
>
> —ARNOLD H. GLASGOW, AMERICAN PSYCHOLOGIST

FROM A FOCUS ON EFFICIENCY TO A FOCUS ON EFFECTIVENESS To operations managers, **efficiency** means producing a product at the *lowest cost*. **Effectiveness** means producing products that *create value* by providing customers with goods and services that offer a better relationship between price and perceived benefits. In other words, effectiveness means finding ways to give customers more for their money—while still making a profit.

In the 1960s, the focus of operations management was mainly on efficiency. The goal was to keep costs low so the firm could make a profit while keeping prices competitive. In today's highly competitive global markets, efficiency remains important. But operations managers now realize that keeping costs (and prices) low are only part of the equation. Customers usually buy goods that offer the best value—and these aren't always the same as the goods that sell for the lowest price. A product that offers better features, more attractive styling and higher quality may provide more value—and attract more customers—than a product with a lower price. Thus, today's operations managers have broadened their focus to look at benefits as well as costs.

> "NOTHING IS LESS PRODUCTIVE THAN TO MAKE MORE EFFICIENT WHAT SHOULD NOT BE DONE AT ALL."
>
> —PETER F. DRUCKER

FROM GOODS TO SERVICES Goods are tangible products that you can see and touch. *Durable goods* are expected to last three years or longer; examples include furniture,

operations management Managing all of the activities involved in creating value by producing goods and services and distributing them to customers.

efficiency Producing output or achieving a goal at the lowest cost.

effectiveness Using resources to create value by providing customers with goods and services that offer a better relationship between price and perceived benefits.

goods Tangible products.

cars, and appliances. *Nondurable goods*, such as toothpaste, apples, and paper towels, are used up more quickly and are often perishable. **Services** are activities that yield benefits but don't directly result in a physical product. Examples include legal advice, entertainment, and medical care. Goods are consumed, while services are experienced.

In the 1960s, the U.S. economy was a manufacturing powerhouse, with more than a third of its labor force employed in the goods-producing sector. But over the past 50 years, the American economy has experienced a fundamental shift away from the production of goods and toward the provision of services. By 2014, less than 16% of the nonfarm labor force worked in the goods-producing sector. By contrast, employment in the service sector had risen to 84% of the labor force.[1]

FROM MASS PRODUCTION TO MASS CUSTOMIZATION

Fifty years ago, one common production strategy was to keep costs low by producing large quantities of standardized products. The goal of this *mass production* strategy was to achieve reductions in average cost by taking advantage of specialization and the efficient use of capital. But today's technologies allow many firms to pursue *mass customization*—the production of small quantities of customized goods and services that more precisely meet the needs of specific customers—with very little increase in costs.

FROM LOCAL COMPETITION TO GLOBAL COMPETITION

For the first 25 years after World War II, American firms dominated key markets. This strength was based partly on the fact that the United States possessed a rich base of natural resources, a growing and increasingly well-educated labor force, an excellent infrastructure, and the strong incentive system inherent in a market economy. But it also reflected the fact that the production facilities and infrastructure in many European and Asian nations had been severely damaged during the war.

By the early 1970s, the economies of Japan, Germany, and other war-ravaged nations had been rebuilt, with many of their major companies boasting efficient new production facilities with state-of-the-art technology. In addition, many Japanese firms had adopted new techniques that greatly improved the quality of their products. With lower labor costs, impressive technology, and world-class quality, these foreign producers quickly began to take market share from American firms. In more recent years, firms in Korea, India, and China have also become formidable competitors.

services Intangible products.

FROM SIMPLE SUPPLY CHAINS TO COMPLEX VALUE CHAINS

Over the past 50 years, the increasingly competitive and global nature of markets has brought about major changes in how firms produce and distribute their goods and services. Many supply chains today span multiple organizations located in many different countries. The shift from a cost perspective to a value perspective has led operations managers to extend their

IF THE SOCK FITS, MAKE IT IN THE USA

When Walmart announced in 2013 that it would increase its purchase of U.S.-made merchandise by $5 billion a year, Michael Penner saw an opportunity. Only a decade before, Mr. Penner had shut down three hosiery plants in Canada and started outsourcing to China. Almost overnight, his company, Richelieu Group, went from being a manufacturer of socks to being designer and marketer of socks.

Mr. Penner was not alone. The North Carolina textile industry was also particularly hard hit by offshoring. For nearly a decade, the U.S. Bureau of Labor Statistics has listed textile occupations as some of the fastest declining occupations in the country as well as one of the industry sectors with the fastest declining output in the United States.

The Walmart announcement, however, prompted Mr. Penner to reconsider manufacturing socks in North America. By late 2014, his company, renamed Peds Legwear, was producing socks out of a factory he had purchased in Hildebran, North Carolina. Ninety Italian machines knit yarn into tubes and also added a toe seam. Previously, knitting the tube and closing the sock's toe seam were two separate operations requiring two work stations. By combining the operations, Peds only needs half the production workers and is better able to compete on price.

Peds Legwear is not alone. Freaker USA, Hanesbrands, and Gildan are also contributing to the revival of the sock industry in North Carolina. Penance Hall, a dress sock company, was started by three friends who wanted to manufacture luxury goods in the United States. Their seven-step manufacturing process starts with wool from South Carolina which is sent for dyeing and knitting to a factory in North Carolina. The boxes the socks are packaged in are printed in Pennsylvania. From the wool to the boxes, Penance Hall's entire supply chain is U.S. based.

There are limits, however, to the capabilities of the North Carolinian production facilities, particularly for Peds. The U.S. factories are only set up to produce socks with simple designs that use few colors. More complex patterns, like hearts or animal shapes, are still made in Asia.[2]

Exhibit 17.1
Operations Management: Fifty Years of Change

Characteristics of Operations Management in 1962	Factors Promoting Change	Characteristics of Operations Management in 2012
• Focus on Minimizing Costs • Production of Goods • Mass Production • Simple Supply Chains • Exploit the Environment	• Improvements in Production and Information Technologies • Rise of Global Competition and Global Opportunities • Recognition of Quality as a Source of Competitive Advantage • Adoption of Marketing Perspective and Customer Focus • Recognition of Serious Environmental Problems	• Focus on Creating Value • Provision of Services • Mass Customization • Complex Value Chains • Sustain the Environment

© Cengage Learning®

view beyond the traditional supply chain to encompass a broader range of processes and organizations known as a *value chain*.

FROM EXPLOITING THE ENVIRONMENT TO PROTECTING THE ENVIRONMENT

In the 1960s, many operations managers viewed the natural environment as something to exploit. The emphasis on keeping costs low made it tempting to dispose of wastes as cheaply as possible—often by dumping them into rivers, lakes, or the atmosphere. But the serious consequences of environmental pollution have become increasingly apparent. Operations managers at socially responsible companies have responded by adopting a variety of green practices to produce goods and services in more environmentally responsible ways.

Exhibit 17.1 summarizes the discussion of the key ways in which operations management has changed over the past 50 years. We'll look at these changes in greater detail as we move through this chapter. But first let's take a look at the some of the key tasks operations managers perform.

17-2 WHAT DO OPERATIONS MANAGERS DO?

Understanding the marketing definition of *product* plays a pivotal role in understanding what operations managers do. A product consists of all of the tangible and intangible features (sometimes called the *customer benefit package*) that create value for consumers by satisfying their needs and wants. For example, when you purchase a car made by General Motors, you not only get the physical automobile, you also get (among other things) a warranty and (for many models) up to five years of OnStar services.[3]

Marketing research typically determines which features a product should include to appeal to its target customers. Although operations managers don't normally have the primary responsibility for designing these goods and services, they provide essential information and advice during the product-design process, especially regarding the challenges and constraints involved in creating actual products on time and within budget.

Once the actual goods and services are designed, operations managers must determine the processes needed to produce them and get them to the customer. A **process** is a set of related activities that transform inputs into outputs, thus adding value. Once these processes are designed, operations managers also play a key role in determining where they will be performed, what organizations will perform them, and how the processes will be organized and coordinated.

The most obvious processes are those directly involved in the production of goods and services. But there are many other processes that play necessary "supporting roles." For example, purchasing

process A set of related activities that transform inputs into outputs, thus adding value.

Operations managers oversee the processes needed to produce products and get them to customers, including inventory control, project scheduling, and managing value chains.

and inventory management processes ensure that the firm has an adequate supply of high-quality materials, parts, and components needed to produce the goods without delays or disruptions.

Let's take a closer look at some of the functions that operations managers perform to move goods and services from the drawing board to the final user.

17-2a Process Selection and Facility Layout

Once a product is designed, operations managers must determine the best way to produce it. This involves determining the most efficient processes, deciding the best sequence in which to arrange those processes, and designing the appropriate layout of production and distribution facilities. Well-designed processes and facility layouts enable a firm to produce high-quality products effectively and efficiently, giving it a competitive advantage. Poorly designed processes can result in production delays, quality problems, and high costs.

There are several ways to organize processes. The best approach depends on considerations such as the volume of production and the degree of standardization of the product.

"THE OTHER PART OF OUTSOURCING IS THIS: IT SIMPLY SAYS WHERE THE WORK CAN BE DONE OUTSIDE BETTER THAN IT CAN BE DONE INSIDE, WE SHOULD DO IT."

—ALPHONSO ROY JACKSON, FORMER U.S. SECRETARY OF HOUSING AND URBAN DEVELOPMENT

- Firms often use a *product layout* when they produce goods that are relatively standardized and produced in large volumes. This type of layout organizes machinery, equipment, and other resources according to the specific sequence of operations that must be performed. The machinery used in this type of layout is often highly specialized, designed to perform one specific task *very* efficiently. One classic example of a product layout is an assembly line, where the product being produced moves from one station to another in a fixed sequence, with the machinery and workers at each station performing specialized tasks. Services that provide a high volume of relatively standardized products also use flow-shop processes. For example, fast-food restaurants often use a simple product layout to prepare sandwiches, pizzas, or tacos in a standard sequence of steps.

- A *process layout* is used by many firms that need to produce small batches of goods that require a degree of customization. This approach arranges equipment according to the type of task performed. For example, in a machine shop, all of the drills may be located in one area, all of the lathes in another area, and all of the grinders in yet another. Unlike assembly lines and other product layouts, a process layout doesn't require work to be performed in a specific sequence; instead, the product can be moved from one type of machinery to another in whatever sequence is necessary. Thus, process layouts can be used to produce a variety of products without the need for expensive retooling. But this flexibility sometimes comes at the cost of longer processing times and more complex planning and control systems. Also, because the machinery and equipment used in a process layout is usually more general-purpose in nature and may be used to produce a greater variety of goods, the process layout requires workers to be more versatile than those employed in a product layout.

- A *cellular layout* falls between the product layout and the process layout. It groups different types of machinery and equipment into self-contained cells. A production facility might have several cells, each designed to efficiently produce a family of parts (or entire products) that have similar processing requirements. Like an assembly line, the product moves from one station in the cell to the next in a specific sequence. However, unlike most assembly lines, cells are relatively small and are designed to be operated by a few workers who perform a wider array of tasks than assembly-line workers.

■ A *fixed position layout* is used for goods that must be produced at a specific site (such as a building or a dam) or that are so large and bulky that it isn't feasible to move them from station to station (such as a ship or commercial airplane). Even some services, such as concerts or sporting events that are performed at a specific location, use this approach. In a fixed position layout, the good or service stays in one place, and the employees, machinery, and equipment are brought to the fixed site when needed during various stages of the production process.

17-2b Facility Location

There is an old saying in real estate that the three most important factors determining the value of a property are "location, location, and location." There is no doubt that the location is also important to operations managers. The location of facilities can have an important influence on the efficiency and effectiveness of an organization's processes.

For some types of facilities, the location decision is dominated by one key consideration. A coal mine, for instance, must be located where there's coal. But for many other types of facilities, the decision is more complex. Exhibit 17.2 identifies some key factors that operations managers evaluate when they decide where to locate a facility, but the importance of each factor varies depending on the specific industry. For instance, many service firms place primary interest on locating close to their markets, while manufacturing firms are often more concerned about the cost and availability of land and labor and access to highways, railways, and port facilities.

17-2c Inventory Control: Knowing When to Hold 'Em

Inventories are stocks of goods or other items held by an organization. Manufacturing firms usually hold inventories of raw materials, components and parts, work in process, and finished goods. Retail firms don't normally hold work in process or raw materials, but they do hold inventories of the finished goods they sell as well as basic supplies that they need.

Deciding how much inventory to hold can be a real challenge for operations managers because increasing (or decreasing) the amount of inventory involves both benefits and costs. For example, benefits of holding larger inventories include:

■ **Smoother Production Schedules:** A candy maker might produce more candy than it needs in August and September and hold the excess in

> **inventory** Stocks of goods or other items held by organizations.

EXHIBIT 17.2	FACTORS THAT AFFECT LOCATION DECISIONS
General Location Factors	**Examples of Specific Considerations**
Adequacy of Utilities	Is the supply of electricity reliable?
	Is clean water available?
Land	Is adequate land available for a facility?
	How much does the land cost?
Labor Market Conditions	Are workers with the right skills available?
	How expensive is labor?
Transportation Factors	Is the location near customers and suppliers?
	Is appropriate transportation nearby?
Quality-of-Life Factors	What is the climate like?
	Are adequate healthcare facilities available?
Legal and Political Environment	Does the local government support new businesses?
	What are the local taxes, fees, and regulations?

© Cengage Learning®

inventory so that it can meet the surge in demand for Halloween treats without investing in more production capacity.

- **Protection against Stock-Outs and Lost Sales:** Holding larger inventories reduces the chance of stock-outs and lost sales due to supply disruptions or unexpected surges in demand.

- **Reduced Ordering Costs:** Every time a company orders supplies, it incurs paperwork and handling costs. Holding a larger average inventory reduces the number of orders the firm must make and thus reduces ordering costs.

But holding larger inventories involves costs as well as benefits:

- **Tied-Up Funds:** Items in inventory don't generate revenue until they're sold, so holding large inventories can tie up funds that could be better used elsewhere within the organization.

- **Additional Holding Costs:** Bigger inventories require more storage space, which can mean extra costs for heating, cooling, taxes, insurance, and more.

- **Increased Risk:** Holding large inventories exposes the firm to the risk of losses due to spoilage, depreciation, and obsolescence.

Operations managers determine the optimal amount of inventory by comparing the costs and benefits associated with different levels of inventory. In our discussion of lean manufacturing, we'll see that one recent trend has been toward finding ways to reduce inventory levels at every stage of the supply chain.

17-2d Project Scheduling

Projects such as constructing a new production facility, developing a new commercial airliner, or filming a movie are complex and expensive endeavors. It's vital to monitor them carefully to avoid major delays or cost overruns. The **critical path method (CPM)** is one of the most important tools that operations managers use to manage such projects. We can illustrate the basic idea behind this tool by looking at a simple example in which a theater company wants to stage a play. Exhibit 17.3 presents the steps involved in this project.

critical path method (CPM) A project-management tool that illustrates the relationships among all the activities involved in completing a project and identifies the sequence of activities likely to take the longest to complete.

EXHIBIT 17.3   ACTIVITIES INVOLVED IN PRESENTING A PLAY

Activity	Description	Immediate Predecessor(s)	Estimated Completion Time (Weeks)
A	Select Play	None	2
B	Select Cast	A (must know play to know what roles are available)	4
C	Design Sets	A (must know play before sets can be designed)	4
D	Design Costumes	A (must know play to determine what costumes are needed)	5
E	Buy Materials for Sets	C (set must be designed to determine types and quantities of materials needed to build it)	2
F	Buy Materials for Costumes	D (costumes must be designed before materials for costumes are determined)	2
G	Build Sets	E (must have materials in order to build the sets)	4
H	Make Costumes	B, F (must have materials in order to make the costumes, and must know actors' sizes to ensure that costumes fit)	6
I	Initial Rehearsals	B (actors must be selected for each role before they can rehearse their parts)	2
J	Final (Dress) Rehearsal	G, H, I (costumes and sets must be completed, and initial rehearsals performed, before the final rehearsal can occur)	1
K	Perform Play (end of project)	J	N/A

© Cengage Learning®

Notice that Exhibit 17.3 identifies **immediate predecessors** for all of the activities except activity A. *Immediate predecessors* are activities that must be completed before another activity can begin. For example, it is clear that the cast for the play cannot be determined until the play has been selected, so activity A (selecting the play) is an immediate predecessor to activity B (selecting the cast). Similarly, since sets can't be built without lumber, paint, and other materials, activity E (buying materials for the sets) is an immediate predecessor for activity G (building the sets).

USING THE CRITICAL PATH METHOD TO FOCUS EFFORTS

Now look at Exhibit 17.4, which is a CPM network for the theater project. This network shows how all of the activities in the theater project are related to each other. The direction of the arrows shows the immediate predecessors for each activity. Notice that arrows go from activities B (selecting the cast) *and* F (purchasing material for the costumes) to activity H (making the costumes). This indicates that *both* of these activities are immediate predecessors for activity H—the costumes can't be made without material, and they must be made in the correct sizes to fit the actors. But also notice that no arrow links activities B and C. This shows that these are independent activities; in other words, the theater company doesn't have to select the cast before it designs the sets (or vice versa).

We can use Exhibit 17.4 to illustrate some basic concepts used in CPM analysis. A *path* is a sequence of activities that *must be completed in the order specified by the arrows* for the overall project to be completed. You can trace several paths in our example by following a series of arrows from start to finish. For example, one path is A → B → I → J → K, and another path is A → C → E → G → J → K.

The **critical path** consists of the sequence of activities that takes the longest to complete. A *delay in any activity on a critical path is likely to delay the completion of the entire project*. Thus, operations managers watch activities on the critical path very carefully and take actions to help ensure that they remain on schedule. We've shown the critical path for the theater project (A → D → F → H → J → K) with red arrows on our diagram.

Distinguishing between the critical path and other paths can help operations managers allocate resources more efficiently. Activities that aren't on the critical path can be delayed without causing a delay in the overall completion of the project—as long as the delay isn't too great. In CPM terminology, these activities have *slack*. When operations managers see delays in critical path activities, they may be able to keep the project on track by diverting manpower and other resources from activities with slack to activities on the critical path.

17-2e Designing and Managing Value Chains

Perhaps the most important function of operations management is the design and management of value chains. A **value chain** is the network of relationships that channels the flow of inputs, information, and financial

---

Exhibit 17.4

A CPM Network for Staging a Play

© Cengage Learning®

---

immediate predecessors Activities in a project that must be completed before some other specified activity can begin.

critical path The sequence of activities in a project that is expected to take the longest to complete.

value chain The network of relationships that channels the flow of inputs, information, and financial resources through all of the processes directly or indirectly involved in producing goods and services and distributing them to customers.

resources through all of the processes directly or indirectly involved in producing goods and services and distributing them to customers.

An organization's value chain clearly includes its supply chain, which consists of the organizations, activities, and processes involved in the physical flow of goods, from the raw materials stage to the final consumer. In fact, some organizations use the terms *value chain* and *supply chain* interchangeably. But a value chain is a broader concept; in addition to the supply chain, it includes activities and processes involved in *acquiring customers*—such as contract negotiations and customer financing—as well as activities and processes involved in *keeping customers* by providing services after the sale, such as performing warranty repairs, offering call center assistance, and helping customers recycle used goods. In a value chain, the main focus is on the customer; in contrast, the supply chain is more oriented toward traditional production relationships.[4]

One of the most important issues that operations managers examine when they design value chains is the tradeoff between vertical integration and outsourcing. **Vertical integration** occurs when a firm attempts to gain more control over its value chain by either developing the ability to perform processes previously performed by other organizations in the chain or by acquiring those organizations. **Outsourcing** is essentially the opposite of vertical integration; it involves arranging for other organizations to perform value chain functions that were previously performed internally.

In recent years, the trend in value chain design has been to rely more on outsourcing and less on vertical integration. Outsourcing allows a firm to shed functions it doesn't perform well in order to focus on its areas of strength. It also frees people, money, and other resources that had been tied up in the outsourced activities, allowing these resources to be employed in more profitable ways.

Even when a firm decides to perform processes itself, it still faces a choice: should it perform these functions domestically, or should it offshore these activities? **Offshoring** means moving processes previously performed domestically to a foreign location. It is important to realize that offshoring is *not* the same thing as outsourcing processes to other organizations. Offshoring doesn't require outsourcing; a firm often offshores processes by directly investing in its

Offshoring involves moving activities previously performed domestically to a foreign location.

own foreign facilities. Similarly, outsourcing doesn't require a firm to go offshore; activities can be outsourced to other *domestic* firms. Despite this distinction, many firms have combined these approaches by hiring organizations in other countries to perform some of the processes that they previously performed at their own domestic facilities.

It is also worth noting that offshoring can go in both directions. Just as American firms offshore processes to other countries, some foreign companies offshore some of their processes to the United States. For example, several Japanese, European, and Korean automakers now have extensive design and production facilities in the United States.

One common reason for offshoring by U.S. firms is to take advantage of less expensive labor. But other factors can also play a role. Land and other resources also may be less expensive in developing nations than in the United States. And some foreign governments, eager to attract American investments, may offer financial incentives or other inducements. In addition, many foreign markets are growing much more rapidly than the relatively mature U.S. market. Firms often find it advantageous to locate production facilities close to these rapidly growing markets.

While foreign outsourcing can often reduce costs, it also can complicate value chains and create coordination problems. And it can expose the firm to certain types of risks. When a firm outsources important functions, it may have to entrust others in its value chain with confidential information and intellectual property, such as copyrighted material or patented designs. These strategic assets have less legal protection in some countries than in the United States, so providing access to foreign firms may increase the risk that the firm's intellectual property will be pirated

vertical integration
Performance of processes internally that were previously performed by other organizations in a supply chain.

outsourcing
Arranging for other organizations to perform supply chain functions that were previously performed internally.

offshoring Moving production or support processes to foreign countries.

or counterfeited. This issue has been of greatest concern when firms have outsourced some of their supply chain functions to organizations in China.[5]

Given the trend toward offshoring and outsourcing, value chains (and the supply chains at their core) have become increasingly complex, often involving many different organizations and processes located in many different countries. Modern operations managers rely on sophisticated *supply chain management software* to streamline the communications among supply chain participants and to help them plan and coordinate their efforts.

The newest versions of **enterprise resource planning (ERP)** software take supply chain management to its highest level. ERP initially focused on integrating the flow of information among *all* aspects of a single organization's operations—accounting, finance, sales and marketing, production, and human resources. But the newest versions go beyond a single organization to help manage activities along an entire supply chain or value chain. The common information system makes it easier for organizations throughout the chain to communicate and coordinate their activities.

ERP systems do have some drawbacks. They are complex, expensive, and difficult to implement, and they require users to learn new ways to enter and access data. Productivity can actually fall until users become accustomed to these new methods. But despite these challenges, ERP systems have become very popular. And they continue to evolve and take advantage of new technologies. One of the newest developments is the arrival of web-based ERP systems that can be "rented" from online providers—a strategy that reduces the need to invest in new hardware and software. The use of web-based ERP services is an example of cloud computing discussed in Chapter 16.[6]

17-3 IMPLICATIONS OF A SERVICE-BASED ECONOMY: RESPONDING TO DIFFERENT CHALLENGES

Exhibit 17.5 illustrates how services differ from tangible goods. These differences present a number of challenges to service providers. One key challenge arises because customers often participate in the provision of services, which means that service providers have less control over how the process is carried out, how long it takes to complete, and whether the result is satisfactory. For instance, the accuracy of a doctor's diagnosis depends on how honestly and completely the patient answers the

EXHIBIT 17.5 DIFFERENCES BETWEEN GOODS AND SERVICES

Goods	Services
Are tangible: They have a physical form and can be seen, touched, handled, etc.	Are intangible: They can be "experienced," but they don't have a physical form.
Can be stored in an inventory.	Must be consumed *when* they are produced.
Can be shipped.	Must be consumed *where* they are provided.
Are produced independently of the consumer.	Often require the customer to be actively involved in their production.
Can have at least *some* aspects of their quality determined objectively by measuring defects or deviations from desired values.	Intangible nature means quality is based mainly on customer perceptions.

© Cengage Learning®

doctor's questions. And the amount of time the doctor spends with each patient will depend on the seriousness of the problem and the complexity of the diagnosis and treatment.

17-3a Designing the Servicescape

Because of the interaction between customers and service providers, the design of service facilities often must take the experiences of the participants into account. A **servicescape** is the environment in which the customer and service provider interact. A well-designed servicescape can have a positive influence on the attitudes and perceptions of both the customer and those who provide the service. A poor servicescape can have the opposite effect.[7]

The design of servicescapes centers on three types of factors: ambience; functionality; and signs, symbols, and artifacts.

- *Ambience* refers to factors such as decor, background music, lighting, noise levels, and even scents. For example, massage therapists often use low light, soothing background music, and pleasant scents to create a relaxing atmosphere for a massage.

- *Functionality* involves how easy is

enterprise resource planning (ERP) Software-based approach to integrate an organization's (and in the sophisticated versions, a value chain's) information flows.

servicescape The environment in which a customer and service provider interact.

it for the customers to move through the facility and find what they are looking for.

- *Signs, symbols,* and *artifacts* convey information to customers and create impressions. Obviously, signs like "Place Your Order Here" and "Pick Up Your Order Here" provide useful information that helps consumers maneuver through the service encounter. But other signs and symbols can be used to create favorable impressions. For instance, lawyers and accountants often prominently display their diplomas, professional certifications, and awards in their offices to communicate their qualifications and accomplishments to their clients.

17-3b How Big Is Big Enough?

Because services are intangible and often must be experienced at the time they are created, service providers can't produce the service in advance and store it to meet temporary surges in demand. This can create challenges for operations managers because the demand for many types of services varies significantly, depending on the season, the day of the week, or the time of day. During peak lunch and dinner hours, popular restaurants tend to be very busy—often with crowds waiting to get a table. The same restaurants may be nearly empty during the mid-afternoon or late at night. Given such fluctuations in demand, the selection of *capacity*—the number of customers the service facility can accommodate per time period—becomes a crucial consideration.

If the capacity of a service facility is too small, customers facing long waits during periods of peak demand may well take their business elsewhere. But a facility large enough to handle peak capacity is more expensive to build; costs more to heat, cool, and insure; and may have substantial excess capacity during off-peak periods. Operations managers must weigh these drawbacks against the ability to handle a larger number of customers during peak hours.

Many service firms try to minimize this tradeoff by finding ways to spread out demand so that big surges don't occur. One way to do this is to give customers an incentive to use the service at off-peak times. Many bars and restaurants have "happy hours" or "early-bird specials." Similarly, movie theaters have lower prices for matinée

automation Replacing human operation and control of machinery and equipment with some form of programmed control.

robot A reprogrammable machine that is capable of manipulating materials, tools, parts, and specialized devices in order to perform a variety of tasks.

showings, and resort hotels offer reduced rates during their off seasons.

17-4 THE TECHNOLOGY OF OPERATIONS

Now let's take a close look at how technology has revolutionized operations management. Some of the new technologies involve the increasing sophistication of machinery and equipment. Others involve advances in software and information technology. The impact of these technological advances is greatest when the automated machinery is directly linked to the new software running on powerful new computers.

17-4a Automation: The Rise of the Machine

For the past half century, one of the biggest trends in operations management has been increased **automation** of many processes. Automation means replacing human operation and control of machinery and equipment with some form of programmed control. The use of automated systems has become increasingly common—and increasingly sophisticated.

Automation began in the early 1950s with primitive programmed machines. But in recent decades, **robots** have taken automation to a whole new level. Robots are reprogrammable machines that can manipulate materials, tools, parts, and specialized devices in order to perform a variety of tasks. Some robots have special sensors that allow them to "see," "hear," or "feel" their environment. Many

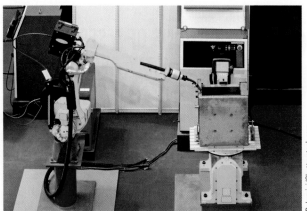

Balonici/Shutterstock.com

Automation involves programming machines and equipment to carry out tasks previously performed by humans.

robots are mobile and can even be guided over rugged terrain.

Robots offer many advantages to firms:

- They often perform jobs that most human workers find tedious, dirty, dangerous, or physically demanding.

- They don't get tired, so they can work very long hours while maintaining a consistently high level of performance.

- They are flexible; unlike old dogs, robots *can* be taught new tricks because they are reprogrammable.

Robots are most commonly used for tasks such as welding, spray painting, and assembling products, but they can do many other things ranging from packaging frozen pizza to disposing of hazardous waste.

17-4b Software Technologies

Several types of software have become common in operations management, and as the processing power of computers has improved, the capabilities of these applications have become increasingly sophisticated. Some of the most common examples include:

- **Computer-aided design (CAD)** software provides powerful drawing and drafting tools that enable users to create and edit blueprints and design drawings quickly and easily. Current CAD programs allow users to create 3-D drawings.

- **Computer-aided engineering (CAE)** software enables users to test, analyze, and optimize their designs through computer simulations. CAE software can help engineers find and correct design flaws *before* production.

- **Computer-aided manufacturing (CAM)** software takes the electronic design for a product and creates the programmed instructions that robots and other automated equipment must follow to produce that product as efficiently as possible.

Today, **computer-aided design and computer-aided manufacturing** software are often combined into a single system, called **CAD/CAM**. This enables CAD designs to flow directly to CAM programs, which then send instructions directly to the automated equipment on the factory floor to guide the production process.

> "CUSTOMERS DON'T EXPECT YOU TO BE PERFECT. THEY DO EXPECT YOU TO FIX THINGS WHEN THEY GO WRONG."
>
> —DONALD PORTER, VICE PRESIDENT, BRITISH AIRWAYS

When a CAD/CAM software system is integrated with robots and other high-tech equipment, the result is **computer-integrated manufacturing (CIM)**, in which the whole design and production process is highly automated. The speed of computers, the ability to reprogram computers rapidly, and the integration of all these functions make it possible to switch from the design and production of one good to another quickly and efficiently. CIM allows firms to produce custom-designed products for individual customers quickly and at costs almost as low as those associated with mass-production techniques, thus allowing firms to pursue the strategy of mass customization mentioned at the beginning of this chapter.

17-5 FOCUS ON QUALITY

Almost everyone agrees that quality is important. But the concept of quality is tough to define—even expert opinions differ. For our purposes, we'll adopt the view that quality is defined in terms of how well a good or service satisfies customer preferences.

Why is quality so important? First, better quality clearly improves effectiveness (creates value) since consumers perceive high-quality goods as having greater value than low-quality goods. But finding ways to increase quality can also lead to greater efficiency because the cost of poor quality can be very high. When a firm detects defective products, it must scrap, rework, or repair

computer-aided design (CAD) Drawing and drafting software that enables users to create and edit blueprints and design drawings quickly and easily.

computer-aided engineering (CAE) Software that enables users to test, analyze, and optimize their designs.

computer-aided manufacturing (CAM) Software that takes the electronic design for a product and creates the programmed instructions that robots must follow to produce that product as efficiently as possible.

computer-aided design/computer-aided manufacturing (CAD/CAM) A combination of software that can be used to design output and send instructions to automated equipment to perform the steps needed to produce this output.

computer-integrated manufacturing (CIM) A combination of CAD/CAM software with flexible manufacturing systems to automate almost all steps involved in designing, testing, and producing a product.

Amazon Prime Air: Drones!

Amazon.com first revolutionized online shipping costs by offering free shipping on orders of $25 or more. Then, with the introduction of Amazon Prime, which cost $99 annually, Amazon began offering *two-day shipping*—at no extra charge—on millions of products. Today, Amazon continues to upgrade shipping options by expanding the number of distribution centers it has so it can roll out *same-day shipping*, including Sunday delivery (in partnership with the U.S. Postal Service).

AP Images/Peter Endig/picture-alliance/dpa

According to Amazon CEO Jeff Bezos, the next step in revolutionizing Amazon delivery will come from Prime Air, which will deliver packages of five pounds or less (86% of all Amazon purchases) using automated delivery via small, GPS-enabled drones. At the warehouse, an item will be boxed, picked up by a small flying robot, and delivered right to the customer's front door, all in about 30 minutes. Bezos says, "I know this looks like science fiction. It's not. It could be a ten-mile radius from a fulfillment center. So, in urban areas, you could actually cover very significant portions of the population."

While critics call Prime Air a PR stunt, mining companies already use drones with high-def cameras to calculate how much material has been removed from work sites. Likewise, drones are now being used for surveying work to map terrain, or in films, to provide flyover action shots in James Bond and Harry Potter movies. In Japan, farmers have been using drones for two decades to spray fertilizer and pesticides on rice fields.

Amazon will conduct research to roll out Prime Air, and activate it after the FAA enacts airspace regulations.[8]

---

them. And the costs of poor quality can be even higher when a firm *doesn't* catch defects before shipping products to consumers. These costs include handling customer complaints, warranty repair work, loss of goodwill, and the possibility of bad publicity or lawsuits. In the long run, firms often find that improving quality reduces these costs by more than enough to make up for their investment.

These ideas aren't especially new. W. Edwards Deming, viewed by many as the father of the quality movement, first proposed the relationship between quality and business success in the early 1950s. His ideas, which came to be known as the *Deming Chain Reaction*, are summarized in Exhibit 17.6.

17-5a Waking Up to the Need for Quality

In the years immediately after World War II, most Japanese goods had a reputation for being cheap and shoddy. But during the 1950s, many Japanese firms sought advice from Deming and other U.S. quality gurus. They learned to view quality improvement as a *continuous* process that was the responsibility of all employees in the organization. During the 1950s and 1960s, the quality of Japanese goods slowly but steadily improved.

By the early 1970s, many Japanese firms had achieved a remarkable turnaround, with quality levels that exceeded those of companies in most other countries (including the United States) by a wide margin. This improved quality was a major reason why Japanese firms rapidly gained global market share, often at the expense of American firms that had faced little competition in years immediately following World War II.

17-5b How American Firms Responded to the Quality Challenge

When operations managers at American firms realized how far they trailed the Japanese in quality, they made a real effort to change their ways. Like the Japanese a few decades earlier, American business leaders began to view improving the quality of their goods and services as a key to regaining international competitiveness.

TOTAL QUALITY MANAGEMENT The first result of this newfound emphasis on quality was the development of an approach called **total quality management**, better known as TQM. There are several

total quality management (TQM) An approach to quality improvement that calls for everyone within an organization to take responsibility for improving quality and emphasizes the need for a long-term commitment to continuous improvement.

Exhibit 17.6

The Deming Chain Reaction: Improved Quality Helps the Business's Bottom Line

Improve quality

Costs decrease because of less rework, fewer mistakes, fewer delays and snags, and better use of time and materials

Productivity improves

Capture the market with better quality and lower price

Stay in business

Provide jobs and more jobs

© Cengage Learning®

variations, but all versions of TQM share the following characteristics:

- **Customer Focus:** TQM recognizes that quality should be defined by the preferences and perceptions of customers.

- **Emphasis on Building Quality throughout the Organization:** TQM views quality as the concern of every department and every employee.

- **Empowerment of Employees:** Most TQM programs give teams of workers the responsibility and authority to make and implement decisions to improve quality.

- **Focus on Prevention Rather Than Correction:** The TQM philosophy agrees with the old adage that an "ounce of prevention is worth a pound of cure." Thus, TQM pursues a strategy of preventing mistakes that create defects.

- **Long-Run Commitment to Continuous Improvement:** TQM requires firms to adopt a focus on making improvements in quality a way of life.

In many cases, American firms using TQM attempt to reduce defects by using **poka-yokes**—the Japanese term for "mistake proofing." Poka-yokes are simple procedures built into the production process that either prevent workers from making mistakes or help workers quickly catch and correct mistakes if they do occur. One simple example of a poka-yoke would be providing assembly workers with "kits" that contain exactly enough parts to complete one unit of work at a time. If the worker completes an assembly and sees a part left over, it's clear that a mistake has been made, and he or she can correct it on the spot.[9]

THE MOVE TO SIX SIGMA During the 1990s, another approach to quality improvement, known as **Six Sigma**, became increasingly popular. Six Sigma shares some characteristics with TQM, such as an organization-wide focus on quality, emphasis on finding and eliminating causes of errors or defects (prevention rather than correction), and a long-term focus on continuous quality improvement. Also like TQM, it relies on teams of workers to carry out specific projects to improve quality. At any given time, a firm may have several Six Sigma projects under way, and the goal of each is to achieve the Six Sigma level of quality.

But Six Sigma differs from TQM in other respects. Unlike TQM, it has a single unifying measure: to reduce defects of any operation or process to a level of no more than 3.4 per million opportunities. Attaining this level of quality represents a rigorous and challenging goal. Six Sigma also differs from TQM in its reliance on extensive (and expensive) employee training and reliance on expert guidance. The techniques used in the Six Sigma approach are quite advanced, and their application requires a high level of expertise.

17-5c Quality Standards and Initiatives

Another way firms try to improve quality is to launch programs designed to achieve certification or recognition from outside authorities. Two common approaches are participation in the Baldrige National Quality Program and seeking certification under the International Organization for Standardization's ISO 9000 standards.

THE BALDRIGE NATIONAL QUALITY PROGRAM Congress passed the Malcolm Baldrige National Quality

poka-yokes Simple methods incorporated into a production process designed to eliminate or greatly reduce errors.

Six Sigma An approach to quality improvement characterized by very ambitious quality goals, extensive training of employees, and a long-term commitment to working on quality-related issues.

At UPS, Orion Refines the Delivery Process for Efficiency

Throughout its history, UPS has studied and dissected the process of package delivery down to the smallest detail. Drivers have long been trained to walk briskly (not run) and avoid left turns (they're less efficient than right turns).

From the receipt of a package to its delivery, having a refined process is critical for UPS. It is the world's largest package delivery company, operating in 200 countries and territories. Its drivers cover 55,000 routes per day in the United States alone.

As the number of routes is increasing, the type of delivery on each route is changing. Previously, UPS focused on commercial deliveries. Drivers would deliver and pick up multiple packages at a single business location. By 2018, however, UPS estimates that half of all deliveries will be residential (one package, one house) thanks to the explosion in e-commerce.

AP Images/David Goldman

To add further complexity, UPS's "My Choice" service allows customers to choose the time and location of their deliveries. When any of the 12.9 million subscribers to My Choice makes a change in delivery preferences, it affects the route planned by the driver delivering the package. Each driver makes an average of 120 stops each day, so reshuffling deliveries throughout the day for each change wreaks havoc on the driver's schedule and efficiency.

At the same time, the company knows that it can save $50 million per year by reducing each of its routes by an average of just a single mile per day.

Enter ORION (On-Road Integrated Optimization and Navigation). A team of 50 UPS engineers wrote the 1,000-page algorithm that searches for the best possible way for drivers to organize their routes and calculates the most efficient path between a variety of points. Every time a change to a driver's route is needed, ORION considers up to 200,000 options before indicating the best scheduling alternative. ORION then reorganizes the entire route to accommodate the change and maintain efficiency and consistency.

Currently 40% of domestic UPS routes use ORION technology to schedule deliveries. By 2017, UPS expects all 55,000 routes to be using ORION, saving the company $300 million to $400 million annually—even with a few left turns.[10]

> "QUALITY IS MORE IMPORTANT THAN QUANTITY. ONE HOME RUN IS MUCH BETTER THAN TWO DOUBLES."
> —STEVE JOBS, CO-FOUNDER OF APPLE

Improvement Act of 1987 in an effort to encourage American firms to become more competitive in the global economy by vigorously pursuing improvements in quality and productivity. Winners of the Baldrige Award must demonstrate excellence in seven areas: leadership; strategic planning; customer and market focus; measurement, analysis, and knowledge management; human resource focus; process management; and business results.

Firms that participate in the **Baldrige National Quality Program** receive benefits even if they don't win the award. Every participating firm receives a detailed report prepared by expert evaluators identifying areas of strength and areas where improvement is needed. Considering the normal fees that high-powered consulting firms charge for similar reports, the information and advice a firm gets for the fee charged to participate in the Baldrige program (which for manufacturing, service, and small businesses is $9,600 to $18,000) are a tremendous bargain![11]

ISO 9000 CERTIFICATION Founded in 1947, ISO is a network of national standards institutes from more than 160 nations that have worked together to develop over 18,500 international standards for a wide array of industries. ISO standards ensure that goods produced in one

Baldrige National Quality Program A national program to encourage American firms to focus on quality improvement.

Leaner and Meaner

Having sold nearly six million vehicles, Toyota is the dominant player in Japan's hybrid car market. At a million cars, Honda is a distant second. Honda hopes to close that gap, however, through advanced robotics and high-tech assembly line processes in its brand-new factory in Yorii, Japan, which is 30% more efficient than the facility it replaces. Honda will not only be able to produce more hybrid Fit hatchbacks (up to

Nataliya Hora/Shutterstock.com

250,000 per year), it will be able to sell them at lower prices than the Toyota Aqua, against which it competes.

So what produced Honda's increased efficiency? New high-speed presses and die swapping machines, which stamp out body panels, are 40% faster. New machinery in the paint shop uses 40% less energy. Robots, instead of workers, now install windows, seats, and doors. Likewise, ten welding robots, which attach panels to the car body, weld 126 attachment points compared to the 16 old robots that only welded 94 attachment points—and they do so at twice the speed. Overall, the assembly line has 9% fewer steps, which reduced the time to assemble a car by 40 minutes. Together, these improvements produced a hyper-efficient factory that makes great cars at a great price.

Honda President Takanobu Ito concludes, "For Honda to progress, we must advance the technology of manufacturing, not just the technology of our products."[14]

country will meet the requirements of buyers in another country. This benefits buyers by giving them the ability to purchase from foreign sellers with confidence, thus giving them a wider array of choices. It also benefits sellers by allowing them to compete more successfully in global markets.[12]

Most of the standards established by the ISO are industry-specific. But in 1987, the ISO developed and published the **ISO 9000** family of standards. The goal of this effort was to articulate an international consensus on good quality-management practices that could be applied to virtually any company. Similar to the other quality initiatives we've discussed, ISO 9000 standards define quality in terms of the ability to satisfy customer preferences and require the firm to implement procedures for continuous quality improvement.

There are several standards in the ISO 9000 family, but the most basic—and the only one for which organizations can be certified—is ISO 9001, which specifies the requirements for a quality-management system. (Other ISO 9000 standards are concerned with the documentation, training, and the economic and financial aspects of quality management.) As of 2012, over 1.1 million organizations worldwide had earned ISO 9001 certificates, but the number of U.S. firms with ISO 9001 certification lags that of several other nations. Only about 26,000 U.S. organizations

had been certified in 2012, compared to over 334,000 in China and 137,000 in Italy.[13]

 17-6
THE MOVE TO BE LEAN AND GREEN: CUTTING COST AND CUTTING WASTE

Lean production refers to a set of strategies and practices to eliminate waste, which is defined as any function or activity that uses resources but doesn't create value. Eliminating waste can lead to dramatic improvements in efficiency. For example, Louis Vuitton produces some of the most expensive handmade bags and purses in the world. To increase productivity, it switched to teams of 6 to 12 workers who learned to complete multiple production steps. So instead of having 3 workers separately gluing, stitching, and finishing the edges of a flap over and over, 1 worker would do all three steps. Because of that, says CEO Ives Carcelle, "We were able to hire 300 new people without adding a factory."[15]

> **ISO 9000** A family of generic standards for quality management systems established by the International Organization for Standardization.
>
> **lean production** An approach to production that emphasizes the elimination of waste in all aspects of production processes.

17-6a Reducing Investment in Inventory: Just-in-Time to the Rescue

One of the hallmarks of lean systems is a tight control on inventories. In part, this reflects recognition of the costs of holding large inventories that we discussed earlier. But the lean approach also offers another reason for minimizing inventories. Large inventories serve as a buffer that enables a firm to continue operations when problems arise due to poor quality, faulty equipment, or unreliable suppliers—making it easier for firms to live with these problems rather than correct them. Advocates of lean production argue that, in the long run, it is more efficient to improve quality, keep equipment in good working order, and develop reliable supply relationships than to continue compensating for these problems by holding large inventories.

Lean manufacturing avoids overproduction and holding large inventories of finished goods by using **just-in-time (JIT) production** methods. JIT produces only enough goods to satisfy current demand. This approach is called a *pull system* because actual orders "pull" the goods through the production process. The workers at the end of the production process produce just enough of the final product to satisfy actual orders and use just enough parts and materials from preceding stages of production to satisfy their needs. Workers at each earlier stage are expected to produce just enough output at their workstations to replace the amount used by the processes further along in the process—and in so doing they withdraw just the needed amount of parts and other supplies from even earlier processes.

JIT techniques obviously result in very small inventories of finished goods and work in process. But lean firms also hold only small inventories of materials and parts, counting on suppliers to provide them with these items as they need them to meet current demand. In a lean system, *all* organizations in the supply chain use the JIT approach, so that inventories are minimized at each stage. Clearly, this type of system requires incredible coordination among all parts of the supply chain; in fact, the movement toward JIT is a key reason why supply chain management has become so crucial.

JIT does have some potential drawbacks. The most serious problem is that it can leave producers vulnerable to supply disruptions. If a key supplier is unable to make deliveries due to a natural disaster, labor strike, or other problem, the firms further along the supply chain may quickly run out of parts or materials and have to shut down production.

17-6b Lean Thinking in the Service Sector

Employing lean principles in the service sector can be quite a challenge because customers often participate in providing the service. This means a service firm usually has less control over how processes are conducted. But many service firms have benefited from creatively applying lean techniques. Kroger supermarkets used lean thinking to reduce checkout waiting times. Kroger uses Vision, a network of infrared sensors, to count the customers in a store and then determine how many checkout aisles should be opened now and in the next 30 minutes. The system dramatically slashed average checkout times from four minutes a few years ago to just 26 seconds today. As a result, customer satisfaction with checkout speed is up 42%, while sales are up nearly 10%. Kroger Vice President Marnette Perry said, "There are 7 million shoppers at Kroger stores today—we'll save them 25 million minutes today."[16]

17-6c Green Practices: Helping the Firm by Helping the Environment

Many of today's leading firms have also tried to become "greener" by finding environmentally friendly ways to carry out the processes needed to produce and

Green practices aim to achieve sustainability by finding ways to meet the organization's current objectives while protecting and preserving the environment.

---

just-in-time (JIT) production A production system that emphasizes the production of goods to meet actual current demand, thus minimizing the need to hold inventories of finished goods and work in process at each stage of the supply chain.

distribute their goods and services. Green practices include designing facilities to be more energy efficient; using renewable energy sources such as wind, solar, or geothermal power when possible; making use of recyclable materials; switching to paints, lubricants, cleaning fluids, and solvents that are less harmful to the environment; and even providing labeling to help consumers find out which products are the most environmentally friendly.

The long-term goal of many green practices is to achieve *sustainability*, which means finding ways to meet the organization's current objectives while protecting and preserving the environment for future generations. One impediment to even greater acceptance of sustainability initiatives is that some sustainability efforts—such as switching to renewable sources of energy—add to costs.[17] But many firms have found that other sustainability efforts can actually benefit the bottom line. A recent study by Aberdeen Group, a well-known technology research firm, found that firms employing best-in-class sustainability practices not only saw an 8% drop in sustainability-related costs but also experienced a 16% increase in customer retention.[18]

In the late 1990s, the International Organization for Standardization developed a set of standards called **ISO 14000**. This new set of standards focuses on environmental management. As with ISO 9000, the term ISO 14000 actually refers to a family of standards. The broadest of these is ISO 14001. In order to receive ISO 14001 certification, a firm must:

- demonstrate the ability to identify and control the environmental impact of their activities;

- make a commitment to continually improve their environmental performance;

- implement a systematic approach to setting environmental targets and to achieving those targets.

It is important to note that ISO 14000 standards do not establish specific goals for environmental performance; doing so would be very difficult, since ISO is intended to be a generic set of standards that apply to all industries, and each specific industry faces different environmental challenges.[19]

> **ISO 14000** A family of generic standards for environmental management established by the International Organization for Standardization.

The BIG Picture

Operations managers are responsible for "putting it all together" by developing and implementing the processes needed to produce goods and services and distribute them to the target market. Their decisions affect both revenues and costs, going a long way toward determining whether a firm makes a profit or suffers a loss.

The responsibilities of operations managers require them to work closely with other managers throughout their organizations. For example, they must work with marketers and designers to ensure that the desired goods and services move from the drawing board to the final customer on time and within budget. They must work closely with financial managers to ensure that the company invests in the capital goods needed to produce goods and services in the most

efficient manner. And they must work effectively with human resource managers to attract and develop workers who possess the knowledge and skills needed to become world-class competitors. Operations managers must even go beyond their own organization and work effectively with the suppliers and distributors who comprise the firm's value chain.

Operations managers must continuously adapt to changes in technology and in competitive conditions. Key challenges in recent years have centered on the need to continuously improve product quality while finding ways to reduce costs and protect the environment. You can expect the goals of becoming ever leaner—and ever greener—to remain a major focus of operations managers in years to come.

Careers in Operations Management

Plant Supervisor

Responsible for supervising production and warehouse crews, monitoring and maintaining a safe working environment, timely completion of paperwork and records, keeping lines of communication open between the plant, management, scheduling, and sales, coordinating overtime and reviewing production schedules to make sure each piece of equipment has the appropriate manpower, and cross-training employees for multiple tasks and jobs. The ideal candidate has a bachelor's degree, two to four years of manufacturing experience, strong interpersonal, communication, and team-building skills, good analytical and problem-solving skills, ability to analyze cost performance data to improve operations and reduce costs, and be willing to work evenings, night shifts, weekends, and holidays. For more information on this career and other possible careers in operations management, check out Career Transitions.

STUDY TOOLS 17

LOCATED AT BACK OF THE TEXTBOOK

☐ Rip Out Chapter Review Card

LOCATED AT WWW.CENGAGE.COM/LOGIN

☐ Review key term flashcards and create your own using StudyBits

☐ Create and complete practice quizzes based off of your notes and StudyBits

☐ Complete Online activities such as Matching, Fill-in-the-Blank, and Drag and Drop exercises

☐ View chapter highlight box content, including CEO Profiles, What Would You Do Cases, and chapter videos

☐ Track your knowledge and understanding of key concepts in business using 4LTR Online

YOUR FEED- BACK YOUR BOOK

Our research never ends. Continual feedback from you ensures that we keep up with your changing needs.

Personal Finance Appendix

Personal financial management issues affect all of us, young and old alike. How successfully we manage our financial resources affects where we live, how well we can provide for our families, and when (or perhaps even if) we'll be able to retire comfortably. The financial decisions you make and habits you develop now will affect your personal and financial future.

New laws and regulations have changed the way many financial markets operate in recent years. The Dodd-Frank Wall Street Reform and Consumer Protection Act of 2010, passed in the wake of the financial crisis of 2008 and 2009, includes several provisions intended to protect the financial rights of consumers. But many of the law's requirements did not go into effect until mid-2011, so it is too soon to evaluate its long-term impact on consumer rights.

One key provision of the Dodd-Frank Act was the establishment of the Consumer Financial Protection Bureau (CFPB). One early goal of the CFPB was to eliminate confusing and potentially deceptive banking practices related to mortgages, credit cards, and other loan agreements.[1]

budget (personal) A detailed forecast of financial inflows (income) and outflows (expenses) in order to determine your net inflow or outflow for a given period of time.

A-1 YOUR BUDGET

One of the first steps in getting control over your financial situation is to develop a **budget**, which is a detailed forecast of your expected cash inflows (income) and cash outflows (expenditures). You can use your budget to develop your financial plan and to monitor your progress toward achieving your financial goals.

A-1a How Do I Get Started?

You can get a good handle on what should be included in your budget by carefully tracking and analyzing all of your financial transactions for several weeks. This takes discipline and careful record keeping, but once you know where your money comes from and where it goes, you'll have what you need to prepare your budget.

There are many approaches to setting up your budget. If you don't want to build your budget from scratch, you can check out several free online personal finance sites that can help you get started. Two of the most popular are Mint .com (http://www.mint.com) and Yodlee.com (http://www .yodlee.com). If you want more bells and whistles—and more

"THE SAFE WAY TO DOUBLE YOUR MONEY IS TO FOLD IT ONCE OVER AND PUT IT IN YOUR POCKET."

—FRANK "KIN" HUBBARD, CARTOONIST, HUMORIST, AND JOURNALIST

support—than the free sites provide, you can purchase a commercial program such as Quicken, Moneydance, or AceMoney. Basic versions of these programs typically cost less than $50 and provide a wide range of features, such as online banking services, financial calculators, and stock quotes. Most also give you the ability to export data into tax preparation software, making tax filing much simpler.

If you are comfortable with Excel (or other spreadsheet software), another option is to build your own budget. Excel includes budget templates to help you get started, and even more are available online. These templates are generic, so you may want to tweak them to suit your own circumstances. You won't get all of the features provided by the commercial packages, but that isn't necessarily a bad thing. Some people actually find all of the bells and whistles in the commercial applications overwhelming and prefer the straightforward simplicity of a spreadsheet template. Also, the process of "building" the budget yourself may give you a sense of personal satisfaction and a greater appreciation for the budget relationships than you'd get using online sites or commercial software packages.

ASSESSING REVENUES: WHERE DOES MY MONEY COME FROM?

A budget starts with a forecast of your income—the money you bring in. This can come from many different sources. For many people, the paycheck from their job is their primary source of income. But the major source of income for entrepreneurs may be the profits they earn from their businesses. Some people also derive a substantial amount of income from financial investments, such as stocks and bonds, while others earn rental income. Retirees often depend on pensions, Social Security, and private investments for much of their income.

ASSESSING EXPENSES: WHERE DOES IT ALL GO?

Once you have identified the amount of income you expect to receive from various sources, you can turn your focus to the spending side of your budget. To set up your budget, you'll need to be very specific about where your money goes. As we've already mentioned, carefully tracking your expenditures over a period of several weeks can help you identify your spending patterns. Many people who do this are surprised by the habits they uncover. You may find that you're spending a lot more than you thought on video games, music downloads, or clothes. Once you discover your spending patterns, you'll be in a better position to determine the categories of spending to include in your budget and to estimate the amount you'll spend in each category.

UNDERSTANDING YOUR SPENDING HABITS Your expenditures can be classified into discretionary and nondiscretionary categories. The payments you have the most control over are called your **discretionary payments**. Perhaps you like dining out, nightclubbing, or shopping. Perhaps you just have expensive taste in coffee. David Bach, author of *The Automatic Millionaire,* challenges us to look at our "latté factors," meaning the little vices we each find hard to resist. You'll find that something as seemingly minor as a $4 cup of coffee each workday costs you $1,040 each year ($4 × 5 days per week × 52 weeks). Once you realize the true cost of these "latté factors," you'll have a greater incentive to bring them under control.[2] Your budget can be helpful in imposing the discipline you need to accomplish this goal.

Nondiscretionary payments are those you have little control over, such as your monthly rent or car payment, which are set by contract. Your lifestyle may also lock you into other costs that are at least partly nondiscretionary. Given your need to get to school and work, you may have to spend a significant amount of money on gas and car maintenance every month. But with a little flexibility and creativity, you may find that such costs aren't *completely* nondiscretionary. For instance, you might be able to significantly reduce your expenses for gas and car maintenance by carpooling or using mass transit.

You may also want to consider your attitude toward spending. Are you most likely to spend too much money when you are depressed or stressed out? Look at this aspect carefully, and try to be as honest as possible with yourself. The final thing

PathDoc/Shutterstock.com

Setting up a budget requires you to be very specific about where your money goes.

you should consider is who you are with when you spend money. You may find that you tend to spend much more money while hanging out with certain friends.

After you have prepared your budget, you'll need to keep track of your actual expenses and compare them to your budget. And you'll need to adjust your budget periodically to reflect significant changes in your lifestyle, employment status, and financial goals.

A-2 YOUR SAVINGS: BUILDING A SAFETY NET

A **savings account** is an interest-earning account that is intended to satisfy obligations that your checking account cannot handle. Think of your savings account as a "safety net" for unexpected financial challenges, such as a major plumbing repair, the need to replace your car's transmission, or even the loss of your job. Many financial experts suggest that you have enough money in your savings to cover six months of your expenses. The good news is that if you're lucky enough to avoid major problems, your savings account will earn you a bit of interest income.

One technique for establishing a sizable savings balance is to "pay yourself first." This concept, popularized

Vectordiv/Shutterstock.com

---

discretionary payments
Expenditures for which the spender has significant control in terms of the amount and timing.

nondiscretionary payments
Expenditures that the spender has little or no control over.

savings account An interest-bearing account holding funds not needed to meet regular expenditures.

EXHIBIT A.1 WHAT FICO CREDIT SCORES MEAN

Score	Creditworthiness	Percentage of Consumers
Below 500	Very poor	2%
500–599	Poor to below average	13%
600–699	Below average to fair	27%
700–799	Fair to good	45%
800 or Better	Excellent	13%

by David Bach, suggests that you have a predetermined amount from each paycheck automatically deposited into your savings account. Once you've accumulated enough in your savings account to provide an adequate safety net, you can use the "pay yourself first" approach to achieve other financial goals.[3]

Interest rates on savings accounts vary from bank to bank, so you should shop around to find the best rate. In recent years, online savings banks have often provided higher interest rates than traditional banks. Just be sure to look for reputable banks that are insured by the **Federal Deposit Insurance Corporation (FDIC)**. The FDIC is an independent agency created by Congress to maintain stability and public confidence in the nation's financial system, primarily by insuring bank deposits. The FDIC insures individual deposits up to $250,000 per account in FDIC-insured banks.[4]

A-3 YOUR CREDIT: HANDLE WITH CARE!

Credit refers to your ability to obtain goods or resources without having to make immediate payment. One of the most important determinants of the amount of credit you can obtain is your **credit score**, which is a numerical indicator of your creditworthiness. Currently, the most commonly used credit scoring system is the Fair, Isaac and Company (FICO) scale. The FICO scale runs from 300 to 850.

Your individual FICO score is based on several factors, including your payment history, the amount you owe, the type of credit used, and the length of time you've held various credit accounts.[5] As Exhibit A.1 shows,

> "RATHER GO TO BED WITHOUT DINNER THAN TO RISE IN DEBT."
> —BENJAMIN FRANKLIN

about 72% of all Americans have scores between 600 and 800; only 2% have scores below 500, and 13% have scores above 800. A high score makes it easier to get credit on favorable terms.[6] On a $250,000, 30-year fixed mortgage, a borrower with a below-average credit score of 620 will pay $87,422 more interest because of higher interest rates than a borrower with a fair to good credit score of 780.[7]

A-3a Credit Cards: Boon or Bane?

Now let's look at a specific source of credit that is near and dear to many college students' hearts: the **credit card**. A credit card allows its holder to make a purchase now and pay the credit card issuer later.

There are several benefits to having and using credit cards. The most obvious is that credit cards are more convenient and safer than carrying a lot of cash. Credit cards also make it easy to track your expenditures, since you have access to a monthly summary of charges. And many cards offer perks, such as discounts on certain products, extended warranties on purchases, or frequent-flier miles. Another benefit of the *responsible* use of credit cards is that it can improve your credit score by allowing you to establish a history of prompt payments. This can make it easier for you to borrow money when you really need it—such as when you want to buy a car or your first home.

Federal Deposit Insurance Corporation (FDIC) An independent agency created by Congress to maintain stability and public confidence in the nation's financial system, primarily by insuring bank deposits.

credit Allows a borrower to buy a good or acquire an asset without making immediate payment, and to repay the balance at a later time.

credit score A numerical measure of a consumer's creditworthiness.

credit card A card issued by a bank or finance company that allows the cardholder to make a purchase now and pay the credit card issuer later.

One downside of having a credit card is that the "buy now, pay later" aspect of credit card use makes it hard for some people to maintain financial discipline. Another problem is that interest rates on unpaid card balances tend to be very high. Many card issuers also impose a variety of fees that can make a noticeable dent in your wallet. And making late payments or failing to pay what you owe can damage your credit history, hurting your chances of getting additional credit when you need it.

A-3b The Devil in the Details—Understanding Your Credit Card Agreement!

Before you accept a credit card, make sure you read the credit card agreement and understand the main conditions for using that card. Some things to look for include:

- **Grace period:** The period of time that you have to pay your balance before interest or fees are assessed. Some credit card companies expect to receive their payment within 21 days of the credit card statement date. So, it becomes very important to get these bills paid as soon as possible to avoid the interest and other fees.

- **APR (annual percentage rate):** The percentage financing cost charged on unpaid balances. The higher the APR, the greater your interest expense on unpaid balances. Your credit card company may charge different APRs for different types of transactions.

- **Late fees:** May also be assessed if a payment is not received within the grace period. Federal law now caps late fees at $25 for a first offense and $35 for additional late payments.[8]

- **Other fees:** Include *annual fees* (a charge just for the privilege of having a card, whether you use it or not), *over-the-credit-limit fees* if your charges exceed your credit limit, and *balance-transfer fees* if you transfer a balance from one card to another. This isn't a complete list, but it does reflect many of the most common types of fees you might incur. Not all cards are subject to all of these charges; the specific types and amounts of fees can vary considerably from one issuer to another—which is why reading the fine print is important!

grace period The period of time that the credit card holder has to pay outstanding balances before interest or fees are assessed.

annual percentage rate (APR) The interest expense charged on a credit card, expressed as an annual percentage.

IF YOU OWE $5,000 ON A CREDIT CARD BUT ONLY MAKE MINIMUM PAYMENTS, YOU'LL BE REPAYING FOR 273 MONTHS, AND PAY $6,923 IN INTEREST!

—BANKRATE.COM

A-3c Protection for Consumers: New Laws and Regulations

Two recent laws have had a significant impact on credit card practices. The Credit Card Accountability, Responsibility and Disclosure Act of 2009 (often called the CARD Act) requires issuers to give a 45-day notice before making significant changes to credit agreements and prohibits them from raising interest rates on existing balances unless the borrower is more than 60 days late in making required payments. It also requires anyone under the age of 21 who applies for a credit card to either verify proof of income or have an older adult cosign the application. And it places caps on certain types of fees that credit card issuers can charge.

As mentioned at the beginning of this appendix, the Dodd-Frank Act created the Consumer Financial Protection Bureau. One focus of the CFPB's early efforts has been to make it easier for consumers to compare the features and costs of various credit cards so that they can select the ones that best meet their needs. The Dodd-Frank Act also requires lenders, insurance companies, and others who reject your application to provide you with a free copy of your credit score.[9]

A-3d Using Credit Cards Wisely: The Need for Discipline

Although many young adults manage their credit cards without major problems, others are stunned when the credit card bill arrives. Many never read their credit card agreements, so they are taken by surprise by higher-than-expected interest charges and fees. Others simply lack discipline. They succumb to the temptations of a "buy now, pay later" mentality and run up big bills that they can't afford to pay.

The first rule when you have credit card difficulties is to "PUT THE CARD DOWN!" When you find yourself in trouble, stop using the card so you don't compound your difficulties. Make sure you don't use the card again until you've gotten your spending habits under control.

Once you've eliminated the temptation to dig a deeper hole, the next step is to make sure you consistently pay a substantial amount each month toward retiring the debt on that card. Given how high APRs are on the unpaid balances for most credit cards, it is usually a good idea to place a *very* high priority on eliminating these balances as quickly as possible.

If you just can't seem to shake the habit of overspending, consider using cash or a **debit card** instead of a credit card. While a debit card looks like a credit card, there is a big difference. When you use a debit card, money is immediately withdrawn from your bank account, so you "feel the pain" just as if you'd paid in cash. Many people spend less when they use cash or debit cards than when they use credit cards.

Marie C Fields/Shutterstock.com

> "THE BEST TIME TO PLANT A TREE WAS 20 YEARS AGO. THE NEXT BEST TIME IS NOW."
>
> —CHINESE PROVERB

<div class="circle">A-4</div> ## YOUR INVESTMENTS: BUILDING FOR THE FUTURE

Investing involves reducing consumption today in order to acquire assets that build future wealth. In a very real way, investing is like the concept of sowing and reaping. A farmer plants a seed (makes an investment) in anticipation of a harvest (return) that will be much larger than the seed that was planted. When it comes to investing, early is better than late—but late is better than never.

A-4a Building Wealth: The Key IsConsistency— and an Early Start!

Don't talk yourself out of investing just because you don't have much to invest. Even if you start with a small amount, your wealth will eventually grow to a significant amount as long as you stick with it. And the earlier you start the better off you'll be. To see this, take a look at Exhibit A.2, which compares how big your retirement nest egg will be at age 65 for different monthly investment amounts beginning at different ages (and assuming you earn an annual return of 8%). A 30-year-old who invests $60 per month will end up with $137,633 at age 65. Compare this to someone who begins investing $60 per month at age 20, and the results are startling. The investor who starts at age 20 only directly invests $7,200 more ($60 per month for 120 more months) than the investor who starts at age 30. But the earlier investor ends up with a nest egg of $316,472—almost $179,000 more than that of the investor who started at age 30.

The reason for this result is that, over time, you earn interest not only on the money you

debit card A card issued by the bank that allows the customer to make purchases as if the transaction involved cash. In a debit card purchase, the customer's bank account is immediately reduced when the purchase is made.

investing Reducing consumption in the current time period in order to build future wealth.

EXHIBIT A.2	GROWING YOUR INVESTMENT: STARTING EARLY MAKES A DIFFERENCE			
	Starting Age			
Monthly Savings	**20**	**30**	**40**	**50**
$30	$158,236	$68,816	$28,531	$10,381
$60	$316,472	$137,633	$57,062	$20,762
$90	$474,709	$206,449	$85,592	$31,143
$120	$632,945	$275,266	$114,123	$41,525
$150	$791,181	$344,082	$142,654	$51,906

Note: Figures in the table show the amount accumulated at age 65. Results are based on an assumed annual rate of return of 8% compounded monthly.

directly invest but also on the *interest* you've earned in *previous* years—a process known as *compounding*. The earlier you begin investing, the more powerful the compounding effect becomes. By the time an investor reaches age 65, any dollars invested at age 20 have been compounded for a *very long* time, resulting in a big increase in the nest egg. The message of Exhibit A.2 is clear: an early start to investing can lead to dramatically more money when it comes time to retire.

FINANCIAL SECURITIES: WHAT ARE MY INVESTMENT OPTIONS?

Now that we've demonstrated the importance of investing, let's look at some specific types of financial instruments you might want to include in your investment portfolio. Our brief discussion can't hope to cover all of the possibilities, so we'll focus only on some of the most common choices. Keep in mind that, in addition to the financial instruments we describe in this section, many people also hold much of their wealth in other assets. The largest single asset for many households is the equity they have in their home.

Let's begin by looking at *common stock*, which represents ownership in a corporation. Common stock offers the possibility of two types of financial returns. The first, called a *dividend,* is a distribution of profits paid out to the stockholders. Dividends are paid only if the corporation's board of directors declares them—and there is no legal requirement for them to do so. If a corporation is in poor financial shape, its board of directors may decide that it is unable to pay a dividend. But even if a company is highly profitable, its board may decide to reinvest (retain) its profits rather than pay dividends to stockholders.

Investors can earn a second type of return, called a capital gain, if the market price of their stock rises relative to the price they paid for it. But stock prices can go down as well as up—as many investors have painfully discovered in recent years! Thus, it is possible for investors to experience *capital losses* as well as capital gains. Clearly, investing in common stock entails a significant degree of risk. But historically the average rate of return on stocks has been better than the return on many other types of investments.

In addition to common stock, some corporations also offer another type of stock, called *preferred stock.* The two types of stock have some important differences. From the perspective of many investors, the most important distinction is that owners of preferred stock are more likely to receive a dividend than owners of common stock. Preferred stock is normally issued with a stated dividend, and common stockholders can't be paid

any dividend until the preferred dividend is paid in full. Still, even preferred stockholders have no guaranteed legal right to receive a dividend.

A *corporate bond* is another type of corporate security, but it is quite different from stock. A bond is a formal IOU issued by a corporation. While stockholders are the owners of a corporation, bondholders are its creditors. Most bonds are long-term debts that mature (come due) 10 to 30 years after they are issued, though bonds with shorter and longer maturities are sometimes issued.

As creditors, bondholders are legally entitled to receive interest payments from the issuing corporation every year until the bond matures, and to receive an amount known as the *principal* (or "face value") when the bond matures. But bondholders don't have to hold their bonds until they mature. Like stocks, bonds can be bought and sold on securities markets, and their price can rise and fall. So, like stockholders, bondholders can experience capital gains or losses.

Because the issuing corporation is legally required to pay interest and principal on a fixed schedule, the returns on bonds are more predictable than returns on stocks. However, even bonds pose some risk. During the recent economic downturn, many firms defaulted on (failed to make) their legally required bond payments.

Government securities are IOUs issued by government entities when they borrow money. As with corporate bonds, government securities normally pay their holders a stated rate of interest until they mature. State and local governments often issue bonds. In fact, many investors like to invest in municipal bonds because interest income earned on these bonds is usually exempt from federal income taxes. But the biggest single issuer of government securities is the federal government. The U.S. Treasury markets a variety of securities, from long-term bonds that mature in 30 years, to short-term treasury bills (popularly called "T-bills") that can mature in as little as four weeks. Historically, securities issued by the federal government have been viewed as very safe investments. But in recent years, the rapid growth in federal debt has led some securities rating services to question this view.[10]

Certificates of deposit are offered by banks and other depository institutions like credit unions. They are similar to savings accounts but are issued for a fixed term—which could be as short as three months or as long as five years. The rate of interest paid on CDs is often higher than the rate on a regular savings account but usually lower than the interest rate on corporate bonds and most government securities. CDs with longer maturities typically earn a higher interest rate than CDs that have shorter terms. You can cash in a CD before it matures, but you'll incur a substantial penalty if you do.

One advantage of CDs is that they are insured by the FDIC. Because of this insurance and their predictable rate of return, CDs are considered to be among the safest investment options. The tradeoff is that they offer lower returns than most other types of investments.

Mutual funds sell shares to investors and pool the resulting funds to invest in financial instruments such as corporate stocks, corporate bonds, government securities, or other assets. Some mutual funds invest mainly in bonds, others invest mainly in stocks, and others in government securities. Some invest in specific sectors of the economy, such as technology, energy, or healthcare, while others invest in broader portfolios.

Most mutual funds are professionally managed, with the fund's manager selecting the specific securities that the fund will hold. This professional management appeals to many investors who don't have the time or expertise to evaluate investment alternatives. But it is also expensive—mutual funds charge fees to cover the cost of managing the fund and to meet other expenses. Investors must pay these fees even if the funds perform poorly.

Exchange Traded Funds (ETFs) are similar to mutual funds in that they represent ownership in a broad portfolio of securities. However, unlike most mutual funds, they are bought and sold just like shares of corporate stock. ETFs are a relatively new investment vehicle (first marketed in 1993), but they have become quite popular in recent years.

Full-service brokers provide financial planning, tax advice, and research to identify good investment opportunities.

svetikd/iStockphoto.com

A-4b Acquiring Financial Assets: The Role of a Broker

Investors normally acquire many of their financial assets, including shares of common and preferred stocks, corporate bonds, and certain other financial assets (such as ETFs), by purchasing them in securities markets. However, individual investors can't directly participate in these markets. Instead, they normally rely on the services of a brokerage firm to buy and sell securities.

When choosing a broker, it's important to consider both the costs and the level of service. In addition to carrying out your trades, a *full-service broker* provides a wide range of services—such as research to identify good investment opportunities, financial planning, and tax advice. Most full-service brokerage firms charge commissions based on the dollar value of the orders their clients place. They also charge fees for the services they provide.

In contrast, *discount brokers* buy and sell securities for their clients but offer few additional services. The commissions and fees charged by discount brokers are usually significantly lower than those of full-service brokers. Many discount brokerage firms charge flat fees of a few dollars per trade for simple transactions.

In recent years, competition among brokerage firms has blurred the distinction between full-service and discount brokers. Many full-service firms have lowered their commissions, while many discount brokers have begun offering investment advice and other services. Most major brokerage firms now offer their clients both discount and full-service options.

Before entrusting a brokerage firm with your financial transactions, you should check out its background. The Financial Industry Regulatory Authority's (FINRA's) BrokerCheck website (http://www.finra.org/Investors/ToolsCalculators/BrokerCheck/) is a good place to start. This site offers very detailed background information on over 1.3 million current and former FINRA-registered brokers and over 17,400 FINRA-registered brokerage firms.

A-4c Building a Portfolio: A Few Words about Diversification, Risk, and Return

The financial securities we've described are not mutually exclusive. It is possible—and usually desirable—to invest in a diversified financial portfolio consisting of a variety of stocks, bonds, CDs, government securities, and other assets.

The main advantage offered by diversification is that it reduces your risk. If you put a large part of your wealth into one specific investment, you could be wiped out if that investment goes sour. If you invest in several different assets, then losses in some are likely to be offset by gains in others. But diversification also has a downside—it not only reduces risk but also reduces the possibility of earning exceptionally high returns.

One widely accepted financial principle is that a trade-off exists between risk and return; in other words, investments with the potential for generating high returns tend to be riskier than investments that offer lower returns. For example, stock prices sometimes decline sharply, so investing in stocks is considered quite risky. But historically, the long-run average return on stocks has been significantly higher than the average return on bonds, which offer safer, more predictable returns.

In general, younger investors are less concerned about risk than older investors. When you are young, you have more time to recover from adverse results, so you may be willing to take more risks and be more aggressive in pursuit of higher returns. If you invest mostly in stocks when you are young, and the stock market crashes, you still have time to recoup your losses and take advantage of future increases in stock prices. But older investors who hold a lot of stock might find that the same crash wiped out much of the wealth just when they were counting on it to supplement their retirement income. Older investors often become more conservative, adjusting their portfolio to include a greater percentage of relatively safe assets such as government securities, bonds of corporations with strong credit ratings, and CDs.

A-4d But What Is My Best Investment? (Hint: Look in the Mirror!)

So far, we have focused on investing in financial assets. But in many ways, the most important investment you can make is in yourself, by devoting your time, effort, and money to your education, training, health, and fitness. The Bureau of Labor Statistics reports that the median weekly earnings of high-school graduates in the fourth quarter of 2015 was $664, while for workers with bachelor's degrees, the figure was $1,131—a difference of $467.[11] Over a typical worker's 40-year career, this amounts to a difference in earnings of over $970,000! And higher education not only increases your income, it also gives you more job security. In 2015, the unemployment rate for

IRA An individual retirement account that provides tax benefits to individuals who are investing for their retirement.

workers with a high-school education was 5.3% while the unemployment rate for workers with at least a bachelor's degree was 2.5%.[12]

STRATEGIES TO BECOME MORE MARKETABLE

One way to increase your marketability and your starting salary is to secure an internship during your college years. Such internships usually offer little or no monetary compensation, but they pay off in other ways. They give students a chance to gain first-hand experience that supplements what they learn in the classroom and helps them determine whether a specific career is right for them. And the internship experience looks great on a résumé. But in 2010, the U.S. Department of Labor issued a ruling that makes it more difficult for profit-seeking firms to offer unpaid or low-wage internships. Many educators, business leaders, and politicians have called on the Department of Labor to modify its stance to make internships easier to establish. But unless and until such modifications are adopted, internships may remain difficult to find.[13]

OTHER WORK OPPORTUNITIES Don't despair if you are unable to secure an internship. There are other ways to gain experience in your field of interest. Consider taking a (gulp) pay cut from your temporary *job* to get experience in your *career* field. Or perhaps consider doing volunteer work in that field—not only will you be doing a good deed, you'll also be learning the ropes in your chosen field. Taking a temporary pay cut to gain relevant work experience often pays for itself many times over when you leave college and pursue a full-time position.

A-4e Investing for the Long Term: Planning for Your Retirement

One of the most important reasons people invest is to build up a nest egg for retirement. While your retirement might seem like it is a long way off, investing for your golden years now can really pay off, since it allows you to take advantage of the compounding effects we talked about earlier.

One of the most popular ways to build wealth for retirement is to set up an individual retirement account, or **IRA**. There are several types of IRAs; the two most popular are the *traditional IRA* and the *Roth IRA*. Both types of IRAs are individual investments—you make the decisions about how much to invest (subject to maximum allowable contributions) and what specific investments to make. You can put your IRA money into stocks, government securities, CDs, mutual funds, or other types of financial securities.

Feeling Too Broke to Save? You're Not Alone.

After decades of increasing debt, Americans are saving again. In fact, increasing savings was the number one financial resolution for 2015.

Millennials are leading the charge. Indeed, 39% of millennials are using spending plans to meet their savings goals. However, that still means that 61% of millennials don't!

If you're among that 61%, here are some suggestions to curb spending and increase savings:

- **Set Saving Goals:** Be specific. You can't track progress toward your goal unless you know what it is.

- **Use Direct Deposit:** Automatically divert a percentage of your regular income into a savings account.

- **Kick the Habit:** E-commerce subscriptions to services like Birchbox are as popular and addictive as Starbucks.

ProStockStudio/Shutterstock.com

Canceling can put $100 to $600 (or more) back in your pocket per year.

- **Save Windfalls:** From income tax refunds to monetary gifts from family, put some or all of every windfall into your savings account.

- **Price Things in Work Hours:** Before buying anything, calculate how many work hours it will take to pay for it (Don't forget sales taxes!). This helps you prioritize purchases and reduce excessive or unnecessary spending.

- **Gamify Saving:** See how long you can make a $20 bill last. Or compete with friends to see who can save the most and spend the least each month.

It's undeniably easier to accumulate debt than savings. It can take less than an hour to get $1,000 by opening a new credit card, but nearly a year to save $1,000 by banking $20 a week. A few simple changes like these, however, can jumpstart the process.[14]

Both traditional and Roth IRAs offer tax advantages intended to provide an incentive for people to invest for their retirement. But the nature and timing of the tax advantages are different. With a traditional IRA, the contributions you make reduce your taxable income in the same tax year, and the earnings on your contributions are tax deferred, allowing them to grow more rapidly.[15] But you must pay taxes on the money received from a traditional IRA when you begin making withdrawals. On the other hand, the contributions you make to a Roth IRA are *not* tax deductible at the time you make them, but earnings on these contributions are tax-free, and you pay no taxes on the distributions you receive from a Roth IRA after you retire.

One drawback to both traditional and Roth IRAs is that the amount that individuals can contribute each year is relatively small. In 2015, the maximum contribution for both types of plans was $5,500. (Individuals over the age of 50 could contribute up to $6,500.)

401(k), 403(b), and 457 plans are employee-contribution retirement plans that are named for the sections of the IRS tax code where they are described. These plans are similar in many respects; the main differences are in who qualifies for each type of plan. 401(k) plans are offered to employees of private-sector businesses, while 403(b) plans are for employees of certain types of nonprofit organizations such as schools, religious organizations, and charities. The 457 plans are primarily for state and local government employees and nonprofit organizations. Some employees in the nonprofit sector qualify for both 403(b) and 457 plans.

Unlike IRAs, all of these plans are implemented through a payroll-deduction process. Also, these plans have much higher contribution limits than traditional and Roth IRAs. In 2014, for example, employees could contribute up to $18,000 in a 401(k) plan, with individuals over 50 allowed to contribute up to an additional $6,000 *if* their employer's plan contained a "catch-up" provision. Other potential advantages of these plans include:

- **Tax advantages:** Any income employees invest in traditional 401(k), 403(b), and 457 plans is tax deductible, and the earnings on these investments are tax deferred. This reduces current taxes and allows the funds to grow more rapidly. However, retirees must pay taxes on funds

> **401(k), 403(b), and 457 plans** Employee payroll-deduction retirement plans that offer tax benefits.

distributed from their fund when they make withdrawals. As with IRAs, there are Roth versions of these plans. Employees who choose the Roth version pay taxes on the income they contribute, but earnings on these contributions and distributions after retirement are tax exempt.

■ **Company matching:** Some employers match employee contribution either dollar for dollar or with a percentage of each dollar you contribute up to a limit. This can be a big advantage of these plans over IRAs. If your company matches your 401(k) or 403(b) or 457 contributions, you should consider contributing as much as you can up to the maximum your company will match—it's like getting free money for your retirement.

EpicStockMedia/Shutterstock.com

A key to a comfortable retirement is to start saving early.

There are also some important restrictions on these plans. First, not all employers offer these plans. Second, if your employer does offer a plan that offers matching contributions, you won't be entitled to all of the matching funds unless you've remained employed with the company for a stated period of time called the **vesting period**. The length of time for full vesting varies depending on the employer, but it is usually several years. Finally, keep in mind that these are *retirement* plans. There are restrictions on withdrawing the money in these plans prior to retirement, and you may pay significant penalties if you do.

company matching An amount contributed by the employer to an employee's retirement account, matching the employee's retirement contributions either dollar-for-dollar or based on a percentage of each dollar contributed by the employee.

vesting period A specified period of time for which an employee must work for an employer in order to receive the full advantage of certain retirement benefits.

The BIG Picture

Making sound personal financial decisions requires careful thought and discipline. You should start by establishing a budget; doing so will help you understand your current financial situation, plan for the future, and monitor your progress toward achieving your goals. One of your first goals should be to set aside enough savings to provide adequate protection against unforeseen financial challenges. One good strategy to build your savings is to "pay yourself first." Another key to financial success is to make careful decisions with respect to your use of credit cards and other forms of credit. Next, you should turn your attention to investing to build your wealth over time. You'll discover many different investment opportunities, each with their own pros and cons. No single investment strategy is foolproof, but two principles that have stood the test of time are: (1) start investing early to take full advantage of compounding, and (2) diversify your investments to protect against risk.

STUDY TOOLS APPENDIX

LOCATED AT BACK OF THE TEXTBOOK

☐ Rip Out Chapter Review Card

LOCATED AT WWW.CENGAGE.COM/LOGIN

☐ Review key term flashcards and create your own using StudyBits

☐ Create and complete practice quizzes based off of your notes and StudyBits

☐ Complete Online activities such as Matching, Fill-in-the-Blank, and Drag and Drop exercises

☐ View chapter highlight box content, including CEO Profiles, What Would You Do Cases, and chapter videos

☐ Track your knowledge and understanding of key concepts in business using 4LTR Online

ENDNOTES

1

1. 10 Trends for 2015, December 2014 Trend Briefing, Trendwatching.com, HYPERLINK "http://trendwatching.com/trends/10-trends-for-2015/" \l "slide-7" http://trendwatching.com/trends/10-trends-for-2015/#slide-7, accessed February 1, 2015.

2. Improving labor market could be cause of drop in total new business creation rate in 2012, March 17, 2013, Kauffman website, http://www.kauffman.org/newsroom/2013/04/entrepreneurial-activity-declines-as-jobs-rise-in-2012-according-to-kauffman-report, accessed February 2, 2015.

3. State of Entrepreneurship Address, January 19, 2010, Kauffman Foundation website, http://www.kauffman.org/newsroom/entrepreneurs-expect-to-limit-hiring-in-2010-according-to-new-kauffman-foundation-poll.aspx, accessed January 13, 2011.

4. Lululemon Athletica chairman quits after firestorm over his fat-thighs comment, by Cheryl Chumley, Washington Times, December 10, 2013, Washington Times website, http://www.washingtontimes.com/news/2013/dec/10/lululemon-athletic-wear-chair-quits-over-firestorm/, accessed January 11, 2014.

5. The biggest corporate blunders of 2013, CNBC website, http://www.cnbc.com/id/101283178/page/2, accessed February 2, 2015.

6. Mistakes in advertising, English Learning Network website, http://www.learnenglish.de/mistakes/HorrorMistakes.html, accessed February 2, 2015.

7. Ubernomics: Fortune's Editor's Desk, by Alan Murray, January 1, 2015, Fortune magazine, Fortune.com http://www.latimes.com/, accessed February 4, 2015; Upstart Uber outraces other tech models, by Tracey Lien and Andrea Chang, December 5, 2014, Los Angeles Times, accessed February 4, 2015.

8. On the Nonprofit Sector and Community Solutions Act of 2010, by Leonard Jacobs, June 18, 2010, The Clyde Fitch Report, The Clyde Fitch Report website, http://www.clydefitchreport.com/2010/06/introducing-hr-5533-the-nonprofit-sector-and-community-solutions-act-of-2010/, accessed January 16, 2011; 7.2% of Americans work for nonprofit groups, study finds, by Suzanne Perry, December 19, 2006, The Chronicle of Philanthropy website, http://philanthropy.com/free/update/2006/12/2006121901.htm, accessed January 19, 2009; Wages in the nonprofit sector: management, professional, and administrative support occupations, by Amy Butler, October 28, 2008, Bureau of Labor Statistics website, http://www.bls.gov/opub/cwc/cm20081022ar01p1.htm, accessed January 19, 2008; Occupational Employment and Wages, 2007, May 9, 2008, Bureau of Labor Statistics website, http://www.bls.gov/news.release/pdf/ocwage.pdf, accessed January 19, 2009; Nonprofit sector needs to be better understood, by Todd Cohen, February 22, 2010, Inside Philanthropy Blog, Philanthropy Journal website, http://philanthropyjournal.blogspot.com/2010/02/nonprofit-sector-needs-to-be-better.html, retrieved March 23, 2010.

9. GNI Per Capita 2007 World Bank Data, revised October 17, 2008, http://siteresources.worldbank.org/DATASTATISTICS/ Resources/GNIPC.pdf, accessed January 19, 2009; CIA World Factbook China, updated December 18, 2008, https://www.cia.gov/library/publications/the-world-factbook/geos/ch.html, accessed January 19, 2009; CIA World Factbook Russia, updated December 18, 2008, https://www.cia.gov/library/publications/the-world-factbook/geos/rs.html, accessed January 19, 2009; CIA World Factbook Hong Kong, updated December 18, 2008, https://www.cia.gov/library/publications/the-world-factbook/geos/hk.html, accessed January 19, 2009.

10. American Customer Satisfaction Index, 2011 Results, ACSI website, http://www.theacsi.org/index.php?option=com_content&view=article&id=12&Itemid=110, accessed January 14, 2012.

11. Why Webvan drove off a cliff, by Joanna Glasner, Wired News, July 10, 2001, http://www.wired.com/techbiz/media/news/2001/07/45098.

12. Honey, I shrunk the iPod. A lot. by Steven Levy, September 19, 2005, Newsweek magazine; Behind Apple's strategy: be second to market, by John Boddie, August 29, 2005, Harvard Business School Working Knowledge, http://hbswk.hbs.edu/item.jhtml?id=4970&t=technology; What's to become of Microsoft's answer to the iPod? by John Letzing July 29, 2009, Marketwatch website, http://www.marketwatch.com/story/microsofts-zune-continues-to-struggle-2009-07-29, accessed April 1, 2010.

13. See note 12 above.

14. Comparative Cumulative Stock Market Returns and Comparative Annualized Stock Market Returns, Great Place to Work website, http://www.greatplacetowork.com/our-approach/what-are-the-benefits-great-workplaces, accessed January 8, 2014; Why investors should demand employee satisfaction, by Daniel Ferry, July 5, 2012, The Motley Fool, http://beta.fool.com/catominor/2012/07/05/why-investors-should-demand-employee-satisfaction/6603/, accessed January 9, 2013; Employee Satisfaction & Stock Performance, by Jeffrey Henning on Fri, August 6, 2010, Voice of Vovici Blog, http://blog.vovici.com/blog/?Tag=Employee%20Satisfaction%20Surveys, accessed January 17, 2011; Giving employees what they want: the returns are huge, May 4, 2005, Knowledge@Wharton, Human Resources, http://knowledge.wharton.upenn.edu/article/1188.cfm, accessed January 19, 2009; How Investing in Intangibles—Like Employee Satisfaction—Translates into Financial Returns, January 9, 2008, Knowledge@Wharton website, http://knowledge.wharton.upenn.edu/article.cfm?articleid=1873, accessed January 19, 2009.

15. 10,000—Baby Boomers Retire, Pew Research Center, January 17, 2011, Pew Research website, http://pewresearch.org/databank/dailynumber/?NumberID=1150, accessed January 11, 2011.

16. Four things that worry business, by Geoff Colvin, October 27, 2014, Fortune website, http://fortune.com/2014/10/09/dom-barton-four-things-that-worry-business/, accessed February 5, 2015.

17. Retail E-Commerce Update, by Jeffrey Grau, December 2008, eMarketer website, http://www.emarketer.com/Reports/All/Emarketer_2000545.aspx, accessed January 19, 2009; eMarketer: E-Commerce Expected to Grow Double Digits through 2012, by David Kaplan, PaidContent website, March 17, 2011, http://paidcontent.org/article/419-emarketer-e-commerce-expected-to-grow-double-digits-through-2012/, accessed January 15, 2012.

18. In trendy world of fast fashion, styles aren't made to last, March 11, 2013, NPR website, http://www.npr.org/2013/03/11/174013774/in-trendy-world-of-fast-fashion-styles-arent-made-to-last, accessed February 3, 2015; 5 truths the fast fashion industry doesn't want you to know, by Shannon Whitehead, October 14, 2014, Huffington Post website, http://www.huffingtonpost.com/shannon-whitehead/5-truths-the-fast-fashion_b_5690575.html, accessed February 3, 2015.

19. U.S. Census Bureau projections show a slower growing, older, more diverse nation a half century from now. Census Bureau Press Release, December 12, 2012. http://www.census.gov/newsroom/releases/archives/population/cb12-243.html, accessed January 9, 2013; Net Migration from Mexico falls to zero and perhaps less, Pew Hispanic Center Report, 2012, http://s3.documentcloud.org/documents/346357/mexican-migration.pdf, accessed January 9, 2013; U.S. Population Projections: 2005–2050, February 11, 2008, by Jeffrey S. Passel and D'Vera Cohn, Pew Research Center website, http://pewhispanic.org/files/reports/85.pdf, accessed January 17, 2011.

20. New Mexico QuickFacts, U.S. Census, December 6, 2012, http://quickfacts.census.gov/qfd/states/35000.html; Mississippi QuickFacts, U.S. Census, December 6, 2012, http://quickfacts.census.gov/qfd/states/28000.html; Hawaii QuickFacts, U.S. Census, December 6, 2012, http://quickfacts.census.gov/qfd/states/15000.html, all accessed January 9, 2013; State and County Quick Facts, Mississippi, U.S. Census Bureau website, http://quickfacts.census.gov/qfd/states/28000.html, last revised February 23, 2010, retrieved March 30, 2010; Hawaii's Asian population at 55% is highest proportion in nation, May 1, 2009, Hawaii 24/7 website, http://www.hawaii247.org/2009/05/01/hawaiis-asian-population-at-55-is-highest-proportion-in-nation/, retrieved March 30, 2010; State and County Quick Facts, New Mexico, U.S. Census Bureau website, http://quickfacts.census.gov/qfd/states/35000.html, last revised February, 23, 2010, retrieved March 30, 2010.

21. "The Lorax" Presents on Premio Lo Nuestro, Univision website, http://corporate.univision.com/case-studies/%E2%80%9Cthe-lorax%E2%80%9D-presents-on-premio-lo-nuestro/#.Us-GtrRpghA, accessed January 9, 2014; Lynx helped Panasonic become a major player in the Hispanic market, Lynx Hispanic Marketing Website Case Studies, 2013, http://www.lynxhispanicmarketing.com/case-studies/panasonic.php, accessed January 9, 2013; Translating Hispanic Marketing into Shareholder Value, Hispanic PR Wire/Business Wire, December 4, 2006, http://www.hispanicprwire.com/print.php?l=in&id=7660; Kraft Aims Kool-Aid Ads at

a Growing Hispanic Market, by Andrew Adam Newman, May 26, 2011, *New York Times* website, http://www.nytimes.com/2011/05/27/business /media/27adco.html, accessed January 16, 2012.

22. Diversity Awareness, Hershey Foods Corporation website, accessed October 4, 2005, https://www.hersheyjobs.com/Career/ControlPanel .aspx?ModuleCategoryID=1999999.

23. Attitudes of young people toward diversity, CIRCLE fact sheet, February 2005, http://www .civicyouth.org/PopUps/FactSheets/Attitudes% 202.25.pdf.

24. U.S. Census Bureau projections show a slower growing, older, more diverse nation a half century from now. Census Bureau Press Release, December 12, 2012. http://www.census.gov/newsroom /releases/archives/population/cb12-243.html, accessed January 9, 2013; China seeks ways to manage ageing population crisis, September 21, 2012, BBC News Website, http://www.bbc.co.uk /news/world-asia-china-19662365, accessed January 9, 2013; U.S. Population Projections: 2005–2050, February 11, 2008, by Jeffrey S. Passel and D'Vera Cohn, Pew Research Center website, http://pewhispanic.org/files/reports/85.pdf, accessed January 17, 2011; China's concern over population aging and health, by Toshiko Kaneda, Population Reference Bureau website, http://www.prb.org/Articles/2006/ChinasConcern OverPopulationAgingandHealth.aspx, accessed January 17, 2011.

25. Amazon, Google employees ranked as "least loyal," by Taylor Soper, July 24, 2013, GeekWire website, http://www.geekwire.com/2013/amazon -google-employees-ranked-least-loyal/#disqus _thread, accessed January 9, 2014; Pending job flexibility act received mixed reviews, by Sue Shellenbarger, WSJ Career Journal, http://www.careerjournal.com/columnists /workfamily/20010426-workfamily.html, accessed October 4, 2005; Bad attitudes in the workplace, by Les Christie, Sept 6, 2005, CNNMoney, http://money.cnn.com/2005/08/24/pf/workplace _morale/?section=money_pf; Inspiring worker loyalty one tough job, by John Ellis, July 1, 2005, *East Bay Business Times* website, http://www .bizjournals.com/eastbay/stories/2005/07/04 /focus1.html; Employee loyalty is at a three-year low, by Laura Petrecca, March 28, 2011, *USA Today*, website, http://www.usatoday.com /money/workplace/2011-03-26-employees-less -loyal.htm, accessed January 16, 2012.

26. Sustainability: Balancing Opportunity and Risk in the Consumer Products Industry, 2007 Report, Deloitte website, http://www.deloitte.com /dtt/cda/doc/content/us_cb _sustainability-study _june2007opt.pdf, accessed January 20, 2009; While Everything Else Stops, Green Still Means Go, by Sarah Fister Gale, January 19, 2009, Green-Biz website, http://www.planetthoughts.org/?pg=pt /Whole&qid=2675, accessed June 1, 2011.

27. China's manufacturing wages rise to $7,000 per year: Baidu benefits, by Marc Weirsum, April 22, 2014, Market Realist website, http://marketrealist. com/2014/04/chinas-manufacturing-wages-rise -7000-per-year-baidu-benefits/, accessed February 5, 2015; Wages in China, June 10, 2013, China Labor Bulletin website, http://www.clb.org.hk/en/content /wages-china, accessed January 10, 2014; Even as Wages Rise, China Exports Grow, by Keith Bradsheir, January 9, 2014, *The New York Times* website, http://www.nytimes.com/2014/01/10 /business/international/chinese-exports-withstand -rising-labor-costs.html?hpw&rref=business& _r=0, accessed January 10, 2014; United States Average Hourly Wages in Manufacturing, January 11, 2014, Trading Economics website, http://www

.tradingeconomics.com/united-states/wages-in -manufacturing, accessed January 10, 2014; Factory jobs gain but wages retreat, by Louis Uchitelle, December 29, 2011, *New York Times* website, http:// www.nytimes.com/2011/12/30 /business/us-manufacturing-gains-jobs-as-wages -retreat.html?pagewanted=all, accessed January 9, 2013; For Mexico, and Edge on China by David Luhnownad Bob Davis, September 16, 2012, *The Wall Street Journal* website, http://online.wsj.com /article/SB10000872396390444318104577587191288101170.html, accessed January 9, 2013; How Rising Wages Are Changing the Game in China by Dexter Roberts, March 27, 2006, *BusinessWeek* website, http://www.businessweek.com/magazine /content/06_13/b3977049.htm, accessed January 20, 2009; Good Luck Competing Against Chinese Labor Costs, Mfg. Job Growth in China Is Headed Up, Not Down; 109 Million Mfg. Workers in China Dwarfs Number in U.S., by Richard McCormack, May 2, 2006, Manufacturing and Technology News website, http://www.manufacturingnews.com /news/06/0502/art1.html, accessed January 20, 2009; Cost of Chinese labor is on the rise by Scott Tong, July 6, 2007, Marketplace website, http://marketplace. publicradio.org/display/web/2007/07/06/cost_of _chinese_labor_is_on_the_rise/, accessed January 20, 2009; Manufacturing in China Today: Employment and Labor Compensation, by Judith Banister, September 2007, The Conference Board website, http://www.conference-board.org/economics /workingpapers.cfm, accessed January 20, 2009; The End of Cheap Labor in China, by Bill Powell, June 26, 2011, *Time* magazine website, http://www .time.com/time/magazine/article/0,9171,2078121,00 .html, accessed January 16, 2012.

28. Asian tsunami devastates Sri Lankan fishing industry, by Jason Beaubien, January 10, 2005, NPR Morning Edition, http://www.npr.org /templates/story/story.php?storyId=4276161; Phuket tourism industry crippled by mass cancellations, by Sally Pook, January 8, 2005, Cyber Diver News Network, http://www.cdnn.info/news /travel/t050111.html; Homeland security scuffle, by Veronique de Rugy, October 15, 2004, *National Review* website, http://www.nationalreview.com /comment/rugy200410150840.asp; Bush brushes aside rebuilding cost concerns, September 19, 2005, Reuters News Service, MSNBC website, http://www.msnbc.msn.com/id/9374106/.

29. Pomp and Circumspect, by Daniel Pink, June 4, 2005, *The New York Times* website, http:// select.nytimes.com/gst/abstract.html?res =F60C1FFD3F5C0C778CDAF0894DD404482. Pg. 12 Fact: The Internet Big Picture World Internet Users and Population Stats, World Internet Stats website, http://www.internetworldstats.com /stats.htm, accessed September 2014. Pg. 15 Fact: http://www.thedailybeast.com/newweek /2007/12/22/the-rise-of-a-fierce-yet-fragile -superpower.html, accessed November 2012.

2

1. B–1.—Gross domestic product, 1959–2008, Economic Report of the President: 2009 Spreadsheet Tables, updated January 14, 2009, Government Printing Office website, http://www .gpoaccess.gov/eop/tables09.html, accessed January 20, 2009.

2. How much is a trillion dollars? The Mansfield North Central Ohio Tea Party Association website, http://americaneedsyounow.org/howmuch.htm, accessed July, 2013.

3. U.S. Foreclosure Activity Decreases 14 Percent in June to Lowest Level Since December 2006

Despite 34 Percent Jump in Judicial Scheduled Foreclosure Auctions, July 11, 2013, Realty Trac website, http://www.realtytrac.com/Content /foreclosure-market-report/midyear-2013-us -foreclosure-market-report-7794, accessed January 12, 2014; More Foreclosures Expected in 2011 by Amy Hoak, December 12, 2010, *The Wall Street Journal* website, http://online.wsj.com/article /SB10001424052748703518604576014011451160994.html?mod=googlenews_wsj, accessed January 24, 2011; RealtyTrac's James J. Saccacio to Discuss Foreclosure Crisis Fallout at AFSA State Government Affairs Forum by RealtyTrac staff, RealtyTrac website, October 1, 2008, http://www .realtytrac.com/ContentManagement/pressrelease .aspx? Chan-nelID=9&ItemID=5284&accnt =64847, accessed January 22, 2009; REALTYTRAC® Year-end Report Shows Record 2.8 Million U.S. Properties With Foreclosure Filings in 2009, RealtyTrac Staff, January 14, 2010, RealtyTrac website, http://www.realtytrac.com /contentmanagement/pressrelease.aspx ?itemid=8333, accessed April 21, 2010; RealtyTrac: 2011 National Foreclosure Rate Lowest Since 2007, January 12, 2012, Commercial Record website, http://www.commercialrecord.com/news148166 .html, accessed January 18, 2012; *CoreLogic National Foreclosure Report*, January 2014, Core-Logic website, http://www.corelogic.com/research /foreclosure-report/national-foreclosure-report -january-2014.pdf, accessed February 6, 2015.

4. 7.9 million jobs lost—many forever by Chris Isidore, July 2, 2010, CNNMoney website, http: //money.cnn.com/2010/07/02/news/economy/jobs _gone_forever/index.htm, accessed, January 24, 2011.

5. Credit Crisis—The Essentials, Updated January 20, 2009, *The New York Times* website; Automakers say if they go, millions of jobs will vanish, by Sharon Silke Carty and Barbara Hagenbaugh, Updated November 21, 2008, *USA Today* website, Auto Industry Bailout Overview, Updated January 20, 2009, *The New York Times* website, http:// topics.nytimes.com/topics/reference/timestopics /subjects/c/credit_crisis/index.html, accessed January 21, 2009; http://www.usatoday.com /money/2008-11-17-automakers-bailout -impact_N.htm, accessed January 21, 2009; http:// topics.nytimes.com/top/reference/timestopics /subjects/c/credit_crisis/auto_industry/index .html, accessed January 21, 2009.

6. TARP Bailout to Cost Less Than Once Anticipated, by Jackie Calmes, *The New York Times* website, October 1, 2010, http://dealbook .nytimes.com/2010/10/01/ tarp-bailout-to-cost -less-than-once-anticipated/.

7. One Trillion Dollars, by Micheal Grunwald, January 26, 2009, Time, pp. 27–31, http://www .time.com/time/politics/article/0,8599,1871769,00 .html, accessed February 5, 2011; Economy adds jobs at fastest pace in three years, by Jeannine Aversa and Christopher S. Rugaber, April 2, 2010, *Associated Press*, http://www.google.com /hostednews/ap/article/ALeqM5gNiyJ905Ho0 Ur96V2TQhsBX19lGwD9ER6P402, accessed April 20, 2010; Bernanke declares "recession is very likely over," by Greg Robb, September 15, 2009, MarketWatch website, http://www.marketwatch .com/story/bernanke-declares-the-recession -over-2009-09-15, accessed, April 20, 2010.

8. Debt ceiling FAQs: What you need to know, by Jeanne Sahadi, May 18, 2011, CNN Money Website, http://money.cnn.com/2011/01/03 /news/economy/debt_ceiling_faqs/index.htm, accessed January 20, 2013; Cliff Dweller, by Michael Grunwald Monday, January 14, 2013,

Time website, http://www.time.com/time/magazine/article/0,9171,2132749,00.html, accessed January 20, 2013.

9. A Message to Obama and Congress: Kill the Cent and Save a Pretty Penny, by Mike Fuljenz, September 1, 2013, Money News website, http://www.moneynews.com/MikeFuljenz/penny-cent-circulation-money/2013/09/01/id/523353, accessed January 15, 2014; Is the penny going away? Not yet, by Amy Bowen, March 3, 2013, *USA Today* website, http://www.usatoday.com/story/news/nation/2013/03/02/penny-not-going-away-yet/1958995/, accessed January 15, 2014.

10. Bridging the gap, June 28, 2014, *The Economist*, http://www.economist.com/news/united-states/21605932-country-where-everyone-drives-america-has-shoddy-roads-bridging-gap, accessed February 7, 2015; America's most dangerous urban bridges, by William Pentland, November 4, 2011, *Forbes* website, http://www.forbes.com/sites/williampentland/2011/11/04/americas-most-dangerous-urban-bridges/, accessed February 7, 2015.

11. Historical Changes of the Target Federal Funds and Discount Rates, Federal Reserve Bank of New York website, http://www.newyorkfed.org/markets/statistics/dlyrates/fedrate.html, accessed January 22, 2009.

12. Workers on tap, January 3, 2015, *The Economist*, http://www.economist.com/news/leaders/21637393-rise-demand-economy-poses-difficult-questions-workers-companies-and, accessed February 8, 2015.

13. 'Peak oil' debunked, again, December 5, 2014, *The Wall Street Journal* website, http://www.wsj.com/articles/peak-oil-debunked-again-1417739810, accessed February 7, 2015.

14. OK Federal Government, excluding Postal Services, U.S. Department of Labor Bureau of Labor Statistics website, March 12, 2008, http://stats.bls.gov/oco/cg/cgs041.htm, accessed August 16, 2008; Postal Service Workers, U.S. Department of Labor Bureau of Labor Statistics website, December 18, 2007, http://stats.bls.gov/oco/ocos141.htm, accessed August 16, 2008; Job Opportunities in the Armed Forces, U.S. Department of Labor Bureau of Labor Statistics website, December 18, 2007, http://stats.bls.gov/oco/ocos249.htm, accessed August 16, 2008.

15. Russia's flat tax miracle, by Daniel J. Mitchell, PhD, The Heritage Foundation, March 24, 2003, http://www.heritage.org/Press/Commentary/ed032403.cfm; Russians do taxes right by Deroy Murdock, *National Review Online*, March 1, 2002, http://www.nationalreview.com/murdock/murdock030102.shtml; Russia: income taxes and tax laws, July 2005, Worldwide-Tax website, http://www.worldwide-tax.com/russia/russia_tax.asp; History of the U.S. tax system, U.S. Treasury website, http://www.ustreas.gov/education/fact-sheets/taxes/ustax.html,accessed March 9, 2006.

16. CIA World FactBook, updated January 14, 2013, https://www.cia.gov/library/publications/the-world-factbook/geos/us.html, accessed January 21, 2013.

17. Labor Force Statistics from the Current Population Survey, Bureau of Labor Statistics website, http://data.bls.gov/timeseries/LNS14000000; http://data.bls.gov/timeseries/LNU04000000?years_option=all_years&periods_option=specific_periods&periods=Annual+Data, accessed January 14, 2014; The Flat Paycheck Recovery, by Rana Foroohar, January 13, 2014; *Time* website, http://content.time.com/time/magazine/article/0,9171,2161670,00.html, accessed January 14, 2014. News and Trends in Management, by

Leslie Kwoh, February 13, 2012, *The Wall Street Journal Online*, http://online.wsj.com/article/SB100014240529702046426045772153720 10543642.html, accessed January 21, 2013; Graduates warned of record 70 applicants for every job by Jeevan Vasagar, July 6, 2010, *The Guardian* website, http://www.guardian.co.uk/education/2010/jul/06/graduates-face-tougher-jobs-fight, accessed January 26, 2011.

18. Labor Force Statistics from the Current Population Survey: Unemployment Rate Table, U.S. Department of Labor Bureau of Labor Statistics website, http://data.bls.gov/PDQ/servlet/SurveyOutputServlet?data_tool=latest_numbers&series_id=LNS14000000, accessed January 22, 2009.

19. Table of Historical Inflation Rates by Month and Year (1914–2013), January 16, 2013, U.S. Inflation Calculator website, http://www.usinflationcalculator.com/inflation/historical-inflation-rates/, accessed January 21, 2013.

Pg. 26 Fact: Open the Door and Let 'Em In by Rana Foroohar, July 22, 2013, *Time Magazine*, http://content.time.com/time/magazine/article/0,9171,2147289,00.html, accessed September 2014.

Pg. 33 Fact: Parents Projected to Spend $245,340 to Raise a Child Born in 2013, According to USDA Report. August 18, 2014, USDA News Report, http://www.usda.gov/wps/portal/usda/usdahome?contentidonly=true&contentid=2014/08/0179.xml, accessed September 2014.

3

1. CIA—The World Economy Overview, The World Factbook website, updated February, 2011, https://www.cia.gov/library/publications/the-world-factbook/geos/xx.html, accessed February 5, 2011; Global Economic Outlook 2012, The Conference Board, January 2012, Conference Board website, http://www.conference-board.org/data/globaloutlook.cfm, accessed February 2, 2012; World Economic Situation and Prospects 2014: Global Economic Outlook (Chapter 1), December 18, 2013, United Nations website, http://www.un.org/en/development/desa/publications/wesp2014-firstchapter.html, accessed February 22, 2015.

2. Rank Order Estimates, CIA—The World Factbook website: https://www.cia.gov/library/publications/the-world-factbook/rankorder/2003rank.html?countryName=India&countryCode=in&regionCode=sas&rank=35#in, https://www.cia.gov/library/publications/the-world-factbook/rankorder/2003rank.html?countryName=Algeria&countryCode=ag&regionCode=afr&rank=139#ag, https://www.cia.gov/library/publications/the-world-factbook/2119rank.html?countryName=Angola&countryCode=ao&regionCode=afr&rank=59#ao, all accessed January 22, 2013.

3. Where in the World Are There No McDonald's? by Jessica Naudziunas, August 1, 2013, The Salt, NPR website, http://www.npr.org/blogs/thesalt/2013/07/25/205547517/where-in-the-world-are-there-no-mcdonalds, accessed March 2, 2015; Where Wal-Mart Isn't: Four Countries the Retailer Can't Conquer, by Susan Berfield, October 10, 2013, Bloomberg website, http://www.bloomberg.com/bw/articles/2013-10-10/where-walmart-isnt-four-countries-the-retailer-cant-conquer, accessed March 2, 2015.

4. ABI: Africa's Mobile Market to Pass 80% Subscriber Penetration in Q1 Next Year; 13.9% of Global Cellular Market by 2017, by Natasha Lomas,

November 28, 2012, TechCrunch website, http://techcrunch.com/2012/11/28/abi-africas-mobile-market-to-pass-80-subscriber-penetration-in-q1-next-year-13-9-of-global-cellular-market-by-2017/, accessed January 24, 2013; 1B Cell Phone Users and no Apple iPhone in India's Breakneck Mobile-Apps Market by Pia Heikkila, September 15, 2012, *International Business Times* website, http://www.ibtimes.com/1b-cellphone-users-and-no-apple-iphone-indias-breakneck-mobile-apps-market-789460, accessed, January 24, 2013; Bringing toilets and dignity to India's poor by Sumnina Udas, September 17, 2012, CNN website, http://www.cnn.com/2012/09/17/world/asia/india-open-toilets-udas/index.html, accessed January 24, 2013.

5. Insperiences, Trendwatching newsletter, http://www.trendwatching.com/trends/insperience.htm, accessed January 12, 2006; Ten Key Trends for Chocolate Products, January 23, 2012, Food and Drink Europe website, http://www.foodanddrinkeurope.com/Consumer-Trends/10-key-trends-for-chocolate products?utm_source=copyright&utm_medium=OnSite&utm_campaign=copyright, accessed February 3, 2012.

6. WTO sees gradual recovery in coming months despite cut in trade forecasts, September 19, 2013, WTO press release, WTO website, http://www.wto.org/english/news_e/pres13_e/pr694_e.htm, accessed January 16, 2014; Trade to expand by 9.5% in 2010 after a dismal 2009, WTO reports, WTO 2010 Press Release, March 26, 2010, WTO website, http://www.wto.org/english/news_e/pres10_e/pr598_e.htm, accessed February 9, 2010; CIA, The World Factbook, The World Economy: Overview, CIA Website, https://www.cia.gov/library/publications/the-world-factbook/geos/xx.html, updated February 2010, accessed February 9, 2010; The CIA World Factbook, Economy, updated January 26, 2012, CIA Factbook website, https://www.cia.gov/library/publications/the-world-factbook/geos/xx.html, accessed February 3, 2012.

7. Currency Cost U.S. Companies at Least $4 Billion in Second Quarter, by Emily Chasan, September 19, 2013, *The Wall Street Journal* website, http://blogs.wsj.com/cfo/2013/09/19/currency-cost-u-s-companies-at-least-4-billion-in-second-quarter/, accessed January 16, 2014; P&G Only One of Many Hit by Foreign Exchange Rates (PG, PEP, KMB, CL, KO, PM, MCD, F, CCL), by Paul Ausick, June 20, 2012, 24/7 *The Wall Street Journal* website, http://247wallst.com/2012/06/20/pg-only-one-of-many-hit-by-foreign-exchange-rates-pg-pep-kmb-cl-ko-pm-mcd-f-ccl/, accessed January 25, 2013.

8. What is countertrade? by Neha Gupta, *Barter News Weekly* website, March 11, 2010, http://www.barternewsweekly.com/2010/03/11/what-is-counter-trade-1851/, accessed February 10, 2010; Countertrade—an innovative approach to marketing, by Dan West, Chairman American Countertrade Association, *BarterNews* issue #36, 1996, http://barternews.com/approach_marketing.htm; Global Offset and Countertrade Association website, http://www.globaloffset.org/index.htm, accessed January 27, 2006.

9. Have Car, Need Briefs? In Russia, Barter Is Back, by Ellen Barry, February 8, 2009, *The New York Times* website, http://www.nytimes.com/2009/02/08/world/europe/08barter.html?pagewanted=all, accessed January 25, 2013.

10. Greenpeace: China-made kids' clothes carry toxic risk, by Calum Macleod, December 17, 2013, *USAToday* website, http://www.usatoday.com/story/news/world/2013/12/17/china-toxic-clothing-greenpeace/4049853/, accessed

January 16, 2014; Mattel Issues New Massive China Toy Recall, Associated Press, MSNBC website, August 14, 2007, http://www.msnbc.msn.com/id/20254745/ns/business-consumer_news/, accessed February 10, 2010; As More Toys Are Recalled, Trail Ends in China by Eric S. Lipton and David Barboza, June 19, 2007, *The New York Times* website, http://www.nytimes.com/2007/06/19/business/worldbusiness/19toys.html, accessed January 29, 2009.

11. Yellin, E. (2009). Your call is (not that) important to us. New York: Simon Schuster, Inc.; Outsourced call centers return, to U.S. homes, by Carolyn Beeler, NPR website, August 25, 2010, http://www.npr.org/templates/story/story.php?storyId=129406588, accessed February 10, 2010.

12. More businesses exporting "Made in USA" again, by Heesun Wee, May 12, 2014, CNBC website, http://www.cnbc.com/id/101646468, accessed March 2, 2015.

13. Fiat Nears Stake in Chrysler That Could Lead to Takeover, by Stacy Meichtry and John Stoll, *The Wall Street Journal* website, January 20, 2009, http://online.wsj.com/article/SB123235519459294991.html, accessed February 10, 2010; eBay to acquire Skype, Press Release, September 12, 2005, Skype website, http://www.skype.com/company/news/2005/skype_ebay.html, accessed February 10, 2010.

14. Intel to Build Advanced Chip-Making Plant in China, by David Barboza, March 27, 2007, *The New York Times* website, http://www.nytimes.com/2007/03/27/technology/27chip.html, accessed January 30, 2009.

15. Santa's real workshop: The town in China that makes the world's Christmas decorations, by Oliver Wainwright, December 19, 2014, *The Guardian* website, http://www.theguardian.com/artanddesign/architecture-design-blog/2014/dec/19/santas-real-workshop-the-town-in-china-that-makes-the-worlds-christmas-decorations, accessed March 2, 2015.

16. Rethink the value of joint ventures by Cynthia Churchwell, Harvard Business School Working Knowledge, May 10, 2004, http://hbswk.hbs.edu/item.jhtml?id=4113&t=globalization.

17. Hyundai grows up, by Michael Schuman, Time Global Business, July 2005, http://www.time.com/time/globalbusiness/article/0,9171,1074141,00.html; At 5 feet 10 inches, I was too tall for Tokyo, by Cathie Gandel, My Turn, *Newsweek*, December 12, 2005. Hyundai Bets Big On India and China by Moon Ihlwan, January 30, 2008, BusinessWeek website, http://www.businessweek.com/globalbiz/content/jan2008/gb20080130_061205.htm, accessed January 30, 2009; Maruti, Hyundai, Tata Motors Lose Market Share to Smaller Firms in 2010, April 10, 2011, *India Times* website, http://articles.economictimes.indiatimes.com/2011-04-10/news/29403269_1_market-share-car-segment-passenger-car, accessed February 6, 2012.

18. What Pizza Hut's Crown Crust Pizza Says about Global Fast Food Marketing, by Ted Burnham, May 2, 2012, NPR website, http://www.npr.org/blogs/thesalt/2012/05/01/151781785/what-pizza-huts-crown-crust-pizza-says-about-global-fast-food-marketing, accessed January 25, 2013; McDonald's International: Top Ten Most Unusual Around the World, by Nina Africano, September 3, 2010, AOL Travel website, http://news.travel.aol.com/2010/09/03/mcdonald-s-international-top-ten-most-unusual-around-the-world/, accessed January 25, 2013; McDonald's country/market sites, http://www.mcdonalds.com./countries.html, accessed February 10, 2011; http://www.dominos.com/Public-EN/Site+Content/Secondary

/Inside+Dominos/Pizza+Particulars/International+Speciality+Toppings/; http://slice.seriouseats.com/archives/2008/02/crazy-weird-asian-pizza-crusts-japanese-korean-hong kong.html; http://recipes.howstuffworks.com/fresh-ideas/dinner-food-facts/favorite-pizza-toppings-in-10-countries.htm; http://slice.seriouseats.com/archives/2008/02/crazy weird-asian-pizza-crusts-japanese-korean-hong-kong.htm; McDonald's No Match for KFC in China as Colonel Rules Fast Food, by William Mellor, January 26, 2011, Bloomberg website, http://www.bloomberg.com/news/2011-01-26/mcdonald-s-no-match-for-kfc-in-china-where-colonel-sanders-rules-fast-food.html, accessed February 6, 2012; Morocco Loving the McArabia, by Erik German, May 30, 2010, Global Post website, http://www.globalpost.com/dispatch/morocco/090825/morocco-loving-the-mcarabia, accessed February 6, 2012.

19. Rural Market India Brand Equity Foundation, updated December 10, 2010, IBEF website, http://www.ibef.org/artdispview.aspx?art_id=27581&cat_id=938&in=78, accessed February 10, 2010; Selling to rural India, Springwise Newsletter, June 2003, http://www.springwise.com/newbusinessideas/2003/06/shakti.html; Red herring: selling to the poor, April 11, 2004, The Next Practice website, http://www.thenextpractice.com/news/red_herring_selling_to_the_poor.php; Are you ready for globalization 2.0? by Tim Weber, January 28, 2005, BBC News website, http://news.bbc.co.uk/1/hi/business/4214687.stm.

20. World Internet Statistics Website, June 30, 2012, http://www.internetworldstats.com/stats.htm, accessed January 26, 2013.

21. World Bank. 2014. Doing Business 2015: Going Beyond Efficiency. Washington, DC: World Bank. DOI: 10.1596/978-1-4648-0351-2, http://www.doingbusiness.org/~/media/GIAWB/Doing%20Business/Documents/Annual-Reports/English/DB15-Chapters/DB15-Report-Overview.pdf, accessed March 2, 2015.

22. Water Works, by Will Sarni, 2012, Interbrand Website, http://www.interbrand.com/en/best-global-brands/Best-Global-Green-Brands/2012-Report/water-works.aspx, accessed January 26, 2013; 2030: China's coming water crisis, by Brian Dumaine, December 14, 2012, *Fortune* magazine website, http://tech.fortune.cnn.com/2012/12/14/2030-chinas-coming-water-crisis/, accessed January 26, 2013; WaterFacts, 2012, Water.Org, http://water.org/water-crisis/water-facts/water/, accessed January 26, 2013.

23. Shadow Market: 2011 Global Software Piracy Study, May 2012, Business Software Alliance website, http://portal.bsa.org/globalpiracy2011/downloads/study_pdf/2011_BSA_Piracy_Study-Standard.pdf, accessed January 26, 2013.

24. China Levies 6.5% Tariff on U.S. Solar-Panel Materials, by Wayne Ma, September 18, 2013, *The Wall Street Journal* website, http://online.wsj.com/news/articles/SB10001424127887323527004579079070572200630, accessed January 19, 2014; Nations rush to establish new barriers to trade, by John W. Miller, February 6, 2009, *The Wall Street Journal Online*, http://online.wsj.com/article/SB123388103125654861.html, accessed January 26, 2013; U.S. Moves to Impose Tariffs on Chinese Tires, by William Mauldin, November 24, 2014, *The Wall Street Journal* website, http://www.wsj.com/articles/u-s-moves-to-impose-tariffs-on-chinese-tires-1416866855, accessed March 2, 2015.

25. USTR releases 2002 inventory of trade barriers, Press Release, April 2, 2002, http://www.useu.be/Categories/Trade/Apr0202USTRReport

ForeignTradeBarriers.html; U.S. targets non-tariff barriers to global trade, News Release, April 3, 2002, http://www.usconsulate.org.hk/pas/pr/2002/040301.htm.

26. Debt Relief under the Heavily Indebted Poor Countries Initiative Fact Sheet, January 10, 2013, IMF website, http://www.imf.org/external/np/exr/facts/hipc.htm, accessed January 26, 2013; Debt Relief Under the Heavily Indebted Poor Countries (HIPC) Initiative, Factsheet, December 16, 2010, International Monetary Fund website, http://www.imf.org/external/np/exr/facts/hipc.htm, accessed February 11, 2010.

27. Top 10 Exporting Countries Causing the US Trade Deficit, by Daniel Workman, April 27, 2010, Suite101 website, http://www.suite101.com/content/top-10-exporting-countries-causing-the-us-trade-deficit-a226747, accessed February 11, 2011.

28. CIA The World Factbook European Union: The Economy Overview: CIA website, https://www.cia.gov/library/publications/the-world-factbook/geos/ee.html, updated February 2011, accessed February 11, 2011.

29. California's Economic Collision Course: Immigration and Water, by Thomas del Beccaro, August 19, 2014, *Forbes* website, http://www.forbes.com/sites/thomasdelbeccaro/2014/08/19/calfiornias-economic-collision-course-immigration-and-water/, accessed March 3, 2015; Brown's California Overtakes Brazil with Companies Leading World, by Michael Marois and Shin Pei, January 15, 2015, Bloomberg Business website, http://www.bloomberg.com/news/articles/2015-01-16/brown-s-california-overtakes-brazil-with-companies-leading-world, accessed March 3, 2015.
Pg. 40 Fact: http://www.cnn.com/2012/09/17/world/asia/india-open-toilets-udas/index.html, accessed November 2012.
Pg. 41 Fact: Asia will have most millionaires by 2014, September 26, 2013, ABC Website, http://www.abc.net.au/news/2013-09-26/an-more-asian-millionaires/4983886, accessed September 2014.
Pg. 52 Fact: http://www.globalissues.org/issue/2/causes-of-poverty, accessed November 2012.

4

1. For the first time in a decade, lying, cheating, and stealing among American students drops, November 20, 2012, Josephson Institute website, http://charactercounts.org/pdf/reportcard/2012/ReportCard-2012-PressRelease-HonestyIntegrityCheating.pdf, accessed February 6, 2012; High school students cheating less, survey finds, by Cathy Payne, November 25, 2012, *USA Today* website, http://www.usatoday.com/story/news/nation/2012/11/25/high-school-students-cheating/ 1719297/, accessed February 6, 2013.

2. Forget ethics training: Focus on empathy, by Craig Downden, June 21, 2013, Financial Post website, http://business.financialpost.com/2013/06/21/forget-ethics-training-focus-on-empathy/, accessed January 24, 2014.

3. Big Three auto CEOs flew private jets to ask for taxpayer money, by Josh Levs, November 19, 2008, CNN website, http://www.cnn.com/2008/US/11/19/autos.ceo.jets/, accessed February 2, 2009.

4. Lawmakers, Questioning Fed Bailout, Seek AIG "Junket" Refund, by Ryan J. Donmoyer, October 9, 2008 Bloomberg website, http://www.bloomberg.com/apps/news?pid=newsarchive&sid=aPlPYw6JXIBU&refer=us, accessed February 21, 2011.

5. Why We'll Miss the Disney Trial, by Barney Gimbel, *Fortune*, December 27, 2004, retrieved

from CNNMoney website, http://money.cnn.com /magazines/fortune/fortune_archive/2004/12/27 /8217949/index.htm; Disney's Basket Cases, by Peter Bart, *Variety*, March 7, 2004, http://www .variety.com/article/VR1117901299.html? categoryid=1&cs=1.

6. Exhibit 4.3 Ethics at Work; Tufts President Lawrence S. Bacow awarded Pierre Omidyar an honorary degree during the University's 155th Commencement ceremonies on Sunday, May 22, 2011, February 24, 2013, TuftsNow website, http://now.tufts.edu/commencement-2011 /pierre-omidyar, accessed February 24, 2013; Merrill CEO departs with $160 million, by Walter Hamilton and Kathy M. Kristof, October 31, 2007, *Los Angeles Times* website, http://articles .latimes.com/2007/oct/31/business/fi-merrill31, accessed February 24, 2013; Thain Says He'll Repay Remodeling Costs, by Peter Edmonston, January 26, 2009, *The New York Times* website, http://www.nytimes.com/2009/01/27/business /27bank.html?_r=0, accessed February 24 2013; Whole Foods Is Hot, Wild Oats a Dud—So Said 'Rahodeb', by David Kesmodel and John Wilke, July 12, 2007, *The Wall Street Journal Online*, http://online.wsj.com/article/SB118418782959963745 .html, accessed February 24, 2013.

7. National Business Ethics Survey: How Employees View Ethics in Their Organizations, 1994–2005, Ethics Resource Center, October 12, 2005, http://www.ethics.org/research/2005-press -release.asp; Ethics Resource Center, 2009 National Business Ethics Survey, http://www.ethics.org/nbes /files/nbes-final.pdf, accessed May 14, 2010; 2011 NBES Key Findings, Ethics website, http://www .ethics.org/nbes/findings.html, accessed February 26, 2012.

8. The role of tone from the top, by Bob Lane, December 28, 2009, Ethisphere website, http://ethisphere.com/the-role-of-tone-from-the -top/, accessed February 21, 2011.

9. Supplemental Research Brief, Ethics and Employee Engagement, 2009 National Business Ethics Survey, Ethics Resource Center, http://www .ethics.org/files/u5/NBESResearchBrief2.pdf, accessed February 6, 2013.

10. Exhibit 4.5 Social Responsibility at Work Clorox Courts Sierra Club, and a Product Is Endorsed by Felicity Barringer, March 26, 2008, *The New York Times* website, http:// www.nytimes.com/2008/03/26/business /businessspecial2/26cleanser.html, accessed February 24, 2013; Tyson Foods home page, http://www.tyson.com/About-Tyson.aspx, accessed February 24, 2013 Will Supreme Court Hear Farmer's Case Against Tyson Foods? by Andrea Tse, January 24, 2011, *The Street* website, http://www.thestreet.com/story/10982877/1/will -supreme-court-hear-farmers-case-against-tyson -foods.html, accessed February 24, 2011; Kraft Limits on Kids' Ads May Cheese Off Rivals, by Sarah Ellison, *The Wall Street Journal*, January 13, 2005, http://www.aef.com/industry/news/data /2005/3076, accessed February 24, 2013; Bailed Out Bank of America Sponsors Super Bowl Fun Fest, by Megan Chuchmach, February 2, 2009, ABC News website, http://abcnews.go.com /Blotter/story?id=6782719&page=1, accessed February 24, 2013; Crash That Led To Toyota Recall "Inconclusive", by Jane Akre, December 8, 2009, Legal Examiner website, http://news .legalexaminer.com/crash-that-led-to-toyota-recall -inconclusive.aspx?googleid=275542, accessed February 24, 2013.

11. Complaining Customers Are Good for Business, by Bob Leduc, Virtual Marketing Newsletter, May 11, 2004, http://www .marketingsource.com/newsletter/05-11-2004.html.

12. O.B. Ultra Tampons Are Coming Back, and the Company Apologizes with a Song, by Jeannine Stein, December 8, 2011, *Los Angeles Times* website, http://articles.latimes.com/2011/dec/08 /news/la-heb-ob-tampons-return-20111208, accessed February 29, 2012; o.b. video apology message, http://articles.latimes.com/2011/dec/08 /news/la-heb-ob-tampons-return-20111208, accessed February 29, 2012.

13. Open letter to iPhone customers, Apple website, http://www.apple.com/hotnews /openiphoneletter/, accessed February 3, 2009; Apple's customer satisfaction up despite struggling industry, by Jeff Smykil, August 19, 2008, Ars Technica website, http://arstechnica.com/apple /news/2008/08/apples-customer-satisfaction-up -despite-struggling-industry.ars, accessed February 3, 2009; The American Customer Satisfaction Index Scores by Company, Personal Computers through 2011, the ACSI website, http://www.theacsi .org/index.php?option=com_content&view =article&id=149&catid=&Itemid=214&c =Apple+, accessed March 20, 2012.

14. Tim Cook Apologizes for Mapocalypse Debacle, by Christina Bonnington, September 28, 2012, Wired website, http://www.wired.com /gadgetlab/2012/09/tim-cook-apologizes-for-maps/, accessed February 4, 2013; Apple shares slide as iPhone misses Christmas sales forecast, by Juliette Garside, January 23, 2013, the *Guardian* website, http://www.guardian.co.uk/technology/2013 /jan/24/apple-results-iphone-sales, accessed February 4, 2013.

15. Making Good, Plus a Profit, by Gill Saporito, March 22, 2015, *Time* magazine, http://time.com /author/bill-saporito/, accessed March 15, 2015.

16. Giving USA 2014 Highlights, http://www .dfwonline.org/userdata/userfiles/file/WI%20Gives /Giving%20USA%202014%20Highlights.pdf, accessed March 15, 2015.

17. Patagonia Fills Payroll with People Who Are Passionate by Todd Henneman, November 5, 2011, Workforce website, http://www.workforce .com/articles/patagonia-fills-payroll-with-people -who-are-passionate, accessed January 25, 2013.

18. Starbucks Focuses Hiring Strategy on Veterans and Military Spouses, November 6, 2013, Starbucks Website, http://news.starbucks.com/news/starbucks -focuses-hiring-strategy-on-veterans-and-military -spouses, accessed January 25, 2014.

19. Recycling in the Restaurant, McDonald's website: http://www.aboutmcdonalds.com/mcd /sustainability/library/policies_programs /environmental_responsibility/recycling_in_the _restaurant.html, accessed February 5, 2013.

20. "Carbon Footprint" Gaining Business Attention, October 18, 2006, Press Release, Conference Board website, http://www.conference -board.org/UTILITIES/pressDetail.cfm?press _ID=2985, accessed February 4, 2009; Green goal of "carbon neutrality" hits limit, by Jeffery Ball, December 30, 2008, *The Wall Street Journal* website, http://online.wsj.com/article /SB123059880241541259.html, accessed February 4, 2009; How green is my orange? by Andrew Martin, January 22, 2009, *The New York Times* website, http://www.nytimes .com/2009/01/22/business/22pepsi.html? _r=1&scp=1&sq=How%20green%20is%20my %20orange&st=cse, accessed February 4, 2009.

21. The oddest, worst and most memorable CEO apologies of the year, by Jena McGregor, December 23, 2014, *The Washington Post* website, http:// www.washingtonpost.com/blogs/on-leadership /wp/2014/12/23/the-oddest-worst-and-most -memorable-ceo-apologies-of-the-year/, accessed March 15, 2015; Lululemon co-founder steps down in wake of 'women's bodies' remark, by Eun Kyung Kim, December 10, 2013, *Today Money* website, http://www.today.com/money/lululemon-co -founder-steps-down-wake-womens-bodies-remark -2D11721314, accessed March 15, 2015.

22. The Scoop on Scope 3 Emissions, by Debra Shepard, June 16, 2011, SustainServ website, http://www.sustainserv.com/de/easyblog/entry /the-scoop-on-scope-3-emissions.html, accessed February 5, 2012; U.S. Corporations Size Up Their Carbon Footprints, by Rachel King, June 1, 2009, Bloomberg *BusinessWeek*, BusinessWeek website, http://www.businessweek.com /technology/content/jun2009/tc2009061_692661 .htm, accessed February 24, 2011.

23. Cheating's Surprising Thrill, by Jan Hoffman, October 7, 2013, *The New York Times* sebsite, http://well.blogs.nytimes.com/2013/10/07/in-bad -news-cheating-feels-good/, accessed January 28, 2014; Is There a "Cheater's High"? by Romeo Vitelli, October 14, 2013, *Psychology Today* website, http://www.psychologytoday.com/blog /media-spotlight/201310/is-there-cheaters-high, accessed January 28, 2014; The Cheater's High: The Unexpected Affective Benefits of Unethical Behavior, September 2, 2013, *Journal of Personality and Social Psychology*, http://www.apa.org /pubs/journals/releases/psp-a0034231.pdf, accessed March 16, 2015

24. Plug-in hybrid sales soar; all-electric cars stay in low gear, by Jerry Hirsch, July 21, 2012, *Los Angeles Times* website, http://articles.latimes .com/2012/jul/21/business/la-fi-0721-autos -electric-vehicles-20120721, accessed February 6, 2013; Marketing, Business and Sustainable Development: A Global Guide, Business and Sustainable Development website, http://www .bsdglobal.com/markets/green_marketing.asp, accessed February 4, 2009.

25. Corruptions Perceptions Index 2013, Transparency International website, http://www .transparency.org/cpi2013/results, accessed January 26, 2014; Corruption Perceptions Index 2012, Transparency International Index website, http://www. transparency.org/cpi2012/results, accessed February 6, 2013.

26. Has Ralph Lauren Learned that Bribery is a Bad Business Strategy in Latin America? by Nathaniel Parish Flannery, April 24, 2013, Forbes website, http://www.forbes.com/sites/nathanielparishflannery /2013/04/24/bribery-a-bad-business-strategy-in -latin-america/, accessed January 26, 2014; Walmart Is Now Under Investigation in Mexican "Bribery Aisle" Scandal, by Juan Gonzalez and Amy Goodman, December 21, 2012, truth-out website, http://truth-out.org/news/item/13469-the-bribery -aisle-how-walmart-used-payoffs-to-bribe-its-way -through-expansion-in-mexico, accessed February 6, 2013; Prosecutors Ask to Meet Jung in Avon Bribe Probe, by Joe Palazzolo, Emily Galzer, and Joann Lublin, July 29 2012, *The Wall Street Journal* Online, http://online. wsj.com/article/SB1000087239 63904448401045775536834065426666.html, accessed February 6, 2013; Bribe Payers Index 2011, Transparency International website, http://bpi.transparency.org/results/, accessed March 24, 2012; Not just Wal-Mart: Dozens of U.S. companies face bribery suspicions, by Stephen Gandel, April 26, 2012, *Fortune* website, http://fortune. com/2012/04/26/not-just-wal-mart-dozens-of-u-s -companies-face-bribery-suspicions/, accessed March 16, 2015.

27. In Emerging Markets, Unilever Finds a Passport to Profit, by Matthew Boyle, January 3, 2013, Businessweek website, http://www.businessweek.com/articles/2013-01-03/in-emerging-markets-unilever-finds-a-passport-to-profit, accessed January 28, 2014; Values in Tension: Ethics Away from Home, by Thomas Donaldson, *Harvard Business Review*, September/October 1996.

28. Selling to the Poor, by Kay Johnson, Time Bonus Section, May 2005; The Payoff for Investing in Poor Countries, by C. K. Prahalad and Allen Hammond, Harvard Business School Working Knowledge website, http://hbswk.hbs.edu/item.jhtml?id=3180&t=nonprofit&noseek=one.

29. Gap, Inc. Social Reporting Award, December 20, 2004, Business Ethics website, http://www.business-ethics.com/annual.htm#Gap%20Inc.

Pg. 70 Fact: Recycling Stats, GreenWaste website, http://www.greenwaste.com/recycling-stats, accessed September 2014.

5

1. Fooled by 'The Onion': 9 Most Embarrassing Fails, by Kevin Fallon, November 27, 2012, The Daily Beast website, http://www.thedailybeast.com/articles/2012/09/29/fooled-by-the-onion-8-most-embarrassing-fails.html, accessed February 2, 2014; Fox Falls For Fake Story About Obama Personally Funding Muslim Museum During Shutdown, by Mike Burns, October 5, 2013, Media Matters website, http://mediamatters.org/blog/2013/10/05/fox-falls-for-fake-story-about-obama-personally/196304, accessed March 21, 2015.

2. Body Language Tactics That Sway Interviewers, by Eugene Raudsepp, *The Wall Street Journal Career Journal*, December 5, 2002, http://www.careerjournal.com/jobhunting/interviewing/20021205-raudsepp.html.

3. Down the Manhole: State Officials Grapple with Gender-Neutral Language, by Katy Steinmetz, February 5, 2013, *Time* magazine, http://swampland.time.com/2013/02/05/down-the-manhole-state-officials-grapple-with-gender-neutral-language/, accessed February 2, 2014.

4. Lance Armstrong blew his last chance experts say, January 19, 2013, *Advertising Age* website, http://adage.com/article/media/lance-armstrong-blew-chance-experts/239295/, accessed February 20, 2013; Dominance and Empathy, by Brigid Schulte, February 13, 2013, *The Washington Post* website, http://www.washingtonpost.com/local/body-language-experts-say-obama-exuded-dominance-and-empathy/2013/02/13/7755207e-7590-11e2-95e4-6148e45d7adb_story.html, accessed March 21, 2015.

5. The Listener Wins, by Michael Purdy, *Monster* contributing writer, Monster.com, http://featuredreports.monster.com/listen/overview/, accessed August 22, 2006; The Human Side of Business, by Stephen D. Boyd, *Agency Sales* magazine, February 2004, page 35, accessed via Infotrac College Edition.

6. We Learn More by Listening Than Talking, by Harvey Mackay, *The Daily Herald*, January 16, 2005, page E6[SB14], http://old.heraldextra.com/modules.php?op=modload&name=News&file=article&sid=45313; Listening Factoids, International Listening Association, http://www.listen.org/pages/factoids.html, accessed August 22, 2006.

7. The Human Side of Business, by Stephen D. Boyd, *Agency Sales* magazine, February 2004, page 35, accessed via Infotrac College Edition; Learn to Listen: Closing the Mouth and Opening the Ears

Facilitates Effective Communication, by Marjorie Brody, Incentive, May 2004, page 57, accessed via Business and Company Resource Center.

8. Number of Employers Passing on Applicants Due to Social Media Posts Continues to Rise, According to New CareerBuilder Survey, June 26, 2014, CareerBuilder website, http://www.careerbuilder.com/share/aboutus/pressreleasesdetail.aspx?sd=6%2F26%2F2014&id=pr829&ed=12%2F31%2F2014, accessed March 22, 2015; Twitter's Growth Will Continue to Slow, Says New Forecast, May 27, 2014, *Forbes* website, http://www.forbes.com/sites/jeffbercovici/2014/05/27/twitters-growth-will-continue-to-slow-says-new-forecast/, accessed March 22, 2015; Twitter was the fastest growing social network in 2012, by Shea Bennet, MediaBistro website, http://www.mediabistro.com/alltwitter/social-networks-growth-2012_b35076, accessed February 21, 2013.

9. Say What? The Best Chinglish from Two Years in China, Ferreting out the Fun website, http://www.ferretingoutthefun.com/2013/12/04/best-chinglish-signs/, accessed January 31, 2014; Shanghai officials say they're winning the war on the quirky Chinglish signs embarrassing their city (and which we all can't help finding funny), by Leon Watson, Daily Mail Online, http://www.dailymail.co.uk/news/article-2183023/Shanghai-says-winning-war-embarrassing-Chinglish-signs-plague-city-Brits-help-finding-funny.html, accessed February 20, 2013; Shanghai Is Trying to Untangle the Mangled English of Chinglish, by Andrew Jacobs, *The New York Times*, May 2, 2010, *The New York Times* website, http://www.nytimes.com/2010/05/03/world/asia/03chinglish.html?pagewanted=1, accessed May 20, 2010; China Clamping Down on Bad English Translations, by Peter Leo, March 17, 2012, *Pittsburgh Post-Gazette* website, http://www.post-gazette.com/stories/local/morning-file/china-clamping-down-on-bad-english-translations-455101/, accessed May 20, 2012.

10. Tech Etiquette: 21 Do's and Don'ts for 2015, by Kevin Sintumuang, January 2, 2015, *The Wall Street Journal* website, http://www.wsj.com/articles/tech-etiquette-21-dos-and-donts-for-2015-1420222724, accessed March 22, 2015.

11. Edward P. Bailey, *Writing and Speaking at Work* (Prentice Hall, 2005), pages 82–89.

12. Presenting Effective Presentations with Visual Aids, U.S. Department of Labor, Occupational Safety and Health Administration, http://www.osha.gov/doc/outreachtraining/htmlfiles/traintec.html, accessed August 22, 2006.

13. Bringing the cloud with you, by Philip Tucker, March 31, 2008, Google Docs Blog, http://googledocs.blogspot.com/2008/03/bringing-cloud-with-you.html, accessed February 13, 2009; Living in the Clouds, by Brian Braiker, June 10, 2008, *Newsweek* website, http://www.newsweek.com/id/140864, accessed February 13, 2009; Comparing Google Docs with competing cloud computing applications, by Michael Miller, February 9, 2009, InformIT website, http://www.informit.com/articles/article.aspx?p=1323244&seqNum=3, accessed February 13, 2009.

6

1. Why States Should Adopt the Revised Uniform Limited Liability Company Act (2006), National Conference of Commissioners on Uniform State Laws website, http://www.nccusl.org/Update/uniformact_why/uniformacts-why-ullca.asp, accessed January 28, 2011.

2. U.S. Census Bureau. The 2012 Statistical Abstract of the United States Tables 743 and 744: http://www.census.gov/compendia/statab/2012/tables/12s0744.pdf, accessed April 6, 2015.

3. U.S. Census Bureau. The 2012 Statistical Abstract of the United States Tables 743 and 744: http://www.census.gov/compendia/statab/2012/tables/12s0744.pdf, accessed April 6, 2015.

4. U.S. Census Bureau. The 2011 Statistical Abstract of the United States Table 743: http://www.census.gov/compendia/statab/2011/tables/11s0744.pdf, accessed January 23, 2011.

5. Joann Lublin, "Smaller Boards Get Bigger Returns," *Wall Street Journal*, August 26, 2014, http://www.wsj.com/articles/smaller-boards-get-bigger-returns-1409078628?KEYWORDS=joann+lublin+boards, accessed February 21, 2015; Joann Lublin, "For Older Board Members, The Pressure to Move On: Asset Managers and Activists Urge Companies to Adopt Director Tenure Policies," *Wall Street Journal*, December 23, 2014, http://www.wsj.com/articles/for-older-board-members-the-pressure-to-move-on-1419362515?KEYWORDS=joann+lublin+boards, accessed February 21, 2015; Angela Chen, "Wal-Mart Adds Former American Airlines CEO Horton to Board," *Wall Street Journal*, November 24, 2014, http://www.wsj.com/articles/wal-mart-adds-former-american-airlines-ceo-horton-to-board-1416839479?KEYWORDS=board+of+director+size, accessed February 21, 2015.

6. About Us. Delaware Division of Corporations, http://www.corp.delaware.gov/aboutagency.shtml, accessed April 6, 2014.

7. Setting Up a One Person Corporation by Karen Klein, November 7, 2007, *Business Week* website, http://www.businessweek.com/smallbiz/content/nov2007/sb2007117_803605.htm.

8. Time Warner Spinning Off Time Inc. Magazines, by R. Yu, USA Today, March 7, 2013, http://www.usatoday.com/story/money/business/2013/03/06/time-warner-spinoff/1969205/.

9. F. O'Connor. "Google Fear a Factor behind Orbitz-Expedia Deal," *Computerworld*, February 13, 2015, http://www.computerworld.com/article/2883920/google-fear-a-factor-behind-orbitz-expedia-deal.html, accessed February 21, 2015; T. Catan & A. Efrati, "U.S. Clears Google's Travel Deal, with Conditions," *The Wall Street Journal*, April 9, 2011, http://www.wsj.com/articles/SB10001424052748704415104576250883736634482, accessed February 21, 2015; J. Nicas, "Google Roils Travel: Flight Searches, Which Place Google at Top, Anger Web Rivals," *The Wall Street Journal*, December 27, 2011, http://www.wsj.com/articles/SB10001424052970203686204577116700668483194, accessed February 21, 2015; D. Fitzgerald, "Antitrust Paradox Hangs over Expedia," *The Wall Street Journal*, 17 February 2015, B3.

10. Why States Should Adopt the Revised Uniform Limited Liability Company Act (2006), National Conference of Commissioners on Uniform State Laws website, http://www.nccusl.org/Update/uniformact_why/uniformacts-why-ullca.asp, accessed January 22, 2011.

11. At Dunkin', Western Expansion Back on Menu, by A. Gasparro, *The Wall Street Journal*, January 13, 2014, http://online.wsj.com/news/articles/SB10001424052702303819704579316922836915570#printMode, accessed March 26, 2014; Vietnam Gets Its First Taste of McDonald's, by V. Trong Kahn, *The Wall Street Journal*; J. Jargon, "Starbucks Shifts in Europe," by J. Jargon, *The Wall Street Journal*, November 30, 2013, B3;

Starbucks Eyes More German Store Openings in European Push, by N. Schimroszik and V. Bryan, Reuters, November 13, 2013.

12. Why States Should Adopt the Revised Uniform Limited Liability Company Act (2006), National Conference of Commissioners on Uniform State Laws website, http://www.nccusl.org /Update/ uniformact_why/uniformacts-why-ullca .asp, accessed January 22, 2011.

13. Franchise Business Outlook: 2013, prepared by IHS Global Insight for the International Franchise Association Educational Foundation, IFA website, http://www.franchise.org/uploadedFiles /Franchise_Business_Outlook_12-17-2012.pdf, accessed February 17, 2013; Census Bureau's First Release of Comprehensive Franchise Data Shows Franchises Make Up More Than 10% of Employer Businesses, U.S. Census Bureau website, http://www .census.gov/newsroom/releases/archives/economic _census/cb10-141.html, accessed February 17, 2013.

14. McDonald's: At a Glance, http://www .entrepreneur.com/franchises/mcdonalds /282570-0.html, accessed April 7, 2015; Subway: At a Glance, http://www.entrepreneur.com /franchises/subway/282839-0.html, accessed April 7, 2015; 7-11: At a Glance, http://www .entrepreneur.com/franchises/7eleveninc /282052-0.html, accessed April 7, 2015.

15. K. Taylor, "Women in Franchising: An Enthusiastic Minority," http://www.entrepreneur .com/article/229675, accessed April 7, 2015.

16. G. Moran, 3 Women to Watch in the Franchising Sector, http://www.entrepreneur. com/slideshow/240847, accessed April 7, 2015. Franchising Attracts More Women, Minorities by Julie Bennett, Startup Journal, accessed through Entrepreneur.com website, http://www.entrepre- neur.com/franchises/franchisezone/startupjournal /article61324.html; Female Franchisors Few and Far Between by Julie M. Young, e-magnify.com website, https://www.e-magnify.com/resources _articlearchiveresults. asp?categoryID=18;

17. "Franchised Business Ownership: By Minority and Gender Groups," International Franchising Association, http://emarket.franchise.org/Minority- Report2011.pdf, 2011, accessed April 7, 2015.

18. J. Bourdow & M. Brewer, "Inclusion is a Growth Strategy," *Franchising World*, June 2013, 15–17.

19. "Diversity in Franchising," International Franchise Association, http://www.franchise.org /industrysecondary.aspx?id=40970, accessed March 24, 2014; DiversityFran Participating Companies, International Franchise Organization, http://ifatest.c30d.com/sites/default/files/October _%202014_DiversityFran%20Participating%20 Companies.pdf, accessed April 7, 2015.

20. Subway, Entrepreneur.com website, http:// www.entrepreneur.com/franchises/subway /282839-2.html.

21. C. Dulaney, "Wendy's to Sell Another 500 Stores to Franchisees," *The Wall Street Journal*, February 3, 2015, www.wsj.com/articls/wendys-to -sell-another-500-stores-to-franchisees-1422965356, accessed February 21, 2015; J. Maze, "Wendy's Franchisee Files Counterclaim over Remodeling," *Nation's Restaurant News*, February 20, 2015, http://nrn.com/corporate-news/wendy-s-franchisee -files-counterclaim-over-remodels, accessed February 21, 2015; A. Kelso, "Wendy's Accelerates Store Reimaging, Undergoes Employee 'Reboot.'" QSRweb.com, January 20, 2012, http://www.qsrweb .com/articles/wendys-accelerates-store-reimaging -undergoes-employee-reboot/, accessed February 21, 2015; "Wendy's Sues One of Its Largest, Oldest

Franchisees," *Dayton Business Journal*, January 2, 2015, http://www.bizjournals.com/dayton/blog /morning_call/2015/01/wendys-sues-one-of-its -largest-oldest-franchisees.html, accessed February 21, 2015; *The Wendy's Company* 2013 Annual Report, available online at http://ir.wendys.com /phoenix.zhtml?c=67548&p=quarterlyearnings #9294433, accessed April 7, 2015.

22. Franchise Rule Compliance Guide, Federal Trade Commission website, http://www.ftc.gov /bcp/edu/pubs/business/franchise/bus70.pdf, pages 20, 102–103, and 121.

Pg. 98 Fact: *The Weekly Standard*, April, 2012, http://www.weeklystandard.com/blogs/ge-filed -57000-page-tax-return-paid-no-taxes-14 -billionprofits_609137.html.

7

1. Entrepreneurial Activity Declines Again in 2013 as Labor Market Strengthens, according to Kauffman Report, by Dane Stangler, April 9, 2014, Kauffman Foundation website, http://www .kauffman.org/newsroom/2014/04/entrepreneurial -activity-declines-again-in-2013-as-labor-market -strengthens, accessed July 3, 2014; New business formation bounces back; posts first increase since the recession, by J. D. Harrison, July 31, 2013, *The Washington Post* website, http://articles .washingtonpost.com/2013-07-31/business /40931691_1_job-growth-new-firms-small -business, accessed February 5, 2014; New Business Startups Declined in 2011, Annual Kauffman Study Shows, March 19, 2012, Kauffman website, http://www.kauffman.org /research-and-policy/kiea-2012-infographic.aspx, accessed June 12, 2012.

2. A drop-off in start-ups: Where are all the entre- preneurs? by Walter Hamilton, September 7, 2014, *Los Angeles Times* website, http://www.latimes .com/business/la-fi-entrepreneurs-20140907-story .html#page=1, accessed April 5, 2015.

3. The Forbes 400, edited by Matthew Miller and Duncan Greenberg, September 17, 2008, *Forbes* website, http://www.forbes.com/2008/09/16 /forbes-400-billionaires-lists-400list08_cx_mn _0917richamericans_land.html, accessed February 15, 2009.

4. Discover Polls Reveal True Character of the American Entrepreneur, October 22, 2007, Press Release, Discover Financial Services website, http://investorrelations.discoverfinancial .com/phoenix.zhtml?c=204177&p=irol -newsArticle&ID=1065373&highlight=, accessed February 15, 2009.

5. The Big Fat Story, The Geek Kings, by *Newsweek* staff, June 5, 2011, *Newsweek* website, http://www.newsweek.com/big-fat-story -geek-kings-67969, accessed February 5, 2013; *Forbes* 400 Richest Americans, September 2013, *Forbes* website, http://www.forbes.com/profile/ dustin-moskovitz/, accessed February 19, 2014; Surprising Past Jobs of Successful Entrepreneurs, by Jason Nazar, October 31, 2013, *Business Insider* website, http://www.businessinsider.com/surprising -past-jobs-of-successful-entrepreneurs-2013-10, accessed April 5, 2015.

6. More than Half of Small Business Owners Work at Least Six-Day Weeks, Still Find Time for Personal Life, Wells Fargo News Release, August 9, 2005, https://www.wellsfargo.com/press/20050809 _GallupPersonalLife; Discover Polls Reveal True Character of the American Entrepreneur, October 22, 2007, Press Release, Discover Financial

Services website, http://investorrelations .discoverfinancial.com/phoenix.zhtml?c=204177&p =irol-newsArticle&ID=1065373&highlight=, accessed February 15, 2009; Small Business Owners Working Longer Hours, May 26, 2009, Rent to Own website, http://rtoonline.com/Content /Article/may09/smal-business-owners-work-hours -survey-052609.asp, accessed June 12, 2012.

7. Entrepreneurial Risk and Market Entry, by Brian Wu and Anne Marie Knott, SBA Office of Advocacy, January 2005, http://www.sba.gov/advo /research/wkpbw249.pdf.

8. The 6 Attributes Shared by Young Millionaires, by Peter Voogd, February 11, 2015, *Entrepreneur* website, http://www.entrepreneur.com/article /242736, accessed April 6, 2015.

9. Failure: Use It as a Springboard to Success, U.S. SBA Online Library, no at-tribution, http://www .sba.gov/library/successXIII/19-Failure-Use-it.doc, accessed December 28, 2005.

10. Rejection Letters: The Publishers Who Got It Embarrassingly Wrong…, by Alice E. Vincent, November 7, 2012, Huffington Post, http://www.huffingtonpost.co.uk/2012/05/16 /publishers-who-got-it-wrong_n_1520190. html#slide=more226527, accessed March 15, 2013; Failure: Use It as a Springboard to Success, U.S. SBA Online Library, no attribution, http://www .sba.gov/library/successXIII/19-Failure -Use-it.doc, accessed December 28, 2005.

11. What Makes Them Tick, by Keith McFarland, Inc 500, 2005, Inc website, http://www.inc.com /resources/inc500/2005/articles/20051001/tick .html; Bootstrap-ping Your Startup? Make Money Before You Spend It, by Kwame Kuadey, June 12, 2012, Young Entrepreneurs Council website, http://theyec.org/bootstrapping-your -startup-make-money-before-you-spend-it/, accessed June 12, 2012.

12. Starved of Financing, New Businesses Are in Decline, by Benjamin Ryan, September 4, 2014, Gallup Business Journal website, http://www.gallup. com/businessjournal/175499/starved-financing-new -businesses-decline.aspx, accessed April 5, 2015.

13. The Inspiration Paradox: Your Best Creative Time Is Not When You Think, by Cindi May, March 6, 2012; *Scientific American* website, http://www.scientificamerican.com/article/your -best-creative-time-not-when-you-think/, accessed February 6, 2014. Creativity Happens When You Least Expect It, by Sian Beilock, February 8, 2012, *Psychology Today* website, http://www .psychologytoday.com/blog/choke/201202 /creativity-happens-when-you-least-expect-it, accessed March 17, 2013.

14. How to finance a new business, April 2008, *Consumer Reports* website, http://www .consumerreports.org/cro/money/credit-loan /how-to-finance-a-new-business/overview/how-to -finance-a-new-business-ov.htm, accessed March 18, 2011.

15. Credit Cards Replace Small Business Loans, by John Tozzi, August 20, 2008, *Business Week* website, http://www.businessweek.com/smallbiz /content/aug2008/sb20080820_288348.htm ?chan=smallbiz_smallbiz+index+page_top+small +business+stories, accessed February 15, 2009.

16. What Do Small Businesses Need Banks for, Anyway? By Patrick Clark, September 10, 2013, *Businessweek* website, http://www.businessweek .com/articles/2013-09-10/what-do-small-businesses -need-banks-for-anyway, accessed February 6, 2014.

17. Start-up Information, updated April 28, 2008, Delaware Small Business Devel-opment Center website, http://www.delawaresbdc.org

/DocumentMaster.aspx?doc=1003#6, accessed February 15, 2009.

18. San Diego's Investing Angels by Mike Freeman, January 32, 2013, *San Diego Union Tribune* website, http://www.utsandiego.com /news/2013/jan/31/Tech-Coast-Angels-fund-local -start-ups/?page=1#article-copy, accessed March 24, 2013; Financial Assistance, Small Business Administration website, http://www.sba .gov/services/financialassistance/index.html, accessed February 15, 2009.

19. Press release from the University of New Hampshire Center for Venture Research, November 18, 2014, https://paulcollege.unh.edu/sites /paulcollege.unh.edu/files/webform/Q1Q2%20 2014%20Angel%20Market%20Press%20Release. pdf, accessed April 8, 2015.

20. The Angel Investor Market in Q1Q2 2011: A Return to the Seed Stage, by Jeffrey Sohl, Center for Venture Research, October 11, 2011, University of New Hampshire website, http://wsbe.unh .edu/sites/default/files/q1q2_2011_analysis_report .pdf, accessed June 12, 2012; Angel Investments Up 40%, by Abby Tracy, March 13, 2012, Inc. website, http://wire.inc.com/2012/03/13/angel -investments-up-40/, accessed June 12, 2012.

21. The Steady, Strategic Assent of jetBlue Airways, Strategic Management Knowledge at Wharton, December 14, 2005–January 10, 2006, http://knowledge.wharton.upenn.edu/article/1342 .cfm; Charging Ahead, by Bobbie Gossage, January 2004, Inc. Magazine, http://www.inc.com /magazine/20040101/gettingstarted.html.

22. Amplestuff website, http://www.amplestuff .com/; Kazoo v. Walmart, *Reveries* magazine, November 29, 2005, http://www.reveries.com/?p=232.

23. Odd Jobs: Prosthetic Dog-Testicle Maker, by Eric Spitznagel, April 25, 2012, Bloomberg Businessweek website, http://www .businessweek.com/articles/2012-04-25/odd -jobs-prosthetic-dog-testicle-maker#disqus _thread, accessed June 14, 2012; 6 Weird But Successful Small Business Ideas, by Heather Levin, September 11, 2011, MoneyCrashers website, http://www.moneycrashers.com/weird-successful -small-business-ideas/, accessed June 13, 2012; Romantic disappointment sparks a business, by Tina Traster, July 6, 2012, Crain's New York Business, http://www.crainsnewyork.com/article /SMALLBIZ/120709950/romantic-disappointment -sparks-a-business#, accessed July 16, 2014; Weird Companies That Work by Patty Simone, October 28, 2010, Entrepreneur website, http://www .entrepreneur.com/article/217476, accessed April 10, 2015.

24. E-Commerce Award—June 2002, Anything Left-Handed website, http://www.anythingleft -handed.co.uk/pressreleases.html.

25. Focus on Success, Not Failure, by Rhonda Abrams, May 7, 2004, USA Today website money section, http://www.usatoday.com/money /smallbusiness/columnist/abrams/2004-05-06 -success_x.htm.

26. Is Entrepreneurship for You? U.S. Small Business Administration, http://www.sba.gov /starting_business/startup/areyouready.html, accessed December 15, 2005.

27. Committee Examines Ways to Ease Growing Regulatory Burden on Small Businesses, July 30, 2008, U.S. House of Representatives Press Release, House of Representatives website, http://www.house.gov/smbiz/PressReleases /2008/pr-7-30-08-regulatory.html, accessed February 15, 2009.

28. How Obamacare affects businesses—large and small, by David Nather, September 30, 2013,

Politico website, http://www.politico.com /story/2013/09/how-obamacare-affects-businesses -large-and-small-97460.html, accessed February 6, 2014; Entrepreneurship in the 21st Century, Conference Proceedings, March 26, 2004, SBA Office of Advocacy and the Kauffman Foundation, http://www.sba.gov/advo/stats/proceedings_a .pdf; Health Care Costs Surface in Economic Stimulus Debate, by Sharon McLoone, February 10, 2009, *Washington Post* website, http://voices .washingtonpost.com/small-business/2009/02 /health_care_costs_surface_in_e.html, accessed February 15, 2009.

29. Business Plan Basics, U.S. SBA, http://www .sba.gov/starting_business/planning/basic.html, accessed February 15, 2009.

30. Frequently Asked Questions, SBA Office of Advocacy, updated September 2009, SBA website, http://www.sba.gov/advo/stats/sbfaq.pde, accessed June 3, 2010.

31. Inventor of the Week, Lemulson-MIT website, http://web.mit.edu/invent/iow/epperson.html, accessed March 15, 2013; Top 10 Accidental Inventions, Science Channel website, http://science .discovery.com/brink/top-ten/accidental-inventions /inventions-01.html, accessed March 22, 2011.

32. Frequently Asked Questions, SBA Office of Advocacy, Updated September 2008, SBA website, http://www.sba.gov/advo/stats/sbfaq.pdf, accessed February 17, 2009.

33. Frequently Asked Questions, SBA Office of Advocacy, Updated September 2008, SBA website, http://www.sba.gov/advo/stats/sbfaq.pdf, accessed February 17, 2009.

34. Small Business Drives Inner City Growth and Jobs, News Release, October 11, 2005, U.S. SBA Office of Advocacy, http://www.sba.gov/advo /press/05-32.html.

35. Global Entrepreneurship Monitor, 2008 Executive Report, by Niels Bosma, Zoltan J. Acs, Erkko Autio, Alicia Coduras, and Jonathan Levie, Babson College and London School of Economics, http://www.gemconsortium.org /article.aspx?id=76, published January 15, 2009, accessed February 17, 2009.

Pg. 120 Fact: http://www.forbes.com/sites /johngreathouse/2012/06/05/business-tips-from -college-dropouts-zuckerberg-jobs-gates-dell -ellison-branson-and-disney/, and http://www .gemconsortium.org/docs/download/260, accessed November 2012.

Pg. 123 Fact: Global Entrepreneurship Monitor Report 2012, by Siri Roland Xavier, Donna Kelley, Jacqui Kew, Mike Herrington, and Arne Vorderwülbecke, January 17, 2013, GEM Consortium website, http://www.gemconsortium .org/docs/download/2645, accessed March 15, 2013.

8

1. J. Novack, "How SEC's New RoboCop Profiles Companies for Accounting *Fraud*," Forbes, August 9, 2013, http://www.forbes.com /sites/janetnovack/2013/08/09/how-secs-new -robocop-profiles-companies-for-accounting -fraud/, accessed October 10, 2013.

2. A. Ross Sorkin, "Graphic: A Long Line of Accounting Scandals," Dealbook, *The New York Times*, November 20, 2012, http:// dealbook.nytimes.com/2012/11/20/graphic-a -long-line-of-accounting-scandals/, accessed March 5, 2013.

3. E. Chancellor, "The Bookkeeper of Venice," *The Wall Street Journal*, November 7, 2012, http://

online.wsj.com/article/SB100014240529702037076 04578092813119816922.html, accessed March 17, 2013; J. Gleeson-White, "Double Entry: How the Merchants of Venice Created Modern Finance," October 1, 2012: W.W. Norton & Company.

4. T. Fairless, "Huge Profit Stokes Concerns over Starbucks's Tax Practices in Europe," *The Wall Street Journal*, April 6, 2015, http://www.wsj.com /articles/starbuckss-tax-practices-draw-european -scrutiny-1428363189?mod=WSJ_hpp_sections _business, accessed April 10, 2015; D. Hakim, "Europe Takes Aim at Deals Created to Escape Taxes," *The New York Times*, November 14, 2014, A1; J. Masters, "U.S. Corporate Tax Reform," Council on Foreign Relations, April 5, 2012, accessed April 10, 2015, http://www.cfr.org/united -states/us-corporate-tax-reform/p27860; *Starbucks Fiscal 2014 Annual Report*, p. 4, http://investor .starbucks.com/phoenix.zhtml?c=99518&p=irol -reportsAnnual, accessed April 10, 2015.

5. "Cell Phone and Smartphone Ownership Demographics," Pew Research Center Internet Project Survey, January 9–12, 2014, http://www .pewinternet.org/data-trend/mobile/cell-phone-and -smartphone-ownership-demographics/; M. Gottfried, "Verizon's Double-Edged Growth," *The Wall Street Journal*, January 27, 2015, http://www.wsj.com /articles/verizons-double-edged-growth-heard-on -the-street-1422306300, accessed April 9, 2015; C. Morran, "Verizon CFO: Getting Rid of Phone Subsidies Is A Mistake," *Consumerist*, March 10, 2014; F. Norris, "New Standards for Companies' Revenue Accounting Will Begin in 2017," *The New York Times*, May 28, 2014, http://dealbook .nytimes.com/2014/05/28/regulators-set-new-rules -for-companies-revenue-accounting/?_r=0; T. Gryta, "As Phone Subsidies Fade, Apple Could Be Hurt," *The Wall Street Journal*, April 21, 2014, http://www .wsj.com/articles/SB10001424052702304049904579 516103768847882.

6. Mission statement on PCAOB website, http://www.pcaobus.org/index.aspx.

7. "B Corporation 2012 Annual Report," B Corporation, http://www.bcorporation.net /news-and-media/annual-report-2012, accessed March 29, 2014; B. Collins, "Ice Cream Dream," *Inside Counsel*, December 2, 2012, 55; B. Halsey, S. Tomkowicz, and J. Halsey, "Benefit Corporation Concerns for Financial Service Professional," *Journal of Financial Service Professionals*, January 2013, 74–82; A. Loten, "When Profits Can Take a Back Seat," *The Wall Street Journal*, January 18, 2012, http://online.wsj.com /article/SB1000142405297020373530457716859 1470161630.html, accessed March 29, 2014.

8. *The Essentials of Finance and Budgeting*, Harvard Business School Press, Boston, MA, 2005, pp. 177–181.

9. Albrecht, Stice, Stice, and Swain, *Accounting Concepts and Applications*, 9th ed. (Cengage Learning), p. 758.

Pg. 138 Fact: Securities and Exchange Commission: A Beginner's Guide to Financial Statements, SEC website, http://www.sec.gov/investor/pubs /begfinstmtguide.htm, accessed March 29, 2009. ("Read The Footnotes" finished seventh in the 2004 Kentucky Derby.)

9

1. See, for example, Moyer, McGuigan, and Rao, *Fundamentals of Contemporary Financial Management*, 2nd ed. (South-Western, Cengage Learning), p. 3; Brigham and Houston,

Fundamentals of Financial Management, 11th ed. (Cengage Learning), p. 2.

2. Numbers, *Business Week,* February 9, 2009, p. 13.

3. "Industry Browser - Services - Restaurants Industry - Company List," Yahoo! Finance, http://finance.yahoo.com/q/ks?s=MCD+Key +Statistics, accessed April 9, 2015; "McDonald's Corporation Financials," *The Wall Street Journal,* http://quotes.wsj.com/MCD/financials/Ratios, accessed April 9, 2015; "McDonald's Financial Ratios MCD," The Motley Fool, http://www.fool .com/quote/nyse/mcdonalds/mcd/financial-ratios, accessed April 9, 2015; "McDonald's Visual Financials," ADVFN, http://www.advfn.com/stock -market/NYSE/MCD/financials, accessed April 9, 2015; "Overview Industry Profile: Fast-Food & Quick-Service Restaurants," First Research, http:// mergent.firstresearch-learn.com/industry_detail .aspx?pid=433&chapter=7, accessed April 9, 2015.

4. J. Mackey, M. Friedman, and T. Rodger, "Rethinking the Social Responsibility of Business," *Reason,* October 1, 2005, http://reason.com/archives/2005/10/01 /rethinking-the-social-responsi, accessed March 25, 2013.

5. The approximate "finance charge" of not taking the discount on credit can be computed using the following formula:

Cost of Not Taking discount

$$= \frac{\% \text{ discount}}{(100-\% \text{ discount})}$$
$$\times \frac{365}{(\text{Credit\_Period-Discount\_Period})}$$

where % discount is the discount the buyer receives for paying on or before the last day the discount is available, the Credit Discount Period is the number of days before payment of full invoice amount is due.

6. Financial Services Used by Small Businesses: Evidence from the 2003 Survey of Small Business Finances, by Traci Mack and John D. Wolken, *Federal Reserve Bulletin,* October 2006, p. A181.

7. Annual Asset-Based Lending and Factoring Surveys, 2011, Commercial Finance Association website, https://www.cfa.com/eweb/upload /CFA_Member_ABLFactoring_2011_Reports.pdf, accessed March 24, 2013.

8. M. Pilon, "What Is Commercial Paper and Why Does It Matter?" *The Wall Street Journal,* October 7, 2008, http://blogs.wsj.com/wallet /2008/10/07/what-is-commercial-paper-and-why -does-it-matter/tab/print/, accessed March 24, 2013.

9. V. Monga, "Cash Hoard Helps Apple Avoid Commercial Paper Backstop—The CFO Report," *The Wall Street Journal,* http://blogs.wsj.com/cfo /2014/06/10/cash-hoard-helps-apple-avoid -commercial-paper-backstop/, accessed April 9, 2015.

10. J. White, "Cash Managers Favored Commercial Paper in January," *The Wall Street Journal,* February 6, 2013, http://blogs.wsj.com /cfo/2013/02/06/cash-managers-favored-commercial -paper-in-january/, accessed March 24, 2013; J. Willhite, "Finance Execs Dumped Commercial Paper in December—The CFO Report, http:// blogs.wsj.com/cfo/2015/01/22/finance-execs -dumped-commercial-paper-in-december/?KEYW -ORDS=%22commercial+paper%22, January 22, 2015, accessed April 9, 2015.

11. "Google Financials," Google Finance, December 31, 2014, http://www.google.com/finance ?q=NASDAQ%3AGOOGL&fstype=ii&ei=FRUsVc -HYIeSPsgeS14DoCw.

12. Table B-90: Corporate Profits with Inventory Valuation and Capital Consumption Adjustments,

1964–2012, Economic Report of the President, March 2013, U.S. Government Printing Office, http://www.gpo.gov/fdsys/pkg/ERP-2013/pdf/ERP -2013-table90.pdf, accessed March 24, 2013.

13. Berkshire Hathaway Inc., Historical Prices, Google Prices, http://www.google.com/finance /historical?q=NYSE:BRK.A, accessed April 13, 2015.

14. Why do companies issue debt and bonds? Can't they just borrow from the bank?, Investopedia website, http://www.investopedia.com/ask/answers /05/reasonforcorporatebonds.asp, accessed on March 28, 2013.

15. A. Scaggs, "One Firm's Perk Is Another's Slap," *The Wall Street Journal,* January 29, 2015, B6; P. Wilson, "Richmond Won Stone Brewing— With a Bit of Drama, Too," *The Virginian-Pilot,* December 29, 2014, http://hamptonroads. com/2014/12/richmond-won-stone-brewing-bit -drama-too, accessed February 27, 2015; M. Hipolit, "Richmond Restaurant Owners Speak Out Against City Funding for Stone Brewing," WTVR.com, December 8, 2014, http://wtvr. com/2014/12/08/richmond-restaurant-owners-not -happy-about-financing-for-stone-brewing-bistro/, accessed February 27, 2015; Stone Brewing Company website, http://www.stonebrewing.com /press/facts.aspm, accessed February 27, 2015; J. Schulz, "Stone Brewing on Why It Picked Richmond," *Columbus Business First,* October 9, 2014, http://www.bizjournals.com/columbus/blog /2014/10/stone-brewing-on-why-it-picked- richmond.html?page=2, accessed February 27, 2015; Virginia Sales Tax Rate—2015, http://www .tax-rates.org/virginia/sales-tax, accessed April 13, 2015.

16. Twitter 2013 Annual Report, pp. 41, 45, https://investor.twitterinc.com/annuals.cfm, accessed February 27, 2015; Twitter Inc., *The Wall Street Journal,* http://quotes.wsj.com/TWTR?mod =DNH_S_cq, accessed February 27, 2015; Facebook 2013 Annual Report, p. 39, http:// investor.fb.com/annuals.cfm, accessed February 27, 2015; Y. Koh, "Twitter's Biggest Battle: Indifference," *The Wall Street Journal,* February 10, 2014, B1; L. Popelka, "What We Learned from Twitter's IPO: The Value of Innovation Is at an All-Time High," *Bloomberg Businessweek,* November 18, 2013, http://www .businessweek.com/articles/2013-11-18/what-we -learned-from-twitter-s-ipo-the-value-of-innovation -is-at-an-all-time-high, accessed December 1, 2013.

17. Financial Sectors' New Buzzword Is Deleverage, by Chris Arnold, NPR website, http://www.npr.org /templates/story/story.php?storyId=94795760, accessed August 9, 2009; Deleveraging, Now Only in Early Stages, Will Transform the Banking Industry, by James Saft, *The New York Times* website, http:// www.nytimes.com/2008/06/26/business/worldbusiness /26iht-col27.1.14006619.html?_r=1, accessed August 9, 2009; Deleveraging: A Fate Worse than Debt, *Economist* website, http://www.economist .com/businessfinance/displaystory.cfm?story _id=12306060, accessed August 9, 2009.

18. Brief Summary of the Dodd-Frank Wall Street Reform and Consumer Protection Act. United States Senate Committee on Banking, Housing and Urban Affairs website, http://banking.senate.gov /public/_files/070110_Dodd_Frank_Wall_Street _Reform_comprehensive_summary_Final.pdf.

19. "Honoring Innovation," *Pet Business,* December 1, 2012, http://www.petbusiness.com /articles/2012-12-01/Honoring-Innovation, accessed March 30, 2014; B. Arnold, "Meet the Doginton Post Awards Winners!" Dogintonpost.com, February 4, 2013, http://dogingtonpost.com/meet-the

-dogington-post-awards-winners/, accessed March 30, 2014; S. Needleman, "When Banks Won't Back Your Startup," *The Wall Street Journal,* March 9, 2014, http://online.wsj.com/news/articles /SB10001424052702304360704579417082607640414, accessed March 30, 2014.

20. Getting Tough with Customers, by Matthew Boyle and Olga Kharif, *Business Week* March 9, 2009, p. 30.

21. Honda Profit Tumbles: Thai Floods Hit U.S. Output, by Y. Takahashi and M. Ramsey, *Dow Jones NewsPlus,* October 31, 2011, http://www .djnewsplus.com/rssarticle/SB132004240725505903 .html, accessed June 11, 2012.

22. U.S. Energy Information Administration, *Table F2: Jet Fuel Consumption, Price, and Expenditure Estimates 2013,* http://www.eia.gov/state/seds /sep_fuel/html/pdf/fuel_jf.pdf, accessed February 27, 2015; J. Nicas & S. Carey, "Suddenly Flush Airlines Debate How to Use Cash," *The Wall Street Journal,* January 22, 2015, http://www.wsj .com/articles/suddenly-flush-airlines-debate-how -to-use-cash-1421970174, accessed February 27, 2015; J. Nicas, "Delta Says Fuel-Savings Will Be Used to Pay Down Debt, Reward Investors," *The Wall Street Journal,* January 20, 2015, http://www .wsj.com/articles/delta-results-helped-by-falling -fuel-prices-1421759622, accessed February 27, 2015; International Air Transport Association, "Fuel Price Analysis, February 13, 2015," available online at http://www.iata.org/publications/economics /fuel-monitor/Pages/price-analysis.aspx; T. Hoium, "OPEC's Oil Price War Is Paying Off, But It's Far from Over," The Motley Fool, February 28, 2015, online at http://www.fool.com/investing/general /2015/02/28/opecs-oil-price-war-is-paying-off-but -its-far-from.aspx, accessed February 27, 2015; C. Ngai & J. Dastin, "Exclusive—U.S. Airlines Confront Cheap Oil's Flip Side: Cost Hedges," Reuters, http://www.reuters.com/article/2014/12/23 /us-oil-hedging-airlines-idUSKBN0K10AJ20141223, December 23, 2014, accessed April 13, 2015; T. Maxon, "American Airlines Dumps Its Fuel Hedges—And Saves," *Dallas Morning News,* July 16, 2014, http://www.dallasnews.com/business /airline-industry/20140716-american-airlines- dumps-its-fuel-hedges--and-saves.ece, accessed April 13, 2015; L. Lloyd, "American Airlines to Reap Benefits from Oil-Price Decline," January 4, 2015, http://articles.philly.com/2015-01-04/ business/57637327_1_american-airlines-southwest -airlines-jet-fuel, accessed April 13, 2015.

Pg. 148 Fact: Nielsen: 50% of Global Consumers Surveyed Willing to Pay More for Goods, Services From Socially Responsible Companies, Up From 2011, August 6, 2013, http://www.nielsen.com /content/corporate/us/en/press-room/2013/nielsen -50-percent-of-global-consumers-surveyed-willing -to-pay-more-fo.html.

10

1. Financial Accounts of the United States: Flow of Funds, Balance Sheets, and Integrated Macroeconomic Accounts, Table L.110, Federal Reserve Statistical Release, March 12, 2015, http://www .federalreserve.gov/releases/z1/Current/z1.pdf, accessed April 13, 2015.

2. D. Michaels, S. Mamudi, and M. Phillips, "Breaking Bad," *Bloomberg Businessweek,* Sept. 30–Oct. 6, 2014, 53–54; J. Bunge, "Nasdaq Takes Blame for Stock Halt—In Shift, Exchange Says Its Performance Surrounding Outage Was 'Unaccept-able,'" *The Wall Street Journal,* August 30, 2013, C1; J. Bunge, "Earlier Glitch Cued Talk,

No Action—Committee Overseeing Feed at Heart of Nasdaq Outage Made No Changes Before Problems Resurfaced," *The Wall Street Journal*, October 31, 2013, C1; S. Patterson, A. Ackerman, and J. Strasburg, "Shutdown Bares Stock Exchange Flaws," *The Wall Street Journal*, August 24, 2013, A1.

3. How is a Credit Union Different Than a Bank? MyCreditUnion.gov, http://www.mycreditunion .gov/about-credit-unions/Pages/How-is-a-Credit -Union-Different-than-a-Bank.aspx, accessed March 30, 2013.

4. Financial Accounts of the United States: Flow of Funds, Balance Sheets, and Integrated Macroeconomic Accounts, Table L.114, Federal Reserve Statistical Release, March 12, 2015, http://www .federalreserve.gov/releases/z1/Current/z1.pdf, accessed April 13, 2015.

5. 2012 Dogs of the Dow, Dogsofthedow.com, http://www.dogsofthedow.com/dogs2012.htm, accessed March 30, 2013; In Dividends We Trust, by J. Buckingham, *Forbes*, November 21, 2011, p. 80; Dividends for 100 Years, by S. Marnjian, October 2, 2009, http://www.fool.com/investing/dividends -income/2009/10/02/dividends-for-100-years.aspx, accessed June 15, 2012; "Dogs" Strategy Paid Dividends for Second Year in a Row, by S. Russolillo and B. Conway, *The Wall Street Journal*, January 3, 2012, http://online.wsj.com/article/SB10001424052 9702044644045771150841303933306.html, accessed March 30, 2013.

6. Mortgage Debt Outstanding, Board of Governors of the Federal Reserve System, March 2015, http://www.federalreserve.gov/econresdata /releases/mortoutstand/current.htm, accessed April 13, 2015.

7. The Cost of the Savings and Loan Crisis, by Timothy Curry and Lynn Shibut, FDIC Review December 2000, accessed on FDIC website, http:// www.fdic.gov/bank/analytical/banking/2000dec /brv13n2_2.pdf, accessed March 30, 2013.

8. FDIC: Deposit Insurance FAQs, https://www .fdic.gov/deposit/deposits/faq.html, accessed April 13, 2015.

9. Public Company Accounting Oversight Board website, http://pcaobus.org/Pages/default.aspx.

10. Brief Summary of the Dodd-Frank Wall Street Reform and Consumer Protection Act, United States Senate Committee on Banking, Housing and Urban Affairs website, http://banking.senate .gov/public/_files/070110_Dodd_Frank_Wall _Street_Reform_comprehensive_summary_Final .pdf, accessed April 13, 2015.

11. Brief Summary of the Dodd-Frank Wall Street Reform and Consumer Protection Act, United States Senate Committee on Banking, Housing and Urban Affairs website, http://www.banking.senate .gov/public/_files/070110_Dodd_Frank_Wall _Street_Reform_comprehensive_summary_Final .pdf, accessed April 13, 2015.

12. Some preferred stock contains a "participating" feature on its dividend. This means that if the dividend paid to common stockholders exceeds some specified amount, the board must also raise the dividend to preferred stockholders. See Participating Preferred Stock, Investopedia website, http://www.investopedia .com/terms/p/participatingpreferredstock.asp, accessed April 13, 2015.

13. Are Bond Buyers This Crazy? by Dan Caplinger, Motley Fool website, http://www.fool.com/investing /dividends-income/2010/08/26/are-bond-buyers-this -crazy.aspx; Investors, Issuers Plan for 2112 with "Century" Bonds, by A. Gara, *Forbes*, April 12, 2012, http://www.forbes.com/sites/thestreet/2012 /04/12/investors-issuers-plan-for-2112-with-century -bonds/, accessed June 15, 2012.

14. The Coming Bond Default Wave, by Richard Lehmann, *Forbes* magazine website, http://www .forbes.com/forbes/2008/1013/130.html.

15. C. Stein, "Stockpickers Say They'll Be Back," *Bloomberg Businessweek*, March 8, 2015, 39–40; J. Cahill, "Corporate Chicago's Billion-Dollar Addiction," *Crain's Chicago Business*, February 14, 2015, http://www.chicagobusiness.com/article/20150214 /ISSUE10/302149992/corporate-chicagos-billion -dollar-addiction, accessed April 13, 2015; "Buybacks Grow 50% Year-Over-Year; Near Pre-Recession Highs," FactSet Insight, June 19, 2014, http:// www.factset.com/insight/2014/6/buyback_6.18.14, accessed April 13, 2015; "2013 Buybacks for S&P 500 Companies Grow Nearly 25% Year-Over-Year," FactSet Insight, May 27, 2014, http://www.factset .com/insight/2014/3/buyback_3.25.14, accessed April 13, 2015; M. Murphy & J. Kester, "CFO Journal: Buybacks Accelerate But Meet Cynicism," *The Wall Street Journal*, October 28, 2014, B1; J. Clements, "The Downside to Share Buybacks," *The Wall Street Journal*, October 26, 2014, 1.

16. C. Chang, W. Nelson, and D. White, Do Green Mutual Funds Perform Well? *Management Research Review* 35 (2012): 693–708; M. Orlitzky, Payoffs to Social and Environmental Performance, *Journal of Investing* 14 (2005): 403–441; M. Orlitzky, F. Schmidt, and S. Rynes, Corporate Social and Financial Performance: A Meta-Analysis, *Organization Studies* 24 (2003): 403–441; V. Vyvyan, C. Ng, and M. Brimble, Socially Responsible Investing: The Green Attitudes and Grey Choices of Australian Investors, *Corporate Governance* 15 (2007): 370–381.

17. Quick Facts, NYSE EURONEXT, http://www .nyx.com/en/who-we-are/quick-facts, accessed March 30, 2013; Markets, NASDAQ OMX, http://www.nasdaqomx.com/aboutus/ourmarkets/, accessed March 30, 2013.

18. Vanguard Total Stock Market Index Fund Investor Shares, Vanguard, https://personal .vanguard.com/us/funds/fees?FundId=0085 &FundIntExt=INT#tab=2, accessed March 23, 2014; K. Grind, How Low Can Fund Fees Go? *The Wall Street Journal*, December 15, 2012, http://online.wsj.com/article/SB10001424127887324 29660457817729254065504.html, accessed March 31, 2013; N. Huang, How to Pick the Best Index Funds, *Kiplinger's Person Finance*, February 2013, http://www.kiplinger.com/article /investing/T041-C000-S002-how-to-pick-the-best -index-funds.html, accessed March 31, 2013; P. Merriman, 10 Ways Index Funds Can Save Your Retirement, Market Watch, December 19, 2012, http://www.marketwatch.com/story/10-ways -index-funds-can-save-your-retirement-2012-12 -19, accessed March 31; "Low Investment Fees and Costs Mean You Keep More for You," Vanguard, https://investor.vanguard.com/investing /investment-fees, accessed 28 February 2015; K. Damato, "3 Reasons to Pay Commissions, Not Fees, To a Financial Advisor," *Wall Street Journal*, February 18, 2015, http://blogs.wsj.com /totalreturn/2015/02/18/3-reasons-to-pay -commissions-not-fees-to-a-financial-adviser/, accessed February 28, 2015; M. Reiman, "Study: Only 24% of Active Mutual Fund Managers Outperform the Market Index," NerdWallet.com, March 27, 2013, http://www.nerdwallet.com/blog /investing/2013/active-mutual-fund-managers -beat-market-index/.

19. D. Benoit, "CEOs' Test: Contending with Activist Investors: Executives Devise Strategies to Deal with Shareholders, Who Are More Assertive Since Financial Crisis," *The Wall Street Journal*, November 25, 2014, http://www.wsj.com/articles /ceos-test-contending-with-activist-investors -1416957944?tesla=y, accessed February 27, 2015; D. Berman, "A Radical Idea for Activist Investors: What If the Goal Were More Investment with an Eye on the Long Term?" *The Wall Street Journal*, January 27, 2015, http://www.wsj.com/articles /a-radical-idea-for-activist-investors-1422370260, accessed February 27, 2015.

11

1. War and Peace in 30 Seconds: How Much Does the Military Spend on Ads? by Derek Thompson, January 30, 2012, The *Atlantic* website, http:// www.theatlantic.com/business/archive/2012/01 /war-and-peace-in-30-seconds-how-much-does-the -military-spend-on-ads/252222/, accessed February 9, 2014; Army to Use Webcasts From Iraq for Recruiting, by Stuart Elliott, November 10, 2008, *The New York Times* website, http://www.nytimes .com/2008/11/11/business/media/11adco.html, accessed February 22, 2009; Army Strong! Army Smash! October 11, 2006, Armchair Generalist website, http://armchairgeneralist.typepad.com/my _weblog/2006/10/army_strong_arm.html, accessed April 19, 2011; U.S. Army Searches New Agency, Defines Hispanic Market as Key Target, August 12, 2010, Portada website, http://www.portada-online .com/article.aspx?aid=6604, accessed April 19, 2010; U.S. Army Puts Marketing in Play, by Andrew McMains, August 11, 2010, *AdWeek* website, http://www.adweek.com/news/advertising-branding /us-army-puts-marketing-play-103040, accessed June 16, 2012.

2. What marketers can learn from Obama's campaign, by Al Ries, November 5, 2008, *Advertising Age* website, http://adage.com/moy2008/article? article_id=131810, accessed February 22, 2009.

3. Vegas FAQs, Updated 3/2015, Las Vegas Conventions and Visitors Authority website, http:// www.lvcva.com/includes/content/images/media /docs/2014-Vegas-FAQs.pdf, accessed April 18, 2015; Major investments continue reinvention of Las Vegas, April 4, 2013, Las Vegas Convention and Visitors Authority website, http://www.lvcva.com /article/major-investments-continue-reinvention -las-vegas/895/, accessed February 9, 2014; Vegas turns to reality show amid recession, by Natalie Zmuda, January 2009, *Advertising Age* website, http://adage.com/abstract.php?article_id=134193, accessed February 22, 2009.

4. American Customer Satisfaction Index Quarterly Scores, Q1–Q4 2008, ASCI website, http://www .theacsi.org/index.php?option=com_content&task =view&id=13&Itemid=31, accessed February 24, 2009.

5. Eight reasons to keep your customers loyal, by Rama Ramaswami, January 12, 2005, Mulitchannel Merchant website, http://multichannelmerchant .com/opsandfulfillment/advisor/Brandi-custloyal, accessed February 24, 2009.

6. The psychology of color in marketing, by June Campbell, accessed March 19, 2005, UCSI website, http://www.ucsi.cc/webdesign/color -marketing.html; Color psychology in marketing, by Al Martinovic, June 21, 2004, ImHosted website, http://developers.evrsoft.com/article/web-design /graphics-multimedia-design/color-psychology -in-marketing.shtml; Colors that sell, by Suzanne Roman, November 29, 2004, ImHosted website, http://developers.evrsoft.com/article/web-design /graphics-multimedia-design/colors-that-sell.shtml; Reinvent Wheel? Blue Room. Defusing a Bomb? Red Room, by Pam Belluck, February 6, 2009, *The New York Times* website, http://www.nytimes

.com/2009/02/06/science/06color.html, accessed February 26, 2009.

7. Nike's China Problem, by Trefis Team, March 20, 2014, Trefis website, http://www.trefis.com /stock/nke/articles/229536/marynikes-china -problem/2014-03-20, accessed April 18, 2015; Shoe makers gunning for Olympian feat, by Andria Cheng, May 9, 2008, Market Watch website, http:// www.marketwatch.com/news/story/story .aspx?guid={781CC2E2-2B3F-4FF5-A0C5 -0FB962D7E204}, accessed February 24, 2009; Nike Climbs to Record as Orders Surge, Profit Rises, by Matt Townsend and Robert Fenne, September 24, 2010, Bloomberg website, http:// www.businessweek.com/news/2010-09-24/nike -climbs-to-record-as-orders-surge-profit-rises.html, accessed April 12, 2011; In China, Nike Sets Out to Alter Sports Mindset by Laurie Burkitt, *The Wall Street Journal* website, http://online.wsj.com /article/SB1000142405297020445080457662490009 968790.html, accessed June 17, 2012.

8. Four Ways Technology Will Soon Update Your Wardrobe, by Kyle Stock, February 7, 2014, *Businessweek* website, http://www.businessweek .com/articles/2014-02-07/four-ways-technology -will-soon-update-your-wardrobe#r=nav-fst, accessed February 11, 2014.

9. Facebook: Friend, Foe, or Frenemy? May 27, 2010, *Newsweek* website, http://www.newsweek .com/blogs/techtonic-shifts/2010/05/26/facebook -friend-foe-or-frenemy-.html, accessed April 11, 2010.

10. The Top 10 Social Media Fails of 2014, by Rebecca Borison, December 10, 2014, Inc website, http://www.inc.com/rebecca-borison/top-10-social -media-fails-2014.html, accessed April 19, 2015; Don't tell customers they're fat: 2013's biggest corporate goofs, by Anthony Volastro, February 3, 2014, NBC website, http://www .nbcnews.com/business/business-news/dont-tell -customers-theyre-fat-2013s-biggest-corporate -goofs-f2D11785316, accessed February 9, 2014; Abercrombie & Fitch Refuses To Make Clothes For Large Women by Ashley Lutz, May 3, 2013, Business Insider website, http://www.businessinsider .com/abercrombie-wants-thin-customers-2013-5, accessed February 9, 2014; The 20 Biggest Brand Fails of 2012, by Tim Nudd, December 20, 2012, *AdWeek* website, http://www.adweek.com/news -gallery/advertising-branding/20-biggest-brand -fails-2012-146137?page=9&js=1&view_name =news_gallery&view_display_id=node_content _1&view_args=146137&view_path=node %2F146137&view_base_path=node %2F146137&view_dom_id=1&pager_element =0#peta-11, accessed March 20, 2013; Why This Nivea For Men Ad Is "Uncivilized," by Jerry Barrow, August 17, 2011, *The Urban Daily* website, http://theurbandaily.com/1485855/why -this-nivea-for-men-ad-is-uncivilized-opinion/, accessed June 17, 2012; Marketing Muck-Ups: The Biggest Follies of 2011, December 12, 2011, *AdvertisingAge* website, http://adage.com/article /special-report-book-of-tens-2011/marketing -muck-ups-biggest-follies-2011/231468/, accessed June 17, 2012.

11. From Obligation to Desire: More than 2 Billion Aspirational Consumers Mark Shift in Sustainable Consumption, October 3, 2013, BBMG, http://bbmg.com/news/obligation-desire-2-5-billion -aspirational-consumers-mark-shift-sustainable -consumption/, accessed April 19, 2015; Can Walmart Get Us to Buy Sustainable Products? by Andrew Winston, February 25, 2015, *Harvard Business Review* website, https://hbr.org/2015/02 /can-walmart-get-us-to-buy-sustainable-products, accessed April 19, 2015.

12. Environment a fair-weather priority for consumers, June 3, 2008, Penn, Schoen & Bergland Press Release, Penn, Schoen & Bergland website, http://www.psbresearch .com/press_release_Jun3-2008.htm, accessed February 24, 2009; Green Fashion: Is It More Than Marketing Hype? by Gloria Sin, May 28, 2008, *Fast Company* website, http://www .fastcompany.com/articles/2008/05/green-fashion -hype.html, accessed February 24, 2009; "Green Fashion," Formerly Hippie, Now Hip! February 21, 2008, CBS News website, http://www .cbsnews.com/stories/2008/02/21/earlyshow /living/beauty/main3855868.shtml, accessed February 24, 2009.

Pg. 201 Fact: Facebook Posts Get Half Their Reach Within 30 Minutes of Being Published, November 2, 2012, MarketingCharts Website, http://www.marketingcharts.com/online/facebook -posts-get-half-their-reach-within-30-minutes-of -being-published-24453/, accessed September 2014.

12

1. The Ultimate Energy Drink: Cocaine? by Melissa Sowry, September 18, 2006, ABCNews Website, http://abcnews.go.com/Health/story?id=2459718 &page=1#.UU45fjcwok9, accessed March 20, 2013; Top 25 Biggest Product Flops of All Time, DailyFinance website, http://www.dailyfinance .com/photos/top-25-biggest-product-flops-of-all -time/#slide=3662621, accessed March 20, 2013.

2. Characteristics of a Great Name, The Brand Name Awards, by Brighter Naming, http://www .brandnameawards.com/top10factors.html, accessed April 10, 2005.

3. Brand Extensions: Marketing in Inner Space, by Adam Bass, Brand Channel website, http://www .brandchannel.com/papers_review.asp?sp_id= 296 ac-cessed March 25, 2007; Brand Extensions We Could Do Without, by Reena Jana, August 7, 2006, *BusinessWeek* website, http://www.businessweek .com/magazine/content/06_32/b3996420.htm; The 20 Worst Product Failures, Sales HQ website, http:// saleshq.monster.com/news/articles/2655-the -20-worst-product-failures, accessed June 20, 2012.

4. Private Label Growing Rapidly by Alex Palmer, September 22, 2009, BrandWeek website, http:// www.brandweek.com/bw/content_display/news -and-features/packaged-goods/e3i7c69fb437bbee1 5e35345c87bdf679fe, accessed June 14, 2010; Ten Private Label Trends that Shook North America, PlanetRetail website, http://www1.planetretail .net/_data/assets/pdf_file/0016/43063/10-PL-Trends -That-Shook-North-America-Final.pdf, accessed May 2, 2011; IRI: Fewer Shoppers Buying Private Label Versus Last Year, Store Brands Decisions website, http://www.storebrandsdecisions.com /news/2011/04/05/iri-fewer-shoppers-buying -private-label-versus-last-year, accessed April 5, 2011; Private Brand Sales Outpace National Brands—PLMA's 2013 Private Label Yearbook, by Christopher Durham, June 28, 2013, My Private Brand website, http://mypbrand. com/2013/06/28/private-brands-sales-outpace -national-brands-plmas-2013-private-label -yearbook/, accessed February 12, 2014.

5. The USA Apparel Market Research Report, June 2010, Fashion, http://www.infomat.com/fido /getpublication.fcn?&type=research&SearchString =apparel&id=737870ST0000927&start=1&tr =17Infomat, accessed June 14, 2010.

6. Not on the List? The Truth about Impulse Purchases, January 7, 2009, Knowledge@Wharton website, http://knowledge.wharton.upenn.edu

/article.cfm?articleid=2132, accessed February 28, 2009.

7. 3M: Commitment to Sustainability, GreenBiz Leaders website, 1999.

8. Wacky Warning Labels 2009 Winners Announced, August 16, 2009, Foundation for Fair Civil Justice website, http://www .foundationforfairciviljustice.org/news/in_depth /wacky_warning_labels_2009_winners_announced/, accessed June 14, 2010; Wacky Warning Labels Show Toll of Frivolous Lawsuits, by Bob Dorigo Jones, June 8, 2012, Bob Dorigo Jones website, http://www.bobdorigojones.com/, accessed June 20, 2012; Deadline for Entering 15th Annual Wacky Warning Labels™ Contest Is May 15, by Bob Dorigo Jones, May 7, 2012, Bob Dorigo Jones website, http://www.bobdorigojones .com/, accessed June 20, 2012.

9. Binge-viewing is transforming the television experience by Dawn C. Chmielewski, February 1, 2013, *Los Angeles Times* website, http://articles .latimes.com/2013/feb/01/entertainment/la-et-ct -binge-viewing-20130201, accessed March 20, 2013; Americans spend 34 hours a week watch-ing TV, according to Nielsen numbers, by David Hinkley, September 19, 2012, *Daily News* website, http://www.nydailynews.com/entertainment/tv -movies/americans-spend-34-hours-week-watching -tv-nielsen-numbers-article-1.1162285, accessed March 20, 2013; How people spend their time online, by Stine Thorhauge, May 24, 2012, Mind-Junpers website, http://www.mindjumpers .com/blog/2012/05/time-spend-online/, accessed March 20, 2013; U.S. Consumer Online Behavior Survey Results 2007_Part One: Wireline Usage, International Data Corporation website, February 19, 2008, http://www.idc.com/getdoc .jsp?containerId=prUS21096308, accessed March 3, 2009; Why Video On Demand Is Still Cable's Game to Lose, by Dan Frommer, September 5, 2008, The Business Insider website, http://www.businessinsider.com/2008/9/why -video-on-demand-is-still-cable-s-game-to-lose, accessed March 3, 2009; Streaming vids boost Netflix profits, by Glenn Abel, January 29, 2009, Download Movies 101 website, http:// downloadmovies101.com/wordpress-1/2009/01/29 /streaming-vids-boost-netflix-profits/, accessed March 3, 2009; Casting the Big Movie Download Roles, September 7, 2007, eMarketer website, http://www.emarketer.com /Article.aspx?id=1005346, accessed March 3, 2009; Time Watching TV Still Tops Internet posted, by Clark Fredricksen, December 15, 2010, eMarketer Blog, http://www.emarketer.com/blog/index.php /time-spent-watching-tv-tops-internet/, accessed May 4, 2011; Average time spent online per U.S. visitor in 2010, posted January 11, 2011, ComScore Data Mine website, http://www .comscoredatamine.com/2011/01/average-time -spent-online-per-u-s-visitor-in-2010/, accessed May 4, 2011; How People Watch TV Online and Off, by Erick Schonfeld, January 8, 2012, TechCrunch website, http://techcrunch.com /2012/01/08/how-people-watch-tv-online/, accessed June 20, 2012.

10. Permission Marketing, by William C. Taylor, December 18, 2007, Fast Company website, http:// www.fastcompany.com/magazine/14/permission .html, accessed March 3, 2009.

11. Budweiser's Clydesdale wins Ad Meter by a nose, by Bruce Horowitz, February 4, 2013, *USAToday* website, http://www.usatoday.com /story/money/business/2013/02/04/clydesdale-ad -wins-by-a-nose/1889693/, accessed March 20, 2013; "Two nobodies from nowhere" craft winning

Super Bowl ad, by Bruce Horovitz, February 4, 2009, *USA Today* website, http://www.usatoday.com/money/advertising/admeter/2009admeter.htm, accessed March 4, 2009.

12. Professor Paul Herbig, Tristate University, International Marketing Lecture Series, Session 6, International Advertising, http://www.tristate.edu/faculty/herbig/pahimadvstg.htm, accessed June 1, 2005; Taking Global Brands to Japan, by Karl Moore and Mark Smith, The Conference Board website, http://www.conference-board.org/worldwide/worldwide_article.cfm?id=243&pg=1, accessed June 1, 2005.

13. Mobile Gets One Out of Five Paid Search Clicks, May 6, 2013, eMarketer website, http://www.emarketer.com/Article/Mobile-Gets-One-of-Five-Paid-Search-Clicks/1009865, accessed February 13, 2014, Steady gains for mobile paid search, eMarketer website, http://www.emarketer.com/Article/Steady-Gains-Mobile-Paid-Search/1009686, accessed March 20, 2013. Search Marketing Trends: Back to Basics, eMarketer website, February 2009, http://www.emarketer.com/Report.aspx?code=emarketer_2000559, accessed June 18, 2010; eMarketer: Display ad growth catching up with search, posted by Leah McBride Mensching on December 16, 2010, sfnblog, http://www.sfnblog.com/advertising/2010/12/emarketer_display_ad_growth_catching_up.php, accessed May 11, 2011; US Online Ad Spend Poised to Grow 20% in 2011, June 8, 2011, eMarketer website, http://www.emarketer.com/Article.aspx?R=1008431, accessed June 20, 2012.

14. Mobile requires revamped SEO, SEM strategy, April 18, 2013, eMarketer website, http://www.emarketer.com/Article/Search-Gets-Mobile-Makeover/1009822, accessed February 13, 2014; EMarketer: Among online ads, search to gain most new dollars in 2011, by Pamela Parker, June 11, 2008, SearchEngine Land website, http://searchengineland.com/emarketer-among-online-ads-search-to-gain-most-new-dollars-in-2011-80707, accessed March 20, 2013; eMarketer: Search Is Vital in a Recession, by Adweek staff, February 25, 2009, Brandweek website, http://www.brandweek.com/bw/content_display/news-and-features/digital/e3i195c363ab252f976a2dabde4d8ef2549, accessed March 3, 2009.

15. Online Video Advertising Moves Front and Center, Mary 14, 2013, eMarketer website, http://www.emarketer.com/Article/Online-Video-Advertising-Moves-Front-Center/1009886, accessed February 13, 201; U.S. Online Advertising Video Spending 2007–2013, August 2008, eMarketer website, http://www.marketingcharts.com/television/emarketer-revises-online-video-ad-spend-projections-downward-5679/emarketer-online-video-ad-spend-us-2007-2013jpg/, accessed June 18, 2010; Promises, promises: Will online video ads deliver this year? posted by David Hallerman, December 9, 2010, The eMarketer Blog, http://www.emarketer.com/blog/index.php/promises-promises-online-video-ads-deliver-year/, accessed May 11, 2011; US Online Ad Spend Poised to Grow 20% in 2011, June 8, 2011, eMarketer website, http://www.emarketer.com/Article.aspx?R=1008431, accessed June 20, 2012.

16. Social media claims more of our attention. But email's not dead yet, posted August 2, 2010 by Meghan Keane, eConsultancy website, http://econsultancy.com/us/blog/6366-social-media-might-claim-a-lot-of-our-attention-but-email-s-not-dead-yet, accessed May 11, 2011; Social Media ROI Examples & Video, by Erik Qualman, posted November 12, 2009, Socialnomics, Social Media Blog, http://socialnomics.net/2009/11/12/social-media-roi-examples-video/, accessed June 28, 2010; The ROI of Social Media: 10 Case Studies,

by Lauren Fisher, July 16, 2011, The Next Web website, http://thenextweb.com/socialmedia/2011/07/16/the-roi-of-social-media-10-case-studies/, accessed June 21, 2012.

17. Infographic: Native Advertising Grows Despite Budget and Transparency Concerns, February 16, 2015, *Adweek* website, http://www.adweek.com/news/technology/infographic-native-advertising-grows-despite-budget-and-transparency-concerns-162963, accessed April 25, 2015.

18. Brandchannel's 2004 Product Placement Awards, by Abram Sauer, February 21, 2005, http://www.brandchannel.com/start1.asp?fa_id=251; A Product Placement Hall of Fame, by Dale Buss, *Business Week* Online, June 22, 1998, http://www.businessweek.com/1998/25/b3583062.htm.

19. 'Transformers: Age of Extinction' Tops 2015 Product Placement Awards, by Angie Han, March 4, 2015, SlashFilm website, http://www.slashfilm.com/transformers-age-of-extinction-tops-2015-product-placement-awards/, accessed April 25, 2015. Announcing the 2013 BrandCameo Product Placement Award Winners, by Abe Sauer, February 25, 2013, BrandChannel website, http://www.brandchannel.com/home/post/2013/02/25/Brandchannel-9th-Brandcameo-Product-Placement-Awards-022513.aspx, accessed March 20, 2013. Apple tops 2010 film product placement awards, by Eric Slivka, February 22, 2011, MacRumors website, http://www.macrumors.com/2011/02/22/apple-tops-2010-film-product-placement-awards/, accessed May 11, 2011.

20. Product placement sees global rise as fans face saturated entertainment, by Abe Sauer, April 24, 2013, BrandChannel website, http://www.brandchannel.com/home/post/2013/04/24/Product-Placement-On-The-Rise-042413.aspx, accessed February 13, 2014; Announcing the 2013 BrandCameo Product Placement Award Winners, by Abe Sauer, February 25, 2013, BrandChannel website, http://www.brandchannel.com/home/post/2013/02/25/Brandchannel-9th-Brandcameo-Product-Placement-Awards-022513.aspx, accessed March 20, 2013; PQ Media Market Analysis Finds Global Product Placement Spending Grew 37% in 2006; Forecast to Grow 30% in 2007, Driven by Relaxed European Rules, Emerging Asian Markets; Double-Digit Growth in U.S. Decelerates, PQ Media website, March 14, 2007, http://www.pqmedia.com/about-press-20070314-gppf.html, accessed September 4, 2008; DVR Households Swelling Ranks, by Jose Fermoso, December 16, 2008, Portfolio website, http://www.portfolio.com/views/blogs/the-tech-observer/2008/12/16/dvr-households-swelling-ranks, accessed March 4, 2009; FCC opens inquiry into stealthy TV product placement, June 26, 2008, *USA Today* website, http://www.usatoday.com/life/television/2008-06-26-fcc-advertising_N.htm, accessed March 4, 2009; DVRs now in 30.6% of U.S. Households, by Bill Gorman, April 30, 2009, TV by the Numbers website, http://tvbythenumbers.com/2009/04/30/dvrs-now-in-306-of-us-households/17779, accessed June 16, 2010; Product Placement Dipped Last Year for the First Time, by Andrew Hampp, June 29, 2010, AdAge website, http://adage.com/article/madisonvine-news/product-placement-dipped-year-time/144720/, accessed May 11, 2011; DVR Penetration grows to 39.7% of households, 42.2% of viewers, by Robert Seidman, March 23, 2011, TV by the numbers website, http://tvbythenumbers.zap2it.com/2011/03/23/dvr-penetration-grows-to-39-7-of-households-42-2-of-viewers/86819/, accessed May 11, 2011; Product Placement Grows in Music Videos, by

Joseph Plambeck, July 5, 2010, *The New York Times* website, http://www.nytimes.com/2010/07/06/business/media/06adco.html?_r=1, accessed June 21, 2012; DVRs and Streaming Prompt a Shift in the Top-Rated TV Shows, by Bill Carter and Brian Stelter, March 4, 2012, *The New York Times* website, http://www.nytimes.com/2012/03/05/business/media/dvrs-and-streaming-prompt-a-shift-in-the-top-rated-tv-shows.html?pagewanted=all, accessed June 21, 2012.

21. Ford, Coke & AT&T Pay More to Sponsor American Idol, by Susan Gunelius, January 18, 2008, Bizzia website, http://www.bizzia.com/brandcurve/ford-coke-att-pay-more-to-sponsor-american-idol/, accessed March 4, 2009; Global Paid Product Placement to Reach $7.6 billion by 2010: Report, by Amy Johannes, August 17, 2006, PromoMagazine website, http://promomagazine.com/research/paidplacementreport/, accessed June 16, 2010.

22. Expand your brand with advergames, SoInteractive website, http://www.sointeractive.co.za/blog/expand-your-brand-with-advergames/, accessed February 13, 2014; Global In-Game Advertising Market to Reach US$2.67 Billion by 2017, According to a New Report by Global Industry Analysts, Inc., February 13, 2014, PRWeb website, http://www.prweb.com/releases/in_game_advertising_IGA/static_dynamic_advergames/prweb8857045.htm, accessed February 13, 2014; Global ad spending in video games to top $7.2B in 2016, by Dean Takahashi, September 12, 2011, Venture Beat Website, http://venturebeat.com/2011/09/12/global-ad-spending-in-video-games-to-top-7-2b-in-2016/, accessed March 20, 2013; eMarketer: In-Game Advertising Spending to Reach $650 million in 2012, by Melissa Campanelli, March 6, 2008, eMarketing and Commerce website, http://www.emarketingandcommerce.com/article/emarketer-game-advertising-spending-reach-650-million-2012/1#, accessed March 20, 2013; Number of U.S. Video Game Players Falls, by Angela Moscaritolo, September 5, 2012, *PC Magazine* website, http://www.pcmag.com/article2/0,2817,2409313,00.asp, accessed March 20, 2013; All Time High: 72% of U.S. Population Plays Video Games, by Matt Peckham, April 3, 2008, *PC World* website, http://blogs.pcworld.com/gameon/archives/006748.html, accessed March 5, 2009; Video Game Advertising report, eMarketer website, http://www.emarketer.com/Report.aspx?code=emarketer_2000485, accessed March 5, 2009.

23. Crocs get a stylish make-over as brand hopes to DOUBLE sales in five years—but can the foam shoe move on from its ugly past? by Margot Peppers, July 19, 2013, *Daily Mail* website, http://www.dailymail.co.uk/femail/article-2370360/Crocs-stylish-make-brand-hopes-DOUBLE-sales-years--foam-shoe-ugly-past.html, accessed February 15, 2013; Pizza and A Movie, Time Pop Chart, June 3, 2013, *Time* website, http://content.time.com/time/magazine/article/0,9171,2144105,00.html, accessed February 15, 2014.

24. Number of U.S. Video Game Players Falls, by Angela Moscaritolo, September 5, 2012, *PC Magazine* website, http://www.pcmag.com/article2/0,2817,2409313,00.asp, accessed March 20, 2013; Advertisers support games through new placements like branded virtual goods and opt-in videos, December 12, 2012, eMarketer website, http://www.emarketer.com/Article/US-Gamers-Race-Mobile/1009543, accessed March 20, 2013; Massive Summary Research—Significant Findings, Massive website, http://www.massiv-eincorporated.com/casestudiesa.html, accessed March 4, 2009;

Google to Buy Adscape, by Nick Gonzalez, TechCrunch website, February 16, 2007, http://www.techcrunch.com/2007/02/16/google-to-buy-adscape-for-23-million/, accessed March 5, 2009; IN-game advertising is a massive market, May 15, 2011, *The Telegraph* website, http://www.telegraph.co.uk/technology/news/5312188/In-game-advertising-is-a-massive-market.html, accessed May 16, 2011; Report: Video Game Ads to Reach $1 Bil. by 2012, by Mike Shields, March 4, 2008, AdWeek website, http://www.adweek.com/news/television/report-video-game-ads-reach-1-bil-2012-95119, accessed June 21, 2012; Let the Games Begin Advertising! April 6, 2007, eMarketer website, http://www.emarketer.com/Article.aspx?1004739&R=1004739, accessed June 21, 2012.

25. Fitness First—Wait Watching, by Lisa Evans, March 17, 2009, The Cool Hunter website, http://www.thecoolhunter.co.uk/article/detail/1504/fitness-first--wait-watching, accessed March 30, 2013; UNICEF Finland: Mom, March 31, 2009, I Believe in Advertising website, http://www.ibelieveinadv.com/2009/03/unicef-finland-mom/, accessed March 30, 2013. Kid Nabbing, by Melanie Wells, February 2, 2004, *Forbes* website, http://www.forbes.com/free_forbes/2004/0202/084.html; Tremor website, http://tremor.com/index.html, accessed March 5, 2009; General Mills, Kraft Launch Word of Mouth Networks, by Elaine Wong, October 5, 2008, BrandWeek website, http://www.brandweek.com/bw/content_display/news-and-features/packaged-goods/e3i2db03fb29d573ec52722456845f5c274, accessed March 5, 2009.

26. Beards Trim P&G's Sales as "Movember" Fuels Hairy Look, by Lauren ColemanLochner, January 25, 2014, Bloomberg website, http://www.bloomberg.com/news/2014-01-24/p-g-says-growing-beard-popularity-is-trimming-grooming-sales.html, accessed February 15, 2014; Facial hair trend hurts Procter & Gamble, by Tiffany Hsu, January 24, 2014, *Los Angeles Times* website, http://articles.latimes.com/2014/jan/24/business/la-fi-grooming-funk-20140125, accessed February 15, 2014.

27. Economic Uncertainty To Slow Sponsorship Growth In 2012, January 11, 2012, ieg website, http://www.sponsorship.com/About-IEG/Press-Room/Economic-Uncertainty-To-Slow-Sponsorship-Growth-In.aspx, accessed March 20, 2013; Sponsorship Spending To Rise 2.2 Percent in 2009, IEG Press Release, February 11, 2009, Sponsorship.Com website, http://www.sponsorship.com/About-IEG/Press-Room/Sponsorship-Spending-To-Rise-2.2-Percent-in-2009.aspx, accessed March 5, 2009; Sponsorship Spending To Rise 2.2 Percent in 2009, August 28, 2009, Sommerville Baddley Marketing website, http://www.sbmktg.net/2009/08/sponsorship-spending-to-rise-22-percent-in-2009/ (accessed June 16, 2010); Sponsorship Spending: 2010 Proves Better Than Expected; Bigger Gains Set For 2011, IEG Press Release, January 12, 2011, http://www.prweb.com/releases/2011/01/prweb4958744.htm, accessed May 15, 2011; Economic Uncertainty to Slow Sponsorship Growth in 2012, January 11, 2012, IEG website, http://www.sponsorship.com/About-IEG.aspx, accessed June 22, 2012.

28. 23 hilariously unfortunate ad placements, March 18, 2013, MSN Website, http://now.msn.com/bad-ad-placement-funny-photos-show-awkward-ad-choices, accessed April 5, 2013.

29. Making Sense of a World of Difference: How Consumers Perceive Sustainability in the US, China, and Beyond, by Alex Murray and Emma Hrustic,

Interbrand Best Global Green Brands Report, http://www.interbrand.com/en/best-global-brands/Best-Global-Green-Brands/2013/articles/world-of-difference.aspx, accessed February 16, 2014.

30. Publicity from Thin Air (Don't Just Wait for News to Happen), by Bill Stoller, Article Point website, http://www.articlepoint.com/articles/public-relations/publicity-from-thin-air.php, accessed June 15, 2005.

31. The Employment Situation – April 2011, Bureau of Labor Statistics News Release, May 6, 2011, Bureau of Labor Statistics website, http://www.bls.gov/news.release/pdf/empsit.pdf, accessed May 16, 2011.

Pg. 221 Fact: Social Media Video 2013 by Erik Qualman, January 1, 2013, Socialnomics Website, http://www.socialnomics.net/2013/01/01/social-media-video-2013/, accessed September 2014.

13

1. Supermarket Facts, Industry Overview 2008, Food Marketing Institute website, http://www.fmi.org/facts_figs/?fuseaction=superfact, accessed June 30, 2010.

2. Wholesale Distribution Industry Outlook: Drones, by Sebastian Valencia, August 27, 2014, Clarkson Consulting website, http://clarkstonconsulting.com/blog/wholesale-distribution-industry-outlook-drones/, accessed April 27, 2015; Amazon's Drone Delivery: How Would It Work? by Doug Gross, December 2, 2013, CNN website, http://www.cnn.com/2013/12/02/tech/innovation/amazon-drones-questions/, accessed April 27, 2015.

3. Apparel Drives US Retail Ecommerce Sales Growth, April 20, 2012, eMarketer website, http://www.emarketer.com/newsroom/index.php/apparel-drives-retail-ecommerce-sales-growth/, accessed February 17, 2014; Walmart Website Error Allowed Customers to Buy $600 Electronics for $8.85, by Susanna Kim, November 6, 2013, ABC News website, http://abcnews.go.com/Business/walmart-super-low-prices-website-glitch/story?id=20804317, accessed February 26, 2014; Healthy Growth for Ecommerce as Retail Continues Shift to Web, March 17, 2011, Emarketer Newsletter, http://www.emarketer.com/Article/Healthy-Growth-Ecommerce-Retail-Continues-Shift-Web/1008284, accessed April 6, 2013; Report: Online retail could reach $156B in 2009, by Rachel Metz, January 29, 2009, The Industry Standard website, http://www.thestandard.com/news/2009/01/29/report-online-retail-could-reach-156b-2009, accessed March 13, 2009; eMarketer revises e-commerce forecast, by Jeffrey Grau, March 5, 2009, eMarketer website, http://www.emarketer.com/Article.aspx?id=1006948, http://www.emarketer.com/Article.aspx?id=1006948; Inside the Secret World of Trader Joes, by Beth Kowitt, August 23, 2010, *Fortune* website, http://money.cnn.com/2010/08/20/news/companies/inside_trader_joes_full_version.fortune/index.htm, accessed May 30, 2011; Healthy Growth for Ecommerce as Retail Continues Shift to Web, eMarketer Blog, March 17, 2011, http://www.emarketer.com/Article.aspx?R=1008284, accessed May 30, 2011; http://mashable.com/2011/02/28/forrester-e-commerce/.

4. Fireclick Index, Top Line Growth, Fireclick website, http://index.fireclick.com/fireindex.php?segment=0, accessed March 13, 2009; L.L. Bean Once Again Number One in Customer Service, According to NRF Foundation/American Express Survey, January 13, 2009, National Retail Federation website, http://www.nrf.com/modules.php?name=News&op=viewlive&sp_id=653, accessed

May 30, 2011; Amazon.com Tops in Customer Service, According to NRF Foundation/American Express Survey, January 17, 2012, National Retail Federation website: http://www.nrf.com/modules.php?name=News&op=viewlive&sp_id=1293, accessed June 23, 2012.

5. 30 Bizarre Vending Machines from Around the World, by Christian Storm, November 10, 2014, *Business Insider* website, http://www.businessinsider.com/most-unique-vending-machines-2014-11, accessed April 27, 2015.

6. Sales soften at Costco, March 4, 2009, Retail Analysis IGD website, http://www.igd.com/analysis/channel/news_hub.asp?channelid=1&channelitemid=9&nidp=&nid=5616, accessed March 13, 2009.

7. Loss Leader Strategy, Investopedia website (a Forbes Digital Company), http://www.investopedia.com/terms/l/lossleader.asp, accessed March 14, 2009; Walmart not crying over spilt milk by Al Norman, August 22, 2008, The Huffington Post website, http://www.huffingtonpost.com/al-norman/wal-mart-not-crying-over_b_120684.html, accessed March 14, 2009.

8. Pricing Errors on the Web Can Be Costly, by Bob Tedeschi, *The New York Times* website, http://partners.nytimes.com/library/tech/99/12/cyber/commerce/13commerce.html, accessed July, 2013; Dell Axim mis-pricing sparks customer furore, by Matt Loney November 26, 2003, ZD-NetWebsite, http://www.zdnet.com/dell-axim-mis-pricing-sparks-customer-furore-3039118131/, accessed July 3, 2014; All You Ever Wanted To Know About the Travelocity "Guarantee", FlyerTalk Forum, http://www.flyertalk.com/forum/online-travel-booking-bidding-agencies/552951-all-you-ever-wanted-know-about-travelocity-guarantee.html, accessed July 2013.

9. Keeping a sparkle, as soda fizzles, by Anne VanderMey, May 1, 2014, *Fortune* website, http://fortune.com/2014/05/01/keeping-a-sparkle-as-soda-fizzles/, accessed April 27, 2015; 15 Facts About Coca-Cola That Will Blow Your Mind, by Kim Bhasin, June 9, 2011, *Business Insider* website, http://www.businessinsider.com/facts-about-coca-cola-2011-6, accessed April 27, 2015.

10. How Apple plays the pricing game, by Ben Kunz, October, 6, 2010, Bloomberg Business Week website, http://www.nbcnews.com/id/38980367/ns/business-us_business/t/how-apple-plays-pricing-game/#.UWInbjcwok9, accessed April 7, 2013.

11. How Costco Became the Anti Walmart, by Steven Greenhouse, July 17, 2005, *The New York Times* website, http://www.nytimes.com/2005/07/17/business/yourmoney/17costco.html?adxnnl=1&pagewanted=1&adxnnlx=1122004143-8Vfn2DFl1MJfernM1navLA; Why Costco is so addictive, by Matthew Boyle, October 25, 2006, CNNMoney website, http://money.cnn.com/magazines/fortune/fortune_archive/2006/10/30/8391725/index.htm, accessed March 14, 2009.

Pg. 242 Fact: Russian proverb.

14

1. The surprising first jobs of 10 famous CEOS, Fast Company website, http://www.fastcompany.com/3027074/dialed/the-surprising-first-jobs-of-10-famous-ceos#1, accessed May 1, 2015; First jobs of the rich and famous, *Parade*, http://www.parade.com/celebrity/slideshows/flashback/stars-first-jobs.html#?slideindex=0, accessed April 7, 2013; Ten teachers who made a mark in another field,

February 16, 2009, Encyclopedia Britannica website, http://www.britannica.com/blogs/2009/02/lbj-gene-simmons-of-kiss-ten-teachers-who-made-a-mark-in-another-field/, accessed April 7, 2012; The Importance of Being Richard Branson, Leadership and Change, Knowledge@Wharton, January 12, 2005, http://knowledge.wharton.upenn.edu/article/1109.cfm; Ambition: Why Some People are Most Likely to Succeed, by Jeffrey Kluger, *Time* magazine, November 14, 2005, pp. 48–59, http://www.time.com/time/archive/preview/0,10987,1126746,00.html; Jeff Bezos, Reference for Business website, 2nd Edition, http://www.referenceforbusiness.com/businesses/A-F/Bezos-Jeff.html, accessed June 24, 2012; The Roller Coaster Ride of Mark Zuckerberg, by Matt Melvin, 2011, Teen Ink website, http://www.teenink.com/nonfiction/academic/article/292887/The.., accessed June 24, 2012; Reagan Trail Days, The Ronald Reagan Trail website, http://www.ronaldreagantrail.net/Pages/ReaganTrail.php?city=2&page=Dixon, accessed June 24, 2012.

2. It Seemed Like a Good Idea at the Time: 7 of the Worst Business Decisions Ever Made, by Erika Anderson, October 4, 2013, *Forbes* website, http://www.forbes.com/sites/erikaandersen/2013/10/04/it-seemed-like-a-good-idea-at-the-time-7-of-the-worst-business-decisions-ever-made/, accessed March 1, 2014; The Worst Business Decisions of All Time, October 17, 2012, 24/7 *The Wall Street Journal* website, http://247wallst.com/2012/10/17/the-worst-business-decisions-of-all-time/3/, accessed April 7, 2013; Top Ten Bad Business Decisions, October 10, 2010, Business Excellence website, http://www.bus-ex.com/article/top-ten-bad-business-decisions, accessed June 24, 2012.

3. The Importance of Being Richard Branson, Leadership and Change, Knowledge@Wharton, January 12, 2005, http://knowledge.wharton.upenn.edu/article/1109.cfm.

4. Hot Topic, Inc. Reports Fourth Quarter EPS Increases 19% to $0.32 Per Diluted Share; Provides Guidance for the 1st Quarter of 2009, March 11, 2009, News Blaze website, http://newsblaze.com/story/2009031112554500001.pz/topstory.html, accessed March 25, 2009.

5. Motivate Your Staff, by Larry Page, How to Succeed in 2005, Business 2.0 magazine, December 1, 2004, http://money.cnn.com/magazines/business2/business2_archive/2004/12/01/8192529/index.htm.

6. A New Game at the Office: Many Young Workers Accept Fewer Guarantees, by Steve Lohr, *The New York Times* website, December 5, 2005, http://select.nytimes.com/gst/abstract.html?res=F00F12FE38550C768CDDAB0994DD404482.

7. 100 Best Companies to Work for, January 2014, *CNNMoney* website, http://money.cnn.com/magazines/fortune/best-companies/2014/snapshots/6.html?iid=BC14_lp_arrow1, accessed March 2, 2014; The Inside Experience, Great Rated website, http://us.greatrated.com/, accessed March 2, 2014.

8. 100 Best Companies to Work for 2015, *Fortune* website, http://fortune.com/best-companies/google-1/, accessed May 1, 2015.

9. Zuckerberg Claims "We Don't Build Services to Make Money," by Larry Magid, February 1, 2012, *Forbes* website, http://www.forbes.com/sites/larrymagid/2012/02/01/zuckerberg-claims-we-dont-build-services-to-make-money/ accessed April 7, 2013; This CEO Gives Every Employee His Cell Number (Seriously), by Venessa Wong, October 22, 2012, Bloomberg *BusinessWeek* website, http://www.businessweek.com/articles/2012-10-22/this-ceo-gives-every-employee-his-cell-number-seriously, accessed April 7, 2013.

10. Don't Get Hammered by Management Fads, by Darrell Rigby, *The Wall Street Journal*, May 21, 2001.

11. A Generation of Slackers? Not So Much, by Catherine Rampell, May 28, 2011, *The New York Times* website, http://www.nytimes.com/2011/05/29/weekinreview/29graduates.html, accessed June 29, 2011.

12. Managing Generation Y—Part 1, Book Excerpt, by Bruce Tulgan and Carolyn A. Martin, *BusinessWeek* online, September 28, 2001, http://www.businessweek.com/smallbiz/content/sep2001/sb20010928_113.htm; Managing Generation Y—Part 2, Book Excerpt, by Bruce Tulgan and Carolyn A. Martin, *BusinessWeek* online, October 4, 2001, http://www.businessweek.com/smallbiz/content/oct2001/sb2001105_229.htm; Generation Y: They've Arrived at Work with a New Attitude, by Stephanie Armour, *USA Today*, November 6, 2005, http://www.usatoday.com/money/workplace/2005-11-06-gen-y_x.htm; The Facebook Generation vs. the Fortune 500, by Gary Hamel, March 24, 2009, *The Wall Street Journal* Blogs website, http://blogs.wsj.com/management/2009/03/24/the-facebook-generation-vs-the-fortune-500/, accessed March 30, 2009; What Gen Y Really Wants, by Penelope Trunk, July 5, 2007, *Time* magazine website, http://www.time.com/time/magazine/article/0,9171,1640395,00.html, accessed March 30, 2009; Managing Generation Y as they change the workforce, by Molly Smith, January 8, 2008, Reuters website, http://www.reuters.com/article/pressRelease/idUS129795+08-Jan-2008+BW20080108, accessed March 30, 2009; Millennial Branding Survey Reveals that Gen-Y Is Connected to an Average of 16 Co-Workers on Facebook, by Dan Schawbel, January 9, 2012, Millennial Branding website, http://millennialbranding.com/2012/01/millennial-branding-gen-y-facebook-study/, accessed June 23, 2012; On Pay Gap, Millennial Women Near Parity—For Now, December 11, 2013, Pew Research website, http://www.pewsocialtrends.org/2013/12/11/on-pay-gap-millennial-women-near-parity-for-now/, accessed March 3, 2014.

13. The cow in the ditch: How Anne Mulcahy rescued Xerox, Special Section: Knowledge at Wharton, November 16–29, 2005, http://knowledge.wharton.upenn.edu/index.cfm?fa=viewArticle&id=1318&specialId=41.

14. Unused vacation days at 40-year high, by Amy Langfield, October 23, 2014, CNBC website, http://www.cnbc.com/id/102110867, accessed May 4, 2015; Relax! You'll Be More Productive, by Tony Schwartz, February 9, 2013, *The New York Times* website, http://www.nytimes.com/2013/02/10/opinion/sunday/relax-youll-be-more-productive.html?pagewanted=all&_r=0, accessed April 8, 2013.

15. Semco: Insanity That Works, by Kevin and Jackie Freiberg, Freiberg's website, http://www.freibergs.com/about/, accessed May 8, 2015.

15

1. Southwest Airlines CEO is defining himself as a leader—without bag fees, by Cheryl Hall, April 19, 2010, DallasNews website, http://www.dallasnews.com/business/columnists/cheryl-hall/20100417-Southwest-Airlines-CEO-is-defining-himself-5278.ece, accessed April 8, 2013; Gary Kelly Southwest Airlines CEO on the Business of Building Trust, by Kate McCann, October 11, 2005, McCombs School of Business website, http://www.mccombs.utexas.edu/news/pressreleases/lyceum05_kelly_wrap05.asp,

accessed July 2, 2010; Southwest Airlines Reports Fourth Quarter Profit and 37th Consecutive Year of Profitability, January 21, 2010, PRNewsWire website, http://www.prnewswire.com/news-releases/southwest-airlines-reports-fourth-quarter-profit-and-37th-consecutive-year-of-profitability-82241197.html, accessed July 2, 2010; 1106 HR Magazine: Views from the Top, November 1, 2006, SHRM website, http://www.shrm.org/Publications/hrmagazine/EditorialContent/Pages/1106ceoex.aspx, accessed July 5, 2011.

2. America's jobless recovery. Not again. June 3, 2011, *Economist* website, http://www.economist.com/blogs/freeexchange/2011/06/americas-jobless-recovery, accessed July 5, 2011; A New Game at the Office: Many Young Workers Accept Fewer Guarantees, by Steve Lohr, *The New York Times*, December 5, 2005, http://select.nytimes.com/gst/abstract.html?res=F00F12FE38550C768CDDAB0994DD404482.

3. Report: CEOs Earn 331 Times as Much as Average Workers, 774 Times as Much as Minimum Wage Earners, by Kathryn Dill, April 15, 2014, *Forbes* website, http://www.forbes.com/sites/kathryndill/2014/04/15/report-ceos-earn-331-times-as-much-as-average-workers-774-times-as-much-as-minimum-wage-earners/, accessed Mary 10, 2015.

4. 18 Weird Jobs Celebrities Had Before They Became Famous, by Samantha Cortez, June 26, 2012, *Business Insider* website, http://www.businessinsider.com/weird-jobs-celebs-had-before-becoming-famous-2012-7?op=1, accessed May 10, 2015; First jobs of the rich and famous, from CareerBuilder.com, September 15, 2005, CNN website, http://www.cnn.com/2005/US/Careers/09/16/first.job/, accessed April 9, 2013; The Official Website of Sean Connery.Com, April 10, 2013, http://www.seanconnery.com/biography/, accessed April 9, 2013; The Humbling First Jobs of 25 Very Successful Celebrities and Business Leaders, by HR World Editors, September 24, 2010, Focus website, http://www.focus.com/fyi/humbling-first-jobs-25-very-successful-celebrities-and-busin/, accessed June 27, 2012; Celebrities' First Jobs, Oprah's website, November 3, 2009, http://www.oprah.com/entertainment/Oprahs-Live-Newscast-and-Celebrities-First-Jobs/1, accessed June 27, 2012.

5. CEO pay is 380 times average worker's—AFL-CIO, by By Jennifer Liberto, April 19, 2012, CNNMoney website, http://money.cnn.com/2012/04/19/news/economy/ceo-pay/index.htm, accessed April 9, 2013; CEO pay vs. performance—Still a roll of the dice, (WSJ) by Dionysus on April 1, 2010, posted on Economatrix website, http://www.economatrix.com/ceo-pay-vs-performance-still-a-roll-of-the-dice-wsj, accessed September 6, 2011; Figure 3AE from Lawrence Mishel, Jared Bernstein, and Heidi Shierholz, The State of Working America 2009/2009. An Economic Policy Institute Book. Ithaca, NY: ILR Press, An Imprint of Cornell University Press, 2009, http://www.stateofworkingamerica.org/tabfig/2008/03/SWA08_Chapter3_Wages_r2_Fig-3AE.jpg, accessed July 1, 2010; We Knew They Got Raises. But This? by Pradnya Joshi, July 2, 2011, *The New York Times* website, http://www.nytimes.com/2011/07/03/business/03pay.html, accessed July 5, 2011; U.S. CEO's Pay 231 Times Higher Than That of Average Workers, by Marla Dickerson, May 2, 2012, *Los Angeles Times* website, http://articles.latimes.com/2012/may/02/business/la-fi-mo-us-ceo-pay-231-times-more-than-average-workers-20120502, accessed June 30, 2012; CEO Pay Moves with Corporate Results, by Scott Thurm, May 23, 2012, *The Wall Street Journal* website, http://online.wsj.com/article/SB1

0001424052702304019404577416210712022298
.html, accessed July 2, 2012.

6. In 2011 The Baby Boomers Start To Turn
65: 16 Statistics About The Coming Retirement
Crisis That Will Drop Your Jaw, December 30,
2010, The American Dream website, http://
endoftheamericandream.com/archives/in-2011
-the-baby-boomers-start-to-turn-65-16-statistics
-about-the-coming-retirement-crisis-that-will
-drop-your-jaw, accessed July 5, 2011.

7. Facing Young Workers' High Job Expectations,
from Associated Press, Los Angeles Times, June
27, 2005; Not Everyone Gets a Trophy, by Bruce
Tulgan, San Francisco: Jossey-Bass (Wiley imprint),
2009.

8. How Corporate America Is Betraying
Women, by Betsy Morris, Fortune, January 10,
2005; Jane Drain—women leaving your workforce,
Smart Manager website, http://www
.smartmanager.com.au/web/au/smartmanager/en
/pages/89_jane_drain—women_leaving_workforce
.html, accessed July 5, 2011; Educated Women Quit
Work as Spouses Earn More, by Tiziana Barghini,
March 8, 2012, Reuters website, http://www
.reuters.com/article/2012/03/08/us-economy
-women-idUSBRE8270AC20120308, accessed June
25, 2012; Highly Achieved Women Leaving the Traditional Workforce Final Report March 2008, U.S.
Department of Labor, http://www.choose2lead
.org/Publications/Are%20We%20Losing%20
the%20Best%20and%20the%20Brightest.pdf,
accessed June 25, 2012.

9. Featured Employee Rap Sheet, Hot Topic
website, http://www.hottopic.com/community
/rapsheets/emp_jodi.asp?LS=0&, accessed April
11, 2006; A New Game at the Office: Many Young
Workers Accept Fewer Guarantees, by Steve Lohr,
The New York Times, December 5, 2005, http://
select.nytimes.com/gst/abstract.html?res=F00F12
FE38550C768CDDAB0994DD404482; Work-life
benefits fall victim to slow economy, by Andrea
Shim, April 4, 2009, Los Angeles Times website,
http://www.latimes.com/business/la-fi-flexible4
-2009apr04,0,4344887.story, accessed April 4,
2009; Pending Job Flexibility Act Received Mixed
Reviews, by Sue Shellenbarger, WSJ Career Journal,
http://www.careerjournal.com/columnists
/workfamily/20010426-workfamily.html, accessed
August 9, 2005; Work-life benefits fall victim to
slow economy by Andrea Shim, April 4, 2009,
Los Angeles Times website, http://www.latimes.com
/business/la-fi-flexible4-2009apr04,0,4344887
.story, accessed April 4, 2009.

10. Why We Hate HR, by Keith W. Hammonds,
December 19, 2007, Fast Company website,
http://www.fastcompany.com/magazine/97/open
_hr.html?page=0%2C1, accessed April 4, 2009.

11. One-third of young people have a bachelor's,
by Mary Beth Marklein, November 5, 2012, USA-
Today website, http://www.usatoday.com/story/news
/nation/2012/11/05/college-graduates-pew
/1683899/, accessed April 9, 2013; Table 1. The
30 fastest growing occupations covered in the 2008–
2009 Occupational Outlook Handbook, Economic
News Release, December 18, 2007, Bureau of
Labor Statistics website, http://www.bls.gov/
news.release/ooh.t01.htm, accessed April 7, 2009;
Census Bureau Data Underscore Value of College
Degree, U.S. Census Bureau News, October 26,
2006, Census Bureau website, http://www.census
.gov/Press-Release/www/rel-eases/archives
/education/007660.html, accessed April 7, 2009;
Increasing Share of Adults Have College Degrees,
Census Bureau Finds, by Derek Quizon, April 26,
2011, The Chronicle of Higher Education website,

http://chronicle.com/article/Increasing-Share-of
-Adults/127264/, accessed July 5, 2011.

12. SHRM Human Capital Benchmarking
Study, 2008 Executive Summary, page 14,
SHRM website, http://www.shrm.org/Research
/Documents/2008%20Executive%20Summary
_FINAL.pdf, accessed April 7, 2009; Effective
Recruiting Tied to Stronger Financial Performance,
Watson Wyatt Worldwide news release, August 16,
2005, Watson Wyatt Worldwide website, http://
www.watsonwyatt.com/news/press.asp?ID=14959,
accessed April 7, 2009.

13. Top Five Resume Lies, by Jeanne Sahadi,
December 9, 2004, CNN Money website, http://
money.cnn.com/2004/11/22/pf/resume_lies/.

14. You're Hired. At Least for Now, by Anne Kates
Smith, March 2010, Kiplinger website, http://www
.kiplinger.com/magazine/archives/employers-choose
-temps-contract-workers.html accessed July 13,
2010; Special Report on Contingent Staffing—The
Future of Contingent Staffing Could Be Like
Something Out of a Movie, by Irwin Speizer,
October 19, 2009, Workforce Management website,
http://www.workforce.com/section/recruiting
-staffing/feature/special-report-contingent-staff-
ingthe-future-contingent/, accessed July 5, 2011; The
Rise of the Independent Work Force, by Alexandra
Levit, April 14, 2012, The New York Times
website, http://www.nytimes.com/2012/04/15/jobs
/independent-workers-are-here-to-stay.html,
accessed June 25, 2012.

15. The Questions: How Not to Answer, compiled
by Barry Shamis of Selecting Winners, Inc.,
FacilitatorGuy Resume Resource Center, http://
resume.bgolden.com/res/interview-bloopers
.php, accessed September 1, 2005; Interview
Bloopers: What Not to Do! by Maureen Bauer,
Channel 3000 website, http://html.channel3000
.com/sh/employment/stories/employment—
20001002-144946.html, accessed September 1,
2005; More Interview Bloopers, by Maureen Bauer,
Channel 3000 website, http://html
.channel3000.com/sh/employment/stories
/employment—20001002-152818.html.

16. Orientation: Not Just a Once-over-Lightly
Anymore, by Matt DeLuca HRO Today,
April/May 2005, http://www.hrotoday.com
/Magazine.asp?artID=928; New Emphasis on
First Impressions, by Leslie Gross Klaff,
March 2008, Workforce Management
website, http://www.workforce.com/archive
/feature/25/41/58/index.php?ht=, accessed
April 7, 2009; Show and Tell—Disney Institute's
Four-Day Seminar on HR Management, by Leon
Rubis, HR magazine, April 1998; New Employee
Experience Aims for Excitement Beyond the
First Day, by Daryl Stephenson, Boeing Frontiers
Online, May 2002, http://www.boeing. com/news
/frontiers/archive/2002/may/i_mams.html.

17. Labor-Intensive, by Sean McFadden, Boston
Business Journal, November 19, 2004, http://www
.bizjournals.com/boston/stories/2004/11/22
/smallb1.html; The Costco Way; Higher Wages
Mean Higher Profits. But Try Telling Wall Street,
by Stanley Holmes and Wendy Zelner, Business-
Week, April 12, 2004; Study: Moderation in
Hiring Practices Boosts Business Performance,
by Todd Raphael, Workforce Management,
August 19, 2005, http://www.workforce.com
/section/00/article/24/14/03.html.

18. Appreciating Benefits as Times Gets Tough,
by Carroll Lachnit, March 24, 2009, Blog: The
Business of Management, Workforce Management
website, http://www.workforce.com/article

/20090324/BLOGS02/303249999/appreciating
-benefits-as-times-gets-tough, accessed April
9, 2009.

19. Perking Up: Some Companies Offer Surprising
New Benefits, by Sue Shellenbarger, March 18,
2009, The Wall Street Journal website, http://
online.wsj.com/article/SB123733195850463165
.html, accessed April 9, 2009.

20. Questions and Answers about Flexible Work
Schedules: A Sloan Work and Family Research
Network Fact Sheet, updated September 2008,
Sloan Work and Family Research Network website,
http://wfnetwork.bc.edu/pdfs/flexworksched.pdf,
accessed April 9, 2009; Work-life benefits fall victim
to slow economy, by Andrea Shim, April 4, 2009,
Los Angeles Times website, http://www.latimes.com
/business/la-fi-flexible4-2009apr04,0,4344887.story,
accessed April 4, 2009.

21. Whitewater Rafting? 12 Unusual Perks,
January 20, 2012, http://money.cnn.com/magazines
/fortune/best-companies/2012/benefits/unusual
.html, accessed April 10, 2013.

22. One In Five Americans Work From Home,
Numbers Seen Rising Over 60%, by Kenneth
Rapoza, February 18, 2013, Forbes website,
http://www.forbes.com/sites/kenrapoza
/2013/02/18/one-in-five-americans-work-from
-home-numbers-seen-rising-over-60/, accessed
March 30, 2014; The work-from-home tug of war,
by Rick Hampson, March 11, 2013, USA Today
website, http://www.usatoday.com/story/news
/nation/2013/03/11/the-work-from-home-tug-of
-war/1979457/, accessed March 30, 2014; Global
Workplace Analytics and the Telework Research
Network, http://www.teleworkresearchnetwork.
com/pros-cons, accessed April 10, 2013; The
hard truth about telecommuting, by Mary C.
Noonan and Jennifer L. Glass, Monthly Labor
Review, June 2012, http://www.bls.gov/opub
/mlr/2012/06/art3full.pdf, accessed April 10,
2013; Give telecommuting the green light, by Ted
Samson, June 7, 2007, InfoWorld website, http://
www.infoworld.com/d/green-it/give
-telecommuting-green-light-628, accessed April 10,
2009; Home Sweet Office: Telecommute Good for
Business, Employees, and Planet, by Brendan
I. Koerner, September 22, 2008, Wired website,
http://www.wired.com/culture/culturereviews
/magazine/16-10/st_essay, accessed April 10, 2009;
Skype: More companies allow telecommuting,
by Ginger Christ, April 5, 2011, Dayton Business
Journal website, http://www.bizjournals.com
/dayton/news/2011/04/05/more-companies-allow
-telecommuting.html, accessed July 5, 2011;
Costs and Benefits, Advantages of Telecommuting for Companies, Telework Research Network
website, http://www.teleworkresearchnetwork.
com/costs-benefits, accessed July 5, 2011.

23. The New Job Sharers, by Michelle V. Rafter, May
2008, Workforce Management website, http://www
.workforce.com/archive/feature/25/53/28/index.php,
accessed April 10, 2009; Study Attempts To Dispel
Five Myths of Job Sharing, by Stephen Miller, May
9, 2007, Society for Human Resource Management
website, http://moss07.shrm.org/Publications
/HRNews/Pages/XMS_021497.aspx, accessed April
10, 2009.

24. 5.1 million jobs lost in this recession so far,
by Rex Nutting, April 3, 2009, MarketWatch
website, http://www.marketwatch.com/news/story
/51-million-jobs-lost-recession/story. aspx?guid
={CF54164C-6F7B-4501-B6FB-D7D1C8D710B9}&
dist=msr_8, accessed April 10, 2009; Boost
Employee Morale After Layoffs, Workforce
Management website, http://www.workforce.com

/archive/article/22/14/10.php, accessed April 10, 2009.

25. Are Your Coworkers REALLY Sick? by Diane Stafford, October 11, 2012, The Weather Channel website, http://www.weather.com/health/cold-flu/sick-days-20121011, accessed March 30, 2014.

26. 10 Unusual Jobs That Pay Surprisingly Well, by Jacquelyn Smith, May 23, 2013, Forbes website, http://www.forbes.com/sites/jacquelynsmith/2013/05/23/10-unusual-jobs-that-pay-surprisingly-well/, accessed March 30, 2014; Employed as a Psychic: Earn $110 to $60 Hourly, by Jane Genova, October 11, 2010, aoljobs website, http://jobs.aol.com/articles/2010/10/11/psychic-earn-110-to-60-hourly/, accessed April 10, 2013; 8 Wacky Jobs at Best Companies, 100 Best Companies to Work for 2011, Fortune website, http://money.cnn.com/galleries/2011/pf/jobs/1101/gallery.best_companies_craziest_jobs.fortune/index.html, accessed July 5, 2011; 8 Wacky Jobs, Fortune website, http://money.cnn.com/galleries/2011/fortune/1105/gallery.fortune500_fun_jobs.fortune/index.html, accessed July 5; Strangest jobs in the world; Odd travel industry jobs include bath sommelier, dog surf instructor, by Katrina Brown Hunt and Darrin Tobias, June 13, 2011, New York Daily News website, http://www.nydailynews.com/lifestyle/2011/06/13/2011-06-13_strangest_jobs_in_the_world_odd_travel_industry_jobs_include_bath_sommelier_dog_.html, accessed July 12, 2011; Unusual Jobs and Their Paydays, by Jason Daniels, May 17, 2012, PayDayOne website, http://news.paydayone.com/general-finance/jobs-and-their-paydays/, accessed June 27, 2012; Unusual Jobs That Pay Surprisingly Well, by Jaquelyn Smith, May 25, 2012, Forbes website, http://www.forbes.com/sites/jacquelynsmith/2012/05/25/unusual-jobs-that-pay-surprisingly-well/.

27. Sexual Harassment Charges, EEOC & FEPAs Combined: FY 1997–FY 2008, EEOC website, updated March 11, 2009, http://www.eeoc.gov/stats/harass.html, accessed April 10, 2009.

28. Sexual Harassment, updated March 11, 2009, http://www.eeoc.gov/types/sexual_harassment.html, accessed April 10, 2009.

Pg. 266 Fact: Women at Work: A Guide for Men, by Joanne Lipman, December 12, 2014, http://www.wsj.com/articles/women-at-work-a-guide-for-men-1418418595, accessed September 24, 2015.

Pg. 267 Fact: Frivolous Lawsuits, America's Best website, April 2008, http://www.americasbestcompanies.com/magazine/articles/frivolous-lawsuits.aspx, accessed November 27, 2012.

Pg. 270 Fact: Few Firms Recruiting Liberal Arts Majors, by Walter hamilton, May 21, 2014, Los Angeles Times website, http://www.latimes.com/business/la-fi-companies-hiring-liberal-arts-majors-jobs-20140521-story.html, accessed May 10, 2015.

Pg. 278 Fact: Occupational Safety and Health Administration Statistics, https://www.osha.gov/oshstats/commonstats.html, accessed September 2014.

16

1. The iPad in Your Hand: As Fast as a Supercomputer of Yore, by John Markoff, The New York Times website, May 9, 2011, http://bits.blogs.nytimes.com/2011/05/09/the-ipad-in-your-hand-as-fast-as-a-supercomputer-of-yore/, accessed April 2, 2013; M. Grothaus, iPad2 Would Have Bested 1990s-era Supercomputers, TUAW, May 9,

2011, http://www.tuaw.com/2011/05/09/ipad-2-would-have-bested-1990s-era-supercomputers/, accessed April 2, 2013; S. Stein, "iPad Air 2" review–CNET, October 21, 2014, http://www.cnet.com/products/apple-ipad-air-2/, accessed April 14, 2015.

2. "Global Internet Phenomena Report: 1H 2014," Sandvine Intelligent Broadband Networks, https://www.sandvine.com/downloads/general/global-internet-phenomena/2014/1h-2014-global-internet-phenomena-report.pdf, accessed April 14, 2015.

3. The Size of the World Wide Web (The Internet), WorldWideWebSize.com, April 14, 2015, http://www.worldwidewebsize.com/, accessed April 14, 2015.

4. K. Zichurh and A. Smith, "Home Broadband 2013," Pew Research Internet Project, August 26, 2013, http://www.pewinternet.org/2013/08/26/home-broadband-2013/, accessed March 31, 2014.

5. About Us, Internet2 website, http://www.internet2.edu/about-us/, accessed April 14, 2015; J. Burt, "Fog Computing Systems Aim to Reduce Processing Burden of Cloud Systems," eWeek.com, November 20, 2014, http://www.eweek.com/print/networking/fog-computing-aims-to-reduce-processing-burden-of-cloud-systems.html, accessed April 17, 2015; I. Barker, "Cloud Adoption Still on the Rise as IT Departments Take the Lead," Cloud News, February 21, 2015, http://www.itproportal.com/2015/02/21/cloud-adoption-still-rise-it-departments-take-lead/, accessed April 17, 2015; C. Mims, "Forget 'The Cloud'; 'The Fog' Is Tech's Future," The Wall Street Journal, May 18, 2014; C. Boulton, "Exposing the Hidden Waste and Expense of Cloud Computing," The Wall Street Journal, February 17, 2015, B4; Right Scale 2015 State of the Cloud Report, http://www.rightscale.com/lp/2015-state-of-the-cloud-report?campaign=701700000012UP1, accessed April 17, 2015; S. Lawson, "Cisco Unveils 'Fog Computing' to Bridge Clouds and the Internet of Things," PCWorld, January 29, 2014, http://www.pcworld.com/article/2092660/cisco-unveils-fog-computing-to-bridge-clouds-and-the-internet-of-things.html, accessed April 17, 2015.

6. S. McCartney, The Middle Seat: Boarding Gate Makeover: Purgatory No More, The Wall Street Journal, August 23, 2012, D3; Nassauer, Screens Get a Place at the Table, The Wall Street Journal, May 31, 2012, D1.

7. "Communities & Groups: Internet2," http://www.internet2.edu/communities-groups/members/, accessed April 14, 2015.

8. Muse website, http://k20.internet2.edu/about/goals.

9. Seeking Safety in Clouds, by J. Bussey, The Wall Street Journal, September 15, 2011, http://online.wsj.com/article/SB10001424053111904060604576572930344327162.html, accessed June 16, 2012.

10. Seeking Safety in Clouds, by J. Bussey, The Wall Street Journal, September 15, 2011, http://online.wsj.com/article/SB10001424053111904060604576572930344327162.html, accessed June 16, 2012.

11. S. Ovide & C. Boulton, "Flood of Rivals Could Burst Amazon's Cloud, The Wall Street Journal, July 26, 2014, B4.

12. E. Rusli, Next in Tech: Research Labs Jump to Cloud–Startups Use Software, Robots to Slash Costs for Basic Experiments, The Wall Street Journal, July 1, 2014, B4.

13. N. Singer, "Bring Big Data to the Fight Against Benefits Fraud," The New York Times, February 20, 2015, http://www.nytimes.com

/2015/02/22/technology/bringing-big-data-to-the-fight-against-benefits-fraud.html, accessed April 15, 2015.

14. Management Information Systems, 5th ed., by Effy Oz, Course Technology, Cengage Learning, 2006, pp. 332–338; Expert Systems, AlanTuring.Net, http://www.cs.usfca.edu/www.AlanTuring.net/turing_archive/pages/Reference%20Articles/what_is_AI/What%20is%20AI07.html.

15. Experiencing MIS, by David M. Kroenke, Pearson Prentice Hall, 2008, pp. 340–341; What Are Expert Systems? Thinkquest.org website, http://library.thinkquest.org/11534/expert.htm, accessed May 24, 2009.

16. Derek Markham, "14 Healthy Living Apps to Help You Kick Off a New Year," Tree Hugger, January 8, 2015, http://www.treehugger.com/gadgets/healthy-living-apps-kick-new-year.html.; Kayla Matthews, "8 Unique Apps to Help You Save Gas Money," Make Use Of, February 20, 2015, http://www.makeuseof.com/tag/8-unique-apps-help-save-gas-money/;

17. D. Nations, "What Is Enterprise 2.0? Enterprise 2.0 Explained," About Tech, http://webtrends.about.com/od/office20/a/enterprise-20.htm, accessed April 16, 2015; D. Nation, "What Is Web 2.0—How Web 2.0 Is Defining Society," About Tech, http://webtrends.about.com/od/web20/a/what-is-web20.htm, accessed April 16, 2015.

18. "Q3 2014 Internet Advertising Revenues Hit $12.4 Billion, Making It the Highest Quarter on Record," IAB, December 18, 2014, http://www.iab.net/about_the_iab/recent_press_releases/press_release_archive/press_release/pr-121814, accessed April 16, 2015; "IAB Internet Advertising Revenue Report: 2014 First Six Months Results," IAB, October 2014, http://www.iab.net/media/file/IAB_Internet_Advertising_Revenue_Report_HY_2014_PDF.pdf, accessed April 16, 2015; "IAB Internet Advertising Revenue Report: 2013 Full Year Results," IAB, October 2014, http://www.iab.net/media/file/IAB_Internet_Advertising_Revenue_Report_FY_2013.pdf, accessed April 16, 2015.

19. "About PayPal," PayPal.com, https://www.paypal-media.com/about, accessed April 16, 2015.

20. C. Palmeri, "Disney Bets Big on Visitor-Tracking Technology," Bloomberg Businessweek/MSN Money, March 10, 2014, http://money.msn.com/technology-investment/post--disney-bets-big-on-visitor-tracking-technology, accessed March 31, 2014.

21. J. Schectman, "Botched RFID Launch Made Penney Target for Thieves," Wall Street Journal, November 22, 2013, http://blogs.wsj.com/cio/2013/11/22/botched-rfid-launch-made-penney-target-for-thieves/ accessed December 11 2013; "RFID News: JC Penney's Sudden Retreat from RFID Led to Rash of Store Thefts," Supply Chain Digest, December 3, 2013, http://www.scdigest.com/ontarget/13-12-03-1.php?cid=7637&ctype=content, accessed December 11, 2013.

22. Spammers Target Email Newsletters, by David Utter, January 19, 2007, WebProWorld Security Forum, http://www.securitypronews.com/insiderreports/insider/spn-49-20070119Spammers TargetEmailNewsletters.html; Spammers Turn to Images to Fool Filters, by Anick Jesdanun, USA Today, June 28, 2006, http://www.usatoday.com/tech/news/computer security/wormsviruses/2006-06-28-spam-images_x.htm.

23. Pharming: Is Your Trusted Website a Clever Fake? Microsoft website, January 3, 2007, http://www.microsoft.com/protect/yourself/phishing/pharming.mspx; Online Fraud: Pharming,

Symantic website, http://www.symantec.com /norton/cybercrime/pharming.jsp, accessed May 24, 2009; Advisory: Watch Out for Drive-by-Pharming Attacks, Pharming.org website, http://www .pharming.org/index.jsp, accessed May 24, 2009.

24. M. Huffman, "Smishing" Emerges as New Threat to Cell Phone Users, *Consumer Affairs*, http://www.consumeraffairs.com/news04/2006/11 /smishing.html, accessed May 22, 2009; E. Millis, "SMiShing" Fishes for Personal Data Over Cell Phone, CNet, February 24, 2009, http://news .cnet.com/8301-1009_3-10171241-83.html, accessed April 2, 2013; L. Musthaler, How to Avoid Becoming a Victim of SMiShing (SMS phishing), NetworkWorld, March 7, 2013, http://www .networkworld.com/newsletters/techexec/2013 /030813bestpractices.html, accessed April 2, 2013.

25. J. Steinberg, "Avoid These Holiday Shopping Cyber-Scams," *Forbes*, November 27, 2013, http:// www.forbes.com/sites/josephsteinberg/2013/11/27 /avoid-these-holiday-shopping-cyber-scams/, accessed December 12, 2013.

26. Create Strong Passwords, Microsoft Safety & Security Center, http://www.microsoft.com/security /online-privacy/passwords-create.aspx, accessed April 2, 2013.

27. K. Waldman. "Facebook's Unethical Experiment," *Slate*, June 28, 2014, http://www.slate.com /articles/health_and_science/science/2014/06 /facebook_unethical_experiment_it_made_news _feeds_happier_or_sadder_to_manipulate.html, accessed April 16, 2015; R. Hotz, "Facebook Feelings Found Contagious," *The Wall Street Journal*, March 13, 2014, A3; T. Lewis, "Emotions Can Be Contagious on Online Social Networks," *Scientific American*, July 1, 2014, http://www .scientificamerican.com/article/facebook-emotions -are-contagious/, accessed April 16, 2015; V. Goel, "Facebook Tinkers with Users' Emotions in News Feed Experiment, Stirring Outcry," *The New York Times*, June 29, 2014, http://www.nytimes .com/2014/06/30/technology/facebook-tinkers-with -users-emotions-in-news-feed-experiment-stirring -outcry.html?_r=0, accessed April 16, 2015.

28. M. Tabini, "1Password 4 for Mac," Macworld, October 14, 2013, http://www.macworld.com /article/2053261/1password-4-for-mac-review-state -of-the-art-password-management-for-everyone .html, accessed March 31, 2014; What Makes a Password Stronger: With Concern about Hackers, Tools for Remembering So Many Codes, by S. Woo, *The Wall Street Journal*, June 23, 2011, p. D2.

29. Passport RFIDs Cloned Wholesale by $250 eBay Shopping Spree, by Dan Goodin, *The Register* website February 2, 2009, http://www.theregister .co.uk/2009/02/02/low_cost_rfid_cloner/; Life With Big Brother: Radio Chips Coming Soon to Your Driver's License? by Bob Unruh, World Net Daily website February 28, 2009, http://www .worldnetdaily.com/index.php?fa=PAGE .view&pageId=90008; RFID Driver's Licenses Debated, by Mark Baard, *Wired* website October 6, 2004, http://www.wired.com/politics/security /news/2004/10/65243; A Threat Analysis of RFID Passports, by A. Ramos, W. Scott, W. Scott, D. Lloyd, K. O'Leary, and J. Waldo, Communications of the ACM, December 2009, pp. 38–42.

30. Ibid.

31. "The Compliance Gap: BSA Global Software Survey," BSA: The Software Alliance, June 2014, http://globalstudy.bsa.org/2013/downloads/studies /2013GlobalSurvey_Study_en.pdf, accessed April 16, 2015.

32. Sikdar, L. Madhavan, S. Lakshmi, & M. Nagappan, "The LInk Between Pirated Software and Cybersecurity Breaches: How Malware in Pirated Software Is Costing the World Billions, National University of Singapore and IDC, March 2014, http://news.microsoft.com/download /presskits/dcu/docs/idc_031814.pdf, accessed April 16, 2015.

17

1. Establishment Data: Historical Employment-Table B-1a. Employees on Nonfarm Payrolls by Industry Sector and Selected Industry Detail, Seasonally Adjusted, Bureau of Labor Statistics, December 2014, http://www.bls.gov/opub/ee/2014 /ces/table1a_201412.pdf, accessed April 17, 2015.

2. *Table 1.5 Fastest Declining Occupations, 2012 and Projected 2022*, U.S. Bureau of Labor Statistics, December 29, 2013, online at http://www.bls.gov /emp/ep_table_105.htm, accessed February 28, 2015; James R. Hagerty, "Wal-Mart Entertains a Pitch—Made In the U.S.A.," The Wall Street Journal, October 6, 2013, http://www.wsj .com/articles/SB100014240527023034925045791 15783923496354; James R. Hagerty, "A Decimated U.S. Industry Pulls Up Its Socks," *The Wall Street Journal*, December 24, 2014, online at http://www .wsj.com/articles/a-decimated-u-s-industry-pulls -up-its-socks-1419440433; Julie Taboh, "'Made in America' Socks Get a Toehold in Online Fashion Market," *Voice of America*, August 27, 2014, online at http://www.voanews.com/content/made -in-america-socks-get-a-toehold-in-online-fashion -market/2430371.html, accessed February 28, 2015; Samantha Hurst, "Brief: 'Shark Tank' Contestant Freaker USA Launches Kickstarter Campaign for Made in the USA Socks," *Crowdfund Insider*, January 2, 2015, online at http://www .crowdfundinsider.com/2015/01/60525-shark -tank-contestant-freaker-usa-launches-kickstarter -campaign-made-usa-socks/, accessed February 28, 2015; Paul Wiseman, "When the Textile Mill Goes, So Does a Way of Life," *USA Today*, March 11, 2010, online at http://usatoday30.usatoday.com /money/economy/employment/2010-03-09-textile -jobs-lost-mount-airy_N.htm, accessed 28 February 2015; http://www.peds.com/brands/peds-boys/; http://www.penancehall.com/our-story1/.

3. A. Martonik, "GM Now Offering OnStar Remote Start and Door Unlock Free for 5 Years," Android Central, June 5, 2013, http://www .androidcentral.com/gm-now-offering-onstar -remote-start-and-door-unlock-free-5-years, accessed April 1, 2014.

4. *OM*, 2nd ed. by David A. Collier and James R. Evans, Mason, OH: South-Western, Cengage Learning, 2010, pages 27–28.

5. Outsourcing: Ripoff Nation, BW Smallbiz Front Line, Winter 2006, *Business Week* website, http://www.businessweek.com/magazine/content /06_52/b4015435.htm?chan=rss_topStories_ssi_5; Outsourcing in China: Five Basic Rules for Reducing Risk, by Steve Dickinson, ezinearticles .com website, http://ezinearticles.com/? Outsourcing-in-China:-Five-Basics-for -Reducing-Risk&id=17214.

6. ERP and Cloud Computing: Delivering a Virtual Feast, by David Stodder, Information Week website, May 20, 2010, http://www. informationweek .com/news/software/bi/224701329, accessed December 6, 2011.

7. Servicescapes: The Impact of Physical Surroundings on Customers and Employees, by M. J. Bitner, *Journal of Marketing*, April 1992, pp. 57–71.

8. G. Bensinger, "Corporate News: Amazon Developing Delivery Drones," *The Wall Street Journal*, December 2, 2013, B8; A. Chang, "With Prime Air, Amazon Plans to Deliver Purchases via Drones," *Los Angeles Times*, December 2, 2013, http:// www.latimes.com/business/technology/la-fi-tn -amazon-prime-air-20131202,0,6889414.story #axzz2plD7WHJm, accessed December 12, 2013; J. Nicas, "From Farms to Films, Drones Find Commercial Uses," *The Wall Street Journal*, March 11, 2014, B1.

9. Steven Rosenbush and Laura Stevens, "At UPS, the Algorithm Is the Driver—Turn Right, Turn Left, Turn Right: Inside Orion, the 10-year Effort to Squeeze Every Penny From Delivery Routes," *The Wall Street Journal*, February 17, 2015, B1, B4; http://www.pressroom.ups.com/Media+Kits /ORION; Alex Konrad, "Meet ORION, Software That Will Save UPS Millions by Improving Drivers' Routes," *Forbes*, November 1, 2013, http://www .forbes.com/sites/alexkonrad/2013/11/01/meet-orion -software-that-will-save-ups-millions-by-improving -drivers-routes/?partner=yahootix, accessed February 27, 2015.

10. Poka Yoke Mistake Proofing, by Kerri Simon, iSixSigma website, http://www.isixsigma.com /library/content/c020128a.asp; Make No Mistake, by Mark Hendricks, *Entrepreneur* magazine, October 1996, http://www.entrepreneur.com /magazine/entrepreneur/1996/october/13430.html, accessed July 30, 2007.

11. "Baldrige Award Process Fees," Baldrige Performance Excellence Program, http://www.nist .gov/baldrige/enter/award_fees.cfm, accessed April 17, 2015.

12. About ISO, ISO website, http://www.iso.org /iso/about.htm, accessed April 6, 2013; ISO Standards, ISO website, http://www.iso.org/iso /iso_catalogue.htm, accessed April 6, 2013.

13. "The ISO Survey of Management System Standard Certifications—2012," International Organization for Standardization, http://www .iso.org/iso/iso_survey_executive-summary.pdf, accessed April 1, 2014; "World Distribution of ISO 9001 Certificates in 2012," International Organization for Standardization, http://www.iso .org/iso/home/standards/certification/iso-survey .htm?certificate=ISO%209001&countrycode =IT#countrypick, accessed April 1, 2014.

14. H. Greimel, "Honda's New Plan Takes Manufacturing to the Next Level," *Automotive News*, December 1, 2013, http://www.autonews .com/article/20131201/OEM01/312029986 /hondas-new-plant-takes-manufacturing-to-the -next-level#axzz2o0wHTJPO, accessed December 12, 2013; Y. Kageyama, "Honda Counts on Lean Production for Fit," Yahoo! News, November 19, 2013, http://news.yahoo.com/honda-counts-lean -production-hybrid-fit-060208142--finance.html, accessed December 12, 2013.

15. At Vuitton, Growth in Small Batches—Luxury-Goods Maker's New French Factory Adds to Capacity but Sticks to Strategy of Tight Rein, *The Wall Street Journal*, June 27, 2011, p. B1.

16. A. Coolidge, "New Technology Helps Kroger Speed Up Checkout Times," *USA Today*, June 20, 2013, http://www.usatoday.com/story/money /business/2013/06/20/new-technology-helps -kroger-speed-up-checkout-times/2443975/, accessed April 1, 2014.

17. One reason renewable energy is more expensive than energy from carbon-based sources such as coal or oil is that the market prices of such carbon-based sources do not reflect their environmental costs.

18. Sustainability Initiatives Cut Costs 6–10%, Environmental Leader website, http://www

.environmentalleader.com/2009/06/09/sustainability-initiatives-cut-costs-by-6-10/, accessed April 6, 2013.

19. ISO 14000—Environmental management—ISO, http://www.iso.org/iso/home/standards/management-standards/iso14000.htm, accessed April 17, 2015.

Personal Finance Appendix

1. About Us, Consumer Finance Protection Bureau, http://www.consumerfinance.gov/the-bureau/, accessed April 21, 2013.

2. Bach, David, *The Automatic Millionaire*, New York: Broadway Books, 2004.

3. Bach, David, *The Automatic Millionaire*, New York: Broadway Books, 2004.

4. FDIC: What's Covered, https://www.fdic.gov/deposit/covered/, accessed April 18, 2015; FDIC: How Are My Deposit Accounts Insured by the FDIC?, https://www.fdic.gov/deposit/covered/categories.html, accessed April 18, 2015.

5. What's In Your FICO Score? myFICO.com, http://www.myfico.com/CreditEducation/WhatsInYourScore.aspx, accessed April 18, 2015; P. Curry, "How Credit Scores Work, How a Score Is Calculated," Bankrate.com, http://www.bankrate.com/brm/news/credit-scoring/20031104a1.asp, April 21, 2013.

6. About Credit Scores, Money-Zine.com, http://www.money-zine.com/financial-planning/debt-consolidation/about-credit-scores/, accessed April 18, 2015.

7. How Your Credit Score Affects Your Mortgage, U.S. News and World Report, March 2, 2011, http://money.usnews.com/money/blogs/my-money/2011/03/02/how-your-credit-score-affects-your-mortgage, accessed April 21, 2013.

8. S. Ladika, "Feds Cap Credit Card Late Fees at $25," Creditcards.com, http://www.creditcards.com/credit-card-news/feds-cap-credit-card-late-payment-fee-25.php, accessed April 21, 2013; L. McFadden, "Does Law Cap Credit Card Rates?" BankRate.com, http://www.bankrate.com/finance/credit-cards/does-law-cap-credit-card-interest-rates.aspx, accessed April 21, 2013.

9. L. McFadden, "What the Dodd-Frank Law Means for You," Bankrate.com, June 25, 2010, http://www.bankrate.com/financing/credit-cards/what-the-dodd-frank-act-means-for-you/, accessed April 21, 2013.

10. C. Lee and J. Hook, "Fresh Downgrade Threat to U.S. Debt," The *Wall Street Journal*, June 9. 2011, http://online.wsj.com/article/SB100014240527023047783045763739927117 72366.html, accessed April 21, 2013.

11. Table 5. Quartiles and Selected Deciles of Usual Weekly Earnings of Full-Time Wage and Salary Workers by Selected Characteristics, Fourth Quarter 2014 Averages, Not Seasonally Adjusted, Economic News Release, Bureau of Labor Statistics, January 21, 2015, http://www.bls.gov/news.release/wkyeng.t05.htm, accessed April 18, 2015.

12. Table A-4. Employment Status of the Civilian Population 25 Years and Over by Educational Attainment, Economic News Release, Bureau of Labor Statistics, April 3, 2015, http://www.bls.gov/news.release/empsit.t04.htm/, accessed April 18, 2015.

13. U.S. Department of Labor Advisory, by Janet Oates (Assistant Secretary, Employment and Training Administration) and Nancy Leppink (Deputy Administrator, Wage and Hour Division), U.S. Department of Labor website, http://wdr.doleta.gov/directives/attach/TEGL/TEGL 12-09acc.pdf; The Unpaid Intern, Legal or Not by Steven Greenhouse, *The New York Times* website, http://www.nytimes.com/2010/04/03/business/03intern.html.

14. M. Quinn, "37% of Americans Think They're Too Broke to Save," GoBankingRates.com, January 5, 2015, http://www.gobankingrates.com/personal-finance/37americans-think-theyre-broke-save/, accessed April 18, 2015; S. Woolley, "Millennials Are Getting Surprisingly Good at Saving: Young People Are Building Their Nest Eggs at a Faster Rate Than Last Year," *Bloomberg Businessweek*, February 23, 2015, http://www.bloomberg.com/news/articles/2015-02-23/millennials-are-getting-surprisingly-good-at-saving, accessed April 18, 2015; S. Tompor, "Young Adults: More Credit Card Debt Than Savings," *USA Today*, February 28, 2015, http://www.coshoctontribune.com/story/money/columnist/tompor/2015/02/28/tompor-credit-card-debt-savings/24169635/, accessed April 18, 2015; Mac and Gaydos, "Six Simple Ways to Save Money," KTAR News, February 25, 2015, http://ktar.com/95/1810820/Six-simple-ways-to-save-money, accessed April 18, 2015.

15. While earnings on traditional IRA contributions are always tax deferred, there are income-based limits on the deductibility of contributions. Thus, high-income taxpayers are unable to deduct any money they contribute to a traditional IRA. For more specifics, see the IRS guidelines at: http://www.irs.gov/Retirement-Plans/Individual-Retirement-Arrangements-(IRAs)-1, accessed April 28, 2014.

Pg. 324 Fact: Bankrate.com credit card calculator—How much will the minimum credit card payment cost me?, http://www.bankrate.com/calculators/credit-cards/credit-card-payoff-calculator.aspx

GLOSSARY

401(k), 403(b), and 457 plans
Employee payroll-deduction retirement plans that offer tax benefits.

absolute advantage
The benefit a country has in a given industry when it can produce more of a product than other nations using the same amount of resources.

accounting
A system for recognizing, organizing, analyzing, and reporting information about the financial transactions that affect an organization.

accounting equation
Assets = Liabilities + Owners' Equity

accredited investor
An organization or individual investor who meets certain criteria established by the SEC and so qualifies to invest in unregistered securities.

accrual-basis accounting
The method of accounting that recognizes revenue when it is earned and matches expenses to the revenues they helped produce.

acquisition
A corporate restructuring in which one firm buys another.

active listening
Attentive listening that occurs when the listener focuses his or her complete attention on the speaker.

active voice
Sentence construction in which the subject performs the action expressed by the verb (e.g., The accountant did the taxes.). The active voice works better for the vast majority of business communication.

activity-based costing (ABC)
A technique to assign product costs based on links between activities that drive costs and the production of specific products.

administrative law
Laws that arise from regulations established by government agencies.

advergaming
Video games created as a marketing tool, usually with brand awareness as the core goal.

advertising
Paid, nonpersonal communication, designed to influence a target audience with regard to a product, service, organization, or idea.

affirmative action
Policies meant to increase employment and educational opportunities for minority groups—especially groups defined by race, ethnicity, or gender.

agent
A party who agrees to represent another party, called the principal.

agents/brokers
Independent distributors who do not take title of the goods they distribute (even though they may take physical possession on a temporary basis before distribution).

angel investors
Individuals who invest in start-up companies with high growth potential in exchange for a share of ownership.

annual percentage rate (APR)
The interest expense charged on a credit card, expressed as an annual percentage.

applications software
Software that helps a user perform a desired task.

apprenticeships
Structured training programs that mandate that each beginner serve as an assistant to a fully trained worker before gaining full credentials to work in the field.

arbitration
A process in which a neutral third party has the authority to resolve a dispute by rendering a binding decision.

articles of incorporation
The document filed with a state government to establish the existence of a new corporation.

asset management ratios
Financial ratios that measure how effectively a firm is using its assets to generate revenues or cash.

assets
Resources owned by a firm.

autocratic leaders
Leaders who hoard decision-making power for themselves and typically issue orders without consulting their followers.

automation
Replacing human operation and control of machinery and equipment with some form of programmed control.

balance of payments
A measure of the total flow of money into or out of a country.

balance of payments deficit
Shortfall that occurs when more money flows out of a nation than into that nation.

balance of payments surplus
Overage that occurs when more money flows into a nation than out of that nation.

balance of trade
A basic measure of the difference in value between a nation's exports and imports, including both goods and services.

balance sheet
A financial statement that reports the financial position of a firm by identifying and reporting the value of the firm's assets, liabilities, and owners' equity.

Baldrige National Quality Program
A national program to encourage American firms to focus on quality improvement.

Banking Act of 1933
The law that established the Federal Deposit Insurance Corporation (FDIC) to insure bank deposits. It also prohibited commercial banks from selling insurance or acting as investment banks.

behavioral segmentation
Dividing the market based on how people behave toward various products. This category includes both the benefits that consumers seek from products and how consumers use the products.

benefits
Noncash compensation, including programs such as health insurance, vacation, and childcare.

bias
A preconception about members of a particular group. Common forms of bias include gender bias; age bias; and race, ethnicity, or nationality bias.

board of directors
The individuals who are elected by stockholders of a corporation to represent their interests.

bond
A formal debt instrument issued by a corporation or government entity.

boycott
A tactic in which a union and its supporters and sympathizers refuse to do business with an employer with which they have a labor dispute.

brand
A product's identity—including product name, symbol, design, reputation, and image—that sets it apart from other players in the same category.

brand equity
The overall value of a brand to an organization.

brand extension
A new product, in a new category, introduced under an existing brand name.

breach of contract
The failure of one party to a contract to perform his or her contractual obligations.

breakeven analysis
The process of determining the number of units a firm must sell to cover all costs.

broadband Internet connection
An Internet connection that is capable of transmitting large amounts of information very quickly.

budget (personal)
A detailed forecast of financial inflows (income) and outflows (expenses) in order to determine your net inflow or outflow for a given period of time.

budget deficit
Shortfall that occurs when expenses are higher than revenue over a given period of time.

budget surplus
Overage that occurs when revenue is higher than expenses over a given period of time.

budgeted balance sheet
A projected financial statement that forecasts the types and amounts of assets a firm will need to implement its future plans and how the firm will finance those assets. (Also called a pro forma balance sheet.)

budgeted income statement
A projection showing how a firm's budgeted sales and costs will affect expected net income. (Also called a pro forma income statement.)

budgeting
A management tool that explicitly shows how a firm will acquire and use the resources needed to achieve its goals over a specific time period.

business
Any organization or activity that provides goods and services in an effort to earn a profit.

business buyer behavior
Describes how people act when they are buying products to use either directly or indirectly to produce other products.

business cycle
The periodic contraction and expansion that occur over time in virtually every economy.

business environment
The setting in which business operates. The five key components are: economic environment, competitive environment, technological environment, social environment, and global environment.

business ethics
The application of right and wrong, good and bad, in a business setting.

business format franchise
A broad franchise agreement in which the franchisee pays for the right to use the name, trademark, and business and production methods of the franchisor.

business intelligence system
A sophisticated form of decision support system that helps decision makers discover information that was previously hidden.

business law
The application of laws and legal principles to business relationships and transactions.

business marketers (also known as business-to-business or B2B)
Marketers who direct their efforts toward people who are buying products to use either directly or indirectly to produce other products.

business plan
A formal document that describes a business concept, outlines core business objectives, and details strategies and timelines for achieving those objectives.

business products
Products purchased to use either directly or indirectly in the production of other products.

business technology
Any tools—especially computers, telecommunications, and other digital products—that businesses can use to become more efficient and effective.

business-to-business (B2B) e-commerce
E-commerce in markets where businesses buy from and sell to other businesses.

business-to-consumer (B2C) e-commerce
E-commerce in which businesses and final consumers interact.

buzz marketing
The active stimulation of word-of-mouth via unconventional, and often relatively low-cost, tactics. Other terms for buzz marketing are "guerrilla marketing" and "viral marketing."

C corporation
The most common type of corporation, which is a legal business entity that offers limited liability to all of its owners, who are called stockholders.

cafeteria-style benefits
An approach to employee benefits that gives all employees a set dollar amount that they must spend on company benefits, allocated however they wish within broad limitations.

cannibalization
When a producer offers a new product that takes sales away from its existing products.

capital budgeting
The process a firm uses to evaluate long-term investment proposals.

capital gain
The return on an asset that results when its market price rises above the price the investor paid for it.

capital structure
The mix of equity and debt financing a firm uses to meet its permanent financing needs.

capitalism
An economic system—also known as the private enterprise or free market system—based on private ownership, economic freedom, and fair competition.

carbon footprint
Refers to the amount of harmful greenhouse gases that a firm emits throughout its operations, both directly and indirectly.

case law (also called common law)
Laws that result from rulings, called precedents, made by judges who initially hear a particular type of case.

cash budget
A detailed forecast of future cash flows that helps financial managers identify when their firm is likely to experience temporary shortages or surpluses of cash.

cash equivalents
Safe and highly liquid assets that many firms list with their cash holdings on their balance sheet.

cause-related marketing
Marketing partnerships between businesses and nonprofit organizations, designed to spike sales for the company and raise money for the nonprofit.

certificate of deposit (CD)
An interest-earning deposit that requires the funds to remain deposited for a fixed term. Withdrawal of the funds before the term expires results in a financial penalty.

channel intermediaries
Distribution organizations—informally called "middlemen"—that facilitate the movement of products from the producer to the consumer.

channel of distribution
The network of organizations and processes that links producers to consumers.

Chapter 7 bankruptcy
A form of bankruptcy that discharges a debtor's debts by liquidating assets and using the proceeds to pay off creditors.

Chapter 11 bankruptcy
A form of bankruptcy used by corporations and individuals that allows the debtor to reorganize operations under a court-approved plan.

Chapter 13 bankruptcy
A form of bankruptcy that allows individual debtors to set up a repayment plan to adjust their debts.

Civil Rights Act of 1964
Federal legislation that prohibits discrimination in hiring, firing, compensation, apprenticeships, training, terms, conditions, or privileges of employment based on race, color, religion, sex, or national origin.

closed shop
An employment arrangement in which the employer agrees to hire only workers who already belong to the union.

cloud computing
The use of Internet-based storage capacity, processing power, and computer applications to supplement or replace internally owned information technology resources.

cobranding
When established brands from different companies join forces to market the same product.

code of ethics
A formal, written document that defines the ethical standards of an organization and

gives employees the information they need to make ethical decisions across a range of situations.

cognitive dissonance
Consumer discomfort with a purchase decision, typically for a higher-priced item.

collective bargaining
The process by which representatives of union members and employers attempt to negotiate a mutually acceptable labor agreement.

commercial banks
Privately owned financial institutions that accept demand deposits and make loans and provide other services for the public.

commercial paper
Short-term (and usually unsecured) promissory notes issued by large corporations.

common market
A group of countries that have eliminated tariffs and harmonized trading rules to facilitate the free flow of goods among the member nations.

common stock
The basic form of ownership in a corporation.

communication
The transmission of information between a sender and a recipient.

communication barriers
Obstacles to effective communication, typically defined in terms of physical, language, body language, cultural, perceptual, and organizational barriers.

communication channels
The various ways in which a message can be sent, ranging from one-on-one in-person meetings to Internet message boards.

communism
An economic and political system that calls for public ownership of virtually all enterprises, under the direction of a strong central government.

company matching
An amount contributed by the employer to an employee's retirement account, matching the employee's retirement contributions either dollar-for-dollar or based on a percentage of each dollar contributed by the employee.

comparative advantage
The benefit a country has in a given industry if it can make products at a lower opportunity cost than other countries.

compensation
The combination of pay and benefits that employees receive in exchange for their work.

compensatory damages
Monetary payments that a party who breaches a contract is ordered to pay in order to compensate the injured party for the actual harm suffered by the breach of contract.

compressed workweek
A version of flextime scheduling that allows employees to work a full-time number of hours in less than the standard workweek.

computer-aided design (CAD)
Drawing and drafting software that enables users to create and edit blueprints and design drawings quickly and easily.

computer-aided design/computer-aided manufacturing (CAD/CAM)
A combination of software that can be used to design output and send instructions to automated equipment to perform the steps needed to produce this output.

computer-aided engineering (CAE)
Software that enables users to test, analyze, and optimize their designs.

computer-aided manufacturing (CAM)
Software that takes the electronic design for a product and creates the programmed instructions that robots must follow to produce that product as efficiently as possible.

computer-integrated manufacturing (CIM)
A combination of CAD/CAM software with flexible manufacturing systems to automate almost all steps involved in designing, testing, and producing a product.

computer virus
Computer software that can be spread from one computer to another without the knowledge or permission of the computer users by attaching itself to emails or other files.

conceptual skills
The ability to grasp a big-picture view of the overall organization, the relationships among its various parts, and its fit in the broader competitive environment.

conglomerate merger
A combination of two firms that are in unrelated industries.

consideration
Something of value that one party gives another as part of a contractual agreement.

constitution
A code that establishes the fundamental rules and principles that govern a particular organization or entity.

consumer behavior
Description of how people act when they are buying, using, and discarding goods and services for their own personal consumption. Consumer behavior also explores the reasons behind people's actions.

consumer marketers (also known as business-to-consumer or B2C)
Marketers who direct their efforts toward people who are buying products for personal consumption.

consumer price index (CPI)
A measure of inflation that evaluates the change in the weighted-average price of goods and services that the average consumer buys each month.

consumer products
Products purchased for personal use or consumption.

consumer promotion
Marketing activities designed to generate immediate consumer sales, using tools such as premiums, promotional products, samples, coupons, rebates, and displays.

consumerism
A social movement that focuses on four key consumer rights: (1) the right to be safe, (2) the right to be informed, (3) the right to choose, and (4) the right to be heard.

contingency planning
Planning for unexpected events, usually involving a range of scenarios and assumptions that differ from the assumptions behind the core plans.

contingent workers
Employees who do not expect regular, full-time jobs, including temporary full-time workers, independent contractors, and temporary agency or contract agency workers.

contract
An agreement that is legally enforceable.

contraction
A period of economic downturn, marked by rising unemployment and falling business production.

controlling
Monitoring performance and making adjustments as needed.

convertible security
A bond or share of preferred stock that gives its holder the right to exchange it for a stated number of shares of common stock.

copyright
The exclusive legal right of an author, artist, or other creative individual to use, copy, display, perform, and sell their own creations and to license others to do so.

corporate bylaws
The basic rules governing how a corporation is organized and how it conducts its business.

corporate philanthropy
All business donations to nonprofit groups, including money, products, and employee time.

corporate responsibility
Business contributions to the community through the actions of the business itself rather than donations of money and time.

corporation
A form of business ownership in which the business is considered a legal entity that is separate and distinct from its owners.

cost
The value of what is given up in exchange for something.

countertrade
International trade that involves the barter of products for products rather than for currency.

coupon rate
The interest paid on a bond, expressed as a percentage of the bond's par value.

covenant
A restriction lenders impose on borrowers as a condition of providing long-term debt financing.

craft union
A union comprising workers who share the same skill or work in the same profession.

credit
Allows a borrower to buy a good or acquire an asset without making immediate payment, and to repay the balance at a later time.

credit card
A card issued by a bank or finance company that allows the cardholder to make a purchase now and pay the credit card issuer later.

credit score
A numerical measure of a consumer's creditworthiness.

credit union
A depository institution that is organized as a cooperative, meaning that it is owned by its depositors.

crime
A wrongful act against society, defined by law and prosecuted by the state.

critical path
The sequence of activities in a project that is expected to take the longest to complete.

critical path method (CPM)
A project-management tool that illustrates the relationships among all the activities involved in completing a project and identifies the sequence of activities likely to take the longest to complete.

crowdfunding
The process of funding ventures by raising money from a large number of investors via the Internet.

current yield
The amount of interest earned on a bond, expressed as a percentage of the bond's current market price.

customer benefit
The advantage that a customer gains from specific product features.

customer loyalty
When customers buy a product from the same supplier again and again—sometimes paying even more for it than they would for a competitive product.

customer relationship management (CRM)
The ongoing process of acquiring, maintaining, and growing profitable customer relationships by delivering unmatched value.

customer satisfaction
When customers perceive that a good or service delivers value above and beyond their expectations.

cybermediary
An Internet-based firm that specializes in the secure electronic transfer of funds.

data
Raw, unprocessed facts and figures.

data mining
The use of sophisticated statistical and mathematical techniques to analyze vast amounts of data to discover hidden patterns and relationships, thus creating valuable information.

data warehouse
A large, organization-wide database that stores data in a centralized location.

database
A file consisting of related data organized according to a logical system and stored on a hard drive or some other computer-accessible media.

debit card
A card issued by the bank that allows the customer to make purchases as if the transaction involved cash. In a debit card purchase, the customer's bank account is immediately reduced when the purchase is made.

debt financing
Funds provided by lenders (creditors).

decision support system (DSS)
A system that gives managers access to large amounts of data and the processing power to convert these data into high-quality information, thus improving the decision-making process.

deflation
A period of falling average prices across the economy.

degree of centralization
The extent to which decision-making power is held by a small number of people at the top of the organization.

demand
The quantity of products that consumers are willing to buy at different market prices.

demand curve
The graphed relationship between price and quantity from a customer demand standpoint.

democratic leaders
Leaders who share power with their followers. While they still make final decisions, they typically solicit and incorporate input from their followers.

demographic segmentation
Dividing the market into smaller groups based on measurable characteristics about people, such as age, income, ethnicity, and gender.

demographics
The measurable characteristics of a population. Demographic factors include population size and density, as well as specific traits such as age, gender, and race.

departmentalization
The division of workers into logical groups.

depository institution
A financial intermediary that obtains funds by accepting checking and savings deposits and then lending those funds to borrowers.

depression
An especially deep and long-lasting recession.

direct channel
A distribution process that links the producer and the customer with no intermediaries.

direct cost
Costs that are incurred directly as the result of some specific cost object.

direct investment
(or foreign direct investment) When firms either acquire foreign firms or develop new facilities from the ground up in foreign countries.

discount rate
The rate of interest that the Federal Reserve charges when it loans funds to banks.

discretionary payments
Expenditures for which the spender has significant control in terms of the amount and timing.

disinflation
A period of slowing average price increases across the economy.

distribution strategy
A plan for delivering the right product to the right person at the right place at the right time.

distributive bargaining
The traditional adversarial approach to collective bargaining.

distributorship
A type of franchising arrangement in which the franchisor makes a product and licenses the franchisee to sell it.

divestiture
The transfer of total or partial ownership of some of a firm's operations to investors or to another company.

Dodd-Frank Act
A law enacted in the aftermath of the financial crisis of 2008–2009 that strengthened government oversight of financial markets and placed limitations on risky financial strategies such as heavy reliance on leverage.

Dow Jones Industrial Average (DJIA)
An index that tracks stock prices of 30 large, well-known U.S. corporations.

dynamic delivery
Vibrant, compelling presentation delivery style that grabs and holds the attention of the audience.

e-commerce
The marketing, buying, selling, and servicing of products over a network (usually the Internet).

economic system
A structure for allocating limited resources.

economics
The study of the choices that people, companies, and governments make in allocating society's resources.

economy
A financial and social system of how resources flow through society, from production, to distribution, to consumption.

effectiveness
Using resources to create value by providing customers with goods and services that offer a better relationship between price and perceived benefits.

efficiency
Producing output or achieving a goal at the lowest cost.

electronic bill presentment and payment
A method of bill payment that makes it easy for the customer to make a payment, often by simply clicking on a payment option contained in an email.

electronic communications network (ECN)
An automated, computerized securities trading system that automatically matches buyers and sellers, executing trades quickly and allowing trading when securities exchanges are closed.

e-marketplace
A specialized Internet site where buyers and sellers engaged in business-to-business e-commerce can communicate and conduct business.

embargo
A complete ban on international trade of a certain item, or a total halt in trade with a particular nation.

employment at will
A legal doctrine that views employment as an entirely voluntary relationship that both the employee and employer are free to terminate at any time and for any reason.

enterprise resource planning (ERP)
Software-based approach to integrate an organization's (and in the sophisticated versions, a value chain's) information flows.

entrepreneurs
People who risk their time, money, and other resources to start and manage a business.

environmental scanning
The process of continually collecting information from the external marketing environment.

Equal Employment Opportunity Commission (EEOC)
A federal agency designed to regulate and enforce the provisions of Title VII.

equilibrium price
The price associated with the point at which the quantity demanded of a product equals the quantity supplied.

equity financing
Funds provided by the owners of a company.

equity theory
A motivation theory that proposes that perceptions of fairness directly affect worker motivation.

ethical dilemma
A decision that involves a conflict of values; every potential course of action has some significant negative consequences.

ethics
A set of beliefs about right and wrong, good and bad.

European Union (EU)
The world's largest common market, composed of 28 European nations.

everyday-low pricing (EDLP)
Long-term discount pricing, designed to achieve profitability through high sales volume.

exchange rate
A measurement of the value of one nation's currency relative to the currency of other nations.

exchange traded fund (ETF)
Shares traded on securities markets that represent the legal right of ownership over part of a basket of individual stock certificates or other securities.

expansion
A period of robust economic growth and high employment.

expectancy theory
A motivation theory that concerns the relationship among individual effort, individual performance, and individual reward.

expenses
Resources that are used up as the result of business operations.

expert system (ES)
A decision support system that helps managers make better decisions in an area where they lack expertise.

exporting
Selling products in foreign nations that have been produced or grown domestically.

external locus of control
A deep-seated sense that forces other than the individual are responsible for what happens in his or her life.

external recruitment
The process of seeking new employees from outside the firm.

extranet
An intranet that allows limited access to a selected group of stakeholders, such as suppliers or customers.

factor
A company that provides short-term financing to firms by purchasing their accounts receivables at a discount.

factors of production
Four fundamental elements—natural resources, capital, human resources, and entrepreneurship—that businesses need to achieve their objectives.

federal debt
The sum of all the money that the federal government has borrowed over the years and not yet repaid.

Federal Deposit Insurance Corporation (FDIC)
A federal agency that insures deposits in banks and thrift institutions for up to $250,000 per customer, per bank.

Federal Deposit Insurance Corporation (FDIC)
An independent agency created by Congress to maintain stability and public confidence in the nation's financial system, primarily by insuring bank deposits.

Federal Reserve Act of 1913
The law that established the Federal Reserve System as the central bank of the United States.

finance
The functional area of business that is concerned with finding the best sources and uses of financial capital.

financial accounting
The branch of accounting that prepares financial statements for use by owners, creditors, suppliers, and other external stakeholders.

Financial Accounting Standards Board (FASB)
The private board that establishes the generally accepted accounting principles used in the practice of financial accounting.

financial budgets
Budgets that focus on the firm's financial goals and identify the resources needed to achieve these goals.

financial capital
The funds a firm uses to acquire its assets and finance its operations.

financial diversification
A strategy of investing in a wide variety of securities in order to reduce risk.

financial leverage
The use of debt in a firm's capital structure.

financial markets
Markets that transfer funds from savers to borrowers.

financial ratio analysis
Computing ratios that compare values of key accounts listed on a firm's financial statements.

Financial Services Modernization Act of 1999
An act that overturned the section of the Banking Act of 1933 that prohibited commercial banks from selling insurance or performing the functions of investment banks.

firewall
Software and/or hardware designed to prevent unwanted access to a computer or computer system.

first-line (supervisory) management
Managers who directly supervise nonmanagement employees.

fiscal policy
Government efforts to influence the economy through taxation and spending.

fixed costs
Costs that remain the same when the level of production changes within some relevant range.

flextime
A scheduling option that allows workers to choose when they start and finish their workdays, as long as they complete the required number of hours.

foreign franchising
A specialized type of foreign licensing in which a firm expands by offering businesses in other countries the right to produce and market its products according to specific operating requirements.

foreign licensing
Authority granted by a domestic firm to a foreign firm for the rights to produce and market its product or to use its trademark/patent rights in a defined geographical area.

foreign outsourcing
(also contract manufacturing) Contracting with foreign suppliers to produce products, usually at a fraction of the cost of domestic production.

franchise
A licensing arrangement under which a franchisor allows franchisees to use its name, trademark, products, business methods, and other property in exchange for monetary payments and other considerations.

franchise agreement
The contractual arrangement between a franchisor and franchisee that spells out the duties and responsibilities of both parties.

Franchise Disclosure Document (FDD)
A detailed description of all aspects of a franchise that the franchisor must provide to the franchisee at least 14 calendar days before the franchise agreement is signed.

franchisee
The party in a franchise relationship that pays for the right to use resources supplied by the franchisor.

franchisor
The business entity in a franchise relationship that allows others to operate its business using resources it supplies in exchange for money and other considerations.

free-rein leaders
Leaders who set objectives for their followers but give them freedom to choose how they will accomplish those goals.

free trade
An international economic and political movement designed to help goods and services flow more freely across international boundaries.

General Agreement on Tariffs and Trade (GATT)
An international trade agreement that has taken bold steps to lower tariffs and promote free trade worldwide.

general partnership
A partnership in which all partners can take an active role in managing the business and have unlimited liability for any claims against the firm.

generally accepted accounting principles (GAAP)
A set of accounting standards that is used in the preparation of financial statements.

geographic segmentation
Dividing the market into smaller groups based on where consumers live. This process can incorporate countries, cities, or population density as key factors.

goods
Tangible products.

grace period
The period of time that the credit card holder has to pay outstanding balances before interest or fees are assessed.

green marketing
Developing and promoting environmentally sound products and practices to gain a competitive edge.

grievance
A complaint by a worker that the employer has violated the terms of the collective bargaining agreement.

gross domestic product (GDP)
The total value of all final goods and services produced within a nation's physical boundaries over a given period of time.

hacker
A skilled computer user who uses his or her expertise to gain unauthorized access to the computer (or computer system) of others, sometimes with malicious intent.

hardware
The physical tools and equipment used to collect, input, store, organize, and process data and to distribute information.

high/low pricing
A pricing strategy designed to drive traffic to retail stores by special sales on a limited number of products, and higher everyday prices on others.

horizontal analysis
Analysis of financial statements that compares account values reported on these statements over two or more years to identify changes and trends.

horizontal merger
A combination of two firms that are in the same industry.

human resource (HR) management
The management function focused on maximizing the effectiveness of the workforce by recruiting world-class talent, promoting career development, and determining workforce strategies to boost organizational effectiveness.

human skills
The ability to work effectively with and through other people in a range of different relationships.

hyperinflation
An average monthly inflation rate of more than 50%.

immediate predecessors
Activities in a project that must be completed before some other specified activity can begin.

implicit cost
The opportunity cost that arises when a firm uses owner-supplied resources.

importing
Buying products domestically that have been produced or grown in foreign nations.

income statement
The financial statement that reports the revenues, expenses, and net income that resulted from a firm's operations over an accounting period.

independent wholesaling businesses
Independent distributors that buy products from a range of different businesses and sell those products to a range of different customers.

indirect costs
Costs that are the result of a firm's general operations and are not directly tied to any specific cost object.

industrial union
A union comprising workers employed in the same industry.

inflation
A period of rising average prices across the economy.

information
Data that have been processed in a way that make them meaningful to their user.

infrastructure
A country's physical facilities that support economic activity.

initial public offering (IPO)
The first time a company issues stock that may be bought by the general public.

institutional investor
An organization that pools contributions from investors, clients, or depositors and uses these funds to buy stocks and other securities.

integrated marketing communication
The coordination of marketing messages through every promotional vehicle to communicate a unified impression about a product.

intellectual property
Property that is the result of creative or intellectual effort, such as books, musical works, inventions, and computer software.

intercultural communication
Communication among people with differing cultural backgrounds.

interest-based bargaining
A form of collective bargaining that emphasizes cooperation and problem solving in an attempt to find a "win–win" outcome.

internal locus of control
A deep-seated sense that the individual is personally responsible for what happens in his or her life.

internal recruitment
The process of seeking employees who are currently within the firm to fill open positions.

International Monetary Fund (IMF)
An international organization of 188 member nations that promotes international economic cooperation and stable growth.

Internet
The world's largest computer network; essentially a network of computer networks all operating under a common set of rules that allow them to communicate with each other.

Internet2 (I2)
A new high-tech Internet with access limited to a consortium of member organizations (and other organizations these members sponsor). I2 utilizes technologies that give it a speed and capacity far exceeding the current Internet.

intranet
A private network that has the look and feel of the Internet and is navigated using a web browser, but which limits access to a single firm's employees (or a single organization's members).

inventory
Stocks of goods or other items held by organizations.

investing
Reducing consumption in the current time period in order to build future wealth.

investment bank
A financial intermediary that specializes in helping firms raise financial capital by issuing securities in primary markets.

IRA
An individual retirement account that provides tax benefits to individuals who are investing for their retirement.

ISO 9000
A family of generic standards for quality management systems established by the International Organization for Standardization.

ISO 14000
A family of generic standards for environmental management established by the International Organization for Standardization.

job analysis
The examination of specific tasks that are assigned to each position, independent of who might be holding the job at any specific time.

job description
An explanation of the responsibilities for a specific position.

job enrichment
The creation of jobs with more meaningful content, under the assumption that challenging, creative work will motivate employees.

job specifications
The specific qualifications necessary to hold a particular position.

joint ventures
When two or more companies join forces—sharing resources, risks, and profits, but not actually merging companies—to pursue specific opportunities.

just-in-time (JIT) production
A production system that emphasizes the production of goods to meet actual current demand, thus minimizing the need to hold inventories of finished goods and work in process at each stage of the supply chain.

Labor–Management Relations Act (Taft–Hartley Act)
Law passed in 1947 that placed limits on union activities, outlawed the closed shop, and allowed states to pass right-to-work laws that made union shops illegal.

labor union
A group of workers who have organized to work together to achieve common job-related goals, such as higher wages, better working conditions, and greater job security.

laws
Rules that govern the conduct and actions of people within a society that are enforced by the government.

leading
Directing and motivating people to achieve organizational goals.

lean production
An approach to production that emphasizes the elimination of waste in all aspects of production processes.

leverage ratios
Ratios that measure the extent to which a firm relies on debt financing in its capital structure.

liabilities
Claims that outsiders have against a firm's assets.

licensing
Purchasing the right to use another company's brand name or symbol.

limit order
An order to a broker to buy a specific stock only if its price is below a certain level, or to sell a specific stock only if its price is above a certain level.

limited liability
When owners are not personally liable for claims against their firm. Owners with limited liability may lose their investment in the company, but their other personal assets are protected.

limited liability company (LLC)
A form of business ownership that offers both limited liability to its owners and flexible tax treatment.

limited liability partnership (LLP)
A form of partnership in which all partners have the right to participate in management and have limited liability for company debts.

limited partnership
A partnership that includes at least one general partner who actively manages the company and accepts unlimited liability and one limited partner who gives up the right to actively manage the company in exchange for limited liability.

line-and-staff organizations
Organizations with line managers forming the primary chain of authority in the company, and staff departments working alongside line departments.

line extensions
Similar products offered under the same brand name.

line managers
Managers who supervise the functions that contribute directly to profitability: production and marketing.

line of credit
A financial arrangement between a firm and a bank in which the bank pre-approves credit up to a specified limit, provided that the firm maintains an acceptable credit rating.

line organizations
Organizations with a clear, simple chain of command from top to bottom.

liquid asset
An asset that can quickly be converted into cash with little risk of loss.

liquidity ratios
Financial ratios that measure the ability of a firm to obtain the cash it needs to pay its short-term debt obligations as they come due.

lockout
An employer-initiated work stoppage.

logistics
A subset of supply chain management that focuses largely on the tactics involved in moving products along the supply chain.

loss
When a business incurs expenses that are greater than its revenue.

loss-leader pricing
Closely related to high/low pricing, loss-leader pricing means pricing a handful of items—or loss leaders—temporarily below cost to drive traffic.

M1 money supply
Includes all currency plus checking accounts and traveler's checks.

M2 money supply
Includes all of M1 money supply plus most savings accounts, money market accounts, and certificates of deposit.

macroeconomics
The study of a country's overall economic dynamics, such as the employment rate, the gross domestic product, and taxation policies.

malware
A general term for malicious software, such as spyware, computer viruses, and worms.

management
Achieving the goals of an organization through planning, organizing, leading, and controlling organizational resources including people, money, and time.

management development
Programs to help current and potential executives develop the skills they need to move into leadership positions.

managerial (or management) accounting
The branch of accounting that provides reports and analysis to managers to help them make informed business decisions.

market makers
Securities dealers that make a commitment to continuously offer to buy and sell the stock of a specific corporation listed on the NASDAQ exchange or traded in the OTC market.

market niche
A small segment of a market with fewer competitors than the market as a whole. Market niches tend to be quite attractive to small firms.

market order
An order telling a broker to buy or sell a specific security at the best currently available price.

market segmentation
Dividing potential customers into groups of similar people, or segments.

market share
The percentage of a market controlled by a given marketer.

marketing
An organizational function and a set of processes for creating, communicating, and delivering value to customers and for managing customer relationships in ways that benefit the organization and its stakeholders.

marketing concept
A business philosophy that makes customer satisfaction—now and in the future—the central focus of the entire organization.

marketing mix
The blend of marketing strategies for product, price, distribution, and promotion.

marketing plan
A formal document that defines marketing objectives and the specific strategies for achieving those objectives.

marketing research
The process of gathering, interpreting, and applying information to uncover marketing opportunities and challenges, and to make better marketing decisions.

Maslow's hierarchy of needs theory
A motivation theory that suggests that human needs fall into a hierarchy and that as each need is met, people become motivated to meet the next-highest need in the pyramid.

mass customization
The creation of products tailored for individual consumers on a mass basis.

master budget
A presentation of an organization's operational and financial budgets that represents the firm's overall plan of action for a specified time period.

matrix organizations
Organizations with a flexible structure that brings together specialists from different areas of the company to work on individual projects on a temporary basis.

maturity date
The date when a bond will come due.

mediation
A method of dealing with an impasse between labor and management by bringing in a neutral third party to help the two sides reach agreement by reducing tensions and making suggestions for possible compromises.

merchant wholesalers
Independent distributors who take legal possession, or title, of the goods they distribute.

merger
A corporate restructuring that occurs when two formerly independent business entities combine to form a new organization.

microeconomics
The study of smaller economic units such as individual consumers, families, and individual businesses.

middle management
Managers who supervise lower-level managers and report to a higher-level manager.

mission
The definition of an organization's purpose, values, and core goals, which provides the framework for all other plans.

mixed economies
Economies that embody elements of both planned and market-based economic systems.

modes of transportation
The various transportation options—such as planes, trains, and railroads—for moving products through the supply chain.

monetary policy
Federal Reserve decisions that shape the economy by influencing interest rates and the supply of money.

money
Anything generally accepted as a medium of exchange, a measure of value, or a means of payment.

money market mutual funds
A mutual fund that pools funds from many investors and uses these funds to purchase very safe, highly liquid securities.

money supply
The total amount of money within the overall economy.

monopolistic competition
A market structure with many competitors selling differentiated products. Barriers to entry are low.

monopoly
A market structure with one producer completely dominating the industry, leaving no room for any significant competitors. Barriers to entry tend to be virtually insurmountable.

multichannel retailing
Providing multiple distribution channels for consumers to buy a product.

multilevel marketing (MLM)
Involves hiring independent contractors to sell products to their personal network of friends and colleagues and to recruit new salespeople in return for a percentage of their commissions.

mutual fund
An institutional investor that raises funds by selling shares to investors and uses the accumulated funds to buy a portfolio of many different securities.

national brands
Brands that the producer owns and markets.

National Labor Relations Act (Wagner Act)
Landmark pro-labor law enacted in 1935. This law made it illegal for firms to discriminate against union members and required employers to recognize certified unions and bargain with them in good faith.

natural monopoly
A market structure with one company as the supplier of a product because the nature of that product makes a single supplier more efficient than multiple, competing ones. Most natural monopolies are government sanctioned and regulated.

negligence
An unintentional tort that arises due to carelessness or irresponsible behavior.

net asset value per share
The value of a mutual fund's securities and cash holdings minus any liabilities, divided by the number of shares of the fund outstanding.

net income
The difference between the revenue a firm earns and the expenses it incurs in a given time period.

net present value (NPV)
The sum of the present values of expected future cash flows from an investment, minus the cost of that investment.

noise
Any interference that causes the message you send to be different from the message your audience understands.

nondiscretionary payments
Expenditures that the spender has little or no control over.

nonprofit corporation
A corporation that does not seek to earn a profit and differs in several fundamental respects from C corporations.

nonprofits
Business-*like* establishments that employ people and produce goods and services with the fundamental goal of contributing to the community rather than generating financial gain.

nonverbal communication
Communication that does not use words. Common forms of nonverbal communication include gestures, posture, facial expressions, tone of voice, and eye contact.

North American Free Trade Agreement (NAFTA)
The treaty among the United States, Mexico, and Canada that eliminated trade barriers and investment restrictions over a 15-year period starting in 1994.

observation research
Marketing research that does not require the researcher to interact with the research subject.

odd pricing
The practice of ending prices in numbers below even dollars and cents in order to create a perception of greater value.

offshoring
Moving production or support processes to foreign countries.

oligopoly
A market structure with only a handful of competitors selling products that can be similar or different. Barriers to entry are typically high.

on-the-job training
A training approach that requires employees to simply begin their jobs—sometimes guided by more experienced employees—and to learn as they go.

open market operations
The Federal Reserve function of buying and selling government securities, which include treasury bonds, notes, and bills.

open shop
An employment arrangement in which workers are not required to join a union or pay union dues.

operating budgets
Budgets that communicate an organization's sales and production goals and the resources needed to achieve these goals.

operational planning
Very specific, short-term planning that applies tactical plans to daily, weekly, and monthly operations.

operations management
Managing all of the activities involved in creating value by producing goods and services and distributing them to customers.

opportunity cost
The opportunity of giving up the second-best choice when making a decision.

organization chart
A visual representation of the company's formal structure.

organizing
Determining a structure for both individual jobs and the overall organization.

orientation
The first step in the training and development process, designed to introduce employees to the company culture and provide key administrative information.

outsourcing
Arranging for other organizations to perform supply chain functions that were previously performed internally.

out-of-pocket cost
A cost that involves the payment of money or other resources.

over-the-counter (OTC) market
The market where securities that are not listed on exchanges are traded.

owners' equity
The claims a firm's owners have against their company's assets (often called "stockholders' equity" on balance sheets of corporations).

par value (of a bond)
The value of a bond at its maturity; what the issuer promises to pay the bondholder when the bond matures.

partnership
A voluntary agreement under which two or more people act as co-owners of a business for profit.

passive voice
Sentence construction in which the subject does not do the action expressed by the verb; rather the subject is acted upon (e.g., The taxes were done by our accountant.). The passive voice tends to be less effective for business communication.

patent
A legal monopoly that gives an inventor the exclusive right over an invention for a limited time period.

penetration pricing
A new product pricing strategy that aims to capture as much of the market as possible through rock-bottom prices.

performance appraisal
A formal feedback process that requires managers to give their subordinates

feedback on a one-to-one basis, typically by comparing actual results to expected results.

personal selling
The person-to-person presentation of products to potential buyers.

pharming
A scam that seeks to steal identities by routing Internet traffic to fake websites.

phishing
A scam in which official-looking emails are sent to individuals in an attempt to get them to divulge private information such as passwords, usernames, and account numbers.

physical distribution
The actual, physical movement of products along the distribution pathway.

picketing
A union tactic during labor disputes in which union members walk near the entrance of the employer's place of business, carrying signs to publicize their position and concerns.

planned obsolescence
The strategy of deliberately designing products to fail in order to shorten the time between purchases.

planning
Determining organizational goals and action plans for how to achieve those goals.

poka-yokes
Simple methods incorporated into a production process designed to eliminate or greatly reduce errors.

positioning statement
A brief statement that articulates how the marketer would like the target market to envision a product relative to the competition.

preferred stock
A type of stock that gives its holder preference over common stockholders in terms of dividends and claims on assets.

present value
The amount of money that, if invested today at a given rate of interest (called the discount rate), would grow to become some future amount in a specified number of time periods.

primary data
New data that marketers compile for a specific research project.

primary securities market
The market where newly issued securities are traded. The primary market is where the firms that issue securities raise additional financial capital.

principal
A party who agrees to have someone else (called an agent) act on his or her behalf.

principal–agent relationship
A relationship in which one party, called the principal, gives another party, called the agent, the authority to act in place of, and bind, the principal when dealing with third parties.

private placement
A primary market issue that is negotiated between the issuing corporation and a small group of accredited investors.

privatization
The process of converting government-owned businesses to private ownership.

probationary period
A specific time frame (typically three to six months) during which a new hire can prove his or her worth on the job before he or she becomes permanent.

process
A set of related activities that transform inputs into outputs, thus adding value.

producer price index (PPI)
A measure of inflation that evaluates the change over time in the weighted-average wholesale prices.

product
Anything that an organization offers to satisfy consumer needs and wants, including both goods and services.

product consistency
How reliably a product delivers its promised level of quality.

product differentiation
The attributes that make a good or service different from other products that compete to meet the same or similar customer needs.

product features
The specific characteristics of a product.

product life cycle
A pattern of sales and profits that typically changes over time.

product line
A group of products that are closely related to each other, either in terms of how they work, or the customers they serve.

product mix
The total number of product lines and individual items sold by a single firm.

product placement
The paid integration of branded products into movies, television, and other media.

productivity
The basic relationship between the production of goods and services (output) and the resources needed to produce them (input) calculated via the following equation: output/input = productivity.

profit
The money that a business earns in sales (or revenue), minus expenses, such as the cost of goods, and the cost of salaries. Revenue – Expenses = Profit (or Loss).

profit margin
The gap between the cost and the price of an item on a per-product basis.

profitability ratios
Ratios that measure the rate of return a firm is earning on various measures of investment.

promotion
Marketing communication designed to influence consumer purchase decisions through information, persuasion, and reminders.

promotional channels
Specific marketing communication vehicles, including traditional tools, such as advertising, sales promotion, direct marketing, and personal selling, and newer tools such as product placement, advergaming, and Internet minimovies.

property
The legal right of an owner to exclude nonowners from having control over a particular resource.

protectionism
National policies designed to restrict international trade, usually with the goal of protecting domestic businesses.

psychographic segmentation
Dividing the market into smaller groups based on consumer attitudes, interests, values, and lifestyles.

public offering
A primary market issue in which new securities are offered to any investors who are willing and able to purchase them.

public relations (PR)
The ongoing effort to create positive relationships with all of a firm's different "publics," including customers, employees, suppliers, the community, the general public, and the government.

publicity
Unpaid stories in the media that influence perceptions about a company or its products.

pull strategy
A marketing approach that involves creating demand from the ultimate consumers so that they "pull" your
products through the distribution channels by actively seeking them.

pure competition
A market structure with many competitors selling virtually identical products. Barriers to entry are quite low.

pure goods
Products that do not include any services.

pure services
Products that do not include any goods.

push strategy
A marketing approach that involves motivating distributors to heavily promote—or "push"—a product to the final consumers, usually through heavy trade promotion and personal selling.

quality level
How well a product performs its core functions.

quality of life
The overall sense of well-being experienced by either an individual or a group.

quotas
Limitations on the amount of specific products that may be imported from certain countries during a given time period.

radio frequency identification (RFID)
A technology that stores information on small microchips that can transmit the

information when they are within range of a special reader.

recession
An economic downturn marked by a decrease in the GDP for two consecutive quarters.

recovery
A period of rising economic growth and employment.

registration statement
A long, complex document that firms must file with the SEC when they sell securities through a public offering.

reserve requirement
A rule set by the Fed, which specifies the minimum amount of reserves (or funds) a bank must hold, expressed as a percentage of the bank's deposits.

retailers
Distributors that sell products directly to the ultimate users, typically in small quantities, that are stored and merchandized on the premises.

retained earnings
The part of a firm's net income it reinvests.

revenue
Increases in a firm's assets that result from the sale of goods, provision of services, or other activities intended to earn income.

revolving credit agreement
A guaranteed line of credit in which a bank makes a binding commitment to provide a business with funds up to a specified credit limit at any time during the term of the agreement.

right-to-work law
A state law that makes union shops illegal within that state's borders.

risk
The degree of uncertainty regarding the outcome of a decision.

risk-return tradeoff
The observation that financial opportunities that offer high rates of return are generally riskier than opportunities that offer lower rates of return.

robot
A reprogrammable machine that is capable of manipulating materials, tools, parts, and specialized devices in order to perform a variety of tasks.

S corporation
A form of corporation that avoids double taxation by having its income taxed as if it were a partnership.

salaries
The pay that employees receive over a fixed period, most often weekly or monthly.

sale
A transaction in which the title (legal ownership) to a good passes from one party to another in exchange for a price.

sales promotion
Marketing activities designed to stimulate immediate sales activity through specific

short-term programs aimed at either consumers or distributors.

Sarbanes-Oxley Act
Federal legislation passed in 2002 that sets higher ethical standards for public corporations and accounting firms. Key provisions limit conflict-of-interest issues and require financial officers and CEOs to certify the validity of their financial statements.

savings account
An interest-bearing account holding funds not needed to meet regular expenditures.

savings and loan association
A depository institution that has traditionally obtained most of its funds by accepting savings deposits, which have been used primarily to make mortgage loans.

scope of authority (for an agent)
The extent to which an agent has the authority to act for and represent the principal.

SCORE (Service Corps of Retired Executives)
An organization—affiliated with the Small Business Administration—that provides free, comprehensive business counseling for small business owners from qualified volunteers.

secondary data
Existing data that marketers gather or purchase for a research project.

secondary securities market
The market where previously issued securities are traded.

Securities Act of 1933
The first major federal law regulating the securities industry. It requires firms issuing new stock in a public offering to file a registration statement with the SEC.

Securities and Exchange Act of 1934
A federal law dealing with securities regulation that established the Securities and Exchange Commission to regulate and oversee the securities industry.

Securities and Exchange Commission
The federal agency with primary responsibility for regulating the securities industry.

securities broker
A financial intermediary that acts as an agent for investors who want to buy and sell financial securities. Brokers earn commissions and fees for the services they provide.

securities dealer
A financial intermediary that participates directly in securities markets, buying and selling stocks and other securities for its own account.

services
Intangible products.

servicescape
The environment in which a customer and service provider interact.

sexual harassment
Workplace discrimination against a person based on his or her gender.

Six Sigma
An approach to quality improvement characterized by very ambitious quality goals, extensive training of employees, and a long-term commitment to working on quality-related issues.

skimming pricing
A new product pricing strategy that aims to maximize profitability by offering new products at a premium price.

Small Business Administration (SBA)
An agency of the federal government designed to maintain and strengthen the nation's economy by aiding, counseling, assisting, and protecting the interests of small businesses.

Small Business Development Centers (SBDCs)
Local offices—affiliated with the Small Business Administration—that provide comprehensive management assistance to current and prospective small business owners.

social audit
A systematic evaluation of how well a firm is meeting its ethics and social responsibility goals.

social responsibility
The obligation of a business to contribute to society.

socialism
An economic system based on the principle that the government should own and operate key enterprises that directly affect public welfare.

sociocultural differences
Differences among cultures in language, attitudes, and values.

software
Programs that provide instructions to a computer so that it can perform a desired task.

sole proprietorship
A form of business ownership with a single owner who usually actively manages the company.

spam
Unsolicited email advertisements usually sent to very large numbers of recipients, many of whom may have no interest in the message.

span of control
Span of management; refers to the number of people a manager supervises.

specific performance
A remedy for breach of contract in which the court orders the party committing the breach to do exactly what the contract specifies.

speed-to-market
The rate at which a new product moves from conception to commercialization.

sponsorship
A deep association between a marketer and a partner (usually a cultural or sporting event), which involves promotion of the sponsor in exchange for either payment or the provision of goods.

spontaneous financing
Financing that arises during the natural course of business without the need for special arrangements.

spyware
Software that is installed on a computer without the user's knowledge or permission to track the user's behavior.

staff managers
Managers who supervise the functions that provide advice and assistance to the line departments.

stakeholders
Any groups that have a stake—or a personal interest—in the performance and actions of an organization.

Standard & Poor's 500
A stock index based on prices of 500 major U.S. corporations in a variety of industries and market sectors.

standard of living
The quality and quantity of goods and services available to a population.

statement of cash flows
The financial statement that identifies a firm's sources and uses of cash in a given accounting period.

statute of frauds
A requirement that certain types of contracts must be in writing in order to be enforceable.

statute of limitations
The time period within which a legal action must be initiated.

statutory close (or closed) corporation
A corporation with a limited number of owners that operates under simpler, less formal rules than a C corporation.

statutory law
Law that is the result of legislative action.

stock (or securities) exchange
An organized venue for trading stocks and other securities that meet its listing requirements.

stock index
A statistic that tracks how the prices of a specific set of stocks have changed.

stockholder
An owner of a corporation.

store brands
Brands that the retailer both produces and distributes (also called private-label brands).

strategic alliance
An agreement between two or more firms to jointly pursue a specific opportunity without actually merging their businesses. Strategic alliances typically involve less formal, less encompassing agreements than partnerships.

strategic goals
Concrete benchmarks that managers can use to measure performance in each key area of the organization.

strategic planning
High-level, long-term planning that establishes a vision for the company, defines long-term objectives and priorities, determines broad action steps, and allocates resources.

strategies
Action plans that help the organization achieve its goals by forging the best fit between the firm and the environment.

strike
A work stoppage initiated by a union.

structured interviews
An interviewing approach that involves developing a list of questions beforehand and asking the same questions in the same order to each candidate.

supply
The quantity of products that producers are willing to offer for sale at different market prices.

supply chain
All organizations, processes, and activities involved in the flow of goods from the raw materials to the final consumer.

supply chain management (SCM)
Planning and coordinating the movement of products along the supply chain, from the raw materials to the final consumers.

supply curve
The graphed relationship between price and quantity from a supplier standpoint.

survey research
Marketing research that requires the researcher to interact with the research subject.

sustainable development
Doing business to meet the needs of the current generation, without harming the ability of future generations to meet their needs.

SWOT analysis
A strategic planning tool that helps management evaluate an organization in terms of internal strengths and weakness, and external opportunities and threats.

system software
Software that performs the critical functions necessary to operate the computer at the most basic level.

tactical planning
More specific, shorter-term planning that applies strategic plans to specific functional areas.

target market
The group of people who are most likely to buy a particular product.

tariffs
Taxes levied against imports.

technical skills
Expertise in a specific functional area or department.

telecommuting
Working remotely—most often from home—and connecting to the office via phone lines, fax machines, or broadband networks.

Theory X and Theory Y
A motivation theory that suggests that management attitudes toward workers fall into

two opposing categories based on management assumptions about worker capabilities and values.

time value of money
The principle that a dollar received today is worth more than a dollar received in the future.

title
Legal ownership.

Title VII
A portion of the Civil Rights Act of 1964 that prohibits discrimination in hiring, firing, compensation, apprenticeships, training, terms, conditions, or privileges of employment based on race, color, religion, sex, or national origin for employers with 15 or more workers.

top management
Managers who set the overall direction of the firm, articulating a vision, establishing priorities, and allocating time, money, and other resources.

tort
A private wrong that results in physical or mental harm to an individual, or damage to that person's property.

total quality management (TQM)
An approach to quality improvement that calls for everyone within an organization to take responsibility for improving quality and emphasizes the need for a long-term commitment to continuous improvement.

trade credit
Spontaneous financing granted by sellers when they deliver goods and services to customers without requiring immediate payment.

trade deficit
Shortfall that occurs when the total value of a nation's imports is higher than the total value of its exports.

trade promotion
Marketing activities designed to stimulate wholesalers and retailers to push specific products more aggressively over the short term.

trade surplus
Overage that occurs when the total value of a nation's exports is higher than the total value of its imports.

trademark
A mark, symbol, word, phrase, or motto used to identify a company's goods.

trading bloc
A group of countries that have reduced or even eliminated tariffs, allowing for the free flow of goods among the member nations.

underwriting
An arrangement under which an investment banker agrees to purchase all shares of a public offering at an agreed-upon price.

unemployment rate
The percentage of people in the labor force over age 16 who do not have jobs and are actively seeking employment.

Uniform Commercial Code (UCC)
A uniform act governing the sale of goods, leases, warranties, transfer of funds, and a variety of other business-related activities.

union shop
An employment arrangement in which a firm can hire nonunion workers, but these workers must join the union within a specified time period to keep their jobs.

universal ethical standards
Ethical norms that apply to all people across a broad spectrum of situations.

U.S. Treasury bills (T-bills)
Short-term marketable IOUs issued by the U.S. federal government.

utility
The ability of goods and services to satisfy consumer "wants."

value
A customer perception that a product has a better relationship than its competitors between the cost and the benefits.

value chain
The network of relationships that channels the flow of inputs, information, and financial resources through all of the processes directly or indirectly involved in producing goods and services and distributing them to customers.

variable costs
Costs that vary directly with the level of production.

venture capital firms
Companies that invest in start-up businesses with high growth potential in exchange for a share of ownership.

vertical integration
Performance of processes internally that were previously performed by other organizations in a supply chain.

vertical merger
A combination of firms at different stages in the production of a good or service.

vesting period
A specified period of time for which an employee must work for an employer in order to receive the full advantage of certain retirement benefits.

viral marketing
An Internet marketing strategy that tries to involve customers and others not employed by the seller in activities that help promote the product.

voluntary export restraints (VERs)
Limitations on the amount of specific products that one nation will export to another nation.

wages
The pay that employees receive in exchange for the number of hours or days that they work.

Web 2.0
Websites that incorporate interactive and collaborative features to create a richer, more interesting, and more useful experience for their users.

wheel of retailing
A classic distribution theory that suggests that retail firms and retail categories become more upscale as they go through their life cycles.

whistle-blowers
Employees who report their employer's illegal or unethical behavior to either the authorities or the media.

wholesalers
Distributors that buy products from producers and sell them to other businesses or nonfinal users such as hospitals, nonprofits, and the government.

World Bank
An international cooperative of 188 member countries, working together to reduce poverty in the developing world.

World Trade Organization (WTO)
A permanent global institution to promote international trade and to settle international trade disputes.

World Wide Web
The service that allows computer users to easily access and share information on the Internet in the form of text, graphics, video, apps, and animation.

worm
Malicious computer software that, unlike viruses, can spread on its own without being attached to other files.

INDEX

3M Corporation, 212
7-Eleven Supermarkets, 233
9/11 terrorist attacks, 15
20th Century Fox, 249
24 Hour Fitness, 187
52-week range, in stock quote, 182
"100 Best Companies to Work for in America" (Fortune magazine), 10

A

ABC (activity-based costing), 143
Abercrombie & Fitch, 199
Aberdeen Group, 317
absolute advantage, 41
accessory equipment, 207
accidental inventions, 122
accountants, 144
accounting, 126–143
   accrual-basis, 134
   balance sheet, 130–133
   benefit corporations, 138
   budgeting, 139–141
   comparative financial statements, 138–139
   defined, 126
   double-entry bookkeeping, 131
   ethics in, 129
   financial, 128
   Financial Accounting Standards Board (FASB), 128–129
   GAAP, 128, 129
   income statement, 133–134
   managerial (management), 141–143
   notes to financial statements, 137–138
   RoboCop, 129
   statement of cash flows, 134–135
   statement of retained earnings, 135
   stockholder's equity statement, 135
   types of accountants, 127–128
   users of, 126–127
accounting equation, 130
accounting fraud, 129
Accounting Quality Model (AQM), 129
accounting scandals, 129, 137
accounts receivable, 131
accounts receivable management, 161–162

accredited investors, 177
accrual-basis accounting, 133–134
accumulated depreciation, 131
acquisitions, 101
active listening, 77–78
active voice, 81
activity-based costing (ABC), 143
activity ratios, 149–150
actual product, 206
Adams, J. Stacy, 251
Adidas, 195
Adler, Fred, 135
Ad Meter consumer ranking, 217–218
administrative (general) expenses, 134
Adobe, 252
AdScape, 220
AdventureCenter.com, 193
advergaming, 220–221
adverse opinion, 136
advertising, 216–218
   defined, 222
   Internet, 218–219, 291–292
   measured media spending on, 222, 223
   media category advantages and disadvantages, 224
   native, 219
affirmative action, 278–279
African Americans, 12–13
age bias, 81
agents/brokers, 233, 234
aging population, 13–14
AIG, 21, 60, 64
AirbnB, 275
airlines, hedges and, 163
Allan, Donald Jr., 173
AllBusiness.com, 121
Allen, Paul, 111
Allstate, 173
Amazon, 9, 236
Amazon Prime, 284, 312
Amazon Prime Air, 232, 312
ambience, 309
Amelio, Gilbert, 75
American Airlines, 163
American Forest and Paper Association, 70
American Idol, 220

American Marketing Association, 186
American Recovery and Reinvestment Act, 21
Americans with Disabilities Act (1990), 278
Andreessen, Marc, 113
angel investors, 116
anti-theft tags, 294
Anything Left-Handed, 118
Anytime Fitness, 106
Apple, 9, 10, 93, 97, 210
   commercial paper and, 155
   foreign outsourcing, 44
   iPhone price, 65
   Maps program, 5, 65
   ownership utility and, 187
   pricing tricks, 243
   product design, 204
   product placement and, 219, 220
   skimming pricing, 240–241
   social responsibility and, 65
   speed-to-market and, 10
   stock buybacks, 173
applications (job), 269–270
applications software, 284
apprenticeships, 272
AQM (Accounting Quality Model), 129
Archer, Baroness Mary, 132
Armstrong, Lance, 77
Arthur Andersen, 64
articles of incorporation, 91
artifacts, 310
Ash, Mary Kate, 112
Asian population, 12, 13
ask price, 178
assembly line, 5
asset-backed commercial paper, 155
asset management, 149–150
asset management ratios, 149–150
assets, 131–132
As You Sow, 71
A to Z Wineworks, 66
Audi, 9
audience (communication), 78, 79, 86
auditor's report, 136–137
audits, external, 136–137
augmented product, 206
autocratic leaders, 260
auto industry bailout, 21
automation, 310–311

Autonomy (software company), 129
average collection period, 150, 151
Avon Corporation, 69
Avon Walk for Breast Cancer, 189

B

B2B e-commerce, 289, 290,
    292–293
B2B marketer, 192
B2C e-commerce, 289–292
B2C marketer, 192
baby boomers, 10–11
background checks, 270–271
Bailey, Edward P., 83–84
balance of payments, 42
balance of payments deficit, 42
balance of payments surplus, 42
balance of trade, 42
balance sheet, 130–133
Baldridge National Quality
    Program, 313–314
bank failures, 25
Banking Act of 1933, 169–170
bank loans, 25
    short-term, 154–155
    term loans, 156
Bank of America, 60, 64, 96
banks, 25, 167
Barger, David, 117
Barrett, Michael, 296–297
Barton, Dominic, 11
Bean, Chuck, 6
Bear Stearns, 21
behavioral segmentation, 193
benefit corporations, 138
benefits, 274–275
Berkshire Hathaway, 156, 171
Bernanke, Ben, 23
Bernbach, Bill, 216
Best Buy, 238
best effort approach, 178
Bewkes, Jeff, 99
Bezos, Jeff, 232, 248, 312
bias, communication and, 80–81
bid and ask, in stock quote, 182
bid/ask spread, 178
bid price, 178
Bidwell, Matthew, 270
Bierce, Ambrose, 92
big idea, promotion and, 217–218
Big Lots, 9
Bill and Melinda Gates Foundation,
    61, 242
Birch, David, 118
B Lab, 138
Black Friday deals, 240
"black hat hackers," 296

bleeding-edge firms, 10
BlendTec, 219
block paragraphs, 84
Blue Light Specials, 240
Blustein, Steven, 161
board of directors
    role of, 97–98
    size of, 96
Board of Governors, 23, 24–25
body language barriers to
    communication, 75
body language, nonverbal commu-
    nication and, 76–77
body scan tailoring, 196
Boeing, 93
Bogusky, Alex, 219
Bolivia, 40
Bond, James, 219–220
bonds, 172–173
Bose, 217
bottom-up budgeting, 139–140
Braiker, Brian, 87
brand champions, 9
brand, defined, 210
branded governments, 3
brand equity, 210
brand extensions, 210
branding, 210
brand managers, 203
brand name, 210, 211
brands, global brand champions,
    2014, 9
Branson, Richard, 248, 251
Brazil, 39, 221, 226
breakeven analysis, 241–242
bribery, 48
Brin, Sergey, 111
Britt, Steuart Henderson, 222
broadband Internet connection,
    284–285
broadcast television, 223, 224
brokers, 178–179
Brolick, Emil, 107
Brooks, Bill, 227
budgetary slack, 140
budget deficit, 22
budgeted balance sheet, 140, 151–152
budgeted financial statements,
    130–139
budgeted income statement, 140,
    151–152
budgeting, 139–141
budget surplus, 22
Budweiser, 218
Buffett, Warren, 156, 180, 248
bulleted lists, 85
Burger King, 47, 199, 221
Burton (snowboards), 12

Bush, George W., 23
business(es)
    defined, 4
    factors of production, 7–8
    history of, 4–6
    mistakes made by, 5
    trends in, 2–4
business buyer behavior, 198
business communication, 74–88
    active listening, 77–78
    active voice, 81
    bias and, 80–81
    block paragraphs, 84
    communication barriers, 75–76
    communication channels, 78, 79
    digital manners, 83
    email, 84, 85
    gender neutral language, 77
    grammar, 83–84
    headings and bulleted lists for,
        84–85
    high-impact messages, 82–85
    nonverbal communication, 76–78
    presentations, 85–88
    right tone for, 83
    using right words for, 78–81
business cycle, 33–34
business economists, 35
business environment, 8–15
    competitive environment, 9–11
    economic environment, 8–9
    global environment, 14–15
    social environment, 12–14
    technological environment, 11–12
business ethics, 56–62. See also
        social responsibility
    in accounting, 129
    actions of business leaders, 61
    code of ethics, 62
    defined, 58
    ethical dilemmas, 58–59
    in the global arena, 68–71
    the individual and, 60
    legal issues and, 57, 58
    legal systems and, 57
    monitoring, 71
    organizational culture and, 61–62
    organization's influence on, 60
    as relative, 57
    universal ethical standards, 57–58
    whistle-blowers, 62
business format franchises, 104
business intelligence systems, 288
business marketers, 192
business market segmentation, 193
business ownership. See forms of
        business organization
business plans, 120–121

business product categories, 207
business products, 206–207
business services, 207
Business Software Alliance, 49, 298
business technology, 11
business-to-business (B2B)
    e-commerce, 289–290, 292–293
business-to-business (B2B)
    marketer, 192
business-to-consumer (B2C)
    e-commerce, 289–292
business-to-consumer (B2C)
    marketer, 192
BusinessWeek top 10 global brands,
    210
Butler, Nicholas Murray, 91
buy-and-hold strategy, 181
buzz marketing, 221
Byrne, Michael, 157

C

cable television advertising, 223, 224
cafeteria-style benefits, 275
California, 53
Canada, NAFTA and, 51–52
Cancer Patient's Aid Association,
    217
cannibalization, 209–210
CAN-SPAM Act (2003), 295
capital, 7
capital budgeting, 162–164
capital expenditure budget, 140
capital gain, 171
capitalism, 26–30
capital structure, 156
carbon footprint, 67–68
Carcelle, Ives, 315
CareerBuilders.com survey, 80
careers
    brand manager, 203
    business economist, 35
    clothing company founder, 124
    ethics officer, 72
    financial analysts, 165
    franchise store managers, 109
    human resources managers, 279
    information technology support
        specialist, 299
    international sports marketing
        manager, 54
    manager of new media, 16
    odd jobs, 278
    pharmaceutical sales
        representative, 229
    plant supervisors, 318
    public relations manager, 89

staff accountant, 144
    stock brokers, 183
    warehouse manager, 244
CareOne, 219
Case, Steve, 111
cash and carry wholesalers, 234
cash budget, 140, 152
cash equivalents, 160
cash flow statements, 134–135
cash management, 160–161
catalogs, 236
Caterpillar, 129
cause-related marketing, 66
C corporations, 96–97, 98–100
cell phones
    end of "free" smartphones, 137
    GDP growth and use of, 39–40
    listening and, 78
    quality indicators, 208
cellular layout, 304–305
centralization, 257–258
century bonds, 172
CEOs (chief executive officers)
    board of directors and, 98
    mistakes made by, 68
    wage gap and, 265–266
    worries of, 11
certificate of deposit (CD), 163
certified fraud examiners, 128
certified management accountants,
    128
certified public accountant, 128
Chandler, Asa, 249
channel intermediaries, 231
channel of distribution, 230
"cheater's high," 69
Chen, Amy, 67
child labor, 70
China
    aging population in, 13
    cell phone use in, 40
    Chinglish used in, 82
    "Christmas village" in, 46
    corruption score, 68–69
    factors of production and, 7–8
    GDP growth, 39
    migration of jobs to, 14
    problems with products produced
        in, 44
Chinglish, 82
Chrysler bailout, 21
Civil Rights Act of 1964, 277
claim on assets, 172
Clayton Antitrust Act (1914), 28
clear beer, 208
Clorox Company, 64
closed-end fund, 174

closing, of verbal presentations, 86
clothing company founder, 124
cloud computing, 286–287
cloud services, 285
cobranding, 211
Coca-Cola, 9, 13, 97, 172, 210, 211,
    220, 242, 249
Cocaine Energy Drink, 208
code of ethics, 62
Code of Vendor Conduct (Gap
    Inc.), 71
codes of conduct, 70–71
Coffee News, 106
cognitive dissonance, 198
Coldwater Creek, 212
Colgate-Palmolive, 190
color psychology, marketing and,
    194
commercial banks, 23, 167
Commercial Finance Association,
    154
commercial paper, 155
common market, 51
common stock, 97, 171
communication, 74. *See also* busi-
    ness communication
communication barriers, 75–76
communication channels, 78, 79
communism, 31
Communist Manifesto (Marx), 31
comparative advantage, 41
comparative financial statements,
    138–139
compensation, 273–274
competition, in capitalist system,
    27–28
competitive advantage, international
    trade and, 41–42
competitive environment, 9–11, 196
component parts and processed
    materials, 207
compressed workweek, 275–276
computer-aided design (CAD), 311
computer-aided design and computer-
    aided manufacturing (CAD/
    CAM), 311
computer-aided engineering (CAE),
    311
computer-aided manufacturing
    (CAM), 311
computer-based training, 272–273
computer-integrated manufacturing
    (CIM), 311
computer viruses, 294
conceptual skills, 248
conglomerate merger, 101
consultive selling, 228

consumer behavior, 197–198
consumerism, 63–64
consumer marketers (B2C), 192
consumer market segmentation, 192–193
consumer price index (CPI), 35
consumer pricing perceptions, 243–244
consumer product categories, 207
consumer products, 206–207
consumer promotion, 223, 225
consumer rights, 63–65
contests, 225–226
contingency planning, 254
contingent workers, 271
continuous innovation, 212
contraction (business cycle), 33
controlling, 247, 262
Controlling the Assault of Non-Solicited Pornography and Marketing Act (2003), 205
convenience products, 207
convenience store, 235
convertible securities, 173–175
Cook, Tim, 96
Cooper, Eric, 286–287
corporate bonds, 156
corporate bylaws, 97
corporate philanthropy, 66
corporate responsibility, 66
corporate responsibility reports, 201–202
corporate restructuring, 100–102
corporations
    advantages of, 98
    benefit, 138
    board of directors role, 97–98
    C corporations, 96–97, 98–100
    defined, 91
    disadvantages of, 98–100
    forming, 97
    nonprofit, 100
    number of business organizations using, 92
    restructuring, 100–102
    S corporations, 99
    statutory close (closed) corporations, 100
    stock ownership in, 97
corruption, 9, 48, 68–69
cost-based pricing, 242–243
Costco, 239
cost, defined, 141
countertrade, 43
coupon rate, 173
coupons, 225
covenants, 156

credit unions, 168
Cringely, Robert, 240
critical path, 307
critical path method (CPM), 306–307
Crocs, 221
crowdfunding, 116
Crystal Pepsi, 208
cultural barriers to communication, 75
cultural environment, 196–197
cumulative feature of preferred stock, 172
current assets, 131
current liabilities, 132
current ratio, 149, 151
current yield, 172–173
customer-based segmentation, 193
customer behavior, marketing and, 197–198
customer benefit, 209
customer benefit package, 303
customer loyalty, 191
customer relationship management (CRM), 190
customer satisfaction, 190–191
customer service, 237
cybermediary, 292
cybersecurity, 11
cyclic unemployment, 33

D

Dairy Queen, 211
Dancing with the Stars, 216
Darwin, Charles, 2
data, 287–288
databases, 288
data mining, 288
data warehouse, 288
DavCo, 107
David Weekly Homes, 252
Dayal, Ashvin, 70
days' range, in stock quote, 182
debt ceiling, 22
debt financing, 156–158
debt-to-asset ratio, 150, 151
Decca Records, 249
decision support system (DSS), 288
Deere, 61
default (on bonds), 173
deflation, 34
degree of centralization, 257–258
Dell Inc., 67, 217, 219
Dell, Michael, 111, 266
Delta Airlines, 6, 163
demand, 29

demand-based pricing, 243
demand curve, 29
Deming chain reaction, 312, 313
Deming, W. Edwards, 312
democratic leaders, 260
demographics, 12
demographic segmentation, 192
departmentalization, 258–259
department store, 235
depository institutions, 167–168
depreciation, 131
depression (economic), 33
Desai, Mihir, 45–46
Dettol, 3
diffusion, product, 213–214
direct channel, 230
direct costs, 143
direct investments, 45–46, 155–156
direct mail advertising, 224
direct response retailing, 236
direct selling, 236
Dirksen, Everett, 20
discontinuous innovation, 212
discount brokers, 178–179
discount rate, 25
discount store, 235
disease, 15
disinflation, 34
Disney, Walt, 112, 115
Disney World, 293
displays, 225
disposable underwear, 117
distribution and pricing, 230–244
    breakeven analysis, 241–242
    consumer pricing perceptions, 243–244
    distribution strategy, 230–231
    distributor role, 231–233
    everyday-low pricing (EDLP), 239
    fixed margin pricing, 242–243
    high/low pricing, 239
    loss-leader pricing, 239–240
    odd pricing, 243–244
    penetration pricing, 239
    physical distribution, 237–238
    pricing mistakes, 241
    pricing objectives and strategies, 238–241
    pricing tricks, 243
    proactive supply chain management, 238
    retailers, 233, 234–237
    skimming pricing, 240–241
    timing and, 240
    transportation decision, 238
    wholesalers, 233–234

distribution strategy, 194, 230–231
distributors, 231–233
distributorships, 104
DiversityFran, 105
diversity of American population, 12–13
divestitures, 101–102
dividends, 171, 172, 183
Dodd-Frank Act, 160, 170, 171
dog food tasters, 278
"Doing Business" report, 48
Dollar General, 235
dollar, U.S., 42–43
domestic corporation, 98
Dominos, 221
door-to-door sales, 236
Doritos, 217–218
double-entry bookkeeping, 131
Double Fusion, 220
double taxation, 99
Dow Jones Industrial Average (DJIA), 181–182
drones, 232, 312
Dropbox, 284, 286
drop shippers, 233
Dr, Pepper, 220
Drucker, Peter, 259
drug testing, 270
DSS (decision support system), 288
Dunkin' Donuts, 103
durable goods, 301–302
Düsseldor Airport, Germany, 4
DVRs (digital video recorders), 220
dynamically continuous innovation, 212
dynamic delivery, 88

E

early bird specials, 240
earnings before interest and taxes (EBIT), 158
earnings per share (EPS), 150, 151
Easy Taxi, 3
eBay, 173, 284
echo-boomers, 256
Eck-Witty Corporation, 158–159
e-commerce, 11–12, 289–293
economic depression (2008), 8
economic differences, international trade and, 46–48
economic environment, 8–9, 196
economics, 18–35
    budget surplus/deficit, 22
    business cycle, 33–34
    capitalism, 26–30
    communism, 31

debt ceiling, 22
defined, 18
employment level, 32–33
federal debt, 22–23
fiscal cliff, 22
fiscal policy, 21–22
GDP (gross domestic product), 32
global economic crisis, 19–21
macroeconomics/microeconomics, 18–19
mixed economies, 31–32
monetary policy, 23–26
on-demand economy, 30
price levels, 34–35
productivity, 35
socialism, 30–31
economic system, 26
economists, business, 35
economy
    defined, 18
    federal debt, 22–23
    fiscal policy, 21–22
    supply and demand, 28–30
EDLP (everyday-low pricing), 239
EEOC (Equal Employment Opportunity Commission), 277
effectiveness, 301
efficiency, 301
Eisner, Michael, 95
electronic bill presentment and payment, 292
electronic communication networks, 178
Eli Lilly, 96
Elson, Charles, 138
email, 79, 84, 85
email greeting cards, 296
eMarketer, 218
e-marketplaces, 293
embargoes, 49
Emerson, Bill, 253
Emerson, Ralph Waldo, 81
employee-referral programs, 269
employees
    accounting and, 126–127
    calling in sick, 277
    compensation, 273–274
    evaluating, 273
    leaving companies, 276
    older workers, 266
    recruiting, 268–269
    responsibility toward, 63
    rising expectations of, 14
    sexual harassment of, 279
    social media and potential, 80
    training, 271–273

women, 267
    work-life balance, 267
    younger workers, 266–267
employee satisfaction, 10–11
employee selection, 269–271
employee termination, 276
employment benefits, 274–275
employment interviews, 270, 271
employment legislation, 277–278
employment testing, 270
enforceable contracts, 9
Engats, John, 286
Engskov, Kris, 103
Enron, 64, 149
enterprise resource planning (ERP), 309
entrepreneurs
    characteristics of, 112–115
    defined, 4, 111
    eccentric, 113
entrepreneurship, 7. See also small business and entrepreneurship
entrepreneurship era, 5
environment
    business's responsibility to, 66–68
    green practices, 315–317
    protection of, 303
EPS (earnings per share), 183
Equal Employment Opportunity Commission (EEOC), 277
Equal Pay Act (1963), 277
equilibrium price, 29–30
equity financing, 156, 158
equity theory, 251–252
E.T. (film), 219
e-tailing, 235–236
ethical dilemmas, 58–59
ethical issues with information technology, 297–298
ethical lapses, 58–59
ethics, 14, 56–57. See also business ethics
ethics officers, 72
Ethics Resource Center (ERC), 61
ethnicity bias, 81
Euronext, 177
European Union (EU), 39, 52–53
euro, the, 42–43, 51–52
evaluations, 273
event marketing, 190
everyday-low pricing (EDLP), 239
exchange rates, 42–43
exchange-traded funds (ETFs), 174, 175–176
Excite (search engine), 249
exclusive distribution, 234–235
expansion (business cycle), 34

expectancy theory, 251
expenses, 134
expert systems (ES), 288–289
explicit costs, 142
exporting, 44
external audits, 136–137
external locus of control, 113
external recruitment, 269
extranets, 286, 292–293
ExxonMobil, 93
eye contact, 76

F

Facebook, 9, 64, 196–197, 212, 256, 297
face-to-face meetings, 79
facial expressions, 76
facility layout, 304–306
facility location, 305
factor, 154
factors, 161
factors of production, 7–8, 41
Fair Labor Standards Act (1938), 277
fake charity websites, 296
Family and Medical Leave Act (1993), 278
Fannie Mae, 21
fast fashion, 12
fast-laning, 3
federal debt, 22–23
Federal Deposit Insurance Corporation (FDIC), 25
Federal Highway Administration, 24
Federal Open Market Committee, 24–25
Federal Reserve (the Fed), 8, 19, 21, 23, 24, 26, 169
Federal Reserve Act of 1913, 169
Federal Reserve banks, 23
Federal Trade Commission (FTC), 108
FedEx, 112, 173
Fiat, 45
fiduciary duty, 147
Field, Pamela, 265
FIFA World Cup, (2014), 3–4
finance, 146–164
    accounts receivable management, 161–162
    budgeting financial statements, 151–152
    capital budgeting, 162–164
    cash budget, 152–153
    cash management, 160–161

debt financing, 156–158
    defined, 147
    equity financing, 158
    financial capital, 146
    financial leverage, 158–160
    financial planning tools, 151–153
    fund sources, 153–156
    inventory management, 162
    planning process, 150–151
    public monies, 157
    ratio analysis, 149–150
    risk-return tradeoff, 148–149, 164
    shareholder wealth and, 147–148
    social responsibility and, 147–148
financial accounting, 128, 141
Financial Accounting Standards Board, 137
financial analysts, 165
financial budgets, 140
financial capital, 146
financial diversification, 174–175
financial leverage, 150
financial markets, 166–183
    bonds, 172–173
    common stock, 171
    convertible securities, 173–175
    defined, 166
    depository institutions, 167–168
    exchange traded funds, 175
    "green" investments, 174
    index funds, 179
    mutual funds, 174–175
    nondepository financial institutions, 168–169
    personal investing, 178–181
    preferred stock, 172
    primary securities market, 176–177
    regulations, 169–170
    secondary securities markets, 177–178
    tracking performance of investments, 181–183
financial ratio analysis, 149–150
financial regulation, 169–170
Financial Services Modernization Act of 1999, 170
Financial Stability Oversight Council, 160, 170
financial statements, 130–139
Fink, Laurence, 168
firm commitment approach, 176
first-line (supervisory) management, 247, 248–249
fiscal cliff, 22
fiscal policy, 21–22
FitBit, 196

Fitness First, 221
fixed costs, 142–143
fixed margin pricing, 242–243
fixed position layout, 305
flavorists, 278
Fleischmann, Isaac, 115
flexible budget, 141
flextime, 275
fog systems, 285
Ford, Henry, 5, 46, 112
Ford Motor Company, 9, 13, 21, 97, 112, 219
foreclosures, 20–21
Foreign Corrupt Practices Act (1977), 69
foreign direct investment, 45–46
foreign franchising, 45
foreign licensing, 45
foreign outsourcing, 43–44, 265, 308–309
Form 10-K, 100
forms of business organization
    C corporations, 96–97, 98–100
    corporations, 91, 92–93, 96–102
    definitions, 90–92
    franchising, 104–108
    LLCs (limited liability companies), 91–92, 102–104
    LLPs (limited liability partnerships), 95–96
    nonprofit corporations, 100
    partnerships, 90–91, 93, 94–96
    S corporations, 100
    sole proprietorships, 90, 92, 93–94
    statutory closed corporations, 100
    total net income by, 92–93
    total number of businesses by, 92–93
form utility, 187
Fortune magazine "100 Best Companies to Work for in America," 10
Fox Nation, 76
franchise agreements, 106–108
Franchise Disclosure Document (FDD), 108
franchisees, 45, 104
franchises, 104–108
    advantages of, 105
    current trends in, 104–105
    disadvantages of, 105–106
    pros and cons, 120
franchise store managers, 109
franchisor, 45, 104
fraud, accounting, 129
Freddie Mac, 21

"Free Doritos" ad, 217–218
free market system (capitalism), 26–30
free-rein leaders, 260
free trade, 14–15, 50–53
frictional unemployment, 33
Friedman, Milton, 153
Fry, Art, 122
FTSE 100, 182
FuelBand, 196
full-service brokers, 178, 179
full-service merchant wholesalers, 233
functionality, 309–310
funding options for small businesses, 115–117
funky french fries, 208

G

GAAP (generally accepted accounting principles), 128, 129, 136, 137
Galbraith, John Kenneth, 19
Gap Inc., 32, 71, 199, 237
garbage analysis, 200
Gates, Bill, 61, 111
GATT (General Agreement on Tariffs and Trade), 14–15, 50
GDP (gross domestic product), 32, 38, 39–40
gender bias, 80–81
gender neutral language, 77
Genentech, 252
General Agreement on Tariffs and Trade (GATT), 14–15, 50
General Electric (GE), 9, 93, 201–202, 210, 217, 218
general (administrative) expenses, 134
generally accepted accounting principles (GAAP), 128, 129, 136, 137
General Mills (GM), 13
General Motors (GM), 21
general partnerships, 91
Generation Y, 110, 256
geographic segmentation, 192, 193
geopolitics, 11
gestures, 76
Giving USA Foundation, 66
Glancey, Jonathan, 127
Glass-Steagall Act (1933), 169–170
global brand champions, 9
global economic crisis, 19–21
Global Entrepreneurship Model (GEM), 123

global environment, 14–15
ethics/social responsibility and, 68–71
Global Insight, 104
globalization gaffes, 40
global marketing environment, 199
global marketing mix, 195
global marketplace. See world marketplace
global trade. See international trade
GM bailout, 21
GoDaddy, 275
Godin, Seth, 205
Goldberg, Whoopie, 266
goods, 301–302
goods manufactured, 134
goods sold, 134
Google, 9, 10, 102, 155, 196, 210, 212, 218, 249, 252
Google Docs, 286
GoogleMaps, 5
Google mission statement, 255
Google Presentations, 87
government accountants, 127
Graham, Paul, 113
grammatical errors, 83–84
Gramm-Bliley-Leach Act (1999), 170
graphical user interface, 284
Great Depression, 33, 34
Great Recession, 21
green apps, 290–291
greenhouse gas emissions, 67
green investments, 174
green marketing, 68, 202
Green Mountain Power of Vermont, 66
green practices, 315–317
Greenspan, Alan, 23
Green Works, 64
greeting cards, email, 296
Greifeld, Robert, 168
Gretzky, Wayne, 3
gross domestic product (GDP), 32, 38, 39–40
gross profit, 134
guerilla marketing, 221

H

hackers, 296–297
Hale & Hearty, 199
Hamm, Jon, 266
hardware, 283
Harley-Davidson, Inc., 255
Harris, Danita, 117
Harrison, Jonathan, 138

Harsono, Christine, 159
Hazlitt, Henry, 22
headings (business communication), 84–85
health insurance, 275
health insurance costs, 119
HealthSouth, 129
hedges, 163
Heritage Glass, 44
Hermes, 9
Hershey, Milton, 208
Hewlett-Packard, 47, 129
high/low pricing, 239
highly leveraged firms, 150, 158, 159–160
Hilton, 3
Hilton, Paris, 188
Hispanic population, 12, 13
history of business, 4–6
H&M, 12, 43
Hoag, Jay, 96
Hoban, Russell, 74
Hollender, Jeffrey, 57
Homan, Dzana, 104
Home Depot, 217
Honda, 209
Hong Kong, 7
horizontal analysis, 139
horizontal mergers, 101
hot dog vendors, 278
Hot Topic, 251
House of Cards, 220
House Price Index, 20
HR management. See human resource management
Hsieh, Tony, 112, 261
HTC One, 206
HTML, 284
HuluPlus, 216
human resource management, 264–279
affirmative action, 278–279
assessing employee performance, 273
benefits, 274–275
challenges to building top-quality workforce, 265–267
compensation, 273–274
defined, 265
hiring, 269–271
importance of, 264–265
legal issues, 277–279
perception problem of HR professionals, 267–268
planning, 268–276
recruitment, 268–269
scheduling options, 275–276

human resource managers, 279
human resources, 7
human skills, 248
humor, in advertising, 217–218
Huntington, Eileen, 104
Hurricane Katrina, 15
Hurricane Sandy, 15
Huu Truc, Nguyen, 40
Hyatt, 3
hybrid departmentalization, 259
hyperinflation, 34
Hypertext Markup Language (HTML), 284
Hyundai, 219

I

IBM, 9, 97, 172, 173, 210
idea marketing, 188–189
IKEA, 255
Image Activation, 107
immediate predecessors, 307
Immigration Reform and Control Act (1986), 278
implicit costs, 142
importing, 44
inactivity fees, 178
income, investing for, 180
income statements, 133–134
independent auditor's report, 136–137
independent wholesaling business, 233
index funds, 175, 179
India
    cell phone use in, 40
    corruption score, 68–69
    GDP growth, 39
    migration of jobs to, 14
    Unilever, 47
indiegogo.com, 116
indirect costs, 143
Indonesia, 39
Industrial Revolution, 4–5
inflation, 34
information, 287–288
information technology, 282–298
    challenges and concerns from new technologies, 293–298
    cloud computing, 285, 286–287
    cloud computing/fog systems, 285
    data ad information, 287–288
    decision making and, 288
    e-commerce and, 289–293
    expert systems, 288–289
    green apps, 290–291
    hackers, 296–297
    hardware and software, 283–284
    Internet/Internet2, 284–286
    intranets and extranets, 286
    malware, 294–295
    networks, 284–286
    overview, 282–283
    role of IT department, 286
    scams, 296
    spam, phishing, and pharming, 295
information technology support specialist, 299
infrastructure
    defined, 48
    international trade and, 48
infrastructure problems, 24
initial public offering (IPO), 176
inner-city establishments, 122
innovation, 212, 213
    international trade and, 41
in-person presentations, 79. *See also* verbal presentations
insider trading, 170
installations, 207
instant skills, 2–3
institutional investors, 97, 169
intangible assets, 131
integrated marketing communication, 216–217
intellectual property, 298
intensive distribution, 234
intercultural communication, 75–76
internal auditors, 127
internal locus of control, 113
internal recruitment, 268–269
Internal Revenue Service (IRS), 92, 93, 95, 127
International Franchising Association (IFA), 104
International Franchising Association Education Foundation, 104
International Listening Association, 77
International Monetary Fund, 51
International Organization for Standardization ISO 9000 standards, 313, 314–315
international sports marketing manager, 54
international trade. *See also* world marketplace
    growth rate, 42
    reasons for, 41–42
Internet, 118, 284–286
Internet2 (I2), 285
Internet advertising, 218–219, 223, 224, 291–292
interviews, job, 270, 271
intranets, 286
inventions, accidental, 122
inventory, 131
    reducing investment in, 316
inventory control, 237, 305–306
inventory management, 162
inventory turnover ratio, 149, 151
investing activities, cash flows from, 134–135
investing for growth, 181
investing for income, 180
investment banks, 169
investors, company responsibility to, 65–66
iPad, 219
ISO 9000 standards, 313, 314–315
ISO 14000, 317
iTunes, 284

J

Jackson, Alphonso Roy, 304
Japan, 41
JC Penney, 294
jetBlue Airways, 117
Jiffy Lube, 104, 106
job analysis, 268
job applications, 269–270
job description, 268
job enrichment, 250–251
job interviews, 270, 271
job offers, 270–271
job sharing, 276
job specifications, 268
Jobs, Steve, 65, 115, 266
Johnson & Johnson, 65
Johnson & Johnson Credo, 62
The Joint, 106
joint ventures, 45
Jordan, Michael, 195
just-in-time (JIT) production, 316

K

Kapor, Mitchell, 293
Karp, David, 113
Kazoo & Company, 117
Kelleher, Herb, 264
Kellogg, John Harvey, 13
Kelly, Gary, 163, 264
Kennedy, John F., 63
Kentucky Fried Chicken (KFC), 47
kickstarter.com, 116
Kimley Horn, 252–253
Kirchner, Nestor, 51

K-Mart, 240
Knapp, David, 40
Knight, Phil, 111
Kraft, 64
Kroc, Ray, 106, 115
Kroger supermarket, 316
Krugman, Paul, 30, 159

L

Lady Gaga, 220
laggards, 213
landfills, clothing in, 12
Lane, Robert, 61
language barriers to communication, 75
last trade, in stock quote, 182
Lavigne, Avril, 220
laws/regulations, international trade and, 48
lawsuits, 267
layoffs, 265
leadership, 260–261
leading, 246–247
leading-edge firms, 6, 9, 10, 13
lean production, 315–317
legal differences, international trade and, 48–50
legal environment, 197
legal-ethical matrix, 58
legal issues
    human resources, 277–278
    information technology, 297–298
legally binding requirement, 156
legal system, ethics and, 57
Legere, John, 68
The Lego Movie, 220
Lehrer, Jonah, 231
leverage ratios, 150
Levi Strauss, 70, 257
Lewis, Craig, 129
liabilities, 132
licensee, 45
licensing, 210–211
licensor, 45
Liddy, Edward, 60
limited liability, 91
limited liability company (LLC)
    advantages of, 102–103
    defined, 91–92
    disadvantages of, 103–104
    forming, 102
    managing, 102
    taxation and, 93
limited liability partnerships (LLPs), 95–96
limited partnerships, 95

limited-service merchant wholesalers, 233
limit orders, 179
line-and-staff organizations, 259–260
line extensions, 210
line managers, 259–260
line of credit, 154
line organization, 259
line organizations, 259
LinkedIn, 212
liquid assets, 149
liquidity ratios, 149
listening skills, 77–78
LLC. See limited liability company (LLC)
LLP (limited liability partnership), 95–96
loans, 116
logistics, 237
London, Jack, 213
long-term debt, 156
long-term funding sources, 155–156
long-term liabilities, 132
The Lorax (film), 13
loss, 4
loss-leader pricing, 239–240
low pricing, 239
Lucas, George, 249
Lululemon, 5, 68
Lumia 900, 208
Lyft, 6

M

M1 money supply, 24
M2 money supply, 24
MacDougall, Alice Foote, 186
Mackey, John, 61, 153
macroeconomics, 18–19
Madoff, Bernard, 129
magazine advertising, 223, 224
MagicBrands, 293
Maine Lobster Game, 236
maintenance, repair, and operating products, 207
Malcolm Baldrige National Quality Improvement Act (1987), 313–314
malware, 206, 294–295
management accountants, 127
management, defined, 246
management development, 273
management hierarchy, 247–248
management, motivation, and leadership, 246–262
    controlling, 262

current motivation practices, 252–253
examples of motivation among high achievers, 248
leadership, 260–261
management hierarchy, 247–248
management skills, 248–249
motivation theories, 250–252
organizing, 257–260
overview, 246–247
planning, 253–257
poor decisions by managers, 249
management skills, 248–249
managerial (management) accounting, 141–143
manager of new media, 16
managing information and technology. See information technology
manufacturers' brands, 211–212
market basket, 175
market cap, in stock quote, 182
marketing, 186–202. See also promotion
    business market segmentation, 192, 193
    color psychology and, 194
    consumer behavior, 197–198
    consumer market segmentation, 192–193
    customer loyalty, 191
    customer relationship management (CRM), 190
    customer satisfaction, 190–191
    defined, 186
    evolution of, 189
    historical overview, 189
    marketing environment, 195–197
    marketing mix, 193–195
    marketing strategy, 191–197
    mistakes, 199
    scope of, 187–189
    social responsibility, 201–202
    technology and, 202
marketing concept, 189
marketing environment, 195–197
marketing era, 5–6
marketing gaffes, 199
marketing mix, 193–195
marketing plan, 191
marketing research, 198–201
marketing strategy, 191–197
market makers, 177–178
market niche, 117
market orders, 179
market segmentation, 191
market share, 196
market timing, 180

Marks & Spencer, 5
Marx, Karl, 31
Mary Kay Cosmetics, 236
Maslow, Abraham, 250
Maslow's hierarchy of needs theory, 250
Massage Envy, 104
mass customization, 202, 302
Massive, 220
mass production, 302
master budgets, 140, 141
materials handling, 237
matrix organizations, 260
maturity date, 173
Maugham, William Somerset, 147
McDonald's, 9, 47, 104, 210
    advertising, 216–217
    average collection period, 150
    balance sheet for, 130, 131–132
    common stock, 182
    current ratio of, 149
    debt-to-asset ratio of, 150
    in global market, 40
    income statement for, 133, 134
    inventory turnover ratio, 150
    ratio analysis of, 149, 150
    recycling by, 67
    statement of cash flows, 134, 135
    stock buybacks, 173
    stock ownership, 97
McGregor, Douglas, 250
McKinsey, 11
memos/reports, 79
Mercedes-Benz, 9, 210, 220
merchant wholesalers, 233
mergers, 101, 102
Merrill Lynch, 61
Mexico
    NAFTA, 51–52
Meyer, Stephanie, 112
microeconomics, 19
Microsoft, 9, 28, 97, 210
middle management, 247, 249
millennials, 256
Miller, Greg, 117
Milligen, Spike, 175
Milsom, Keith, 118
minority franchising, 105
mission, 254
missionary selling, 227
mission statements, 254, 255
mixed economies, 31–32
M-LAW, 214
MLM (multilevel marketing), 236
modes of transportation, 238
monetary policy, 23–26
money, defined, 23

money market mutual funds, 161
money supply, 23–24, 25
monopolistic competition, 27–28
monopoly, 28
Moonfruit, 221
Moscovitz, Dustin, 113
Motel 6, 189, 220
Motorola, 173
Mulcahy, Anne, 257
multichannel retailing, 234
multilevel marketing (MLM), 236
mutual funds, 174–175

N

NAFTA (North American Free Trade Agreement), 15, 51–52
NASD (National Association of Securities Dealers), 177
NASDAQ, 168, 177
NASDAQ Composite, 182
NASDAQ OMX, 177
National Association of Securities Dealers (NASD), 177
national brands, 211
National Conference of Commissioners on Uniform State Laws, 104
national debt clock, 22
National Do Not Call list, 236
nationality bias, 81
National Minority Franchising Initiative (NMFI), 105
National Report, 76
National Retail Federation (NRF), 236
native advertising, 219
natural disasters, 15
natural monopoly, 28
natural resources, 7, 31
Neeleman, David, 117
Neiman Marcus, 212
Nestle, 13
net asset value per share (NAVPS), 174
Netflix, 96, 216, 284
net income, 134
net operating income, 134
net present value (NPV), 164
networks, 284–286
Neuticles, 117
newly issues stock, 155
new product development, 212–214
news media, 76
newspaper advertising, 223, 224
New York Stock Exchange (NYSE), 177

Nike, 12, 195
Nikkei 225, 182
Nintendo, 217
Nissan, 9
noise, 75
Nokia, 208
nondepository financial institutions, 168–169
nondurable goods, 302
nonprofit corporations, 100
nonprofit organizations, 188
Nonprofit Roundtable, 6
nonprofits, 6, 7–8
nonstore retailers, 235–237
nonverbal communication, 76–78
North American Free Trade Agreement (NAFTA), 15, 51–52
Northwestern Mutual, 9
Noseworthy, Graeme, 6
notes in financial statements, 136, 137–138
NYSE, 168

O

Oakley, 196
Obama, Barack, 8, 21, 188
observation research, 199–200
Occupational Safety and Health Act (1970), 278
odd jobs, 278
odd pricing, 243–244
offshoring, 308–309
off-the-job training, 272
older workers, 266
oligopoly, 28
Olympus, 129
Omidyar, Pierre, 61
on-demand economy, 30
O'Neal, Stanley, 61
The Onion (website), 76
online retailing, 235–236
on-the-job training, 272
open-end mutual fund, 174
opening, of verbal presentations, 86
open market operations, 24–25
operating activities, cash flows from, 134
operating budgets, 140
operating expenses, 134
operational planning, 253
operations management, 300–317
    automation, 310–311
    changes in, 300–303
    critical path method (CPM), 306–307
    defined, 300, 301

operations management *(Continued)*
   facility location, 305
   green practices, 315–317
   inventory control, 305–306
   just-in-time (JIT) production, 316
   lean production, 315–317
   operations manager roles, 303–309
   process selection/facility layout, 304–305
   project scheduling, 306–307
   quality and, 311–315
   service-based economy, 309–310
   servicescape, 309–310
   technology and, 310–311
   value chain design, 307–309
opportunity cost, 41
oral presentations, 85–88
order processing, 237
Ore-Ida, 208
organization chart, 256
organizing, 246, 257–260
orientation, 272
Orman, Suze, 266
outdoor advertising, 223, 224
outlet store, 235
out-of-pocket costs, 142
outsourcing, 265, 308
Overstock.com, 236
over-the-counter market, 178
owner's (or stockholder's) equity, 133
ownership utility, 187
Oze-Moore, 152, 158, 159

P

PacificCare, 148
Pacioli, Luca, 131
packaging, 212
Page, Larry, 111
paid search advertising, 218
paid sick days, 274
paid vacation/holidays, 274
Pampered Chef, 236
Papa John's, 106
PareUp, 3
participatory (bottom-up) budgeting, 139–140
partnerships, 45
   advantages of, 94–95
   defined, 90–91
   disadvantages of general, 95
   formation of general, 94
   limited, 95
   number of business organizations using, 92

par value (bond), 173
passive voice, 81
"pass through" (tax), 95, 100, 103
Patagonia, 66, 68
Peds Legwear, 302
peer-to-peer lending, 116
Penance Hall, 302
penetration pricing, 239
Penner, Michael, 302
people marketing, 188
People's Daily Online, 76
PepsiCo, 67
P/E (price-to-earnings) ratio, 182
perceived value, 190
perceptual barriers to communication, 75
performance appraisals, 273
Perry, Marnette, 316
personal investing, 178–181
personality testing, 270
personal selling, 226–228
Pertew, Takek, 275
Peters, Tom, 236
Pew Internet and American Life Project, 284
P&G, 222
pharmaceutical sales representative, 229
pharming, 295
philanthropy, corporate, 66
phishing, 295
physical barriers to communication, 75
physical distribution, 230, 237–238
physical exams, 270
pipeline (transportation mode), 238
piracy of intellectual property, 298
piracy rates, 49
Pizza Hut, 47
place marketing, 188
place utility, 187
plane (transportation mode), 238
planned economies, 30–31
planned obsolescence, 65
planning, 246, 253–257
plant supervisors, 318
P&L statement, 133
poka-yokes, 313
political differences, international trade and, 48–50
political environment, 197
Popelka, Larry, 159
population
   aging, 13–14
   diversity in U.S., 12–13
Post-it-Notes, 122
posture, 76

PowerPoint, 87
PPI (producer price index), 35
Prahalad, C.K., 47, 70
pre-employment testing, 270
preemptive right, 171
preferred stock, 97, 172
premium (bond), 223, 225
prepaid expenses, 131
presentations, 79, 85–88
present value, 163–164
Prezi, 87
price levels, 34–35
price-to-earnings, in stock quote, 182
pricing. *See* distribution and pricing
pricing mistakes, 241
pricing objectives, 238–241
pricing strategy, 194
pricing tricks, 243
PrideBites, 159
primary data, 198–199
primary research tools, 199–200
primary securities markets, 176–177
Prius, 68
privacy issues, information technology and, 297–298
private enterprise system (capitalism), 26–30
private labels, 211–212
private placement, 176, 177
privatization, 32
proactive supply chain management, 238
probationary period, 271
process, 303–304
process layout, 304
process selection, 304
producer price index (PPI), 35
product, 204–228. *See also* promotion
   branding, 210–212
   business product categories, 207
   consumer product categories, 206–207
   definitions, 204
   features and benefits, 209
   goods and services spectrum, 206
   innovation types, 212, 213
   new product development, 212–214
   packaging, 212
   product adoption and diffusion, 213–214
   product differentiation, 207–208
   product layers, 206
   product life cycle, 214–216
   product line, 209–210

product (*Continued*)
   product lines, 209–210
   product mix, 209
   product quality, 208–209
   services, 205–206
   warning labels, 214
product adoption categories, 213
product consistency, 208–209
product differentiation, 207–208
product diffusion rates, 213–214
product features, 209
production era, 5
productivity, 35
product layers, 206
product layout, 304
product life cycle, 214–216
product lines, 209–210
product, marketing definition of, 303
product mix, 209
product placement, 219–220
product quality, 208–209
product quality indicators, 208
product strategy, 193–194
product warning labels, 214
profitability, pricing objectives and, 238–239
profitability ratios, 150
profit and loss statement, 133
profit, defined, 4
profit margin, 242–243
pro forma financial statements, 152
project scheduling, 306–307
promissory notes, 154, 155
promotion
   advergaming, 220–221
   advertising, 222
   buzz marketing, 221
   choosing right promotional mix, 228
   coordinating marketing messages, 217
   integrated marketing communication, 216–217
   international perspective, 218
   Internet advertising, 218–219
   native advertising, 219
   personal selling, 226–228
   positioning statement, 217–218
   product placement, 219–220
   public relations, 226
   sales promotion, 223, 225–226
   social media, 219
   sponsorships, 222
   technological changes and, 216
promotional channels, 218–228
promotional message, 217–218
promotional mix, 218–228

promotional products, 225
promotion strategy, 195
property, plant, equipment category on balance sheet, 131–132
Prosper.com, 116
protectionism, 49
psychics, 278
psychographic segmentation, 192–193
public accountants, 127
Public Company Accounting Oversight Board (PCAOB), 137
publicity, 226
public offerings, 176
public relations (PR), 226
public relations manager, 89
public speaking. *See* verbal presentations
pull strategy, 228
pull system, 316
Purcell, Paul, 252
pure competition, 27
pure goods, 206
pure services, 206
Purina, 13
push strategy, 228

Q

qualified opinion, 136
quality
   operations management and, 311–315
   price and, 243
quality indicators, 208
quality level, 208
quality of life, 4
Qualman, Erik, 219
questions, during presentations, 87
Quicken Loans, 253
quotas, 49

R

race bias, 81
Rackspace, 286
radio advertising, 223, 224
radio frequency identification (RFID), 293, 297–298
rail (transportation mode), 238
Ralph Lauren Corporation, 69
ratio analysis, 149–150
ratios, financial, 149–150, 151
raw materials, 207
Ray-Ban, 196
Reagan, Ronald, 21
RealtyTrac, 20

Reavis, Jim, 286
rebates, 225
Rebus puzzles, 201
recalls, product, 44
recession, 19–21, 33
recovery (business cycle), 33
recruitment, 268–269
Redbox, 187
Redux Beverages, 208
Reese's Pieces, 219
references, 270
referrals, 269
registration statement, 176
Reiman, Tonya, 77
relationship era, 6
Report Card on the Ethics of American Youth, 59
reports/memos, 79
reserve requirement, 25–26
residual claim, 171
retailers, 233
retained earnings, 155–156
retirement programs, 275
return-on-equity (ROE), 150
return on equity ratio, 151
revenue, 133–134
Revised Uniform Limited Liability Company Act, 104
revolving credit agreement, 154–155
RFID technology, 293, 294, 297–298
Rhoads, Terry, 195
Richelieu Group, 302
right to dividends, 171
risk
   defined, 148
   international trade and, 41
risk-return tradeoff, 148–149, 164
RoboCop, 129
Robolove, 4
robots, 311–312
Rock, Chris, 248
Romano, Ray, 128
Rosenblum, Paula, 294
Rowling, J.K., 115
Russell 2000, 182
Russia, 7

S

Saks Fifth Avenue, 212
salaries, 274
sales budget, 140
sales promotion, 223, 225–226
samples (products), 225
Samsung, 9, 210

Sandberg, Sheryl, 64
Sarbanes-Oxley Act (2002), 65, 137, 170
savings and loans association, 168
scams, Internet, 296
scandals, accounting, 129, 137
scanner data (observation research), 200
SCM (supply chain management), 237
SCORE (Service Corps of Retired Executives), 120
S corporations, 100
search engine optimization (SEO), 218
seasonal unemployment, 33
secondary data, 198–199
secondary securities markets, 176, 177–178
Securities Act of 1933, 170
Securities and Exchange Commission (SEC), 127, 129, 168, 170, 176
securities brokers, 169
securities dealers, 169
Securities Exchange Act of 1934, 170
securities information processor (SIP), 168
security, 238
selective distribution, 234
self-lacing sneakers, 196
selling expenses, 134
Semler, Ricardo, 261
services, 205–206, 302
servicescape, 309–310
sexual harassment, 279
shareholder value, social responsibility and, 147–148
Shaw, George Bernard, 85
Sherman Antitrust Act (1890), 28
ship (transportation mode), 238
shopping products, 207
short-term bank loans, 154–155
short-term funding sources, 153–155
Sidecar, 6
Sierra Club, 64
signs, 310
Silver, Spencer, 122
Simmons, Gene, 248
Sintumuang, Kevin, 83, 84
Six Sigma, 313
Skeel, David, 158
skills testing, 270
skimming pricing, 240–241
Skype, 284

Small Business Administration (SBA), 9, 119, 120, 121
small business and entrepreneurship, 110–123
    advantages of, 110–112
    around the world, 122–123
    buying a franchise, 120
    buying an established business, 120
    characteristics of millionaire entrepreneurs, 114
    drop in rate of, 110
    entrepreneural characteristics, 112–115
    entrepreneurial mindset, 112
    funding options for, 115–117
    market niches, 117
    new business survival rates, 118
    opportunities for, 117–118
    role in the economy, 121–122
    starting a business from scratch, 120
    threats for, 118–119
    tools for business success, 119–121
Small Business Development Centers (SBDCs), 120
smart fashion, 196
smart purses, 196
SMiShing, 295
Smith, Adam, 26
Smith, Fred, 112
Smith, Mike, 249
SMS phishing, 295
Snapchat, 68
Snapple, 217
social audit, 71
social contagion, 297
social environment, 12–14, 196–197
socialism, 30–31
social media, 80, 219
social responsibility, 14
    consumer rights, 63–64
    defined, 56, 62
    examples of company actions, 64
    foreign outsourcing and, 44
    in the global arena, 68–71
    "green" investments, 174
    marketing and, 201–202
    monitoring, 71
    responsibility to customers, 63–65
    responsibility to employees, 63
    responsibility to investors, 65–66
    shareholder value and, 147–148
    spectrum of business approaches, 62, 63
    stakeholder approach, 63
    Whole Foods Market, 153

sociocultural differences, international trade and, 46
software, 283
software technologies, 311
Soh, Jeffrey, 116
sole proprietorships
    advantages of, 93
    defined, 90
    disadvantages of, 93–94
    number of business organizations using, 92
Solso, Tim, 96
Sony, 209
Southwest Airlines, 211, 264
S&P 500, 175, 181, 182
spam, 295
span of control, 258
specialty products, 207
specialty store, 235
speech anxiety, 87–88
speed-to-market, 10–11
Spencer, Percy, 122
Spiegel, Evan, 68
"spin-offs," 101–102
sponsorships, 222
spontaneous financing, 154
spread, 169, 178
spyware, 294
SSE Composite, 182
staff accountant, 144
staff managers, 260
stakeholder approach, 63–68
stakeholders, 63
standard of living, 4
Standard & Poor's 500, 175, 181, 182
Starbucks, 6, 9, 66, 103, 201–202, 233
Star Citizen (game), 116
Star Wars films, 249
Starwood, 3
statement of cash flows, 134–135
statement of retained earnings, 135
static budget, 140
Statista, 219
statutory close (closed) corporations, 100
Stewart, Martha, 112
stock brokers, 183
stock buybacks, 173
stock (securities) exchanges, 177–178
stockholders, 97, 126
stockholder's equity, 133
stockholder's equity statement, 135
stock indices, 181–182

stock symbol, 182
Stoller, Bill, 226
Stone Brewing Company, 157
store brands, 211–212
store retailers, 234
strategic alliances, 45–46
strategic goals, 255
strategic planning, 253–257
strategies, 255–257
structural unemployment, 33
structured interviews, 270
StubHub, 199
subprime mortgages, 19–20
Subway, 104, 106
Super Bowl ads, 217–218
supercenters, 235
Supercuts, 104, 106
supermarkets, 235
supply, 29
supply and demand, 28–30
supply chain, 237, 292–293
supply chain management, 237
supply curve, 29
Survey of Small Business Finances, 152
survey research, 200
sustainability, 14, 200, 316–317
sustainable development, 67
Sweetgreen, 275
SWOT analysis, 254–255
symbols, 310
sympathetic pricing, 3–4
system software, 283–284

T

Taco Bell, 235
tactical planning, 253
Target, 199, 201–202
target market, 191–192
tariffs, 49
TARP (Troubled Assets Relief Program), 21
taxation
  C corporations, 99
  double, 99
  fiscal policy and, 21–22
  limited liability companies (LLCs) and, 92, 93, 103
  sole proprietorships and, 93
tax pass through, 95, 100, 103
T-bills, 160–161
team selling, 228
technical skills, 248
technological environment, 11–12, 197

technology
  digital manners and, 83
  entertainment media changes and, 216
  marketing and, 202
  small business opportunities through, 118
  trends in, 2–3
  as worry of CEOs, 11
telecommuting, 276
telegraph, the, 249
telemarketing, 236
Telephone (Lady Gaga), 220
telephone conversations, 79
television advertising, 222, 223, 224
termination, employee, 276
term loans, 156
terrorism, 15
testing, 270
textile industry, 302
texting, 79
T.G.I. Friday's, 211
Thain, John, 60
Thaler, Richard, 176
Theory X and Theory Y, 250, 251
The Smashing Place, 117
Thomas, Jordan, 64
Thompson, Scott, 61
thrifts, 168
Time, Inc., 99
time utility, 187
time value of money, 160–161
Time Warner, 96, 99
Title VII, Civil Rights Act of 1964, 277
T-Mobile, 68, 137
Tome, Carol, 173
tone (business writing), 83
tone of voice, 76
top-down budgeting, 139
top management, 249, 251
total quality management, 312–313
Toyota, 9, 13, 68, 210
TQM (total quality management), 312–313
trade credit, 151–152
trade deficit, 42
trade promotion, 225–226
trade shows, 225
trade surplus, 42
trading blocs, 51
traditional promotional tools, 222–226
traffic counters, 200
training and development, 271–273
Transparency International, 68
transportation, 237–238

Treasury bills, 160–161
Trendwatching.com, 2–4
trillion dollars, 20
triple bottom line, 136
Troubled Assets Relief Program (TARP), 21
trough (business cycle), 33, 34
truck (transportation mode), 238
truck jobbers, 234
Truc, Nguyen Huu, 40
Truman, Harry, 33
Trump, Donald, 167
Tufts University Micro Finance Fund, 61
Tupperware, 236
Twain, Mark, 8, 78
Twilight franchise, 112
Twitter, 80
Twitter stock, 157
Typhoon Haiyan, 15

U

Uber, 6
UGG Australia, 187
Ulrich, David, 252
underwriting, 176
underwriting syndicate, 176
unemployment rate, 21, 32–33
Unilever, 47, 70
United Continental, 161
United States
  corruption score, 68–69
  GDP growth, 39
universal ethical standards, 57–58
unqualified ("clean") opinion, 136
unsought products, 207
UPS, 238
UPS Store, 106
Urban Outfitters, 233
U.S. Bureau of Labor Statistics, 268
U.S. Census Bureau, 268
U.S. Department of the Treasury, 21
U.S. dollar, 42–43
U.S. Small Business Administration, 116
U.S. Treasury bills (T-bills), 158–159
utility, 186–187

V

vacation days, 274
value, 2
  defined, 190
  distributor role and, 231–233
  perceived *vs.* actual, 180

value chain, 307–308
value chain design, 307–308
value investing, 180–181
Vanguard's Total Stock Market Index (VTSMI), 179
variable costs, 143
Vegetable Jello, 208
vending machines, 236–237
venture capital firms, 116–117
verbal presentations, 85–88
Verizon Communications, 135
Veronic Mars (film), 116
vertical integration, 308
vertical mergers, 101
vestibule training, 272
Viagra, 122
videoconferencing, 79
viral marketing, 221, 292
Virgin Atlantic, 217
Virgin Group, 251
visual aids, for presentations, 87
voice mail, 79
Volkswagon, 9
voluntary export restraints (VERs), 49
voting rights, 171
Vuitton, Louis, 315
VW Beetle, 213

W

Wacky Warning Label Contest, 214
wage gap, 265–266
wages, 69, 70, 274
The Wall Street Journal, 182, 253
WallStreetJournal.com, 193
The Wall Street Journal's Career Journal, 76
Walmart, 40, 69, 93, 96, 97, 200, 239
Walt Disney Company, 112
Walton, Sam, 251
warehouse clubs, 235
warehouse manager, 244
warehousing, 237

warning labels, 214
Washington Mutual, 21
Waste Management, 129
water shortage, 49
Watkins, Sherron, 61
Watson, Liz, 77
wearable chic, 196
Web 2.0, 290–291
WebVan, 10
Weinstein, Shel, 117–118
Wendy's Company, 104, 107
Western Union, 249
Wetpaint/Altimeter Study, 219
wheel of retailing, 235
whistle-blowers, 62
Whole Foods Market, 153, 209, 235
wholesalers, 233–234
Wilshire 5000, 175, 182
Wilson, Chip, 68
Winfrey, Oprah, 77, 266
Winston, Andrew, 200
Winterton, Grant, 48–49
W.L. Gore, 252
women franchises, 104
women workers, 267
worker expectations, 14
workforce. *See* employees
workforce advantage, 10–11
work-life balance, 267
World Bank, 48, 50–51
WorldCom, 129, 149
world marketplace, 38–53
  balance of payments, 42
  balance of trade, 42
  barriers to international trade, 46–50
  changes in American fast-food franchises, 47
  competitive advantage and, 41–42
  countertrade, 43
  direct investment, 45–46
  economic differences, 46–48
  European Union (EU), 52–53
  exchange rates, 42–43

  exporting, 44
  foreign outsourcing, 43–44
  franchises in, 104
  free trade, 50–53
  GATT, 50
  GDP growth, 38, 39–40
  growth rate of global trade, 42
  importing, 43, 44
  International Monetary Fund (IMF), 51
  international trade restrictions, 49–50
  NAFTA, 51–52
  population statistics, 38–39
  reasons for international trade, 41–42
  sociocultural differences, 46
  World Bank, 50–51
  World Trade Organization (WTO), 50
World Trade Organization (WTO), 50
World Wide Web, 11, 284
worms, 294–295
Wyatt, Watson, 80

Y

Yahoo!, 61
Yellen, Janet, 23
Yergin, Daniel, 30
Yiwu, China, 46
younger workers, 266–267
You Sow, 71
YouTube, 284
Yunis, Muhammad, 40

Z

Zappos.com, 193, 232–233, 236, 275
Zara, 12
Zarrella, Dan, 200
Zuckerberg, Mark, 60, 112, 113, 117, 247, 248, 253

WHAT'S INSIDE:

Key Topics in this Chapter: *Definitions of business, the history of business, the role of nonprofits, factors of production, six dimensions of the current business environment, personal success, careers.*

LEARNING OBJECTIVES

1-1 Define business and discuss the role of business in the economy

1-2 Explain the evolution of modern business

1-3 Discuss the role of nonprofit organizations in the economy

1-4 Outline the core factors of production and how they affect the economy

1-5 Describe today's business environment and discuss each key dimension

1-6 Explain how current business trends might affect your career choices

CHAPTER OUTLINE

Business Now: Moving at Breakneck Speed
Business Basics: Some Key Definitions

The History of Business: Putting It All in Context

Nonprofits and the Economy: The Business of Doing Good

Factors of Production: The Basic Building Blocks

The Business Environment: The Context for Success
The Economic Environment
The Competitive Environment
The Workforce Advantage
The Technological Environment
The Social Environment
The Global Environment

Business and You: Making It Personal

4LTR ONLINE

Have students access their 4LTR Press Online account in order to…

- Create StudyBits
- Review key terms and create flashcards
- Create practice quizzes from their StudyBits
- Complete assessment content: matching, drag and drop, and fill-in-the-blank problems
- View Chapter Highlight Boxes: videos, What Would You Do cases, key exhibits/tables

VIDEO

Graeter's
Run time 6:04 minutes

Established in 1870, Graeter's is a fourth-generation Cincinnati-based family business that primarily makes ice cream, as well as candy and baked goods. The firm started out as a small open-air establishment in Cincinnati and is now headed by the founder's great-grandson, Richard Graeter II, who is now the company's CEO. He describes how the firm has stuck to its roots by providing quality over quantity. Graeter's began expanding its businesses to cities outside Cincinnati in 2002, when mail order sales shot up nearly ten times after the company was featured on *Oprah*.

Ask Your Students:

1. Briefly explain how Graeter's manages to produce a product that is personal to both the consumer and the company itself.

2. Briefly explain the role the media played in the expansion of Graeter's as a business.

VIDEO SEGMENT SUMMARY

Urban Farmz—What Do You Mean … This Kind of Business?

Urban Farmz is not your typical farm. Founders Jake, an MBA graduate, and his free-spirited vegan cousin, Caleb, recently started this organic and sustainable farming cooperative on their grandfather's small farm upstate. In this first scenario, we see Jake and Caleb, sitting with their business advisor, Sylvie, and Grandpa Richardson. Sylvie is presenting the current financial picture of the company after its first six months in business. So far, things are running well—but there are so many details to worry about.

LECTURE EXAMPLE

Nissan recently announced that it was making a shift from selling luxury cars to selling cheaper cars (priced under $3000) in developing countries. Such a shift in the core business model isn't restricted to Nissan but can be seen in retail companies such as Amazon, eBay, and Walmart. Tried and tested models simply do not work in today's environment. For the most part, companies are forced to change and adapt to suit the changing environment. The main concern is not adapting, but finding a sustainable business model in the new environment.

Source: "Your Business Model is Obsolete," CNN Money, retrieved 03-13-13, http://management.fortune.cnn.com/2013/02/25/business-model-obsolete/ .

CHAPTER PREP 1

KEY TERMS

value, 2
business, 4
Profit, 4
loss, 4
entrepreneurs, 4
standard of living, 4
quality of life, 4
nonprofits, 6
factors of production, 7
business environment, 8
Speed-to-market, 10
business technology, 11
World Wide Web, 11
e-commerce, 11
demographics, 12
free trade, 14
General Agreement on Tariffs and Trade (GATT), 14

DISCUSSION QUESTIONS

1. When did American business begin to concentrate on customer needs? Why?
2. How do nonprofit organizations compare to businesses? What role do nonprofits play in the economy? How do they interact with businesses?
3. What are some key strategies for developing a competitive edge in today's competitive global market? How important is customer satisfaction?

GROUP ACTIVITY

Break into groups of three to five people. Choose a product or service that you all buy on a regular basis. Write a brief description of how the product is positioned in the marketplace relative to its competition. Then work together to figure out why you are loyal customers and how the competition could dislodge you over the next five years. Write a one-page plan to solidify your position in the marketplace; consider changing everything from the product features to the advertising venues. Share your plan with the class, and gather feedback about how well it might work.

ASSIGNMENTS

Most successful businesses today actively develop loyal customers who buy their brands again and again. After all, getting current customers to buy more is much easier than constantly seeking new customers. Think of three brands that you buy on a regular basis. Why do you stick to these products? How could another company dislodge you?

WHAT'S NEW

- Updated section 1-1, "Business Now: Moving at Breakneck Speed"
- Updated box feature "Not Every Dumb Move Is an Utter Disaster..."
- New box feature, "Traffic Jams and Parking Woes – A Problem of the Past?"
- Updated Exhibit 1.2, "2014 Global Brand Champions and the Ones to Watch, Interbrand"
- New box feature, "High-Level Worries"
- New box feature, "Fast Fashion – Doesn't Look So Hot Lining Our Landfills"

WHAT'S INSIDE:

Key Topics in this Chapter: *Why economics is relevant to your students, macroeconomics versus microeconomics, global economic crisis (how it happened and the aftermath), fiscal policy (including fiscal cliff), monetary policy, capitalism, the four degrees of competition, fundamentals of supply and demand, socialism, communism, mixed economies, GDP, unemployment, phases of the business cycle, inflation, productivity, careers.*

CHAPTER OUTLINE

Economics: Navigating a Crisis
Global Economic Crisis: How Did This Happen?
Moving in a Better Direction

Managing the Economy Through Fiscal and Monetary Policy
Fiscal Policy
Debt Ceiling/Fiscal Cliff
Monetary Policy

Capitalism: The Free Market System
The Fundamental Rights of Capitalism
Four Degrees of Competition
Supply and Demand: Fundamental Principles of a Free Market System

Planned Economies: Socialism and Communism
Socialism
Communism

Mixed Economies: The Story of the Future

Evaluating Economic Performance: What's Working?
Gross Domestic Product
Employment Level
The Business Cycle
Price Levels
Productivity

LEARNING OBJECTIVES

2-1 Define economics and discuss the evolving global economic crisis

2-2 Analyze the impact of fiscal and monetary policy on the economy

2-3 Explain and evaluate the free market system and supply and demand

2-4 Explain and evaluate planned market systems

2-5 Describe the trend toward mixed market systems

2-6 Discuss key terms and tools to evaluate economic performance

4LTR ONLINE

Have students access their 4LTR Press Online account in order to…

- Create StudyBits
- Review key terms and create flashcards
- Create practice quizzes from their StudyBits
- Complete assessment content: matching, drag and drop, and fill-in-the-blank problems
- View Chapter Highlight Boxes: videos, What Would You Do cases, key exhibits/tables

VIDEO

Nederlander Concerts
Run time 9:45 minutes

Nederlander is one of the most respected concert management companies in the United States. Headquartered in Los Angeles, the company owns and operates such award-winning venues as the Greek Theatre, Santa Barbara Bowl, and the San Jose Civic Center. One of few family-run businesses in all of entertainment, Nederlander takes pride in its ability to book big acts in its small to mid-sized venues. Artists rocking out Nederlander stages range from Pearl Jam and Jimmy Buffett to Dave Matthews and 30 Seconds to Mars. While bands get most of the attention, the behind-the-scenes planning for Nederlander shows falls to 60 full-time employees, who staff the company's marketing, talent buying, finance, and development departments. Hundreds of seasonal workers join in each year to provide support for concert events and concessions. While many businesses view international expansion as the key to growth, Nederlander prefers its regional approach. Today's global entertainment world is full of flash-in-the-pan promoters, but Nederlander has delivered a century's worth of great entertainment simply by being the best in its space.

Ask Your Students:

1. Explain the role of capitalism in the 100-year growth of Nederlander Concerts.
2. Why is Nederlander able to charge higher prices for small theatre performances when audiences could pay less at stadium concerts?

VIDEO SEGMENT SUMMARY

Urban Farmz—A Twenty Won't Even Fill Your Car!

In this scene, the new business partners consider making a deal with a Fair Trade cooperative to buy organic coffee produced in Ethiopia. The coffee is great, but is it great enough? It sells for $18 a pound wholesale and $22 a pound retail. Jake thinks that's too high, especially in the aftermath of the recession. "Why would Urban Farmz's customers pay that much for coffee when they can buy it for $8 a pound at Walmart?" he argues. "A twenty won't even fill up your car today," he says.

CHAPTER PREP 2

KEY TERMS

economy, 18

Economics, 18

Macroeconomics, 18

Microeconomics, 19

Fiscal policy, 21

budget surplus, 22

budget deficit, 22

federal debt, 22

Monetary policy, 23

commercial banks, 23

money supply, 23

money, 23

M1 money supply, 24

M2 money supply, 24

Open market operations, 24

Federal Deposit Insurance Corporation (FDIC), 25

discount rate, 25

reserve requirement, 25

economic system, 26

capitalism, 26

pure competition, 27

monopolistic competition, 27

oligopoly, 28

monopoly, 28

natural monopoly, 28

Supply, 29

supply curve, 29

Demand, 29

demand curve, 29

equilibrium price, 30

socialism, 30

communism, 31

mixed economies, 32

privatization, 32

gross domestic product, 32

unemployment rate, 32

business cycle, 33

Contraction, 33

recession, 33

depression, 33

recovery, 33

expansion, 34

inflation, 34

hyperinflation, 34

disinflation, 34

deflation, 34

consumer price index (CPI), 35

producer price index (PPI), 35

Productivity, 35

LECTURE EXAMPLE

Apple Inc. was one of the few companies that managed to beat the recession. In fact, the Apple juggernaut gained steam during the recession and opened new stores all across the world. Dozens of companies around the globe had to lay off employees, cut costs, and reduce production. But Apple went on to do the exact opposite. How did Apple manage to navigate the recession? The allure of Apple products hasn't diminished anywhere around the world, and it continues to expand operations even in countries like Spain, which have been hard hit by recession. Despite the "mean" decline in spending power, consumers are willing to spend on Apple products thanks to the company's brand building efforts.

Source: "Apple's 'recession-proof' in Europe," retrieved 03-13-13, http://articles.timesofindia.indiatimes.com/2012-02-09/telecom/31041279_1_dixons-retail-plc-john-browett-apple; "8 Big Companies That Beat the Recession," Huffington Post, retrieved 03-13-13, http://www.huffingtonpost.com/2010/08/02/8-big-companies-that beat_n_667099.html#s121372&title=Apple_.

DISCUSSION QUESTIONS

1. Compare and contrast microeconomics and macroeconomics. How do the two approaches interrelate? Use a specific example to explain.

2. What are the fundamental elements of the free market economic system? How can businesses thrive within this system?

3. Why do most countries have neither "pure" market nor "pure" planned economies? Is the trend toward the market end of the spectrum likely to continue? Why?

GROUP ACTIVITY

Research four industries—past or present—that represent the four degrees of competition (pure competition, monopolistic competition, oligopoly, and monopoly). For each example, describe the industry, explain how it came to embody that type of competition, and describe how difficult it would be for an entrepreneur to enter the industry. Finally, provide your opinion regarding whether certain industries are better suited to certain degrees of competition, or if all industries should strive toward one single type of competition in particular.

ASSIGNMENTS

With the current size of the U.S. federal debt, you might think that it has been around forever, but the outsized federal debt is actually a fairly recent phenomenon. Use the Internet to research the history of the federal debt. What triggered the periods of growth and decline? How do you think the federal debt will affect you? Do you believe it will ever go down to zero? Why or why not?

WHAT'S NEW

- Updated Exhibit 2.2, "Federal Government Revenue and Expenses"
- New box feature, "Are Bad Roads Driving You Around the Bend?"
- New box feature, "Waste Not, Want Not"
- New box feature, "The Sky Is Falling! The Sky Is Falling!"

WHAT'S INSIDE:

Key Topics in this Chapter: *U.S. business opportunities in a global market, benefits of global trade, competitive advantage, measuring the impact of international trade, exchange rates, global strategies and their risks and potential rewards, trade barriers and restrictions, advances toward free trade, careers.*

LEARNING OBJECTIVES

3-1   Discuss business opportunities in the world economy

3-2   Explain the key reasons for international trade

3-3   Describe the tools for measuring international trade

3-4   Analyze strategies for reaching global markets

3-5   Discuss barriers to international trade and strategies to surmount them

3-6   Describe the free-trade movement and discuss key benefits and criticisms

CHAPTER OUTLINE

An Unprecedented Opportunity

Key Reasons for International Trade
Competitive Advantage

Global Trade: Taking Measure
Balance of Trade
Balance of Payments
Exchange Rates
Countertrade

Seizing the Opportunity: Strategies for Reaching Global Markets
Foreign Outsourcing and Importing
Exporting
Foreign Licensing and Foreign
    Franchising
Foreign Direct Investment

Barriers to International Trade
Sociocultural Differences
Economic Differences
Political and Legal Differences

Free Trade: The Movement Gains Momentum
GATT and the World Trade
    Organization
The World Bank
The International Monetary Fund
Trading Blocs and Common Markets

4LTR ONLINE

Have students access their 4LTR Press Online account in order to...

■   Create StudyBits

■   Review key terms and create flashcards

■   Create practice quizzes from their StudyBits

■   Complete assessment content: matching, drag and drop, and fill-in-the-blank problems

■   View Chapter Highlight Boxes: videos, What Would You Do cases, key exhibits/tables

VIDEO

Brazil
Run time 2:46 minutes

Brazil is considered an emerging market; the country is going through economic development and economic reform. Imports from China have increased 60%, and Brazil, with its abundant supply of natural resources, will supply China with iron ore and other raw materials. To that end, the Açu Superport, also known as the "Highway to China," located off the coast of Rio de Janeiro, will be able to service the *Chinamax*, a vessel capable of shipping huge amounts of natural resources.

Ask Your Students:

1. Do you think the efforts of Brazil's government to keep the economy growing will be successful? Why or why not?

2. What downsides might Brazil experience by implementing quotas and tariffs?

VIDEO SEGMENT SUMMARY

Urban Farmz—Urban Farmz Goes Global

Urban Farmz "goes global" after Grandpa and Jake make a trip to Paris. There they meet a woman, Ami, who makes delectable jams and mustards for her café. She would like to export them to America. Better yet, after looking at Urban Farmz's products on its website, Ami decides she wants to import some of them to Paris as part of her business. So, not only will Urban Farmz be directly importing products, but it will also be directly exporting them. Now the business needs to jump through regulatory import-export hoops it hasn't encountered before. Grandpa explains to Caleb what they must do.

CHAPTER PREP 3

KEY TERMS

opportunity cost, 41

absolute advantage, 41

comparative advantage, 41

balance of trade, 42

trade surplus, 42

trade deficit, 42

Balance of payments, 42

balance of payments surplus, 42

balance of payments deficit, 42

exchange rates, 42

countertrade, 43

Foreign outsourcing, 43

Importing, 44

Exporting, 44

Foreign licensing, 45

Foreign franchising, 45

Direct investment, 45

Joint ventures, 45

partnership, 45

strategic alliance, 45

Sociocultural differences, 46

Infrastructure, 48

protectionism, 49

Tariffs, 49

Quotas, 49

Voluntary export restraints (VERs), 49

embargo, 49

free trade, 50

General Agreement on Tariffs and Trade (GATT), 50

World Trade Organization (WTO), 50

World Bank, 50

International Monetary Fund (IMF), 51

trading bloc, 51

common market, 51

North American Free Trade Agreement (NAFTA), 51

European Union (EU), 52

LECTURE EXAMPLE

Today's dynamic business environment has no national borders, and many of today's global brands are making use of this by looking for cheaper options for production in countries across the world. Since its inception in 1964, sporting-goods company Nike has come a long way—from being just an importer of Japanese running shoes to a global sporting-goods retailer. In fact, Nike is one of the many sporting-goods brands with production centers in the less-developed parts of the world.

Places such as Indonesia, Honduras, Vietnam, and China became attractive opportunities due to their low labor and distribution costs. With manufacturing centers in more than 50 countries, Nike takes advantage of the beneficial exchange rates and greater cost-to-profit ratios through globalization.

Source: Richard. M. Locke, "The Promise and Perils of Globalization: The Case of Nike," Massa-chusetts Institute of Technology, IPC Working Paper Series, retrieved on 03-11-13, http://web.mit.edu/ipc/publications/pdf/02-007.pdf.

DISCUSSION QUESTIONS

1. What countries represent the largest global business opportunities for the next decade? What factors determine the size of the opportunity?

2. Explain the meanings of "strong" currency and "weak" currency. What are the advantages and disadvantages of each?

3. What are the key elements of sociocultural barriers to trade? How can companies overcome these barriers?

GROUP ACTIVITIE

Separate into groups of no more than five. As a group, you have $10,000 to invest in the foreign exchange market. You will leave the market (that is, convert all your holdings to the U.S. dollar) in exactly 20 years from today. Decide which currencies you would invest in—and how much of the $10,000 you would invest in each—to maximize your long-term earnings. In a paragraph, describe what your decision—and the exercise as a whole—tells you about exchange rates as a measure of global trade.

ASSIGNMENTS

Many multinational companies market products under different brand names when conducting business overseas. For example, Unilever's Axe Body Spray is called Lynx in the United Kingdom and Australia. Research some of your favorite brands (or products that you buy on a regular basis), and list if and how they use alternate product names when conducting business in foreign markets. Then, explain why a company might use a different brand name abroad.

WHAT'S NEW

- Updated Exhibit 3.1, "Selected Population and GDP Figures"

- Updated box feature, "The World Isn't Every Company's Oyster"

- New box feature, "Santa's Workshop – Chinese Style"

- Updated box feature, "Veggie Surprise, Anyone?"

- New box feature, "Golden State or Leaden Weight?"

WHAT'S INSIDE:

Key Topics in this Chapter: Universal ethical standards, framework for ethical decision making, code of ethics, whistle-blowers, social responsibility, responsibility to stakeholders (consumers, employees, investors, community), Sarbanes-Oxley Act of 2002, corporate philanthropy, environmental responsibility, ethics in global business, social audits, careers.

CHAPTER OUTLINE

Ethics and Social Responsibility: A Close Relationship

Defining Ethics: Murkier Than You'd Think

Universal Ethical Standards: A Reasonable Goal or Wishful Thinking?

Business Ethics: Not an Oxymoron

Ethics: Multiple Touchpoints

Ethics and the Individual: The Power of One

Ethics and the Organization: It Takes a Village

Creating and Maintaining an Ethical Organization

Defining Social Responsibility: Making the World a Better Place

The Stakeholder Approach: Responsibility to Whom?

Ethics and Social Responsibility in the Global Arena: A House of Mirrors?

Monitoring Ethics and Social Responsibility: Who Is Minding the Store?

LEARNING OBJECTIVES

4-1   Define ethics and explain the concept of universal ethical standards

4-2   Describe business ethics and ethical dilemmas

4-3   Discuss how ethics relates to both the individual and the organization

4-4   Define social responsibility and examine the impact on stakeholder groups

4-5   Explain the role of social responsibility in the global arena

4-6   Describe how companies evaluate their efforts to be socially responsible

4LTR ONLINE

Have students access their 4LTR Press Online account in order to…

- Create StudyBits
- Review key terms and create flashcards
- Create practice quizzes from their StudyBits
- Complete assessment content: matching, drag and drop, and fill-in-the-blank problems
- View Chapter Highlight Boxes: videos, What Would You Do cases, key exhibits/tables

VIDEO

Zappos

Run time 7:31 minutes

Opening in 1999, online retail store Zappos deals in a wide variety of shoes and related products. Although Zappos has grown and expanded greatly from its roots in San Francisco, the company lays an emphasis on fostering social responsibility by building relationships with charities and charitable organizations. This facet of Zappos forms a significant part of what Zappos stands for as an organization. By building up their charitable giving and volunteer engagement programs, Zappos has moved on from what used to be a process of writing a few checks to random charities in the area, to cultivating long-lasting relationships with charitable organizations that see a direct involvement on the part of the employees at Zappos.

Ask Your Students:

1. Briefly explain how Zappos has implemented social responsibility programs into its business.

2. How have charitable giving and volunteer engagement programs helped Zappos foster social responsibility?

VIDEO SEGMENT SUMMARY

Urban Farmz—Greenwashing?

Caleb gets an up-close-and-personal look at greenwashing when a producer tries to pass off its products to Urban Farmz as certified organic when really they're not. "That kind of bull is going to ruin us," says Caleb, who is disgusted by the producer's lack of honesty. "Too many big corporations are using terms like *green* and *natural* to scam the public," he claims. "Corporate responsibility is real. You can't just say you're something you're not." Or can you?

CHAPTER PREP 4

KEY TERMS

ethics, 56

universal ethical standards, 57

business ethics, 58

ethical dilemma, 58

code of ethics, 62

whistle-blowers, 62

social responsibility, 62

stakeholders, 63

consumerism, 63

planned obsolescence, 65

Sarbanes-Oxley Act, 65

corporate philanthropy, 66

cause-related marketing, 66

corporate responsibility, 66

sustainable development, 67

carbon footprint, 67

green marketing, 68

social audit, 71

LECTURE EXAMPLE

Shell Petroleum Corporation, a subsidiary of the Shell Corporation in Nigeria, has faced its fair share of controversies. Despite spending millions on its CSR agenda in Nigeria, building schools and hospitals in the country, Shell's overall corporate image remains as sketchy and controversial as ever. Social activists in Nigeria often target Shell with claims of malpractice and exploitation of the local communities. While the debate rages on, the importance of social responsibility and ethical business practices becomes all the more apparent.

Source: Esther Hennchen, "A Critical Eye on Shell's CSR Practices in Nigeria." Retrieved 03-11-13, http://www.esadeknowledge.com /view/the-role-of-oil-mayors-in-supporting-sustainable-peace-and -development-in-nigeria-the-case-of-royal-dutch-shell-54840.

DISCUSSION QUESTIONS

1. Compare the role of the individual and the role of the organization in ethical decision making. How can business promote an ethical climate?

2. When might the need for social responsibility conflict with the need to maximize profits? When the needs conflict, how should a firm decide which path to pursue?

3. How can domestic companies that outsource manufacturing to foreign factories ensure that their vendors adhere to ethical standards?

GROUP ACTIVITY

Break into groups of about five students. Work with your team to develop a corporate philanthropy concept for each of the businesses listed below. Choose ideas that are likely to help the business serve the community, build employee morale, *and* build long-term profitability. Keep in mind that the best programs feature a close link between the firm's product or customers and the needs of the community. To find the most creative ideas, spend a few moments brainstorming with your teammates about each business before you finalize your plan.

- A city newspaper
- A hip-hop music label
- A computer repair service
- A local hot dog stand
- A leading brand of frozen pizza
- A national department store chain

ASSIGNMENTS

Find a small business in your community that takes social responsibility seriously. (Your local chamber of commerce can probably help you identify a candidate.) Interview the owner to learn more about the firm's programs. Did the owner actively choose how to contribute, or did he or she simply respond to opportunities that arose on an ad hoc basis? How does the firm balance the need for short-term profitability with the need for social responsibility? What other options are available for small firms to contribute to your community without undermining their bottom line?

WHAT'S NEW

- Updated section 4-2, "Business Ethics: Not an Oxymoron"
- Updated Exhibit 4.5, "Social Responsibility at Work"
- Updated section 4-4, "Defining Social Responsibility: Making the World a Better Place"
- New box feature, "Profits and Then Some"
- New box feature, "Sorry! So, So Sorry!"

WHAT'S INSIDE:

Key Topics in this Chapter: *The invisible advantage of effective communication, communication barriers, effective nonverbal communication, active listening, listening dos and don'ts, analyzing the audience, communication channels, choosing the right words, shaping the message, delivering successful verbal presentations, careers.*

LEARNING OBJECTIVES

5-1   Explain the importance of excellent business communication

5-2   Describe the key elements of nonverbal communication

5-3   Compare, contrast, and choose effective communication channels

5-4   Choose the right words for effective communication

5-5   Write more effective business memos, letters, and emails

5-6   Create and deliver successful verbal presentations

CHAPTER OUTLINE

Excellent Communication Skills: Your Invisible Advantage
Communication Barriers: "That's Not What I Meant!"

Nonverbal Communication: Beyond the Words
Active Listening: The Great Divider

Choose the Right Channel: A Rich Array of Options
Consider the Audience: It's Not about You!

Pick the Right Words: Is That Car Pre-Loved or Just Plain Used?!
Analyze Your Audience
Be Concise
Avoid Slang
Avoid Bias
Use the Active Voice Whenever Possible

Write High-Impact Messages: Breaking through the Clutter
Strike the Right Tone
Don't Make Grammar Goofs
Use Block Paragraphs
Use Headings and Bulleted Lists Wherever Appropriate

Create and Deliver Successful Verbal Presentations: Hook 'Em and Reel 'Em In!
Opening
Body
Close
Questions
Visual Aids
Google Presentations
Handling Nerves
Handling Hostility
Incorporating Humor
A Spot on the Back Wall?
Delivery

4LTR ONLINE

Have students access their 4LTR Press Online account in order to...

- Create StudyBits
- Review key terms and create flashcards
- Create practice quizzes from their StudyBits
- Complete assessment content: matching, drag and drop, and fill-in-the-blank problems
- View Chapter Highlight Boxes: videos, What Would You Do cases, key exhibits/tables

VIDEO

Plant Fantasies
Run time 7:14 minutes

Can companies really Twitter their way to profits? Is Facebook replacing face-to-face meetings? Do handwritten business letters have any place in the digital age? If New York's Plant Fantasies is any indication, reports on the death of traditional business communication have been greatly exaggerated. The urban landscaping company began in 1987 and quickly developed a reputation as the gardener of choice for New York City's top real-estate moguls. Although the company's growth occurred side-by-side with the rise of the Internet, founder Teresa Carleo has maintained a preference for traditional face-to-face meetings and phone calls.

According to Carleo, the key to effective communication is to match the right methods with the right business needs. Some tasks at Plant Fantasies focus on the labor of gardening, while other situations involve professional collaborations with landscape architects and clients. Each situation has its own requirements. In the end, good business communication is about using time wisely and making positive connections with people.

Ask Your Students:

1. Which communication channels are most common at Plant Fantasies?

2. Using the concept of channel richness, explain why leaders at Plant Fantasies place a high value on face-to-face communication.

VIDEO SEGMENT SUMMARY

Urban Farmz—One Joking Text ...

Caleb was joking on a text conversation to Sylvia about her "meddling" in their business with a customer, and Sylvia's feelings were hurt by the text. Caleb forwarded the text to Jake, who takes Sylvia's side and wants Caleb to apologize.

Caleb exclaims, "We can all joke around or whatever, but one joking text and everyone gets all intense."

CHAPTER PREP 5

KEY TERMS

communication, 74

noise, 75

communication barriers, 75

intercultural communication, 75

nonverbal communication, 76

active listening, 77

communication channels, 78

bias, 80

active voice, 81

passive voice, 81

dynamic delivery, 88

LECTURE EXAMPLE

Motorola is one of many companies that failed in the Chinese market. China has emerged as one of the most attractive markets in the world, but many multinational companies fail to replicate their global success in China. Cross-cultural communication through advertising plays an important role in defining whether a company is successful or not. In order to be "trendy," Motorola used an advertising campaign that featured models sporting Mohawks and colorful clothes. However, a vast majority of the Chinese population did not perceive the message as intended and failed to relate to the advertisement campaign. Such a basic communication failure on Motorola's part contributed to its disastrous performance in China.

Source: Shaun Rein, "Three Dumb Things Foreign Companies Do in China," retrieved 03-11-13, http://www.forbes.com/2009/12/01/china-three-mistakes-leadership-managing-marketing.html.

DISCUSSION QUESTIONS

1. What are the six main barriers to effective communication? Which barriers are easiest to surmount? Why?
2. What factors should you consider when you choose a communication channel for your messages? Should you always use the richest channel? Why or why not?
3. Why do so many people ignore or delete email messages? How can you boost the chances that your target audience will read your message?

GROUP ACTIVITY

Break into teams of roughly four so that there is an even number of students on each team. Your instructor will direct you to write down a well-known phrase, event, book, movie, or song title on a piece of scrap paper, and will then collect and redistribute your responses. When you receive a stack of responses from another team, pass one out to each member of your team, but don't look at any besides your own. As a team, you may want to review the rules of Charades, such as the common gestures for movies, songs, and books. In turn, each team member should act out the phrase he or she received without making any noises or mouthing words. The rest of the group will then guess the phrase being acted out. When all four team members have succeeded (or given up), reform as a class to discuss your findings.

ASSIGNMENTS

Choose a favorite actor, musician, businessperson, political figure, or athlete with a Twitter page. Scan through his or her Twitter feed until you have a good understanding of the types of tweets he or she makes. In a paragraph or two, analyze your celebrity's use of Twitter as a communication medium. For example, does he or she use effective language to convey messages to the audience? Do those messages tend to focus on self-promotion, general musings, or conversation? When does your celebrity post? Does that timing have an impact on how messages are received?

WHAT'S NEW

- Updated box feature, "If You See It in the News, It's Got to Be True…Psych!"
- Updated Exhibit 5.2, "Communication Channels"
- Updated box feature, "Oops! Flushthatjobdownthetoilet"
- New box feature, "Mind Your Digital Manners! Not as Easy as You Might Think"

WHAT'S INSIDE:

Key Topics in this Chapter: *Sole proprietorships, general partnerships, corporations, limited liability companies, stockholders, S corporations, statutory close corporations, nonprofit corporations, mergers and acquisitions, forming and managing an LLC, franchising, careers.*

CHAPTER OUTLINE

Business Ownership Options: The Big Four

Advantages and Disadvantages of Sole Proprietorships
Advantages
Disadvantages

Partnerships: Two Heads (and Bankrolls) Can Be Better than One
Formation of General Partnerships
Advantages of General Partnerships
Disadvantages of General Partnerships
Limited Partnerships
Limited Liability Partnerships

Corporations: The Advantages and Disadvantages of Being an Artificial Person
Forming a C Corporation
Ownership of C Corporations
The Role of the Board of Directors
Advantages of C Corporations
Disadvantages of C Corporations
Other Types of Corporations: Same but Different
Corporate Restructuring

The Limited Liability Company: The New Kid on the Block
Forming and Managing an LLC
Advantages of LLCs
Limitations and Disadvantages of LLCs

Franchising: Proven Methods for a Price
Franchising in Today's Economy
Advantages of Franchising
Disadvantages of Franchising
Entering into a Franchise Agreement

LEARNING OBJECTIVES

6-1 Describe the characteristics of the four basic forms of business ownership

6-2 Discuss the advantages and disadvantages of a sole proprietorship

6-3 Evaluate the pros and cons of the partnership as a form of business ownership

6-4 Explain why corporations have become the dominant form of business ownership

6-5 Explain why limited liability companies are becoming an increasingly popular form of business ownership

6-6 Evaluate the advantages and disadvantages of franchising

4LTR ONLINE

Have students access their 4LTR Press Online account in order to…

- Create StudyBits
- Review key terms and create flashcards
- Create practice quizzes from their StudyBits
- Complete assessment content: matching, drag and drop, and fill-in-the-blank problems
- View Chapter Highlight Boxes: videos, What Would You Do cases, key exhibits/tables

VIDEO

Two Men and a Truck—Franchising
Run time 6:15 minutes

Two Men and a Truck has a franchise-based business plan. The plan allows franchisees to create their own benchmarks, which provide a continual assessment of the franchisees' performance and direction. The challenges in setting up a successful franchise include finding the right office space in an optimal geographic location. Franchising, as opposed to the running of tight-knit family businesses, allows for a higher level of brand recognition, which translates into more customers utilizing the service provided. Franchising does come with its cons, however. Although there is an entrepreneurial angle to the way business is conducted in a franchise, it still falls under an overall system that is bound by its own rules and regulations.

Ask Your Students:

1. Briefly explain the challenges faced by franchisees of Two Men and a Truck when setting up a new operation.

2. What advantages do franchisees of Two Men and a Truck have over people setting up an independent business?

VIDEO SEGMENT SUMMARY

Urban Farmz—Just Like Before, But Now with Tax Breaks!

Sylvie sits down with Jake. The good news is that Urban Farmz is making money. However, Sylvie now thinks the business needs to be restructured. Currently it's a limited liability company, but an S corporation would be better. The question is whether Caleb will be on board with the change. Sylvie and Jake know he is reluctant to let Urban Farmz get "too corporate." Surprisingly, they discover that Caleb supports the plan. He has been researching corporate ownership structures and agrees that an S corporation would be better than a C corporation. "[We can] avoid all that double taxation stuff with the C corp. No personal liability, just like before, but now with tax breaks," he exclaims. "Cool!"

LECTURE EXAMPLE

Starting a new firm isn't as daunting as it seems. Today's business world is filled with entrepreneurial success stories, and new businesses have the option of choosing from several business models. Start-ups can use different entry methods, such as sole proprietorships, partnerships, and franchises.

Franchising has become synonymous with the fast-food industry, and some of the world's biggest retail chains such as KFC and Subway are increasingly using the system to expand both domestically and internationally. Franchising has become a popular option because franchisors do not have to use their own resources, and it provides instant brand recognition for the franchisee.

Source: Jeff Haden, "The Best Way to Start a Small Business," Money-watch, retrieved 03-11-13; Ilan Alon, "Service Franchising: A Global Perspective," retrieved 03-11-13, http://www.cbsnews.com/8301 -505143_162-57336572/the-best-way-to-start-a-small-business/; http://books.google.co.in/books?hl=en&lr=&id=tyeA7U8m11UC& oi=fnd&pg=PP8&dq=franchising+scholarly+articles+subway&ots=No AdZyyUKK&sig=1n9u0crF2s4lZbLtqX4tEAJRtVg#v=onepage&q&f=false.

CHAPTER PREP 6

KEY TERMS

sole proprietorship, 90

partnership, 90

general partnership, 91

corporation, 91

articles of incorporation, 91

limited liability, 91

limited liability company (LLC), 91

limited partnership, 95

limited liability partnership (LLP), 95

C corporation, 96

corporate bylaws, 97

stockholder, 97

Institutional investors, 97

board of directors, 98

S corporations, 100

Statutory Close (or Closed) Corporation, 100

nonprofit corporations, 100

horizontal merger, 101

vertical merger, 101

conglomerate merger, 101

acquisition, 101

merger, 101

divestiture, 101

franchise, 104

franchisor, 104

franchisee, 104

distributorships, 104

business format franchises, 104

franchise agreement, 106

Franchise Disclosure Document (FDD), 108

DISCUSSION QUESTIONS

1. How do limited partnerships and limited liability partnerships differ from general partnerships and from each other?

2. What advantages help explain why virtually all large companies are organized as C corporations?

3. What is a Franchise Disclosure Document (FDD), and why is it important?

GROUP ACTIVITY

As homework, ask your students to research the costs and benefits of becoming a franchisee for a specific franchise. (Basic information on costs and benefits is usually available at the franchise websites and also at websites such as Entrepreneur.com.) Students should come to class prepared to discuss the following questions:

1. From the student's perspective, what do they like about the franchise? Has the franchise been "in the news" for any reason (good or bad) recently?

2. What is the franchise fee for the franchise? What other start-up costs would a franchisee incur? What are the royalties and other ongoing fees that franchisees must pay?

3. Does the franchisor offer any help with financing? If so, what type?

4. What types of training and support does the franchisor offer?

Divide the class into small groups of three to five students. Have students in each group discuss the franchises they have researched, and select the one they view as the best investment opportunity. Each group should provide a brief oral report giving the reasons for its recommendation.

ASSIGNMENTS

It might surprise you to know that limited partnerships can be formed by families as well as companies. Use the Internet to find out how to set up a family limited partnership. Who would be the general partners and who would be the limited partners—and why? What advantages would this type of arrangement have for the family? What has the IRS said about family limited partnerships?

WHAT'S NEW

- New box feature, "When It Comes to Boards, Bigger Isn't Always Better"

- Updated Exhibit 6.3, "Stock Ownership in Selected Major U.S. Corporations"

- New box feature, "Merger Makes for Unwelcome Competition"

- Updated Exhibit 6.6, "Types of Mergers and Acquisitions"

- Updated section 6-6a, "Franchising in Today's Economy"

- Updated Exhibit 6.7, "Franchisee Costs for Selected Franchises"

- New box feature, "Wendy's Restaurants Sued by 152-Store Franchisee"

WHAT'S INSIDE:

Key Topics in this Chapter:

Entrepreneurs, advantages of business ownership, common entrepreneurial characteristics, funding options, opportunities versus threats, pros and cons of various launch options, tools for business success, SBA, economic impact of small business, global entrepreneurship, careers.

CHAPTER OUTLINE

Launching a New Venture: What's in It for Me?
Greater Financial Success
Independence
Flexibility
Challenge
Survival

The Entrepreneur: A Distinctive Profile
The Entrepreneurial Mindset: A Matter of Attitude
Entrepreneurial Characteristics

Finding the Money: Funding Options for Small Businesses
Personal Resources
Loans
Crowdfunding
Angel Investors
Venture Capital

Opportunities and Threats for Small Business: A Two-Sided Coin
Small Business Opportunities
Small Business Threats

Launch Options: Reviewing the Pros and Cons
Making It Happen: Tools for Business Success

Small Business and the Economy: An Outsized Impact
Entrepreneurship Around the World

LEARNING OBJECTIVES

7-1   Explain the key reasons to launch a small business

7-2   Describe the typical entrepreneurial mindset and characteristics

7-3   Discuss funding options for small business

7-4   Analyze the opportunities and threats that small businesses face

7-5   Discuss ways to become a new business owner and tools to facilitate success

7-6   Explain the size, scope, and economic contributions of small business

4LTR ONLINE

Have students access their 4LTR Press Online account in order to…

- Create StudyBits
- Review key terms and create flashcards
- Create practice quizzes from their StudyBits
- Complete assessment content: matching, drag and drop, and fill-in-the-blank problems
- View Chapter Highlight Boxes: videos, What Would You Do cases, key exhibits/tables

VIDEO

The Entrepreneurial Life: KlipTech
Run time 6:25 minutes

Washington-based entrepreneur Joel Klippert founded KlipTech when he stumbled upon what he thought was a revolutionary concept in the sustainable building products industry. Joel first created building material for skateboard ramps, and then moved on to making counter tops and building claddings out of the very same material. Joel explains that getting the company to this stage was not an easy feat, and that he was laughed at and turned away by many financial institutions that simply did not believe his business plan was viable. However, Joel recognized that if he was not able to be the leader in an already established market, then the next best step to take was to create a market

for himself—in this case, using sustainable and reusable material to create his product.

Ask Your Students:

1. What are the main challenges faced by entrepreneurs like Joel Klippert who are looking to establish a start-up?

2. What, according to Joel, are the advantages of carving out a market segment as opposed to competing with other firms or organizations in an established market?

VIDEO SEGMENT SUMMARY

Urban Farmz—Just Me and My Cousin Jake

Urban Farmz may be structured as an S corporation for tax purposes, but at its heart, it is still a small business started by a couple of entrepreneurs. "Everyone is just sort of a freelancer," Caleb says about the Urban Farmz team when a writer from *Growing Green* magazine contacts him to do a story about it. "We can't really do salaries," he says. However, even though Urban Farmz is a local company, it is on the Web and can sell everywhere. "And no, Urban Farmz doesn't have any franchises yet," Caleb tells the writer. "Its advertising budget is also limited at this point—mostly just word of mouth."

CHAPTER PREP 7

KEY TERMS

entrepreneurs, 111

internal locus of control, 113

external locus of control, 113

Angel investors, 116

Venture capital firms, 116

market niches, 117

Small Business Administration (SBA), 119

Small Business Development Centers (SBDCs), 120

SCORE (Service Corps of Retired Executives), 120

business plan, 121

LECTURE EXAMPLE

A start-up need not necessarily be a traditional company or in fact a company at all. It can be something as simple and innovative as a stress-busting, plate-smashing center. The Venting Place, a Tokyo-based start-up, provides frustrated people the opportunity to smash crockery against the wall in order to relieve stress. Surprisingly, or not so surprisingly, The Venting Place attracts countless visitors on a daily basis. This start-up is a prime example of an entrepreneur taking advantage of people's basic needs. Entrepreneurship is essentially about taking an idea and implementing it on a sustainable scale rather than overreaching beyond necessary or sustainable means.

Source: Danielle Demetriou, "Stressed Japanese workers smash plates to ease recession blues," The Telegraph, retrieved 03-11-13, http://www.telegraph.co.uk/news/newstopics/howaboutthat/3909595/Stressed-Japanese-workers-smash-plates-to-ease-recession-blues.html.

DISCUSSION QUESTIONS

1. Review the benefits an entrepreneur might seek in starting a new business. Which benefits are most appealing to you? Why?

2. Review the definition of niche marketer, and cite three examples of niche marketers. How has technology affected niche marketing?

3. What are the key contributions of small business to the U.S. economy? Rank the benefits in terms of importance, and provide the reasons for your ranking.

GROUP ACTIVITY

Take a moment to write down three to five things that you find frustrating about daily life on a fairly regular basis. Be honest, and use real problems. Then break into groups of three to five students and exchange papers. Take about three minutes to choose one problem on the list that you received, and to develop a product or service idea that could solve that problem. Then, together with your team, review each person's idea, and choose the one with the most potential. Working together, further develop the idea into a business concept. Create a logo and a slogan for your business, and present your idea to the class, along with the problem that your business will solve.

ASSIGNMENTS

Identify a person in your neighborhood who started a business from scratch, a person who bought an existing business, and a person who bought a franchise (your local chamber of commerce can probably help you identify candidates). Interview each of the entrepreneurs to learn more about their experiences. What were the pros and cons of each approach? Would they use the same approach if they could do it over again? Why or why not? What are their long-term goals? How did the actual experiences of the entrepreneurs you interviewed compare to the material in the book? Did you hear anything surprising?

WHAT'S NEW

- Updated box feature, "Eccentric Entrepreneurs"
- New box feature, "How to Make a Million Dollars"
- New section 7-3c, "Crowdfunding"
- Updated box feature, "Nutty Market Niches"

WHAT'S INSIDE:

Key Topics in this Chapter: *The importance of accounting and key users, the accounting profession, financial accounting, GAAP, FASB, accounting ethics, balance sheets, income statements, statement of cash flows, auditor's reports, Sarbanes-Oxley Act, interpreting financial statements, managerial accounting, cost concepts, budgeting, careers.*

CHAPTER OUTLINE

Accounting: Who Needs It—and Who Does It?
Accounting: Who Uses It?
Accounting: Who Does It?

Financial Accounting: Intended for Those on the Outside Looking In
Role of the Financial Standards Accounting Board
Ethics in Accounting

Financial Statements: Read All about Us
The Balance Sheet: What We Own and How We Got It
The Income Statement: So, How Did We Do?
The Statement of Cash Flows: Show Me the Money
Other Statements: What Happened to the Owners' Stake?

Interpreting Financial Statements: Digging Beneath the Surface
The Independent Auditor's Report: Getting a Stamp of Approval
Checking Out the Notes to Financial Statements: What's in the Fine Print?
Looking for Trends in Comparative Statements

Budgeting: Planning for Accountability
Preparing the Budget: Top-Down or Bottom-Up?
Developing the Key Budget Components: One Step at a Time
Being Flexible: Clearing Up Problems with Static

Inside Intelligence: The Role of Managerial Accounting
Cost Concepts: A Cost for All Reasons
Assigning Costs to Products: As (Not So) Simple as ABC?

LEARNING OBJECTIVES

8-1 Define accounting and describe how accounting information is used by a variety of stakeholders

8-2 Identify the purposes and goals of generally accepted accounting principles

8-3 Describe the key elements of the major financial statements

8-4 Describe several methods stakeholders can use to obtain useful insights from a company's financial statements

8-5 Explain how the budget process can help managers plan, motivate, and evaluate their organization's performance

8-6 Explain the role of managerial accounting and describe the various cost concepts identified by managerial accountants

4LTR ONLINE

Have students access their 4LTR Press Online account in order to…

- Create StudyBits
- Review key terms and create flashcards
- Create practice quizzes from their StudyBits
- Complete assessment content: matching, drag and drop, and fill-in-the-blank problems
- View Chapter Highlight Boxes: videos, What Would You Do cases, key exhibits/tables

VIDEO

B2B CFO—Financial Statements
Run time: 7:00 minutes

B2B CFO is a firm that provides CFO services to small and medium-sized businesses that cannot yet afford to hire a full-time CFO. With over 20 years of experience, B2B CFO helps business owners keep track of their finances. The company did just that with Hosco Finishing System Components, a firm that recently broke away from its parent company, and has repositioned itself with Tom Murray and his partners at the helm. Sheri Pawlik, on behalf of B2B CFO, helps Tom Murray and Hosco to take care of the cash and profit calculations, and to identify the causes that drive profitability, which allows Hosco to pinpoint the areas the company needs to focus on to help maximize profits.

Ask Your Students:

1. What are the advantages of hiring a temporary CFO for small and medium-sized businesses?
2. How does B2B CFO help companies like Hosco get capital from financial institutions in order to survive?

VIDEO SEGMENT SUMMARY

Urban Farmz—I'm Not Cut Out for This Kind of "Number Crunching"

Sylvie asks her friend, Dan, a CPA, to look at Urban Farmz's accounting numbers. "The debt-to-income ratio is way off," Dan tells her after taking a look at them. "I thought you said these guys were doing well."

"They are just growing so fast that I can't control their day-to-day spending, most of which is actually necessary," Sylvie confirms.

Dan says Urban Farmz is taking too long to collect from its customers. He suggests maybe its accounts should be sent to a collections agency.

CHAPTER PREP 8

KEY TERMS

accounting, 126

financial accounting, 128

Generally Accepted Accounting Principles (GAAP), 128

Financial Accounting Standards Board (FASB), 128

balance sheet, 130

accounting equation, 130

assets, 131

liabilities, 132

owners' equity, 133

income statement, 133

Revenue, 133

accrual-basis accounting, 134

Expenses, 134

Net income, 134

statement of cash flows, 134

horizontal analysis, 139

budgeting, 139

operating budgets, 140

financial budgets, 140

master budget, 140

managerial (or management) accounting, 141

cost, 141

out-of-pocket cost, 142

implicit costs, 142

fixed costs, 142

variable costs, 143

direct cost, 143

indirect costs, 143

Activity-Based Costing (ABC), 143

LECTURE EXAMPLE

Innovation and success are generally considered to go hand in hand. However, sometimes a company's innovation is not restricted to its products or its marketing strategies. Enron is an example of an innovative and successful company that collapsed due to "innovative accounting."

While the generally accepted accounting principles (GAAP) are used by most companies, companies that manipulate the books are always around. The need for straightforward and transparent accounting has never been more important than it is in today's globalized world. The example of Enron further emphasizes the need for application of international auditing standards and restoration of investor faith in the financial markets.

Source: Elisa S. Moncarz, Raúl Moncarz, Alejandra Cabello, Benjamín Moncarz, "The Rise and Collapse of Enron: Financial Innovation, Errors and Lessons," retrieved 03-11-13, http://www.ejournal.unam.mx /rca/218/RCA21802.pdf.

DISCUSSION QUESTIONS

1. State the "accounting equation" and define each of its terms. What is the logic behind this equation? How is the structure of the balance sheet related to this equation?

2. Describe the three basic categories of cash flows reported by a statement of cash flows and give examples of specific cash flows included in each category.

3. What is the purpose of budgeting? What is the master budget, and what are its major components? How does a top-down budgeting process differ from a bottom-up approach, and what are the advantages and disadvantages of each?

GROUP ACTIVITY

Pick out several publicly traded corporations, taking care to include some that you know are doing very well financially and others that are struggling. Print out the most recent comparative financial statements for each company. (Links to these statements are available on most financial websites.) Break the class into small groups and give each group the financial statements for one of the corporations. Tell the group to work together to find out what has happened over the past two years to the firm's total liabilities and stockholder's equity, revenues, expenses, net income, and cash position, and discuss what these figures tell them about the company's financial performance. Have each team report its findings to the class, and let the class interpret the results.

ASSIGNMENTS

The past several years have seen a number of significant accounting scandals uncovered across the business world, in companies ranging from tech companies like Hewlett-Packard and Groupon, to snack companies like Diamond Foods, and camera and medical equipment maker Olympus. Research online news sites to find a recent accounting scandal, and using concepts and terms from this chapter, describe the violations committed by the company.

WHAT'S NEW

- New box feature, "Foreign Tax Havens for Multinationals"
- Updated Exhibit 8.3, "McDonald's Statement of Cash Flows"
- Updated section 8-3c, "The Statement of Cash Flows: Show Me the Money"
- Updated box feature, "Beyond the Numbers: Why You Should Read the Annual Report"

WHAT'S INSIDE:

Key Topics in this Chapter: *Determining what motivates financial decisions, shareholder value, risk and return, evaluating and planning financial needs, ratio analysis, budgeted financial statements and cash budget, short-term financing, long-term funds, pros and cons of debt financing and equity financing, financial leverage, managing cash, managing accounts receivable, managing inventories, capital budgeting, time value of money, careers.*

LEARNING OBJECTIVES

9-1 Identify the goal of financial management and explain the issues financial managers confront as they seek to achieve this goal

9-2 Describe the tools financial managers use to evaluate their company's current financial condition and then develop financial plans

9-3 Evaluate the major sources of funds available to meet a firm's short-term and long-term financial needs

9-4 Identify the key issues involved in determining a firm's capital structure

9-5 Describe how financial managers acquire and manage current assets

9-6 Explain how financial managers evaluate capital budgeting proposals to identify the best long-term investment options for their company

CHAPTER OUTLINE

What Motivates Financial Decisions?
Shareholder Value and Social
   Responsibility: Does Good
   Behavior Pay Off?
Risk and Return: A Fundamental
   Tradeoff in Financial Management

**Identifying Financial Needs:
Evaluation and Planning**
Using Ratio Analysis to Identify Current
   Strengths and Weaknesses
Planning Tools: Creating a Road Map
   to the Future
Basic Planning Tools: Budgeted
   Financial Statements and the Cash
   Budget

Finding Funds: What Are the Options?
Sources of Short-Term Financing:
   Meeting Needs for Cash
Sources of Long-Term Funds:
   Providing a Strong Financial Base

**Leverage and Capital Structure:
How Much Debt Is Too Much Debt?**
Pros and Cons of Debt Financing
Pros and Cons of Equity Financing
Financial Leverage: Using Debt to
   Magnify Gains (and Losses)

**Acquiring and Managing Current
Assets**
Managing Cash: Is It Possible to Have
   Too Much Money?
Managing Accounts Receivable: Pay
   Me Now or Pay Me Later
Managing Inventories: Taking Stock of
   the Situation

4LTR ONLINE

Have students access their 4LTR Press Online account in order to…

- Create StudyBits
- Review key terms and create flashcards
- Create practice quizzes from their StudyBits
- Complete assessment content: matching, drag and drop, and fill-in-the-blank problems
- View Chapter Highlight Boxes: videos, What Would You Do cases, key exhibits/tables

VIDEO

Moonworks and the Bank of Rhode Island
Run time: 6:40 minutes

Moonworks is a home-improvement products business established in 2008. The company relies on funding from the Bank of Rhode Island, a community bank with $1.6 billion in assets. The bank initially examined Moonworks' management techniques and business plans in order to ensure that it would be repaid on time, regardless of the economic environment. With a guarantee from Jim Moon, the president and founder of Moonworks, the Bank of Rhode Island was able to justify the grant of the initial loan. By building a healthy relationship with the Bank of Rhode Island over the years, Moonworks was able to expand its business, and it is

currently one of the fastest-growing start-ups in America.

Ask Your Students:

1. What aspects do financial institutions like the Bank of Rhode Island assess before granting funding to businesses?

2. What options are available to start-ups like Moonworks in order to obtain funding grants?

VIDEO SEGMENT SUMMARY

Urban Farmz—It's Just Part of Being in Business

Dan, who has been brought on as Urban Farmz's new chief financial officer, asks Jake and Caleb what kind of access the business has to credit. "We have some low-interest credit cards and accounts with some of our vendors, but frankly, I'm a little freaked that we're getting in too deep [in debt]," Jake tells him. "Every company finances its growth with debt. It's just a part of being in business," Dan explains to him and Caleb. "A 10-year loan to pay for capital improvements the company desperately needs and a line of credit to meet its short-term cash flow requirements would be cheaper than using a credit card," he says. Caleb wonders if the debt will ruin his and Jake's credit.

Capital Budgeting: In It for the Long Haul
Evaluating Capital Budgeting Proposals
Accounting for the Time Value of Money
The Risk-Return Tradeoff Revisited
Net Present Value: A Decision Rule for
   Capital Budgeting

CHAPTER PREP 9

KEY TERMS

Financial capital, 146

finance, 147

risk, 148

risk-return tradeoff, 148

financial ratio analysis, 149

liquid asset, 149

liquidity ratios, 149

Asset management ratios, 149

financial leverage, 150

leverage ratios, 150

profitability ratios, 150

budgeted income statement, 151

budgeted balance sheet, 151

cash budget, 152

trade credit, 153

spontaneous financing, 154

factor, 154

line of credit, 154

revolving credit agreement, 154

commercial paper, 155

retained earnings, 155

covenant, 156

equity financing, 156

debt financing, 156

capital structure, 156

Dodd-Frank Act, 160

cash equivalents, 160

U.S. Treasury bills, or (T-bills), 160

money market mutual funds, 161

Capital budgeting, 162

time value of money, 163

certificate of deposit (CD), 163

present value, 163

net present value (NPV), 164

LECTURE EXAMPLE

Traditionally, maximizing shareholder value is the aim of most companies. However, this might not always be feasible, and it isn't as simple as it sounds. Companies are not legally required to maximize shareholder value. In an article by Antony Page and Robert Katz, the myth of such a duty has been debunked. In pursuit of profit, some CEOs will concentrate on maximizing profits and pay less attention to ethical and social responsibilities. These days, however, many leaders are shifting their focus from maximizing shareholder via profits to maximizing shared value, which balances profits with social responsibility.

Source: Mark Kramer, "What's Wrong with Maximizing Shareholder Value," Guardian Sustainable Business Blog, retrieved 03-11-13, http://www.guardian.co.uk/sustainable-business/blog/maximising-shareholder-value-irony.

DISCUSSION QUESTIONS

1. What are the key questions financial planning must answer? What role does the budgeted income statement and budgeted balance sheet play in finding answers to these questions?

2. Name and describe four commonly used sources of short-term financing.

3. Is it possible for a firm to have too much money? Explain. What role do cash equivalents play in a financial manager's strategy to manage cash balances?

GROUP ACTIVITY

Divide the class into small groups and ask them to do research on four or five different financial instruments in which companies can invest with their cash on hand. These might include savings accounts, CDs, mutual funds, stocks, bonds, and such. Ask the students to prepare a brief report on the investments they have chosen with a specific focus on the risk-return tradeoff. The groups should identify which investment has the most and least risk, and which investment has the most and least return. They should also discuss what type of company a certain investment is most appropriate for, due to the risk-return balance.

ASSIGNMENTS

Suppose that soon after earning your bachelor's degree you are accepted into an MBA program at a prestigious university. It is an intensive program that would require you to be a full-time student for about 18 months. What are the major financial costs and benefits of enrolling in this program? [Hint: Be sure to consider not just the out-of-pocket costs, but also any other financial sacrifices you might have to make if you become a full-time student.] Describe how you could evaluate whether enrolling in this program is a good financial decision. [Hint: Keep in mind that the benefits of your education will be in the form of higher cash flows over your entire career.]

WHAT'S NEW

- Updated section 9-2, "Identifying Financial Needs: Evaluation and Planning"

- Updated box feature "Just Because They Can, Doesn't Mean They Should"

- New box feature, "Decisions, Decisions – How Airlines Are Spending Their Cash from Fuel Savings"

WHAT'S INSIDE:

Key Topics in this Chapter: *Types of financial markets, regulation of financial markets, common stock, preferred stock, bonds, primary securities markets, secondary securities markets, tips for personal investing, mutual funds, tracking investment performance, stock indices, interpreting stock quotes on financial websites, careers.*

CHAPTER OUTLINE

The Role of Financial Markets and Their Key Players
Depository Institutions
Nondepository Financial Institutions

Regulating Financial Markets to Protect Investors and Improve Stability
Financial Regulations: Early Efforts
Deregulation during the 1980s and 1990s: Temporarily Reversing Course
Recent Developments: Reregulation in the Aftermath of Financial Turmoil

Investing in Financial Securities: What Are the Options?
Common Stock: Back to Basics
Preferred Stock: Getting Preferential Treatment
Bonds: Earning Your Interest
Convertible Securities: The Big Switch
Exchange Traded Funds: Real Basket Cases (and We Mean That in a Good Way)

Issuing and Trading Securities: The Primary and Secondary Markets
The Primary Securities Market: Where Securities Are Issued
Secondary Securities Markets: Let's Make a Deal

Personal Investing
Choosing a Broker: Gaining Access to the Markets
Buying Securities: Let's Make a Deal
Strategies for Investing in Securities

Keeping Tabs on the Market
Stock Indices: Tracking the Trends
Tracking the Performance of Specific Securities

LEARNING OBJECTIVES

10-1 Explain the role of financial markets in the U.S. economy and identify the key players in these markets

10-2 Identify the key laws that govern the way financial markets operate and explain the impact of each law

10-3 Describe and compare the major types of securities that are traded in securities markets

10-4 Explain how securities are issued in the primary market and traded on secondary markets

10-5 Compare several strategies that investors use to invest in securities

10-6 Interpret the information provided in the stock quotes available on financial websites

4LTR ONLINE

Have students access their 4LTR Press Online account in order to…

- Create StudyBits
- Review key terms and create flashcards
- Create practice quizzes from their StudyBits
- Complete assessment content: matching, drag and drop, and fill-in-the-blank problems
- View Chapter Highlight Boxes: videos, What Would You Do cases, key exhibits/tables

VIDEO

Morgan Stanley
Run time: 10:23 minutes

Since its founding in 1935, Morgan Stanley has been a leader in investment management. The company provides a wide range of financial services for individuals as well as institutional investors. Morgan Stanley investment advisors educate clients at all stages of life in the benefits and risks of investing in mutual funds, stocks, and bonds. Working with clients, they help determine investment strategies based on goals and objectives, the time horizon for investing, and risk tolerance. In this video, a Morgan Stanley financial advisor discusses personal investing.

Source: www.morganstanley.com

Ask Your Students:

1. How has Morgan Stanley adapted to the changing climate in the securities industry?

2. Discuss the impact of changes in securities industry regulations and how they affect the competitive environment.

VIDEO SEGMENT SUMMARY

Urban Farmz—We Paid $300…for Nothing!

Jake is ready to "Occupy Wall Street," so to speak. He has had it with Urban Farmz's bank after being stuck on the phone on hold again, waiting for customer service. "I'm so fed up with this bank," he rants to Caleb. "Just this month alone, we've paid—get this—$300 in fees for nothing. We've given them all of our business. We pay our bills on time. No overdrafts. I don't get it."

CHAPTER PREP 10

KEY TERMS

Financial markets, 166

Depository institutions, 167

Credit unions, 167

Savings and loan association, 168

Securities broker, 169

Securities dealer, 169

Investment bank, 169

Federal Reserve Act of 1913, 169

Banking Act of 1933, 169

Securities Act of 1933, 170

Securities Exchange Act of 1934, 170

Securities and Exchange Commission, 170

Financial Services Modernization Act of 1999, 170

common stock, 171

capital gain, 171

preferred stock, 172

bond, 172

maturity date, 172

par value (of a bond), 172

coupon rate, 172

current yield, 172

convertible securities, 173

Financial diversification, 174

mutual fund, 174

net asset value per share, 174

exchange-traded fund (ETF), 175

primary securities market, 176

secondary securities market, 176

public offering, 176

private placement, 176

initial public offering (IPO), 176

underwriting, 176

registration statement, 176

accredited investor, 177

stock (or securities) exchange, 177

market maker, 177

over-the-counter (OTC) market, 178

electronic communications networks (ECNs), 178

Market order, 179

Limit order, 179

stock index, 181

Dow Jones Industrial Average (DJIA), 181

Standard & Poor's (S & P) 500, 182

LECTURE EXAMPLE

Common stock is perhaps the most traded form of ownership in the world, and a person can buy shares in any company listed in the stock market. Due to several global scandals in recent years, investor confidence has waned, and people are increasingly wary of investing in banks, financial institutions, and global stock markets. While commercial banks have traditionally been viewed as good investment options, other options such as mutual funds, stock market investments, and bonds are available to long-term investors as well.

Source: Stacy Curtin, "Why Investors Shouldn't Lose Faith in Stocks: Motley Fool Co-Founders," retrieved 03-11-13, http://finance.yahoo.com/blogs/daily-ticker/why-investors-shouldn-t-lose-faith-stocks-motley-132309326.html.

DISCUSSION QUESTIONS

1. Describe the basic rights of common stockholders. What are the key differences between common and preferred stock?

2. What is the key difference between the primary and secondary securities markets? Why are the trades that occur on the secondary market important to a firm's management?

3. What is a mutual fund? How does a closed-end mutual fund differ from an open-end fund? Why do such funds appeal to investors?

GROUP ACTIVITY

Divide your class into groups of four to five students. Tell them that they have been given $100,000 from a rich aunt, but with one condition—they must first invest the money in the stock market for three months before they can spend one penny. Ask each group, then, to spend some time researching which stocks they will buy with their money. They can buy shares of one company, or several, but they must spend the entire $100,000.

Over the next few weeks have students periodically check the price, volume, and market capitalization of their stocks and update the performance in class. At the end of the time period, ask your students to compute the percentage capital gain (or loss) that each group earned or lost with their initial investment.

ASSIGNMENTS

Use the Internet to investigate a career in investment banking. [Hint: Good starting places are websites such as The Princeton Review Career Profile, and Career Overview.com.] What education would you need? What are this career's potential risks and rewards? Is this a career that appeals to you? Why or why not?

WHAT'S NEW

- Updated section 10-1a, "Depository Institutions"
- New box feature, "Are Stock Buy Backs Good for Companies?"
- Updated box feature, "Index Funds Certainly Aren't Average"
- New box feature, "Just Because They Can, Doesn't Mean They Should"
- Update Exhibit 10.3, "Yahoo! Finance Quote for a Stock"

WHAT'S INSIDE:

Key Topics in this Chapter: *Marketing objectives, process, scope, marketing utilities, marketing strategies and tactics, four U.S. marketing eras, CRM, value, customer satisfaction and loyalty, marketing plans, market segmentation, target markets, B2C versus B2B, marketing mix, global considerations, marketing environment, consumer behavior, marketing research, social responsibility, marketing technology, careers.*

CHAPTER OUTLINE

Marketing: Getting Value by Giving Value
The Scope of Marketing: It's Everywhere!
The Evolution of Marketing: From the Product to the Customer

The Customer: Front and Center
Customer Relationship Management (CRM)
Perceived Value versus Actual Value
Customer Satisfaction
Customer Loyalty

Marketing Strategy: Where Are You Going, and How Will You Get There?
Target Market
Consumer Markets versus Business Markets
Consumer Market Segmentation
Business Market Segmentation
The Marketing Mix
The Global Marketing Mix
The Marketing Environment
The Global Marketing Environment

Customer Behavior: Decisions, Decisions, Decisions!
Consumer Behavior
Business Buyer Behavior

Marketing Research: So What Do They Really Think?
Types of Data
Primary Research Tools
An International Perspective

Social Responsibility and Technology: A Major Marketing Shift
Marketing and Society: It's Not Just about You!
Technology and Marketing: Power to the People!

LEARNING OBJECTIVES

11-1 Discuss the objectives, the process, and the scope of marketing
11-2 Identify the role of the customer in marketing
11-3 Explain each element of marketing strategy
11-4 Describe the consumer and business decision-making process
11-5 Discuss the key elements of marketing research
11-6 Explain the roles of social responsibility and technology in marketing

4LTR ONLINE

Have students access their 4LTR Press Online account in order to…

- Create StudyBits
- Review key terms and create flashcards
- Create practice quizzes from their StudyBits
- Complete assessment content: matching, drag, and drop and fill-in-the-blank problems
- View Chapter Highlight Boxes: videos, What Would You Do cases, key exhibits/tables

VIDEO
The Nederlander Organization
Run time: 8:09 minutes

The Nederlander Organization is a theater management firm that deals with Broadway-type shows in the U.S. and the U.K. The company owns theater establishments and concert venues, and promotes shows across the countries. With its "Audience Rewards" program, Nederlander aims to bring value-added services to customers by providing them a viable alternative to a traditional discount. The program not only provides incentives to theater-goers to revisit these shows, but also provides Nederlander with an umbrella under which it can market multiple shows and events.

The "Audience Rewards" program also provides room for partnership with other large firms and organizations that are looking to gain access to Nederlander's customer demographic.

Ask Your Students:

1. Briefly explain the "Value-Added Services" system the Nederlander Organization provides to its customers.
2. How has the Nederlander Organization incorporated innovation in its marketing strategy?

VIDEO SEGMENT SUMMARY
Urban Farmz—We Can't Make This Stuff Grow!

Value Mart has dropped Urban Farmz as one of its suppliers because it couldn't meet the company's minimum order. Instead, Value Mart is contracting with a national supplier that gives it a yearly price and quantity guarantee. Caleb is furious.

Sue, the supplier Urban Farmz has hired, tries to put things into perspective for Caleb. "Value Mart was never meant to be our customer," she tells him. "If you try to please too many people, you fail everyone."

CHAPTER PREP 11

KEY TERMS

marketing, 186

utility, 186

marketing concept, 189

Customer relationship management (CRM), 190

value, 190

customer satisfaction, 190

Customer loyalty, 191

marketing plan, 191

market segmentation, 191

target market, 191

consumer marketers (also known as business-to-consumer or B2C), 192

business marketers (also known as business-to-business or B2B), 192

demographic segmentation, 192

geographic segmentation, 192

psychographic segmentation, 192

behavioral segmentation, 193

marketing mix, 193

environmental scanning, 196

market share, 196

consumer behavior, 197

cognitive dissonance, 198

business buyer behavior, 198

marketing research, 198

secondary data, 198

primary data, 198

Observation research, 199

Survey research, 200

green marketing, 202

mass customization, 202

LECTURE EXAMPLE

Increasing the market share of a product is difficult when a large segment of the market is already using the product. For example, Mintel, a market research firm, has found that 96% of women already use moisturizers. In order to get these women to use more moisturizer, Unilever brand Vaseline has resorted to focusing on the concerns of current users. Since women often skip using lotion due to time constraints, the brand has introduced a moisturizing spray called Spray & Go. Spray & Go positions itself as a quick-and-easy solution for the skin-care needs of the time-pressed woman.

Source: Andrew Adam Newman, "Now a Little Spray Will Quickly Moisturize You," retrieved 03-11-13, http://www.nytimes.com/2013/03/08/business/media/vaseline-adds-a-body-lotion-spray-to-its-line.html?_r=0.

DISCUSSION QUESTIONS

1. What are the key categories of nontraditional marketing? Do you expect these areas to grow over the next decade? Why or why not?

2. What are the key characteristics of a high-potential target market? Is the biggest target market always the best? Why or why not?

3. What are the key differences between primary and secondary data? Compare the benefits and drawbacks of each.

GROUP ACTIVITY

Break into groups of five to seven students and consider this scenario: You and your teammates are partners in the ownership of a medium-sized fast-food chain in the Midwest. You own 41 outlets, most of them in small towns. The mainstays of your menu are hamburgers and seasoned French fries, a couple of sandwiches, various chips, soft-serve ice cream, and sodas. Your most important customers are men aged 18 to 34 (they account for about 20% of your customers and about 55% of your sales), but since restaurant options are limited in most of the towns where you operate, you serve customers across a wide demographic range. Sales in the past two years have been dropping at an accelerating rate. You think the issue may be a national focus on low-carb diets—not a great fit with your local focus on sandwiches, French fries, and ice cream. Eager to rejuvenate the business, you are about to meet with your partners to discuss potential solutions.

Spend about 10 minutes brainstorming possible strategies with your team. Be sure to consider all of the possibilities, including doing nothing ("This will all blow over . . ."). Then choose your best option, and identify the potential risks and benefits (e.g., If you made changes to attract new customers, would you alienate your current core customers?). How does your solution compare to ideas from other teams? What are the ethical implications of your approach?

ASSIGNMENTS

Leaf through a handful of magazines and identify five different car ads. After examining the ads, identify the target market for each car, using as much detail as possible. What elements in each ad led to your assumptions about the target market? Which segmentation variables (demographic, geographic, psychographic, behavioral) do you think the marketers used to segment their target markets? Do you think any of the carmakers would benefit from changing their target markets? Why or why not?

WHAT'S NEW

- Updated section 11-1, "Marketing: Getting Value by Giving Value"
- Updated Exhibit 11.4, "Analyzing Promotional Strategies"
- Updated box feature, "Smartphones Are So Yesterday – Smart Fashion is Truly Tomorrow"
- Updated section 11-3f, "The Global Marketing Mix"
- Updated box feature, "If You Can't Be a Good Example, Then You'll Just Have to Serve As a Horrible Warning"
- New box feature, "Walmart and the World"

WHAT'S INSIDE:

Key Topics in this Chapter: *Definitions of products and services, product layers, consumer and business product categories, product differentiation, quality, product lines, product mix, cannibalization, branding, licensing, packaging, six stages of new product development, product life cycle, the power of promotion, integrated marketing communication, developing a strong promotional message, positioning statements, international considerations, emerging and traditional promotional tools, personal selling, developing the right promotional mix, careers.*

CHAPTER OUTLINE

Product: It's Probably More Than You Thought
Services: A Product by Any Other
    Name
Goods versus Services: A Mixed Bag
Product Layers: Peeling the Onion
Actual Product
Product Classification: It's a Bird, It's a
    Plane…

Product Differentiation and Planning: A Meaningful Difference
Product Quality
Features and Benefits
Product Lines and the Product Mix
Branding
Packaging

Innovation and the Product Life Cycle: Nuts, Bolts, and a Spark of Brilliance
Types of Innovation
The New Product Development
    Process
New Product Adoption and Diffusion
The Product Life Cycle: Maximizing
    Results over Time

Promotion: Influencing Consumer Decisions
Promotion in Chaos: Danger or
    Opportunity?
Integrated Marketing Communication:
    Consistency and Focus
Coordinating the Communication

LEARNING OBJECTIVES

12-1 Explain "product" and identify product classifications

12-2 Describe product differentiation and the key elements of product planning

12-3 Discuss innovation and the product life cycle

12-4 Analyze and explain promotion and integrated marketing communications

12-5 Discuss development of the promotional message

12-6 Discuss the promotional mix and the various promotional tools

4LTR ONLINE

Have students access their 4LTR Press Online account in order to…

- Create StudyBits
- Review key terms and create flashcards
- Create practice quizzes from their StudyBits
- Complete assessment content: matching, drag and drop, and fill-in-the-blank problems
- View Chapter Highlight Boxes: videos, What Would You Do cases, key exhibits/tables

VIDEO
Pepe's Pizzeria
Run time: 6:58 minutes

Pepe's Pizzeria has grown quickly from its beginnings in New Haven as a small bakery that used to serve pizzas on the weekends. Pepe's now gives customers a handcrafted product that stays true to the company's rustic Italian roots, the basis of its customer loyalty. Pepe's loyal customer base is both a benefit and a challenge for the company, as loyal customers are also very particular about the products and services they receive at a Pepe's establishment. By maintaining aspects that are familiar to customers, such as the restaurant's ambience and the employees' uniforms, Pepe's has successfully diversified into other locations, creating new markets and customers, while retaining loyal ones.

Ask Your Students:

1. What are the disadvantages local establishments like Pepe's Pizzeria face when expanding into different areas?

2. How has Pepe's Pizzeria helped its loyal customers retain their sense of belonging with the brand, even after diversifying to different locations?

VIDEO SEGMENT SUMMARY
Urban Farmz—I Believe the Term Is Co-branding

Urban Farmz needs an integrated marketing communications plan, one that reaches its customers on the Web as well as its retail, restaurant, and grocery customers. Grandpa thinks such a plan could get too expensive. "How are you going to reach all of those people? I'm not sure you boys should be spending all that on advertising," he tells Caleb and Jake.

Sylvie assures Grandpa that reaching all of Urban Farmz's customers is possible using the right promotion mix. She asks Sue and Caleb to explain to Grandpa how the integrated marketing plan the two of them have developed will work.

A Meaningful Message: Finding the Big Idea
An International Perspective

The Promotional Mix: Communicating the Big Idea
Emerging Promotional Tools:
    The Leading Edge

Traditional Promotional Tools:
    A Marketing Mainstay
Choosing the Right Promotional Mix:
    Not Just a Science

CHAPTER PREP 12

KEY TERMS

product, 204

pure goods, 206

pure services, 206

Consumer products, 206

business products, 207

product differentiation, 207

quality level, 208

product consistency, 208

product features, 209

customer benefit, 209

product line, 209

product mix, 209

cannibalization, 209

brand, 210

brand equity, 210

line extensions, 210

brand extensions, 210

licensing, 210

cobranding, 211

national brands, 211

store brands, 211

product life cycle, 214

promotion, 216

integrated marketing communication, 216

positioning statement, 217

promotional channels, 218

product placement, 219

advergaming, 220

buzz marketing, 221

sponsorships, 222

advertising, 222

Sales promotion, 223

consumer promotion, 223

trade promotion, 225

public relations (PR), 226

publicity, 226

personal selling, 226

push strategy, 228

pull strategy, 228

LECTURE EXAMPLE

In February 2012, as part of its 75th anniversary, Lay's launched a nationwide social media campaign called "Do Us a Flavor." The brand invited its followers on Facebook to submit new flavor ideas for Lay's chips. The winning entry will be introduced as a new variety of Lay's chips and also fetch $1 million as prize money. The campaign garnered an enthusiastic response and received over 3.8 million entries. Initiatives such as this provide an opportunity for companies to make their consumers a part of their brand-building process. Almost all companies have now started to widely tap the benefits of social media to foster lasting relationships with their customers.

Source: Christine Champagne, "How Lay's Got Its Chips to Taste Like Chicken and Waffles," retrieved 03-11-13, http://www.fastcocreate.com/1682425/how-lays-got-its-chips-to-taste-like-chicken-and-waffles.

DISCUSSION QUESTIONS

1. Review the marketing definition of *product*. Why do you think marketers define product so broadly? How does the definition of product affect quality?

2. What are the three different levels of product innovation? Which is most common? Can a business survive long term with only continuous innovation? Why or why not?

3. How has marketing promotion evolved over the past decade? How has technology contributed to the changes?

GROUP ACTIVITY

Gather a variety of basic household and/or office items (examples: serving fork/spoon, ruler, hair brush, paper clip, etc.). Divide the class into groups of three or four students, and give one item to each group at random. Each group should develop an alternate use for their object and a "Big Idea" for how to promote the new use. Each team should then share ideas with the class and vote on the best idea.

ASSIGNMENTS

Choose a grocery store product with a bland or badly designed package. Keeping in mind that the typical shopper passes about 300 items per minute, redesign the package so that it grabs consumer attention, highlights key product features, and differentiates your product from its competitors. Draw or construct your new package, and if possible, take a photo of it with the competition. Share the results with your classmates.

WHAT'S NEW

- Updated section 12-1e, "Product Classification: It's a Bird, It's a Plane…"
- Updated Exhibit 12.2, "Product Quality Indicators"
- Updated Exhibit 12.4, "Business Week/Interbrand Top Ten Global Brands 2014"
- Updated box feature, "Wacky Warnings"

WHAT'S INSIDE:

Key Topics in this Chapter: *Distribution strategy, distribution channels, the role of distributors, retailers versus wholesalers, nonstore retailing, wholesaling options, multichannel retailing, wheel of retailing theory, supply chain management, physical distribution, modes of transportation, pricing strategy, breakeven analysis, profit margin, consumer perceptions in pricing, careers.*

CHAPTER OUTLINE

Distribution: Getting Your Product to Your Customer
The Role of Distributors: Adding Value

Wholesalers: Sorting Out the Options
Merchant Wholesalers
Agents and Brokers

Retailers: The Consumer Connection
Store Retailers
Nonstore Retailers

Physical Distribution: Planes, Trains, and Much, Much More
Transportation Decisions
Proactive Supply Chain Management

Pricing Objectives and Strategies: A High-Stakes Game
Building Profitability
Boosting Volume
Matching the Competition
Creating Prestige

Pricing in Practice: A Real-World Approach
Breakeven Analysis
Fixed Margin Pricing
Consumer Pricing Perceptions:
  The Strategic Wild Card

LEARNING OBJECTIVES

13-1 Define distribution and differentiate between channels of distribution and physical distribution

13-2 Describe the various types of wholesale distributors

13-3 Discuss strategies and trends in store and nonstore retailing

13-4 Explain the key factors in physical distribution

13-5 Outline core pricing objectives and strategies

13-6 Discuss pricing in practice, including the role of consumer perceptions

4LTR ONLINE

Have students access their 4LTR Press Online account in order to…

- Create StudyBits
- Review key terms and create flashcards
- Create practice quizzes from their StudyBits
- Complete assessment content: matching, drag and drop, and fill-in-the-blank problems
- View Chapter Highlight Boxes: videos, What Would You Do cases, key exhibits/tables

VIDEO

GaGa's Inc.
Run time: 7:30 minutes

After losing his job as a TV news anchor after 9/11, Jim King, together with his wife Michele, established GaGa's, a frozen desserts business. Jim began the business out of his own kitchen, supplying local grocery stores with the product. Jim says that GaGa's is essentially a marketing agency that gets in touch with stores and other retailers via brokers, who facilitate the process. GaGa's has avoided associating itself with major dessert manufacturers, established supermarket chains, and home shopping networks, because the shipping and handling costs involved are very high and do not guarantee returns on the firm's investment. GaGa's aims to establish itself as an umbrella brand that will, over time, have more products such as SherBetter in its portfolio.

Ask Your Students:

1. Briefly explain the role of GaGa's Inc. as a marketing agency.
2. According to GaGa's Inc., what are the disadvantages faced by similar firms looking to associate their products with already-established manufacturers and supermarket chains?

VIDEO SEGMENT SUMMARY

Urban Farmz—Potatoes, Onions, Apples…

Rick and Caleb determine that they may need to change their distribution strategy. "I'm noticing a lot of waste," Rick tells Caleb. "You're getting complaints about damage and bad produce." Perhaps a dual distribution channel might be the solution, Caleb suggests: one for the hardier vegetables and one for items more easily damaged, such as herbs. He and Rick also come up with a just-in-time inventory plan that will allow chefs in the city to purchase Urban Farmz's herbs the same day they plan to use them.

CHAPTER PREP 13

KEY TERMS

distribution strategy, 230

channel of distribution, 230

physical distribution, 230

direct channel, 230

channel intermediaries, 231

retailers, 233

wholesalers, 233

independent wholesaling businesses, 233

merchant wholesalers, 233

agents/brokers, 233

multichannel retailing, 234

wheel of retailing, 235

multilevel marketing (MLM), 236

supply chain, 237

supply chain management (SCM), 237

Logistics, 237

modes of transportation, 238

Penetration pricing, 239

everyday-low pricing (EDLP), 239

high/low pricing, 239

loss-leader pricing, 239

skimming pricing, 240

breakeven analysis, 241

profit margin, 242

odd pricing, 243

LECTURE EXAMPLE

Online retail giant Amazon is constantly innovating, finding new ways to reduce its shipping times and improve its speed of delivery of purchased products. For instance, customers already have the option of ordering a product online and collecting it later from automated lockers installed at select convenience stores in Seattle, New York, and the United Kingdom. The company has also acquired Kiva systems, a maker of automated warehouse-robots that can reduce errors and improve shipping times. Over the next few years, Amazon aims to make next-day service or same-day delivery the default shipping options on most of its products.

Source: Farhad Manjoo, "I Want It Today," retrieved 03-11-13, http://www.slate.com/articles/business/small_business/2012/07/amazon_same_day_delivery_how_the_e_commerce_giant_will_destroy_local_retail_.html.

DISCUSSION QUESTIONS

1. Explain the difference between a channel of distribution and physical distribution.
2. What is the key difference between merchant wholesalers and agents/brokers? What are the risks and benefits of each approach for producers?
3. Why is price such a difficult variable for marketers to control? What factors must they consider in setting prices?

GROUP ACTIVITY

Break into groups of three to five students. With your teammates, choose a cheap product that you all know and like. How much would the product cost if the price increased by 20%? Develop recommendations for how to improve the product to offer enough additional value to justify a 20% price increase. After about 15 minutes, reconvene as a class, and share your ideas. Look for patterns among the recommendations. Discuss the feasibility of implementation.

ASSIGNMENTS

Investigate the prices of the following products at a minimum of three distribution outlets (and don't forget the Internet):

- An MP3 player
- A cup of coffee
- A car
- A washing machine
- A hamburger
- A pair of Levi's 501 blue jeans
- A book

What patterns do you notice? Do different distribution outlets include different levels of service with the product? Do you see a relationship between the brand name and the price? Which distribution outlet represents the best value for each product? Explain your answers.

WHAT'S NEW

- New box feature, "It's a Bird… It's a Plane… It's Superwoman… Wait, No – It's a Drone!"
- New box feature, "Timing is Everything"
- New box feature, "Coca Cola: It's Everywhere You Want to Be; and Some Places You May Not Want to Be…"

WHAT'S INSIDE:

Key Topics in this Chapter: *Role of managers, management skills and levels, motivation theories and real-world practice, strategic planning, tactical planning, operational planning, contingency planning, defining a mission, SWOT analysis, creating an organizational structure and chart, modern organization models, leadership styles, control process, careers.*

CHAPTER OUTLINE

Bringing Resources to Life
Management Hierarchy: Levels of Responsibility
Management Skills: Having What It Takes to Get the Job Done

Motivation: Lighting the Fire
Theories of Motivation
Theory X and Theory Y
Motivation Today

Planning: Figuring Out Where to Go and How to Get There
Strategic Planning: Setting the Agenda

Organizing: Fitting Together the Puzzle Pieces
Key Organizing Considerations
Organization Models

Leadership: Directing and Inspiring
Leadership Style

Controlling: Making Sure It All Works

LEARNING OBJECTIVES

14-1 Discuss the role of management and its importance to organizational success

14-2 Explain key theories and current practices of motivation

14-3 Outline the categories of business planning and explain strategic planning

14-4 Discuss the organizing function of management

14-5 Explain the role of managerial leadership and the key leadership styles

14-6 Describe the management control process

4LTR ONLINE

Have students access their 4LTR Press Online account in order to…

- Create StudyBits
- Review key terms and create flashcards
- Create practice quizzes from their StudyBits
- Complete assessment content: matching, drag and drop, and fill-in-the-blank problems
- View Chapter Highlight Boxes: videos, What Would You Do cases, key exhibits/tables

VIDEO

Camp Bow Wow
Run time: 6:08 minutes

Sue is the owner of Camp Bow Wow, a premier dog daycare and dog-boarding firm in Boulder, Colorado. Sue bought the camp close to two-and-a-half years ago and started out with a very flat organizational structure, in which she played a hands-on role in the camp's day-to-day activities. However, she emphasizes that she chose to keep the work culture relaxed—not just for her employees, but for herself as well. Later, Sue started mentoring and promoting promising managerial candidates, thus creating a more vertical organizational structure that allows for more control over the camp's inner workings.

Ask Your Students:

1. What are some of the key skills required to be an effective manager at a Camp Bow Wow franchise?
2. Briefly explain how the Camp Bow Wow franchise in Boulder, Colorado, changed its organizational structure to better serve the firm's needs.

VIDEO SEGMENT SUMMARY

Urban Farmz—Who's Their Boss … I Don't Know

Urban Farmz has made it through its first year, grown 50% during that time, and has 25 employees and even an IT system. However, there is a problem, Jake and Sylvie tell Caleb. Nobody knows who is in charge, including the company's drivers, warehouse workers, and the farmers it works with.

CHAPTER PREP 14

KEY TERMS

management, 246

planning, 246

organizing, 246

leading, 246

controlling, 247

top management, 247

middle management, 247

first-line (supervisory) management, 247

technical skills, 248

human skills, 248

Conceptual skills, 248

Maslow's Hierarchy of Needs Theory, 250

Theory X and Theory Y, 250

Job enrichment, 250

expectancy theory, 251

equity theory, 251

strategic planning, 253

tactical planning, 254

operational planning, 254

contingency planning, 254

mission, 254

SWOT analysis, 254

Strategic goals, 255

Strategies, 255

organizational chart, 257

degree of centralization, 257

span of control, 258

Departmentalization, 258

line organizations, 259

line-and-staff organizations, 259

Line managers, 259

Staff managers, 260

Matrix organizations, 260

Autocratic leaders, 260

Democratic leaders, 260

Free-rein leaders, 260

LECTURE EXAMPLE

Nike CEO Mark Parker believes that a company survives best when it knows how to keep up with the changing times. Nike, which captured the top slot on Fast Company's 2013 list of Most Innovative Companies, is constantly reinventing itself with new products and technology. In 2012, the company introduced Fuelband, an electronic bracelet that keeps track of a person's calorie expenditure through the day. The same year, it launched the ultra-lightweight Flyknit Racer, born out of revolutionary manufacturing technology. Mark's emphasis on constant innovation has led to a 60% increase in revenue for the company since he took over as its CEO in 2006.

Sources: Austin Carr, "Death to Core Competency: Lessons from Nike, Apple, Netflix," retrieved 03-11-13, http://www.fastcompany.com/3005850/core-competency-dead-lessons-nike-apple-netflix.

DISCUSSION QUESTIONS

1. How has the role of the manager changed in the last couple of decades? What forces have driven the changes?
2. What is the purpose of a mission statement? Why are the most effective mission statements simple, vivid, and compelling?
3. What are the characteristics of effective leaders? What leadership style do most effective leaders use?

GROUP ACTIVITY

Before you begin this project, gather plenty of newspapers and enough masking tape so that each group of three to five students has its own roll. The purpose is for each group of students to use the newspaper and tape to build the best-possible tower in 15 minutes. As a class, determine the potential criteria for "best" tower (e.g., tallest, widest, wackiest), and vote on three to five standards to use for the project. Then break into small groups. Earmark one student per group to be the observer, and let the building begin!

Ask the observer from each group to present the tower and to comment on the group process. Did a leader emerge? What style did the leader use? What seemed to motivate the group to perform? How much time did the group spend planning their approach versus actually building the tower? How did the group resolve conflict?

ASSIGNMENTS

Examine your own skill set, drawing on your work experience, schooling, travel, sports, hobbies, and extracurricular activities. Cluster your skills into each key management category: technical skills, human skills, and conceptual skills. Which skill set is the strongest? How could you develop your weaker areas? How might your strengths and weaknesses impact your career plans?

WHAT'S NEW

- New box feature, "Starting Early and Staying Strong"
- Updated section, 14-2c, "Motivation Today"
- Updated box feature, "Wanna Be More Productive? Relax!"
- New box feature, "Power to the People"

WHAT'S INSIDE:

Key Topics in this Chapter: *The importance of a quality workforce, challenges facing today's HR managers, HR perception problems and solutions, HR planning process, effective recruitment and selection, training and development for a competitive edge, evaluations and feedback, employee benefits, federal legislation that affects HR, affirmative action, sexual harassment, careers.*

CHAPTER OUTLINE

Human Resource Management: Bringing Business to Life

Human Resource Management Challenges: Major Hurdles
Layoffs and Outsourcing
Wage Gap
Older Workers
Younger Workers
Women Workers
Work–Life Balance
Lawsuits

Human Resources Managers: Corporate Black Sheep?
The Problem
The Solution

Human Resource Planning: Drawing the Map
Recruitment: Finding the Right People
Selection: Making the Right Choice
Training and Development: Honing the Competitive Edge
Evaluation: Assessing Employee Performance
Compensation: Show Me the Money
Benefits: From Birthday Cakes to Death Benefits
Separation: Breaking Up Is Hard to Do

Legal Issues: HR and the Long Arm of the Law
Affirmative Action: The Active Pursuit of Equal Opportunity
Sexual Harassment: Eliminating Hostility

LEARNING OBJECTIVES

15-1 Explain the importance of human resources to business success

15-2 Discuss key human resource issues in today's economy

15-3 Outline challenges and opportunities that the human resources function faces

15-4 Discuss human resource planning and core human resources responsibilities

15-5 Explain the key federal legislation that affects human resources

4LTR ONLINE

Have students access their 4LTR Press Online account in order to…
- Create StudyBits
- Review key terms and create flashcards
- Create practice quizzes from their StudyBits
- Complete assessment content: matching, drag, and drop, and fill-in-the-blank problems
- View Chapter Highlight Boxes: videos, What Would You Do cases, key exhibits/tables

VIDEO
Zappos
Run time: 8:06 minutes

Zappos.com, one of the nation's leading online retailers, has had to retool its job designations, roles, and work ethic to better serve its customer base. In comparison to traditional brick-and-mortar establishments, online retailing requires a keener eye for detail and better logistical control, along with prompt and efficient customer service. Zappos uses workflow analysis and job design to divide the work involved into distinct jobs, resulting in greater productivity, better customer service, and prompt service delivery. It offers customers a hassle-free shopping experience, with no charges on shipping and delivery, and emphasizes prompt deliveries. The firm has a 24/7 helpline to address any issues that the customer may have. Zappos has thus created a mix of jobs and responsibilities that fosters maximization of productivity.

Ask Your Students:

1. How do workflow analysis and job design improve efficiency at Zappos?

2. Explain how flexible work scheduling benefits both the employees and the management of Zappos.

VIDEO SEGMENT SUMMARY
Urban Farmz—I Was Thinking Something More Managementish

Caleb and Jake begin taking applications to hire additional help. That's when their star produce supplier, Sue, applies for a job. However, Sue is not interested in a job as a driver or warehouse worker. She has a managerial position in mind. "I know all the organic and natural certification processes and rules, and I have a great network of farmers all over the country," she tells them.

CHAPTER PREP 15

KEY TERMS

human resource (HR) management, 265

job analysis, 268

job description, 268

job specifications, 268

Internal recruitment, 268

external recruitment, 269

structured interviews, 270

probationary period, 271

contingent workers, 271

orientation, 272

on-the-job training, 272

apprenticeships, 272

Management development, 273

performance appraisal, 273

compensation, 273

Wages, 274

Salaries, 274

Benefits, 274

cafeteria-style benefits, 275

flextime, 275

compressed workweek, 275

telecommuting, 276

Civil Rights Act of 1964, 277

Title VII, 277

Equal Employment Opportunity Commission (EEOC), 277

affirmative action, 278

Sexual harassment, 279

LECTURE EXAMPLE

In 2012, Internet search engine giant, Google, captured the first position on Fortune's annual *Best Companies to Work For* list for the fourth time. The company has numerous programs in place to ensure that its employees remain happy, healthy, and productive. One of its popular initiatives is the "20 Percent Time" program. The program allows Google engineers to spend one day a week on company tasks that are not a part of their typical work responsibilities. Engineers can hence contribute to projects that interest them and also build their knowledge base.

Source: Surojit Chatterjee, "Top 5 Reasons Why Google is the Best Company to Work for," retrieved 03-11-13, http://www.ibtimes.com /top-5-reasons-why-google-best-company-work-553844.

DISCUSSION QUESTIONS

1. Review the challenges that human resource departments face in today's business environment. Which issues are most daunting? Why?

2. Compare and contrast computer-based training and classroom training. From a business perspective, which do you think is more effective? Why?

3. Which pieces of federal labor legislation do you believe are most important? Why?

GROUP ACTIVITY

Before beginning the project, students should take a couple of minutes to write down their three most positive qualities. Next, ask five other students to name what they see as your single best quality. Remember that while you might not know each other well, you surely know each other better than an interviewer would upon first meeting, and interviewers often make decisions based on first impressions. Then reconvene as a class and check your lists. Did most of you find consistency between the qualities you see in yourselves and qualities others see in you? What were some of the surprises?

ASSIGNMENTS

The Michelin Man isn't exactly known for his svelte figure, but if you work at Michelin North America, you'd better not model your figure after his, or you may end up paying up to $1,000 more per year for health premiums than your leaner-waisted co-workers. In fact, a growing number of firms are either offering incentives for employees to engage in healthier behavior, or imposing penalties for less healthy behavior. Supporters insist that these policies are the most effective way to encourage employees to proactively manage their own health, but detractors label such policies coercive and invasive. What do you think of companies offering financial incentives or penalties for certain health-related behaviors? Explain your thinking.

WHAT'S NEW

- Updated section 15-2b, "Wage Gap"
- Updated section 15-4a, "Recruitment: Finding the Right People"
- Updated box feature, "Wacky Benefits"

WHAT'S INSIDE:

Key Topics in this Chapter: *Dramatic changes in the basic elements of computer technology, Internet2, cloud computing, decision making with information technology, the impact of information technology on e-commerce, Web 2.0, B2B e-commerce, solutions to the challenges sparked by rapid technological advances, ethical and legal concerns, careers.*

LEARNING OBJECTIVES

16-1 Explain the basic elements of computer technology—including hardware, software, and networks—and describe key trends in each area

16-2 Discuss the reasons for the increasing popularity of cloud computing

16-3 Describe how data become information and how decision support systems can provide high-quality information that helps managers make better decisions

16-4 Explain how Internet-based technologies have changed business-to-consumer and business-to-business commerce

16-5 Describe the problems posed by the rapid changes in Internet-based technologies, and explain ways to deal with these problems

CHAPTER OUTLINE

Information Technology: Explosive Change
Hardware and Software
Networks
The Role of the IT Department

Cloud Computing: The Sky's the Limit!

Information Technology and Decision Making: A Crucial Aid
Data and Information
Characteristics of Good Information
Using Information Technology to Improve Decision Making
Expert Systems

Information Technology and the World of e-Commerce
Using Information Technology in the B2C Market
Using Information Technology in the B2B Market

Challenges and Concerns Arising from New Technologies
Malware
Spam, Phishing, and Pharming
Hackers: Break-ins in Cyberspace
Ethical and Legal Issues

4LTR ONLINE

Have students access their 4LTR Press Online account in order to…

- Create StudyBits
- Review key terms and create flashcards
- Create practice quizzes from their StudyBits
- Complete assessment content: matching, drag and drop, and fill-in-the-blank problems
- View Chapter Highlight Boxes: videos, What Would You Do cases, key exhibits/tables

VIDEO

New Balance Hubway
Run time: 6:45 minutes

Hubway is an Internet-based self-serve bike-sharing system. With over 100 stations and 1,000 bikes, Hubway offers residents and tourists an eco-friendly and efficient method of personal transport. Hubway has devised a system by which all customer communication occurs via the Internet and direct mail. Users can sign up for an annual membership or simply walk up to a station, swipe their credit card, and have a bike released to them. Hubway utilizes social media platforms such as Facebook and Twitter, and updates on these platforms provide information to users in a particular area. With the number of users in their initial year of operation exceeding expectations, Hubway has successfully implemented core e-business strategies and intuitive customer interaction to create a service that is both eco- and customer-friendly.

Ask Your Students:

1. How has Hubway incorporated core e-business concepts in its operations?

2. How has Hubway used social media platforms like Facebook and Twitter to its advantage?

VIDEO SEGMENT SUMMARY
Urban Farmz—One Portal! Exactly!

Caleb, Rick, and their friend Emily agree that it would be great to have all the merchandise for the wholesale business go through one portal on the Web—it would be easier to keep track of everything that way. Emily says she is aware of a company that can custom-design an information system for Urban Farmz that does just that. "They'll spend like a week learning your business and come up with something that will rock your world," she assures Caleb and Rick.

CHAPTER PREP 16

KEY TERMS

hardware, 283

software, 283

system software, 283

applications software, 284

internet, 284

broadband Internet connection, 284

Internet2 (I2), 285

intranet, 286

extranet, 286

Cloud computing, 286

Data, 287

information, 287

databases, 288

decision support systems (DSS), 288

business intelligence systems, 288

data warehouse, 288

data mining, 288

expert system (ES), 289

E-commerce, 289

business-to-consumer (B2C) e-commerce, 289

business-to-business (B2B) e-commerce, 289

Web 2.0, 291

viral marketing, 292

cybermediary, 292

electronic bill presentment and payment, 292

e-marketplaces, 293

radio frequency identification (RFID), 293

malware, 294

spyware, 294

computer virus, 294

worms, 294

spam, 295

phishing, 295

pharming, 295

hacker, 296

firewall, 297

Intellectual property, 298

LECTURE EXAMPLE

According to analyst firm Gartner, customer relationship management (CRM) software will form a major proportion of the IT expenditure of companies around the world in the next few years. Companies are planning new strategies to attract, retain, and measure customer satisfaction and are banking on effective CRM software for this purpose. Popular CRM software like Zoho CRM, Salesforce.com, and Microsoft Dynamics are helping thousands of companies gain customer insights from popular social media sites like Twitter, Facebook, LinkedIn, and YouTube. They also facilitate team collaboration and communication, organization of information, and easier tracking of leads from networks.

Sources: Chris Kanaracus, "Gartner: CRM Software Top Priority for IT Spending in 2013–14," retrieved 03-11-13, and "Part 2: Who Actually Uses CRM?," retrieved 03-11-13, http://www.computerworld.in/news/gartner-crm-software-top-priority-it-spending-2013-14-78822013; http://www.worketc.com/CRM_101/Part_2_Who_actually_uses_CRM.

DISCUSSION QUESTIONS

1. What are the characteristics of the Web 2.0 approach to B2C e-commerce? Describe a real-world website you are familiar with that does a particularly good job of using this approach, and explain why it is so effective.

2. What is RFID technology? How can firms use this technology to improve the supply chain management of firms? How else are RFID chips used? Who objects to these uses—and why?

3. What is phishing? How does pharming differ from phishing, and why is it more dangerous? How can you protect yourself from these scams?

GROUP ACTIVITY

Divide the class into small groups, and ask each group to identify two companies that they think are using social media effectively, and two companies that are not using social media effectively. Each group should prepare a brief report describing the reasons why they feel a company is using social media well or poorly. They should consider issues such as what the purpose of the social media presence is, how the company uses social media to connect with customers, how active the company is on social media, and how much helpful information the company provides through social media. Each group should also come up with ideas of how the poorly performing companies can improve their social media effectiveness. Allow each group to provide a brief summary of their ideas to the class.

ASSIGNMENTS

Does the current way information technology is distributed and used contribute to unequal opportunities within our society? Do some research on the Internet to learn about the digital divide. What is this divide, and why should we be concerned about it? How has this divide changed over the years? How can the divide be bridged?

WHAT'S NEW

- New box feature, "Forget the Cloud – The Computing Forecast Calls for Fog"
- Updated section 16-2, "Cloud Computing: The Sky's the Limit!"
- Updated box feature, "Want to Go Green? There are Apps for That!"
- New box feature, "Facebook – Just Because They Can, Doesn't Mean They Should"

WHAT'S INSIDE:

Key Topics in this Chapter: *The role of operations management, efficiency to effectiveness, goods versus services, what operations managers do, process selection and facility layout, strategies for inventory control, project scheduling tools, managing value chains, servicescape, operations technology, quality improvement, Baldrige National Quality Program, Six Sigma, lean and green production, careers.*

LEARNING OBJECTIVES

17-1 Define operations management and describe how the role of operations management has changed over the past 50 years

17-2 Discuss the key responsibilities of operations managers

17-3 Describe how operations managers deal with the special challenges posed by the provision of services

17-4 Explain how changes in technology have revolutionized operations management

17-5 Describe the strategies operations managers have used to improve the quality of goods and services

17-6 Explain how lean and green practices can help both the organization and the environment

CHAPTER OUTLINE

Operations Management: Producing Value in a Changing Environment
Responding to a Changing Environment

What Do Operations Managers Do?
Process Selection and Facility Layout
Facility Location
Inventory Control: Knowing When to Hold 'Em
Project Scheduling
Designing and Managing Value Chains

Implications of a Service-Based Economy: Responding to Different Challenges
Designing the Servicescape
How Big Is Big Enough?

The Technology of Operations
Automation: The Rise of the Machine
Software Technologies

Focus on Quality
Waking Up to the Need for Quality
How American Firms Responded to the Quality Challenge
Quality Standards and Initiatives

The Move to Be Lean and Green: Cutting Cost and Cutting Waste
Reducing Investment in Inventory: Just-in-Time to the Rescue
Lean Thinking in the Service Sector
Green Practices: Helping the Firm by Helping the Environment

4LTR ONLINE

Have students access their 4LTR Press Online account in order to…

- Create StudyBits
- Review key terms and create flashcards
- Create practice quizzes from their StudyBits
- Complete assessment content: matching, drag and drop, and fill-in-the-blank problems
- View Chapter Highlight Boxes: videos, What Would You Do cases, key exhibits/tables

VIDEO

Numi Organic Tea
Run time: 7:22 minutes

Brian Durkee, the Director of Operations at Numi Organic Tea, describes the firm as a triple-bottom-line company, its primary areas of focus being people, planet, and profit. Numi has a close relationship with the tea factories that it does business with, and Brian's role involves making sure that the factories operate in accordance with Numi's pre-existing policies. The "organic" element is also carried over to other aspects of the supply chain, such as the packaging and transport of products. By working with third-party partners outside the U.S., Numi has eliminated the need for additional capital and equipment and does not have to worry about output volume and economy-specific factors like fluctuating costs.

Ask Your Students:

1. What are the challenges that Numi faces in trying to move its operations overseas?

2. How does Numi incorporate its sustainable ethos in its supply-chain operations?

VIDEO SEGMENT SUMMARY

Urban Farmz—Another Spike in Traffic

Business continues to boom for Urban Farmz. It has five new restaurants to supply, it has started four new online markets, and it will attract even more customers once the article about it comes out in *Growing Green* magazine. That sounds like a great situation, right? "Maybe not," says Rick, Urban Farmz's operations manager. "We're growing too fast," he tells Jake, noting that the business doesn't have enough workers or delivery vans, nor an accurate inventory system. "How are we going to fill all these orders? How are we going to ensure that we don't cut corners trying to keep up?" he asks. Fortunately, he has a plan for improving the capacity, accuracy, and efficiency of Urban Farmz's operations.

CHAPTER PREP 17

KEY TERMS

operations management, 301

efficiency, 301

effectiveness, 301

goods, 301

services, 302

process, 303

Inventory, 305

critical path method (CPM), 306

immediate predecessors, 307

critical path, 307

value chain, 307

Vertical integration, 308

Outsourcing, 308

Offshoring, 308

enterprise resource planning (ERP), 309

servicescape, 309

automation, 310

robot, 310

Computer-aided design (CAD), 311

Computer-aided engineering (CAE), 311

Computer-aided manufacturing (CAM), 311

computer-aided design and computer-aided manufacturing CAD/CAM, 311

computer-integrated manufacturing (CIM), 311

total quality management (TQM), 312

poka-yokes, 313

Six Sigma, 313

Baldrige National Quality Program, 314

ISO 9000, 315

Lean production, 315

just-in-time (JIT) production, 316

ISO 14000, 317

LECTURE EXAMPLE

Achieving cost-effective management and overall organizational efficiency is a challenge, considering the global nature of today's business. However, an ineffective operations management system is likely to erode profits. Companies achieve their operational targets in many ways. Companies such as Motorola and General Electric use Six Sigma (process effectiveness indicators) tools to determine their effectiveness and also to eradicate any defects in the processes. These process indicators provide information and solutions for creating a seamless operations system across borders.

Sources: Source: Pat O'Sullivan, "Operations Management: Effective-ness and Efficiency," retrieved 03-11-13, http://www.mentors.ie/blog/operations-managementeffectiveness-and-efficiency/.

DISCUSSION QUESTIONS

1. Explain the relationship between the operations management goals of "efficiency" and "effectiveness."

2. How does offshoring differ from outsourcing? What are the advantages and disadvantages of offshoring?

3. What is automation? Describe the major hardware and software components of a computer-integrated manufacturing system.

GROUP ACTIVITY

Divide your class into several small groups for a research project. As a way of introduction, show them recent reporting indicating that the costs of labor in China have increased dramatically. That, along with the rising cost of fuel, has convinced many companies that a new outsourcing location is needed to stay profitable. Present each group with one of the following countries, and ask them to prepare a report that shows the benefits and drawbacks of investing in that country for outsourcing: Myanmar, India, Bangladesh, Mexico, Estonia, or Thailand. Their reports should include information on the financial benefits that companies would gain as well as the potential costs that the company may not face elsewhere.

ASSIGNMENTS

The auto company you work for is about to open a new factory in one of two locations, the United States or China. Do some research about the costs involved in operating a factory in both countries, such as labor, meeting government regulations, dealing with competition, and transportation. Which location would you choose and why?

WHAT'S NEW

- New box feature, "At UPS, ORION Refines the Delivery Process for Efficiency"
- New box feature, "If the Sock Fits, Make It in the USA"

APPENDIX PREP
Personal Finance

WHAT'S INSIDE:

Key Topics in this Appendix: *Budgets, assessing your revenues and expenses, spending habits, savings accounts, building credit, credit card laws and regulations, abusing credit, investments, different investment options, acquiring financial assets, building a portfolio, retirement planning, careers.*

LEARNING OBJECTIVES

A-1 Apply the principles of budgeting to your personal finances

A-2 Identify strategies to help build a sufficient savings

A-3 Explain the importance of using credit wisely

A-4 Discuss key wealth-building principles and the financial instruments that may be part of a wealth-building strategy

CHAPTER OUTLINE

Your Budget
How Do I Get Started?

Your Savings: Building a Safety Net

Your Credit: Handle with Care
Credit Cards: Boon or Bane?
The Devil in the Details —
    Understanding Your Credit Card
    Agreement!
Protection for Consumers: New Laws
    and Regulations
Using Credit Cards Wisely: The Need
    for Discipline

Your Investments: Building for the Future
Building Wealth: The Key Is
    Consistency—and an Early Start!
Acquiring Financial Assets: The Role of
    a Broker
Building a Portfolio: A Few Words
    about Diversification, Risk, and
    Return
But What Is My Best Investment? (Hint:
    Look in the Mirror!)
Investing for the Long Term: Planning
    for Your Retirement

4LTR ONLINE

Have students access their 4LTR Press Online account in order to…
- Create StudyBits
- Review key terms and create flashcards
- Create practice quizzes from their StudyBits
- Complete assessment content: matching, drag and drop, and fill-in-the-blank problems
- View Chapter Highlight Boxes: videos, What Would You Do cases, key exhibits/tables

VIDEO
Living Debt Free
Run time: 2:35 minutes

Danny Kofke, a special needs teacher, supports his family on an annual salary of slightly over $40,000, one of the few families in the U.S. that are currently living debt-free. Kofke's salary is almost $10,000 less than the average U.S. household's, and his wife has not had to work in the past 7 years to add to the family's income. Despite the necessity for maintaining a stringent budget, Kofke's family has appliances such as a huge flat-screen TV, a washer/dryer, and two cars. With the average U.S. family facing an average debt balance of $14,500, this is a rare occurrence. Kofke attributes these purchases to the savings system.

Ask Your Students:
1. Is all debt bad? When does going into debt make sense?
2. Why is it so important for people to save and invest when they are young?

VIDEO SEGMENT SUMMARY
Urban Farmz—Retirement? Please!

In this scene, Dan talks to Aron, one of Urban Farmz's employees, about a new baby he has on the way and his plans to try to attend college. "If you want, I can take a look at your finances, get you into a good college savings plan, and maybe convert some of your retirement to a 529 [plan]," Dan tells him. "Retirement? Please," replies Aron. "All I've got is a few thousand in the bank for emergencies." Dan wonders if Urban Farmz has the means to create a 401(k) plan for its employees. He agrees to talk to Caleb and Jake about it. Aron says he will talk to his co-workers to see if they would use such a plan if it were available.

APPENDIX PREP

KEY TERMS

budget (personal), 320

discretionary payments, 322

nondiscretionary payments, 322

savings account, 322

Federal Deposit Insurance Corporation (FDIC), 323

credit, 323

credit score, 323

credit card, 323

grace period:, 324

annual percentage rate (APR), 324

debit card, 325

Investing, 325

IRA, 328

401(k), 403(b), and 457 plans, 329

company matching, 330

vesting period, 330

LECTURE EXAMPLE

As Robert Arnott said, "In investing, what is comfortable is rarely profitable." Managing personal finances is a hard but not an impossible task. With the help of online tools such as SimpliFi and Voyant, one can create a financial plan with ease. Creating a budget is a good way to control expenditure and something as simple as a spreadsheet could be useful. Understanding the basics of investment by identifying viable options is an all-important step in the whole process. Long-term savings are feasible and indeed necessary, and building a safety net is essential for adequately managing your finances.

Sources: "A Step By Step Guide to Gaining Control of Your Financial Life," CNN Money, retrieved 03-12-13, http://money.cnn.com/magazines/moneymag/money101/ .

DISCUSSION QUESTIONS

1. What is the difference between discretionary costs and nondiscretionary costs? Illustrate the difference by giving examples. Why is this distinction important?

2. Why is it important to begin investing early? Why is it important to diversify your investments? How is the return you expect to earn on various investments related to their risk?

3. How are 401(k), 403(b), and 457 retirement plans similar and how do they differ? How do Roth plans differ from traditional plans? What are the key advantages of these plans compared to IRAs?

GROUP ACTIVITY

In groups, have students peruse the stock pages of *The Wall Street Journal* or other financial newspaper. Use the actual paper rather than going online at this point. The students will only be reviewing the pages to identify publicly traded companies, so even month-old papers are okay for this purpose. In consulting the paper, student teams will select a basket of stocks that they want to purchase. You can give them a budget of $100,000 (or more or less) if you want to create specificity to the project.

Once students have identified their basket of stocks, they should divide the companies among team members and then research whether the companies whose stocks they have chosen pay dividends. If they do, students should find out if the companies offer dividend reinvestment programs (DRIPs). If they do not, students should research the companies' valuation curves— over a period of time that you specify.

ASSIGNMENTS

Go to a website such as Creditcards.com or Creditcardguide.com (http://www.creditcardguide.com/), and click on the link to student credit cards. Look at the list of recommended cards. Which card would you most like to hold? What is the initial APR on this card—and how long does the introductory rate apply? What is the regular APR? Does the card have an annual fee? What type of "perks" does it offer? How good does your credit have to be to qualify for this card?

WHAT'S NEW

- New box feature, "Too Broke to Save"
- Updated section A-4d, "But What Is My Best Investment? (Hint: Look in the Mirror!)"

WHAT'S INSIDE:

Key Topics in this Appendix: *Labor unions, organization of unions, U.S. labor laws, collective bargaining, distributive bargaining, interest-based bargaining, strikes, lockouts, picketing, boycotting, mediation, arbitration, unions and compensation, job security, productivity, and challenges that unions face.*

LEARNING OBJECTIVES

A1-1 Describe how unions in the United States are organized

A1-2 Discuss the key provisions of the laws that govern labor–management relations

A1-3 Explain how labor contracts are negotiated and administered

A1-4 Evaluate the impact that unions have had on their members' welfare and the economy, and explain the challenges that today's unions face

CHAPTER OUTLINE

The Basic Structure of Unions

Labor Laws in the United States

Collective Bargaining: Reaching an Agreement
Subjects of Bargaining: What It's All About
Approaches to Collective Bargaining
Dealing with Impasse
Administering a Collective Bargaining Agreement

The State of the Unions: Achievements, Problems, and Challenges
Unions and Compensation
Unions and Job Security
Unions and Productivity
The Challenge of Declining Union Membership

4LTR ONLINE

Have students access their 4LTR Press Online account in order to…

- Create StudyBits
- Review key terms and create flashcards
- Create practice quizzes from their StudyBits
- Complete assessment content: matching, drag and drop, and fill-in-the-blank problems
- View Chapter Highlight Boxes: videos, What Would You Do cases, key exhibits/tables

VIDEO

Unite Here Local 1 Chicago
Run time: 10:01 minutes

Unite Here Local 1, is a part of the Unite Here International Union, which represents U.S. and Canadian workers in the gaming, food service, manufacturing, hotel, textile, distribution, and airport industries. Unite Here addresses the issues such as wages, benefits, and working conditions. The union encourages employees to enforce their contracts and ensure that no violations of the contract occur. In Chicago, Unite Here engages in constant negotiation over issues such as extended contract periods, better health benefits, increased wages, and the prevention of job subcontracting. If negotiations come to a standstill, Unite Here members go on strike in an effort to obtain an appropriate response from management.

Ask Your Students:

1. What are the primary concerns and issues addressed by the representatives at Unite Here Local 1?

2. How does Unite Here Local 1 use collective bargaining and other negotiating techniques to better serve the employees it represents?

VIDEO SEGMENT SUMMARY

Urban Farmz—Why Not Start with a Clear Contract?

Aron, one of Urban Farmz's employees, talks to Thalia, Jake and Caleb's lawyer, about the merits of the firm's workers joining the United Farm Workers union. But Jake is totally against the idea. "Do I not treat you guys with the utmost respect? I mean, this is just going to cause problems," he tells Aron.

ONLINE APPENDIX PREP 1

KEY TERMS

labor union, A1-2

craft unions, A1-2

Industrial union, A1-2

employment at will, A1-4

National Labor Relations Act (Wagner Act), A1-4

Labor–Management Relations Act Taft–Hartley Act, A1-5

closed shop, A1-5

union shop, A1-5

right-to-work law, A1-5

open shop, A1-5

collective bargaining, A1-6

distributive bargaining, A1-6

Interest-based bargaining, A1-6

strike, A1-7

lockout, A1-7

picketing, A1-7

boycott, A1-7

mediation, A1-8

arbitration, A1-8

grievance, A1-8

LECTURE EXAMPLE

When France's second-largest car maker, Renault SA, announced that a few of its factories in France might be shut down in response to a weakening economy and declining sales, a series of negotiations ensued between the management and the labor unions. Finally, the company proposed a nation-wide deal in February 2013 that allowed it to eliminate 7,500 jobs by 2016 and freeze salaries in 2013. Despite being tough on the workers, two of the three labor unions have agreed to back the deal. In return, the automobile giant has promised to increase productivity and not close any auto plants.

Sources: Mathieu Rosemain, "Renault Gains Union Backing To Eliminate 7500 Positions," Retrieved 03-11-13, http://www.bloomberg.com/news/2013-03-06/renault-gains-union-backing-to-eliminate-7-500-positions.html.

DISCUSSION QUESTIONS

1. What is a labor union? What is the difference between a craft union and an industrial union? What is the AFL-CIO and how is it related to unions?

2. What is the difference between distributive bargaining and interest-based bargaining? Under what conditions is interest-based bargaining likely to be most effective?

3. How are mediation and arbitration similar? What is the key difference between them?

GROUP ACTIVITY

Divide into groups of approximately nine students. Then, assign each group member at random to one of three subgroups. Have the first subgroup play the role of union organizers (2 members), the second play the role of managers at the printing company (2 members), and the third play workers at the same company (the rest of the group). Allow the union reps and managers 3 minutes each to present their case to the workers. Then, have the workers vote in a mock certification election to decide whether to unionize or not (union reps and managers cannot vote). After all workers have voted, rejoin as a class to compare your results. How many voted in favor of the union? Ask the workers in each group to explain briefly why they voted the way they did.

ASSIGNMENTS

Using the Internet, research five labor unions not covered in the appendix. Briefly describe each of these unions in a short paragraph. For example, describe what crafts or industries they represent, when they were formed, whether they are private or public, what their major goals are, and how many members they have.

WHAT'S NEW

- Updated section, A1-1, "Labor Laws in the United States"

- Updated Exhibit A1.2, "Right-to-Work Laws"

- Updated Exhibit A1.3, "Trends in Work Stoppages: 1970-2014"

- Updated Exhibit A1.4, "Union vs. Nonunion Median Weekly Earnings in Selected Industries (2014)"

- Updated section, A1-4, "The State of the Unions: Achievements, Problems, and Challenges"

- New box feature, "Businesses Tire of Waiting, Find Alternate Routes to Avoid West Coast Ports"

WHAT'S INSIDE:

Key Topics in this Appendix:
Constitutional law, statutory law, administrative law, case law, civil law, criminal law, contracts, breach of contract, sales of transferring ownership, titles, principal–agent relationships, bankruptcy, intellectual property, patents, trademarks, and copyrights.

LEARNING OBJECTIVES

A2-1 Explain the purposes of laws and identify the major sources of law in the United States

A2-2 Describe the characteristics of a contract and explain how the terms of contracts are enforced

A2-3 Describe how both title and risk pass from the seller to the buyer when a sale occurs

A2-4 Provide an overview of the legal principles governing agency, intellectual property, and bankruptcy

CHAPTER OUTLINE

The Purpose and Origin of Laws
Sources of Law
Civil versus Criminal Law

Contracts: The Ties that Bind
What Makes a Contract Enforceable?
What Happens When a Party Fails to Satisfy the Terms of a Contract?

Sales: Transferring Ownership
How and When Does a Title Pass from Seller to Buyer?
Which Party Assumes Risk of Loss During the Process of Transferring Title from Seller to Buyer?

Other Legal Principles: What the Law Says about Agency, Intellectual Property, and Bankruptcy
Principal–Agent Relationships
Bankruptcy
Intellectual Property

4LTR ONLINE

Have students access their 4LTR Press Online account in order to…

- Create StudyBits
- Review key terms and create flashcards
- Create practice quizzes from their StudyBits
- Complete assessment content: matching, drag and drop, and fill-in-the-blank problems
- View Chapter Highlight Boxes: videos, What Would You Do cases, key exhibits/tables

VIDEO

Real World Legal—Pharzime
Run time: 3:59 minutes

Two executives from a fan manufacturing company discuss the various safety issues associated with a particular product design. They discuss the likelihood of product failures based on product tests, and the likelihood of danger to customers as a result of malfunctions. Although the majority of testing conducted on the product reveals no defects, testing the products at high intensities revealed a few products to be dangerously flawed—enough to put potential customers at risk. The executives try to determine the necessity for a product recall, evaluating the pros and cons—the safety of potential customers versus the loss of a potential long-term contract.

Ask Your Students:

1. Considering that 80% of the initial tests run on the TF-300 were without incident, is the company shown in the video justified in allowing the production of the TF-300 to commence?

2. In what ways can customers protect themselves from unethical practices such as the one implied in the video?

VIDEO SEGMENT SUMMARY

Urban Farmz—No, We Aren't Going to Be Patient

Thalia, the lawyer for Urban Farmz, is contacting the lawyer of Whittendale Markets, which has filed for Chapter 11 bankruptcy and still owes Urban Farmz $35,000. Urban Farmz feels they've been taken advantage of by extending the line of credit and still not getting paid by Whittendale Markets.

Thalia states that Urban Farmz will not take a reduced payment, since they're a small business and are paying interest on the line of credit given to Whittendale Markets. The conversation between Thalia and the other lawyer ends by her saying, "We'll just have to see what the bankruptcy court decides."

ONLINE APPENDIX PREP 2

KEY TERMS

laws, A2-2

constitution, A2-3

statutory law, A2-3

Uniform Commercial Code (UCC), A2-3

administrative laws, A2-4

case law (also called common law), A2-4

tort, A2-5

negligence, A2-5

crime, A2-5

Business law, A2-6

contract, A2-6

consideration, A2-6

statute of frauds, A2-6

breach of contract, A2-7

statute of limitations, A2-7

compensatory damages, A2-7

specific performance, A2-7

sale, A2-7

title, A2-7

principal–agent relationship, A2-8

principal, A2-8

agent, A2-8

scope of authority (for an agent), A2-8

Chapter 7 bankruptcy, A2-9

Chapter 11 bankruptcy, A2-9

Chapter 13 bankruptcy, A2-9

property, A2-10

intellectual property, A2-10

patent, A2-10

trademark, A2-11

copyright, A2-11

LECTURE EXAMPLE

Apple's recent victory over Samsung regarding the infringement of intellectual property may be a good thing for the industry. This case could possibly force Apple's competitors to create completely original products, and which will benefit consumers. The courts ruled that Samsung had infringed several of Apple's patents, including the distinctive round edges and several other design functions found in its products. Samsung was told to pay around a billion dollars in damages to the American technology giant. Samsung plans to appeal the verdict but Apple's victory is sure to discourage other competitors from mimicking designs. Moreover, it forces firms to invest in long-term innovation and protects intellectual property as well.

Sources: Nick Wingfield, "Apple's Case Muddies the Future of Innovations," The New York Times, retrieved 03-12-13, http://www.nytimes.com/2012/08/27/technology/apple-samsung-case-muddies-future-of-innovation.html.

DISCUSSION QUESTIONS

1. What is a contract? Name and briefly describe the four characteristics of a valid contract. What can one party in a contract do if the other party fails to honor the terms of a contract?

2. Define a sale. Describe how the Uniform Commercial Code deals with key issues involved in the sale of goods.

3. What is the purpose of a copyright? What would happen if copyright protection were not available? How would this affect the incentives of authors, songwriters, and playwrights?

GROUP ACTIVITY

For this project, students will work in teams to create a unique company name and mark. Prepare by creating a deck of cards, each with a different industry written on it. Some options are:

- Aerospace
- Apparel
- Automotive
- Beauty
- Construction
- Consumer Products
- Education

Assign students to teams, then give each team a card at random so that each team has a different industry. Each team will need to come up with a new product or service for their industry, describe it generally, and give it a name. Each team will subdivide into pairs and research the existence of their brand name in the USPTO.gov database. The USPTO database can be challenging to navigate, so by sending students to research in pairs, the entire team is likely to pull together the needed information. Students will likely find a company with a similar or same name, if not in their industry, then in another.

ASSIGNMENTS

Use the Internet to find out more about Chapter 7 bankruptcies. How does a debtor file for a voluntary bankruptcy? How do creditors file an involuntary bankruptcy? What is the purpose of the "means test" and how is it applied? What role does the trustee play? Which assets are protected from creditors' claims in your state? Which debts can be discharged under Chapter 7, and which debts remain intact?

WHAT'S NEW

- New box feature, "And Then There Were Two. No – One"